MW01054408

The History of the Panzerkorps
Panzerkorps
Großdeutschland
Volume 3

Helmut Spaeter

Translated by David Johnston

The History of the Panzerkorps
Großdeutschland
Volume 3

By Helmut Spaeter
An English Translation by David Johnston

Originally Published in German as
Die Geschichte des Panzerkorps "Großdeutschland", Band 3
in Bielefeld (Germany)

English Edition Published by
J.J. Fedorowicz Publishing, Inc.
104 Browning Boulevard
Winnipeg, Manitoba

Printed in Canada
ISBN 0 - 92991 - 50 - 9

Printed by
Friesens Printers

Publishers' Acknowledgements

This book is dedicated to the memory of Helmut Spaeter who passed away as the final preparations for the English edition were being made...*wir hatten einen Kameraden.*

Our thanks are also extended to David Johnston for his usual excellent translation work and to Matt Lukes for a superb signing box.

We wish to apologise for the quality of some of the maps and diagrams offered in this book. We had to work with a book that is nearly 40 years old with none of the original artwork available. As a result, we had to scan the graphics out of the printed book. Despite the poor quality, we thought the maps and organizational diagrams were of interest and deserved to be published anyway. We hope you understand.

We wish to thank you, the reader, for purchasing this book and all of you who have written us with kind words of praise and encouragement. It gives us the impetus to continue translating the best available German-language books and also produce original titles. Our catalog of books is listed on the following pages and can be viewed on our web site at

www.jjfpub.mb.ca.

John Fedorowicz, Mike Olive and Bob Edwards

Other Titles
by
J.J. Fedorowicz Publishing

The Leibstandarte (1. SS-Panzer-Division): Volumes I, II,
    III, IV/1 and IV/2
European Volunteers (5. SS-Panzer-Division)
Das Reich (2. SS-Panzer-Division): Volumes I and II
The History of Panzer-Korps "Großdeutschland": Volumes
    1 and 2
Otto Weidinger
Otto Kumm
Manhay, The Ardennes: Christmas 1944
Armor Battles of the Waffen-SS, 1943-1945
Tiger: The History of a Legendary Weapon, 1942-1945
Hitler Moves East
Tigers in the Mud
Panzer Aces
Footsteps of the Hunter
History of the 12. SS-Panzer-Division "Hitlerjugend"
Grenadiers, the Autobiography of Kurt Meyer
Field Uniforms of German Army Panzer Forces
    in World War 2
Tigers in Combat, Volumes I and II
Infanterie Aces
Freineaux and Lamormenil—The Ardennes
The Caucasus and the Oil
East Front Drama—1944
The History of the Fallschirm-Panzer-Korps
    "Hermann Göring"

Michael Wittmann and the Tiger Commanders
    of the Leibstandarte
The Western Front 1944: Memoirs of a
    Panzer Lehr Officer
Luftwaffe Aces
Quiet Flows the Rhine
Decision in the Ukraine: Summer 1943
Combat History of the schwere Panzer-
    Jäger-Abteilung 653
The Brandenburgers—Global Mission
Field Uniforms of Germany's Panzer Elite
Soldiers of the Waffen-SS: Many Nations, One Motto
In the Firestorm of the Last Years of the War
The Meuse First and Then Antwerp
Jochen Peiper: Commander, Panzer-Regiment
    "Leibstandarte"
Sturmgeschütze vor! Assault Guns to the Front!
Karl Baur: A Pilot's Pilot
Kharkov
Panzer Aces 2
Panzertaktik! German Small-Unit Armor Tactics
Panzer Soldiers for "God, Honor, Fatherland":
    The History of Panzerregiment "Großdeutschland"
Tigers in Combat I (revised edition)

J.J. Fedorowicz Publishing

Signing Box by Matt Lukes

Table of Contents

Part I
Panzerkorps Großdeutschland
Formation – Organization – Strengths
Chapter 1

Panzerkorps
Großdeutschland   *Command Post, December 1944*
Order of the Day

> *Soldiers of the Panzerkorps Großdeutschland!*
>
> *The Führer has ordered that the Pz.Gren.-Division Großdeutschland and the former Jäger-Division Brandenburg form the Panzerkorps GD!*
>
> *At the same time he has ordered me to be the commanding general of this Panzerkorps.*
>
> *In doing so I assume command of two divisions of the army, which since the start of the war have fought gloriously and honorably in every theater. The army looks to you full of pride, the German people with great trust; but the Führer makes the highest demands of you!*
>
> *We will do justice to all expectations!*
>
> *The actions of those who gave their lives for us while wearing the armband, the great reputation of both divisions and the knowledge that we have to defend the holy soil of our fatherland at the hotspots of the front, make us ready for any sacrifice!*
>
> *Most faithful allegiance to the Führer, unshakeable faith in our victory, iron comradeship with one another, unconditional obedience and honor shall be the inner qualities of every one of us!*
>
> *So I salute you all and know that there will be no task that we cannot master, no enemy that we will not defeat!*
>
> *Long live the Führer!*
>
> *Long live the Panzerkorps GD!*
>
> *von Saucken*
>
> *General der Panzertruppen*

This order of the day from General von Saucken set in motion a development for the former Pz.Gren.-Division Großdeutschland which in some ways was similar to that of the Infantry-Regiment GD in the first months of 1942, but which also showed a fundamental change in the structure of the German Army at the turn of the year 1944-45. There is no denying the fact that by this time the days of military successes with the occupation of enemy territory and the destruction of enemy armies were long gone and that instead the entire world had risen up to destroy the aggressor Germany. The multi-front war had brought the German armed services to the extreme limits of their ability to fight, driven the German population into desperate resistance, and led the German command to senseless, restricted actions.

The overpowering armies of the enemy stood everywhere on the German frontiers, ready to launch their final offensive whose goal was Berlin. Used to its dictatorial commands being carried out immediately, the state leadership—which since Christmas 1941 had been one with the supreme military command—once again scraped together everything in men, materiel and inner will to resist that could still be summoned from the war-weary German population. Everyone who could carry or operate a weapon was placed in new and existing battle formations; *Luftwaffe* units which could no longer fly were sent into action as ground formations, navy personnel without ships were assigned to existing army divisions to serve as infantry. All of this served to bring the units of the German Army ringing the frontiers back up to full strength in personnel. But in spite of all the personal and forced sacrifices no decisive battle accomplishments could be expected from men unaccustomed to fighting and not ready for a war of attrition. At this time the military command once again placed its hopes in the few remaining intact veteran divisions, which had so many battle-tested men in their ranks that it was still possible to expect some fighting spirit even at this stage of the final battle. These units were sent all available war materiel, their strength was bolstered through the addition of convalescents and recruits, and they were organized based on experience in order to commit them as potent fighting units at the expected hot spots of the battles to come. The few veteran soldiers were expected to fight as if the war had just begun, with no thought to their diminished will to fight as a result of years of punishing service.

Among the units which the German command expected to be at a high state of combat readiness even in the most difficult situations were the Pz.Gren.Div. *Großdeutschland* and the *Brandenburg* Division. Consequently they were to be placed under a unified command, which was of course expected to result in an increase in performance. But there may have been several other factors. One of these can probably be found in the development of the *Waffen-SS* divisions, whose greatly increased numbers were used to form the *6. SS-Pz.Armee* at this time. Even though little thought was given any more at the end of 1944 as to whether the *Waffen-*

SS was a parallel organization to the army, since concerns about the state of the army were taking center stage, the constant penetration of *Waffen-SS* officers into the highest command positions of the *Wehrmacht* may perhaps have prompted the concentration of suitable German divisions into larger formations. Where the *Großdeutschland* units were concerned, there was also the fact that in the second half of 1944 not just a corps, but also a *Führer-Grenadier-* and a *Führer-Begleit-Brigade* had been formed, while the former *Wach-bataillon Großdeutschland* had been expanded into a regiment—and all of this from a single personnel reservoir: the *Pz.Gren.-Ersatz-Brigade GD* at Cottbus and Guben. But this also meant that, more and more, convalescents and men recovered from wounds no longer returned to their old units, but instead were assigned to new formations as cadre personnel. The Pz.Gren.Div. GD could see how it would deal with the replacements in its ranks. These measures must undoubtedly damage the homogeneity of this oldest of GD units, which would inevitably have an effect on its fighting morale and steadfastness.

One positive addition—and this must be stressed at this point—was the arrival of the *Brandenburg* Division from the southeast area, where until the end of 1944 it had been engaged against partisans. Unit by unit it was moved into the *Panzerkorps Großdeutschland*'s assembly area. Its battalions and Kampfgruppen were characterized by outstanding fighting spirit and were extremely familiar with the fighting methods of the Soviets and the Soviet-led partisan units of the southeast (Balkans), however they were not used to participating in division-size operations. This was in no small part due to the fact that it had been formed from numerous special units. When the German armies were forced back to their starting positions in Germany in 1944 there was no longer any requirement for these missions and the *Brandenburg* Division was converted into a panzer-grenadier division with the organization, equipment and armament of such a formation. For the *Brandenburg* Division this marked the end of a special development that had begun in 1939 with the "*Deutsche Kompanie.*"

At first the *Brandenburg* Division had little in common with its new sister division, the Panzer-Grenadier Division GD, in terms of the origins of its personnel or the nature of its tactical employment. At the time it joined the Pz.Korps GD in December 1944 its personnel strength was extremely low as a result of its fierce actions in the fighting retreat in Romania, Yugoslavia, Greece and Hungary. It did, however, have at its disposal two full-strength replacement training units, the *Lehr-Rgt. Brandenburg* and the *Ausbildungs-Btl. Brandenburg* at Brandenburg/Havel. These units were able to provide the personnel needed to fill the gaps in the division's ranks. When the division was reorganized, however, its number of regiments shrank from the previous four to two *Jäger* regiments, and these had just two battalions each.

When the SS took over the responsibilities of the Abwehr's Amt II, approximately 1,800 members of the former *Lehr-Rgt. Z.b.V. 800*

Brandenburg voluntarily elected to join the SS, however the bulk of the former members of *Brandenburg* remained with the division and went with it into the *Panzerkorps Großdeutschland*. When it was reorganized as a panzer-grenadier division, several new units were added that had never been part of the *Brandenburg* Division: the Pz.Stu.Pi.Btl. BR (armored assault pioneer battalion), elements to supplement the future Pz.Art.Rgt. BR (armored artillery regiment), elements of the Pz.A.A. BR (armored reconnaissance battalion) and so on. As well, units such as the Fsch.Jäg.Btl. BR (parachute battalion) and the *Küstenjäger* (marine commandos) left and were assigned to or became part of other units.

The initial orders for the formation of the *Pz.Korps Großdeutschland* had been issued by headquarters in September 1944. Thus on 13 September the command of the *Brandenburg* Division received a *Führer* order decreeing that the unit was being subordinated to the Pz.Korps GD as its second division. The GD division command received a similar order at the beginning of October. General Staff Obstlt. Bleicken was replaced as Ia of the Pz.Gren.Div. GD by General Staff *Major* Adler; as future chief-of-staff of the corps, Bleicken went to the organizational department in Zossen to learn the initial details of the reorganization and reformation. Individual discussions with *Generaloberst* Guderian and General Staff *Oberst* Thomale were principally aimed at moving the divisions into a quiet formation area.

Since both units were initially still heavily engaged in the northeast and southeast areas, their immediate withdrawal was not possible. Instead, the first move was to form those new units which would have to be assigned to the two divisions as part of the new organization. Moreover, preparations were made to reduce the division strengths to approximately 10,000 men each, which was to be achieved primarily by disbanding the third battalions and removing them from the organization. This move made it possible to fill gaps in unit personnel.

The command positions were filled as follows:

Pz.Korps Großdeutschland

Commanding General	General der Panzertruppen von Saucken
Chief-of-Staff	General Staff Oberst Bleicken
Ia (Operations Officer)	General Staff Major Beck-Broichsitter (wounded)
	General Staff Major Usener
Quartermaster	General Staff Major Usener
	General Staff Major Volkmar

Pz.Gren.Div. GD

Div. Commander	GenMaj. Lorenz
Ia (Operations Officer)	General Staff Major Adler
Ib (Logistics officer)	General Staff Major Friesenhausen

Pz.Gren.Div. Brandenburg

Div. Commander	GenMaj. Schulte-Heuthaus
Ia (Operations Officer	General Staff Major Erasmus
Ib (Logistics officer)	General Staff Major Uhl (missing)
	General Staff Major Volkmar
	General Staff Major Spaeter

The formation of the *Pz.Korps Großdeutschland*, the reorganization of the two divisions and the assignment of new units took place from mid-December 1944 until about 10 January 1945. The first days of January were used to reorganize the units of the Pz.Gren.Div. *Brandenburg* arriving late from the southeast.

Several corps units were also formed during the course of these reorganizations, in particular a signals battalion, combat engineers, artillery, medical units and supply units. In detail the formation took place as follows:

Korps-Begleit-Kp. GD	*Oblt.* Säuberlich
(corps escort company)	Strength: Roughly one motorcycle platoon (insufficient time for any more)
Korps-Nachr.Abt. GD	*Major* Seek
(signals battalion)	Strength: 1 telephone and 1 radio company

Pz.Korps-Füsilier-Rgt. GD (beginning of Jan. 1945)

Commander	*Major* Fabich

Former: III./Pz.Gren. GD = I./Pz.Korps-Füs.Rgt.

Commander	*Hptm.* Buse

Former: both III./Jäg.Rgt. BR = II./Pz.Korps-Füs.Rgt. GD

Commander:	*Major* Plitt, *Hptm.* Sprengel

(Thus the oldest GD battalion—the III./Pz.Gren.Rgt. GD—was disbanded and incorporated into the Pz.Korps-Füs. Rgt. GD.)

Korps-Pz.Pi.Btl. 500 GD (corps armored pioneer battalion)

Commander:		*Hptm.* Eicke
with:	1.Kp. =	*Oblt.* Meier
	2.Kp. =	*Oblt.* Wendt
	3. (Goliath) Kp. =	*Lt.* Meier

Major Chrapkowski was assigned as corps pioneer commander, while Hptm. Richter became *Hauptmann beim Stabe*.

The *Korps-Sanitäts-Kp. GD* (corps medical company)—former 2. San.Kp. GD in place of a BR medical company as second *Korps-San.Kp. GD*.

Korps-Nachschub-Truppen GD (corps supply troops) under the command of *Major* Gericke were supposed to be assembled from elements of the transport capacities of both divisions. Because the corps saw action so soon this did not happen.

Designated Art.Rgt. 500, the *Pz.Korps-Artillerie-Rgt. GD* was formed from units of the Pz.Art.-Rgt. GD (6. (s.F.H. 18) Bttr. and a battery from III. Abteilung) and the Pz.Art.Rgt. *Brandenburg* (one battalion l.F.H. 18). Hptm. Burchardt was named regimental commander and Oblt. Mahnke adjutant. Elements of the Art.Ers.Abt. GD (artillery replacement battalion) Guben were supposed to be sent later. *Major* Hammerich was the anticipated commander, however he did not arrive. In preparation for action the units detached from GD were positioned in the corps area in East Prussia under Hptm. Burchardi, the *Brandenburgers* under Hptm. von Hobe in the Frankfurt/Oder area.

Essentially these are the corps units which came under direct corps command. In some cases only their headquarters or a basic formation was created because events would not allow their completion. The vehicles of the corps headquarters (about 25) as well as a few of those of the corps units wore a tactical emblem consisting of a black helmet on a yellow background to distinguish them from the attached panzer-grenadier divisions. The reorganization was especially painful for the Pz.Gren.Div. GD because considerable elements were taken away from its battle-tested fighting community. Not only did the Panzer-Grenadier Regiment GD's III Battalion become the I Battalion of the Panzer Corps Fusilier Regiment (after a farewell by former regimental commander *Oberst* Heesemann), its sister battalion of the Panzer-Fusilier Regiment GD was disbanded and its personnel assigned to the other two battalions. The *15. (Pz.Jäg)* and *16. (Fla) Kompanien* (anti-tank and anti-aircraft companies) also disappeared and were reassigned to the Pz.Jäg.Abt. GD then being formed and the existing H.-Flak.Abt. GD respectively.

The former Pz.Rgt. GD was allocated the I. (Panther) Abt.; but it had to release the former II. (Pz. IV) Abt. to the *Führer-Begleit-Brigade*. Its establishment remained the same with the existing III. (Tiger) Abt. and the addition of Pz.Abt. (FKL) 302 under *Major* Sahmel in January 1945. The latter unit was equipped with remote-controlled tanks.

While IV./Pz.Art.Rgt. GD, which was supposed to be released to corps, was renamed I./Pz.-Korps-Art.Rgt. GD, for the most part it remained with the Pz.Art.Rgt. GD.

The former Pz.Stu.Pi.Btl. GD was strengthened considerably. It was turned into the Pz.Pi.Rgt. GD under the command of *Major* Korthal and was organized as follows:

Pz.Stu.Pi.Btl. (armored pioneer battalion)
    Commander.: Hptm. Warschnauer

SPW-Pi.Btl. (armored troop carrier battalion)
Commander: Maj. Barthels

The heaviest loss suffered by the Panzer-Grenadier Division GD was the result of the transfer of the Stu.Gesch.-Brigade GD (assault gun brigade) to the Panzer-Grenadier Division *Brandenburg*, since the latter could not be equipped with new armored elements in time. After reequipping with Panthers, the BR's intended armored unit, I./Pz.Rgt. 26 (the battalion associated with the GD since Jassy and Targul Frumos) was likewise assigned to another GD unit in the Frankfurt/Oder area. It already bore the designation I./Pz.Rgt. *Brandenburg*, however it never saw action as part of the Panzer-Grenadier-Division *Brandenburg*.

It is understandable that the reorganization of the Pz.Gren.Div. GD and especially its considerable transfers of personnel to other units caused the division headaches. The division commander, GenMaj. Lorenz, tried desperately to retain the core of his fighting units. He was forced to watch as his veteran fighting force, whose strength was mutual trust, was completely torn apart. He tried with all the means at his disposal to make up for the transferred units with new formations, also to have the lost third battalions reformed. In this he succeeded only partially in the Pz.Gren.Div. GD.

The entire reorganization of the divisions and the panzer corps took place under considerable time constraints, consequently the older, badly battered units were unable to grow together again.

The reorganization of the *Brandenburg* Division into a panzergrenadier division, which was initiated by a top secret order dated 13 September 1944, was carried out from mid-September by a reorganization staff under the direction of Hptm. Witauscheck and his assistant Lt. Biske. The reorganization staff was initially based at Baden near Vienna, from where the units received directives for reorganization as soon as they arrived from their respective areas of operation. This proceeded especially rapidly in the case of the 4th Regiment, which was renamed *Jäger-Rgt. 1* of the Pz.Gren.Div. BR, and also of the Pz.Stu.Pi.Btl. BR. The majority of the personnel of the former 2.Rgt. BR had been killed during the breakthrough near Belgrade; the survivors joined with 1. Rgt. BR near Esseg, Hungary to form a Kampfgruppe *Brandenburg*.

The Pz.A.A. BR (armored reconnaissance battalion) was formed at Wildflecken; the headquarters of the Pz.Art.Rgt. BR (armored artillery regiment) was established at Baden while its I. Abt. (or II. Abt.?) was sent to East Prussia and consisted entirely of releases from the former A.R. 73. There were three batteries each with four guns (light field howitzers). The planned II. Abt. (or I. Abt.?) existed solely on paper; neither personnel nor guns were available at the time of formation. III./Pz.Art. BR under the command of Hptm. Spielvogel consisted of the headquarters battery, one 100-mm cannon battery and two light field howitzer batteries, the bulk of which came from the Pz.Art.Ers.Abt. Guben (armored artillery replacement battalion).

Seen overall, the composition of the former *Brandenburg* Division was planned in such a way that the newly-formed units were concentrated in the area directly north of Rastenburg, while the area of Wiener Neustadt and Baden bei Wien with the reorganization staff served mainly to take in the regiments arriving from the southeast area. The former 3. Rgt. BR, which from about March 1944 was in action in the area around Fiume-Trieste and which later fought as a mountain unit in the Italian Alps, was not released from Italy by the Commander-in-Chief Italy, *Generalfeldmarschall* Kesselring. Instead, after the reorganization order was issued, its personnel were shared out among mountain divisions and the Kesselring Machine-gun Battalion. Thus, with few exceptions, the bulk of the 3. Rgt. BR never did come under the command of the *Panzerkorps GD*.

After being relieved by the returning I./Pz.Rgt. GD in November 1944, I./Pz.Rgt. 26—known to have been under the GD's orders in the Jassy and Targul Frumos area—was transferred first to Hungary, then was moved to Germany to reform and reequip with Panthers. As such it became I./Pz.Rgt. *Brandenburg* under the command of Hptm. Graf Rothkirch. On its way to the division, however, in the Frankfurt/Oder area it fell into the hands of the Pz.Gren.Div. *Kurmark*, another GD unit which was fighting there, and remained with it until the end of the war as *Ausführungs*-Abt./Pz.Rgt. *Kurmark* (BR).

Since about July 1944 the Pz.Abt. z.b.V. 12 (special purpose Panzer battalion) had been the only panzer battalion in the area of *Oberkommando Serbien* and saw action at many localities there. In August 1944 it was renamed II./Pz.Rgt. *Brandenburg* on order of the OKH and roughly in November 1944 was to be sent to the reorganized Pz.Gren. Div. BR. This II./Pz.Rgt. BR had no tanks at that time, however, so that the transfer took place on paper only.

This battalion was reformed at Grafenwöhr at the end of 1944 and was equipped with Panthers. It subsequently tried with all means to reach its division, the Pz.Gren.Div. BR, however this did not happen. When the end came the battalion was in the Hohen Tauen—as II./Pz.Rgt. BR.

Organization:

Commander	Major Waldeck
Adjutant	Hptm. Noeres
Signals Officer	Oblt. Schilken
Abt. V-k	Hptm. Broy
Abt. IVa	Oberzahlm. Wulff
HQ Comp.	Hptm. von Kardorff
4. Kp.	Oblt. Albrecht
5. Kp.	Oblt. Möllmann
6. Kp.	Hptm. Fischer

Workshop Comp. Lt. Hayn

As stated, the two *Jäger* Regiments, which were designated *Jäger-Rgt.* 1 and *Jäger-Rgt.* 2, formed the core of the Pz.Gren.Div. *Brandenburg*. Their first commanders were:

Jäger-Rgt. 1   Oberst von Brückner
Jäger-Rgt. 2   Obstlt. Oesterwitz

Here, in detail, the organization of *Jäger-Rgt.* 2:

Rgt. Commander: Obstlt. Oesterwitz
Rgt. Adj.   Hptm. Vincenz
I./Jäg.Rgt. 2
Commander   Hptm. Steidl
1.-3. (Jäg) Kp. – each with:
    1 assault platoon with 3 squads
    1 platoon with 2 MG 42
    1 sniper squad
    1 anti-tank squad (Ofenrohr = Panzerschreck)
4. (hvy. flat trajectory) Kp. – with:
    1 heavy machine-gun platoon
    1 platoon 75-mm Pak
    1 platoon 20-mm flak (SP)
5. (hvy. high-angle fire) Kp. – with:
    2 platoons 80-mm mortars
    1 platoon 120-mm mortar
II. Btl./Jäg.Rgt. 2
Commander   Major Renner
6.-8. (Jäg.) Kp. – each with:
    1 assault platoon with 3 squads
    1 platoon with 2 MG 42
    1 sniper squad
    1 anti-tank squad (Ofenrohr)
9. (hvy. flat trajectory) Kp. with:
    1 heavy machine-gun platoon
    1 platoon 75-mm Pak
    1 platoon 20-mm flak (SP)
10 (hvy. high-angle fire) Kp. with:
    2 platoons 80-mm mortars
    1 platoon 120-mm mortars

One supply company per battalion.

There were wide variations in the allocation of vehicles. When II. Btl. entrained at least half of all its vehicles were unserviceable. I Battalion's non-commissioned officers and enlisted men came in part from the remnants of the former I./2. (Jäg.) Rgt. BR as well as from the Fsch.Jäg.Btl. BR (parachute battalion) and replacements.

II. Btl. was formed mainly from the former II./3. Rgt. BR and minor elements of the former III./2. (Jäg.) Rgt. BR. The bulk of the latter formation went to the newly-established 8. Kp./II./Jäg.Rgt. 2.

There were supply companies only for the two battalions of Jäg.Rgt. 2; each of these contained the trains of the combat companies of a single battalion. The leader of each supply company was also deputy battalion commander of his respective battalion.

In addition there were the regimental companies, of which the 11. (IG.) Kp. (infantry guns) and the 12. (Pi.) Kp. (combat engineers) should be mentioned.

Containing light and heavy batteries, the H.Flak.-Art.Abt. BR (army flak artillery battalion) emerged from the H.Flak.-Art.Abt. 280 and in August 1944 was sent to *Brandenburg* in the Batschka.

The Pz.Stu.Pi.Btl. BR (armored assault pioneer battalion) was formed at Baden bei Wien, commander Hptm. Müller-Rochholz. The battalion consisted of:

Btl. HQ	
1. Kp.	Oblt. Bank (KIA)
	Lt. Hertkorn (KIA)
	Oblt. Schlosser
3. (gep.) Kp.	Oblt. Laurenz
	Lt. Prieß
Supply Comp.	Hptm. Michaelis
Armored Bridging Column	Oblt. Hasper

Total battalion strength approximately 400 men.

In detail, the battalion was organized into three pioneer platoons and one heavy machine-gun platoon in the first two companies, while the third company was made up of three pioneer platoons and one heavy mortar platoon.

The bringing together of the two divisions in the area north of Rastenburg near Sensburg under the direct command of the Pz.Korps GD ultimately also served to get to know the senior officers and to coordinate mutual intentions. A solstice celebration near Lötzen, which brought together all of the elements of both divisions, was another means to this end. There was also an exchange of officers. For example, the commander of the Pz.Gren.Div. BR was former commander of the Pz.Gren.Ers.Brig. GD and former regimental commander of the Pz.Füs.Rgt. GD, GenMaj. Schulte-Heuthaus, but his Ia was a long-time *Brandenburger*. On the other hand a large number of Jäger from the former *Brandenburg* Division now served in the Pz.Gren.Div. GD, while the former *Brandenburgers* Oblt. Säuberlich and *Major* Plitt led the Korps-Begl.Kp. and II./Pz.Korps-Füs.Rgt. GD respectively.

In order to outwardly identify membership in both units, the Pz.Gren.Div. *Brandenburg* took as its tactical emblem a white steel helmet with the red Brandenburg Eagle. The *Brandenburg* Division was awarded a "*Brandenburg*" cuff band, but the GD insignia was carried on the shoulder boards or straps.

All in all, the time was much too short to weld both units together. Nevertheless, both divisions demonstrated a high fighting morale in the next months even though they never had the opportunity to fight together on one front under one command.

Chapter 2
The Replacement Units

The enormous personnel transfers for the establishment of the Führer-Grenadier and Führer-Begleit Brigades, the expansion of the guard unit in Berlin into the Wach-Regiment-Großdeutschland as of 1 November 1944, and finally making good the losses in the continuing, heavy fighting involving the Pz.Gren.Div. GD placed such demands on the Panzer-Grenadier Replacement Training Brigade Großdeutschland that it was forced to expand its existing companies, establish new replacement units and bring in additional replacements. As well there were increasing numbers of convalescents arriving from hospitals, for whom convalescent and training companies had to be formed in the area around Cottbus and Guben.

In order to make the urgently needed replacements available for the GD units and facilitate their selection for special missions, roughly in November 1944 the *Großdeutschland* Military Camp was established at Gorleben/Elbe near Dannenberg by experienced members of the Pz.Gren.Ersatz-Brigade GD in cooperation with the Reich Youth leadership. Camp leader was Lt. Kalb, formerly of the Pz.Rgt. GD, while his assistants and instructors included Obfw. Rapp, likewise of the Pz.Rgt. GD, Fw. Lehmann of the Wach-Rgt. GD, and Fw. Jaster of the Pz.Füs.Rgt. GD. In this camp, which consisted of labor service barracks, sixteen- and seventeen-year-old youths eligible for military service received pre-military training. Since volunteerism was still valued in the GD units even at this time, efforts were made in this way to convince youth to serve in the GD units.

With about ten instructors from every possible weapons specialty the youths were familiarized with military service based on experience in courses of eight weeks. The training was done with the fact in mind that the students were primarily children, who viewed the training more as sport and games than bitter seriousness. Nevertheless, many of the participants from the east took the training rather more seriously. In spite of the late stage of the war the food in this youth camp was excellent and the atmosphere in the barracks was a friendly one.

At the end of each course boys who had volunteered for service in the GD units were selected to proceed to Cottbus.

In January 1945 the camp was relocated to massive buildings in Buxtehude, where the training continued. The basic training plan consisted of small arms firing, field exercises, small tactical problems, initial infantry training and light athletics. Joint outings, visits to movie theaters and social evenings provided relief from the routine of training and diversion for the participants, many of whom were worried about their relatives in the east. In March 1945 *Oberfeldwebel* Rapp assumed command of the camp and led it until the surrender. Scarcely four weeks later there followed reorganization into a Volkssturm company and transfer to Wesermünde. Out of a sense of responsibility toward the youths Obfw. Rapp disbanded the company before the surrender and released the boys to return home. Only the soldiers were assigned to the 16th Panzer-Grenadier Division, where they remained until the end of the war.

Toward the end of 1944 the Pz.Gren.Ersatz-Brigade GD received a not insignificant addition to its strength when the *Lehr-Regiment Brandenburg*, which was based at Grain, Upper Styria was placed under its command. The *Lehr-Regiment Brandenburg* had been formed at Grain in March 1944, initially with two battalions.

Regimental commander at this time was *Major* Martin, who was relieved by *Major* Pinkert roughly in July 1944. He was followed by *Major* von Goerne. At this time the unit was expanded into a regiment with a total of four battalions, resulting in the following organization by the end of the year:

I./Lehr-Rgt. BR   1.-4. Kp.
II. Btl.   5.-8. Kp.
III. Btl.   9.-12. Kp.
IV. Btl.   13.-16. Kp

plus: 17. and 18. Kp. and 1.-2. Genes.Kp./Lehr-Rgt. BR (convalescent company).

II. Btl.'s command positions were as follows:

II./Lehr-Rgt. BR
Btl. C.O.   Hptm. von Einem-Josten
Adj.   Lt. Ullmann, Lt. Mohrmann
Btl. Med. Officer   Oberarzt Dr. Fischer
Bases:
   Until July 1944 Admont, Styria
   From July 1944 St. Veit, Oberkrain
5. Kp.   Oblt. Gutweniger
6. Kp.   Oblt. Grüber, Lt. Fuchs
7. Kp.   Oblt. Weidmann
8. Kp.   Oblt. Gruber, Oblt. Haut

The training was such that after the recruits were taken in they proceeded with normal infantry and field training, after which the various companies were trained for their special roles in mountain exercises. The companies of II Battalion were sent into action against partisans in the second half of 1944.

In the course of the integration of the Pz.Gren.Div. *Brandenburg* the

Lehr-Rgt. *Brandenburg* was also placed under the command of the Pz.Gren.Ersatz-Brigade GD at Cottbus. At the turn of the year 1944-45 *Major* Petereit and Oblt. Brock were dispatched to the regimental command post in Veldes, Oberkrain, north of Yugoslavia, in order to make preparations for the takeover of the Lehr-Rgt. *Brandenburg*. Only I./Lehr-Rgt. BR was taken over at first, however, and it was sent by rail to Cottbus; the remaining elements of the Lehr-Rgt. *Brandenburg* remained in their quarters and were later placed under the command of Obstlt. Schwarzrock. I./Lehr-Rgt. BR arrived at Cottbus at the beginning of January 1945 and was initially quartered in the Alvensleben Barracks, before the bulk of it was finally sent to the front as part of the operation to reinforce the Pz.Korps GD's front-line units. A small percentage of the men remained at Cottbus as instructors, others were transferred to the Ausb.Btl. *Brandenburg* (training battalion) at Brandenburg-Havel.

This Ausb.Btl. *Brandenburg*, formerly the *Brandenburg* Home Headquarters, included almost 2,500 men in its training, convalescent and trained replacement companies and was housed in the *General-Feldzeugmeister* Barracks. This increase in personnel was mainly due to the steady flow of *Luftwaffe* and *Marine* personnel being sent for retraining as infantrymen but also to the flow of returning convalescents, etc. In addition to replacements for the front-line forces, which benefited both divisions of the Pz.Korps. GD, personnel were also assigned to the Wach-Rgt. GD in Berlin.

At the beginning of 1945 Hptm. Schewe of the Pz.Gren.Ers.Brig. GD was named to command this training battalion and he would lead it until the end of the war. The last intake of recruits took place at the end of February 1945. In March 1945—at the time of the unification with the Pz.Gren.Ers.Brig. GD in Schleswig—the former Ausb.Btl. *Brandenburg* was renamed III. (*Brandenburg*)/Pz.Gren.E.u.A.Rgt. GD (panzer-grenadier replacement and training regiment). It consisted of the 9th-12th Training Companies, special purpose training company, 1st-2nd Conversion Companies and trained replacement company.

The men of the Pz.Gren.Div. *Brandenburg* played a significant role in the success of the *Panzerkorps* GD. Coming from an entirely different milieu, prepared for special missions during the years of the division's existence, in the course of their few months as members of the Pz.Korps GD they became a valuable part of the overall formation.

Part II
The History of Panzer-Grenadier Division Brandenburg

Whoever assigned the name *Brandenburg* for this formation and how this designation ever came to be will probably never be known. One fact remains, however—a more appropriate name could not have been found.

After the war the state of Prussia was chopped up by the victorious powers out of fear of its historical tradition, however the idea of Brandenburg survived. It was the cradle of that Prussia which made our German fatherland a great power in the world, the home of the great family which would then find its way into a new German empire. The contemporaries of the Great Elector spoke of arrogance when his armed merchantmen and frigates carried the white eagle on a white field over the world's oceans in defiance of the sea powers of the day. And they could not suspect that two centuries later the descendants of those who had been stranded far away from home would join together under the same flag beneath which their fathers had once served. For the *Bau-Lehr-Bataillon Brandenburg z.b.V. 800*, which subsequently evolved into a regiment and a division, became the symbol of the great German family whose sons streamed back to the homeland to stand by it in its time of need and protect the cradle of their ancestors. Germans from all over the world came together beneath the red eagle of this unit to risk their blood and lives in a struggle unprecedented in world history.

If one entered the *Brandenburg*'s non-commissioned officer's mess or enlisted men's canteen and closed his eyes for a moment, one might have thought himself in an international coffee house in a large city. All languages were spoken there—English, French, Spanish, Portuguese, many dialects of Arabic, Swahili, Japanese, just to name a few. Of course German was also heard among them. The foreign Germans were not reproached for speaking among themselves in the languages they had grown up with. All professions were also represented. The bank director from Madrid sat next to the settler from Palestine, the factory worker from the States next to the farmer from former German East Africa, the wood cutter from Canada next to the painter from Japan.

The distinguishing features were the *Brandenburger*'s own, however: their German origins, their field gray uniform and the fact that they were volunteers. They had been investigated for their special qualifications at the induction centers where they volunteered, and then if they exhibited the skills that were being sought and also met the physical requirements they were assigned to this unit. There were many remarkable reunions there. The forty-year-old clerk from Buenos Aires suddenly came across one of his younger employees, who because of some successful weapons exercise or because he had come across the great water several months earlier already wore the braid of an non-commissioned officer or the shoulder boards of an officer. There were many other such examples.

It is not surprising that the active officer and the career officer were rather lost in this hodgepodge of a unit; for the getting-together of the recruit-clerk and his lieutenant-employee after duty in the city for a bottle of wine or a glass of beer to talk over old times, with the younger sometimes even picking up the tab, was neither prevented nor discouraged. The atmosphere during daily duties was also rather more relaxed than in the rest of the army. This in no way means that we are dealing with an undisciplined wild herd with only a minimum of training. That was certainly not the case, indeed one could claim the opposite. The intended special missions demanded special training, which in many cases surpassed that of the normal units and placed far greater mental and physical demands on the soldiers than was usually the case. And discipline was entirely comparable to that of the elite units of the army. Seen purely ideally, it could be rated even higher, for it was based on volunteerism. Only the tone was different—the "service" was absent. It was rough, but honest, and one nevertheless had a fine feeling for the now necessary boundaries. It must also be stated here, however, that it was because of the commanders and officer corps that this potential problem never became a real problem.

The concept of life and death held by the *Brandenburgers* was also different than that found elsewhere. They lacked the problematic seriousness with which this question was approached elsewhere in Germany. Thanks to their fundamental understanding of the outside world they were perhaps more deeply aware of the importance of the decisive struggle than the majority of their countrymen, and they also saw the ultimate outcome approaching sooner and more clearly than they. Their sense of duty to the bitter end and their volunteerism should also be rated higher. Nonetheless they approached war and battle less from a military than a sporting aspect, and they were thus made for their special missions—or vice versa, depending on one's point of view. The regiments of the *Brandenburg* Division were the first to learn conventional combat as fought by normal units, if one may put it that way. The combat missions of the first *Brandenburgers* lay in another sector and the accounts of these and their effects today fill many filing cabinets of the intelligence services and other intelligence organizations or of war archives.

The special missions unit described here was certainly not without parallels. England, for example, raised a unit for fast attack operations, the so-called commandos, which consisted of picked troops and which received extensive and varied training for special operations. Unlike the German special unit, however, this British unit was known to the public and was anchored in the consciousness of the general forces. The members of the commandos were picked from the ranks of the regular troops, and after a certain time they also returned there. They enjoyed a high reputation in the army and among the public as daring lone fighters, while the *Brandenburgers* were little known among the regular troops or the German public.

Theirs was a battle employing the element of surprise and military stratagems, and their missions included actions directly behind the enemy front and in the home country of the enemy. Using the tools provided by standard military training alone, they would not have got far. There was more to it, since in most cases the use of weapons was not only unadvisable but even foolish. While battle was the means by which normal troops reached their objective, in the case of the *Brandenburgers* the means consisted of more or less sporting outmaneuvering and deceiving of the enemy. Two things emerge from: on the one hand the *Brandenburgers* were feared and—depending on the mentality of the nation—even hated by the enemy, while on the other they were also acknowledged on account of their accomplishments. A French officer once said of them, "*C'étaient des as!*", while a British officer said, "They were damned good sports!"

Death on the battlefield, the result of the blind chance of an impacting shell or spray fire from an automatic weapon, the mass death on the open battlefield in sight of comrades and superiors was for them a concept which they had to deal with during the course of certain missions—but it was not the norm for them. The death they had to deal with was no turn of fate; for them it meant their own failure or betrayal by a third party, the same for their enemy. To a certain degree they found a personal relationship with Father Hein, the ultimate expression of which was to outmaneuver him to the extent possible while carrying out their assigned mission. And when it happened some of them may have gone down with the words "*Mec toub*" (it is written) on their lips, an indication that they had adopted the beliefs of Oriental or African peoples after their long association with them.

One word, perhaps, may be dedicated to the political attitude of these men who came together under the *Brandenburg* banner. One can confidently leave it to one word—and that was: German. Unconditionally German, perhaps more unconditionally than elsewhere, where this word was mainly associated with party-political concepts. Here a party town leader stood beside a social-democrat from San Francisco, the German nationalist from Tokyo beside the catholic organizer from Rio de Janeiro. They all proudly wore the emblem of the blockade runner on their gray tunics, which had been awarded them because they had broken through the enemy's blockade in times of greatest urgency. Few words were spoken about their attitude toward the regime. And why should they have! They all knew why they had come—and that was enough. For them and the others too.

And so the *Brandenburgers* were actually a community before they were brought together in a unit; and this also explains why this particular unit of volunteers thrown together from all over the world could carry out missions which were beyond other formations. They wrote the name *Brandenburg* with large letters in the book of the history of the Second World War, and those of their opponents who were capable of a clear and factual assessment free of chauvinistic hate came to admit that they were fair and good sports, that they exhibited the virtues which were universally associated with the good soldier and lay in the tradition of the name that they bore. For the characteristic Prussian diligence and honor, which for many years were known around the world as typical German qualities, also had their origins in the Brandenburg cradle of the great Germany which we all preserve in our hearts today.

This spirit of the *Brandenburgers* also enabled them to survive the gloomy and demoralizing years after the total collapse and in spite of all dismemberment will live on as long as a red eagle on a white field is shown and as long as men extend their hands with the greeting that has lasted for centuries:

"Good *Brandenburg* here always"

Chapter 1
Brandenburg z.b.V. 800

The question of the justification of the use of camouflage to approach targets, as employed in many forms by the *Brandenburgers* as well as by the commandos and the special forces of other states, has already been dealt with in the literature of the postwar period.

It is acknowledged in the modern literature on international law outside Germany and in the findings of the Allied tribunal after the Second World War that the camouflaged approach to enemy objects does not represent an offense against Article 23 of the Hague Land Warfare Convention. A German publication[1] has the following to say about this area concerning the Hague Land Warfare Convention:

"The mission of the commando does not permit him to conduct offensive operations in enemy uniform, however he may seize important objects in the enemy's rear, such as bridges, bottlenecks and oil refineries, without fighting, defend them against enemy attack and prevent them from being destroyed.

The commando may only use the enemy's uniform to penetrate into enemy territory without fighting and to approach the target. If they become involved in combat they must identify themselves as German soldiers before opening fire.

Commandos who act according to these rules are not committing a breach of international law. This follows from an analogous use in naval warfare, according to which it is not against the rules for a warship to initially hide its nationality by flying a false flag and only raising its own flag immediately before opening fire.

Commandos captured in enemy uniforms are therefore only considered spies if they conduct intelligence gathering in them. Furthermore, if they have engaged in combat operations—for example opening fire—while in these uniforms they are guilty of war crimes and can be judged accordingly. But if they have used the enemy uniforms neither for intelligence gathering purposes nor in combat but only to approach their assigned targets, if captured they should be treated as prisoners of war.[2]

---

[1] From: Dr. Hans Erasmus. *Der Geheime Nachrichtendienst* (The Secret Intelligence Service), Musterschmidt Verlag, Göttingen.

[2] From: Dr. Paul Leverkuehn. *Der Geheime Nachrichtendienst* (The Secret Intelligence Service), Verlag für Wehrwesen Bernhard & Graefe, Frankfurt/Main

The *Abwehr II* must be seen as the initiator for the formation of the first *Brandenburg* units. The practical idea for this probably originated from *Hauptmann* Dr. von Hippel, an old colonial officer from East Africa and comrade of *General* von Lettow-Vorbeck in the First World War. He envisioned using detachments of versatile fighters—not part of conventional units—for so-called "free chase" missions. The *Abwehr* chief Canaris seized upon these plans, but turned to a conventionally-organized unit.

The result was the first unit of volunteer soldiers, all of whom had to speak foreign languages perfectly, for extraordinary missions. Even when the first unit was expanded it remained under the direct command of the *Chef Abwehr II*. The purpose of this direct command was to make it easier and faster to answer questions about its status as a special unit than in the general unit hierarchy. It must be stressed emphatically that this was the unit's sole connection to the *Abwehr*. The missions carried out by the *Brandenburgers* had nothing to do with special *Abwehr* missions.

The first unit, which consisted mainly of Sudeten-German linguists and other eastern Germans, was formed in autumn 1939. Its first official designation was: *1.Bau-Lehr-Kompanie "Deutsche Kompanie" z.b.V.* (1st Construction Instruction Company "German Company" for Special Missions)

15 October 1939 must be accepted as the date of establishment. The reason behind this action was the notion that standardized training for men engaged in special missions was a requirement for success. As much importance was placed in acquiring men with flawless characters as in training them in the use of the tools of the combat engineer. The ability to speak a foreign language was a requirement. What the unit's creators had in mind was not operations as spies or adventurers in uniforms, but volunteer soldiers for extraordinary missions. And so they consciously drew a clear line between them and the agent in civilian clothes whose mission was espionage. These were later combined into a special unit, the *Kurfürst Regiment*.

The choice to designate the unit stationed at Brandenburg/Havel under Lt. Grabert as a construction instruction company was entirely logical. For among its cadre personnel there were numerous combat engineers who were fully versed in the use of explosives and target reconnaissance. The combination of these combat engineers with the volunteer linguists trained for independent action ultimately produced a group of men who would come to occupy a very unique position in military history under the title *Brandenburger*.

In the last days of 1939 this construction instruction company was expanded to the degree that the formation of a second company was necessary. Finally, at the beginning of January 1940, the units housed in the General-Feldzeugmeister Barracks in Brandenburg/Havel were combined into the *Bau-Lehr-Bataillon z.b.V. 800* under the command of Hptm. Dr.

von Hippel. He was the same one who had only partly succeeded in pushing through his ideas on the formation of a unit for special missions. But he was a man who placed daring above all. His words:

"You are to be a gang of robbers, with which one can fetch the devil from hell."

soon became a motivating factor for all the actions by these men. The battalion initially consisted of two companies with the following designations:

(1.) Bau-Lehr-Kompanie z.b.V. 800   Lt. Grabert
(2.) Bau-Lehr-Kompanie z.b.V. 800   Hptm. Fabian

In addition to training, which only occupied a secondary role anyway, the men were given their first missions, more akin to fantasy than something from the manual. For example, several of them were to acquire the fingerprints of Brandenburg's chief of police as an exercise, which they in fact succeeded in doing. Missions such as this were carried out using every possible trick. One *Leutnant* organized a live hand grenade duel on Lake Quenz—to harden the men under difficult conditions, as he put it—luckily without injury.

The first parachute training using a Junkers W 34 was carried out at Spandau near Berlin, and in no case were safety concerns paramount. Fw. Löber's parachute hung upon the machine as he attempted to jump from the hatch. The pilot brought the aircraft low over the Silo Canal near Brandenburg. Löber finally landed in the water without his parachute, dropping from a height of 100 meters. He set a fine example by reporting for the next practice flight still in his wet clothing and making the jump.

The *2. Bau-Lehr-Kompanie* was initially built around a number of Reich Germans as cadre personnel plus Romanian-Germans from Transylvania and the Banat; there then followed Baltic Germans who had resettled in the Warthe District (formerly part of Poland). These were initially recruited by Fw. Sorgenfrey and were brought to Brandenburg in the early days of 1940. *2. Kompanie* also included several Sudeten Germans and German volunteers from Palestine.

Most of the special training was conducted on the "Quenz Estate", an estate farm near the unit's base at Brandenburg, where the so-called "Witch's Kitchen" was also located. There the men learned to fabricate explosives from readily available materials such as flour, powdered sugar, potash and so on. Another part of the training took place on the pioneer land training ground at Brandenburg, which was used mainly to practice approaching targets and destroying them. The numerous bridges over the Havel were also especially well-suited for this purpose.

All in all, there was created in Brandenburg a unit whose members were unique in their daring as in their boldness, their many stratagems and their knowledge of many foreign lands and the customs of their inhabitants. Its members possessed a generous portion of personal daring which

2. Regiment "BR" z.b.V. 800

made it possible for them to prove themselves in situations where they had only themselves to rely on. Their special missions did not take place in the spotlight of large-scale military actions; their battle was that of the small, mobile band which struck with the element of surprise.

Their emblem consisted of a snake and a sword. They were the unit which employed deception in its actions and the rapid strike.

When Hitler made the decision in January 1940 to carry out a surprise landing in Norway ("Operation Weserübung") plus the occupation of Denmark, which was seen as necessary to secure Germany's contacts with the north, it was the *Brandenburgers* who were probably the first to set foot on Norwegian and Danish soil. On 9 April 1940 a platoon of *Brandenburgers* occupied the bridge over the Grossen Belt in order to take this vital strategic object intact. When "Operation Widar", the attack on Norway, began, *Brandenburgers* had long been in the country when the main invasion force approached the coast.

Most of these early missions were individual actions. They were prepared by the *Abwehr II* and carried out by detachments consisting of single squads to reinforced companies depending on the importance of the object. These were not units in the conventional sense, instead they were put together to match their circumstances. Each detachment, always named after its leader, consisted of linguists, explosives bearers, weapons specialists and men familiar with the local area.

Even while several groups were in action, in Brandenburg preparations were being made to bolster the *Bau-Lehr-Bataillon z.b.V. 800*. The large number of men streaming in, plus the large number of expected missions, led to the expansion to four companies.

The battalion's composition, in this case roughly in March 1940, was as follows:

Bau-Lehr-Bataillon z.b.V. 800

Base: Brandenburg/Havel, Gen.-Feldzeugmeister Barracks

1. to 4. Kompanien

As well, an increasing number of officers were joining the unit, usually attracted by friends already serving there.

24

As early as February-March 1940 the preparations for *"Fall Gelb"* (Case Yellow), war against France, were involving a considerable portion of the *Bau-Lehr-Bataillon z.b.V. 800*. They were closely associated with the *z.b.V. Bataillon 100*, which would have to carry out similar missions. The *Brandenburgers* were to carry out four operations during the course of *"Fall Gelb"*:

Elements of the 3. Kp. were to capture the bridges over the Maas near Massyk intact and hold them until the arrival of German forces.

Elements of the 2. Kp., in particular the 1st Platoon, were to capture the Gennep Bridge intact and hold it until the subsequent capture of the Peel positions.

A further company, the 4. Kp., was order to capture the bridges over the Juliana Canal. These were located at Berg, Urmond, Obicht, Stein, and near the city of Sittard.

The platoon led by Fw. Eggers—under the cover designation Bau-und Lehr-Stab z.b.V. 800 and directly subordinated to Headquarters, VI Army Corps and its 24. I.D.—was to capture intact objects along the Westwall on the border with Luxembourg.

Also set in motion was another mission by a platoon of *Brandenburgers* against the Rhine bridges near Arnhem; this failed, however, because of false statements by Dutch V-men.

The objective of all of these missions by the *Brandenburgers* was the early capture of decisive objects which were to be kept intact until the arrival of German units and thus spare the blood and lives of the attacking German units. Surprise was decisive in each of these missions. The following accounts were provided by men who participated in them directly:

Feldwebel W. Stöhr: the bridges of Gennep by I Platoon/2. Kp.

Unteroffizier Janowski: the bridges near Newport, Belgium by Lt. Grabert's platoon.

The Bridges of Gennep

In mid-February 1940 we changed positions from Brandenburg to the Reichswald between Goch and the village of Asperden on the Rhine. We were completely sealed off, the troops were not allowed out, live training with the sole purpose of preparing us for our mission with the greatest precision. Personnel strength approximately sixty men.

An approximate knowledge of the targets was available from aerial reconnaissance photos, allowing suitable mock-up bunkers to be built. Every single man was familiarized and trained on these down to the last detail. All of our exercises were carried out with live ammunition. Furthermore there was systematic training in the silent approach, which many were ultimately able to do with Indian-like skill. The sharpness of this training exceeded that given to most units by a wide margin; tests of courage were also demanded.

Admiral Canaris, who visited us twice, personally convinced himself of our level of training, allowing him to draw a picture of or general readiness for action. Finding this to be outstanding, he at once donated 200 Reichsmark to the company fund, which of course made a great impression.

The unit itself consisted exclusively of men from the Sudetenland and Upper Silesia, only a few non-commissioned officers from Berlin and some from the Rhineland.

Then, shortly before the start of the war, we were joined by several Dutchmen, so-called Mussert people. A total of about four to five such operations were planned and in some cases carried out at this time.

9 May 1940: Alarm! It was initiated by a code-word, whereupon our actions began. The war in the west became a war of movement. At about 22:00 hours the individual squads set off in the direction of the border.

Our mission team consisted of nine men.

Equipment: we Germans wore our Wehrmacht uniform, but with a coat, which was worn unbuttoned, and no belt. Beneath the coats, jammed into our armpits, we carried the submachine-guns. Egg- and stick-type hand grenades were hidden somewhere in our pockets, pistols in our pants pockets; we also had wire cutters.

The three Dutchmen in our team were dressed as policemen of their nation and were openly armed. They had to create the impression that we were prisoners.

At dawn on 10 May 1940 we were lying in cover approximately 700-800 meters from our objective. A brief rest break. The detachment commander once again explained to each man his mission. Just prior to this at the border we had run into a problem: one of the Dutchmen refused to go along. For better or worse we had to leave one man behind to watch this Dutchman, since there was a danger that he might betray us all—understandable from his standpoint.

And now: march! The reality was much different than what we had imagined. The bridge itself, an imposing iron construction, had a length of approximately 150 meters, and it was protected by defensive installations with bunkers and a constant bunker watch of at least platoon strength. Things worked out differently for thus than we anticipated.

But cheekiness prevails, something that was also proven later. The watching Dutchmen spotted us as we approached the bridge. At first we were met at the near end of the bridge by four Dutchmen. They obviously thought that we were prisoners. Anyway there were no German troops to be seen far and wide. It was time to act! The detachment commander and his Feldwebel suddenly stuck their pistols in the chest of the sentry at the guard hut. It happened so quickly that no one on the other end of the bridge could realize what was going on. While the Oberleutnant kept the sentry in check, I casually walked the two steps to the guard hut, pulled my knife my heart pounding, and cut all the wires I could reach. I did not see what was meanwhile being played out outside, as I had eyes and ears only for the wires.

Apparently one of the Dutchmen had become suspicious and fired. And so we had our first seriously wounded. We others, however, went across the bridge, while the rest of our detachment remained behind to provide cover.

Halfway across the bridge there was another Dutch sentry, but he presented arms and let us pass.

They met us at the other end of the bridge. There we didn't think our lives were worth a nickel, for almost every Dutchman had his weapon trained on us. But none fired. Then they took us in their midst and transported us in the direction of Holland. We were guarded by nine Dutch soldiers. Suddenly low-flying aircraft attacked our small party. That was our salvation. In the resulting confusion we escaped and disappeared on both sides of the railway embankment which passed nearby. We took up a defensive position, the four of us found our way together again after becoming separated during our escape, and attacked desperately. Three bunkers were taken through tricks, surprise and force of arms, approximately forty Dutch soldiers fell into our hands as prisoners.

This action saved the attacking troops about two days, to say nothing of the possible toll in blood. That same day the bulk of two divisions was able to cross the bridge.

25 May 1940 — Grabert Platoon
Action Against the Bridges near Newport, Belgium

From a war report:

The locks and road bridge of Newport in Belgium, taken by surprise attack on 27 May 1940. A squad led by Lt. Grabert and Uffz. Janowski, who were awarded the Iron Cross, First and Second Class respectively for bravery in the face of the enemy in Holland, succeeded in taking and holding the locks, which were defended by a far superior force. Their destruction had resulted in the flooding of Flanders in 1915."

Two weeks special leave after our Holland mission. The Iron Cross I had been awarded was still hanging on its ribbon, and I was preparing to enjoy the comforts of home, my father's tobacco and wine as well as the dishes prepared with motherly love when a telegram ordering me to return to garrison tore me from seventh heaven.

My conscience was so pure, as only a soldier's can be, and nevertheless I could not dispel an uncomfortable feeling in the pit of my stomach. Usually a well-deserved special leave was only interrupted if unforeseen events had taken place, I thought. Was this event of an official or a personal nature? A sip of my father's Asbach (brandy) now and then during the train ride to Brandenburg soon made me immune to any uncomfortable feeling. My astonishment was great when I was met in the station by a cursing driver from my unit. They had expected me to arrive one train earlier. The officer of the watch sent me to the commander, in whose office I met my platoon leader Lt. Grabert and the battalion adjutant.

"Get going Jano, form a new squad from the men in the barracks. Draw uniforms, weapons and so on and be ready to move out in two hours, understood?"

"Understood sir, ready to move out in two hours!"

Sweating and cursing like a Berserker, as I always did in such cases, I soon found 11 good men, some of whom I knew already, raced with them through all the stockrooms, where we were issued new uniforms and weapons. We had no forms—to the consternation of the supply chiefs. But orders are orders, and two hours was barely enough for such a task. Ten minutes short of two hours and my men were standing before me, puffing, steel helmets at an angle, half dressed and chewing. Not a very pretty picture, but after another five minutes we almost looked like soldiers of an elite unit who were about to carry out a special mission. Lt. Grabert appeared, also swallowing the last bites of his meal, and I reported. He replied: "Stand at ease, you may smoke."

What a joy that first cigarette was after all the rushing around. That was my Grabert, permitting smoking in the ranks.

"Men, we're going to Belgium—I and your squad leader were requested by name. No idea what's up; in any event it's a special mission, that's obvious. We scarcely know each other—but I do know your squad leader and he me, which will do for now. It is probably also your first action. You are members of Brandenburg, and I am certain that you will do your unit proud. I am depending on you and you trust us. Fall out."

The waiting truck took us to the D-train at D-train speed. For the first time we had the new submachine-gun in our hands, and my astonishment was great to discover after disassembling and reassembling this lovely new instrument that it functioned flawlessly; no spring or screw was left over. Half an hour weapons instruction in a reserved compartment and then we went to sleep.

They were expecting us in Ghent and we were driven to a big hotel. We scarcely had a chance to clean up a little when we were fetched by an Oberleutnant and driven to a headquarters, where the circle of officers included our commander. The situation was explained briefly: our troops' advance had been halted before the Newport locks.

The enemy probably intended to blow the locks as he had done in 1915 and flood Flanders.

Mission: prevent the lock from being blown up, seize and hold the Ostende-Newport road and canal bridge.

Not bad, our troops halted—we go through with 11 men!

Partial preparations had been made for our mission. We discovered Belgian uniforms and a Belgian autobus on a small farm outside the city. Each of us was given a coat and a cap with a small tassel. Into the bus, windows down, submachine-guns cocked, safeties on, and off. Just beyond Ostende a large number of Belgian soldiers, some with rifles stacked, some marching east. We slowed down—the others shook their heads as they looked at us. I got out of the bus and *headed for a group of Belgians: "What are you doing here?"*

"How come you don't know? The war is over, the king has surrendered." The war over! The king surrendered? We knew nothing about any of this. And then the Fleming continued: "We Flemings are going home to mother, the Walloons have remained with the English. You are probably one of those who wish to carry on. Well, good luck."

"Where are the English?"

"Newport."

"How many?"

"One company."

"In front of or beyond the bridge?"

"Beyond."

"Bridge already blown?"

"Haven't heard anything yet, but if you don't hurry you will hear it soon, and then you won't get across, for it is already prepared for demolition."

"So?"

"But better if you keep your hands off the locks, for if you blow them up it will bring great catastrophe to Belgium."

I returned to the bus and reported to Lt. Grabert.

We drove through Newport town to just short of the big memorial to King Leopold. Suddenly a few ricochets whizzed through the bus. The vehicle pulled off to the left and we all ran out and took cover. Using our binoculars we could make out an infantry company on the road to Newport-Bad, approximately 900 meters behind and to our right. The road and lock bridges were about 150 meters in front of us. Next to me was a large road marker stone on which I could read:

"Here the German army was stopped in 1915."

To the right of the bridge, 7 to 8 meters before the canal and beyond the bank of the canal, a gully, which, if we reach it, will offer us good cover. One by one we worked our way toward this point—and all arrived safe and sound. The English did not appear to have mortars, otherwise they would have begun firing at us long ago. Their machine-guns did, however, make a murderous racket. It must have been about 19:00 hours; we decided to attack as darkness fell. After much debate we reached the decision that Lt. Grabert and I would cross the road bridge, he left I right, and cut the wires leading to the explosives. Once we reached the other side we would both open fire and, trusting in the famous moment of surprise, give the squad the opportunity to follow. An Unteroffizier, a Belgian specialist who had joined us in Ghent, was to lead the rest of the squad to us. After reaching the other side, with each man changing position frequently, the squad would fire everything it had, lobbing hand grenades at the British lying in position 50 to 60 meters from the other bank; meanwhile the demolition wires were to be completely destroyed. It made no sense to think and plan any further, since our chances of reaching the other side of the canal were very slim. But neither Grabert nor I had many opportunities to think, especially since we knew precisely that even the brave heart begins to tremble with the if and but.

The darkness placed its great camouflage net over us. We pulled our belts tighter, checked weapons and ammunition. The English fired white parachute flares at intervals of three to four minutes. Grabert gave me the signal—go! The short, insulated wire cutters in our right pockets, submachine-guns pushed onto our backs, we crawled toward the bridge. The English kept the bridge under continuous fire. Humming and whistling, the tracer rounds whizzed above our heads. Crawl, crawl, meter by meter. Our equipment hung like lead on our bodies, and I had the feeling as if my limbs must become paralyzed. My hands felt for the demolition wires—nothing! Another parachute flare. Nose in the dirt, glance to the left—Grabert was level with me—and between us, who knows how he got there, a dead German Unteroffizier with his motorcycle, still pointing toward home, riddled by a thousand bullets, smeared with blood. Before this parachute flare burned out I made out the ignition wires at the edge of the bridge's pedway. It was a new moon and one could not see the hand in front of one' face. I placed my helmet on my wire cutters and raised it slowly, in order to determine at what height I could move without being hit. For in order to reach the wires I had to get to the pedway, which was about 15 cm higher. When my lower arm was raised vertical from the elbow there was a ping and my helmet spun on the tip of the cutters like a carousel. That was 30 cm, high enough to avoid getting shot, for which I did not feel the least desire. My faithful wire cutters went click and an ignition wire was gone. If only Grabert had found his wire too! When the next parachute flare went up he called to me, "have it!" The danger of a trip to heaven was not gone yet, however, for these wires undoubtedly led only to the charge in the socket, which we had already left behind us. Oh cursed fear! Did we still have a chance, even if the opposite end of the bridge went up? This and a thousand other thoughts shot through my brain while I had to lie quietly and wait for the parachute flare to burn out. At the same time we reached the end of the bridge, which now began to drop. No parachute flare now or they must see us. I let myself roll right toward the bank of the canal and lay close to the foundation, in which the second charge must be installed. Suddenly I was able to pray: dear God, one more tiny moment—I'll be done. And he granted me that moment. I had the wires in my hand, and once again my cutters went click. At the same instant a spark shot from the severed wire—they had tried to set off the charges. Lt. Grabert also seemed to have found his line and cut it, for the bridge was standing. No explosion, no trip to heaven!

The English were sitting in the houses opposite; one could see the muzzle flashes clearly. I had taken aim at the muzzle flashes and waited for Grabert's first shot. Nothing! Suddenly he was lying beside me, gasping: "submachine-gun jammed with dirt, fire alone!"

My cannon opened up—continuous fire. One magazine after another, while Grabert caused a hellish racket with his hand grenades. The enemy fire ceased abruptly, which was the signal for the squad to follow. Shouting fierce battle cries they stormed across the bridge—and all made it safely. The enemy had meanwhile regained his composure and raked us with his machine-guns. Seldom have I experienced such heavy fire. Behind me the bullets rang off a metal object; I turned around cautiously and directly behind me saw the base of a lamppost, about 30 cm in diameter.

Our machine-gun was still not firing. As it was positioned close beside me I crawled over to see why Gute wasn't firing. The butt of the machine-gun was lying on his shoulder, the muzzle in the dirt. The noise was too much for my young comrade. I pushed him away from the gun, took the safety off and fired. It barked twice and then jammed. Meanwhile the others were busy changing positions, and repeatedly our weapons fired from various locations. The Tommies must have thought they were facing a German company. From all sides our hand grenades flew toward the enemy machine-gun nests, until the enemy fire suddenly ceased.

The order was given to assemble at the bridge. From all sides they came creeping along the bank of the canal to the bridge.

The enemy seemed to have fled. We cut all the cables we could find at the bridge and then marched off to a corner house which was close to the canal.

While Grabert set up his temporary command post there, a Gefreiter and I went back to the lock gates, whose ignition wires we had cut. On the way back to the command post I suddenly heard the sound of motors, which I was sure I had not heard before. Tanks? Damn it—against them we were powerless. Was everything to come to nothing now, after our surprise attack had succeeded? My comrade had a hand grenade cluster with him. I took it and crept toward the sound of the engine. I had to be within ten meters. But the tank was stationary, not moving. I counted to three and then raced toward the monster with my hand grenade cluster. At the last minute I realized that it was an English ambulance. They had probably started its engine to cover their retreat.

The hellish noise of the fighting had ceased. Only from the interior of the city, several hundred meters away, were the English machine-guns still firing at us. We had succeeded, and although the danger was far from over we felt safe. But with the feeling of safety our over-stressed nerves made their presence felt. In the darkness of the command post the glowing cigarettes held in trembling fingers came to light like fireflies. Suddenly there was a huge crash in the cellar—as if a beer wagon full of bottles had crashed onto the street from the fifth floor. Submachine-guns at the ready, we rushed into the hallway, only to hear a drink-seeking soldier cursing pitifully in every pitch and probably rubbing his head. A Tommy had surely left the hatch in the floor leading to the cellar open, after first having kicked away the ladder. Our comrade had thus unsuspectingly fallen through the opening onto a mountain of empty bottles. His painful action was rewarded, however. He found plenty of brandy and other good things, which quickly helped us back on our feet. We stayed still as mice in case the Tommies should figure out what we were up to. Nothing plays on the nerves more than uncertainty, knowing that the enemy is nearby. He probably feared being out-

flanked by strong forces, for at about 04:00 hours, with morning already beginning to dawn, it became quiet in the city. Three comrades and I undertook a
scouting mission into the interior. A clear day began to rub its sleepy eyes, and
with the beginning light several bullets whizzed over our heads, undoubtedly
from the rear guard in the church tower. Our submachine-guns barked lustily.

On to the other end of the city. Nothing. The city had been evacuated. A fresh
outburst of machine-gun fire revealed to us that the enemy had taken up position
approximately 600 meters from the city in the dunes. I was able to report to my
superior and friend that the enemy had evacuated Newport. We were in high
spirits.

It was my task to lead our troops, of whose position we had no idea, to the
bridge. The bus, which was still on the far side of the locks, was little more than
a wreck, and, since I had no desire to walk, I put to good use the English ambulance which I had mistaken for a tank during the night. Just outside Ostende on
the big beach road I came upon German infantry, motorcycle troops and a heavy
machine-gun platoon. The headquarters was in the city of Ostende itself, where
I reported to the commanding general. He found our operation even more terrific than we, slapped me heartily on the shoulder, issued the necessary orders, and I
led part of the fully motorized force in the direction of Newport. We approached
in battalion strength and were rudely welcomed by the thud of exploding mortar
rounds. Our own mortars went into position and returned fire. Since the enemy
shells were landing too far apart, our infantry was able to deploy and took up
position on the far side of the city. They didn't stay there long, since the Tommies
withdrew in haste soon afterwards—direction Dunkirk.

Our promised special leave came to nothing at first, since we subsequently
had to make our way to Rommel in platoon strength, in order to take part in his
advance. During the Western Campaign Lt. Grabert was promoted to
Oberleutnant and I to Feldwebel. I received the Iron Cross, First Class, and
Grabert received a dressing down because we had not removed the explosives
from the road bridge when the senior staff crossed.

The Eggers platoon, which entrained on 23 March 1940, initially
moved into the forest camp at St. Thomas in the Eifel Mountains near
Kyllberg. Training there was done mainly in the forest, meaning night orientation marches and plenty of sports. Bicycles were issued in mid-April
1940 and the platoon was moved up to the border with Luxembourg in the
area of Ammeldingen an der Our. Target training was carried out there,
with each squad being assigned a bridge or roadblock, which in Case X was
to be occupied and held open. Shortly after nightfall on 9 May the individual squads crossed the Our River, which formed the border, in inflatable
boats. The seizure of the targets was carried out at about 05:35 hours on 10
May 1940; all were taken intact. After the first special missions at the start
of the French campaign most of the detachments returned to their quarters in Brandenburg/Havel. There the first decorations were presented to
the participants. They also returned in the midst of the formation of new

units, which had become necessary for the expansion of the battalion. Individual squads were also prepared for new missions and sent to the front. Things were happening very quickly, and it was difficult for the individual to figure out what was going on.

On 22 May 1940 the former *1. Kp./Bau-Lehr-Bataillon z.b.V. 800*, which by then had been brought up to strength with South-Tyroleans who had arrived in March and which now also included a platoon of Southwest Africans and another of Palestinians, moved to the army mountain school at Fulpmes in the Stubai Valley near Innsbruck for the purpose of forming a mountain unit. In the coming weeks it was followed by another company. The two companies were to form the foundation of *II. Bau-Lehr-Bt. Z.b.V. 800*, which was established under the command of Rittmeister Jakobi with headquarters in the Weilburg in Baden bei Wien.

Other companies were transferred to Aachen, later to Düren, which was the future home base of *III. Bau-Lehr-Btl. z.b.V. 800* which was in the process of being raised. The bases of the individual units were chosen based on the countries of origin of the *Brandenburgers* and their future missions in the various theaters. 8. Kp., which was moved from Brandenburg to Aachen, became the 11. Kp. Its personnel included many well-known and famous mountaineers as well as former participants in Himalayan expeditions. Each battalion—whose frameworks at least were in existence by about July 1940—was initially fully independent. They were not under a unified command, instead in terms of personnel and equipment were under the direct command of the head of the *Abwehr II* in Berlin, General Staff *Oberst* Lahousen. Only in a tactical aspect were the individual units subordinate to the commanders-in-chief of the armies or army groups in whose area they were operating. These subordinations lasted only until the missions were accomplished and the units returned to their bases. The Reich capital increasingly became central to the command of the *Brandenburger* units, especially since the *Abwehr* was based there and all lines of communication came together there in Mattheikirch Square.

Finally, in mid-August 1940, an operations staff was established there, which in future was to concentrate the individual, previously independent battalions and special units under a unified command. From roughly October this operations staff became the headquarters of the

Lehr-Regiment Brandenburg z.b.V. 800,

So that this month should be seen as the formation deadline for the regiment. Its organization at this time was as follows:

Lehr-Regiment Brandenburg z.b.V. 800

Subordinate to:	Amt Abwehr/Ausland
Department Head:	Admiral Canaris
Direct superior:	General Staff Oberst Lahousen
Rgt. Commander:	Major von Aulock
	(only for about 14 days)
	Obstlt. Haehling von Lanzenauer
	(from Nov. 1940)

	I.	II.	III.
	Bau-Lehr. Btl.	Bau-Lehr.Btl.	Bau-Lehr.Btl.
Base:	Brandenburg/Havel	Baden bei Wien	Düren near Aachen

Area of Operations:

east-west	southeast	west
1. to 4. Kp.	5. to 8. Kp.	9. to 12. Kp.

Further companies joined by mid-1941: 13. to 17. Kp.

Nachrichten-Verbände z.b.V. 800

In addition there were further units, detachments and squads. These included signals men, who, in 1939 and 1940, were initially assigned to the individual detachments and companies in small groups and squads.

Not until mid-1940 were the existing signals squads assigned to the various operational groups formed into a signals unit designed to meet the special needs of the *Brandenburg-ers*. It was initially of company strength with two platoons and was based in Spandau near Berlin. One of these platoons was transferred into the East-Dun-kirk area soon afterwards. Its mission was to provide signals support for the planned "Operation Sea Lion".

Gradually, in keeping with the expansion of the unit to division size, this first signals unit, which in November 1940 moved its base to Prützke near Brandenburg and then in January 1941 to Berlin-Zehlendorf ("Krumme Lanke" restaurant, "Krula" for short, and Wolfsschlucht), became the *Nachrichten-Abteilung Brandenburg* (signals battalion). It consisted of three companies: 1. Kp. — Krumme Lanke, 2. Kp. —

Birkenwerder near Berlin, 3. Kp. — Paulsborn.

Only rarely could the missions be carried out with the standard army radio equipment. Therefore in cooperation with the OKW and the *Abwehr* new radio sets were developed, and as well radio procedures and the cipher method (coded messages) were modified to suit the special requirements of *Brandenburg* missions. Of special significance was the short wave band, which was scarcely used by the *Wehrmacht* for radio traffic. With the aid of short waves it was possible to transmit over long ranges up to 4 000 km with minimal power output (and thus minimal size of the radio itself). Using such equipment it was possible for the central radio station in Berlin to stay in contact with even the most distant operational group.

Its duties were: The rapid transmission of orders from Berlin to the units deployed at the front; communications with and between the reconnaissance and Kampfgruppen during the mission.

The radio sets used were not much bigger than the backpack radios of the infantry. They were mainly served by radio operators who maintained the usual contact with neighboring units, while their fellow squad members took part in patrols and commando operations. This comprehensive training usually took place centrally in the *Nachr.Abt. BR*. Their employment with numerous signals units in all of Europe proved a success, although looking after the numerous detached signals platoons and squads sometimes proved rather difficult.

Further missions at numerous places at the front were carried out during the time of expansion into the Lehr-Regiment *Brandenburg* z.b.V. Among them were the preparations for "Operation Sea Lion," the planned invasion of the British Isles, ordered by Hitler on 16 July 1940. Special Unit Hollmann and the bulk of 4. Kp. were assigned to this mission and prepared for the operation. The target of this operation was the entrance to Dover harbor; the British had a steamer standing by to block the entrance to the port. The special unit's tasks were thus as follows: Prevent the planned blocking of the entrance to Dover harbor by the British by seizing the waiting steamer before it could be used; Capture and put out of action the British coastal batteries located on the hills.

Initial plans called for a glider-borne operation, however this was dropped. It was decided to deposit the Kampfgruppen at the foot of the steep cliffs using towed barges and taking advantage of the tide. The necessary preparations were made on the Channel Coast, first in the area of East-Dunkirk, then mainly in the Ostende area, partly involving the *Kriegsmarine*.

In August-September 1940 another detachment, the 11. Kp., moved into the La Chapelle area near Dieppe with some elements going to Lillebonne, and likewise prepared landing operations. Another *Brandenburg* detachment with a strength of nearly 100 men moved into the quartering area of the 26. I.D. (CO GenMaj. Förster)under the cover name

Armee-Pionier-Zug 909. These 100 men, primarily English-speaking foreign Germans, were equipped with Fichtel-Sachs light motorcycles and were dressed in fake uniforms. Their mission was to accompany the first wave of attackers, establish a bridgehead west of Hastings and near St. Leonards, advance into the interior and finally attack from the rear and eliminate the coastal batteries located on the promontory of Beachy Head.

The landing operation, which was dependent on air superiority over England, was never carried out. It was postponed from August to September, scheduled for 21 September and finally cancelled as unfeasible on 12 October as the autumn storms at that time of the year made the success of the operation questionable. Instead, in August 1940 a plan was devised to attack Gibraltar from the land side with improved weapons at the beginning of 1941 with the understanding of Spain. The object of this operation was to close the western entrance to the Mediterranean.

The following details are taken from the *Wehrmacht* Operations Staff Directive No. 18 of 12 November 1940 (O-Abt. L (I) No. 33356/40 Top Secret):

Paragraph 2

Political measures have been initiated in order to secure Spain's early entry into the war. The objective of the German intervention on the Iberian Peninsula (codename: Felix) will be to drive the English out of the western Mediterranean. To this end

Gibraltar will be taken and the straits closed,

the English will be prevented from establishing themselves at another place on the Iberian Peninsula or on the Atlantic islands.

The preparation and execution of the operation are intended as follows:

Phase I:

Scouting teams (officers in civilian clothes) will make the necessary preparations for the action against Gibraltar and for the capture of airfields.

Concerning camouflage and cooperation with the Spanish they are bound to the security measures of the Chief of Foreign Intelligence.

In secret cooperation with the Spanish, special units of the Office of Foreign Intelligence will guard the area of Gibraltar against English attempts to expand the approaches or detect and disrupt the preparations.

The units assigned to the mission will stand ready far back from the French-Spanish border without preliminary briefings. Advance warning will be given three weeks prior to the crossing by the troops of the Spanish-French border (but not until the completion of preparations regarding the Atlantic islands). In view of the limited capacity of the Spanish railroads, the army is to select mainly motorized units for the operation, so that railways are available for supply...

The first meeting between Hitler and the Spanish head of state Franco at Hendaye on the Spanish border on 23 October 1940 brought no agreement on the Gibraltar plan. The operation was subsequently abandoned in December of that year when Franco finally rejected it. Consequently all preparations by the *Brandenburgers*, who were once again to lead the operation, were shelved.

There followed the entry into Albania by Italian troops in October 1940 which soon developed into a defeat for the attackers. As a result of Greek requests British air forces were moved to Crete in November 1940 and from about March 1941 to the Greek mainland. Hitler saw himself compelled to assist the Italians and orders were issued for German troops to enter Greece from Bulgaria (Marita Plan). When on 27 March 1941 the Yugoslavian government fell just 48 hours after joining the Tripartite Pact, Hitler was also forced to conduct a simultaneous assault against Yugoslavia. It began on 6 April 1941.

One of the first steps taken by the German side was the surprise occupation of the Danube narrows at the Iron Gate in order to prevent it from being blocked by Serbian troops. A Kampfgruppe under the command of *Oberst* Bazing and comprising combat engineers, elements of the *Luftwaffe* and special formations, launched a surprise attack at dawn on 6 April 1941 and occupied the banks of the Danube on both sides of Orschowa. It was then able to frustrate all attempts by the Serbs to sink concrete-filled barges in the channel. A fierce firefight developed which ultimately ended in the favor of the Germans. *Brandenburg* involvement consisted of: elements of II. Btl./Lehr.Rgt. BR z.b.V. (whose operational units were transported in by air), as well as a II. Staffel, whose primary mission was to transport supply and replacements by truck via Hungary.

Later, on 17 April 1941, the *Wehrmacht* communiqué provided closer details of this daring operation:

> ...at dawn on 6 April a Kampfgruppe comprising combat engineers, elements of the Luftwaffe and special formations under Oberst Bazing crossed the Danube at the iron gate near Orsova under the most difficult river conditions. The Yugoslavian side was taken in a daring assault, fierce resistance was broken, and all attempts by the enemy to block the channel were frustrated. The determined actions of a few German soldiers thus secured a vital shipping route and guarded it against a planned enemy attack.

Italy had entered the war on Germany's side on 10 June 1940. It soon proved necessary for Germany to help defend Italy's colonial empire, but on the other hand it also represented an opportunity to advance into the neighboring colonial areas held by the Allies. The initial success enjoyed by the Italian troops in North Africa resulted in a British counterattack under General Wavell on 8 December 1940. In the weeks that followed, this led to the loss of important Italian positions in Libya: Sollum fell on 17 December, Bardia was lost on 6 January 1941, Tobruk was surrendered on 22 January, and Benghazi had to be abandoned on 7 February. The loss of Cyrenaica and of nearly 100,000 men finally forced Italy to ask the

German government for its support. In February 1941 followed the formation of the *Deutsche Afrika-Korps* under *General* Rommel, which saw its first action from Tripoli on 24 February. By April the combined efforts of the *Afrika-Korps* and the Italian forces had driven the British back to the Egyptian border, where there was a temporary cessation of activity by both sides.

The first *Brandenburgers* appeared in Africa roughly in June 1941, at first primarily to reconnoiter and scout enemy bases and intentions. One of these operations was carried out under the code name "Operation Dora". Meanwhile, in the homeland special units for service in Africa were formed, one of which was *Sonderverband 287* (special unit), which included *Brandenburgers*. The *11. Kp./III. Btl./Lehr-Rgt. BR z.b.V. 800* was released from the *Lehr-Regiment Brandenburg z.b.V.* and joined the new formation as *1. (Sonder-) Kp.* (1st special company). There it came under the command of *Sonderstab F* (Felmy Desert Brigade, Arabic Legion). This *Brandenburg* company did not return to the regimental formation, instead at the beginning of 1943 it was merged with the I.R. 92, later "Mot.-Brigade 92." The formation of *Sonderverband 287* took place at the Ruinenberg Barracks in Potsdam, and the training for desert operations in southern Greece (Lavrion). A similar sister unit, *Sonderverband 288*, was created a short time later as a fully motorized unit in the style of an independent Kampfgruppe. The mission of these special units was to drive to the Suez Canal, either through the African desert or, following the capture of the Caucasus, through Iran and Iraq, make contact there with the Arab forces supposedly in revolt, and conduct joint operations with the leading elements of the *Afrika-Korps*.

Neither of these scenarios developed as anticipated; both special units were ultimately employed in the anti-partisan role in Greece and Russia as part of the LXVIII. A.K. (*General* Felmy).

Further isolated actions were carried out in North Africa in the first half of 1941 on orders from *Abt. II* of the *Amt Ausland/Abwehr*, however these met with only partial success. Meanwhile at Brandenburg/Havel a tropical company under Oblt. von Koenen was formed (spring 1941) for future operations in Africa. It soon had a strength of almost 300 men. Koenen, a farmer's son from Southwest Africa, always selected his men personally, naturally preferring those from the black areas of the earth. On 28 October 1941 the first two half-companies of the von Koenen tropical company left the mainland via Naples, Italy and landed near Tripoli, where they were placed under the direct command of Rommel's headquarters for special missions. The first missions, which focused on scouting enemy positions, blowing up important objects and spreading unrest in the enemy's rear, were carried out by small teams from the company. Five *Brandenburgers* set out by sea for Alexandria, however they were discovered and captured. Another operation, in which single men were dropped by parachute into the rear, was likewise a failure.

The period of the commando units—on both sides—arrived with the stabilization of the front at the end of 1941 and the withdrawal of the British to the Ain-el-Gazala position at the end of January 1942. The southern flanks of both sides disappeared somewhere in the sand; there, in that no-man's-land, was the true arena for the small war and for special operations to tie down and confuse enemy units. Comparable formations of commandos faced each other there; here the *Brandenburgers* of the von Koenen company, there the British Long Range Desert Group. Both conducted daring operations in an attempt to outdo the other, to root out the other side, to achieve success.

Here is a report on "Operation Salaam", which was supposed to lead to the Nile at Assiut.

Brandenburg at the Nile (Operation Salaam)

OKW planning for 1942 called for Panzer-Armee Afrika to attack Egypt and advance to the Suez Canal. Thorough reconnaissance was of course necessary in order to carry out the planned action. This proved difficult in the area of Egypt because tight security made it almost impossible to insert agents and depositing them from the air was out of the question as the Egyptian airspace was hermetically sealed by British fighters.

But with the stubbornness unique to him, the then Generaloberst Rommel insisted that a solution be found to this problem, which was in the hands of the OKW Amt Ausland/Abwehr. In practical terms there was only one solution: take advantage of the open left flank of the British Army and insert radio-equipped agents into Egypt by having them pass through the Libyan desert.

Execution of this plan, which was dubbed "Operation Salaam", was initiated in November 1941. The question of who should lead the mission was solved when the Hungarian Army made one of its reserve officers, Captain von Almaszy, available for the operation. Almaszy had been a flying instructor in a civilian flying school in Cairo in peacetime. He knew the Libyan desert from years of experience, spoke excellent English and Italian, and had very good relationships with leading Arab personalities. Two potential agents were found serving in an army interpreter school; both had lived in Egypt for many years. Their names were kept secret for certain reasons, as were the names of the other participants in this expedition. With the exception of the agents and the Hungarian captain, all of the participants were members of the Lehr-Regiment BR z.b.V. 800 or were attached to it for the duration of the operation. Their mission was to transport the agents to their drop-off points. With a very few exceptions they were people who had lived in the Orient for a long time, were masters of the local language and customs, and were in such physical condition that they could endure the hardships that lay ahead of them.

The preparations for this operation took approximately 3 months. As a result of the military setbacks that Rommel suffered in the winter of 1941-42 the planned jump-off bases had to be moved back. The end result was that the force would have to cover a distance of about 1 500 kilometers to reach the planned drop-off point, Assuit on the Nile, or approximately 3 000 kilometers there and back with no possibility of replenishing water, fuel or rations. Furthermore, because of ground conditions, the last 300 kilometers (or 600 km there and back) had to follow the British military road from Dachla to Assiut. Since it had to be calculated that the force might have to spend the day in concealment in order to pass this last stretch at the right time, a duration of six weeks was anticipated. This was provided by the Luftwaffe as the army did not have the necessary concentrates. To facilitate crossing the sandy wastes stout rope ladders were developed for the vehicles and manufactured by a Berlin firm with special authorization of the OKW. These rope ladders were to be placed beneath the wheels when they threatened to spin in the soft sand. Furthermore it was necessary to procure a great deal of special equipment; its manufacture ran into difficulties in the third year of the war, however most of these were bureaucratic in nature. Thanks to the restless energy of those involved, these difficulties were also overcome.

One problem of a special nature was the radio sets to be taken along. They had to have a long range but also be suitable for short-range use, and their size and weight could not exceed specified dimensions. The technicians of the OKW's Radio-Outlying Station in Stahnsdorf not only developed a suitable set in the prescribed time, they also manufactured it—an outstanding achievement that should not be forgotten.

In mid-February 1942 the two agents and three radio operators with all the equipment left Berlin under the command of a Wachtmeister, in order to collect Almaszy, who had gone ahead, in Tripoli. They first traveled by train to Naples, from where the Luftwaffe was to fly them to Africa. This proved impossible at first, however, as all cargo space was required for the direct supply of the Afrika-Korps, which was in the middle of its spring offensive. The detachment leader immediately decided to return to Rome, where he obtained the two Ju 52s required to transport his personnel and equipment directly from the air fleet. Thus he was able to arrive in Tripoli on time.

In Tripoli the work on the vehicles began. Captured English vehicles were selected for the mission, two Ford Deluxe cars and three Ford 1 ton troop trucks, so-called Flitzer (runabouts). These vehicles were carefully overhauled and test-driven. Special attention was paid to fuel consumption, which was used to calculate the total quantity of fuel to be taken along. As well Balkenkreuze (crosses) were painted on the vehicles; these were oversprayed with sand so that they were only recognizable from close up. These markings were necessary, because the entire mission was to be carried out in German uniforms in order to prevent those taking part from being shot as spies if captured by the British. This way they would be treated as German soldiers.

On 29 April 1942 all was ready. The stretch to the jump-off point, Audschila Oasis (Gialo), was covered in stages. At El-Agheila airfield the vehicles' compasses were carefully compensated, for the first 1 200 kilometers of the trip went straight across the desert. As well the machine-guns and radios were checked once again. At Gialo there was a further unpleasant stop. The Italian *maps—the only ones available for the area—were wrong. They showed Dachla' Serir', which meant hard, smooth sandy ground, almost all the way to the British military station. Statements by locals, however, indicated that there was a belt of dunes about fifty kilometers east of the Gialo—Kufra track which one could only traverse by the so-called dune corridor, which would mean following a zigzag course at the cost of much time and fuel. This would also upset all the fuel calculations. A reconnaissance flight by Almaszy in an aircraft provided by the Italian air force confirmed the locals' statements. New calculations were therefore made and the necessary augmentations undertaken. Finally the oasis' drinking water proved unusable for carriage over long distances. Luckily there was a well not far away whose water met the requirements and relieved this unfortunate situation.*

On 11 May the group headed out of Gialo into uncertainty. Based on a precisely-laid plan, the light trucks were left behind at intervals to act as filling stations for the return trip, and the last segment from Dachla to Assiut on the English military road was covered with just the two cars. It sounds unlikely, but it is nevertheless a fact, that on the way in on this road the expedition passed two English columns and exchanged greetings in the form of shouts and waves with the English. Apparently none of the British imagined that they would meet German soldiers there, 1 500 kilometers behind their front.

A halt was made on the last hills before Assiut with a view of the Nile. In order to have proof that the objective had been reached, Almaszy had several pictures taken in front of the Assiut road sign. The two agents removed their uniforms and put on local costumes. Then, taking the radio sets and English as well as Egyptian money, they bade farewell to their comrades to begin their voluntary mission. Meanwhile Almaszy and his men set off on the return journey.

They covered the famous three-hundred kilometers in good time, however past Dachla it seemed that the return to their own lines was nearly impossible and that the operation would end in a return to Dachla and surrender to the British. Whether it was a case of compass failure, or whether they had become lost for other reasons, or perhaps that a party from the British Long Range Desert Patrol had been the first to find the parked vehicles with the fuel—whatever the reason, the 1-ton truck had disappeared. Good ideas were hard to come by now. Luckily, however, one of the participants discovered with his binoculars several stationary trucks not far away; they had been pushed together and appeared to have been abandoned in the middle of the desert. The Brandenburgers approached cautiously and found themselves at a refueling station placed by their British opposite numbers. Now they had what they needed and helped themselves accordingly. The rest of the trip proceeded without incident and the other two 1 ton trucks were found according to plan. Almaszy and his men arrived back in Gialo on the morning of 4 June and from there they were able to report their success to the OKW by radio. Regrettably the operation by the agents did not come off as planned. For one thing the radio operator provided by the panzer corps to act as their contact was captured along with his equipment and documents in a surprise advance by the English. In addition the two agents lacked the character for their task, and, as it turned out after the war, they had been picked up by the

41

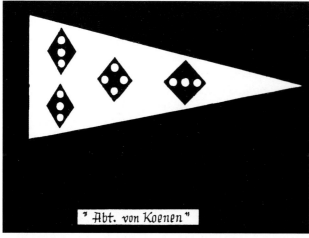

"Abt. von Koenen"

British for this reason even before they could establish contact with their designated backup contact station. But since they were not Brandenburgers this point does not fall back on us. What is left is the memory of this operation, which even the British intelligence service acknowledged as one of the most brilliant feats of the Abwehr and the Lehrregiment Brandenburg z.b.V. 800.

In addition to numerous smaller operations during 1942, one particular operation which took place roughly halfway through the year under the command of Oblt. Konrad of Leipzig is deserving of special mention. Its target was the supply road from the Gulf of Guinea to Port Sudan, which served the British 8th Army. Supplies were trucked to Port Sudan and then shipped by sea to Egypt. Approximately 100 *Brandenburgers* took part in this "Operation Dora II". The vehicles used by this reconnaissance and interdiction unit included 24 captured British trucks, of which 12 were equipped with 40-mm guns, 4 runabouts, radio vehicles, fuel trucks, etc. An intact captured Spitfire was used as a reconnaissance machine.

The column departed Tripoli and set off down the old caravan route, first to Mursuk, which was the site of the base camp. There the formation was divided into three patrols:

Oblt. von Leipzig's patrol: Main group. Was to advance from Mursuk south toward the Tümmo Mountains, from there continue in the direction of the Tassili Plateau, past which led the British supply road.

Feldwebel Stegmann's patrol: Was to set out for Tibesti.

Lt. Becker's patrol: Advance west in the direction of Ghat on the Algerian border.

Even though these three operations brought in important reconnaissance information, in the end they could not bring about any lasting disruption of the British supply system. While the teams crossed the desert expanses, in some cases under frightful conditions, the fighting fronts began moving again, and this alone was enough to limit the success of the operation. Finally, in autumn 1942, the teams returned to their starting point in Tripoli.

One mission that did achieve success was an operation against the rail bridge of Sidi-bou-Baker on the Wadi-el-Kbir far behind the Allied lines, roughly northwest of Gafsa in southern Tunisia, which began on 27 December 1942. Once again it was a small group of *Brandenburgers* who were dropped near the target at night in three gliders and carried out the demolition of the bridge. The operation was concluded by a foot march of more than 180 kilometers to the nearest Italian base at Maknassi.

The von Koenen Battalion, which since January 1943 had grown to four companies and which for the next months was quartered in Hamamet and surrounding villages, carried out numerous operations from there. Success was mixed. The unit's successes were accompanied by sacrifices on the part of the soldiers who had helped achieve them. Here is a list of the fatal casualties suffered by the von Koenen Battalion:

Killed in Action:

Gefr. Reinhold Eichhorn	6/6/1942 Trig el Abd, Libya
Gefr. Ernst Schweim	8/6/1942 Bir el Hacheim, Libya
Gefr. Herbert Vosswinkel	8/6/1942 Bir el Hacheim, Libya
Gefr. Manfred Lawicki	10/6/1942 Bir el Hacheim, Libya
Lt. Otto Müller	10/7/1942 El Alamein rail line, Egypt
Gefr. Hans Lohse	15/7/1942 El Alamein, Egypt
Gefr. Jaspar Lüttje	15/7/1942 El Alamein, Egypt
Gefr. Hein Kleckers	16/7/1942 El Alamein, Egypt
Stabsarzt Dr. Wolfgang König	1/8/1942 Athens hospital
Gefr. Hein Maili	6/8/1942 Quatarra track
Gefr. Hermann Gross	16/1/1943 Beni Illid, Libya
Gefr. Kurt Laske	Jan 1943 inland sea
Uffz. Kurt Herkner	22/2/1943 Hamam Pass, Libya
Gefr. Willi Broch	19/2/1943 Hamam Pass, Libya
Gefr. Josef Dott	19/2/1943 Hamam Pass, Libya
Gefr. Herbert Brabant	22/2/1943 Hamam Pass, Libya
Gefr. Hermann Grube	22/2/1943 Hamam Pass, Libya
Gefr. Herbst	Feb. 1943 Tunisia
Gefr. Josef Taipel	Feb 1943 Tunisia
Uffz. Willi Bieset	1943 Tunisia
Gefr. Georg Kaspar	1943 Tunisia
Uffz. Karl Stephan	1943 Naples hospital
Lt. Hans Brügmann	Aug. 1943 lake region West Africa

The rapidly growing superiority of the Allies in Africa following the American landings in Algeria and Morocco on 7-8 November 1942 forced the *Afrika-Korps* onto the defensive and compelled it to retreat steadily toward the north coast of Africa and abandon the Italian colonies in that area. In February 1943 a German counterattack against the Americans attacking from the west was a success, however the German forces were ultimately forced to defend the Mareth Line south of Gabes (Tunisia). The following account deals with that period:

"Operation Spring Wind"

While as members of the Abwehr station in Tunis, to which we were assigned, we were under the command of Generaloberst von Arnim's panzer corps, we received orders to drive into the area of Generalfeldmarschall Rommel's panzer army southwest of Kairouan in order to undertake an operation as an Abwehr team. Our headquarters promised that this operation would provide intelligence information which would also be of interest to the panzer army.

Our situation in the Tunis bridgehead had not been very envious from the start. The German forces that had landed in Tunisia were so inferior in numbers and materiel to the Anglo-American enemy approaching from Algeria that even in the area of the headquarters we asked ourselves each night before we went to sleep whether we might not perhaps be awakened the next morning by the British military police. The situation is perhaps best characterized by the fact that at Medjez-el-Bab, approximately sixty kilometers away, the Tommies had a concentration of tanks, while for some time the only obstacle on the road between us and those tanks was a single 22-mm anti-tank gun. Not a battalion, not a battery, no—one little cannon! Certainly things had improved somewhat in the meantime, but the many units whose direction signs we had nailed up prominently at every crossroads existed mainly on paper or were still in Italy and would never set foot on African soil. We had a bridgehead which was barely large enough for tactical purposes and which was becoming smaller almost daily as a result of pressure by Montgomery from Tripolitania. The objective was to strike at a place the enemy did not suspect an attack, so as to break open the sack in which we were stuck and thus create room for operational possibilities.

All was ready on the morning of 14 February 1943. The planned attack took place in the early morning hours near Sidi-bou-Zid without the customary artillery barrage. Resistance by the completely surprised Americans was isolated and weak. In some places determined officers rallied their men to resist, but in general it was a headlong flight. After the war American officers confirmed to the writer that on hearing the cry "Rommel's boys are attacking!" the inexperienced American soldiers threw away their weapons and equipment and simply ran as fast as they could. The so-called retreat road to Sbeitla was littered with weapons of every type, equipment and uniforms, but even better booty was to be had, including 27 tanks and armored troop carriers filled to the brim with ammunition and fuel. As well, 23 guns were captured and 700 prisoners taken.

From Sbeitla our Kampfgruppe continued its attack toward Tebessa. The purpose of this advance was to isolate the British 1st Army under Alexander from the Americans and drive it into the Mediterranean. But General Alexander recognized the German intentions in time and sent some of his troops on a forced march to Tebessa, where the British troops halted the fleeing Americans. For lack of sufficient artillery our repeated attacks on the heights around Tebessa and the Kasserine Pass were halted in the face of Anglo-American defensive fire.

We ourselves were not sent in the direction of Tebessa, since our mission was less to take part in the actual fighting than to gather information. Tactical emblems on burnt-out tanks showed us that divisions were deployed in the sector which our intelligence service still suspected were much further to the rear, and furthermore a surprise advance to the Thelepte airfield enabled us to secure valuable maps and command documents.

Since we got the impression that the road and railway from Sbeitla to Feriana had been evacuated by the enemy, we reconnoitered in that direction on our own and found that our suspicions were correct. The hole in the sack had in fact been created. In Gafsa we came upon weak friendly forces, but by the time we arrived they were already facing a relief attack by Montgomery's 8th Army at any hour from the direction of Nefta and the salt lakes. Since we had no radio with us we drove by night and in pouring rain on bottomless and muddy tracks, often up to the axles in mud, to the field marshal's command post, in order to deliver our report. We learned there that our attack near Tebessa had come to a standstill and that the planned success by our units had been taken away at the last minute, so to speak.

Thus the fate of the Tunis bridgehead was finally settled. Theoretically the end could only be a few weeks away, practically it took almost three months to come. The principal reason for this was that Operation Spring Wind had made necessary a reorganization of the American forces: but our small force, which consisted of nothing more than the remnants of several completely battered divisions, had sent running no less than 80,000 completely fresh and excellently equipped Americans, a ratio of perhaps 20 to 1! And once again the Brandenburgers had been there.

The bulk of the von Koenen battalion succeeded in escaping from the African bridgehead on the Cap Bon peninsula in boats and other vessels and regrouped in Italy. After a brief rest and refit period the battalion then saw action in the Balkans, in the struggle against enemy partisans.

The subsequent path of the von Koenen battalion is reflected in the graves of its fallen, whose names are listed below:

Killed in Action von Koenen Battalion:

Lt. Gert Heinitz	24/4/1944	Bela Reka, Serbia
Gefr. Heinz Gorit	Feb. 1944	Bela Reka, Serbia
Gefr. Erhard Möbus	11/6/1944	Kupress, Croatia
Kr.Ing. Hummel	6/7/1944	Livno, Croatia
Uffz. Fritz Schill	6/7/1944	Livno, Croatia
Oblt. Hans Blödorn	2/7/1944	Osin Glavica, Croatia
Uffz Ernst Sandfort	2/7/1944	Osin Glavica, Croatia
Gefr. Bernhard	18/7/1944	Nevesinja, Croatia
Obstlt. Fritz von Koenen	22/8/1944	Vizegrad, Croatia
Gefr. Kurt Sand	22/8/1944	Vizegrad, Croatia
Fw. Mitzel	7/9/1944	Giörisent, Miklos Mts.
Uffz. Herbert Jürgensen	7/10/1944	Klausenburg, Transylvania

Oblt. Willi Klima	7/10/1944	Klausenburg, Transylvania
Obgefr. Erich Treude	7/10/1944	Klausenburg, Transylvania
San.Uffz. Hans Schubert	7/10/1944	Klausenburg, Transylvania
Fw. Helmut Friedrich	13/7/1944	Nevesinje, Croatia
Obfhr. Deppersdorf	1945	Russian internment camp
Obfw. Rolf Koczy	31/1/1945	Regentin, Pomerania
Obfw. Walter Genrich 1	9/1/1945	Lask, Poland
Stabsfw. Rud. Meier	19/1/1945	Lask, Poland
Uffz. Werner Sander	5/2/1945	Kaluga, Russia
Rittm. Ernst Eberhard Frey	11/2/1946	Died in captivity (Sergo-Kadiewka, Russia)

Chapter 2
Brandenburgers in the East

The start of "Operation Barbarossa," the attack on the Soviet Union which began in the early morning hours of 22 June 1941, saw detachments and squads of *Brandenburgers* in action at many points on the German-Soviet border. Preparations for these had begun early on: equipment was procured, teams were assembled, missions assigned and targets issued. Every possible means was employed: captured Soviet trucks, which could transport men to the target without attracting attention; gliders, which could deposit them in the immediate vicinity or even behind the target; and parachute drops from low-flying aircraft, in order to overrun enemy installations from the air. The targets were: to seize and hold bridges over river lines ahead of the German armored spearheads until the tanks arrived; to take and hold important objects such as rail tunnels, rail installations and railway bridges; to eliminate enemy batteries or at least suppress them until relieved by German units of the main attack force.

Among the preparations by Lt. Imhof was a mission carried out during the hours of darkness on the night of 21-22 June 1941 by a team consisting of Lt. Kern plus two ethnic Germans and one V-man. Its objective was the Bobr River near Lipsk, where the men were to capture the bridge intact. Another group of *Brandenburgers* succeeded in capturing the bridge at Viejsieja intact. Another operation was directed against the Josvainai bridge in Lithuania. The following men were killed during the course of this action on 23 June 1941:

Gefreiter Wieser
Jäger   A. Schmidt
Jäger   Sonnhofer
Jäger Taaktmann
Jäger Kurt Weiss

Another target was the big road bridge over the Dvina near Dvinsk, which was approached by a team of *Brandenburgers* from the *8. Kompanie. Major* Gerhard of the 8. Pz.Div. described what took place:

"After the crossing of the East Prussian—Lithuanian border it was of decisive importance for the subsequent advance by the 8. Panzer-Division that the big road bridge over the Dvina near Dvinsk fall into our hands intact.

During the nocturnal advance a car edged into the advance guard, even in front of my own vehicle. As it turned out, the vehicle belonged to the commander of a platoon of the *Regiment z.b.V. Brandenburg 800* which had been assigned to us. The *Oberleutnant*, who was a stranger to me, said nothing about the goal and objective of the assignment. All we knew of this regiment was that it was under the direct command of the OKW, was used for special missions and was shrouded in secrecy.

Then at dawn on 26 June the *Brandenburg* platoon set off toward the east in three captured Soviet trucks, ahead of even our own advance guard. One truck succeeded in crossing the Dvina untouched. Not until it reached the other side was it recognized for what it was and fired on; however, the men inside were able to get away from the truck and take up position. The other captured truck was caught by Soviet heavy machine-guns while still on the bridge and its men were forced to get out prematurely; they linked up with the men on the other side but suffered casualties. In spite of heavy enemy fire the *Brandenburgers* of this platoon were able to hold on the far side of the bridge and keep the crossing open until the arrival of the armored spearhead. Most of the members of this platoon were killed, including the *Oberleutnant* and leader of the operation, almost all of the survivors were wounded. The fallen found their last resting places on the right bank of the river right beside the exit from the bridge.

The following men died hero's deaths there:
Oberleutnant Wolfram Knaak
Oberleutnant Heinz Rösler
Gefreiter Karl Innerhofer
Gefreiter Anton Stauder
Oberschütze Mathias Plattner

The fallen leader of the *Brandenburg* detachment was awarded the Knight's Cross posthumously in spring 1942."

Another operation, this time a parachute drop, was carried out in the same sector on 25 June 1941. In command of the *Brandenburg* detachment was *Leutnant* Lex; with him were about 35 men. His mission: occupy the two bridges (river bridge and road viaduct) on the twin-track rail line from Lida to Molodeszno and prevent their destruction.

The first Junkers aircraft approached the target at about 15:00 hours on 25 June 1941. It immediately came under furious enemy ground fire. Both pilot and radio operator were seriously wounded, one engine was hit. Lt. Lex decided to jump early near the target. It was fortunate that he did, for aerial reconnaissance had just discovered that approximately fourteen Soviet tanks had taken up position nearby. The *Brandenburgers*, who assembled right at the railway embankment, were placed under heavy enemy fire and a fierce battle developed. The Soviets tried to set off the demolition charges on the bridges by concentrating their fire on them; however, the ignition systems had been rendered inoperable by the *Brandenburgers*. The Kampfgruppe was supposed to be relieved at the bridges after an hour at the most, however the leading elements of the advancing panzer divisions were stopped by superior enemy forces in the area west of Traby. The *Brandenburgers* were forced to fight on, in spite of increasing losses, to hold the bridges. This they succeeded in doing, although the cost was very high. The detachment commander (Lt. Lex) was fatally hit, his deputy, a *Feldwebel*, was also killed. Four more men paid for this mission with their lives and sixteen more were wounded, some seriously.

Finally, during the evening hours of 26 June, the detachment was relieved by several armored cars of the motorcycle battalion. The surviving *Brandenburgers*, about 14 in number, were placed under its command and fought with it until the beginning of July 1941. Finally, on 7 July, the last seven were released to return to their base.

Another operation, prepared and carried out by Freg.Kpt. Alexander Celarius in July 1941, was aimed against Oesel Island. *Brandenburgers* under the command of *Hauptmann der Flieger* Benesch also took part. This operation provided an outstanding example of cooperation between gliders and water craft, a combination which made it possible to outflank and silence one of the heaviest batteries on the enemy-occupied island.

Most of these operations and their successes naturally went into the mass of success reports which issued almost hourly from German radio. Their men and detachment leaders were rarely named in *Wehrmacht* communiqués , and when they were there was no mention of the reason for the awarding of the Knight's Cross. But without the men of the *Lehr-Regiment Brandenburg z.b.V. 800* and their daring operations, in many places the element of surprise would have been replaced by heavy fighting, whose toll in human life would have been much greater.

The *Brandenburgers* conducted fewer operations as the German armies advanced rapidly eastward into the depths of the enemy's territory. The element of surprise was primarily exploited by the panzer divisions and their armored advance battalions, while the number of potential targets for special operations dropped.

The German advance gradually lost momentum in the vastness of the Soviet Union; this momentum was not to be regained until October 1941 when, with winter looming on the horizon, an offensive was launched with the goal of taking Moscow. 9. Kp./III. Btl. was temporarily transferred into the central sector of the Eastern Front with the mission of seizing the Isdra dam in front of Moscow and preventing the Russians from blowing it up.

But "General Winter" frustrated this operation when cold and supply difficulties caused the front to freeze.

The *9. Kompanie* was repeatedly used in the infantry role during the subsequent fighting retreat, resulting in heavy casualties. In the spring of 1942 the same company was employed in the anti-partisan role in the Dorogobush-Smolensk and Vyazma areas until in August it was pulled out of action to rest and refit.

Further commando operations by the *Brandenburgers* were required on other fronts of the war, which now encompassed much of the world, with the emphasis being on stealth operations.

In the high north, in Finland, like their German comrades in arms, the Finns were engaged in a tough struggle with the Bolsheviks. Their objective was the Murmansk rail line, over which flowed a significant percentage of the Soviet supplies.

Preparations for the mission in the far north began at the Zossen troop training grounds roughly in October 1941. There a *Leutnant* from Berlin formed a so-called light company, which initially received the designation *15. (Lei.) Kp./Lehr-Rgt. BR z.b.V. 800.* He sought the best skiers from all elements of the *Wehrmacht*, including an Olympic champion from 1936; approximately forty handlers for Polar dogs were attached from the Army Dog School at Sperenberg near Berlin. Marine combat engineers, weapons specialists and so on were brought together at Zossen. The special equipment required for fighting in the Karelian forest was assembled, everything was prepared to the last detail.

Toward the end of 1941 the *Leutnant* and his men reported to the corps headquarters of *General* Dietl, who first asked what they were doing there. The *Leutnant* described his plans: to blow up power plants and bridges in the enemy rear; ambushes and harassing actions against Soviet supply bases; disruption of Soviet supply by blowing the Murmansk rail line and so on. However, at first the 15. (Lei.) Kp. saw no action. *General* Dietl first kept the *Brandenburgers* in a forest camp at Rovaniemi—to become accustomed to the climate and the country. The first mission against Soviet bases and depots near Alakwetti and on the Liza—in the direction of Murmansk—took place sometime in April 1942.

The mission failed in the impenetrable depths of the Karelian forest, and the participants only just managed to make their way back to their base.

An enemy penetration into the German defense line, which was made up of a series of strongpoints, near Kiestinki in May 1942 made it necessary for the *Brandenburgers* to be sent into combat to help halt the enemy. This action was followed by a return to the Rovaniemi forest camp, where the men remained until June 1942 preparing for their next mission.

An *Oberleutnant* from Swabia then took over the company and prepared a secret mission for the summer of 1942; once again the objective was to blow the Murmansk rail line. One day 100 collapsible boats painted red, green and blue were delivered to the company; as well they received small outboard motors to power the boats. The company was joined by native Finns familiar with the forest and selected Russian volunteers.

Finally, in August 1942, all was ready. The company moved into Karelia via Kuusamo, across the narrow Paanajärvi River. Then the men of the company crossed the approximately two-kilometer-wide, fast-flowing river in their collapsible boats. Several men were drowned, however the company finally reached its jump-off base. From a small fishing village somewhere in the desolate spaces of Karelia the *Brandenburgers* continued their eastward trek almost 200 kilometers, crossing lakes, streams and rivers. No humans lived in this desolate area, just wild animals. Finally, on the east bank of the Kotosero, they finally came upon an inhabited village, however a strong Soviet outguard was stationed there. Three selected demolition teams moved past this position in their collapsible boats toward the Murmansk rail line, which was finally within range. The teams were able to place charges at fourteen places without being seen; they were set off at selected intervals. Panic broke out in the Soviet command centers at Polyarni Krug on the Arctic Circle, at Kandalaschka and Louhi. Supply trains were blown up at various times and places, however the Soviets never saw any of the saboteurs. These daring *Brandenburgers* retraced their path to the forest camp at Rovaniemi, where they were welcomed home with appreciative words from *General* Dietl.

At the turn of the year 1941-42 the individual battalions, with the exception of detachments, were still at their bases of Brandenburg/Havel, Baden bei Wien and Düren. They trained in their areas of specialty, evaluating the experiences of returning operational groups and expanding their personnel complement. The eastern theater, which was becoming increasingly important, would be the main area of operations principally of the II. Btl./Lehr.Rgt. *Brandenburg* z.b.V., which was based in the Weilburg in Baden bei Wien.

As a result of the occupation of France by German troops, the abandonment of "Operation Sea Lion", and the cessation of fighting in the west and north, the missions previously carried out by *III. Btl. Lehr-Regiment BR z.b.V. 800* became less important. Instead anti-partisan operations in the southeast area grew in importance. For the time being the only *Brandenburg* unit in combat was I./Lehr-Rgt. B R z.b.V. 800 based at Brandenburg/Havel, which had elements engaged in the central and northern sectors of the Eastern Front.

All battalions used the time at their bases for steady expansion, so that they gradually became regiment-size units. The formation of combined Kampfgruppen became especially important. This was to enable each company to fulfil completely independent combat missions. The division into so-called half-companies, the allocation of heavy and anti-tank weapons, and the assignment of combat engineers bolstered the fighting strength of such a formation, which often comprised 400 to 500 men per company. After returning from the missions against the Dvina bridges and its rest and refit under the command of Oblt. Grabert, in spring 1942 the organization of the *8. Kp./II./Lehr-Rgt. BR z.b.V. 800* was as follows:

8. Kp./II./Lehr-Rgt. BR z.b.V. 800

Comp.Commander	Oblt. Grabert	
Medical officer		
Paymaster		
1st Section:	Lt. Haut	KIA autumn 1944, Yugoslavia

1st Section:	Lt. Grube	KIA Sept. 1942, Malgobek
2nd Section:	Fw. (Lt.) Mihl	KIA 31/10/42, Staro Lesk.
IInd Half Company	Lt. Hiller	KIA 24/7/42, Bataysk
1st Section:	Lt. Prohaska	KIA Aug. 42, Maykop bridge
2nd section:	Fw. (Lt.) Girgenson	KIA Dec. 42, Terek Mts.

Heavy Platoon

Equipment: 2 rifle squads   per section
  1 pioneer squad
  1 80-mm mortar squad   (1st Section) or
  1 50-mm mortar squad   (2nd Section)
  Heavy Platoon   2 hvy. machine-gun squads
  1 squad with Type 41 anti-tank rifles

Vehicles:
  Squad vehicles   Opel Blitz 3.5 ton
  Kitchen vehicle   Opel Blitz 3.5 ton
  Repair vehicle, etc. Opel Blitz 3.5 ton
  Type 41 anti-tank rifle
  Steyr light armored vehicle
  Comp. Commander   Kfz. 15 Kübel
  Medical officer   Kfz. 15 Kübel

Also, motorcycles and motorcycle/sidecar combinations, etc.

The increase in personnel by the various companies made it necessary to also enlarge the quartering areas, so that for example the 5. Kp. under Oblt. Zülich moved to Mödling (part of the town of Hinterbrühl); the 6. Kp., having returned from its missions in the Crimea, likewise moved into the barracks camp near Mödling, while other elements of the battalion completed another high mountain training course lasting several weeks. The designation "Jäger" came to be used more frequently for these men—many were from Styria, Tyrol and other mountain regions—and their external symbol was the Edelweiß which was worn on the right upper sleeve and on the left edge of their mountain caps.

But all preparations by *II./Lehr-Regiment BR z.b.V. 800*, which was intended for service in the southern areas of the east, were aimed at partic-ipation in the operation aimed at the Caucasus and the Terek region planned for the middle of 1942. Its missions remained unchanged, consist-ing of the surprise capture of important objects as well as patrols and reconnaissance advances deep into enemy territory.

Thus the spring of 1942 was spent in feverish preparation for the com-ing mission. At the end of June 1942 the companies of II Battalion assem-bled for the final parade in their quarters. They then departed for Vienna and the departure stations there. II Battalion headquarters set out in for Kishinev on 1 July by way of Heggyes—Halom (Hungary)—Raab—Komorn—Itzani (Buchenwald)—Jassy (Romania); from Kishinev it trav-eled by truck into the Tiraspol area. The companies, which entrained one after another, followed by rail and on 8 July arrived in the Odessa area, where they occupied temporary quarters. In the days that followed they continued towards Nikolayev, where tent camps were occupied on the bank of the River Bug. A company of BR marine pioneers also arrived. The first order for a special mission by *II./Lehr-Regiment BR z.b.V. 800* reached it on 12 July 1942. It was actually meant just for the experienced 8. *Kompanie* under Oblt. Grabert, while the other companies were to remain in their quartering areas. Grabert's orders were to proceed via Kherson, Perekop, Melitopol, Stalino and Mariupol to Taganrog where he would come under the command of the 13. Pz.Div. commanded by *Generalmajor* Herr, part of *Panzergruppe Kirchner* (13. Pz.Div., *SS-Wiking* and a fast Slovakian division). The company was to take part in the capture of Rostov and then carry out its primary mission, to seize the approximately 6000-meter-long raised roadway over the Don delta between the actual city and Bataysk.

On 22 July the half companies of the 8. Kp. drove through Taganrog and subsequently arrived in the town of Sambeck, where they made a temporary halt. At about noon elements of the 13. Pz.Div. had already approached to within 5 to 7 kilometers of the city, where Soviet rear guards were defending stubbornly.

Heavy enemy artillery fire prevented our forces from entering the city in the evening hours. German attack units had to be readied and heavy artillery moved into position before the attack on Rostov could begin. Meanwhile the Grabert company was split up for its special mission against the Bataysk raised roadway; two half-companies led by Oblt. Grabert and Lt. Hiller were to play the decisive roles there.

At about midday on 23 July the leading elements of the German attack force were finally able to enter the suburbs of Rostov; fierce house-to-house fighting broke out while German and Russian aircraft bombed the city center without letup. The enemy hunkered down in every corner of the city center, and consequently the fighting went on through the entire night. Meanwhile, in the houses of the outer suburbs the *Brandenburgers* waited impatiently to begin their mission, which was supposed to begin as soon as the city was taken.

Fighting in Rostov against the remaining Soviet units went on until the early afternoon of 24 July; then, finally, the men of the Grabert Company were able to move out. The *Oberleutnant* and his men were able to cross the first arm of the Don at about 15:00 hours, followed immediately by Lt. Hiller. On the other side the company first assembled near the command post of the Kradschtz.Btl. 43 (motorcycle battalion), commander Obstlt. Stolz. By evening the remaining half-companies and squads of the 8. Kp., including those led by Lt. Haut, Lt. Gruber and Lt. Prohaska, brought inflatable boats, ammunition, rations, equipment, etc across by ferry to the other side—all in preparation for the surprise attack by the Grabert—Hiller groups on the bridges in front of Bataysk. There were approximately five or six bridges crossing the Don delta, and Oblt. Grabert wanted to take advantage of the darkness to advance to the last bridge in front of Bataysk.

An *Unteroffizier* who took part in the action provided the following detailed account:

The Death of Oblt. Grabert near Bataysk

He was as an eyewitness described him and his men in their last battle— always the best.

The Wehrmacht communiqué of 27 July 1942 began with the words: "South of Rostov the strongly fortified and fiercely defended city of Bataysk was stormed and taken by German troops after two days of fighting."

First among the men who achieved this feat were those of the Grabert Platoon, whose leader, in the front ranks as always, laid down his life in the battle for the bridges in front of Bataysk.

There is a huge swampy area between Rostov and Bataysk. Only a single raised embankment, on which there is a road and a railway, bridges it. It is no wonder that the Russian had trained his artillery and mortars on every part of this single line of communication. At dusk the Grabert march group, whose strength was about that of an infantry company, began its advance. The men moved along the embankment in long, widely-spaced ranks. Parachute flares rose constantly, single shots and bursts of machine-gun fire whipped over the embankment. The troopers carrying the heavy weapons panted under their burdens as they moved forward. But today there was no avoiding it, the bridge had to fall into our hands before the Russians could blow it.

Finally we reached the near bridgehead. We moved into a deep ravine right before the river. A few motorcycle troops who for hours had been laying down machine-gun fire in an attempt to prevent the Russians from blowing the bridge greeted us with grateful eyes.

Positions for our weapons were located in no time. The commander got his bearings and briefed his non-commissioned officers. It didn't look good there. The railway bridge 200 meters to our left was blazing fiercely. There must have been a heavy machine-gun in the bridge piling. It fired into our flank repeatedly. The arm of the river in front of us—a good 100 meters wide—was in full view of the enemy. On both sides of the bridge all was swamp. The commander's decision was firm. The bridge had to be in our hands and a bridgehead established before daybreak. At about 01:00 hours furious mortar fire began from over there. The first exploding shells cost deaths. Our own mortars received permission to fire. The squad leader crept out of his observation post into the night like a lynx. There—a muzzle flash. "They've fired!" he shouted loudly as the dull thump from the other side became audible.

The comrades ducked their heads until the shell exploded and the danger was past. Two enemy heavy mortars were spotted, and although we could only hear our own shells landing, they were silenced with thirteen shots. Then something

The Bridges at Bataisk

else happened. Suddenly there was a jet of flame on the bridge. The firing increased dramatically. We held our breath. Were the Russians going to blow up the bridge—half an hour before our assault? The machine-gun fire was furious, but the fire appeared harmless. A truck must have been sitting at the end of the bridge and been set on fire after being hit by a tracer round. We breathed a sigh of relief. The attack began at 02:30 hours. Brief conference with the commander. The point group moved out. Silently, like ghosts, they moved across the bridge— the two platoons followed at a distance. Still the enemy had noticed nothing. With eyes opened wide, the machine-gunners sat behind their weapons, fingers on triggers. There—the Russians opened fire. The din drowned made it impossible to hear anyone. After long, hot minutes the first parachute flares rose up from the other side. Thank God! They had made it. Others followed. Ammunition up—shift fire forward! Here we are! The enemy has been put to flight, the bridgehead established. There was no need to worry about holding it, for our Oberleutnant Grabert was in command over there.

But the Russian did not give up. He knew what he had lost. Early in the morning he showered the river bank with a hail of shells for hours. One after another the machine-guns were put out of action, finally the anti-tank gun as well. The number of wounded increased, too many for the doctor and medics to handle alone. And so other brave men pitched in to help. A tremendous example of comradeship and readiness to help, but the behavior of the wounded themselves was even more impressive. There were no cries, no complaining of pain, just muffled moans. One of the ten I bandaged in a short time had a head wound; the blood soaked two packet dressings. Quite calmly, with childlike eyes, he asked: "Is it bad?"

During a pause in the fighting a shout came from the other side: "Ammunition!" Where was our supply? The heavy weapons had no more. Nevertheless, when the Russians once again gave us some peace, we formed a munitions column with the boxes from the knocked-out machine-guns. But where was supply? We couldn't understand that our comrades behind us should leave us in the lurch. Not until much later did we receive an explanation: immediately after our attack, eight kilometers behind us the enemy had launched a partisan raid from the flank in battalion strength with the objective of overrunning the Don ferry near Rostov in order to cut us off. If they had succeeded we up front could slowly but surely have counted our hours. But that did not happen. The attack was beaten off, but Russian barrage prevented any ammunition from being moved forward all day.

With contact between the two banks repeatedly being broken because of a lack of signal flares, amid all the noise a cry was heard from the other side: "An injection of morphine for the commander!" Stabsarzt Dr. Weber and Uffz. Fohrer quickly decided to swim the river. The pair made it across in spite of heavy sniper fire. The doctor tended to the many wounded while Oblt. Grabert, who had a minor grazing head wound, described the seriousness of the situation to the Unteroffizier. The latter now swam back, pursued by rifle, anti-tank and machine-gun fire, and though slightly wounded he was able to convince the recently arrived commander of an infantry battalion and the forward artillery observer to take the most urgent measures. Then suddenly our Oberleutnant lay before us. He had suffered a serious belly wound while dashing across the bridge under heavy fire. Calm and composed, he asked for morphine. The doctor who dressed his wound tried to console him, but he only answered: "Don't kid me doc-

tor, I am a medical man myself and know that I must die." His few remaining words were dedicated to the course of the battle and the fate of his men. He was proud of them, and it also seemed a blessing to him that he was not to be one of the few to survive this heroic sacrifice.

Meanwhile all hell broke loose again. On our right flank waves of Russians charged through water and swamp. The danger of being cut off loomed large before our eyes. There was only one thing to do—the last round was pulled from the mud, captured weapons were gathered together. And then something like a miracle happened—wounded rose up from every hole, hobbled or crawled over to the embankment and with their bloodied bodies formed the wall to the right. One, an Oberschütze, whose right arm had been shot up hours earlier while he was transporting ammunition, now stood upright in his hole and calmly fired shot after shot from his Russian rifle. On the right a South-Tyrolean sat almost completely in the open at his heavy machine-gun's observation post and sent death and destruction into the enemy. Then, with the first Russians already within 200 meters, our Stukas appeared. Precisely guided by radio, they dove on the Russian attackers. Their bombing was so accurate that we were ourselves showered with dirt and stones. The Russian attack collapsed. Meanwhile, after passing along some personal messages, Oblt. Grabert closed his eyes for the last, long sleep.

And this quiet spread over the entire sector after the attack was smashed. The men lay in their foxholes, completely exhausted, and tried in vain to sleep. Those Jäger who could stand staggered over to say goodbye to their commander. Then we laid him carefully in a gully and covered him with grass and flowers. If we were relieved during the night we intended to take him with us as the Goths once did their dead kings. But we were not to succeed in this. We had to abandon the attempt after three men were wounded and one vehicle was shot up. And so he rested amid his men beneath the piling of his bridge, our Oberleutnant and Knight's Cross wearer Siegfried Grabert. And now tank after tank rolled across this bridge, headed south. Their rumble gratefully thanked the dead heroes who had cleared the way for them through swamp and death. At first the number of our missing was shockingly high, but individuals kept returning well into the night—often seriously wounded. True to his orders, an Unteroffizier had held out all night in the approaches to the bridge, the enemy all around him. When, following a thorough preparatory artillery bombardment, the infantry stormed toward Bataysk the next morning, he went with them and led an assault team until he collapsed under fire. When Lt. Hiller was badly wounded and called out for help, an Unteroffizier medic crawled through the darkness to the most forward position and died with him after being shot in the head. But my thoughts slide back to those carefree days as a student in Tübingen, where we spent so many Sunday mornings.

Total losses suffered by the Grabert company in the operation against the Don bridges before Bataysk were 87 men, specifically: 17 men killed (2 officers, 2 NCOs, 13 enlisted men), 16 men missing (2 NCOs and 14 enlisted men), and 54 men wounded (11 NCOs and 43 enlisted men), of whom 34 were taken to hospital. *8. Kp./II./Lehr-Regiment BR z.b.V. 800* was subsequently pulled out of the line and transferred to the rear to reorganize in peace. After his death Oblt. Grabert was recommended for the Oak Leaves in recognition of his heroic actions. Under the command of Headquarters, 1st Panzer Army and principally employed in the area of III. Pz.Korps commanded by *General* von Mackensen, the individual companies were caught up in the southwards advance by German units through Armavir and Maykop to the Caucasus. They participated in the increasingly fierce fighting, without at first being called upon to undertake further special missions.

The initially rapid German advance into the Caucasus was carried out without regard to remaining Soviet splinter groups and open flanks. As a result, following German reserves, supply columns and Kampfgruppen frequently became involved in heavy fighting with these same Soviet forces. Not infrequently units of *II./Lehr-Regiment BR z.b.V. 800* were also involved, having been deployed as flanking cover. This resulted in casualties which reduced the fighting strengths of the companies.

Accompanying the rapid advance by the 13. Pz.Div. (*General* Herr), elements of the *II./Lehr-Regiment BR z.b.V. 800* finally reached the area approximately five to six kilometers from Maykop, the panzer division's next objective. Black clouds of smoke already hung over the city, the Soviets having set the oil wells on fire. The objective was to seize the city quickly, before further demolitions rendered the oil wells completely unusable.

This was an ideal setting for another special operation by the *Brandenburgers*: the bridges over the Byelya, beyond which extended the city of Maykop. It was to be carried out by Lt. Prohaska and his men. The following is a detailed account of the operation:

Capturing the Bridges over the Byelya before Maykop

Finally prepare for Prohaska action. I drove up again to Oberst Crisolli, commander of the 13. Pz.Div.'s rifle regiment, and six kilometers from Maykop received detailed mission orders. I brought Ernst Prohaska forward. Our men moved like automatons in the blazing heat and it cost me a lot of sweat to get my load moving. Oswald Sommer dropped out immediately, since while leaping from the vehicle he shot himself through the hand with our famous submachine-gun. The mission under Lt. Prohaska started at 17:00 hours. Riding in the lead tank commanded by Oblt. Morell, I led the mission with the special assignment of preventing the tanks from pressing ahead too quickly, as this had so often cost us the success of our missions. We had the men get down from the four captured trucks. It worked perfectly, although several times General Herr came roaring up and wanted to turn the relief tanks loose prematurely. Although our mission group in Maykop lost its way on the way to the bridge, it was able to infiltrate its way into the retreating Russian vehicles without being recognized. As part of this retreating column it slowly rolled to the Byelya bridge with numerous stops.

During the last halt before the bridge one of our Russian-Germans was spoken to by a Russian general, who, standing above the defile that fell away to the bridge, was watching the crossing by his troops. He had formerly served in the forces commanded by this Russian officer and was now recognized by him. Luckily they exchanged words without our men being recognized as Germans. The nervous strain caused by such incidents cannot be described. There was another immediately afterwards: a Russian traffic director was standing right in front of the bridge and stopped our first captured vehicle with his white flag to prevent a stoppage on the bridge. When it was time to move on the starter failed. Our volunteer Russian driver then shouted at the traffic controller, who ran over, cranked the engine and waved us on. Our vehicle rolled across the bridge over the Byelya far below. On the other side the men jumped out quickly and immediately took out a tanker truck sitting at the other end of the bridge with hand grenades and submachine-guns. At the same time the ignition wire for the bridge's explosive charge was cut and an all-round position was set up in the bridgehead. I had given strict orders for the relief tanks not to fire, so as to give us the best possible chance of passing through the city, which was full of enemy troops, to the bridge. Oblt. Morell immediately understood all of these requirements which were so foreign to him. In the terrific confusion of the Russian retreat and the clouds of dust our dirt-covered tanks succeeded in passing through Maykop unnoticed, past Russian march columns sitting ready to go in the side streets. When a shot was accidentally fired from one of the panye wagons behind us, to my great amusement Oblt. Morell said into his throat microphone in a most measured tone and well-articulated radio German: "Don't shoot! Don't shoot! What asshole has started shooting here?" We also briefly became lost just short of the bridge when we could already see the flares fired by Ernst Prohaska, for the correct route to the bridge took an unexpected turn. An old grandmother showed us the way to the bridge at an intersection. We reached the bridge eighteen minutes after it was taken. The bridge, which was of iron construction with a planked driving surface, was completely clogged with vehicles, including those that had driven up behind us. Almost all were abandoned. Right in front of our tank was a panye wagon and in front of it a heavy Soviet Zis limousine. Oblt. Morell drove over the panye wagon with his tank and wanted to do the same to the car. This he was unable to do, however, because the tank's clutch was damaged and could not take the strain. The tank was unable to back up for the same reason and thus the narrow bridge was completely blocked. Almost fifty minutes passed, during which there was a heavy exchange of fire. Ernst Prohaska, who obviously wanted to speed up the proceedings, came running across the bridge through the heavy fire and fell almost right in front of our tank. Unfortunately only then did our vehicle succeed in backing up, clearing the bridge. A following Panzer IV then drove over the Russian car and pushed the remaining vehicles off the other end of the bridge. The tanks rolled across and with the following infantry occupied the bridgehead. The bulk of the enemy troops still in the city escaped by crossing the Byelya downstream and entering the forests that began on the left bank on the road to Tuapse. After darkness fell I assembled our men and had them driven back to Crisolli's command post. At the same time I reported to the Oberst. The otherwise so aloof commander almost hugged me, although it didn't come to that. In any case they had us to thank for the successful seizure of the city of Maykop and its river crossing. (A crude oil brigade whose emblem was a drilling tower arrived at the same time as we.) That would otherwise have held them up for at least four days observed Oberst Cristolli.

Early on 10 August 1942 the fallen of this Maykop bridge operation, including the brave Lt. Prohaska, who was posthumously awarded the Knight's Cross, were laid to rest on the left bank of the Byelya in sight of the still-burning city. Seven comrades had been killed, including several from 5. Kp.: Oblt. Zülch (killed on the advance road near Dondudovs-kaya), Lt. Pils, Walter Perunter, Fw. Schink and three other men. After a brief rest break the southeastwards advance was resumed—toward the Terek region. It seemed as if the *II./Lehr-Regiment BR z.b.V. 800* was spread out among the entire army of the Caucasus.

Voroshilov was passed through on 17 August; rest day in Kruglolesskoye; on through Novo-Georgievsk, Voronzovo—Alexandrovskoye, where on 23 August the march column occupied quarters. Finally on 31 August the advance entered the Terek Valley in order to force the first crossings of the river line. There at the Terek the enemy had established a new defense line; to break through it was the task given the German formations so as to make possible the continuation of the advance. Several panzer divisions were assembled in the area west of Mozdok; these were to force their way through the Soviet Terek front; in their area was *II./Lehr-Regiment BR z.b.V. 800*, which was to capture small bridgeheads across the river line in several special night operations. One such operation was carried out by 5. Kp. near Naurskaya on 8-9 September under the command of Lt. Steidl. It was a success, allowing the waiting Kampfgruppe to advance on Gnadenburg—Malgobek on the south bank of the Terek.

In the weeks that followed there was fierce fighting in the Terek region with Soviet forces which defended their positions grimly. The companies of the *II./Lehr-Regiment BR z.b.V. 800* in particular, were in action day and night. The following is from the diary of 8. *Kompanie*:

10/9/1942: Motorized advance by 8.Kp. into the Mozdok area. Same night crossed the Terek over a temporary bridge.

11/9/1942: Motorized advance by the company through Gnadenburg, south of Pavlodolskaya to Malgobek.

12-17/9/1942: Quartered near Malgobek in a lice-infested system of Soviet positions. Several patrols sent out from there.

19-24/9/1942: Capture of the hill between Nishnikurp and Werchnikurp by the company; several men wounded by heavy Soviet machine-gun fire.

25-27/9/1942: 8. Kp. at rest in Werch. Akbasch.

28/9/1942: Forest march by 8.Kp. with limited enemy contact, then securi-

ty on hills southwest of Illarinovka. Also flak in position there.

29/9-1/10/1942: In same position.

2-7/10/1942: Forest security on Seno mountain west of Samankul. Only Soviet opposition from forest bandits with submachine-guns and hand grenades. The heavy company lost two killed and several wounded here.

On the same day that the 8. Kp. was on security duty on Seno Mountain, the 5. Kp. received orders to attack and take the village of Planovskoye, southwest of Werch. Abkasch, which was heavily occupied by the enemy. The following is an account of the operation by the mission leader:

Operation Planovskoye—25 September 1942

A new, difficult mission lay before us: attack the strongly fortified and manned village of Planovskoye on the Terek. The extended village was surrounded by completely open plains. All around was one position after another. These were occupied by heavy anti-tank guns and countless light and heavy machine-guns; an artillery observation post was also discovered. The Russian air force had command of the air, furthermore an armored train operated as far as Planovskoye. The man formerly in charge of heating deserted to us and told us everything he knew. He said that the village was held by Soviet officer cadets who would defend to the utmost in case of a German attack. We and a pioneer battalion made up the attacking infantry. Tank and armored troop carrier units were to advance further. During a briefing of junior commanders he revealed the honorable mission of sending patrols into the village defenses to find a weak spot so as to enable the other units to carry out a less costly attack. The outskirts of the village were mined. Lt. Unger would lead the mission. He was from my half-company. In the event that he failed I was to follow with the rest of the company. In the afternoon I drove with Louis Unger to the most forward outposts to conduct a final examination of the terrain and discuss the method of attack.

It would be a hard nut, Unger confided to me, but there was confidence in his eyes. He was from South Tyrol and wanted to become an active officer. His bravery in battle and his daring stamped him as an exemplary officer. Sepp had decided to go with Unger. In the evening Hans Weber, my faithful driver, asked to be allowed to come along on the next day's mission. Filled with tension, we lay down to rest and slept a restless sleep until midnight. At 02:00 hours we drove forward to the outpost. Sitting next to me in the car was Louis; he shivered, the cold night wind whistled through the shot-up windshield. Louis was completely calm and collected, although he told me that in two hours he would no longer be alive. I had a similar premonition. We reached the very front lines. The riflemen squatted freezing in their holes and stared into the darkness. It was quiet, now and then a Russian over at the outskirts of the village fired a parachute flare— more out of habit than malice, he had no way of knowing that today was his day. It was 04:00. Louis Unger and his thirty men marched into the darkness toward the vastly superior enemy. Before he left I shook his hand and whispered to him, "Heil und Sieg!" He had 1200 meters to go to the village. When he had stormed one section of the position the pioneers and tanks were supposed to move out. Unger had been gone an hour already. Zülch and I waited tensely for the first sounds of fighting. We had moved 500 meters past the outposts. Beside us was the command vehicle of the artillery observer. My men lay in the ditches by the road and slept. In the east it began to get light. Brief bursts of fire from German and Russian submachine-guns flared up, hand grenades exploded, then it was quiet again in the village. So Unger had made it there. After a few minutes, however, the witch's dance began again. Illumination flares rose high, whistling signal flares rang out, the Russians were alerted and launching a counterattack. The sound of fighting grew louder from minute to minute. Pioneers attempted to get through to Unger. After a short while they came back, covered in blood. They had failed to get through. Zülch and I tried everything to have the armored portion of the attack committed. We failed, as the defensive fire over the open plain was too furious. It was broad daylight. Zülch and I wanted to establish contact with Unger in the town. Perhaps the two of us could make it across the open plain. In a hail of shells we ran upright toward the section of trench on the outskirts of the village where we thought Unger to be. Suddenly bullets began whizzing about us and we clearly saw six Russian machine-guns 200 meters away, firing at us. Burst after burst whistled past, just over our heads; we lay pressed flat against the earth. They were hours of desperation. We could neither move forwards nor backwards. Unger was surrounded in the village, we expected death at any second. The enemy armored train approached slowly from Darg-Koch. I could clearly see its white smoke and the dark barrels of its cannon. Soon it began firing at us. Shells struck the earth with tremendous fury in front of and behind us. Iron fragments howled through the air. In the inferno of this battle Lutz came running and reported: "Lt. Unger is dead, almost everyone else dead or wounded, remainder completely surrounded." There was only one thing for us to do: help those men still alive or go to ground ourselves. I jumped up, ran ten meters, and threw myself down again. I'm not dead yet, was my only thought, even though bullets whizzed and cracked all around me. I threw away my submachine-gun and steel helmet, I was too weak; I had to get back to the corn field and bring relief forces. After a one-kilometer run for my life I did it. Zülch kept up with me. I immediately committed the attack, cost what it may. The pioneers and tanks were too cowardly to attack. I told the commander what I thought, even though he was several ranks higher. Then we stormed off. Shouting, we raced across the open plain. Many were killed, many cried out in pain, but suddenly we were at the edge of the village in front of the Russian positions. Grimly we rolled up hole after hole and destroyed the enemy, who defended desperately. Vladimir Mark and Brune were my best people. With them I was the first to reach Unger's people, whom Sepp Schmied had been leading determinedly for eight hours while completely surrounded. We hugged him. It was impossible to lift one's head above the rim of the trench, there were still snipers on the hill where the observation post was. After some determined work these, too, were destroyed. The armored elements rolled into the village, after I had rolled up the positions. At the south end of the village an anti-tank rifle was still firing along the one-kilometer-long village street. I gathered the bodies of my dead comrades and found among them my driver Hans Weber. It was hard for me to take, there were tears in my eyes. Together with Mark and several soldiers I dug a mass grave at the outskirts of the village. Ignoring our wounded, we buried our fallen comrades, including our brave Lt. Louis Unger, in the warm earth. At the command post Sepp tended to the many wounded. Karl Sauter had a serious chest wound; in spite of this he stood upright, smoked a cigarette and talked enthusiastically about the next mission. He was a one of a kind warrior. Tired and worn out, we fell into a trench, which we shared with the dead Bolsheviks. The Russian artillery fired without pause, I scarcely heard it; the village was in flames, I didn't care, I just wanted to feel no pain for a few hours.

The company stood assembled in an open square once again to say farewell to their dead comrades. The simple soldier's grave was bordered by captured Maxim machine-guns. In the middle lay Louis Unger, left and right his intimates, including Hans Weber, Ladurner, Alfrieder, Huber, Fred and so on. They remained as lookouts on our difficult path, thousands of kilometers away from their homeland. In the south the huge mountains of the central Caucasus gleamed. The company's most difficult and costly operation was behind it.

Only one day after the 8. Kp. took up quarters in Planovskoye, on 9 October another risky operation was initiated under the command of Lt. Lau. The target was the twin bridges (rail and road bridges) over the Terek west of Arik and the operation was a complete success.

The river crossing was an approximately 120-meter-long railway bridge on the oil transport line that ran Baku—Crossni—Rostov. The operation was committed against this object, while we knew too little about the road bridge which the Soviets had recently built farther south, to include it in the operation. And so in terms of men and weapons, planning for the operation was limited to the railway bridge. With the 13. Pz.Div.'s vigorous advance there would only be a few hours in which to complete it. At dawn a force of 35 men succeeded in taking the bridge positions by surprise. They rolled up the earth bunkers and trenches and cut the ignition wires leading to the demolition charges. The enemy was so perplexed and surprised that an immediate further attack from the hedgehog position on the riverbank succeeded in also rendering unusable the ignition wires leading to the road bridge. The Soviet demolition plan for the railway bridge was captured, and it showed that about 4 tons of explosives had been stuffed into three of the supports. In addition, thirty-two aerial bombs were discovered under the first arch of the bridge.

The men who took part in this raid were decorated with the Iron Cross, First or Second Class, while the mission leader, Lt. Lau, received the Knight's Cross. In addition, on 13 December 1942 Headquarters, 1st Panzer Army sent the following telex:

My sincerest congratulations on the Knight's Cross of the Iron Cross awarded to you for your battle-deciding act of bravery.

signed von Mackensen

Headquarters, 1st Panzer Army

After various special missions by *II./Lehr-Regiment BR z.b.V. 800* resulted in the formation of a number of bridgeheads from the east bank of the Terek, at the end of October 1942 German armored units (the 13.Pz.Div. on 29 October 1942) resumed the advance to the south. By this time the individual BR companies had gone over to the defensive in their quarters and along the Terek, and when the German attack to the south was resumed they moved out. They accompanied the armored advance in Kampfgruppe formations. The 8.Kp.'s advance road was:

Giselj (before Ordzhonikidze on the Terek)—Kodachdshin—Alagir, at the foot of the Caucasus, end point of the railway line. The southernmost point that was reached. Karman—Ssindsikau—Digora—Tschikoja—Chrasnidon—Naltschik.

The advance was repeatedly accompanied by heavy fighting, in which the *Brandenburgers* were frequently involved. As always, they also had to carry out special missions against important targets.

On 2 November a mission was planned against the bridge over the Terek near Darg-Koch north of Ardon to be carried out by Oblt. Zülch's 5. Kp.

The mission leader on this operation, Lt. Steidl, succeeded in crossing the intervening ground with a force of thirty men at night and passing the bridge. On the other side, however, Steidl ran into a heavily-manned system of Soviet positions. He described what followed:

A fierce battle broke out for the bunkers. In hand-to-hand combat and pistol duels we succeeded in taking the bunkers, though with casualties. The bulk of the enemy regiment fled in total confusion into the town of Darg-Koch. We turned the cannon and anti-tank rifles around and fired shot after shot into the confused mass. I immediately radioed Zülch: "Bridge in our hands undamaged at 05:00 hours." White recognition flares rose up. Several nearby bunkers were still occupied by the Russians. I was unable to launch an attack against them, my losses were too high. A Russian counterattack was likely in minutes, large gatherings were visible at the outskirts of the town. The artillery on the opposite hills was already laying down direct fire on us. I radioed for rocket artillery support. This proved a failure, however, as the projectiles were short and landed in our positions. I suffered further casualties from friendly fire. Russian tanks and trucks loaded with infantry rolled out of the town toward us. We shot them up. After two hours of fighting ammunition was running low. The Russians had already pressed close to us on a broad front. Relief had still not arrived, the Russians were placing barrage fire on the road from Ardon, over which our relief had to advance. In vain we looked back. All we saw was a few infantry lying flat on the other bank, it had to be Zülch with his people. I trusted that he would help us. But he did not come. The Russians came ever nearer. I was now holding the bridge with ten men. All that we had left was hand grenades and a few rounds of ammunition. We squatted on dead and wounded Bolsheviks in the trench and defended ourselves desperately. Enemy hand grenades were already flying into our holes. Obj. Niederkoster was killed by a shot through the head while standing next to me, Mark received a serious head wound, Trinko too. I applied makeshift dressings to both. There seemed no hope of retreat, the bridge lay under heavy fire, the Russians wanted to blow it. Suddenly a Leutnant and an Oberjäger appeared in the trench. They brought orders from Zülch for me to withdraw immediately to our side of the river since relief could not reach me. So it had all been in vain; the way back was almost impassible in the heavy fire. I tried to rouse and encourage my men. It succeeded. The wounded went first. Only Mark and Trinko made it to the safety of the bank. I had to watch as my wounded were shot up. It was also not possible to bring reinforcements across the railway bridge. Now it was my turn. I lobbed my last hand grenade at the Russians, leapt from the trench and rolled down the 20-meter-high slope to the bridge, jumped up and ran across it. There was firing from all sides. The heel was shot off one of my boots, splinters of wood sprayed in front of me. I stumbled and tripped over a dead body: it was my faithful Magajef. Now there was only one thing to do; I clambered over the railing and jumped from the 15-meter-high bridge into the river. With wild desperation, half unconscious, I reached the bank where the rest of the company was already in position. Under heavy fire, I made it to Zülch through a drainage ditch and made my report. He ordered me to prevent a crossing of the river until nightfall. Relief was coming in the evening. Freezing and hungry, I joined what was left of my men in a hole in the ground. The last of Sepp's emergency rations raised my spirits a little. By evening I had determined my losses. Ganzert, the Romanian-German, had drowned, Fw. Winter, Dorn, Liguda and others had been killed. Many wounded lay in the marsh on the riverbank and could not be recovered until it was dark. In the evening hours the bridge went up before our eyes with a mighty roar. The promised relief arrived, and tired and worn out we returned to our former bivouac near Ardon.

Here we have a shocking example of an initially successful operation ending in failure because relief could not be supplied in time. These were among the most difficult and bitterest experiences of the *Brandenburgers*.

A few days after this operation against the road bridge at Darg-Koch the commander of this successful 5. Kp., Oblt. Zülch, was forced to go to the rear with an ear problem. During the course of a enemy breakthrough into the train area and the subsequent counterattack he was killed by an explosive bullet. Soon afterwards Lt. Steidl was placed in command of the company. The offensive battles in the area of Headquarters, 1st Panzer Army, the army of the Caucasus, continued. In each case they cost further irreplaceable losses and took the *Brandenburgers*, especially II. Btl., deeper into the Caucasus region. But Soviet resistance became ever stronger in association with the imminent encirclement of the German 6. *Armee* in and around Stalingrad.

The enemy breakthroughs on both sides of this city also placed the army group under *Generalfeldmarschall* von Manstein in increasing danger of being separated from its narrow supply base, the most important part of which ran over the road from Kerch and through Rostov. It was there that another *Brandenburg* unit made a name for itself, conducting successful operations, especially early in the fighting: the *Küstenjäger-Kompanie Brandenburg* (coastal commando company). In the beginning its hunting grounds lay in the waters of the Black Sea and the Sea of Azov; its missions were surprise landings from the sea against important enemy-held objects. Formed at Swinemünde in the summer of 1942 at the suggestion of the regimental commander under the cover name of *Leichte Pionier-Kompanie* (light combat engineer company), the unit was familiarized with marine operations at Swinemünde with the help of the *Kriegsmarine*. Equipped with assault boats and pioneer landing craft with light weapons up to 20-mm anti-aircraft guns, it saw its first action in the Strait of Kerch against the Taman Peninsula northwest of Novorossisk. The mission was to eliminate a Soviet observation post situated in the wreck of the beached steamer Gorniak; from there Russian artillery observers were calling down well-directed artillery fire on the crossing point in the Strait of Kerch used by German units. A secondary objective was to destroy a Soviet searchlight position on the mainland near Cape Pekly which illuminated the waterway every night. The operation was prepared in the well-tested manner and ended with the elimination of both targets. Following the conclusion of offensive activities in southern Russia at the end of 1942-early 1943 the *Küstenjäger-Kompanie Brandenburg* moved to Langenargen on Lake Constance, where it made good its losses, pushed ahead with its formation and at the same time was expanded into a *Küstenjäger-Abteilung Brandenburg*. At the turn of the year its organization was as follows:

Battalion headquarters *Küstenjäger-Abteilung Brandenburg*

    1 group of assault boats
    1 pioneer landing craft
    2 light machine-guns
1. (Kst.Jg.) Kp.:
    9 light machine-guns,
    2 light anti-aircraft guns,
    2 medium mortars plus assault boats and
        Type 41 pioneer landing craft
2. (Kst.Jg.) Kp.: same as the 1. Kompanie
3. (Kst.Jg.) Kp.: same as the 1. Kompanie
4. (schw. Kst.Jg.) Kp.:
    14 light machine-guns,
    6 light anti-aircraft guns,
    6 commando boats

Battalion also fully motorized.

The *Küstenjäger-Abteilung Brandenburg* was subsequently employed mainly on anti-partisan operations from the sea, for example on the Côte d'Azur, in the Adriatic and the Mediterranean area, where it carried out a series of daring landing operations against coastal towns and the Greek islands. It also took part in the operations against Fiume and the island of Rhodes with success. In 1944 it became an independent unit and did not become part of the Pz.Gren.Div. BR.

Chapter 3
Anti-Partisan Warfare in the Balkans

The multitude of missions that developed during the course of the war years, the manifold possibilities on land, water and from the air, the widening of the theaters of war in which the *Brandenburgers* fought everywhere, may have prompted the OKW at the end of 1942-beginning of 1943 to consider bringing the widely-scattered units under the unified command of a division headquarters based in Berlin. It was planned to turn away from the previous form of mission and instead suit them to the altered situation at the front. The growing partisan movement in western Russia and in the southeast of Europe made it necessary to guard supply routes which entailed the increasing use of battle-tested German troops. The *Brandenburgers* units were particularly well suited to this role.

In the aftermath of this decision some BR units were withdrawn from their current areas of operation, some of which were already located in the Balkans, and transferred to their home bases for reorganization, expansion and reequipment with conventional weapons. Other BR units, which had spent the last months at their bases, were transferred into new areas of operation after their reorganization.

All in all the expansion of the *Brandenburg* units resulted in a significant bolstering of strength, in which the former Bataillone must be seen as the foundations for future regiments. At first, at the end of 1942 and increasingly in January 1943, these expansions took place under the cover of numberings, and the following units were created:

Sonderverband 800 – for *Brandenburg* home headquarters
Sonderverband 801 – from I. Btl.   – for 1. Rgt. BR
Sonderverband 802 – from II. Btl.   – for 2. Rgt. BR
Sonderverband 803 – from III. Btl.   – for 3. Rgt. BR
Sonderverband 804 – from IV. Btl.   – for 4. Rgt. BR
Sonderverband 805   — for 5. Rgt. BR
(*Sonderverband* = special unit)

In addition, formed from the former Nachr.Kp. BR (signals company) was the *Nachr.Abt./Sonderverband 800*. The *Art.Abt./Sonderver-band 800* (artillery battalion) and various smaller units were formed from scratch. The regiments expanded to sixteen companies.

This reorganization brought many difficulties for numerous *Brandenburg* units, as in many cases it had to be carried out while the units were on deployment. The unit numberings were changed, various commanders, non-commissioned officers and enlisted men were transferred for other new formations. But the command of *Sonderverband 800* sought ways of withdrawing all units still in action as soon as possible and returning them to their bases to carry out their reorganization. This often required great effort, especially since the situation at the front in the spring of 1943 made it difficult to release any unit in action at the front. Nevertheless, on 1 April 1943 the former *Sonderverband 800* was renamed the *Division Brandenburg.*

Division Brandenburg z.b.V.800

Division commander, Ia and adjutant
Base: Berlin – Hohenzollerndamm
        Friedrichstr. 94
        Berlin-Birkenwerder
Tactical Emblem: red eagle on white field
        Wappenschild: black-white-red
1. Regiment:
Created from – I./Lehr.Rgt.
Base: Brandenburg/Havel (home headquarters)
I. Bataillon:
1. – 4. Kp.
II. Bataillon:
5.-7. Kp.
8. Kp. not yet established
III. Bataillon:
9.-11. Kp.
12. Kp. not yet established
Rgt.-Nachr.-Zug (regimental signals platoon)
Rgt.-Batterie – from 1944 (regimental battery)
2. Regiment:
created from II./Lehr.Rgt.
base: Admont (home headquarters)
I. Bataillon: created from 5. Kp./Lehr-Rgt.
1.-3. Kp.
4. Kp. from 1944
II. Bataillon: created from 7. Kp./Lehr-Rgt.
5.-8. Kp.
III. Bataillon: created from 8. Kp./Lehr-Rgt.
9.-11. Kp.
12. Kp. not yet established
Rgt.-Nachr.-Zug
Rgt.-Batterie –from 1944
3. Regiment:
created from III./Lehr-Rgt. (remaining coastal drivers)
    (remaining members of Africa Detachment)
Base: Düren/Rhld. (home headquarters)
I. Bataillon:
1.-3. Kp.

4. Kp. disbanded mid-July 1943
II. Bataillon:
9.-11. Kp.
12.Kp. disbanded mid-July 1943
Rgt.-Nachr.-Zug
Rgt.-Batterie from 1944
Panzer-Kompanie from Feb. 1944
4.Regiment:
created from *Sonderverband H* (remaining Danube drivers)
Base: Brandenburg/Havel (home headquarters)
I. Bataillon:
1.-5. Kp.
II. Bataillon:
6.-8. Kp.
9. Kp. from August 1943
10.Kp. from Sept. 1943
III. Bataillon:
Companies from the von Koenen Abteilung (Africa)
Rgt.-Nachr.-Zug
Rgt.-Batterie from 1944
Panzer-Kompanie from Feb. 1944

Also created were several special units which were not incorporated into the larger formation on account of the nature of their missions.

The organization depicted here was the goal of the reorganization process which was very slow in reaching completion on account of the conditions at the fronts and the missions of the *Brandenburgers*. In January of 1943 the *II./Sonderverband 802* (the former *II. Btl./Lehr-Regiment BR z.b.V. 800*) was involved in heavy fighting during the retreat from the Caucasus toward the Kuban bridgehead. Its path back to the Don is illustrated by the route taken by its *8. Kompanie*:

9 Jan. 1943	Pyatigorsk
11 Jan 1943	Voronzovskaya
15 Jan. 1943	Vordorazdel
17 Jan. 1943	Rodukinskoye
21 Jan. 1943	Koprovski-Armavir
26 Jan. 1943	Gorskaya-Balka
30 Jan. 1943	Yekaterinovskaya
5 Feb. 1943	Azov, on the Don Delta, southwest of Rostov
10 Feb. 1943	Sinyavka, north of the Don Delta
17 Feb. 1943	Troitskoye, in the Mius position

18 Feb. to 3 April 1943 as corps reserve in Troitskoye, west of the Mius position. 4 April 1943: *II./Lehr-Regiment BR z.b.V. 800* entrained for return to the homeland.

This was the route taken by the forces withdrawing from the Caucasus to the Mius position, which for the next while would represent the defense line of the German forces in the south of the Eastern Front.

Stationed in the north of the Eastern Front in the Leningrad area toward the end of 1942 was the *16. (Lei.) Kompanie* (later II./4. Rgt. BR) which had been formed in September 1942. After a short time, during which it saw no action in Russia, this company was transferred to the Balkans for operations against the partisans. Its base there was Milanovac.

Meanwhile, in January 1943 I./1. Rgt. BR was still engaged in reorganization at its current base at Freiburg. Not until 30 January did it receive its first mission: anti-partisan operations in Lithuania and Estonia. It subsequently entrained and was transported via Frankfurt—Kassel—Berlin—Stettin—Königsberg—Insterburg—Tilsit to Idriza, Lithuania, where it was housed in the barracks of an old firing range. A mission order for security duties and the simultaneous engagement of partisan units active in the local area was received on 15 February. In addition to these duties there was still time for training, vehicle maintenance, etc. Finally, on 16 March, I./1. Rgt. BR was loaded aboard trains again and was taken via Dvinsk through Estonia to Kliastizie, from where it traveled by truck into the notorious partisan area around Kresty. No sooner had the unit arrived there when elements of the battalion walked into an ambush which claimed the lives of *Gefreiter* Müller and *Gefreiter* Häsler of 3. *Kompanie*. There were frequent fierce battles in this area with the partisans, who appeared out of nowhere and disappeared just as quickly. Casualties mounted.

At the same time, February-March 1943, at Düren the reorganization of the 3. Rgt. BR, as well as of the III. Btl., which was also based there, was approaching its end. At the beginning of April the regimental headquarters of 3. Rgt. BR entrained together with III. Btl. and was transported into the area south of Karachev, Russia. It was anticipated that the regiment would see action in "Operation *Zitadelle*", the attack in the Kursk salient. Meanwhile the regiment's II. Bataillon remained in the area of operations in southern France, where it went about its special missions until mid-1944. Other elements of this II./3. Rgt. BR transferred to Italy in the summer of 1944 and saw action there.

I./3. Rgt. BR remained at Düren until mid-1943 in order to complete its reorganization and rearmament.

So in April 1943 the *Division Brandenburg z.b.V. 800* was spread out over all of Europe: I./1. Rgt. BR in the Deminez area of Lithuania-Estonia in action against partisans; II./1. Rgt. BR still at Freiburg in the Gallwitz Barracks undergoing reorganization. The bulk of 2. *(Jäger)* Rgt. BR was at its bases in Austria for rest-refit and reorganization. I./3. Rgt. BR was still at Düren in reorganization; II./3. Rgt. BR was in southern France; III./3. Rgt. BR and the regimental headquarters of 3. Rgt. BR was in the area south of Karachev in preparation for "Operation Zitadelle." 4. Rgt. BR was still in the formation process. Understandably, under these conditions a unified command of a division formation was impossible. All that the division commander could do was go on the road and visit each of his units in turn.

Even though the *Division Brandenburg z.b.V. 800* was under the direct command of the OKW/*Wehrmacht* Operations Staff, the individual regiments and battalions inevitably had to be assigned to the command agencies in their respective areas of operation. These agencies had little understanding of these special *Brandenburg* units, however, which usually caused considerable problems. The result was the employment of these *Brandenburg* units as infantry where the fighting was fiercest, which had to lead to their decimation. Of course they were then no longer capable of carrying out their actual missions.

At the beginning of June 1943 I./3. Rgt. BR was transported by express train from Düren to the Pustoshka area, roughly 150 km west of Vitebsk, for anti-partisan duties in the area of Headquarters, 1 Army Corps. A more logical move would have been to send it to join its regiment in the area south of Karachev. Meanwhile, as part of an armored group comprising the 4. Pz.Div. and the 10. Pz.Gren.Div., the regiment's III. Btl. took part in a major anti-partisan operation in the area southwest of Bryansk. The operation was only a modest success, however, for while the partisans were able to escape into the swampy wooded country, the fully-motorized German forces became bogged down. As a result elements of the 3. Regiment BR did not play a direct part in "Operation Zitadelle," instead at the end of July 1943 they became caught up in the general retreat which followed the Soviet counteroffensive in the Orel—Bryansk area, south of Kursk and on both sides of Sinkiw. Elements of the 3. Regiment *Brandenburg* were caught up in this and fought in a purely infantry role in the retreat to the Dniepr.

At the beginning of July 1943 the I./1. Rgt. BR again found itself engaged in anti-partisan operations in the Alolia area and on 9 July it was transported by express train via Pskov—Luga into the Orodesh area, still in Lithuania-Estonia, where it continued its anti-partisan role. Meanwhile on about 15 June the III./1. Rgt. BR was transported from its base to Greece. There it occupied quarters in the Thebes—Amphissa area. Its mission: anti-bandit operations!

Meanwhile, following their rest-refit and reorganization, elements of the 2. Regiment BR were now also on the move again and were transported by rail to Greece. In mid-July 1943 the I./2. (Jäg.) Rgt. BR moved into Ptolemais and saw its first action in and near Olympia on 17 July.

Finally, early in August 1943, on the 5th day of the month to be precise, I./1. Rgt. BR's period of anti-partisan duties in Estonia-Lithuania came to an end. It was transported by rail via Wilna—Posen—Breslau—Ratibor to Ludenburg, Austria and from there by motor vehicle to Neuhaus, Styria, where it occupied quarters. The period that followed was taken up by reorganization, reequipment with new weapons and equipment, including vehicles. This period of rest and reorganization extended undisturbed until 10 September 1943. On the other hand the I./4. Rgt. BR was already in action in the southeast area. It consisted of three rifle companies plus a heavy company. In terms of armament and organization the battalion was largely comparable to a motorized rifle battalion, with the rifle squads equipped with the latest weapons. Each squad was a twelve-man unit with truck transport and armed with rifles, automatic rifles, rifle grenades and MG 42 machine-guns. Each company included *Sturmpioniere* (assault combat engineers), while in addition to heavy machine-gun and heavy mortar platoons, the heavy company was also equipped with 105-mm recoilless guns, 75-mm anti-tank guns and 20-mm anti-aircraft guns. But the II./4. Rgt. BR was also in action in southeastern Europe, especially in the Foca and Podgrab area, where the 6. Kp. in particular distinguished itself in fierce fighting.

Thus with the exception of the 3. Regiment, almost all the battalions of the *Brandenburg* regiments were assembled in southeastern Europe. At the beginning of September 1943 the 3. Regiment's I. Btl. was involved in heavy defensive fighting against superior Russian forces in the area north of Gurki. Its II. Btl. was operating in southern France, while its regimental headquarters and III. Btl. were caught up in the tough fighting withdrawal toward the Dniepr (southwest of Roslavl).

Finally, on 12 September, the rested I./1. Rgt. BR entrained at Neuhaus, Austria for transport into the Balkans. It first detrained in Nish and occupied temporary quarters in the town. On 22 September its rail journey continued through Macedonia, passing through Skoplje, before it finally detrained in Saloniki (Greece). On 28 September it finally arrived in the Levadia area by way of the pass at Thermopylae. There its companies occupied strongpoints and carried out their first patrol operations against partisans.

Everywhere in the Balkans, in Greece, Albania and Yugoslavia, underground forces were at work. Local forces, officially referred to as bandits or partisans, fought to drive out the occupiers or at least make their lives difficult. Most were civilians who took up arms and employed all means to set up new fighting areas behind the fronts so as to tie up German troops and hinder their use at the fronts. They believed in employing all means available: explosives to destroy bridges and tunnels; disruption of rail transport; ambushes at night and in bad weather; the use of the dagger and knife to silently eliminate lone sentries and runners. All of these were employed as well as attacks on German strongpoints. In general the solution was: kill and destroy the German occupiers! The partisans were supported by the Allies, by Soviet Russia, with arms and money. Night after night canisters, parachutes, containers, arms and equipment for the partisans rained down from the skies.

The following is a radio message from the "Red Orchestra" dated 29 September 1943:

Albert to Director (Moscow)—from Werther to Olga:

Since 21 September all rail connections between northern Italy and Germany rendered unusable or occupied except for the Villach—Udine line. Large numbers of Croatian and Slovenian guerillas (??) under the command of Tito are joining with Italian troops of the Fiume, Zara and Laibach districts and are disrupting communications in the German rear, on whose maintenance German troops in Italy are largely dependent. Likewise almost all rail lines and roads between northern Italy and southern France have been cut, so that the German troops sent to Italy are as good as encircled, with no supply of weapons, ammunition or materiel. They would be lost if the heavily-armed Allied army landed in southern Italy would fight like Tito's partisans, who have no air force.

But the German command is counting on the continued slow tempo of the Allies and will seek a way out through the new massed call-up of Austrian reserves for use against Tito's partisans.

In these fierce battles full of tricks and traps, the *Brandenburg* battalions faced the partisans, their objective to destroy them or drive them away. It was a battle without end, for the partisans would appear and give battle, but then they would disappear only to turn up elsewhere the next night. Only by taking this into account can the employment of the *Brandenburgers* in individual battalions out of contact with each other be understood. I./1. Rgt. BR on the Gulf of Corinth, near Levadia; III./1. Rgt. BR in the Larissa area north of the Thermopylae pass; I./2. (Jäg.) Rgt. BR in Albania near Coritza, a Kampfgruppe as part of the 4. Rgt. BR on the Adriatic Sea, somewhere in the area of Banya Luka.

Here is another radio message from the "Red Orchestra" dated 6 October 1943:

Albert to Director (Moscow)—from Werther:

Since 22 September Germans have detected well-equipped regular British and Yugoslav special troops in Montenegro. They are supporting Montenegrins fighting on the Bay of Cattaro. 24 September 1943

Albert to Director (Moscow) – from Olga:

Infantry division No. 87 cut off by partisans near Trieste; because of success of the partisans in Montenegro Bulgarian troops are pulling back through Djakowa.

Heavy fighting in Russia inflicted heavy losses on the elements of the 3. Regiment BR deployed there. II./3. Rgt. BR alone lost seven officers killed in the area between Bryansk and Roslavl in addition to many non-commissioned officers and enlisted men; all other officers were wounded, some seriously. The battalion was finally withdrawn from infantry operations and was moved into the forested area in the rear southeast of Minsk for anti-partisan operations. At this time (roughly October-November 1943) a well-planned patrol succeeded in penetrating 150 kilometers into enemy territory, bringing back valuable intelligence information.

At the beginning of November 1943 the III./1. Rgt. BR was alerted to prepare for participation in a surprise attack on the island of Leros. This island, part of the Italian Dodecanese, had been occupied by the British following Italy's abandonment of the German-Italian alliance. The main British force involved was the 234th Infantry Brigade. The British hoped to gain new air and jump-off bases for future operations to take the place of the lost island of Crete. They had also occupied the islands of Cos, Samos and several others and had begun turning them into powerful strongpoints.

The German command in this theater could not stand idly by in the face of the British plans, however, unless it was prepared to face a constant threat from the British island strongpoints in the near future. In the early days of October 1943 German Kampfgruppen carried out a surprise landing on the British-held island of Cos and quickly eliminated all resistance. Then on 22 October the island of Stampalia, west of Cos, fell into German hands, and the enemy supply shipping as well as the enemy warships operating in the area found themselves losing their bases one by one.

Heavily fortified Leros, from where the British conducted forays into the Aegean, was seen as the key point, however. Continuous attacks by German level bombers and Stukas prepared the way for the landing. On 12 November German Kampfgruppen under the command of Gen.Lt. Müller came ashore in the northern and southern parts of Alinda Bay and established bridgeheads. Almost simultaneously German paratroopers of the II./Fsch.Jäg.Rgt. 2 under the command of *Major* Kühne jumped into the center of Leros east of Burna Bay, immediately establishing hedgehog positions. The fighting lasted several days against an enemy who received reinforcements from the island of Samos, but it was finally decided in favor of the Germans when fresh Kampfgruppen were put ashore on 15-16 November. Among the forces involved in these landings was a Kampfgruppe from the III./1. Rgt. BR, whose leader was wounded at the very start of the fighting. Oblt. Wandrey immediately took command of the Kampfgruppe and together with his men distinguished himself in the storming of Hill 961. He was later awarded the Knight's Cross for his action against this hill.

Just as the operation by a Kampfgruppe of the III./1. Rgt. BR against the island of Leros was an isolated incident, so too the actions by individual battalions of the 2. (Jäg.) Rgt. BR in the mountains of Montenegro (in the Milosevo area) can only be seen from the point of view of independent action. The struggle against the Greek and Yugoslavian partisans, who could not be engaged in an open field battle, was like fighting a hydra. Lengthy preparations, the positioning of heavy weapons and preparatory fire were all out of place as were large envelopment operations aimed at surrounding such groups. Only Indian-like tracking and surprise attacks with available forces, quick reaction when bandit groups launched their sudden attacks and their ruthless destruction with the available means could lead to success. The German units acting out of necessity of war were too few to seize and destroy the entire hydra. They were limited to isolated actions aimed at keeping it down. Repeatedly the struggle in this area had to be viewed in this way, a struggle against an all too often invisible enemy who, although he absorbed blows, could never be finished off.

On 1 and 2 December 1943 the I./2. (Jäg.) Rgt. BR were engaged in preparing for operations in the Milosevo area. At the same time the other two battalions (the II. and III.) assembled in the same area for another joint foray through the Lim Valley near Prijepolje to the west. The objective was the destruction of Tito's main forces, which had dug in in the Montenegrin mountains with front facing east along the Lim, a mountain stream. Elements of the 1. Geb.Div. (mountain division) and the III./2. (Jäg.) Rgt. BR had already moved out to clear the high mountain passes between Sjenica and the area east of Prijepolje. On 2 December their leading elements were heavily engaged west of Gvods, direction of attack west.

The enemy positions were identified in a line approximately Milosevo to the Kosevina ridge to the Lim Valley, opposite which was the 1. Geb.Div. on the Kacevo hills. Rain and snow darkened the sky, the climbing serpentine roads were muddy and difficult to negotiate. Gray swaths of fog rose up from the deep Lim Valley, and only rarely did the visibility extend as far as Prijepolje. According to a Moslem who had fled the city, it was heavily occupied by Tito bandits and renegade Italians equipped with tanks and heavy weapons. The bridge over the Lim had been prepared for demolition and was protected by bunkers.

Success depended on capturing the big bridge over the Lim in Prijepolje, so said *General* von Stettner, who was in command of the entire operation. The plan called for a combined attack by the 1. Geb.Div. from the west and III./2. (Jäg.) Rgt. BR from the north along the valley. This would be preceded by special operations by a roughly two-company-strong Kampfgruppe under the command of Oblt. Steidl of the I./2. (Jäg.) Rgt. BR from the south. The Kampfgruppe of the I. Btl. was comprised of elements of the 1.and 2. Kp., bolstered by captured Italian anti-tank guns. The latter, the only heavy weapons involved in this operation, were commanded by Fw. Plattner.

Early on 3 December this suicide detachment, which had to seize the bridge over the Lim in a surprise raid prior to the main attack, set out with pack animals. It stopped level with the forward outposts near Kocevo for the night. The surprise attack against the bridge crossing, which was about 1200 meters away, was to begin at about 02:00 hours on 4 December.

The leader of the operation described his experiences in this action:

Battle for the Prijepolje Bridge: 4 December 1943

Lt. Mark and his platoon led the way. He veered off to the right, we became separated and marched straight ahead, taking us directly to the Lim. Turning off was impossible on account of the marshy ground, we had to turn around and head north through the group of houses. In the darkness we heard voices speaking Italian. Wladimir Mark was in conversation with the enemy's forward security. We lay flat on the ground. Wladimir gave them to understand that we were Italians; the tension rose, they did not believe us and opened fire. Time was precious for us now, we had to have Prijepolje before dawn. And so I jumped up and began shouting, and we stormed the enemy foxholes and overran them. We had several wounded, whom we carried with us. We hastened down into the Lim Valley, hoping that the enemy in the city had not been alerted. We still had four kilometers to cover, it was already past four, speed was vital, a pale glow began rising over the mountain tops in the east. After one kilometer we began taking fire from the front and right. We rushed the enemy. The last bunker sentry before the bridge lost his life before he realized what was happening. It became light, fog drifted through the valley. A few hundred meters before us lay the city. The big bridge was clearly visible. My heart beat quietly now, the target was in sight, we must succeed. Hunting fever seized us. There was lively traffic on the other side of the Lim. Bunker embrasures over there, only sixty meters away, guns were limbered, the enemy thought we were their own people. We could not be made out clearly in the fog, otherwise none of us would have got out of there alive. We marched in file down a narrow path; to our right was a steep mountain slope, above heavily manned enemy positions, to our left the Lim River and on the other bank more enemy, nothing but enemy. I ordered maximum march tempo and immediate attack from off the move. The first bunker at the outskirts of the town was stormed, and we dashed toward the center of town, from where the street leading to the bridge branched off. Large numbers of armed civilians ran toward us. Furious defensive fire came in from all sides. We passed the bunkers before the bridge, the guards were rushed and overpowered, the ignition wires were cut. On the other side there was a barracks with a stout wall, a veritable fortress. Gasping, I ran across the bridge. Wladimir was already there; deadly bullets ricocheted off the iron railings left and right and whistled past my head. There was no cover, and the unprotected path seemed endless in the furious fire. But it went well. A small bridgehead was established. The hut and the hospital were firmly in our hands. Unfortunately I had lost many people in the bitter close-quarters fighting. All I had there was Heinrich's 2. Kompanie, while Günther was engaged in house fighting on the other side. The enemy was determined and stubborn; he had recovered from his initial shock and was now fighting back with everything at his disposal. We already had several hundred prisoners, nevertheless the enemy launched a heavy counterattack against us. They approached to close-combat distance from all sides. Hand grenades flew in both directions, furious fire thinned my ranks. Heavy machine-guns supported the enemy attack from a big white house. One of my best, Kohlhuber, was hit in the head, his forehead stuck to the wall. The small space filled with wounded. My radio message to the regiment, "Bridge in our hands intact at 06:30 hours, relief urgently needed," went unanswered. For hours we had been fighting a bitter defensive battle. The enemy wanted to reach the bridge, but only over our dead bodies. We ran out of hand grenades. I had thirty men left, all of the others were dead or wounded. Our doctor performed magnificently. With iron calmness he amputated the shattered limbs of my brave soldiers. My Kompanie-Feldwebel was amazing: he killed enemy after enemy with empty bottles and flare pistols, more than fifty dead lay in front of his position alone. The bridge lay under heavy fire and was impassible. Wladimir was wounded in the shoulder. It didn't seem to be so bad, he smoked a cigarette. I walked with him to the window and looked toward the opposite part of the town. Günther was attacking the hills, from where the enemy was firing into our backs. Bullets smacked into the wall beside me and Günther. The next minute he fell down. A bullet had gone through his head, blood streamed from his nose and mouth, his brains spilled out. Another of the best gone forever. I clenched my teeth. I had to hang on no matter what and not weaken. Just eighteen men holding the bridgehead now. More than 800 prisoners were in our hands. The first armored car rolled across the bridge; in it was my regimental commander. The II. Btl. was over in the town, Lt. Haut and a few men had come over the bridge under protection of the armored car to reinforce us. The commander shook my hand and hugged me for joy. I attacked the barracks, which was defended by about 300 men. In vain, I could not get close to it. After several costly attacks I gave up and intended to wait for darkness. We fired into it with tanks, anti-tank guns and recoilless guns, but the enemy was stubborn and returned our fire. My batman Heinrich was still cowering in a niche in a wall between two dead comrades, where he had been since morning.

The regimental commander definitely wanted the heavily-defended barracks in our hands before nightfall. After futile attacks which cost painful losses, I waited for darkness to fall. By now the number of prisoners had risen to 1,200. Armored vehicles transported my wounded back across the bridge, which was still under heavy enemy fire. When darkness came I stormed toward the barracks. My Kompanie-Feldwebel ringed the area to prevent the bandits from escaping and supported me with machine-gun fire. Covered by two tanks, my assault team succeeded in reaching the entrance. Smoke and gasoline bombs were used to overcome the last resistance. 180 enemy dead lay in the house. At 22:00 hours Prijepolje and the west bank of the Lim were firmly in our hands.

The following account was provided by the leader of the captured Italian anti-tank guns:

The following is not intended to be an account of the entire day on which our I. Bataillon took the bridge over the Lim, rather a description of my more or less personal experiences on that day.

Led by Lt. Mark, our 2. Kompanie seized the bridge over the Lim at dawn. I had spent a lot of time in the assembly area with Lt. Mark, a close friend of mine, and had often tried to talk him out of his premonition of death in the coming action and cheer him up. However, I did not entirely succeed in convincing him that all would go well.

When out first group had rushed across the bridge I followed up with our "artillery," an Italian 47-mm anti-tank gun with no aiming mechanism, which was pulled by a mule. In the process we came under heavy fire from the barricaded houses above the bridge. A Gefreiter who was leading the mule was hit in the arm and wanted to abandon the animal. But a loud blast from me and he continued on bravely. Our efforts to get the mule moving again were in vain, however, for it stubbornly stood where it was. It is unbelievable that all of us and the animal were not shot down. Many bullets were stopped or deflected by the iron bridge railings; an explosive bullet exploded against the binoculars in front of my chest without injuring me in any way, though I was blinded for a moment. After we had reached the other end of the approximately 110-meter-long bridge the anti-tank gun was prepared under cover. Then I positioned it on the open road at the end of the bridge. In terms of cover this was an impossible thing, but the only point from which we could place the two enemy-occupied buildings, from where they were shooting at us from the windows, under fire. They were about 60 to 80 meters away from us. Our company had meanwhile taken considerable losses, in part because the promised relief had not arrived (it was not to arrive until many hours later). So we held our tiny and unfavorable hedgehog position as best we could, and I can still remember clearly how I waved to Lt. Mark, who was having a shoulder wound bandaged in a house, as if to say: "You see, it is going well after all and your wound is not serious." Unfortunately I had no way of knowing that a few minutes later, when he himself was convinced of a good outcome, that he would be hit by an explosive bullet fired through a window: it literally blew the front of his forehead off. He had believed he was in cover and that nothing would happen to the rest of us. The loss of so many comrades and friends made us all furious. I served the anti-tank gun myself, took an ammunition canister from cover to the wall of a house, raced across the street with it, opened the breech, set azimuth and elevation, sighted over the barrel (there was after all no aiming mechanism), and fired. A dash back to cover, back to the gun again, soon one high-explosive or armor-piercing round into the breech, fire and away again. It was as if I was standing in the soccer net. Shells and bullets whizzed past the bridge supports and the spar braces of the anti-tank—but I was not hit. I probably sent more than a hundred shells into the house in this way, tearing huge holes and probably also having a devastating effect. After a long time we finally thought that we had relief coming from the mountains: a long column was approaching. I looked through my glasses and saw: Italians, fully armed—Alpini. I hauled the gun around and fired high-explosive shells up the mountain. After several shots I was on target. Men and mules plunged eighty meters down a cliff. Two squads of the 1.Kp. deployed on the Italians' flanks, which were covering us from the other bank of the Lim, helped drive them off. Many years later, in 1947, I chanced to meet two Italian drivers in South Tyrol; they talked about this incident and described it exactly as I had experienced it. I listened and had them repeat it to me. It was indeed the same incident: I told them that it had been I who had fired at them with the anti-tank gun, where-

upon we drank a bottle of wine and I drove home with them in their truck.

Suddenly we were also attacked from the other side, down from the mountain behind us. I hauled the anti-tank gun around again and fired in that direction. My shots seemed to be either high or low. Then a Feldwebel shouted to me from a half-demolished house that I should take cover as quickly as possible as I was taking fire from three sides. The bullets truly were flying, and I looked around for a possible way out. I saw it in an instant: it was the blind spot in a small cement step, which led to the door of a house. A dash, a jump, and while I was still halfway suspended in the air I saw it: I was going to land right in a manure pile that was half covered by mud and snow. Landing hands first, I slid towards it, coming down on my belly. But it was cover, which was vital and made everything else secondary, even the unpleasant smell…

Our situation became more hopeful when, at about 17:00 hours, two small tanks finally arrived. Somewhat later one of them helped me recover two men who had been wounded while crossing the bridge. A volunteer joined me, and in the protection of the small tank we succeeded in reaching the middle of the bridge, where the two lay. Zimmermann had a chest wound, the other a fractured femur. We dragged them behind the tank, laid them on the protected side and in this way brought them back safely. I was especially glad to be able to help Zimmermann, because earlier in Baden bei Wien he had put through many calls with girls for me, something he should not have done.

The Tito people were still defending themselves in the barricaded buildings, and our assault teams were repeatedly beaten off with losses. Among those killed was Lt. Hilpold. An assault led by the regimental commander himself, armed with a submachine-gun and my hand grenades, likewise had no success. Like all the others it did not get far. Finally our company commander lost patience, and he ordered a Feldwebel and me to form an assault team and enter the building. Having learned from the earlier failures, I equipped myself with smoke candles, and under cover of these we finally succeeded in forcing an entrance. When the defenders realized this, all of those still alive beat a retreat through a back door. Almost all were caught by our comrades, who were waiting in position.

With the arrival of mountain troops in the late evening and the breaking of resistance in the area of our bridgehead, our mission was over. This day had cost us heavy losses, however. If I remember correctly, our 2. Kompanie was left with a combat strength of less than twenty men. The enemy's losses were horrific. The shattered bodies of the defenders, including thirty or more members of a women's brigade, lay in heaps in the rooms of the house. They had refused to surrender and all had been killed. Even today I feel great respect for the heroic defenders of the bridge at Prijepolje.

The success at the Prijeploje bridge had cost this Kampfgruppe painful losses, the bulk of which were suffered by 2.Kp./I./2. (Jäg.) Rgt. BR. Those killed were:

Lt. Wladimir Mark	Gefr. Gottlob Tritscher
Obj. Edwin Weich	Gefr. Viktor Keleman

Obgefr. Helmut Schnell   Gefr. Erich Schmögner
Obgefr. Max Kohlhuber

The bulk of the 1. Geb.Div. moved into Prijepolje, *General* von Stettner set up his command post, while early on the morning of 5 December the bulk of the 2. (Jäg.) Rgt. BR left with a motorized Kampfgruppe to pursue the enemy westwards. The first objective was the city of Plevlja, then the advance continued to the Tara River, while the 1. Geb.Div. immediately turned northwest in the direction of Sarajevo. An unbroken stream of soldiers, pack animals, trucks, tractors towing guns, and tanks rolled over the mountain roads leading west and northwest. Great quantities of booty littered both sides of the advance roads, the city of Plevja was simply overrun, and by the evening hours of 5 December the leading elements of 2. (Jäg.) Rgt. BR were on the steep banks of the Tara. The day's *Wehrmacht* communiqué made repeated reference to the successes of this regiment. For leading the attack which captured the vital Prijepolje bridge, Oblt. Steidl was decorated with the Knight's Cross.

Meanwhile the I./1. Rgt. BR, which was based at Atalanti in the southeast of Greece, continued its mission of securing the area, which for the most part consisted of engaging bandit groups operating there. Then on 12 December it was transferred into the Kamena-Wurla area, approximately 30 kilometers south of Lamia, where it carried out similar missions. The battalion remained there until spring 1944.

The turn of the year 1943-44 found the Division *Brandenburg* with its command post in Berlin and its battalions and regiments scattered all over the east: I./1. Rgt. in the Lamia area of southeastern Greece; II./1. Rgt. in the southeast, III./1. Rgt. in the Amphissa—Sperchias Valley area. I. Btl. of the 2. (Jäg.) Rgt. BR was in the Prijeploje area of Montenegro, with II. and III. Btl. on the Tara. The 3. Regiment still did not have its II. Btl., the latter having been on special operations in France for months. I. Btl., which had since arrived from the homeland, was very soon involved in fierce fighting in the Pinsk area of Soviet Russia. The regimental headquarters and III./3. Rgt. had been engaged there for months and had paid a terrible toll in blood.

The I./4. Rgt. arrived in the Banja-Luka area of southern Croatia in January 1944 in order to take part in an operation against the headquarters of the partisan leader Tito ("Operation Jaice"). The turn of the year found the II./4. Rgt. BR involved in operations to surround the partisan-held city of Livno as part of Kampfgruppe Berge (114. Jäg.Div.), which also included II./1. Rgt. BR.

This distribution of *Brandenburg* units and formations over the entire area of the east and southeast naturally diminished the influence of the division command, whose effect on its widely dispersed detachments was reduced to that of an observer. It made repeated efforts to get its units back under its own flag, however it failed to do so or at best enjoyed only partial success until the unit was reorganized as a panzer-grenadier division. With the removal of Admiral Canaris as head of the German intelligence service in February 1944 (transfer of responsibilities to the RSHA) it did, however, lose its founder and benevolent father.

With the solidifying of the fronts, the end of offensive operations and the growing shortage of soldiers for the long fronts the number of missions for the division of course shrank. Its elements were increasingly drawn into the infantry role with the conventional army units at the front.

In June 1944 *Generalmajor* Kühlwein assumed command of the division, while General Staff *Major* Erasmus acted as temporary Ia, both in Berlin. Finally, March 1944 saw the formation of the *Lehr-Regiment Brandenburg* at Krain, Upper Styria, mainly as a replacement and training unit for the battalions and regiments of the Division *Brandenburg* then in action at the fronts.

Its organization was as follows:
I. Bataillon:
    1.-4. Kp.
    Base: Admont/Styria
II. Bataillon:
    5.8. Kp.
    Base: St. Veit/Oberkrain

The recruiting of replacements (excluding those sent by the *Ersatz-Bataillon* at Brandenburg/Havel) was done by training units all over the Reich. Infantry training was a priority as was anti-partisan warfare, in which the bulk of the field battalions had specialized recently. The partisan movement, which was then also becoming noticeable in the territory of Ostmark, made near front-line training necessary, some units having to take responsibility for local defense of their quartering areas, for example. Frequent operations against partisans in the local area and support of local police forces often resulted in wounded and missing personnel.

By the spring of 1944 the situation on the Eastern Front in Romania had become so strained that Hungary, a transit and supply base for the south of the front, tried to reach an accommodation with the Allies. Hungary's intentions were shown in its attempt to withdraw Hungarian fighting units from operations at the front and hold them in reserve for that eventuality. While Reich Administrator von Horthy, Foreign Minister Nagy and the minister in charge of the Hungarian Army were invited to German headquarters for "important" talks, elements of the Division *Brandenburg* (rushed in from Yugoslavia, Slovakia and Austria by road and rail transport) seized the most important bridges and buildings in Hungary's capital.

When the representatives of the Hungarian government returned from *Führer* Headquarters they found themselves faced with a *fait accompli* and were no longer in any position to take countermeasures. The subsequent occupation of the entire country by German troops (for example the reinforced Grenadier-Regiment (mot.) 1029 GD) was the same (with a few exceptions) and there was no bloodshed.

The *Brandenburg* units remained in Hungary for only a few days and then returned to their former areas of operation.

An interesting footnote to this operation is the fact that during the occupation of Budapest the Germans discovered an Italian delegation which had been sent by the Badoglio government.

In March 1944 the area of operations of the battalions and regiments of the Division *Brandenburg* was concentrated in the coastal regions of the Adriatic Sea. I./1. Rgt. moved into barracks in Tirana, Albania on 9 March, relieving III./1. Rgt. From then on it assumed responsibility for security missions in the mountains around the Albanian capital. III./1. Rgt. moved to Dalmatia, with quarters in Skradin. Its schedule of missions is revealed by the pay book of a member of that battalion's 9.Kp., who entered the following as close-combat days:

18 March 1944: "Operation Baumblüte"
28 March 1944: "Operation Bora"
29 March 1944: Assault on D. Ceranje—Hill 214, and ridge to the northwest
6 April 1944:   Assault on Debeljak Mountain near Grabovi
8 April 1944:   Assault on Hill 146 near Cacelezi
14 April 1944: Assault on Hill 181 near Ostrovicke-Licano
18 April 1944: Night engagement near Hill 146 northeast of Vuksic.

The "Proletarski Brigade" and the "Lika Shock Brigade" provided the opposition in most of these engagements.

The 2. (Jäg.) Rgt. BR continued to be deployed in the Prijepolje area of Yugoslavia, while its sister regiment (3. Regiment BR) was forced to release its III. Btl. to Italy. There it conducted operations against bandits in the Abazzia area together with the *Küstenjäger-Abteilung BR.* I./3. Rgt. BR soon followed and fought against bandits in the Udine—Goertz area. Increasingly the *Brandenburg* units concentrated themselves in the mountain country along the Adriatic Sea, having seemingly gained the upper hand against the partisan movement in the interior. But the German Kampfgruppen were still in a precarious position—they were still in control of their own supply lines; but for how long?

A daily report from Italy to the OKH on 27 June 1944 gives some idea of the ferocity of the fighting in the southern area:

Daily Report 27 June 1944

Army Telex Net
Received from: HDVS 28/6/0756

After heavy artillery preparation, at daybreak the enemy resumed his attack west of Lake Trasimeni with far superior forces of armored vehicles and continuous air support; thanks to the heroic efforts of the paratroopers and grenadiers and the outstanding cooperation between the infantry, artillery and rocket units the enemy was repulsed everywhere with heavy losses.

Enemy assaults with tanks and armored cars against the sector held by the Fallsch.Pz.Div. Hermann Göring were smashed by concentrated fire long before they reached the main line of resistance.

(3) Bandit Activity

An operation by III./3. Brandenburg against a bandit strongpoint in area 18/20 led to the destruction of an arms and explosives dump and the freeing of five German soldiers.

And the situation at the fronts at the beginning of 1944? The leading elements of the Allied armies in Italy were at the gates of Rome, on 6 June other Allied armies landed in Normandy, on 9 July powerful Soviet forces drove into Finland on the Karelian Isthmus, mid-June found German divisions engaged in fierce defensive battles and fighting retreats in the Rogachev—Mogilev—Orsha—Vitebsk—Polotsk area, while the Panzer-Grenadier Division *Großdeutschland* was already fighting on Romanian soil in the area of Jassy—Targul Frumos. Fear of Soviet retribution hung over those states of southeastern Europe which had concluded pacts with Germany. Increasing numbers of partisan units were forming in Greece, Yugoslavia and Albania. With its immobile formations, garrison headquarters and only a few combat-ready units, Army Group E under *Generaloberst* Löhr was coming under increasing pressure from enemy actions.

For the battalions of the Division *Brandenburg* the weeks of July and August 1944 passed with continual actions against the growing strength of the partisan units.

While the bulk of the 1. Rgt. BR (I. and III. Btl.) grappled with the bandit groups operating in the Skradin—Drnis—Sebenico area on the Dalmatian Coast, and at the beginning of August I./3. Rgt. BR struggled with the fortress of Osoppo near Udine, III./3. Rgt. BR was withdrawn from the Fiume area on the Italian-French mountain border and transferred to the Magdalene Pass, approximately 45 kilometers east of Grenoble, to secure the German supply lines there. Elements of the II./3. Rgt., which was operating in the south of France, also transferred some elements to Italy. At this time the I./4. Rgt. BR was still in action in the bandit region around Jaice, south of Banja Luka, while other elements carried out their missions in and near Sarajevo. Also in Sarajevo was the bulk of the Fsch.Jg.Btl. BR (parachute battalion), which was joined by elements of the 4. Rgt. BR as reinforcements. Meanwhile the 2. (Jäg.) Rgt. BR continued to fight for the crossings over the Tara in the Plevlja area against increasingly strong bandit formations.

Two events in August 1944 led to changes in the planned areas of operation, however: the rapid advance of the Soviet armored spearheads from the east into Romania—and the internal uprising in Romania with the associated and forced resignation of Antonescu. In mid-August the Germans made every effort to regain control of the uprising spreading from Bucharest in order to prevent unrest in the rear of the shattered German front. For this purpose the elements of the Fsch.Jg.Btl. BR in and near Sarajevo (approx. two companies) as well as elements of the 4. Rgt. BR were hurriedly placed on alert for an airborne operation. A participant in the action provided the following account:

Airborne Operation against Bucharest

Target: Otopeni, 12 km north of Bucharest. With our advance detachment of twelve men in total were the Major and battalion commander, several runners and I. We absolutely had to take off immediately without allowing ourselves to worry about the following elements. Not until we were airborne did we learn the exact plan of operations. Our objective was Otopeni, a city 12 km north of Bucharest. In the afternoon hours of 24 August we neared our destination, the airfield.

Advance detachment at the target! But there we received our first surprise: German Fieseler Storch aircraft appeared, circled the airfield and dropped hand grenades at us. To the side of the runway we found two bunkers in which we were able to take cover. From there we had time for an undisturbed observation of the terrain. Around the airfield there was a vast cornfield, beyond it a mixed forest. Suddenly there was a buzzing in the bunker and the Major picked up the receiver of the field telephone. On the other end was Forest Camp I. We heard German words. Those on the other end of the line were obviously surprised to hear that we were Germans too. They didn't believe that we as Germans had occupied the Otopeni airfield. Our Major argued forcefully and the Luftwaffe female signals auxiliary on the other end of the line hesitantly described the way to the forest camp, which was quite near the road to Bucharest. While we left the other men to stand guard at the airfield, the Major, I and a runner tried to get to the forest camp which was some 2.5 kilometers away. We found a serviceable Opel near the bunker and roared off.

Our eyes fell out of our heads… We were dirty and dusty with sunburned faces. Our astonishment was all the greater, therefore, when we saw twin sentries at the entrance to the forest camp wearing brand-new uniforms. When we looked at them they presented arms snappily as if they were in front of a garrison barracks. It seemed that they had not ceased hostilities there, even though they had to know what was going on. But our eyes nearly fell out of our heads when we reached the command barracks; for when we walked in we found ourselves in an office in which were sitting a General, an Oberst and several female signals auxiliaries. At first they took no notice of us whatsoever. But then the Oberst looked up and asked what we were doing. We learned that we were dealing with the forest camp's Ic, Oberst Rehe. The General introduced himself as Gerstenberg.

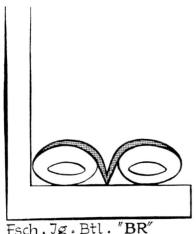

Fsch, Jg. Btl. "BR"

Things livened up when they heard that we were paratroopers and had come as the advance guard of our battalion. The female auxiliaries were ecstatic, the doors opened and even more blitz girls came in.

The new commander... Our Major, who saw what was going on there, now insisted on an immediate explanation of the situation. He and General Gerstenberg retired for consultation, with the result that he was named commander of the Otopeni airfield. The General transferred to him all disciplinary responsibilities as well as command of all available forces. Admittedly they were mostly untrained personnel, who were of little use for land warfare. Our new unit was less than imposing quantitatively or qualitatively; for 2,000 men was not much with which to attack the huge city. So far we had heard nothing from the other units of our parachute battalion. Was it not a great risk to operate with such a hodgepodge force? But the Major wanted to place everything on one card and start a surprise attack. Of course we still lacked weapons and ammunition. These had to be procured somehow, but from where?

Stukas called in!... The time passed with efforts to equip our troops for the attack. Stukas were scheduled for 19:00 hours to support the attack on Bucharest. First, while preparations were still going on, a "Gigant" appeared on the airfield and about 60 boisterous paratroopers of the 1. Kp. left the machine. At 18:45 hours a droning in the sky: Stukas! We watched them approach Bucharest and heard the first bomb bursts in the distance. If everything had gone according to plan, this Stuka attack should have created the conditions for our attack. But how could we attack Bucharest if we had inadequate equipment? At 20:00 hours two more "Gigant" transports came thundering in, disgorging about another 120 paratroopers from their hatches. (The Stuka attack ended without success.) With this the 24th of August 1944 came to an end.

On the morning of 25 August 1944 General Stahel, who had been sent by Führer Headquarters, stepped into our Major's command bunker. He was always sent when difficult situations had to be cleared up. Our question was: is our situation so hopeless that they sent this man here? Was General Stahel's arrival in the midst of the witch's cauldron of Bucharest a glimmer of hope or the symbol of defeat? General Gerstenberg had meanwhile been named the new head of the German military commission in order to restore German ascendancy in Bucharest. But General Stahel soon had to realize that the catastrophe in Romania could not be stopped and that Operation Gerstenberg was doomed to failure before it began.

Meanwhile approximately 200 paratroopers had arrived on the Otopeni airfield. But that was still too few for an attack on Bucharest, especially since the men of the Luftwaffe ground crews, supply units and so on were not troops in the actual sense. General Stahel was with General Gerstenberg in the forest camp and had not issued any more orders after the one to defend the airfield.

Then a heavy American bombing raid on the airfield, with much devastation and many killed and wounded. The last chance of an armed German intervention in Bucharest was smashed. It became increasingly obvious that the German units stationed in and around Bucharest were being surrounded by Romanian troops. Soon the Otopeni airfield and the forest camp lay under Romanian artillery and tank fire. Small groups of combat inexperienced German soldiers began surrendering, removing their shirts and waving them over their heads.

On 30 August Romanian emissaries bearing white flags appeared, in order to begin surrender negotiations.

The leader of the Romanian delegation was a Colonel Ionescu, about fifty years old, wearer of the Iron Cross, Second Class. He promised that we could leave with all our weapons and pass through Romanian troops to the Yugoslavian border. General Stahel asked for 24 hours to consider.

Generale Gerstenberg and Stahel decided to accept the Romanian offer. Colonel Ionescu returned at 19:30 hours and the agreement was sealed. The Germans hoped to be able to save their troops by getting across the Danube to Yugoslavia. The paratroopers were to assume command in the column.

The column moved out at about 02:20 hours on 1 September 1944, accompanied by strong Romanian motorized units. While en route, near a village two Romanian cars bearing white flags approached. Romanian officers got out and requested Generale Gerstenberg and Stahel to accompany them to see the Russians for the purpose of further negotiations. Thus the force was deprived of its leaders. The Russians had rejected the Romanian promise of free passage and insisted that the Germans become prisoners. Meanwhile the Romanians went into combat positions in the open field and prevented the column from moving any farther. Breaking out and continuing on to Yugoslavia was impossible.

Faced with this situation our Major, who had assumed command following the departure of the two generals, decided to surrender.

That evening we marched to the prisoner of war camp at Targoviste.

Thus the attempt to turn around the situation in Bucharest ended with all of the participating German soldiers being made prisoners.

The rapid Soviet advance through Romania and the defection of Romanian troops to the Soviet side forced the German army command to establish new defense lines as far east of the Danube as possible, in order to hold onto the supply lines to Army Group E in Greece and the German troop bases to the south. In spite of growing partisan activity in Yugoslavia and Greece all available German combat troops were pulled out of the

Balkans and moved east in the direction of Belgrade and across the Danube to the east.

The beginning of September 1944 found the following *Brandenburg* units on the march:

I./1. Rgt. BR out of the Skradin Drnis area on 4 September 1944 via Bihac to Sunja. There it entrained and traveled via Brod to Semlin, from there by motor transport to Vaniza near Belgrade. Arrival 12 September 1944. III./1. Rgt. BR from the Skradin area on the march to Belgrade (motor transport) and arrival in Mokri Lug on 16 September.

I./2. (Jäg.) Rgt. BR departed the Prijepolje area of Montenegro on 6 September via motor transport through Kraljewo to Belgrade, where it arrived on the evening of 8 September, quarters in Mokri Lug. II./2. (Jäg.) Rgt. BR and III. Btl. followed. The first *Brandenburg* battalions to have arrived were placed on alert on 10 September—I./2. (Jäg.) Rgt. BR was ordered to continue on in the direction of the Bulgarian border. It set out on 10 September, via Semendria and Petrova. Following a brief firefight with bandits at Petrova it continued in the direction of Bor (copper mines) and Rgotina on the Timok and arrived at about 15:00 hours on 13 September. Moved into Negotin near the Bulgarian—Yugoslavian border. Earlier reports indicated that Soviet tank spearheads were already near the Danube. Terrible scene in Negotin: completely exhausted strongpoint crews, all Romanians, who had only just managed to retreat, female signals auxiliaries who had escaped the clutches of marauding Romanian troops at the last minute, sailors of German Black Sea units who had made their way there—a scene of German troops in complete disarray.

These leaderless soldiers were rounded up, brought together in a refugee column and sent toward the rear. Patrols reported enemy spearheads already on this side of the Danube and enemy groups also in Zajecar, where they inflicted a dreadful bloodbath on the ethnic Germans there. At the last minute another patrol located and secured a fuel dump in Prahovo, north of Negotin, and it was evacuated under enemy fire.

South of Negotin the II./2. (Jäg.) Rgt. BR was deployed to protect the regiment's flank.

From Brza Palanka, on the Negotin—Turnu Severin road, came alarming reports that the German troops manning a strongpoint there had been surrounded. I./JGG was immediately dispatched there to relieve them.

The liberation of this strongpoint was described by the leader of the operation:

Freeing of the Brza-Palanka Strongpoint

The mission was simple: free the garrison, which was surrounded by strong partisan forces. On the north bank of the Danube the Russian divisions were already marching west. The area through which I had to proceed was held by the bandits, the distance to the strongpoint was 60 kilometers. I decided to carry out the operation with vehicles, since there were supposed to be 120 wounded and female signals auxiliaries in Brza-Palanka.

We worked our way through the gorges, repeatedly bridges were blown under our noses; we drove over mines, were shot at, that's how it was day after day. The enemy closed the ring behind us. Like an island in a large sea we drifted slowly towards our objective, grim and determined. We took several wounded with us, the dead we left behind somewhere beside the road.

I had the vehicles halt ten kilometers before Palanka. Adolf Jork and part of his company established all-round security. I pushed ahead over the hills, through the forest to Palanka, and I succeeded in fighting my way through a weak part of the encircling ring into the town.

We found a scene of devastation. Heavy artillery fire was falling on the town. I could clearly see the Romanian batteries firing from the north bank of the Danube. We found cover in a cellar. The local commander was nowhere to be found. The sound of fighting could be heard from the surrounding hills. I found the first members of the garrison in a ravine at the southern exit. They were sailors, who hugged us for joy; they had given up all hope. The wounded lay in blood, some without dressings, in makeshift huts. The local commander, an older Hauptmann, was not in control of the situation and his nerves were shot. A Major and Knight's Cross wearer on his way to Kladvoo joined me in order to assume command of the forces there. The female signals auxiliaries were cowering in foxholes and couldn't believe it when we said that we had come to rescue them.

I began transporting the wounded to the vehicles that night. The recovery effort proved very difficult as there was a shortage of litters and bearers, and the first priority of the men with me was to engage the enemy. I spent the night in Palanka.

In the darkness the Major fell into a drainage ditch and suffered a mild concussion. It began to rain. We found shelter in a pitiful hut. When it became light we moved out of Palanka in a long column—Kieffer in front to provide security, all the women in the middle, I formed the rear guard. We made it to the vehicles without difficulty. There was an engagement during the drive back. Behind me a scout car drove over a mine. The business was soon cleaned up, and in the evening the wounded and the girls were in good hands in Negotin, while I and my battalion remained outside the city on guard.

Of the Brandenburg units that had arrived previously, III./1. Rgt. BR saw action in the Arangjelovac area south of Belgrade in mid-September, intervening in the battle for the Vencac on 19 September. On 24 September it moved to Topola and the southeast, initially to secure the area. On 25 September its sister unit, I./1. Rgt. BR, which had previously been stationed in Vanica near Belgrade, transferred to Sabac on the Save, west of Belgrade, where together with White Russians fighting on the German side it secured to the south and soon made contact with the enemy.

In the meantime it was becoming increasingly clear that the Soviet armies, bolstered by deserting Romanian units, were pouring west against negligible resistance. Their objective was Belgrade and the encirclement of the German units still south and east of the city, which were desperately attempting to establish a cohesive defense line along the Danube. But while individual Kampfgruppen, including elements of 2. (Jäg.) Rgt. BR, the 1. Gebirgs-Div. and the Gren.Brig. (mot.) 92, were still engaged in this, the Soviet armored spearheads continued their steady advance north of the Danube, roughly in the area Hermannstadt—Temesvar—Arad, always heading west. South of Negotin—Kragujevac other Soviet elements sought to reach the Adriatic Sea in order to cut the supply lines of Army Group E (*Generaloberst* Löhr). The entire situation pointed to the encirclement of the German armies in and around Belgrade; a second Stalingrad was beginning. *General* Schneckenburger, the commandant of the city, prepared for the encirclement.

For the Division *Brandenburg* 13 September 1944 was also the day that it became a panzer-grenadier division and was incorporated into the *Panzerkorps Großdeutschland* as its second division and sister division of the *Panzer-Grenadier Division Großdeutschland.*

The OKW/*Wehrmacht* Operations Staff issued a secret order on 13 September 1944 for the reorganization, with the release of some volunteers to other combat units. The majority, however, remained with their units and were taken into the panzer-grenadier division. General Staff *Oberst* Erasmus issued the orders necessary for the reorganization via the OKH's Operations Department and the *Wehrmacht* Operations Staff.

As a result of these, roughly in mid-September 1944 a reorganization staff under Hptm. Witauschek (former IIb of the division) was transferred to Baden bei Wien with orders to undertake the reorganization of the units that had been withdrawn from the front or were arriving from elsewhere.

This took place the fastest with the elements of the former 4. Rgt. BR, the bulk of which would later form the new *Jäger-Rgt. 1.* The Pz.Stu.Pi.Btl. BR under Hptm. Müller-Rochholz meanwhile ended its formation process, while the Pz.A.A. BR (armored reconnaissance battalion) was being established at Wildflecken. The future Pz.Art.Rgt. BR (armored artillery regiment) could thank its existence to the absorption of an artillery battalion of the 1. Pz.Div.'s A.R. 73, while a III. Btl. was formed at Guben from GD replacement units. Much more complicated was the reorganization of the 1. Rgt. BR and 2. (Jäg.) Rgt. BR, both of which became drawn into the Belgrade pocket. It was November-December 1944 before the remnants of the two units could be returned to the Reich for reorganization. Scarcely any of the 3. Rgt. BR, which from about March was last in action against partisans in the Fiume—Trieste area, was taken into the new panzer-grenadier division. Instead the bulk of this regiment remained in northern Italy, where it was divided among several mountain divisions and remained until the end of the war. Incidentally, during the last months of the war the so-called MG.-Btl. Kesselring was created from the 3. Rgt. BR; this unit distinguished itself in numerous actions.

While the future Pz.Rgt. BR was created with two battalions, neither of these two units ever came under the command of the *Panzer-Grenadier Division Brandenburg*. The I./Pz.Rgt. BR was an entirely new formation created from the I./Pz.Rgt. 26 under the command of Hptm. Count Rothkirch and equipped with Panthers (Pz. V). In February 1945, however, it came under the command of the Pz.Gren.Div. *Kurmark* in the Frankfurt/Oder area, where it did its duty as the future II.(BR)/Pz.Rgt. *Kurmark*. In September-October 1944 the II./Pz.Rgt. BR, which was created from the Pz.Abt. z.b.V. (tactical emblem: a devil riding a tank cannon), ended up in the Belgrade pocket and lost all of its Skoda and Italian-made M-15 tanks. The crews were finally employed as alert units in the city of Belgrade itself and most were destroyed. The few who escaped this destructive battle subsequently gathered at Grafenwöhr for the new formation of the II./Pz.Rgt. BR under its commander, *Major* Waldeck, who had previously led the unit with such success. The formation process was never completed, however, and this battalion never found its way to the *Panzer-Grenadier Division Brandenburg*.

The II. and III. Btl. of the 2. (Jäg.) Rgt. BR were likewise engaged in fierce fighting on both sides of the mountains west of Negotin against superior Soviet forces which had meanwhile crossed the Danube. The fighting was desperate. At the end of September 1944 the I./2. (Jäg.) Rgt. BR was in Milanovac (Danube) after a counterattack against Orsova had failed. The battalion was surrounded, but it had orders to hold the town on the west bank, which was seen as one of the cornerposts of a future German main line of resistance, at all costs. Meanwhile, the *Jäger* of this reinforced battalion watched as endless enemy columns moved west farther north on the opposite side of the river.

On the evening of 30 September 1944 the 1. Geb.Div. reported to the Military Commander Serbia, *General der Infanterie* Felber, who had overall command in Serbia, that the division's mission (to clear the bend of the Danube) was no longer possible with the forces available. The division, which consisted of three reinforced regimental groups led by *Major* Eisl (98), *Oberstleutnant* Malter (99) and *Oberst* Pfeiffer (2. (Jäg.) Rgt. BR), faced[1]:

In the Stalag—Negotin—Brza Palanka area: 2 Soviet rifle corps with 5 divisions and 1 tank brigade;

In the Belareka—Slatina area: elements of the IV Mechanized Guards

---

[1] From: Lanz, Hubert: Gebirgsjäger, Die 1. Geb.Div. 1935-45, Podzun Verlag, Bad Nauheim, 1954.

Corps;

In the area between Timok and the Morava: several Tito partisan divisions, including the 23rd and 25th Communist Divisions.

Assessing the situation correctly, *General* von Stettner sent Kampfgruppe *Oberst* Pfeiffer (which included the II. and III./2. (Jäg.) Rgt. BR) via Petrovac and Svilajnac into the Morava Valley to hold this important sector open for the division. On its arrival it was halted by the corps group, which had to establish a rear position beyond the Morava, and was ordered to defend Pozarevac (ESE of Belgrade) and the bridge over the Morava to its southwest.

Meanwhile, in the first days of October 1944 I./4. Rgt. BR, which together with the II./1. Rgt. BR had been deployed in the heart of the Bosnian partisan area with its base of operations at Jaice, approximately 43 kilometers south of Banja Luka, was withdrawn and sent via Travnik, Sarajevo, Doboj and Derventa to the Brod—Belgrade highway. During the course of this motor transport movement the unit reached the town of Indija, approximately 40 kilometers northwest of Belgrade south of Novi Sad, and was initially held there by the Commander-in-Chief Southeast.

The I./2. (Jäg.) Rgt. BR was meanwhile engaged in extremely fierce defensive fighting in Milanovac, where it had been surrounded since 30 September.

Strength: the badly battered I./2. (Jäg.) Rgt. BR

Reisinger mountain battery of the 1. Geb.Div. with 4 guns, pack animals, etc.

1 battalion as garrison of Milanovac

Luftwaffe flak platoon

1 platoon of *Jäger* of the 1. Geb.Div.

1 group of tank landing craft, 1 gunboat, several assault boats

Total strength of the forces in the town: approximately 1,500 men.

Details of the battle in Milanovac until the breakout on 8 October are provided by the diary of one of the participating units, 2. Kp./I./2. (Jäg.) Rgt. BR:

1/10/1944: Secured western exit from Milanovac. At about 22:00 hours crossed the Danube near Svinita. Secured on the east bank during the night hours.

2/10/1944: Secured on the hills northeast of Svinita. Squad led by Ojg. Maschik reconnoitered toward Nova Banja, which was found to be free of the enemy.

At about 19:00 hours road demolitions between Svinita and Berzasca, approximately 3 000 meters west of Svinita.

At about 22:30 hours recrossed to Milanovac. The motor ferry and one gun-

boat sailed to Belgrade during the night taking wounded and sick. It is hoped that they got through.

3/10/1944: Quiet in Milanovac. Combat strength of the 2. Kp.: 3 officers, 11 NCOs and 89 enlisted men.

4/10/1944: Soviet artillery fired on Milanovac, the company had no losses. Otherwise no hostilities.

5/10/1944: Soviet fighters strafed the town at about 09:00 hours. Bombing attacks on Milanovac at about 09:30 and 10:00 hours, also artillery fire. Casualties: two slightly wounded.

6/10/1944: Soviet fire and their bombing raids suggest they are becoming more active. The situation is slowly becoming critical. Our III. Btl. has launched a counterattack to free us. We are also supposed to attack—toward Hill 283—in order to establish contact. (Hill 283, approximately 6 000 meters east of Milanovac. This hill, around which the road to Topolnica leads, is very commanding.)

Hill 283 was taken by storm: 1 Soviet anti-tank gun and several small arms captured; enemy losses: 6 dead, 15 wounded, 2 prisoners. Four enemy counterattacks were beaten off at close quarters as were another two during the night. Further bombing raids on Milanovac.

7/10/1944: Heavy enemy attack from all sides against Hill 283 at about 10:00 hours following artillery and rocket barrage. A platoon from the 1. Kp. fled, leaving behind its weapons and equipment, however the hill was held by the 2.Kp. Heavy casualties, especially in wounded. 2. Kp.'s total losses in the last two days: 4 killed, 24 wounded.

8/10/1944: The 2. Kp. is only 50 meters, in some places only 30 meters, from the Soviet positions. Two enemy attacks on Hill 283 during the night, at 02:00 and 08:00 hours, were repulsed at close quarters. Toward 08:00 the twelfth enemy attack was beaten off at the cost of heavy casualties to us.

Contact with III./2. (Jäg.) Rgt. BR, which is supposed to relieve us, could not be established. At about 12:00 hours the 2. Kp. withdrew from Hill 283 unnoticed by the enemy. Fw. Resch scouted a way back and evacuation of the wounded to Milanovac. The commander of the 2. Kp. (Oblt. Karl Kieffer) and a few men covered the retreat.

The reinforced I. Btl. withdrew from Milanovac at about 22:00 hours. All vehicles had to be left behind, however, and were destroyed. The wounded were taken along through the difficult terrain on pack animals and later were loaded on oxcarts that were found.

All wounded evacuated except one.

The retreat by this Kampfgruppe of the I./2. (Jäg.) Rgt. BR through the difficult terrain, constantly in danger of being destroyed by Soviet troops, finally ended on 11-12 October in Kucevo, where it was taken in by units of the 1. Geb.Div. Losses during the breakout were several men missing.

On 10/10/1944 the I./1. Rgt. BR, which was still surrounded in Sabac, broke out of the besieged city and at dawn managed to cross the bridge over the Danube to Ruma on the Belgrade—Vinkovci rail line. It soon came under heavy enemy pressure, however, and was forced to fight its way through to Belgrade with rear guards heavily engaged. New positions were occupied near Arme. Meanwhile the III./1. Rgt. BR was fighting north of Belgrade.

In the meantime the I./4. Rgt. BR under Hptm. Gerlach, which had been halted in Indija, received orders to advance down the Belgrade—Smederevo road in order to bring relief to the elements of the 2. (Jäg.) Rgt. BR and the 1. Geb.Div. which were surrounded on the Danube. Although the Belgrade—Smederevo road was reported free of the enemy, it was soon discovered that the Soviets had established a bridgehead across the Danube approximately 14 kilometers east of Belgrade on 11 October. German alert units were able to seal this off, but only just. The I./4. Rgt. Breached Smederevo without incident. At dawn the battalion resumed its advance from Smederevo in a southeasterly direction and reached the village of Osipaonica, on the road to Palanka. There it received orders to advance farther south into the Morava Valley in the direction of Vk. Orasje. The reason for this was the belief that such a move could deflect a renewed enveloping attack by the Soviet from the south towards Belgrade. Vk. Orasje was reached by evening and positions occupied there. The 2. Kp. went into position on both sides of the road at the southern exit from the village, while the 3. Kp. and the heavy company occupied positions further back. Scarcely an hour had passed when at about 15:00 hours the sound of tracks was heard from a southerly direction. A strong patrol discovered enemy tank and anti-tank units advancing north. Contact was made with the enemy, however there was no serious fighting. Reinforcements, including the Gren.-Brigade (mot.) 92 and two assault guns, were on the way. An attempted breakthrough during the night by Soviet tanks failed with the loss of one tank. An attack by us to the south on 13 October gained some ground and two T 34s were destroyed with *Ofenrohr* (stovepipe) anti-tank weapons. By evening the enemy had occupied positions approximately 600 meters south of Vk. Orasje on the Vk. Plana—Vk. Orasje road. Meanwhile the I./2. (Jäg.) Rgt. BR which had successfully broken out linked up with III./2. (Jäg.) Rgt. BR which was securing in Pozarevac. It transferred west across the Morava to take up a new rear position on the west bank. The bridges were blown.

The I./1. Rgt. BR, now led by Oblt. Hebler, was caught up in the fighting southeast of Belgrade, where the 3. Kp. succeeded in destroying four anti-aircraft guns, an anti-tank gun and tractor and an armored car during an enemy breakthrough toward the city.

The night of 14-15 October 1944 found the I./4. Rgt. BR under

Hptm. Gerlach engaged in heavy fighting with Soviet armored spearheads attacking in the direction of Vk. Orasje from the south on the west bank of the Morava. There the danger existed that the German positions on the west bank, which faced south, would be rolled up. Elements of the Gren.-Brigade (mot.) 92 and the I./4. Rgt. BR were to stop the advance along the Morava, but in the existing situation with the strength of the enemy this seemed impossible. On 15 October orders came for the battalion to withdraw to Osipaonica, where it linked up with elements of the 1. Geb.Div. and elements of the 2. (Jäg.) Rgt. BR. With the I./4. Rgt. BR acting as rear guard, the units, heavily mixed with units of the 1. Geb.Div., elements of the Gren.Brig. (mot.) 92 etc, marched north toward Semendria, where they were met by heavy artillery fire. The enemy was already north of the Danube and his spearheads were in the suburbs of Belgrade. The Soviets were in the city ahead of them, cutting off their line of retreat. The German units had to fight their way to the north through the enemy troops. Meanwhile heavy fighting raged in the streets and houses of Belgrade. In addition to the trains of several BR units, the I./1. Rgt. BR also defended desperately against Soviet tanks and infantry advancing into the city.

Obfw. Göller of the 3. Kp./I./1. Rgt. BR described the fighting in Belgrade in those days:

During the morning of 14 October we received orders to go into position at the east end of the city of Belgrade. The Russians had pulled back from this part of the city at dawn even though they had had no contact with us.

Apparently they were suspicious of the quiet and probably thought it was a trap, even though no one from the German side was there.

At about 14:00 hours we received orders to undertake a counterattack about 800 meters further south, where enemy elements had established themselves at a crossroads.

This area was retaken at nightfall, however we soon discovered that we had been surrounded: elements of the 1. and 2. Kp./I./1. Rgt. and I with a few men of the 3. Kp., but with no mortars. The only contact with the battalion command post was by radio. We received orders from the battalion commander, Oblt. Hebler, to make our way to the rail station. The explosions as the rail installations were blown up showed us the way there.

After a terrific night march through houses, back yards, cellars and Russians—our interpreter repeatedly negotiated with them—we finally reached the rail station. There was a brief exchange of fire with the pioneers of the demolition team there who opened fire as soon as our interpreter spoke to them. We soon straightened things out, however, and at daybreak we were warmly welcomed by Oblt. Hebler and a Hauptmann of the commandant's staff. They had already written us off, especially since the Russians were in every part of the city with tanks and strong forces. At about 23:00 hours some of these enemy tanks had made a blind advance out of a single side street. Calling out in German "don't shoot, German tanks!" they then proceeded to shoot up and run over the anti-tank and anti-aircraft guns positioned there. Situated at that intersection had been one 75-mm Pak, 4 anti-aircraft guns, one armored car and ammunition vehicles. One Russian tank was knocked out by a Panzerfaust. After our resurrection the surviving members of those platoons were incorporated and saw action with us.

On 15 October the available part of our battalion (I./1. Rgt.) was formed into assault groups of about twenty men each. These were sent into the heart of this very confused situation (in the southeast area) and assigned to the various sector commanders. The forces there were mainly thrown-together alert units made up of sailors, airmen and supply troops, almost all inexperienced in land warfare.

My Kampfgruppe and I were assigned as infantry cover to a Leutnant, who was in position at the Belgrade military transmitter with two anti-tank guns. He was in an ideal defensive position behind a small park and from there commanded four intersections. Several enemy tanks had already been knocked out from there.

The Leutnant and his crews were very happy to receive us as reinforcements, especially since we knew each other from earlier actions in the Balkans. The park itself was crisscrossed by slit trenches, in which we positioned ourselves. The knocked-out tanks and the feeling of being able to trust one another created a good atmosphere.

Two heavy night attacks against our position were repulsed with the help of anti-tank rifles (they had a terrific effect on the houses!).

The Russians attacked again at dawn and lost two of their tanks to the anti-tank guns. The entire enemy assault was halted, part before the park, part inside. In agreement with the anti-tank guns, we subsequently undertook a counterattack as far as the other end of the park with about six men, while the others raked the windows of the houses with submachine-gun and machine-gun fire. We reached the end of the park in one continuous dash. A street separated us from the opposite houses, in which the Russians were sitting. From there, about 40 meters away we could see Russians walking around in an office building with large front windows; it was probably a command post. Two Panzerfaust rounds were fired through the windows; there was a terrible outcry and Russians came flying out. We were waiting with one of our machine-guns on the shoulder and four men with submachine-guns. The Russians ran straight into our fire! When the magazine was empty we returned to our start position—with no loss to ourselves. The entire affair had lasted seven minutes at most and had the result that the Russians withdrew from the houses and did not fire another shot in that place all day.

At about 09:00 hours on 16 October Oblt. Hebler came and brought us cigarettes, chocolate and several bottles of champagne from the opened supply dump. Since it was quiet there, we were relieved by about fifty navy and air force soldiers and after three days and nights were finally able to get some sleep. At about 17:00 hours my group and I were ordered to the high-rise building, as the

Russians had already broken through to there with strong forces.

We were able to hold them up through the night, perhaps because they were surprised to meet resistance; and we were all alone, with no friendly support, no heavy weapons.

During the course of the morning of 17 October we withdrew on orders and were received by an alert unit in position at a crossroads further to the rear. Shortly thereafter I was ordered with a squad to the command post, where two heavy mortars were waiting for us. I had to release the squad and search for two mortar crews. By evening I had collected the necessary people, and with plenty of ammunition, radio sets, etc waited for what was to come.

On 18 October we went into position not far from the transmitter, for the park which was so familiar to us had by then changed hands. The alert unit had disintegrated and fled, the brave anti-tank guns had been shot up. The Russians had infiltrated into the trenches in broad daylight and had overrun the entire outfit.

The firing position for the two mortars was approximately 80 meters away from the park in a ruin; good field of fire, camouflage and avenue of retreat.

I sited the observation post in the fourth floor of a house, from where there was a good view of the entire park. I took a radio and two runners up with me, while one squad from our unit took up position in the lower rooms.

In spite of the close range we soon carried out adjustment fire on the park and were able to fire for effect as if on the practice range. The Russians now put their mortars to use but were unable to root out our firing position; not suspecting us to be so close, they fired too far to the rear.

During the morning the enemy committed strong forces in an attempt to break our resistance, which they failed to do, since each assault into the park collapsed in the fire of our two mortars. Likely encouraged by the mortars, the Kampfgruppen in the neighboring houses also offered spirited resistance.

Inexplicably, at about twelve noon both mortars were put out of action by blockages. Since the crews could not clear the blockages, I decided to go to the firing position myself and repair the damage. I left the runners at the observation post with orders to keep me informed about the enemy and his movements and, if possible, immediately direct fire. On one mortar the striker tip had broken, on the other it was bent. Both were replaced, the barrels quickly cleaned and greased, and firing was resumed immediately using the previous elevation, since the observation post was urgently calling for fire.

Now I wanted to return to my observation post; to do this I had to cross a street which was sometimes in the enemy's view. I aimed for the entrance to the house on the other side, leapt onto the road, and heard the loud bark of a Russian submachine-gun. Hit, I tumbled through the doorway of the house. During the pause in the firing caused by the blockages the enemy had been able to cross the park and get into a house from where he was able to command two further streets.

I went to the battalion command post, where my wound was tended to. This was followed by a wild ride across the Save under fire in a motorcycle-sidecar combination. There I was placed aboard an ambulance train which departed the same evening.

Two days later the city of Belgrade was in Russian hands after a seven-day battle. How many good comrades were killed in that time. My departure from the survivors was difficult, for I sensed that they were facing a difficult time.

While the battle in the city of Belgrade was still raging back and forth, the German elements surrounded south and southeast of the city (the bulk of the 1. Geb.Div., the 2. (Jäg.) Rgt. BR, which had combined its forces into two battalions, under the command of Obstlt. Oesterwitz, elements of the Gren.Brig. (mot.) 92 under *Oberst* Hillebrandt, and other small Kampfgruppen) were engaged in fierce rear guard actions against a hard pressing enemy. Before them the city of Belgrade was in enemy hands, behind them in the Morave Valley strong enemy armored spearheads, from the east attacking enemy forces, from the southwest heavy artillery and shallow angle weapons fire. The units stayed together, marching toward Belgrade with advance and rear guards and security to all sides, in an effort to force a breakthrough. Whenever possible, the wounded were brought along in vehicles. But panic was never far behind them. Fighting off attacks from all sides, the march column moved on.

Everyone knew the situation: we are surrounded. Overpowering enemy, the threat of destruction, death or capture from all sides. All attempts by this surrounded group to break into the southern part of Belgrade in order to break through the enemy's encircling ring to the north, failed.

At about 23:00 hours on 17 October came the order: "Break through to the west!" But that also meant breaking up the previously cohesive Kampfgruppe and attempts to somehow get through to the German lines. Panic seized the men of the units, but somehow everyone came together in order to break through together and with the help of the officers. Others, already separated from their units, sought to escape the chaos alone. Still others resigned themselves to their fate and gave up; they surrendered themselves to their fate: captivity!

The following account is by Obgefr. R. Felhofer, the driver of a heavy car of the 1. Kp./I./2. (Jäg.) Rgt. BR, who with the Auer company had been detached to a sister battalion:

Patrols revealed to us that Belgrade was already occupied by the Russians and that we were encircled. At about 23:00 hours on 17 October 1944 the order came through to destroy as quietly as possible all vehicles and equipment that could not be taken along. Now we realized how far we had to go and began to suspect what lay ahead of us. Everyone went to work, I smashed up the engine with a pickaxe as best I could. Then I packed my things, and it was difficult to part from my Steyr Kübelwagen with which I had gone through so much. But

Panzer-Grenadier-Division "Brandenburg" (as of January 1945)
Divions-Stab = Divisional Staff; Feldgendarmerie-Zug = Military Police Platoon;
Divisions-Begleit-Kompanie = Divisional Escort Company; Stab = Staff; Stabs-
Kompanie = Headquarters Company; 4. (schwere) Kompanie = 4th (Heavy)
Company; Granatwerfer-Kp. = Mortar Company; and, Versorg.-Kompanie = Supply
Company

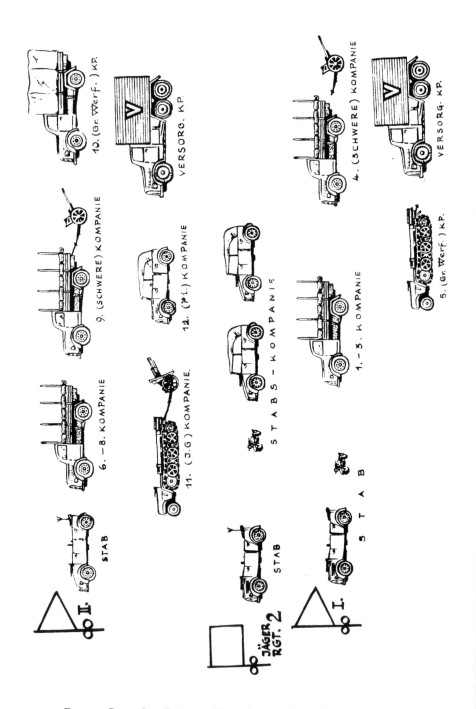

Panzer-Grenadier-Division "Brandenburg" (as of January 1945)
Stab = Staff; 10. (Gr.Werf.) Kp. = 10th (Mortar) Company; 11. (I.G.) Kompanie =
11th (Infantry Gun) Company; and, 12. (Pi.) Kompanie = 12th (Pionier) Company

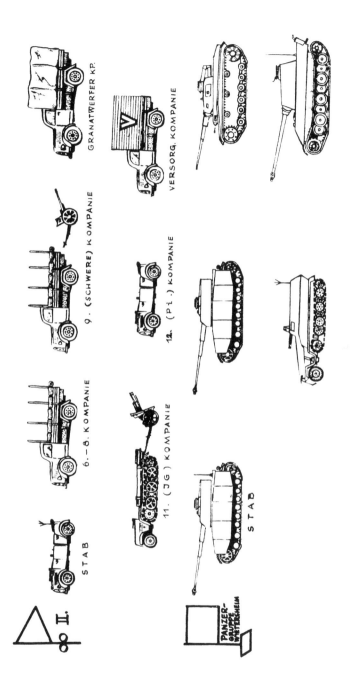

Panzer-Grenadier-Division "Brandenburg" (as of January 1945)
First Battalion with Panzer-Grenadier-Division "Kurmark"
Second Battalion lost at Belgrade

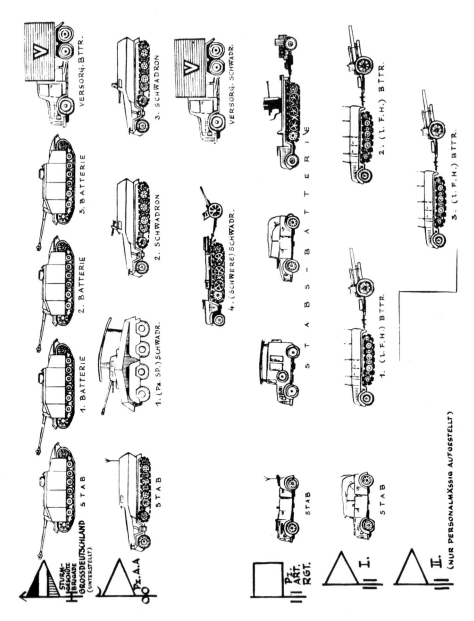

Panzer-Grenadier-Division "Brandenburg" (as of January 1945)

Sturmgeschütz-Brigade "Großdeutschland" unterstelled = attached; 1. Batterie = 1st Battery; Versorg.-Battr. = Supply Battery; 1. (Pz.Sp.) Schwadr. = 1st Armored Reconnaissance Troop; 2. Schwadron = 2nd Troop; 4. (schwere) Schwadr. = 4th (Heavy) Troop; Pz.Art.Rgt. = Armored Artillery Regiment; Stab = Staff; Stabs-Batterie = Headquarters Battery; 1. (l.F.H.) Bttr. = 1st (Light Field Howitzer) Battery; and, II. (nut personalmäßig aufgestellt) = Second Battalion (personnel only)

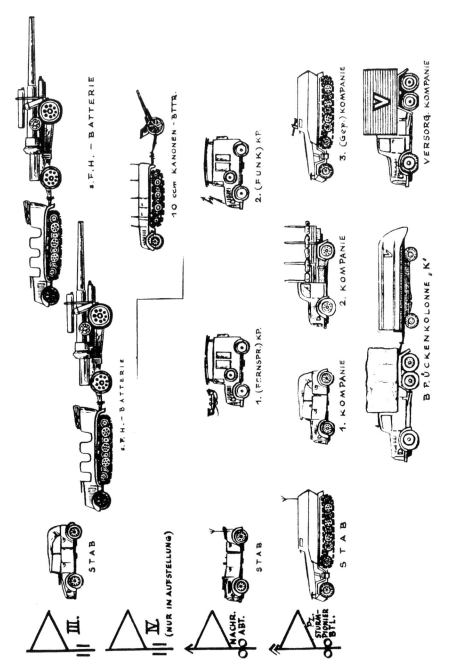

Panzer-Grenadier-Division "Brandenburg" (as of January 1945)
Stab = Staff; s.F.H.-Batterie = Heavy Field Howitzer Battery; 10 cm Kanonen-Bttr. = 10 cm
Cannon Battery; 1. (Fernspr.) Kp. = 1st Wire Company; 2. (Funk) Kp. = 2nd Radio Company;
3. (gep.) Kompanie = 3rd (Armored) Company; Brückenkolonne "K" = Bridging Column "K";
Versorg.-Kompanie = Supply Company

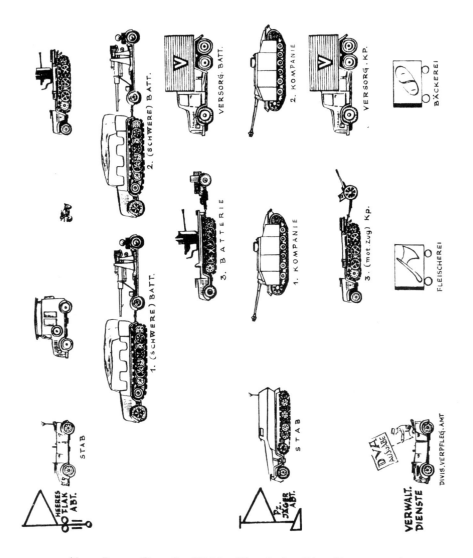

Above: Panzer-Grenadier-Division "Brandenburg" (as of January 1945)
Stab = Staff; 1. (schwere) Batt. = 1st (Heavy) Battery; Versorg.-Batt. = Supply Battery; 3. (mot. Zug) Kp. = 3rd (Motorized Towed) Company; Versorg.-Kp. = Supply Company; Verwalt. Dienste = Administrative Services; Divis.-Verpfleg.-Amt. =Divisional Ration Procurement; Fleischerei = Butcher's; and, Bäckerei = Bakery

Facing Page: Panzer-Grenadier-Division "Brandenburg" (as of January 1945)
Nachscub-Dienste = Logistical Services; Kolonnen = Supply Columns; Feldpost-Amt = Field Post Office; Werkstatt-Kompanie = Maintenance Company; 1. Fahr-Schwadron = 1st Horse-Drawn Troop; Sanitäts-Dienste = Medical Services; Feldlazarett = Field Hospital; 1. (San.) Kp. = 1st Medical Company; 1. Krank.Kw.Zug = 1st Ambulance Platoon; Feldersatz-Bataillon = Field replacement Battalion; and, (abgestellt zur Div. "GD") = (attached to the "GD" Division)

104

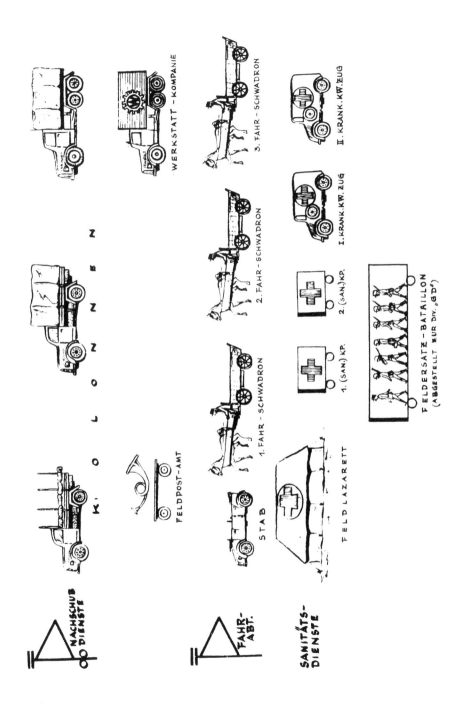

KOLONNEN

NACHSCHUB-DIENSTE

WERKSTATT-KOMPANIE

3. FAHR-SCHWADRON

II. KRANK.KW.ZUG

I. KRANK.KW.ZUG

2. FAHR-SCHWADRON

2. (SAN.)KP.

FELDPOST-AMT

1. FAHR-SCHWADRON

1. (SAN.)KP.

FAHR-ABT.

STAB

FELD LAZARETT

SANITÄTS-DIENSTE

FELDERSATZ-BATAILLON
(ABGESTELLT ZUR DIV. "GD")

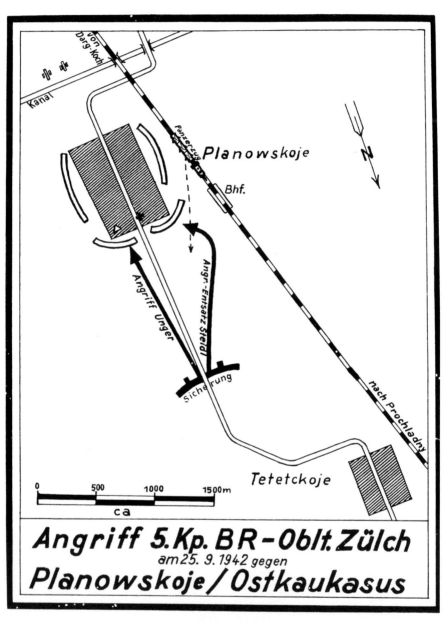

Angriff 5.Kp. BR-Oblt. Zülch
am 25. 9. 1942 gegen
Planowskoje / Ostkaukasus

Attack of the 5th Company "Brandenburg" — Oberleutnant Zülch
on 25 September 1942 against
Planowskoje (East Caucasus)

who had much time for reflection; the Russians had already noticed our work of destruction and sent many salvoes in our direction. The ambulances were filled with wounded, lamenting because they knew that there was nothing more our side could do for them. Everyone had to look after himself, all was confusion. Our officers were in action with the companies. There were about 30,000 men in the pocket, but everyone had to find his own way out.

We formed into a group and set out on our own. I had a compass, another a map, behind us a sea of flames, before us uncertainty: how far would we have to go before we reached our own main line of resistance, and how would we be able to overcome everything? At best each man was armed with a carbine. Toward dawn we met up with elements of our company, and for us things became easier because our Hptm. Steidl was there and he had our complete trust. When we reached the main Nish—Belgrade road the Russians were waiting for us. It was still dark and all of a sudden we heard Russian loudspeakers calling for us to surrender. We were told that there were thirty tanks around us and that any attempt to break through would mean certain death. They gave us two hours to think it over.

Many began digging foxholes for protection. There were soldiers from all branches of the Wehrmacht on the run. I crept forward slowly, and all went well until I came to a ravine. We must have been noticed, for all of a sudden a real fireworks display began. I got through in one piece again, but every moment someone cried out and fell. A few managed to get through this ravine of death, as we called it, and continued in a westerly direction.

At noontime we saw Russians in front of us again. Some tanks roared up and down, and we saw Russian infantry going into position. A Feldwebel from our battalion who spoke perfect Russian had two Panzerfausts, and with these he worked his way up to the Russians. He chased the soldiers from their trenches by calling to them in Russian, and when he was near the tanks he knocked out two. This created confusion among the Russians and we charged, shouting as loud as we could. We had scarcely any ammunition left, but that made us shout all the more. Once again everything worked out, of course many were wounded, but everyone kept going as best he could. Our flight continued and we entered a village, where we found something to eat, including some jam. Suddenly we were ordered to fall in. We were ordered to throw away any unnecessary items we still had with us, in order to make it easier to get away. We would have to cover 60 kilometers in the night to come. Then we resumed our flight; rain sprinkled down, and it was so dark that it was difficult to see the man in front. Anyone who had on a white shirt tore off a piece and stuck it on the back of the man in front of him so that we did not lose contact. We entered a muddy area; we waded through muck which was knee-deep in places. Many lost their boots but we kept moving irresistibly. In spite of our efforts we covered only six kilometers. It was hopeless, the Russians were driving around in front of us in cars. Gradually we gave up hope of getting out alive.

We had to cross another ravine which was lit by searchlights. We waited two

107

hours, then suddenly the searchlights were turned away. It was time to act quickly, and once again it went well. I could no longer walk in my boots since everything was full of mud. So I went on barefoot; it was terrible, but I had to keep up. Thus it went on, with no rest; we were already so hungry that we ate whatever we could find in the turnip fields. There were minor skirmishes with partisans all the way but we kept going.

Toward evening we reached the Save and breathed a sigh of relief. The combat engineers set about constructing rafts from tree trunks in order to get everyone across. As a result we were able to rest for a while. But all of a sudden the Russians came along the Save and frustrated our crossing. Once again it had all been for nothing. Then word came down that we had to reach Sabac, a city on the Save, which was about 60 kilometers away.

We continued at a quick pace. Many comrades stayed here, some because of injured feet or hunger; others had had enough of flight, believing that there was no point to it all. Of course almost all of them were attacked by partisans. Using my last reserves of will power, I hobbled along on two sticks, for my feet were swollen and blue. It was already cold and as well there was the overexertion, mostly cross-country through stubble fields. For each the main thing now was to save his own life.

There was only one uncertainty, whether or not the bridge in Sabac had been blown yet. I crawled the last few kilometers to Sabac on all fours.

Finally the city was in sight, and we soon saw Germans, regular soldiers, we were saved! We were soon given something to eat and we cleaned ourselves up as best we could. The civilian population clapped their hands together in shock, so disheveled were we. That made no difference to us, the main thing was that we had all survived.

We soon moved out again, until we were met by vehicles which took us to the station in Ruma.

They had been difficult days and nights, but now they were over. In those four days and nights we had covered 280 kilometers and had barely escaped the Russians.

The breakout battles by the surrounded elements of the Brandenburgers and the 1. Geb.Div. were focused on the Belgrade—Nish road, where the Soviets had set up strong anti-tank, tank and machine-gun positions in order to prevent their escape. The hills near Bolce, Hill 511 and near Avala—all just southeast of Belgrade—were hard fought for positions which the men tried to get past with the courage of desperation. They succeeded, but only at the cost of many wounded and the last of their strength.

Repeatedly surrounded by Soviet motorized troops, the completely fragmented German Kampfgruppen sought to crack the encircling ring. Ammunition ran low, physical strength deteriorated in the continuous fighting by day and the tension-filled night marches aimed at escaping the enemy. More and more men were captured, many others fell in the difficult mountain and forest terrain around Belgrade.

In terms of sacrifices, casualties and losses the Stalingrad of Belgrade was no less frightful than the battles for the city on the Don. On 20 October 1944 the last remaining German troops in Belgrade surrendered; the battle there was over.

The I./4. Rgt. under the command of Oblt. Schönherr was destroyed. The battalion officers, including Lt. Steeger and Lt. Mundlos, plus the rest of about 20 men were betrayed and captured by the Soviets about 7 kilometers south of the Save. Lt. Seeger was killed by a partisan bullet.

Other elements of the I./1. Rgt. BR under Oblt. Hebler fought their way through to the northwest.

During the course of their breakout to the west on the Save, Kampfgruppen of the 2. (Jäg.) Rgt. BR found their way together again near Sabac, where they fought desperately to save their skins. Oblt. Auer was killed there. They continued west in the direction of Mitroviac, constantly pursued, harried and attacked by Soviet tanks. It was 22 October 1944.

Finally they came upon German troops, who had established a loose rear position north of the Save. Finally a change to again take a break, catch their breath, assemble.

What was left? Who was missing? The steady stream of arriving groups and individuals were immediately assembled and were put aboard trains for transport to the rear.

For the elements of the 2. (Jäg.) Rgt. BR the destination was Esseg in Hungary, where almost the complete train had also assembled. There the men had their first opportunity to rest, reorganize and draw new kit.

Finally, on 27-28 October 1944, the unit moved by motor transport to Darda on the Drau, a border town still on Hungarian soil. There the regiment took in replacements, trained and rested.

The beginning of November 1944. The leading Soviet units were on the Danube near Baja and Apatin but made no move to attack. Near Apatin, due north of the confluence of the Drau and the Danube, the Soviets had established a bridgehead to the west, but for the time being this did not appear particularly threatening. On the other side was the II./1. Rgt. BR, which repeatedly tried to reduce the bridgehead near Apatin. This it failed to do, as it lacked the necessary forces. More was going on farther north, near Mohacs on the west bank of the Danube, where the Soviets had meanwhile created further possible crossings of the river in the seemingly impenetrable marshy terrain along the river. Fighting, at times heavy, was in progress there; for the German side the objective was to eliminate the enemy bridgehead. After its breakout from the Belgrade pocket, the I./1. Rgt. BR received a brief rest and refit and was then sent into action near Apatin.

On 7-8 November 1944 further operational elements of the 2. (Jäg.) Rgt. BR, in particular the I. Btl. under Hptm. Steidl, moved up to the Danube with orders to drive back the enemy forces that had set foot on the west bank of the Danube near Apatin and destroy what was left.

Hptm. Steidl described the entry into the positions in front of the Apatin bridgehead:

Positions had already been prepared at the embankment, and the makeshift occupation of same was completed rapidly. At least here we had contact on both sides and were not sitting in the field with open flanks. Before us was the forest with its many tributaries. The embankment on which we erected the main line of resistance was built against the high water of the Danube. At the foot of the same was a pumping station with a tall chimney, where I installed my command post. The distribution of forces may be seen from the sketch map. We established ourselves comfortably in the pumphouse. While Lt. Simdes was against installing the battalion command post directly in the main line of resistance, I wanted to be up front with my men. I climbed up the inside of the chimney and tried to get a view of the forests. This I was unable to do as several rungs were missing. The machinery in the pumphouse was still intact. Karl had set up his command post in a neighboring building. We had all the advantages on our side: the embankment with commanding position, field of fire, even if only for a few meters, while the enemy squatted in the swamp and had wet feet. Yet every night he tried to break in at some point and during the day snipers in trees cost us casualties. The enemy was very skilled in the use of snipers. During the day we could scarcely raise our heads from our holes. Casualties were unbearable in the long run, each day six to ten men were hit in the head by sniper fire. I received some ammunition for the assault guns under my command and had Lt. Unger, who commanded them, methodically fire on the tree tops. Afterwards I had some peace.

My neighbors, on the left an SS unit and right the battalion commanded by Rittmeister von Mertens, reported relative quiet, while the enemy concentrated in front of my sector, which was about two kilometers wide. Further crossing traffic was reported from the northern strongpoint, which was held by Hungarians. During the night they heard loud cursing, the rolling of horse-drawn wagons and the sound of posts being driven. All of this suggested that we were facing a major attack. Except for the usual shooting all was still quiet. We used the time, improving the positions, stockpiling ammunition and considering all our options in the event of a major attack. A bitter battle was already raging in the north near Mohac. We could hear the barrage fire in the distance. But we made our lives as comfortable as possible. My adjutant learned how to play skat, and we sat comfortably in the pumphouse by candlelight. Karl Kieffer was often there. Goller delivered the supplies partly by rail or came with the senior NCOs on the "rail tretmax." Each day I went through the positions, tipped a bottle of Hennessy with Schmalbruch in his tiny bunker and visited my medical officer Dr. Blut. My mortar people, Obj. Maltwieser and Angeringer, shot two fine deer; we crossed a tributary in a boat and crept through the forest to the downed animals. Rittmeister von Mertens, the old Southwest African, also visited me. Oblt. Hirl was wounded and Oblt. Eagner took his place.

The battalions never did get to attack the bridgehead at Apatin, however, for the enemy was in the process of enlarging his crossing point to the west. Heavy crossing traffic especially at night, increasing artillery fire on the German positions and the steady reinforcement of the Soviet forces on the west bank of the Danube were the first signs of an impending attack.

Finally, on 20-21 November, the German positions, especially those north of the Apatin bridgehead, collapsed when the enemy succeeded in penetrating the German defense lines and rolling up the German main line of resistance to both sides. Kampfgruppen and battalions were hastily pulled out of the quiet sectors and committed to counterattacks, mainly north against the enemy penetration points. The Heine battalion (II. Btl.) fought heroically to the last man in an effort to hold its positions against the Soviet troops attacking from all sides. The effort was in vain, for only Hptm. Heine and his runner survived the battle; the battalion was shattered.

Withdrawal movements were initiated under pressure from Soviet attacks; SS units were supposed to have established a new fall-back line farther to the rear.

Elements of the 1. Rgt. BR under *Oberst* von Brückner were also there, establishing a series of fall-back lines to ensure that the battalions still fighting farther east could be withdrawn. Finally, on 27 November 1944, Fünfkirchen was reached; no one suspected that the enemy was already approaching. Armor-piercing shells whizzed over the assembled vehicle columns. The Soviets also kept them under continuous rifle and machine-gun fire.

That evening the withdrawal, now motorized, resumed in a westerly direction towards Pellerd. The enemy's advance guards were there too, the result of his irresistible drive west. A series of new positions were occupied, but in each case our forces were too weak and the Russians slipped past to reappear behind them. A position was occupied in Gyod—where was this all to lead?

The retreat continued, through the mountains, through ravines and forests to the northwest—hard pressed by enemy armored spearheads.

On 3 December, as so often in the recent past, defensive positions were occupied, this time in the city of Kaposvar (northwest of Pecs). There was fierce close-quarters fighting at the railway station, in the course of which fifteen T 34s were destroyed.

New units were on the way, including the hastily reorganized 1. Geb.Div. They were supposed to reinforce our lines and finally bring the enemy to a halt. But the fighting continued, now along the Kaposvar—

Böhönye road. The enemy continued to press, but over the course of the next days he was halted. On or about 8 December 1944—snow lay in the Puszta, the ground was frozen solid—the unit went over to rest status in the Szenyer area, initially as battle reserve.

Preparations for counterattacks were made with the goal of securing suitable defensive positions. The enemy had largely been brought to a halt in this sector. I./2. (Jäg.) Rgt. BR's new positions were in the Edi—Long. Puszta area. There was now talk of relief, the units were to be refurbished and the long-anticipated reorganization of these elements of the Brandenburgers into a panzer-grenadier division was to become a reality.

Finally, beginning on 16 December, the vehicles of the 2. (Jäg.) Rgt. BR departed the regiment's combat zone and traveled via Nagykanizsa and Steinamanger in the direction of Grosspetersdorf.

Thus after a long tug of war with the command authorities the last elements of the Brandenburgers were released for reorganization. III./1. Rgt. BR was in Rechnitz and had already been reorganized. On 18 December 1944 it entrained for transfer to East Prussia—into the area of the Pz.Korps. GD. There it was quartered in Angerburg.

Other elements of the Brandenburgers arrived even later in East Prussia, but by Christmas Eve almost all were once again assembled in common quarters—for the last time in this war and forever.

Postscript

Whoever has followed the eventful history of the Division Brandenburg to this point, where it left the stage of a special unit and returned its last elements for reorganization into a panzer-grenadier division, will want to reflect for a moment.

The arc spreads wide from the first tentative actions and operations over the glowing accomplishments at the Dvina bridges, at Bataysk, at Maykop, at Prijepolje and other places, to the incorporation of the Kampfgruppen into the defense fronts and the costly and bitter fighting retreats in the southeast.

Lacking any precedent in military tradition, a unit created from the demands of the Second World War a type of soldier unsurpassed in ability, fighting strength, flexibility, inventiveness and willingness to sacrifice. The sense of aloneness of a small party which has left its own lines under cover of darkness and proceeds through enemy territory to reach its objective, is apparent in the combat reports; equally obvious is the degree of mental dexterity, quick reaction, mutual dependence and fighting elan that was required to successfully complete an operation.

The Brandenburgers were active in the entire vast area from the impenetrable forests of Finland across all the fronts of Europe to the desert sands of Africa; operations were planned and carried out on land, on water and in the air. There were successes and failures, the result of specific conditions. But two soldierly virtues shone through all of their varied experiences: the will to fight and readiness for self-sacrifice.

To record the unique history of this unit in a non-dramatic, factual way based on documents and operational reports was the goal of the publisher and his co-workers. A conscious effort was made to avoid over-glorification, which could only have falsified the true picture of this unit. We owe this honesty to the many sacrifices which the Brandenburgers were called upon to make in every theater of the war.

Part III
March Separately–Fight Separately!!

> "…but somehow this great feeling of safety that one had always felt when the "GD" made an expert attack was missing…"
>
> *a member of the GD*

The Panzerkorps Großdeutschland was still in the formation process, with the Pz.Gren.Div. GD as a complete unit in the Rastenburg—Sensburg area and the first arriving units of the Pz.Gren.Div. BR north of Rastenburg in the Angerburg—Lötzen area, when, as a result of the developing situation on the Vistula, it was ordered to move one division into the Willenberg—Chorzele area before the end of the year. Which of the two divisions it was to be was not specified; but the decision was not difficult: the Pz.Gren.Div. Großdeutschland, for it was the only one at full strength and relatively combat ready—even if its reorganization was still not complete. However, there was to be time for that in the new assembly area. The first unit of the division to entrain was the Pz.Aufkl.Abt. GD, on 25 December 1944 at Korschen, East Prussia.

At this time the bulk of the two regiments of the Pz.Gren.Div. BR were still in transport to East Prussia, only the newly-formed units for the BR were on hand. The arrival of the first battalions was not expected much before the beginning of January, with the complete assembly of the Pz.Gren.Div. BR not before 10 January 1945.

The corps headquarters was aware of this situation and remained in its previous area pending the ultimate assembly of its second division. The corps units planned for the establishment, most of which came from the Pz.Gren.Div. GD anyway, were supposed to be separated from their parent unit and assembled, especially since there were firm plans for the entire corps to come together in that area.

This plan would be frustrated by the enemy situation at the Vistula, however…

In the first days of January 1945 the front followed a seemingly regular north-south line, which for the most part followed the course of the river: from the upper course of the Vistula near Baranov downstream past Pulawy—Warsaw to the confluence with the Narev, then along the Narev through Pultusk—Lomza, further along the Bobr, just west of Augustovo and through Goldap—Ebenrode—Schlossberg to the Memel and to its entry into the Baltic Sea. That was the Eastern Front. Courland was being held, as was the city of Memel. The front held by the German armies was bolstered by various armored Kampfgruppen, but there were also

Volkssturm and East Prussian units. The defense sectors of the individual units were so broad that they had neither the personnel nor weapons to withstand a concentrated Soviet attack. The most serious shortcoming was the absence of sufficient mobile reserves—motorized infantry and tank units—which could react quickly to enemy penetrations.

Such units had been pulled out of the Eastern Front at the beginning of December 1944 for participation in the Ardennes offensive in the west. At the beginning of January 1945, contrary to the advice of his closest "command advisors," Hitler ordered a further, unbearable denuding of the front in the east. Even the bulk of the garrisons of the fortifications under construction in the German rear in the east, the result of a proposal by *Generaloberst* Guderian, were withdrawn to prop up the western front following the failure of the Ardennes offensive. Budapest, which had been encircled by the Soviets during Christmas 1944, also demanded relief and led Hitler to dispatch an SS corps with two divisions, likewise taken from the Eastern Front.

Apart from the weak intervention reserves of the armies themselves, there were just twelve panzer and panzer-grenadier divisions, all in reasonably good shape, to serve as a mobile reserve behind the more than 700 kilometers of front. These were used to secure the more threatened positions, specifically between the upper Vistula and Pilica, as well as behind the Narev front and in East Prussia.

The senior command agencies knew that this front was in no way capable of withstanding the Soviet assault that was sure to come. But not only did Hitler ignore the situation reports, he dismissed them with a wave of his hand, calling the Soviet buildup, "the biggest bluff since the time of Ghengis Khan." Nevertheless, everyone did everything possible to avoid falling into the arms of the expected fate and avoid the worst.

The path of the front, alone, clearly showed the expected focal point of the Soviet offensive: the enemy had bridgeheads across the river lines in five places, each large enough to allow the massing of the necessary attack armies. They were: the Baranov—Sandomierz bridgehead on the upper Vistula in the area of the 4. Pz.Armee under *Generaloberst* Balck, later *General der Panzertruppe* Gräser; the somewhat smaller bridgehead at Pulawy, likewise in the area of the 4. Pz.Armee; on its northern wing the Magnuszew bridgehead where the Pilica flowed into the Vistula, which extended dangerously into the area of the 9. Armee commanded by *General* Baron von Lüttwitz south of Warsaw; and the Pultusk bridgehead on the lower Narev, north of Warsaw, in the area of *Generaloberst* Weiss' 2. Armee's southern sector.

The Soviets committed two fronts to pinch off East Prussia[1]: the 3rd White Russian front massed 54 rifle divisions, 2 tank corps and 9 independent tank units on the eastern frontier. Its objective was Königsberg. The Soviet 2nd White Russian Front under Field Marshall Rokossovski, which was roughly comparable in strength, was supposed to break out of the Rozan—Pultusk bridgehead north of Warsaw. drive into East Prussia from the south and by advancing toward a line Elbing—Thorn sever it from the rest of the Reich.

Standing by for a frontal assault on the middle Oder was the Soviet 1st White Russian Front under Marshall Zhukov with 31 rifle divisions, 5 tank corps and 3 independent tank units. The bulk of its forces were in the Magnuszew bridgehead with a somewhat weaker group in the smaller Pulawy bridgehead.

The Soviet 1st Ukrainian Front under Koniev, which was especially strong with 60 rifle divisions, 9 tanks corps and 8 independent tank units, was to drive out of the bridgehead near Baranow. The bulk of its forces were given the task of reaching the Oder near Breslau, while a weaker group was to drive through Cracow and take the industrial region of Upper Silesia. Positioned on its southern flank, the 4th Ukrainian Front under Petrov was to follow this movement south of the upper Vistula.

The German armies were aware of the entire Soviet buildup, betrayed by the obvious signs: the increase in the quantity of enemy artillery, which conducted ranging fire, the insertion of new units into the bridgeheads and the arrival near the front of tank units, and finally the increase in enemy radio traffic. Only the timing was still uncertain.

The Soviets had selected 20 January 1945 as the starting date for their major offensive, however this was moved forward on account of the situation in the west and the British government's assessment of the German Ardennes offensive. With the German attack bogged down, on 6 January 1945 Prime Minister Churchill wired the following to his partner in the east:

The heavy fighting in the west may require major decisions at any time. You know from your own experience how unsettling a situation is in which one must defend a very wide front with a temporary loss of the initiative. General Eisenhower would urgently and necessarily like to know in broad terms what you are planning, since our most important decisions depend on it… I would be grateful if you would advise me whether we can count on a major Russian attack on the Vistula front or somewhere in January… I consider the matter urgent.

Stalin replied the next day:

We definitely must take advantage of our artillery and air superiority over the Germans. For this we need clear weather with no ground fog. We are preparing an attack, but the weather is not in our favor. We have taken the situation of our allies on the western front into consideration, and so the headquarters has

[1] From: von Tippelskirch, Kurt, *Geschichte des zweiten Weltkrieges*, Athenaeum Verlag, Bonn, 1954.

decided to accelerate our preparations and launch a broad offensive against the Germans on the entire central front regardless of weather no later than the second half of January. Rest assured that we will do everything possible to ensure support for our glorious allies.

Even though Stalin rightly assessed the German offensive in the west "as a stupid maneuver on Rundstedt's part carried out for reasons of prestige," he acquiesced to the desires of his British partner and set 12 January 1945 as the first day of the Soviet major offensive.

The alert order was issued in the Willenberg—Chorzele area during the evening hours of 12 January 1945. Get ready! Immediate departure in the direction of Krasnosielc to Stary in order to keep open the bridgeheads over the Orzyc to the east. During the night and throughout 13 January the various units of the Panzer-Grenadier Division *Großdeutschland* marched south.

The Soviet 2nd White Russian Front under Field Marshall Rokossovski had attacked to the west and northwest from the Roza—Pultusk bridgehead. The objective was to bar its path to the west, to bring it to a halt.

At almost the same hour on the following day, 13 January 1945, the units of the Panzer-Grenadier Division *Brandenburg* were also placed on alert. Less than 24 hours later the vehicles set off for the entraining station at Angerburg in East Prussia. The *Führer* order to the *Panzerkorps Großdeutschland* (less one division) read: "Reach the Litzmannstadt (Lodz) area by train, in order to advance south from there and close the breach in Army Group A's front."

At the beginning there were not enough trains available to express transport the entire Panzer-Grenadier Division *Brandenburg* south. Days passed, until 19 January to be precise, until all units were in fact entrained and sent on their way.

This *Führer* order, which split the *Pz.Korps Großdeutschland* (it left its assembly area with just one division and some corps troops, including the Pz.Korps.Pi.Btl. 500 GD, a few transport columns and two medical companies), separated the two panzer-grenadier divisions forever! In the end the Panzer-Grenadier Division GD was in northern East Prussia on German soil, while the Panzer-Grenadier Division BR was in southeastern Czechoslovakia.

Chapter 1
Panzer-Grenadier Division Großdeutschland

Until 11/1/1945: OKH reserve in East Prussia and northern Poland

15/1 — 31/1/1945: Defensive battle and fighting withdrawal in East Prussia

1/2/1945 — 12/3/1945: Attack to restore contact with Königsberg. Defense and positional warfare in Ermland.

Nothing known of the enemy. Heavy artillery fire from the east; enemy spearheads are said to already be between Mackeim and Praschnitz, advancing to the north and west.

That was the situation on 13 January. And so on 13-14 January the vehicles of the Panzer-Grenadier Division GD rolled south. The only thing that was certain was that the Soviet 2nd White Russian Front under Rokossovski had attacked from the Pultusk—Rozan bridgehead (better known as Rozan to the German soldier) and was advancing northwest in the direction of Elbing while its right wing drove toward Ortelsburg, probably with the objective of reaching the Baltic and cutting off Army Group Center.

The Panzer-Grenadier Division *Großdeutschland* had orders to prevent the Soviets from crossing the Orzyc and establish a new defense line there, and in addition to advance south, passing to the southeast of Praschnitz, and drive the enemy forces suspected to be in that area back to their starting position. These orders resulted in the commitment of both of the available regiments: in keeping with its previous rest area just east of Willenberg, the Pz.Füs.Rgt. GD under *Oberst* von Breese-Viniary was assigned the Flammberg—Stegna road, while the Pz.Gren.Rgt. GD under *Oberst* Heesemann was to approach via Praschnitz—Karwazci—Ptoniawy. After a brief stopover in Camp Mielau the I. (Panther)/Pz.Rgt. GD, formerly stationed in Chorzele, moved to Wegrzynowo, approximately 10 kilometers northwest of Mackeim, and sought to make contact with the leading elements of the Pz.Gren.Rgt. in the Helenowo area, southeast of Praschnitz, as it had been subordinated to that regiment for the coming actions. All of these movements took place on Sunday, 14 January 1945.

On the same day Hptm. Buse's I./Pz.Korps Füs.Rgt. GD, which was then under the command of the Pz.Gren.Div. GD in the Willenberg area, moved to Praschnitz and initially stationed itself there at the disposal of the division. The battalions of the Pz.Art.Rgt. GD were allocated to the individual regiments in keeping with their previous assignments.

119

I./Pz.Art.Rgt. GD was subordinated to the Pz.Gren.Rgt. GD, and II. Abt. to the Pz.Füs.Rgt. GD, while the remaining battalions including the I./Pz.Korps.Art.Rgt. GD remained in the hands of the artillery commander so as to enable him to form a point of main effort.

And so on that 14 January the panzer-fusiliers were approaching the bridgeheads over the Orzyc near Krasnosielc and (to its south) Stary in order to keep these open to the east, but also to place a barrier in the path of the expected Soviets. They were the first to make contact with the enemy; the following account of what happened was provided by the commander of 8. (MG.) Kp., Oblt. E. Hoffmann:

Sunday, the 14th of January 1945. We rolled out of our area around Karnia into darkness, heading south to Stegna.

Night march in motorized formation; the drivers tense behind the steering wheels, the commanders and company leaders with maps in hand in the leading vehicles. Forest tracks, narrow roads. Sunday morning, 14 January 1945, we landed in Stegna. An assault battalion of an infantry division was sitting there waiting for mission orders which arrived during the morning. We settled into the quarters it had left. But then it was our turn too. New orders: reach the bridgeheads over the Orzyc near Krasnosielc and Stary. By evening we were in Krasnosielc; heavy Soviet artillery fire greeted us there, trying to hit the bridge over the river. We got down from our vehicles and defended to the south.

Hptm. Zabel, commander of II./Pz.Füs.Rgt. GD, to the regimental command post for orders. The company commanders took over their sectors, heavy infantry weapons moved in, by about 22:00 hours on Saturday everything was in position.

The commander returned at about 2300 hours: tomorrow morning (15 January) attack approximately 6 kilometers southwest. The assault battalion that had arrived in Stegna on the II. Btl.'s left, III./Pz.Füs.Rgt. on the right. What fun! Once again runners trotted off, feeling their way over the darkened roads to the various companies. Assemble—once again two or three hours sleep, then the battalion moved farther west, the rifle companies on foot, the heavy company partly by vehicle. We wound our way through the terrain in long rows. The assault battalion was already in its jump-off position. Behind it we moved farther to the right. The commander of the 8. (MG.) Kp./II./Pz.Füs.Rgt. GD sent the special missions officer ahead on a motorcycle to establish contact with the III./Pz.Füs.Rgt. We had just passed the right wing of the assault battalion when the motorcycle came roaring back. The Leutnant jumped down and shouted: "Herr Oberleutnant, I've been shot at! There are already Russians in front of us!"

"Rubbish!" said the commander. "According to the regimental order III. Btl. should be where you were shot at."

The junior Leutnant shrugged his shoulders and replied in desperation, "but they were definitely Russians!"

"Lovely, gentlemen, according to the army service manual: battle to achieve

a favorable jump-off position. Whose turn is it? You, Herr von Trembecki? Please, two platoons up, right and left of the road, the third platoon behind them as reserve. Fw. Kuhnt, one medium mortar squad in position up front in support, understood? The commander of the heavy company looked around, they nodded and split up.

Soon there began a lively outburst of infantry fire. The rifle company worked its way forward, the medium mortars opened up. Everything else remained in the ruins of a village on the road, which had apparently departed this life in 1939. Von Trembecki did not make any headway; he committed the reserve platoon and then fought his way forward slowly in an area of brush-covered terrain. Hptm. Zabel came back from the regiment, but all that he knew was that the III. Btl. must be there.

The commander of the 8. (MG.) Kp. went forward and a second and third mortar squad were also committed. We fought with front facing west. To commit any more would have made no sense; Trembecki has to remain up front and gain us some breathing room the leader of the heavy company reported to the battalion commander.

And now things opened up from the right too.

"Man," said Zabel, "where is the III. Bataillon? where is the I. Bataillon? This damned radio silence. Is the III. Bataillon shooting at our people up front on the right or what is going on there? Go!! Flares up, recognition signal—hold up a steel helmet!"

None of this did any good.

"Damn it, still not a swine to be seen," the commander of the "Eighth" muttered to himself.

Then the gun commander of the infantry gun platoon was brought to him. He had been hit in the belly.

Out now—even if it is the III. Btl. Now someone's been hit. My gun commander knocked out, that's all I need! Go, infantry gun platoon around to the right; wood 800 meters, lower angle group, six volleys—ready—fire! This had been going on for 90 minutes already. We attacked to the west and southwest—and we were supposed to be attacking south! Gradually it came to us: we were sitting in the middle, surrounded on three sides.

Trembecki was stopped, the battalion took up a hedgehog position and blazed away to all sides. The commander of the heavy company was hailed: "Herr Oberleutnant, an entire battalion marching toward us at an angle!" This time from the south. In fact it was a fat marching column, its objective obviously the town where we had spent the night. The commander of the "Eighth" observed through his binoculars; all right then: "Feldwebel, a fine feast for your machine-gun platoon!"

The guns went into position on the reverse slope in textbook fashion. "Sight 1 000 meters, one squad from the front, one squad from behind; cross fire: one canister per gun—all clear?"

"Jawohl," replied the machine-gun platoon leader.

The boys lay expectantly behind their guns; behind them the Feldwebel and the commander with binoculars raised. The commander nodded.

The Feldwebel's voice rang out above the sound of battle: "Position! Open fire!!" Four MG 42s began to rattle. Over there stumbling and tumbling. The entire battalion was gone—nothing more to be seen.

"Take cover!" shouted the Feldwebel.

The commander merely said, "That did it, but stay here to guard against further attacks."

Another thirty minutes passed; still nothing from the others; the II. Btl. continued to defend grimly against the now hard-pressing enemy.

The enemy artillery pounded our small area again and again. The medic Rosemeyer requested instructions for the evacuation of the wounded; there were already more than thirty. "We've been squatting in the shit for two hours already," declared Zabel. Crouching behind a ruined house, he repeatedly scanned the terrain through his binoculars. The sound of fighting grew ever louder. Were those tank cannon?

The binoculars swept attentively back and forth over the battlefield. Reismann appeared, was told that he and his company would have to hold on the right, and disappeared again"

"There they are," said Fw. Kuhnt, referring to the other side's tanks.

Yes, there they were. Driving slowly and firing, the enemy tanks moved toward the wood that lay on our right. Swarms of Soviet infantry separated from them and advanced on our ruins. And from everywhere in the ruins they were met by rifle fire.

"Man, I could sure use my anti-tank platoons here," moaned the commander of the "Eighth." He stood calmly next to Zabel, his submachine-gun in his hand; then a young soldier rolled down from a wall and lay at the commander's feet.

"Mother, mother," he whispered softly; the commander slowly stroked his face, which gradually relaxed and became quite peaceful. Gone, finished! The youthful face at the feet of the officers now looked quite peaceful and almost happy.

The enemy tanks drew nearer. Fw. Kuhnt, leader of the heavy company's headquarters squad, was the first to put his thoughts into words. "They look more like Tigers than T 34s!"

The glasses were pressed to the eyes.

"Yes,"said the Oberleutnant, "that's what they are; but those are definitely Ivans in front of us; apparently the III. Bataillon is now attacking from there with Tigers."

"About time," muttered Zabel. The news raced along the ruins. Flares rose

into the sky again; none of the Ivans caught in the middle would get out alive. They now ran like hares toward—and into their ruin.

Finally the tanks ceased their fire, the rest took care of the infantry. We were finished, exhausted. The tank attack now passed through us to the south; on the right the III. Btl. attacked, the I. (SPW) Btl. and its mounted troops carried on with the tanks. Objective: the towns of Dworskie and Gasewo!

The Oberst appeared, the regimental commander. "Accompany the attack if you can," he said, more fatherly than commanding. To our left the assault battalion had already moved out. Then we, too, turned about to the left and the ranks of the rifle companies moved into the terrain like strings of pearls. Before us a village which commanded the area as if perched on the lid of a coffin.

Under the eye of the regimental commander the heavy company moved medium mortars forward, and these went into position behind a house. Then they coughed up their first rounds. These were on target immediately, pinning down the enemy garrison while the rifle companies attacked.

An hour later we were in the village. But our strength was gone. We could do no more.

Far ahead of us we saw our tanks and armored troop carriers advancing past the village on the right; behind them on the left was the assault battalion, which also passed the village on the left.

Then the evening twilight came slowly. We set ourselves up for defense, served the captured heavy weapons. And dropped from exhaustion.

Hptm. Zabel returned from the regiment. New mission. And again we got up and moved on. We reached the wood that was our destination and set ourselves up for defense on the hard-frozen ground.

The enemy appeared to have a good artillery observer. He must have seen the last of the battalion entering the wood, for now all hell broke loose.

Up front at the edges of the wood crouched the men, between them heavy machine-gun teams; farther in the woods the heavy mortar squads—but the devil was loose in the entire forest.

A battery of Soviet 152-mm guns, the so-called "Black Pigs," kept the whole thing under constant fire. Salvo after salvo struck the trees; shells bursting in the trees hacked down entire trunks. Black detonations in front of us, behind us, beside us—and we lay on the frozen ground with no possibility of crawling into it. It was the wood between Pienicki and Gasewo! For an hour the commander of the heavy company lay beside his Feldwebel. Now and then one of them raised his face a little beneath his steel helmet to see if the other was still alive. For an hour there was nothing but the sound of incoming and exploding shells. Then, finally, finally, the enemy artillery fire shifted out of the wood to the rear"

"Go ahead and shoot there," murmured the Oberleutnant, "there's no one there." "Look out, up ahead—it's starting up again! Enemy infantry trying to attack across a narrow strip of plowed field." Then—wiped out. Ahead of us

medium mortars intervened. There they are again. "The artillery observer is good," declared the commander of the heavy company, for now the heavy rounds began howling into the middle of the forest again.

Into the fresh craters—a measure of protection at least. Hptm. Zabel came. "I would like to know where the others are. Again there is nothing to our left and right!"

Thirty casualties already and almost all from artillery fire.

The night passed. It was 16 January 1945. And again it rattled like yesterday. Again a series of 152-mm Black Pigs. The commander of the "Eighth" suddenly raised his binoculars. "Good God, entire Soviet regiments! That's why the heavy shells on us here."

The Soviets were already moving two kilometers behind us, and we? Then, hello, there appeared to be some of us still there. MG 42s rattled there, tank cannon roared. The Ivans were caught by surprise, their attack lost its momentum and ground to a halt. And then—then they began to run to the rear, pursued by bursts of machine-gun fire. And now from our right wing at the edge of the forest they began firing at the Ivans. But soon they settled down again, moving into farms and the forest level with us.

"Now we'll get it again," someone said. But no—this time it was different.

A runner from the heavy company came up from behind.

"Commander of the Eighth, commander of the Eighth? Back there the infantry gun platoon has been attacked by enemy tanks, heavy casualties!!" Now this. Incidentally the enemy tanks were heading this way.

"Oh boy!" said Zabel. "Now we're in a pickle; they want to cut us off. But now we get out of here!"

"If we get beyond the road before the enemy tanks reach the curve, then they can kiss our ass!" the commander of the "Eighth" observed laconically but crudely.

The order went from man to man; soldiers rushed past...

"Take your weapons with you." The voices of the platoon leaders and company commanders. "Go, go!" the commander of the Eighth said to the men of his company as they rushed past him. "Go boys, over there. Hey, take your machine-gun mount with you!"

Mortar men loaded down with ammunition, with base plates, heavy machine-gun people—everyone raced past at breakneck speed.

With a few men of his company, one arm bleeding, stuck in his winter uniform, his submachine-gun in the left, the Oberleutnant secured the river crossing until the enemy tanks appeared. Then the last of them also plunged deeper into the forest. Thank God, finally out of the fire. New positions were occupied. The orders were the same as before: stop and hold.

Yes, things went as planned for the Panzer-Füsiliere on 15 January.

After brief preparations, it was to attack together with an assault battalion from the Krasnosielc bridgehead almost parallel to the Orzyc in a southerly direction toward Stary and villages to its east. The second battalion probably strayed too far to the east and ran into the middle of the enemy attack. It was almost surrounded and was only just rescued by the Tigers and armored troop carriers. Taking advantage of the situation, the latter drove farther south and southeast toward Wola Pienicka. The entire regiment was thus united and succeeded in entering the town and the area on both sides of it. While the I. (SPW) and III./Pz.Füs. held the line that had been reached, the men of the II./Pz.Füs.Rgt. GD gained ground with the Tigers as far as the wood southeast of Wola Pienicka and were able to establish themselves at the edges of the forest. The Tigers of III. (Tiger)/Pz.Rgt. GD advanced alone as far as Dworskie.

The Soviets defended stubbornly at first; each had to be blasted from his cover before surrendering. It was a fight to the finish. The leader of the Tiger battalion's reconnaissance platoon, Lt. Bock von Wülfingen, was seriously wounded in the head, others were killed. As darkness fell on that 15 January 1945 three Tigers (Lt. Oertel with a crew of Nadler, Uffz. Müller, Gefr. Wolff and Obgefr. Viess, and Fw. Herwagen with a crew of Uffz. Schreier, Uffz. Maierhofer, Gefr. Etzel and Gefr. Gussone, both of 11. Kp./III./Pz.Rgt. GD, and Fw. Bühler and his crew of 10. Kp./III./Pz.Rgt. GD) entered Gasewo, which lay at right angles to the direction of attack, however they lacked the forces to occupy the entire town. Together with a few fusiliers of the II./Pz.Füs.Rgt. GD they established themselves in one part of the town and tried to hold their positions. The Tigers were almost out of fuel, which severely restricted their freedom of movement. So it happened that as darkness fell there were German soldiers in one part of the town and Soviets in another. No more supplies were getting through, an indication that the Germans were already surrounded. Cook Uffz. Baumann was seriously wounded in the arm while trying to get there and had to abandon the attempt. And so the Tiger crews and the panzer-fusiliers stood constant guard against the other, enemy-occupied half of the town and listened uneasily to the continuous rumble of moving enemy columns in the distance. Obviously the Soviets were unable to demonstrate their strength, the alternative being to drive back and forth with lights on. The isolated Tigers and panzer-fusiliers were pulled out of the town before dawn.

Meanwhile the Panzer-Grenadiere had moved up through Ploniawy to the Orzyc crossing near Leg, followed closely by the I. (Panther)/Pz.Rgt. GD, in order to occupy the assembly area due east of the river for the attack to the east and northeast (in the latter case toward the panzer-fusiliers). Since the bridge at Leg was too weak to bear tanks of this size, there were considerable traffic tie-ups, as a result of which just two companies got across in time.

The preparations at about noon on that 15 January due east of the

Orzyc proceeded in such a way that the II./Pz.Gren.Rgt. GD under Hptm. Sommer took over the attack lanes on the extreme right (also on the far right of the division's sector), while taking up position beside it to the north were the III. Btl. and then the I. (SPW)/Pz.Gren. and the Panthers of the I. (Panther)/Pz.Rgt. GD. The Kampfgruppe's first objective: Goloniwy, southwest of Gasewo, as well as the high ground around Hill Point 109. It was also anticipated that it would establish contact there with the panzer-fusiliers attacking from the north.

The right attack group with II./Pz.Gren.Rgt. GD had as its objective Borowe and the high ground to the north. Due southwest of it, the Kreuzberg west of Kryzewo was already in the area of the 129. I.D. with elements of Inf.Rgt. 427 and several forward observers there.

In the left attack lane the town of Goloniwy was taken very quickly.

The participating III./Pz.Gren.Rgt. GD (including members of the newly formed assault platoon—strength: 3 squads each 1 : 3 with assault rifles and MG 42s—which served as an assault and relief group in the hands of the battalion commander) was forced to fight, as one member of the assault platoon described as follows:

Our Steyr mule had brought us to the jump-off positions; now we advanced in a line of skirmishers while scattered artillery salvoes fell around us, seemingly haphazardly. The zone behind the actual front line was a scene of hectic activity: damaged tanks heading to the rear with wounded sitting and lying on them, ammunition vehicles and runners.

Then we met a few ragged and dismayed soldiers from another infantry unit. They told us that they were the last of their company; they had only managed to save themselves from the Soviet tanks by wading through swamp and chest-deep water. A dressing station had been set up in a half fallen down blockhouse in a ravine; doctors and medics were treating several badly wounded men lying on litters in blood-encrusted camouflage uniforms.

We climbed the other side of the ravine and spread out. Before us spread an almost completely level plain, which according to orders we were now supposed to cross. Farther left the panzer-fusiliers were attacking—we also heard that.

In spite of heavy enemy artillery fire we worked our way forward in short dashes. The ground was frozen rock hard and was only thinly covered with snow. As a result the shells exploded immediately upon impact, spraying their shrapnel low over the ground.

We took our first casualties. As second gunner I was carrying the ammunition boxes and replacement barrels. In spite of the cold my sweat-soaked shirt stuck to my back.

Finally we were through the barrage zone which the enemy artillery had set up in front of us. Beside me a soldier sought cover in an abandoned Russian foxhole. When he jumped in he landed on an Ivan hiding beneath some straw.

III./Pz. Gren.Rgt. GD's assault platoon received orders to provide flanking cover from a Russian position. A steady stream of Russian mortar rounds landed beyond and among us. Uffz. Harz, a longtime member of the GD (and commander of the assault platoon), was seriously wounded in the head and collapsed in his hole. Only with difficulty were we able to recover him. The night of 16 January arrived. At dawn came orders to advance farther. In a skirmishing line we felt our way forwards in the darkness that still covered the ground, again covering the battalion's left flank. We were just passing through a wood when we heard branches snapping farther left. Then the party began. Bursts of submachine-gun fire chirped through the trees, the entire wood echoed with the war cries of the Soviets. My first gunner was already lying behind his machine-gun; I threw myself down beside him and passed him the first belt of ammunition. Although he had been wounded quite badly in the thigh, the gunner remained at his weapon and fired his bursts with ice-cold calm. Those beside us also opened fire, and slowly the shouts of Urray died away. After that all we heard from the other side was the whimpering and moaning of the wounded.

And that's how it went the entire day — advance and then occupy positions — Defend.

At about the same time on 15 January the Panthers of the I./Pz.Rgt. GD advanced east out of the town of Goloniwy with the objective of Dworskie. The tanks had no sooner passed through the town heading east, however, when they were met by a hail of anti-tank and tank shells, mixed with the fire of Stalin Organs. They veered slightly to the north, and, battling the enemy armor (together with the I. (SPW)/Pz.Gren.Rgt. GD under Hptm. Brinken, with III./Pz.Gren.Rgt. GD behind and to its right) advanced steadily towards Hill 109.

During the advance Obfw. Czubaiko of III. Zug/4. Pz.Kp. was killed, while Lt. Sutter's tank of III. Zug/4. Pz.Kp. was hit and set on fire. Sutter managed to reach the main aid station in spite of serious burns. The tanks of Oblt. Vogel and Lt. Reissnerder of the same 4. Kp. were also knocked out. The attack force made a slight turn to the south and succeeded in taking and holding Hill 109.

At about noon the Panzergrenadiere of II./Pz.Gren.Rgt. GD with elements of the following II. Btl. attacked from Goloniwy in the direction of Borowe. The skirmishing lines of the already seriously decimated companies moved out of the town, which lay in a valley, to the edge of a ravine in order to reach the open plain. Former Russian positions offered protection against the Stalin organ barrages which appeared out of nowhere in the midst of the showers of mortar fire. Obfw. Baerwald, platoon leader in the 9. Kp./II./Pz.Gren.Rgt. GD, always at the front and loaded with hand grenades, ran straight into a Soviet counterattack. He fought like a berserker, used his hand grenades and made a hell of a racket. He succeeded in halting the Russians even though he was wounded in the cheek.

When the men settled into the old, abandoned Russian foxholes and bunkers to wait out the night, two members of the company (Obgefr. G. Lorenz and Uffz. Rehfeldt, both mortar men) had a terrific experience which they decided in their favor only through their presence of mind.

The racket was finally over. I stood up, in the process reaching into a pile of straw on the floor of our earth bunker. It began to move. A fright went through me. I stood up, my submachine-gun ready to fire. "Günter, there's one here!" He replied, equally dismayed, "hey, there's more, behind in the hole!"

I moved back until my back was against the wall and then called out loudly, "Russki, hands up! Throw away your weapons!" At the same moment Günter's flashlight came on weakly. There against the wall lay six to eight Ivans on litters; one was lying on the ground, his tunic torn, many bandages, bloody red, moaning: a commissar! Those boys could easily have taken care of we two, no one had noticed them. We bravely began persuading the Russians in a loud voice; then I disarmed them all.

Good gracious, they had ammunition in every pocket and in rucksacks. We kicked open the bunker doors to get more light. I looked more closely at the commissar. A young fellow, about 25 years old. He spoke to me, but I could not understand him. He made the gesture of shooting. I asked again, then one of the other Ivans explained that the commissar was asking to be shot. He had a frightful back wound which was spurting blood.

Günter Lorenz and I looked at each other. Then a hand grenade rolled into our bunker from outside. It went off. We were not hit, but I was half deafened by the explosion. I turned around—then a single shot was fired. Günter screamed, "The swine are shooting!" then we both opened up with our submachine-guns until it was deathly quiet in the bunker. We ran out, to a knocked-out Stalin tank where we sought cover. The night was cloudless, starry—and icy cold. Farther right in front of us—in a barely discernable village—the firing went on all night."

This village (it was Borowe) had been taken by the 5.and 6. (Schtz.) Kp./II. Btl. A heavy machine-gun platoon of the 9. Kp./II. Btl. under the command of Fw. Walter Pfeil, former leader of the combat train, went there as reinforcements. All night long the village was kept under fire by enemy mortars and artillery, as well as by machine-guns and snipers. Hptm. Sommer of II. Btl. had already been wounded early on 15 January; his successor was Oblt. Mackert, who went on to lead the battalion until the end of the war.

The darkness covered the battlefield on which the Pz.Gren.Division GD had suffered so many killed and wounded on the first day of the counterattack.

From right to left: elements of II./Pz.Gren.Rgt. GD in Borowe, other elements of the same battalion in Goloniwy with contact with III. Btl. and I. (SPW)/Pz.Gren.Rgt. GD, also there I./Pz.Rgt. GD on and near Hill 109 with a view to Dworskie and Gasewo, where elements of the

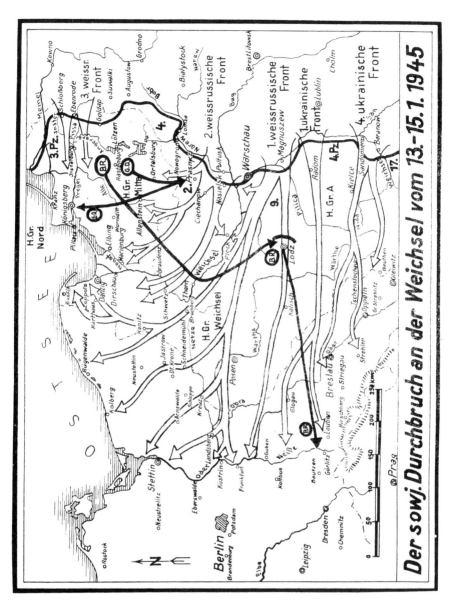

The Soviet breakthrough on the Weichsal from 13 to 15 January 1945.

II./Pz.Füs.Rgt. GD and three Tigers were holding. Wola Pienicka and to the north Krasnosielc were in our hands.

But the tremendous pressure of the enemy superiority continued. The Russians had been halted temporarily, but they had not been brought to a

129

complete stop. The lights of their vehicles, the rumbling in the immediate vicinity, the sound of their tank tracks already revealed their intention to force a breakthrough at any cost.

The brave men of the weak German units in action on this day were worn out, exhausted, reduced to a small number. They knew that there were insufficient numbers of heavy weapons, no reserves in the rear, no relief on its way. They suspected and felt that they were on their own; their carbines and assault rifles, their machine-guns, tanks and field howitzers were the only means available to defend against this vastly superior foe.

But yet they repeatedly pulled themselves together and held desperately in their holes and bunkers—without hope that the morning would bring relief.

At about three in the morning on 16 January 1945 the headquarters of the 2. Armee received a telephone call from the headquarters in Zossen. *General* Wenck, the new chief of the general staff, was on the line demanding to speak to *General* Heidkämper, chief of staff of the 2. Armee. He picked up the receiver and heard the following words: "Pz.Gren.Div. GD is to be pulled out of the line immediately and sent to Army group A."

General Heidkämper pointed out to *General* Wenck that the release of this last reserve would have a catastrophic effect; it would result in an enemy breakthrough against the 2. Armee, which would have no reserves with which to meet it. *General* Wenck replied that the enemy had already achieved a breakthrough south of the Vistula and quick help was needed there most badly. Furthermore it was a *Führer* order; arguments were pointless.

The order was passed on to General Staff *Major* Adler, the Ia of the Pz.Gren.Div. GD, at the division command post in Helenowo, but it did not get through to the various, widely scattered GD units until various times on the morning of 16 January.

Almost simultaneously—partly caused by the ordered withdrawal movements, but also under overpowering pressure from Soviet troops who had attacked early on 16 January—the various units left their positions, in some cases in haste, because the open terrain left them no other choice. On the right the panzer-grenadiers of II./Pz.Gren.Rgt. GD (in particular the 5. and 6. Kp. in Borowe) held until the early evening hours; it was impossible to reach them by runner during the day. Not until the Kreuzberg, already lying almost right behind them, which was stormed from the south by the Soviets and finally had to be abandoned by the elements of the I.R. 427 of the 129. I.D. holding on there, did the men of these two companies leave the village of Borowe to withdraw behind the Orzyc river line in several stages. There they met the sister battalions of the Pz.Gren.Div. GD, which had begun arriving piecemeal by evening. They immediately occupied a new defense line on the ridge on both sides of Leg but already on the west bank of the Orzyc. Contact was sought with the panzer-fusiliers

Kampfraum Praschnitz
Januar 1945

The Praschnitz Area of Operations — January 1945

to the north and this was loosely established.

The right wing of this regiment, the II./Pz.Füs.Rgt. GD, which was still holding out in the exposed wood between Dworskie and Gasewo, was simply blasted out after suffering more than 80 wounded in the hail of concentrated artillery fire which fell on this wood. Faced with imminent destruction, the panzer-fusiliers fled toward the safety of the forest edge on the banks of the Urzyc. Stary was the crossing point for the bulk of the regiment, which had suffered considerable losses. All other GD units also received the order to cease all offensive actions. The I. (Panther)/Pz.Rgt. GD, for example, was on the march in the direction of Krasnosielc when it received the order to turn around. It (along with the I./Pz.Korps Füs.Rgt. GD under Hptm. Buse) was placed under the command of the army and was immediately sent via Praschnitz to Camp Mielau. By the evening of that 16 January new positions had been occupied along the Orzyc; these ran in a straight north-south direction with elements of the 129. I.D. on the right and an infantry division on the left near Krasnosielc. Waves of attacks on these positions by Soviet close-support aircraft caused rising casualties and forced the men to dig into the hard, frozen ground.

Back, back! I staggered, I reeled more than I was able to run; my legs felt heavy as lead. The sun shone brightly on the snow so that anyone moving— Russian or German—was immediately visible. And all the while the shells exploded—the devil knows where they were coming from.

There is my firing position! My God—I saw terrible white holes in the snow, one beside the other, several mortars were completely destroyed; one looked as if it had been blown up.

I saw nothing still of value; but also—thank God—no bodies. There was no one left there; footsteps led into the fir wood over there. My platoon was gone and I was unable to find it by nightfall.

Together with the people of the heavy machine-gun platoon we occupied makeshift holes in the snow at the edge of the forest. Everyone tried to regroup, but my platoon remained missing.

Defensive preparations were made. It was said that rations were being issued somewhere. A runner also knew something about my men and where they were. I said goodbye to Fw. Pfeil to leave and find my platoon. A Russian tank or anti-tank gun was firing in the area, shells exploding in the trees made the area uncomfortable. Moments later Fw. Pfeil was killed in the same hole in which I had smoked a cigarette with him only a few minutes before.

The senior NCO had reached a village with rations, and I finally also found my platoon again.

Thank God, all had gone relatively well. But three direct hits in my mortar positions had destroyed three of the six available. One of my men had been killed, several were wounded.

I formed new teams with the three still serviceable mortars, then we moved into firing positions once again."

It was the night of 16-17 January 1945, Tuesday to Wednesday. But still the men held out in their holes along the Orzyc river line in the snow and cold until new orders to withdraw reached them. Bad news arrived at the command posts. It spoke of an enemy breakthrough and troops pouring into the Ziechenau area on the Nasielsk—Mielau rail line. There on 16 January in the Ziechenau area a recently established Pz.Jäg.Abt.GD (anti-tank battalion) under Hptm. Walle had already been completely destroyed as a result of improper use of its guns and the overwhelming Soviet superiority. More than sixteen anti-tank guns were lost, the bulk of the battalion was scattered, killed or missing. Only about 100 men with three or four guns eventually regrouped in the Allenstein area.

Enemy tanks were already said to be in front of Praschnitz, where the Kampfgruppe commanded by *Major* Fabich, leader of elements of the Pz.Korps-Füs.Rgt. GD was holding on, and large numbers of enemy infantry were moving northwest in trucks and other vehicles. The Praschnitz—Mielau road was already in danger of being cut by enemy armored spearheads. Reconnaissance revealed that Soviet columns were swinging far to the west toward Mielau. The first enemy patrols had also penetrated as far as Mackeim and heavy fighting was going on in the town.

Chapter 2
Retreat to East Prussia

All signs indicated that the enemy had broken through the German position within two days and had penetrated into the German rear area. Columns of infantry and motor vehicles, interspersed with groups of refugees, were moving northwest over the frozen, snow-covered roads. Here an upset car, there an overturned wagon, now and then a truck set on fire by strafing enemy aircraft; the chaos was complete, everything was heading toward the rear.

The German 2. Armee tried with all available means to hold its positions still east of Praschnitz, intercept the Soviet troops advancing deep into German territory, and bring them to a halt. The first GD units to be pulled out of the line and sent from the Praschnitz area along the road to Mielau were I.(Panther)/Pz.Rgt. GD, the I./Pz.Korps-Art.Rgt. GD under Hptm. Maiwald and the elements of the Pz.Füs.Rgt. GD under the command of *Major* Fabich. The Pz.A.A. GD (armored reconnaissance battalion) was constantly in action, sending patrols to the south and southeast of this line in order to clarify the enemy situation.

The I. (Panther)/Pz.Rgt. GD set out from Praschnitz down the road in the direction of Mielau at about 03:30 hours on 17 January. Turning south in Czernice-Borowe, the companies of the battalion drove southwest toward the villages of Lesniewo, Koziczyn and Koziczynek with orders to reconnoiter and secure the area. Shortly after leaving Lesniewo in a southeasterly direction, the 4. Kp./Pz.Rgt. GD encountered six enemy tanks, all of which were destroyed in a brief engagement. Soon afterwards, however, the Vogelsang company (4. Kp.) and the Liebscher company (1.Kp.) received orders by radio instructing them to immediately turn northwest toward Grudusk, as enemy tanks had also been observed there. The companies arrived in Grudusk but found nothing. Lt. Kunze of the battalion established contact with the German infantry positioned there. Meanwhile elements of the I./Pz.Korps-Füs.Rgt. GD marched along the road from Praschnitz to Mielau, during which they were repeatedly forced to leave their vehicles to fend off enemy patrols and advance elements. In each case these disappeared again, leaving the road open. The regiment's orders were to reach Mielau as quickly as possible.

The I. (Panther)/Pz.Rgt. GD spent the night in Grudusk and together with the infantry forces in the town defended it against the growing enemy pressure. It appeared that the Soviets were preparing for an attack.

On this day the two regiments occupied their positions on the west bank of the Orzyc, with II./Pz.Gren.Rgt. GD on the right pulling back from the river and taking over fortified positions on both sides of and in particular west of Ploniawy. The front in part faced south. This bending of the right wing was made necessary by the open right flank, which was the result of the 129. I.D. deployed further south abandoning its positions and the entry of enemy troops into the forest southwest of Helenowo. On 17 January the main line of resistance there was relatively quiet, however, as the enemy's pursuit was hesitant. New withdrawal orders had already been received for the evening.

Repeated counterattacks were launched in an effort to drive the enemy back to his starting positions. Under the command of Hptm. Brinken, the I. (SPW)/Pz.Gren.Rgt. GD attacked without tank support and charged toward the old positions in its armored troops carriers. It managed to get close to these, however immediate counterattacks by superior Soviet forces compelled it to turn back. The wounded had to be left behind, while Obfw. Lucht, Fw. Auf der Mauern and many, many others lost their lives in this courageous action in the heavy snow. It was all for nothing. A short time after the battalion's return Soviet artillery began a heavy barrage. A direct hit on the battalion command post of I. (SPW)/Pz.Gren.Rgt. GD reaped a terrible harvest. Hptm. Brinken, the battalion's brave commander, was killed.

Developments could no longer be halted, however; they now played out faster, gathering speed, and became a stream, a suction in the general direction of the northwest. The tempo of the Soviet advance frustrated all of the desperate efforts to settle down somewhere, occupy new positions, defend some town, regroup, reorganize the defense. The dreaded armored spearheads and motorized columns appeared everywhere, spreading confusion and chaos.

The men gave up and sought safety in flight. The horror was in their eyes; staring fixedly they tried to save their lives. Here and there intact German units continued to offer resistance and tried to halt the enemy. When this happened the enemy usually went round and reappeared in the rear of these Kampfgruppen.

It was becoming crazy; no sooner was a unit in position when the order came to abandon it. The goal was to break through, fight through to the north, out of the encirclement.

For the GD units still holding onto their positions (these were split into two Kampfgruppen—one near Mielau, mainly corps units, and the other, the bulk of the division, in the area northeast of Praschnitz) 18 January 1945 brought orders to withdraw to new positions. Desperately they sought to make contact with their neighbors, to their sister battalions; for to be cut off meant a weakening of one's own fighting strength and then destruction. In situations such as this it was imperative that every single soldier did exactly what his orders prescribed, even if it sometimes made no sense. Only the division command was in a position to view the entire situation and make the decisions.

The avenues of retreat were clearly laid down: for the panzer-grenadiers, who at the time were facing the greatest pressure from the enemy's north-south attacks, it was Ostrowek—Ch. Biernaty—Lipa, for the panzer-fusiliers the forest west of Krasnosielc, with their right wing in constant contact with the panzer-grenadiers, whose withdrawal dictated the pace of the panzer-fusiliers's retreat from their positions. After the III./Pz.Gren.Rgt. GD on its left had been forced back, the II./Pz.Gren. under Oblt. Mackert was withdrawn to new positions in front of the town of Ch.-Kuchny, all the while under heavy artillery fire and assaults by enemy infantry. With the help of III. (Tiger)/Pz.Rgt. GD it was able to settle down again and hold the town. The handful of Tigers, which had been put together in tank squads, conducted repeated counterattacks to facilitate the infantry's withdrawal and regrouping. The light and maneu-verable self-propelled 20-mm flak (mounted on prime movers) made repeated forays from around the corners of forests or hedges, pouring shells into the approaching enemy and forcing him to go to ground. They helped the men of the infantry battalions gain some breathing room and settle into new positions.

During 18 January the I. (SPW)/Pz.Gren.Rgt. GD, whose 3. (SPW) Kp. under Oblt. von Prittwitz had assumed the rear guard role near Leg, moved into new, fortified positions near Ostrowek. In the evening there was fierce fighting there with the pursuing enemy, who was driven back again and again in trench fighting. Meanwhile enemy armor had also attacked the defenders of the small town of Grudusk on the road to Mielau. Eleven of twelve attacking tanks were knocked out without loss by the elements of the I. (Panther)/Pz.Rgt. GD located there. The companies of this battalion then covered the infantry's withdrawal from Grudusk, which was thus abandoned to the enemy. By midday the entire battalion was on the march in the direction of Dembsk, east of Mielau, where, with elements of Kampfgruppe Fabich (elements of the Pz.Korps-Füs.Rgt. GD), it occupied new defensive positions.

The I./Pz.Korps-Art.Rgt. GD had meanwhile also arrived in this area, making it possible for these elements to draw closer together and act in unison. Hptm. Winkler, who had taken the place of the previous com-mander, Hptm. Maiwald, assembled his three light field howitzer batter-ies, which were commanded as follows:

10. Batterie	Oblt. Zänker
11. Batterie	Oblt. Haller
12. Batterie	Oblt. G. Busch
Stabs-Batterie (HQ battery)	Lt. Jansen

The situation there was more uncertain than ever, the Grudusk—Mielau highway was said to have been already cut. Kampfgruppe Fabich, which was near Dembsk, was ordered to launch a counterattack against the road with elements of the I. (Panther)/Pz.Rgt. GD and the I./Pz.Korps-Füs.Rgt. GD (Hptm. Buse) and reopen it. This did not come to pass, however, after the Liebscher company (1./Pz.Rgt. GD) became involved in a fierce fight with enemy tanks near Borowe, halfway between Grudusk and Mielau. The I. (Panther)/Pz.Rgt. GD was immediately sent there in relief with its remaining tanks. Supported by the Pz.Rgt. GD following its return, Kampfgruppe Fabich secured the commanding Hill 192 due south of Dembsk. Toward the evening of 18 January the situation on both sides of this position was completely uncertain. Enemy tanks were driving around the area and both sides of the position. Fears that the enemy had already long since driven past and was advancing down the Mielau—Kuklin—Neidenburg road seemed to be confirmed. There was already fighting on the southern outskirts of Mielau on the evening of this day; the former armored forces school with its huge barrack camps became a battlefield. The enemy had reached Mielau and elements had already driven past the city to the north.

In the Mielau combat zone there was no rest for the Panzer-Korps fusiliers, the tank crews of the I. (Panther)/Pz.Rgt. GD deployed there and the gunners of the I./Pz.Korps-Art.Rgt. GD under Hptm. Winkler during the night of 18-19 January. The confusion was there; to the right of their position in Mielau fierce fighting in the town, heavy artillery and mortar fire, fires against a blood-red sky, all visible from Hill 192. At around midnight the panzer-fusiliers left their hill position near Dembsk and marched northwest towards the Mielau—Neidenburg highway; their objective was Uniszki—Zawaddzkie. They were accompanied by the panzer battalion's mobile reserve, specifically 4. Kp. under Lt. Vogelsang and the remnants of the 2. Kp./Pz.Rgt. GD. After arriving near Uniszki, enemy tanks were sighted to the east and northeast; these were immediately engaged by 4. Kp./Pz.Rgt. GD. But Uniszki could not be held; the enemy was already driving past it to the north and northwest. New defensive positions were occupied along the road to Neidenburg. I./Pz.Korps-Art.Rgt. GD, which was poorly equipped with vehicles, was often the last to pull out, covering the withdrawal with its guns. A serious fuel shortage hindered the movements. A gun crew took shelter in a village somewhere to rest for a few hours; it missed departure and from then on neither it nor its *Leutnant* were heard from again. The retreat to the north went on; nevertheless, the individual armored groups of the I. (Panther)/Pz.Rgt. GD made repeated surprise attacks against the pursuing enemy armor. Lt. Kunze alone accounted for three enemy tanks. During the afternoon, at about 16:45 hours, Kampfgruppe Fabich, with the I./Pz.Korps-Füs.Rgt. GD and led by the tanks of the panzer battalion, resumed its march, setting out from Kuklin for Neidenburg. Near Wetzhausen, halfway to Neidenburg, the point came upon heavily fortified enemy positions with anti-tank guns and tanks. Attack was the only option; they had to get through or be destroyed. The formation closed up, pressed from behind. With little fuel remaining, the tanks attacked again and destroyed three enemy tanks. The brave Lt. Kunze and Fw. W. van Remmen were killed in the assault, however the enemy could not be driven from the road. The Kampfgruppe therefore diverted to the west, losing numerous vehicles, some through enemy action but most from lack of fuel, and advanced north parallel to the road. Some of the panzer-fusiliers walked, mostly during the night, through ice, cold and snow; they required more than 16 hours to finally reach Neidenburg. There the men first assembled and determined who was still present and who was missing. A few men established a blocking line due south of the city so as to at least guard their own quarters and gain time to regroup. But hopes for a breathing space were soon shattered; large numbers of Stalin tanks soon appeared before Neidenburg, pushed between the weak forward lines of security and the artillery firing positions and opened up with a withering barrage. The unit that suffered was the 10. Bttr./I. Abt.Korps-Art.Rgt. GD under Oblt. Zänker; it was completely overrun and lost all its guns. The battery had thus ceased to exist. On 19 January the enemy armored spearheads drove into Neidenburg itself. The garrison and the civilian population fled to the north. The remaining GD elements also moved northeast in the direction of the main body of the Pz.Gren.Div. GD. These elements of the GD Division had left their positions east of Praschnitz and during the night of 18-19 January had withdrawn further to the north. It had to abandon its defense lines as a result of the strong pressure being exerted by enemy advance guards with tank and artillery support through the forest west of the Krasnosielc—Stegna road to the north, as well as outflanking movements through this complex forest terrain.

Moreover, having lost half of their combat strengths, the battalions could only man the line somewhat south of the town of Szlachecki (Panzergrenadiere), Lipa and to the east of it (Panzerfüsiliere) strongpoint style. All that was left was twenty or thirty men per company; the rest were separated, wounded, dead or missing. These few, however, continued to do their seemingly hopeless duty until the oppressive superiority of the Soviets simply blasted them out of their holes. Lone assault guns and Tigers, those that had not been taken to the rear with damage or abandoned and blown up due to lack of fuel, helped hold the positions by carrying out local counterattacks.

The retreat continued into the Swiniary—Rycice—Polon area in the evening hours of 19 January, but once there only temporary guards could be put out. The bulk of the men remained with the vehicles—at 24:00 hours the retreat continued as far as the area south of Flammberg.

The division command post was temporarily in Neufließ, from where the retreat was directed mainly by radio. From there the division also succeeded in assembling its units. Together with the GD corps units under its command, the Pz.Gren.Div. GD spread itself like a screen over the area on the southern East Prussian border in a generally east-west direction. The elements on its right were in or moving into the area northeast of Grünfliess—Muschaken—Gr. Dankheim, in particular the remaining tanks of the I. (Panther)/Pz.Rgt. GD and the remnants of the I./Pz.Korps-Füs.Rgt. GD and Kampfgruppe Fabich, whose direction of retreat was generally north-northeast. There were frequent engagements with Soviet columns and swarms of enemy tanks which had broken through and were streaming into the country from the north. The tanks appeared everywhere, spreading confusion and disappearing again. This Soviet wave repeatedly broke through or bypassed opposition and continued north. They were preceded by heavy air attacks against the German columns, which suffered serious losses in men and vehicles as a result. Refugee columns moved in the same direction, blocking roads and making the chaos complete. On 21 January new positions were occupied along both sides of the Omulef brook in front of Willenberg. Flammberg had been lost the previous day after I./Pz.Gren.Rgt. GD had repulsed numerous enemy attacks. While counterattacks by the few remaining Tigers of III. (Tiger)/ Pz.Rgt. GD against Roggen and enemy tanks sighted there provided temporary relief, against the mass of enemy armor they were no more than pinpricks. Enemy armored spearheads were already sighted in front of Maishöfen south of Passenheim on this day; the I. (Panther)/ Pz.Rgt. GD counterattacked with its few remaining Panthers. This happened only to protect the withdrawal to the north of the supply company and the remaining vehicles, the majority of which were under tow, and prevent the loss of further vehicles. There was no letup in the pressure exerted by the enemy in this area; his spearheads spread across the land like a swarm, outflanking and pursuing the German defenders and driving deep into enemy territory.

Enemy armored spearheads appeared before Willemberg. There was heavy fighting for the city, which was soon turned into a smoking heap of rubble by the heavy artillery fire and continual bombing and strafing attacks. Willemberg was abandoned during the night. Arriving elements of the 24. Pz.Div. provided relief and made it possible for elements of the Pz.Gren.Div. GD to move early to the north, via Ortelsburg—Mensguth—Gr.Rauschken into the area south of Gillau. The Pz.Gren.Rgt. GD established its command post there on 22 January in order to establish another blocking position against the enemy spearheads advancing on Passenheim. The medical units moved into the same area, with 1. San.Kp. GD establishing its main dressing station in Samplatten. At first it had little to do.

On the same day—21 January 1945—the Div.Begl.Kp. GD under the command of Oblt. Kollewe received orders to immediately move to Passenheim and secure to the south, but its primary mission was to secure a fuel-carrying train which was supposedly located there. By evening the Div.Begl.Kp. GD had arrived there and had assumed responsibility for securing the line Scheufelsdorf—Passenheim. Much abandoned and still usable equipment was collected there, as well as gasoline and diesel fuel. Also found were badly needed replacement parts.

Meanwhile the I./Pz.Korps-Füs.Rgt. GD under Hptm. Buse, and with it Kampfgruppe Fabich, fought its way back along the Stabigotten—Allenstein road, frequently halted by the flood of panic-stricken refugees heading in the same direction. The Soviet armored spearheads were pressing hard and during the noon hours of 22 January sought to encircle Allenstein. Panic broke out among the refugees in the city. The streets became blocked, vehicles were abandoned. Men, women and children poured out of the city to the north, intent on getting away from the battle that was starting there. The Soviets occupied the city of Allenstein in the early evening hours of 22 January; there was little resistance, since the presence of large numbers of civilians made this senseless from the very beginning. The I./Pz.Korps-Füs.Rgt. GD occupied new defensive positions in the area of Göttkendorf.

Things also went very wrong south at Passenheim at noontime on 22 January. Seemingly endless tank and infantry columns, including guns, train vehicles and Stalin Organs, rolled north on the road from Gedwangen. They were headed straight for the Div.Begl.Kp. GD which, together with the Helmont battalion, was standing guard along the rail line between Schützendorf and Scheufelsdorf, its main objective to enable the establishment of a new defense line south of Purden Lake. Schützendorf was unable to withstand the heavy pressure from the enemy and was occupied by the Soviets. Scheufelsdorf, located to the northwest, also had to be evacuated, which opened the rail line and road to Allenstein south of Purden Lake to the advancing armored spearheads. II./Pz.Gren.Rgt. GD under Oblt. Mackert, which was defending there, could only let the enemy columns pass by.

Finally, toward evening, approximately 1,000 Soviet infantry entered the Passenheim railway station, near which the Div.Begl.Kp. GD had positioned itself, although south of the city proper. The I. (SPW)/Pz.Füs.Rgt. GD under Hptm. Zügel stood at the southern edge of Passenheim as operational reserve.

At Purden Lake the situation of the II. Btl. and I. (SPW)/Pz.Gren. Rgt. GD, the latter at Krummfuss, had become untenable. Elements of the Pz.Pi.Rgt. GD occupied Gr. Purden and defended the village against enemy-occupied Alt-Märtinsdorf. The Soviet tank and infantry columns rolled further down the highway in the direction of Allenstein. Our own positions along the railway embankment north of the highway lay under extremely heavy enemy mortar and artillery fire, making it impossible for the men to raise their heads. Meanwhile a new group of enemy forces advanced towards Krummfuss; the defending unit, I./Pz.Gren.Rgt. GD, put up fierce resistance, but it was very weak and was unable to prevent the Soviets from entering and occupying the town. II./Pz.Gren.Rgt. GD prepared to withdraw to the northeast to avoid being cut off. During the evening it withdrew along Servent Lake as far as the Graskau area, where it established its command post. The enemy then also pressed hard toward Passenheim and during the course of 22 January entered the city. The city had to be abandoned, new positions were occupied south of Gr. Rauschken. Farther east the battalions of the Pz.Füs.Rgt. GD held on in the Leinau area, were the few remaining serviceable Tigers of the III. (Tiger)/Pz.Rgt. GD had to carry out a relief attack during the evening.

In the area north and northwest of Allenstein the I./Pz.Korps-Füs.Rgt. GD withdrew from Göttkendorf to the north and occupied new positions before Braunswalde. Initially all was quiet; not until the afternoon did the enemy feel his way toward our security, however a daring advance by our lead elements drove him back again.

Farther west—already in the area of the Pz.Gren.Div. GD—elements of the Pz.Pi.Rgt. GD had left their security positions and withdrawn toward Wallen and Klausendorf. But no sooner had they occupied positions there in the afternoon, when Soviet spearheads attacked from the southwest. A brief exchange of fire was enough to cause them to disappear again, however. The situation remained quiet during the night.

On 24 January 1945 the enemy continued to push hard between Servent Lake (II./Pz.Gren. near Graskau) and due north of Passenheim (I. (SPW)/Pz.Füs.Rgt. GD and a few tanks of I. (Panther)/Pz.Rgt. GD). Energetic advances eliminated various penetrations into our positions. *Oberst* Heesemann, commander of the Pz. Gren.Rgt. GD, carried out a successful counterattack near the Graskau forester's house in difficult wooded terrain. I. (SPW)/Pz.Gren.Rgt. GD was able to hold on Hill 159. After its considerable losses of the past few days and the wounding of battalion commander Hptm. Zimmermann, III./Pz.Gren.Rgt. GD was pulled out of the line and sent via Ortelsburg into the area near Wildenau. Arriving replacements were immediately incorporated so as to raise the unit's combat strength—although this hardly translated into an increase in its defensive ability. The forest positions in the deep snow and the sound of combat from all directions made the young men more than nervous.

During the course of 24 January the Tigers of III. (Tiger)/Pz.Rgt. GD had to be moved through Mensguth along the road to Wartenburg since enemy forces had broken through and were moving north unhindered in the area of Hirschberg—Mokainen. Without further ado the Tigers attacked and drove the enemy back in a southwesterly direction, knocking out several enemy tanks in the process. The danger of our retreat road being cut had been eliminated for the time being.

Meanwhile the Pz.A.A. GD was in its element. It conducted wide ranging reconnoitering operations into southern East Prussia. From the area north of Mensguth its patrols drove far to the west and southwest, bringing back valuable information. They also made repeated attacks on isolated enemy spearheads which turned up here and there and prevented them from advancing further. Mainly, however, they watched over the secondary roads with their armored vehicles to see if enemy columns were streaming through and reported their findings by radio to the division, which was able to draw its conclusions. The situation north of Allenstein and in the Wartenburg area was threatening. The Soviets appeared intent on blocking the roads over which the Pz.Gren.Div. GD would retreat. Either a barrier would have to be thrown up as quickly as possible or the withdrawal of our units would have to be accelerated.

On 25 and 26 January the Pz.Gren.Div. GD continued to hold in the general line Graskau—Rauschken—Mensguth, even though the enemy was already advancing far to the north, especially west of this line and in the area north of Allenstein. There, too, the danger appeared the greatest: on 25 January the Tigers had to be committed to a counterattack in the Cronau area to force advancing enemy armor to turn back. The fear that these were advancing further in a northeasterly direction toward the GD Division's retreat roads made necessary increased measures on the division's right flank. The Pz.A.A. carried out numerous counterattacks, including in the line Lengainen—Nickelsdorf, and repeatedly tried to interrupt Soviet road traffic from Allenstein in the direction of Wartenburg—Seeburg. Still farther west, due north of Allenstein, the I./Pz.Korps-Füs.Rgt. GD under Hptm. Buse fought all alone against northwards advancing enemy forces in the Rosgitten area, delaying their advance.

All efforts in this area had been redirected towards forcing the units on the right flank of Rokossovski's army farther to the west and preventing them from breaking into East Prussia from behind at all cost. On the one hand the enemy was advancing in the direction of Elbing, on the other *General* Hossbach, commander-in-chief of the 4. Armee, decided on his own to pull back the German front through Lötzen—Angerburg—Rastenburg toward a new position from Friedland south through Prassen, due west of Korschen. In order to restore contact between the 4. Armee and the 2. Armee an East Prussia pocket formed, whose southern tip was held by the GD in the Mensguth area and whose open exit to the north was in the Brandenburg area on the Baltic. The danger of those units holding in the south, especially the Pz.Gren.Div. GD, of being cut off, was extreme, however.

In light of this situation the order received during 26 January to break contact with the enemy and transfer north into the area north and northwest of Bischofsburg during the night of 27 January is understandable. The units had held on to their positions in the Graskau—Rauschken—Mensguth line and to the south of it during the day, fighting off repeated enemy attacks. The enemy pressure seemed to abate there somewhat, after the bulk of the attackers were redirected to the northwest, where the point of main effort undoubtedly lay. Near Schönau advancing enemy spearheads were once again halted through the intervention of a group of Tigers. At the same time, in the evening hours of 26 January the GD corps units, which were fighting on their own, gathered in the area of Guttstadt and to its southwest. They included the I./Pz.Korps-Art.Rgt. GD with four guns left, elements of the Pz.A.A. GD and somewhat later also the Pz.Korps fusiliers under Hptm. Buse. These units were to launch an attack in a west-southwesterly direction between Glottau and Quetz in order to restore contact with the German front further west near Christburg, this having been severed by enemy armor. Not surprisingly—the enemy was particularly well-prepared to meet flanking attacks here—after good initial success this insufficiently strong attack bogged down in the face of determined resistance. During the night of 26-27 January the individual battalions disengaged from the enemy in the Graskau—Mensguth area and, as per orders, were transported by vehicle to northwest of Bischofsburg. While leaving its positions 3. Kp./I. Btl./Pz.Gren.Rgt. GD was once again subjected to Soviet loudspeaker propaganda.

The noon situation briefing in *Führer* Headquarters at Zossen near Berlin on 27 January provides closer details and reveals the intentions of the German military command in those days. The following are extracts from that briefing:

Situation Briefing in Headquarters—27 January 1945

Guderian*: Army Group North launched its attack this morning and has achieved very good success. The leading elements of these tank destroyers and of ARKO 302 reached halfway between Frauenburg—Elbing (latter was reached by the enemy on 23 January 1945). They were there already this midmorning.*

The armored groups advancing here got this far (shown on map); the 28. Jäg.Div. advanced to Karwinden and to Liebemühl and was heavily engaged by the enemy to the north of it. The Einem Group will be moved up in this direction to force the decision. The 170. Div. and the 131. Div. have also made good progress in their attacks, as the blue arrows here show.

Farther south in the area of the 18. Pz.Div. and the rest of the 229 I.D., however, our attack, which was essentially for the purpose of tying down the enemy, has not won through, rather the units remain on the defensive in this position.

The intention is to renew the advance in order to tie up enemy forces.

Here below an enemy advance has been repulsed.

Großdeutschland, which is temporarily without fuel, has been pulled out of the line, as well as another division.

Hitler*: Großdeutschland is coming there?*

Guderian*: Großdeutschland is coming out up there; the 562. Div. also. The intention is to move the 562. Div. to here in an overland march so as to be able to commit it up there or here if required.*

The withdrawal movements have taken place without pressure from the enemy. The enemy has not followed. Combat sentries and rear guards are far back in contact with the enemy.

Here is a push towards Friedland, without result.

The enemy then launched considerable attacks south of Königsberg. Committed against them were the 547. Division and the remnants of the 61. Division as well as elements of the 2. Division Hermann Göring which capable of movement.

The enemy's main pressure is on the northeast front and north of Königsberg, where the remnants of the 551. Division and the 285. Division have apparently almost lost the last of their fighting strength, and consequently a serious situation has arisen there this morning. It is not entirely certain...

Here are the strength reports:

The 203. Division has 3,400 men, the 451. Division 3,100. "Hannibal"— that is the police group—still has 900 men there, information on Kampfgruppe Hauser and the 21. Division was not available.

Großdeutschland is still in relatively good shape: 2 medium strength, one average, 3 weak battalions; 4 light batteries, 39 heavy artillery pieces. That is the corps artillery and the army artillery. Tank strengths have sunk badly. A total of 25 left...

On 28 January 1945 the various units of the Pz.Gren.Div. GD rested in the area south of Bartenstein. Part of the reason was the absence of fuel for the vehicles; unequivocal orders were issued for these to be blown up except for those needed to transport the weapons and personnel. During the afternoon hours elements of the Pz.Gren.Rgt. GD (II./Pz.Gren. under Hptm. Mackert) had to be deployed east towards Rössel as enemy tanks had broken through there. The men of this battalion remained in position to secure their own rest area and ensure the evacuation of refugees. Toward evening several enemy tanks appeared and opened fire. The only casualty was Gren. Walter of the 6. Kp. who was killed.

The march was resumed during the night, initially north in the direction of Bartenstein, after it became known, more as a rumor than as an order, that the GD was to be deployed to relieve Königsberg.

The division's columns moved over the road in the direction of Pr.-Eylau then veered northwest toward Kreuzburg. It then rested there during the night of 29-30 January.

On 29 January elements of the 1. and 3. Kp./I./Pz.Gren.Rgt. GD were given the task of proceeding to army group headquarters to serve as guard detachment. This happened as a result of a general order issued by Hitler concerning the protection of senior command centers on the Eastern Front against enemy action. This guard detachment under Oblt. von Prittwitz provided a quiet regimental reserve for non-commissioned officers and enlisted men. While their comrades in the battalions were in heavy action, the detachment carried out peacetime duties in Zinten, later near Heiligenbeil and in Neuhäuser near Pillau, with guard duty, cinemas and training. Not until 16 April did the detachment return to the division.

The division's armored reconnaissance battalion was taken from the division and together with the remaining elements of Kampfgruppe Fabich (I./Pz.Korps-Füs.Rgt. GD and I./Pz.Korps-Art.Rgt. GD) was assembled in the area west of Guttstadt for another attempt at a breakthrough toward the west and southwest. After initially gaining ground, the attack bogged down in the line Deppen—Waltersdorf—Liebstadt. While elements of the Kampfgruppe dug in in Liebstadt and held out against overwhelming odds for two days, all attempts to break through the enemy tank and anti-tank barrier near Deppen were hopeless. The elements of the Pz.A.A. GD and Kampfgruppe Fabich remained in heavy fighting there until 30 January.

Serious losses suffered by all the corps units near Liebstadt and Deppen as well as by the Pz.A.A. GD reduced fighting strength even further. During the night of 30-31 January all elements there were pulled out of the line and placed on the move: Kampfgruppe Fabich with I./Pz.Korps-Füs.Rgt. GD and I./Pz.Korps-Art.Rgt. GD moved toward Wormditt as army group reserve, the Pz.A.A. GD into the Zinten area southwest of Kreuzburg, where it was supposed to return to the Pz.Gren.Div.'s command.

On the evening of 29 January the leading elements of the Pz.Gren.Div. GD arrived in front of Kreuzburg, south of Königsberg. The division commander, *General* Lorenz, took up quarters in a wooden shack on the southern outskirts of the city. At that point Kreuzburg was still free of the enemy. The city of Königsberg was also still in our hands, although Soviet tank groups and following infantry had outflanked it to the south. Leading enemy units had reached the Baltic coast near Maulen and Waldburg and had severed communications with Brandenburg. So Königsberg was surrounded. But the enemy forces southwest of Königsberg were still relatively weak. It was vital that an immediate counterattack be launched by the units of the Pz.Gren.Div. GD to open the Brandenburg—Königsberg highway and restore communication links.

On 30 January the Pz.Gren.Div. GD moved its command post to Kobbelbude, while at the time the main line of resistance ran about one thousand meters farther east. The path of the main line of resistance was uncertain, however, and it first had to be won. There did not seem to be any more cohesive Kampfgruppen in this area, and the GD, which simply drove through the weak Soviet ring from the south, was the only combat-capable force there. Right behind the I. (SPW)/Pz.Gren.Rgt. GD under Hptm. Pfau, which advanced through Kobbelbude to VW. Wesdehlen, came the vehicles of the II./Pz.Gren.Rgt. GD. At the Kobbelbude crossroads the men of the battalion left their vehicles and proceeded on foot to VW. Wesdehlen. Several Bolsheviks buzzing about the countryside were caught and brought in as prisoners.

The panzer-fusiliers were moved closer to Brandenburg in order to attack from there (the Soviets had already advanced to the eastern outskirts of the city) along the coast road straight northeast in the direction of Königsberg. All remaining serviceable Tigers of the III. (Tiger)/Pz.Rgt. GD were brought together under the command of Hptm. Bock once again for this attack and committed in the direction of Waldburg—Maulen. It was the last concentrated tank attack by the Pz.Rgt. GD, of which there was little left apart from a few tanks of the I. (Panther)/Pz.Rgt. GD under the command of Oblt. Pohl. The crews without tanks were formed into infantry companies under Vogelsang and Liebscher. In the attack against Maulen on the afternoon of 30 January all operational tanks, armored troop carriers, four-barreled guns, etc were once again formed into an attack wedge. The attackers entered Maulen and put the surprised enemy to flight. These armored elements quickly regrouped and as darkness was falling they launched another attack against Wundlaken. This failed, however, in the face of heavy anti-tank and mortar fire. Maulen was held.

Meanwhile the I. (SPW)/Pz.Gren.Rgt. GD set out from the Wesdehlen area through VW. Wangnicken toward Jäskeim; after heavy fighting the battalion entered the town. The enemy was driven back and a continuous line was established through Seepothen to the panzer-fusiliers near Maulen. The attack got little farther than VW. Wangnicken, however, and was halted by heavy enemy fire.

The 7. (Schtz.) and 8. (MG.) Kp./Pz.Gren.Rgt. GD carried out another advance against Jäskeim, however, finally breaking into the town after heavy fighting. The enemy was cleared from the town in fierce house-to-house fighting and a large number of civilians were freed. Counterattacks, in some cases by Cossacks, were bloodily repulsed. The III. (Tiger)/Pz.Rgt. GD was moved up the southern outskirts of Jäskeim from the south (from Kobbelbude and the railway embankment), however it was unable to establish contact with the men of II. Btl. holding on there.

Chapter 3
Attack and Defense near Jäskeim, East Prussia

All night we had rolled in tight-knit columns, always expecting to run into the enemy, and had reached the town of Kobbelbude on the Königsberg—Elbing rail line. We took up quarters and were about to lie down to get some sleep, which we had been deprived of for days now, when the word came: "Let's go, everyone get ready, we're attacking!" In no time at all my mortar platoon and I were ready to depart, then the motors roared to life and off we went. Deep snow covered the East Prussian countryside, making everything look gray-white. I sat in the cab of the truck beside my driver and stared hard into the darkness of the dawning January morning. The country was one broad plain; in the distance we could see villages burning—and from all sides streams of machine-gun tracer, which were soon swallowed up by the darkness. Then, suddenly, there was a bright flash, and immediately afterwards a house went up in flames; sparks rose into the red tinted sky and the short, sharp crack of tank cannon reached us. That was about all that could be heard above the roar of the engines at full throttle. Once again we drove into uncertainty. The red brake light of the truck in front of us flashed briefly—we stopped.

I jumped out and walked forward to the company commander, Oblt. Hinnerk. The call was already ringing out along the column: "Platoon leaders to the company commander!" I walked with the commander of the light infantry gun platoon, Obfw. Grosse. "Shit," he said, "look at this, we're right in the middle of it again!"

We walked along the waiting trucks, in which our men sat shrouded in blankets, weapons in hand. It was damned cold. The blue-gray clouds hung over us—it was going to snow again today.

The commander sat in his car, bent over the map board. We reported: "Platoon leader, medium mortar, present!" The commander nodded his head wearily for us to come closer: "It's good, Rehfeldt, come over here. The situation is as follows: ... We are on the Kobbelbude—Seepothen road and further to Königsberg. The point is already in contact with the enemy, all that we know of Ivan is that he is in the villages everywhere. Nothing at all is known about his main line of resistance, weapons and so on. There is therefore a chance that we might get clobbered if we should by chance walk into an antitank barricade. But we might be lucky and sneak through a gap in the Ivans somewhere. Tell your men to pay maximum attention to all sides!! Firing positions must be suitable for all-round defense so that there are no awful messes.

He looked at us seriously. "Now have your men get down and make everything ready. I thank you and—see you in Königsberg."

I asked for a map of the area, since I had absolutely no idea where we were. The commander gave me a firing map and I walked back and called to my runner: "Günter, everyone prepare to leave the vehicles, then follow with equipment—two boxes of ammunition per man!" My people now began moving. The squads and platoons formed up. They followed in rows, with large intervals. Our first objective was a farm.

Only a few shots were fired as we neared the farm at dawn; Russians had taken up position there. We cautiously inspected the various houses and cow sheds; there were still Ivans in several of the cellars. My platoon had arrived; I assigned them positions and waited for the order to attack. The infantry advanced slowly through the deep snow. White flakes danced in the air, visibility worsened steadily. A strong wind blew up, the snow became a snowstorm. Large, wet flakes smacked against our faces. Unfortunately the wind was blowing from straight ahead, driving the snow right into our eyes. Visibility was already down to less than 30 meters, and we were supposed to attack in this. Our heavy infantry guns came roaring up, the light infantry guns were already in position, my mortars were ready to fire. But the attack was not to be carried out. Our infantry lay approximately 300 meters in front of a farm—on a hill and in a sand pit. I called my radio operator and asked him if the set was functioning. After a brief radio test one of my squad leaders set out with the radio operators. But after only a few meters contact was lost. The snowstorm was too heavy.

We saw nothing of the Russians and they nothing of us. The ammunition we had laid out by the mortars was soon completely covered by the snow. I had my men fire a few nuisance rounds to let the Ivans know that we were still there. Unobserved, the shells detonated somewhere in the snow. I went forward a few paces to the heavy machine-gun sentry in order to be able to see better. We had difficulty keeping our eyes open, the field glasses were useless, being completely damp and misted over. Suddenly figures came toward us. Russians? I was still unable to make anything out. I pushed the barrel of my submachine-gun forward, released the safety and stared at the snow-covered forms moving slowly towards us. Now they were within ten meters—I recognized women and children. I jumped up: "Over here!" Weeping girls with pale, fearful faces flung their arms around my neck. "Help us, help us!" Children cried "mommy, mommy!" Old men and women stood silently, faces frozen white from cold, their clothing wet from the snow. Shocked, I stood there, holding fast to a young girl who was on the verge of collapsing. From the expressions on their faces I got some idea of the distress, the hardships and the frightful suffering that these East Prussians must have felt after having been driven from home and hearth with nothing but the clothes on their backs. I walked slowly before them. There were about thirty persons—some with no coats, men without shoes, barefoot, the Russians having taken their boots. How happy they were now to have come across German soldiers again. Our battalion medical officer took charge of these people, and they were all led into a house. I returned to my people.

A runner came from battalion: "Non-commissioned officers fall out immediately, they are to advance together with 7. Kp. The 7. Kp. will attack farther right." — "Change of position, load equipment! Follow in line!" The squad leaders reported to me that everyone was accounted for, we moved out.

The snowstorm had abated somewhat by now. We walked down a dirt road toward a farm about 800 meters farther right. Infantry was already in front of the farm, waiting until I went into position with my mortars. I placed four lookouts behind the barn and paid attention to the subsequent advance. There was no sign of Russians from there. Before us beyond a shallow rise lay the village of Jäskeim, of which just the rooftops were visible. We were to find out if there were Russians there. The light infantry guns moved two guns into open firing position for direct aiming.

A three-man patrol came back and reported that the village was weakly occupied by the Russians. Our infantry moved forward in open formation. They were barely visible in their white camouflage suits; not a shot was fired. I had my field glasses to my eyes and carefully observed the rise and the village. There was nothing to be seen. Like small dots, our infantry disappeared behind the rise. Then, suddenly, five mortar rounds detonated in front of us; five black smudges in the snow right where our people had just advanced. They had been lucky!

I looked to the right. There was the Kobbelbude railway property with many freight cars, locomotives and railway installations. I saw lively panye wagon traffic and figures running around. Unsettled, I asked the adjutant: "Who is to the right of us?" — "No one. We are the right flank, that entire side is open." "Excellent," I said. "If the Russians launch a counterattack from there we're in for it." — "Yes, therefore keep an especially good lookout to the right!"

I had two mortars face to the right and observe. Meanwhile my radio operator had fixed the problem with his equipment, and so I sent one squad leader with a radio ahead to the infantry to act as forward observer. Our MG 42s could be heard rattling from the village; so they had made contact with the enemy.

I discussed the entire situation with the battalion adjutant: we had now broken through the Russian ring around Königsberg from behind and wanted into the city. So far we had fought our way through from Praschnitz as a moving pocket. Our right flank was open, we were on the extreme right. Today the garrison of Königsberg was attacking to tie up the Russians. Our breakthrough was to take place this evening.

My two radio operators trudged towards Jäskeim. Ivan fired two more mortar rounds. We saw the two drop to the ground and then move on again slowly. Soon they had disappeared. We established radio communications with them: "Ilona here, Ilona, Ilona, do you read, over." The radios worked perfectly. Soon came a request to move the mortars up to the village.

We moved out with one squad. I ordered the others to follow in succession, which meant that one squad remained in position and fired while the other worked its way forward.

I myself went forward with my runner. Walking was very difficult in the knee-deep snow and our progress was slow. Looking around, I saw that the light infantry guns had been limbered and were following with the two trucks. We reached the first houses and found our forward observer. Engines roaring, the two light infantry guns arrived. Both platoon leaders were looking for the commander. I had my people take cover and by radio ordered the remaining squad to follow. The light infantry guns unlimbered and initially went into open firing position for direct aiming.

The village was a so-called street village, which meant that the houses lay on both sides of a main street. There were no side streets.

With submachine-guns slung carelessly we two platoon leaders went looking for an observation post. One house looked especially favorable. While we sought the suitable windows and briefly inspected the house, frightened civilians, the owners of the house, emerged from a cow shed. The old mother and two daughters of 28 and 18 years. Astonished, we asked if they hadn't seen the Russians. Yes they had, but they had been inside only a short while and had been looking for German soldiers; then they had suddenly fled: "germanski soldat!"

We set up our observation post, assigned observers, and I was just about to return with my runner to select a firing position when a cry rang out through the village: "Cossacks coming!" Everyone looked in the direction of the outstretched hand. It was still snowing lightly.

I stood in front of the house and looked too. Then I saw about twenty Cossacks approaching at a mad gallop, heading straight for us. They were carrying rifles in their right hands, like a suddenly appearing apparition. Everything happened very quickly. Our armored troop carrier battalion had also seen these riders and opened fire with its super-heavy machine-guns. The bursts were too high and struck our village, right where our light infantry guns and my people were standing. They immediately took cover and, standing at the corners of the houses, opened fire with rifles and pistols at the riders as they raced past only a few meters away, heading toward us. It was a real shoot-up. The Ivans fired at us from the saddle with rifles and submachine-guns. A magnificent sight! A bullet smacked loudly into the window right next to me. I jumped back, raised my submachine-gun and aimed carefully at the leading horseman, who had just raised his rifle to his cheek; range about 30 meters. My submachine-gun barked, the barrel rose high, shell casings flew out, powder smoke entered my lungs. I fired an entire magazine, thirty rounds, at the leading horseman. Looking over open sights, I saw him drop his rifle and fall from his horse, which reared up and likewise fell. The following horses tripped over the fallen. A terrific mix-up! I lowered my submachine-gun, ejected the empty magazine, shoved in a fresh one, and was about to continue firing when I heard an artillery piece fire and a shell detonate. Pieces of horses and men whirled through the air. Our light infantry was firing into the confused Cossacks from 80 meters. Rapid fire!

My runner fired at individuals who tried to flee to cover. His automatic rifle cracked at regular intervals. A Russian lay behind his downed horse and fired at us with his pistol. I quickly raised my submachine-gun and fired from the hip. He collapsed. Got him! Of the entire group not a single horse was still standing, and *a few wounded screamed, "Pan, pan!"*

My runner and I cautiously left the cover of the doorway and walked over to the fallen to have a look at them. The apparition had been finished as quickly as it had appeared. I stepped back, the tension drained from my limbs, I laughed at the civilians crouched together in fear in one corner. "They won't hurt you anymore." The 18-year-old girl stared at me, eyes wide: "I was so worried about you." I laughed, "yes, child, it's always like that. Whoever shoots first and has the better aim wins. That was nothing."

Then, suddenly, there was an outburst of firing from the farm from where we had just come. I raised my field glasses to my eyes; then I saw another ten to fifteen Russian horsemen disappear into a gully. A severe shock seized me: what if they run into my following squad? That might end badly. Unsettled, I waited to see if the runner showed up soon. Meanwhile we made the village ready for defense. It was sited rather unfavorably in a shallow valley; at least it was impossible to approach it unseen. The civilians stood in the kitchen, which faced in the direction of the enemy, and observed our activities. They were happy that we were there and asked us worriedly whether the Russians were likely to return. As long as we are here no Russian will come!

I heard someone outside ask, "Is this Unteroffizier Rehfeldt's observation post?"

"Yes, I'm here. What is it?"

A runner stepped inside. He came from Sprengula's second squad and reported that the squad had arrived and was awaiting assignment of a firing position from me. I walked out in front of the house with the runner and showed him where I had in mind for the firing position. There was a hiss and a bang, followed by another bang; we both took cover and jumped back into the doorway of the house.

Damn it, mortar fire! The Russians were announcing their presence again. The runner set off and soon disappeared behind the houses on the other side of the road.

The company commander summoned me: "Rehfeldt, let someone relieve you You're falling asleep on your feet! You still have three NCOs!" I smiled wearily: "Yes, three left." Which meant: yes, three left; allow yourself to be relieved or not? What choice did I have?

"I would like to do it myself, Herr Oberleutnant."

I walked back to the door. There was Uffz. Sprengula, who had led up the second squad.

"Hans, second squad present as ordered; mortars are in position, request target assignment."

"Very good Bruno, sit down." I offered him a cigarette and he sucked the smoke into his lungs.

"I tell you man, that almost went badly. A few confused Russians came gal-

loping towards us; it would have gone bad for us if the Flak hadn't opened fire!"

Outside a couple of "brickbats" hissed overhead and exploded loudly behind our house, rattling the windows and causing the panes to fall out; quick as lightning we got down from the chairs on which we were sitting and kneeled on the floor.

We laughed at each other and sat down on the sofa, stooped slightly to remain beneath the edge of the window as protection against fragments. Ivan sprayed the entire village with light and heavy mortar fire.

"There is no phone; we will just have to set a line of communicators so that I can keep a firm hand on my people," I said.

I gave him several instructions and sent him back to the mortar position. Günter, my runner, had meanwhile filled my empty magazine and was flirting with the 18-year-old girl, who seemed to be amusing him with her typical open East Prussian way of speaking. He was playing the knight who would protect her against all dangers. I said with a laugh, "Don't believe everything Günter tells you; he is quite a bad Casanova." She looked at me wide-eyed, "Oh but Herr Unteroffizier, you are just jealous!"

All three of us laughed. Then—boom! Window panes rattled and shattered; fragments struck the wooden door, blue-gray powder smoke rolled in.

Damn it, that was close! Terrified, the girl squatted on the floor and looked at us questioningly.

"They won't hurt us," we said to her, "they won't go through the roof."

I walked over to the observation post; the commander of the light infantry gun platoon was there. He was just ranging in his guns. It was already dark, so it was just barrage fire. The commander stood beside him. "Place your fire thus, Rehfeldt can do the rest—ah there he is—you begin barrage fire immediately too."

He showed me where he wanted the fire placed.

There was virtually nothing to be seen of the Russians. I ordered my men to prepare to fire and issued the first fire command: "On MKZ 12—range 300, right only—fire!" In the absence of a field telephone each command had to be passed down the line. I had special sentries posted. My barrage fire lay about 150 meters in front of us. I made rough line corrections to the left and right. The commander discovered to his dismay that there was no infantry at all left in our village—all three rifle companies were to the right of us. Our heavy company (8. Kp.) was forced to defend itself. Of course we did not have the necessary people. Thus we were only able to post sentries at the most important points. The heavy machine-guns were in the front line, my people were assigned as security, especially to the right. A forward artillery observer came to us; unfortunately his radio wasn't working, but he spent the night with us. The commander set up his company command post in the house with us, so that we were all close together. Runners and squad and gun commanders came and asked questions, reported this and that. Finally there was a clearly organized plan of defense for the village. For security reasons the light infantry gun was pulled back toward the farm behind us and wire was laid to the command post.

Several men brought two prisoners into the company command post; both were wounded. I questioned them, but we didn't learn much from what they had to say. They probably didn't know anything.

A runner sent back by the forward artillery observer was supposed to take the two prisoners to the rear. They whined and cried loudly, but what were we supposed to do with them? Cursing and complaining, the runner left with them.

Everyone was ordered to remain extremely alert; the commander inspected the positions and then came to me. We would have to stay awake again tonight! We split the night into two halves; the commander and I would stand watch from 20:00 to 01:00, from 01:00 to 06:00 the artillery Leutnant and the commander of the light infantry gun platoon.

By now it was quite dark outside. We blacked out the window and sat down at the table in the feeble light of a petroleum lamp to write our daily reports. Would we get anything to eat today? No one knew for sure. The fire roared in the stove, outside it was cold.

The civilians had laid down in the bedroom. The Leutnant and the commander of our light infantry gun platoon had stretched out on the floor and were snoring loudly. With monotonous regularity the field telephone rang every 15 minutes: line test! At about 22:00 hours I again checked on the alert readiness of the men. Happily the sentry was on the ball. At the corner of the house with our observation post stood an observer, who excitedly came to me and reported that the Russians were working their way towards our village! I picked up my night glasses and stared intently into the darkness. The terrain was flat out to 300 meters in front of us, then it rose to a small hill, beyond which the houses of the village of Seepothen could be seen burning brightly. Against the red illuminated night sky I could clearly see the Ivans coming over the hill singly and in groups. They were walking upright, with rifles or spades slung over their shoulders. Behind a fence, which lay about 200 meters in front of us, I could see figures digging, running back and forth. Sometimes several would stand together, holding hands and stamping their feet. Apparently they were cold too. We watched for a while, then asked the commander for permission to fire. Since I had more ammunition for the mortars than for the light infantry gun, he authorized twenty rounds for the mortars. As I waited I observed the Russians, estimated the range once again, then came the call: "Ready to fire!"

I turned around and gave the command to fire.

The shots rang out in the stillness of the night, but my greatest fear was not realized: there were no muzzle flashes from the mortars. Only once a few sparks from the burning extra charge flew over the house behind which the mortars sat. Four shells were on their way. Filled with tension I watched, field glasses raised, for the impacts. Hissing slightly, they fell before us. Then there were four bright *flashes, the sound reached the houses—good, excellent. I issued a correction, gave the order to fire again. Again the short, sharp crack of firing, then the rounds hissed over us and bright flashes as the shells struck home. It was as if the Russians had disappeared from the face of the earth. Only a few still leapt about. After the last shell impacted there was a lot of shouting from the other side; we had apparently got one. "Look there," I grumbled, "at least we can hear our success there!"*

I exhorted the sentries to be on their toes, to keep their eyes open. Report anything suspicious to me immediately!

I walked back into the house. The commander was sitting at the table, his head had fallen onto his chest—he was asleep. Quietly I sat down on the sofa and reflected: damn it, I could deal with being tired; for days and nights we had run around, driven, fought; every time we thought we were going to get a brief rest there was another skirmish.

There was a rumbling outside the door, then someone stepped inside, blinked in the light. Then I recognized him—our farrier! "Well, have you brought food?" I asked. He nodded. The food was really here! That would cheer up even the most tired soldier. The commander woke up, looked in amazement at the clock, shook his head: "I really did fall asleep!"

Meanwhile the news had spread like wildfire. The food collectors set out. The truck had also brought some ammunition. That was reassuring to me.

Then Günter, my runner, came with a steaming mess tin. Wonderful, the good it did; we were not hesitant with our praise. We were as hungry as wolves. We also ate half of our cold rations straightaway, true to the maxim: perhaps there will be a storm tonight and then everything is shit, better to have done with it.

The commander spoke to the farrier, who had with him a large briefcase full of things to be signed, everything possible that the train behind was supposed do for us. Then there was plenty to do. Finally they were finished, and the next day the senior NCO was to bring a bottle of schnapps as it was my grandmother's birthday. "That is reason to celebrate," laughed the company commander.

"Jawohl, Herr Oberleutnant!"

Then we sat down together; we were both from the same town. We talked about leave, about Hagen and whether we would soon get mail.

We listened—outside a machine-gun rattled. We interrupted our conversation. What was going on?

I walked out to our alert sentry, who was still standing at the corner of the house. "What's going on?"

He informed me that a few Ivans had deserted to our heavy machine-gun crew. I looked once again through my field glasses and again saw the Russians directly in front of us digging in the snow and several walking around. Suddenly the commander was standing behind me. "Well Rehfeldt, if they want to desert, let's give them a little encouragement. You know Russian—call to them." I laughed—why not?

I cupped my hands in front of my mouth and shouted to the Russians: "Russian soldiers! Come here; throw away your weapons! Hands up!"

I yelled in this way for a good half hour until my throat was sore. In fact a few pans did come crawling over; they were picked up by our heavy machine-gun outpost.

Finally I gave up calling to the Russians. Something was going on over where the Ivans were—an anti-tank shell whizzed overhead. The tracer could be seen clearly as it disappeared in the sky.

The Russians continued to fire into the blue at regular intervals; they hurt no one. A glance at the illuminated face of my watch showed that it was 00:15 hours—our watch was over.

I walked into the house, admonished the sentries once again and in passing said to the commander, "Herr Oberleutnant, you can get some sleep now." Praise God and thanks—he lay down on the sofa, close to the stove, and closed his eyes.

I gently opened the door to the bedroom; in the feeble light of a petrol lamp I saw the forward artillery observer and the commander of our light infantry gun platoon lying asleep on the floor.

I woke both to begin their watch and made up a bed for myself; it was pleasantly warm next to the large tiled stove. I slung my steel helmet and submachine-gun within reach on the bedpost, leaving my belt with rations bag and magazine pockets buckled just in case.

The civilians lay on the bed, fully dressed; on the floor lay the two runners and the Uffz.-medic as well as the leader of the company headquarters squad. It was quite dark in the room and I couldn't find anything to put beneath my head. Then a form stood up, rubbed both eyes and stared at me. Then she realized where she was and laughed at me. She had completely forgotten the present situation and was shocked to see all these soldiers in her bedroom. Finally we shared a pillow—it was the small, 18-year-old Maria. She looked at me questioningly: "Do you think the Russians will come in the morning? I am so terribly afraid—and what will you do?" She apologized to me, but what was I supposed to say? "We still want to break through to Königsberg, but at the moment we are surrounded. You must see that you get through to our train; but I don't know yet how things will turn out." That is all that I could say.

She sighed and lay down again, closing her eyes. I had my head propped up on my arm and observed the sleeping girl. In the dim glow of the lamp I could only guess at her facial features; it was a pretty face, framed by long hair. Soon she was sound asleep—I thought of home, of the war.

I fell asleep.

Outside a machine-gun rattled. A parachute flare was fired; I listened, eyes open. Soon it was quiet again and I fell back to sleep.

155

31 January 1945

I woke up to hear someone in the room speaking fast and rather loudly. Daylight was already streaming in through the window. What was happening? I leapt to my feet, submachine-gun in hand. The civilians fled with their belongings to the cellar. I put on my steel helmet, stuck a cigarette in my face and woke the still-sleeping Maria. "Get up, go down to the cellar, Ivan's attacking."

"What are you doing? Are you staying?" she asked me with fear in her voice. "Yes, we're staying for sure. Come, get going! Quickly!" She disappeared through the hatch in the floor.

Outside there was an explosion. Anti-tank shells hissed overhead. This was serious!

An increasing number of mortar rounds dropped on the village.

"Boys, boys, such a racket early in the morning," laughed my runner Günter and wolfed down all of his cold rations. "Well, don't you want one last good meal before a hero's death?"

The Russian machine-guns began to bark, and the first small arms fire was heard.

"Ivan's coming, Ivan's coming!" Everyone was wide awake.

I ran to the rear entrance to the house and shouted firing orders. But now, when speed was all important, of course things went wrong. I raced inside. Finally, finally, ready to fire! "Fire'" Filled with deep satisfaction, I knew my shells were on their way to the enemy. The first shots were too long. I shouted into the din: "One hundred meters less—break; 10 less every five shots—fire!"

Then I waited again for the mortars to fire. There—this time it was twenty shots which left the tubes in rapid succession.

While scanning the terrain, looking in particular for the anti-tank guns that were making our lives miserable, off to the right, beyond the railway embankment, I spotted a large number of Russian infantry who had dug in there and taken up position against us. We had no front in that direction!

Convinced that they would smoke us out properly next time, I fired into the midst of the attacking Russians. But it was probably just a Russian feint attack, for the Ivans came no closer. Perhaps they just wanted to determine our weapons strength.

The commotion gradually died down. The tension eased. I explained to the commander my intention to have a go at the Russians on the right, and he was highly enthused. He also wanted to use the light infantry gun against them.

I called to Uffz. Sprengula, telling him to remain at the observation post, and ran back to the firing position in long strides. The boys were sitting in a house, the sentries stood outside and kept watch. With them were the driver and co-driver of the rations truck. There was no gas. The farrier had gone back on foot to get some. The guards stood concealed behind the houses, but the Russians would eventually see in from the right—well, I would have a go at them.

I asked for a report on the ammunition. I was astonished to learn that there was only 100 rounds on hand. I couldn't believe it. "Didn't we receive more ammunition yesterday evening?" I asked. Yes, but it was still on the truck, no one had unloaded it yet. There was a bit of a row over the failure to unload the ammunition. People were assigned and they quickly got the ammunition down. I was able to count on a stock of 400 rounds. At least that was something. No suitable observation post from which I could see everything on the right could be found. I was therefore forced to fire without cover, from the garden fence. A rabbit hutch prevented me from being seen. The mortar was about 10 meters behind me, thus I was able to pass my corrections directly. The light infantry gun fired on a linesman's shack, suspecting an anti-tank gun to be there.

My first four shots landed smack in the middle of the Russians, as my Berliner Fritze always said. And then there was round after round. Over where the Ivans were a cloud of smoke rose up, soon followed by others, and the snow was stained dark. Now and then articles flew through the air, perhaps pickets or"something similar. "Direct hit, direct hit!" shouted my commander, celebrating like a child. I also enjoyed it. I would probably have expended all the ammunition, but that wouldn't do. Unfortunately I soon had to stop. An entire group of dark figures (Russians) had fled to the left into a gully.

Suddenly there was an approaching hiss, and a shell whistled into the snow about 20 meters from me. Hello, Ivan is hitting back!

Three more came hissing in and I passed the word: "Cease fire—take cover!"

"Bad, bad, Ivan'" I said derisively. Hiss—crack! I lay flat on my belly in a furrow, this could easily go wrong. With a leap I was in the house. Now let the Ivans shoot as they wish. They were surely seeking my firing position.

My radio operator sat in the room tinkering with his set. "Well, will it work?" — "Oh yes, just another minute," came the reply. Soon afterwards we were able to go to receive and speak with my observation post over 150 meters. We were thus able to dispense with the line of communicators and perhaps saved some blood. For the lads no longer had to stand outside.

We rolled ourselves a cigarette, and I sat comfortably on the sofa, thinking good thoughts.

Then an armor-piercing shell crashed into the house. Ivan was hell bent on eliminating my firing position. Each sat where he felt the safest. Not much could happen, for the shells had to penetrate two walls. Furthermore we were great optimists. For variety Ivan now also began firing 150-mm shells into the village. These were very unpleasant things. Between two impacting shells, which detonated right beside the house, a runner came hurrying from the observation post. "Damn it, that one nearly got me," he blurted out. He was breathing hard, no wonder, having run so hard. In his hand he held the tail shaft of a 120-mm mortar shell. "Ivan dropped it right on the kitchen table," he related. "A 120-mm shell," he continued, "landed on the roof of the observation post, flew through and exploded on the floor. There was suddenly a hole in the roof and bang, the thing

lay on the table where we had just been eating. You should have seen their faces,"
he laughed.

*Crack—boom. We were the target once again. Now we had to be careful, and
no sooner thought than another bang outside. Window panes shattered, powder
smoke entered. I slid off the sofa onto the floor like greased lightning—that was
another fine surprise barrage. I looked around and saw that everyone was sitting
on the floor or ducking—it looked downright amusing yet it was deadly serious.*

*Scarcely had this shock passed when another came. Once again we were
incredibly lucky. We listened, no one said anything—what was howling toward
us in the air was something we had not heard before. Quite novel, strange—it
hissed overhead. And then the earth seemed to tremble, the house shook. Plaster,
chalk and mortar fell from the walls. Further shocks jolted us, the air pressure
blew in windows.*

*We looked at one another in astonishment—man, those were big shells! If
they had landed in our village! Approximately 20 to 30 impacts, large black
craters with a diameter of more than ten meters, with huge chunks of dirt thrown
out. They lay up to 300 meters beyond our village. Hopefully there would be no
more of those. I debated whether it might not be better to order a change of position, for we had definitely been spotted. While I was still thinking it over there
was a huge bang followed by a loud rumbling, as if the entire house was about to
collapse.*

*Cautiously someone went outside to see what was going on. He came run-
ning in, shouting, "Go, get out, the house is on fire!" Then we heard the crackling,
smoke rose up.*

*I ordered everyone to immediately move five houses up and go into position
there. My runner and I set out to scout a firing position. But it wasn't that simple. The Russians, who could see anyone moving in front of the houses, fired at
every single man with anti-tank guns, having already got the range. As I was
dashing between two houses they placed a shell right in front of my nose, and I
almost ran into the detonation. Not until I had reached safety behind the house
did I stop and rest.*

*Günter the runner was still in the next house. "Come on, they're not shoot-
ing right now." Cautiously he looked around the corner. There was another sharp
crack and the she'll struck the roof of the house behind which I had taken cover.
Then Günter made his move. He did it like a veteran warrior. One had to move
immediately after the shell landed, for Ivan had to re-aim and load before firing
again. Günter smiled at me. But Ivan had seen him dash, for a new shot detonated against the front wall of the house, causing the bricks to fly.*

*We both waited a moment, then we made a dash across the street to the next
house, always through deep snow. I couldn't complain about being cold; the Ivans
were harrying us too well for that. We looked at one another; my people were
spread out behind several houses and were working their way toward us. Filled
with concern, I watched each one as he made the dash from one house to another.*

The anti-tank fire became more intense. Several houses were already burning and one of the roofs collapsed in a shower of sparks. It was madness to order a change of position in broad daylight in full view of the enemy—but it had to be.

Then another of my people came panting through the snow, a box of ammunition in each hand, the half a hundredweight baseplate on his back. Exhausted he leaned against the wall. At the moment none of my mortars was ready to fire. If only the Russians don't attack now!

I couldn't see either of the two Unteroffiziere anywhere. No one knew where they were.

Still, all had gone well, no casualties in spite of the shooting. All my efforts were dedicated to getting at least one mortar ready to fire as quickly as possible. There was still no contact with the observation post, where was the commander? I would have to act on my own.

I was furious, because I did not get even a little support from the two squad leaders.

Then, suddenly, the company commander of the 7. (Gren.) Kp. came out of a house, behind him several men. I called out to him and asked where the 7. Kp. was. "Here is our command post, we're staying with you," he said. The company commander of the "Seventh" was just in the process of deploying his people to defend the village; I advised him and showed him our own positions. Ivan was now firing everything he had and all around one could hear anti-tank shells bursting without pause. Since the Russians did not know in or behind which house we were situated, now and then he put a few shots into each house.

The fronts of all the houses had been shot up. Concerned about my platoon, I went outside again to check on my men. It seemed almost impossible to get from house to house. My boys stood behind the protecting walls and waited.

So as to finally have at least one mortar ready to fire, I immediately called for a baseplate, a tube and a bipod, whether they belonged together or not, and as much ammunition as could be reached. The first man made the dash. It was Gefr. Bleuel. As mortar commander he came running with the baseplate and immediately went into position on his own behind the schoolhouse. The mortar was soon complete, ammunition also arrived, it was do or die. But one had to be lucky too; we still had no casualties.

I repeatedly asked if anyone knew where the two Unteroffiziere were. Finally someone said to me, "They are in a deep cellar drinking, they found some schnapps." I was furious, but what could I do? "Leave them there. I know what I have to do!" A quiet fury seized me, since I had sent my runner (Gefr. Günter Lorenz, KIA Feb. 1945) into the greatest danger while these fellows drank.

I was very happy when finally a mortar was ready to fire, inside I was very grateful to Bleuel. The lad had guts! "Does Bleuel have the Iron Cross, Second Class already?" I asked. "No, Herr Unteroffizier," was the answer. Well perhaps he soon would.

The number of incoming mortar rounds increased. We listened. That was suspicious. And rightly so—for Russian machine-guns opened up, submachine-guns barked, explosive bullets flitted through the air. I peered cautiously around the corner of the house and looked toward the forefield. Aha, there they come. Lone figures in camouflage clothing were running towards the village firing their rifles. They were already damned close to my former observation post.

Our men fired from every window. Now the shooting also began near me. I raised my submachine-gun and, leaning against the corner of the house, aimed carefully at two onrushing Ivans; range about 150 meters! Beside me someone with an automatic rifle was firing at an enemy machine-gunner. Through my field glasses I observed rifle bullets kicking up snow.

The bullets struck at brief intervals. Three went wide, but with the fourth the pan stumbled and fell forward. He wasn't going to get up again. I looked appreciatively at the shooter; he stuck his head out through the window and grinned at me: "Next please!" Then he resumed firing.

There were fifteen rounds in his magazine. The pans continued to race towards us, screaming loudly: "Urray!!" We had to be very careful; we could not let the Ivans reach the houses. From every window and from behind every corner we fired with submachine-guns, machine-guns and rifles.

Below at my observation post I heard the typical crack of pistols, the Ivans must already be close there.

Two anti-tank shells exploded in the next house. Direct hit! Our heavy machine-gun, which had been firing without pause, fell silent. I had my field glasses raised. Damn, they got it! A single man came running back under heavy enemy fire. In any case the heavy machine-gun was finished.

In the general tumult I suddenly heard mortars firing to the right of me. Astonished, I turned to the side. It was firing independently—and tensely I watched for the impacts. Excellent, they were on target! If only they kept firing. I called to Bleuel: Go, fire! and was happy at how accurate the fire was. The lad's aim was excellent.

Continue firing independently! But only a few more shots rang out before there was silence in the wood. No more ammunition! Then, from behind us a whistling sound followed by a detonation!! Our infantry guns were firing. But they, too, must be almost out of ammunition, for only a single shell was fired each time. Pinpoint fire! They placed just a single shell everywhere, then that was it. There we were, with less than fifty men, and were supposed to defend an entire village against three times as many Russians with heavy weapons support. We had to worry about saving our skins. We let the Ivans come very close. 100 meters—150 meters—but then we opened fire as if on the practice range. Every shot was a hit. More and more Ivans were killed. The rest lay down in the snow and tried to go into position, but that was to do them no good.

Three of us fired simultaneously at a Russian who tried to disappear into the snow. He kept digging with his arms for a little while, then he collapsed and lay *motionless in the snow.*

They were wiped out like that one after the other—the last tried to flee and we got quite a few of them as well. The snow was littered with dark forms. Some continued to move an arm or a leg for a little while; one tried to stand, but he was picked off and fell—for good.

Breathing a sigh of relief, we lowered our rifles and submachine-guns. The attack had been repulsed.

"Rehfeldt, you fired wonderfully with that one mortar! Excellent direct hit! Look, there are the Kanakas, more than 15 dead!" I looked; in fact they were mortar hits.

Good—Bleuel—I was determined that the lad would get the Iron Cross, second Class.

The attack had been beaten off—but what was to come next?

We had expended all of the ammunition for our light machine-guns and the mortars. Our own situation was less than rosy.

I had the equipment removed and disassembled in cover. Now we had to prepare for close-range defense. Every man was used for this, whether he had a rifle or a pistol. I distributed the men as best I could. The first row of houses was abandoned as far as the old observation post to avoid unnecessary casualties.

31 January – 1500 Hours

It was about 15:00 hours. If only the night would come, then ammunition could be brought forward. No one could risk going back in broad daylight. Ivan would get him easily. Submachine-gun between my knees, steel helmet in my hand, I sat beside the commander of the 7. Kp. His face was very serious; the 7. Kp. was down to 22 men. He very much wanted to speak to our commander (8. Kp.), but he was not yet at the observation post. When he stood up and moved toward the door our commander walked in. "Thank God," he said, and sat on the sofa, wiping the sweat from his brow. His hair hung down tangled and wet, his face was covered in stubble.

"The Ivans are shooting at single men with their anti-tank guns, damn them!"

Once again we discussed the entire defense of the village, and the ammunition shortage was raised repeatedly. The boxes of machine-gun ammunition were redistributed, two were unbelted for use as rifle ammunition—everything was in such short supply and no hope of getting more. Miraculously the telephone line to the battalion (II./Pz.Gren.Rgt. GD) was still intact. Our commander wanted to speak to the commander. I called and asked for him to come to the phone—just then the Ivans fired another barrage and their aim wasn't so bad. There was a crackling sound on the line, I called once again, and I noticed how easily the crank turned: the line had been cut! I put down the receiver and said with a wry smile: "troubleshooter—get going!" easily said—I knew exactly what it meant to go out as a troubleshooter now, with everyone in cover, the Russians firing one barrage after another. He would have to search for the damaged area, wire in hand, with clammy fingers, repair the line and come back! Many a troubleshooter never returned from such a mission.

Our two troubleshooters got to their feet. "No, just one," ordered the commander. "Spare people." The two exchanged tools, then one set off. I followed him as far as the door.

At first he advanced at a crouch behind the houses, the line in his hand, then he made several leaps and finally ran as fast as he could—seen by the enemy!

His camouflage suit protected him well; tensely, I followed the operation. Then he stopped for a brief instant to catch his breath; there was an explosion. For seconds there was a small black cloud beside him and he lay motionless in the snow.

Shocked, I thought: dead or badly wounded?

No, he cautiously moved his head, looked around slowly and then pulled in his legs in preparation for a leap. If only it worked.

He jumped to his feet and continued to run along the line.

Crash—boom! This time directly in front of him in the snow! That damned anti-tank gun! If only he is alright! But no, he was probably just knocked down by the blast. He ran on, that brave young man. The Russians knew how important the man was to us. They probably suspected a runner or a signals man. They continued to fire the anti-tank gun at him, the man on whom all our hopes rested. If he fell all contact would be lost. Now he lay as if dead, or feigned it to deceive the Russians. Many more pairs of eyes in addition to my own were trained on the scene of the drama; for he still lay motionless. The anti-tank did not fire again. "Pity about the lad," I said to myself softly. Then someone yelled, "He's alive, he's coming, he's coming!" I turned around, then I saw him laboriously wading through the deep snow towards us.

Everyone followed him with worried eyes. But luckily he reached the protection of the houses again. There he dropped exhausted into the snow. A pair of soldiers walked over to him and carried him into the house.

Just then in the company command post, the telephone operator reported: "Contact restored, Herr Oberleutnant!"

And then the commander got on the line and tried to have reinforcements, ammunition and sleds with which to transport the wounded to the rear sent as quickly as possible. He spoke as I had never heard him do, indeed he almost implored the commander. The latter promised to do whatever he could. With a tired motion of his hand the commander placed the receiver on the field telephone and let himself drop onto the sofa with a sigh. "If something doesn't get here soon, we'll all be done by tomorrow morning; then they will write in the big book: they died, true to their oath of loyalty, all on their own, abandoned and betrayed. Shit, shit!" The last few words he shouted out loudly. Then he turned his head and said, "Felbermeyer, give me a cigarette, or do we have any left." The latter grinned,

162

rummaged in his map case and pulled our a pack of Nordlands. The commander had him pass them around, I held my lighter under his nose." The finest flame-thrower," he laughed and inhaled the smoke pleasurably into his lungs.

"How is the tent where we pitched our tents. May one feel safe there?"

No sooner said than there was a tremendous blow, we felt the air pressure on our ears and lungs. Deathly silence. That was in the house! No one moved a muscle. My hand trembled slightly as I raised the cigarette to my lips. Slowly, with exaggerated calm, I stood up, intent on seeing what had happened. When I stepped out in to the hall everything was covered with mortar, dust and bricks. Pictures lay on the floor, glass shattered beneath my feet. Through the door I saw the next room, which faced the enemy. There was a huge hole in the wall, right next to the window. The shell had penetrated a wall and exploded inside the room. There was just a small hole in the next wall.

That was lucky, I thought laconically, and was just about to go outside when two figures ran around me and plunged at worrying speed through the door of the house.

At the same instant another mortar sell impacted directly behind the house, then another.

"My dear man," laughed the two. They listened hard outside for a while and then ran on. The Russians must have noticed the amount of traffic in and out of our house, for the anti-tank fire grew heavier. Several guns were firing. Most of the houses were already burning. Then there was another fierce barrage of heavy mortar fire and the bursting and cracking of the shells was followed immediately by shouts of "Urray!" as the Bolsheviks launched another attack. They had probably discovered that we no longer had any support from heavy weapons. Once again they pounded the village. One could scarcely stick one's head outside.

The commander came running in, his steel helmet on backwards, a lit cigarette between his teeth. He hastily shoved a magazine into his pistol. Felbermeyer risked a joke in spite of the serious situation: "Does the Herr Oberleutnant intend to shoot at people with his pocket flak?" The commander twisted his face into a bitter smile: "Better than a pop-gun!" he said, looking at his 7.65-mm, which was little more than a child's toy.

Everyone had found a place which offered the best cover. I checked my magazine once again and released the safety on the submachine-gun. Through my field glasses, about 800 meters away I saw approaching a horse-drawn anti-tank tank gun. That would be a target for me—if only we had ammunition.

Our last heavy machine-gun suddenly opened up, I saw snow flying. Good—excellent!

The horse dropped, a man fell to the ground—the horse-drawn vehicle stopped. But the crew had already got down.

Our heavy machine-gun fired furiously—wonderful the way it pinned those fellows down. But then—jam!

The Russians immediately unlimbered the gun and moved it into position. A dangerous flash—bang!!

Snow and dirt whirled about. One direct hit after another on the house in which the heavy machine-gun was positioned.

Not a shot was fired from our side. I saw our soldiers fix bayonets and ready hand grenades. Their faces were deadly serious and pale. Only when the shell impacted too close, sending fragments smacking and whizzing about, did they flinch and duck down. A dangerous silence.

The first Russians, who were wearing long coats, came close to the houses; they carried the long rifles with their three-sided bayonets. Now they advanced hesitantly, as if they did not trust the enemy. I raised my submachine-gun, aimed carefully and curled my finger. The Ivan, who was less than 40 meters away, collapsed in the burst of fire. His small cap flew in his face. I let the barrel drop and sought my next target. As if on command the shots came now in regular succession. All were well-aimed shots—all hits. We had to conserve ammunition.

I had three full magazines left, barely 100 rounds. But what was that when each burst spat out ten to fifteen shots?

Therefore limit fire, shoot accurately; already I heard the sound of pistol shots. To our right the dull thud of hand grenades.

Now it was do or die.

Five Ivans came running at us with submachine-guns rattling; they did not know where we were, for they couldn't see us behind the walls and windows. But they fired like crazy, their bullets smacking into the house walls.

I ducked briefly, raised my submachine-gun to my shoulder and it soon barked its thirty rounds—an entire magazine—at the Ivans. They didn't get far, two pitched forward and moved no more. The rest were more or less seriously wounded. They lay in the snow, moving their arms and legs and twitching.

Got them! Things seemed to be hectic on the right, a real shoot-up there. I took the pans from the flank, and again they dropped and lay still. It was a real storm of fire from every window and doorway and behind every house corner. The Ivans got to the village but not into it. One had to have nerve and stand fast. The heavy weapons could not engage the Russians without endangering our own people. It was a man against man struggle—the lone fighter's war.

There was no point in shooting at individual attacking Russians with the machine-guns; the machine-gunners had therefore picked up rifles and were taking aimed shots.

Concerned, my gaze followed our positions to see if the men would keep their nerve. For if we were forced out of the protection of the wrecked houses we would surely be lost. Without cover we never would have got away through the deep snow. This meant: stay—fight—fall!

The enemy who attacked here had been rudely jolted from his dream of victory—by the crashing and bursting of our shells, the bark of the machine-guns and the loud crack of the tank cannon.

A burst of submachine-gun fire struck the fence behind which I lay in cover, making the pickets fly. Quick as lightning I jumped back, changed cover and inserted a fresh magazine. The last! All empty—empty—no more ammunition! Shocked, I looked around; Günter, my runner, picked up a bullet crusted over with ice and snow, cleaned it off and inserted it into the chamber of his rifle.

The last bullet!

I raised my submachine-gun—the last magazine, Günter! Then I looked into the forefield again; everywhere brown forms lying around in the snow, motionless, with curiously bent limbs. Around me now only scattered rifle fire—it was becoming quieter. There, what is that? The Russians who had survived the attack were retreating. Here and there, singly and in twos, all were falling back. We must have had just enough ammunition. I had six rounds left in my magazine. Günter, my runner, raised his rifle, aimed carefully and fired. His eyes stared at the target. "On target," was all he said and now? My radio operator had twenty rounds left, he gave him five. The calm before the storm!

I once again assigned observation sentries, had what was left of the ammunition distributed equally, then I walked back to the command post.

With a high-pitched whistling sound three light infantry gun shells passed overhead and detonated among the retreating Russians. They were the last three rounds. Who knew where they had found them?

In the room of the command post the two commanders sat facing one another, excited, because telephone communications with the battalion had been cut again. I removed my steel helmet and reported to the commander on the ammunition situation. "Just so you know, no ammunition can be brought up during the day. We must hold out until evening!"

Runners arrived; the news they brought was not encouraging; losses, dead, wounded, no more ammunition, one light machine-gun jammed—broken cartridge case, impossible to repair—even that was not enough to further shock us at that moment. From our observation post came one of my squad leaders, Obgefr. Hans Esser, to report what was happening there. The house had been shot up like a sieve. The only good thing was that the civilians had fled during the previous night.

There were only three men left there. The Russians had managed to get into the area to their right and continued to hold the area even against fierce counterattacks.

What? The Russians were inside our village? They must be driven out again at once!

Through the window we heard a sudden outburst of heavy fighting and exploding hand grenades. We listened; but it quickly quieted down again.

Suddenly we were startled by the ringing of the field telephone, which none of us was expecting. I picked up the receiver: "Rehfeldt here." And then I heard an agitated voice from far away:

"Who is that? Rehfeldt, that's excellent! Are you still in your old position? Are the Ivans still attacking? Do you have enough ammunition? The position must be held at all costs! Do you hear? At all costs! The regimental commander was just here—he expressed his appreciation for you!! But you must hold on!!"

"Jawohl, Herr Hauptmann! I am passing you to Oberleutnant Hinnerks!"

The commander had stood up and now took the receiver. Then I hear him say "yes" several times, "yes, but..."

No buts, our commander spoke as if reading from a book, our commander smiled tiredly, then his eyes suddenly opened wide—his face filled with tension. He seemed to be pleasantly surprised. We looked at him questioningly. "Yes Herr Hauptmann, out!"

The commander let himself fall onto the sofa. "Boys, we're being relieved tonight!"

There would have been a tremendous crash if all the stones that fell from our hearts at that moment had actually dropped onto the wooden floor.

Outside a loud conversation broke out; the hallway door was thrown open, then heavy footsteps came in. They seemed to be carrying someone in. The door opened; two men, sweating with red faces, had the leader of our company head-quarters squad between them. He stood up, teeth clenched, and hobbled painfully to the chair. Exhausted, he sat down and groaned softly.

Questioned by the commander, he answered, "I launched a counterattack with five men to chase the Ivans from the house but the fellows are back in there. I have a pistol bullet in the thigh. The entire heavy machine-gun crew except the Unteroffizier was killed—direct hit from an anti-tank gun."

So the Russians had achieved a penetration; it was clear that from their house they would try to gain control of the village bit by bit.

Another counterattack would have to be made. The commander of the 7. Kp. wanted to lead it himself. Preparations were hastily made and then the men of the assault teams moved out.

Outside it was gradually becoming darker—it was almost 18:00 hours. Now the runners could be dispatched without being seen by the Russians. Soon the first runners also came up from behind. They told us that ammunition was coming! Two sleighs were on the way. They were also to be used to evacuate the wounded. Furthermore relief was on its way.

"Who's coming then?" was our question. "A Volksgrenadier battalion! Great soldiers!" These words did not fill us with confidence, they were all cobblers, tailors, drivers etc. Our only thought: hopefully they will be here soon; it was all the same to us. I sent Günter, my runner, to my squad leaders on account of the daily report. Then the very ones who had got themselves dead drunk arrived. They were still not quite sober. I was going to have them both relieved as soon as the possibility arose.

Obgefr. Esser, who proved invaluable to me, had positioned the rest of my people around the command post to provide close defense. Outside it had become very dark. The fires in the village flickered eerily. Lone runners flitted from house to house like dark shadows. From time to time the Russians fired sudden barrages; then the detonations echoed through the village and for the next few minutes everyone took cover. We hoped that the Russians would not attack yet.

I looked at my watch: 19:40 hours—now the 7. Kp. made its counterattack against the Russian house. I stepped into the open. The clear, starry sky arched over our land. It was very cold.

Then a green flare rose up, and shortly thereafter the sound of exploding hand grenade bundles shattered the stillness of the night. Submachine-guns barked briefly, hand grenades exploded.

This was followed by furious defensive fire from at least four machine-guns. Then the first anti-tank shells crashed into the houses.

I walked back into the room. With an ear-shattering roar a shell blew off half the corner off the house. Sitting next to the stove I wrote my daily report.

Then a soldier came in and asked for me. I said, "Yes, who is it?" "Grenadier Bleuel, Herr Unteroffizier, I've been wounded!" I raised the candle and looked into his face, from which the color was draining. He smiled at me self-consciously. "Full of splinters, Herr Unteroffizier!"

I asked him if it was bad. "Can you still smoke?"

"Yes I can, but I don't have any!" That wasn't what I meant, I gave him three cigarettes; the last I lit for him myself. Then I made sure that he was evacuated on the first sleigh. I looked into his loyal eyes, "Good luck lad!"

The horse in front of the sleigh snorted fearfully, then the vehicle disappeared into the darkness of the night. The wounded moaned and whimpered softly. I tried to bolster their courage: "Wait a little while, then they'll come for you too. Then you'll be warm—just be patient!" The men lying on the ground looked at me with large, fearful eyes. Their silent entreaty to us—just don't leave us, don't forget us.

In the command post the commander was just calling the commander to ask when our relief was coming, in code of course: "When is the Ascension of Christ? Are the disciples coming soon?"

Günter observed: "Herr Oberleutnant, if the Ivans hear that they will surely say, Germanski bible no good, don't know much about it." We laughed loudly.

Relief was on its way, plus the sleigh with ammunition. The sled driver came in. "Where shall I bring in the ammunition?" he asked.

I received 200 rounds for my 80-mm mortars and ammunition for the rifles and submachine-guns as well as hand grenades. The two truck drivers, who were still without fuel, asked about gasoline. The sleigh driver shook his head, no idea. I called the battalion adjutant and asked what we were supposed to do with the trucks without fuel.

Again—thud, boom—surprise barrage!

The enemy anti-tank guns also fired; that's all we needed, hopefully it wasn't the prelude to another attack by the Ivans.

We hastily distributed the ammunition. I had four mortars go into position and prepare to lay down barrage fire on my order. Then suddenly someone called out, "Hello, 8. Kompanie?"

"Over here, over here!!" I called in a hushed voice. Then I saw our relief coming. Leading the way were an officer and a guide from our battalion. Behind them a long line of soldiers, widely spaced. Thank God!! Our relief had arrived!

I called to them again: "8. Kp. command post here!" Then I went into the house and reported to the commander: "Herr Oberleutnant, our relief is here!" Then the officer came in; the platoon and squad leaders remained standing in the doorway.

My commander got up and walked towards them: "Hinnerk, glad to see you. Please sit down." They shook hands, then sat down facing each other. The commander asked about the unit, strength, armament, ammunition and morale of the people; where the men were coming from and everything else possible. Runners from the company headquarters squad had already informed our platoon and squad leaders and they turned up slowly.

The new arrivals were quite a group, precisely as the runner had described them to us. Old, young, all together; very few of them had ever played infantry before. I suspected the worst. They had taken cover in the houses behind us. We were still in charge of guarding the village. The leader of this unit, an officer, spoke quite openly and without shame about his "elite force." He envied my commander for belonging to such a famous unit.

Then he pulled a bottle of schnapps from the pocket of his fur coat and opened it. Felbermeyer produced two schnapps glasses from out of his briefcase—an ideal runner—and then the officers drank to our and their health. Finally the bottle was passed around by us non-commissioned officers.

Finally our commander described the situation, making a sketch on the tabletop with chalk..."and unfortunately the Russians are in the house here below. We attempted two counterattacks, but without ammunition we were unable to drive the fellows out."

We looked at the leader of the relief force; he would rather we stay and throw the Russians out of the house. But our commander wanted to transfer command as quickly as possible and get away from there.

I proposed laying down a surprise barrage with the 200 rounds of ammunition I had just received to smoke out the Russians, then take and occupy the house. I dearly wanted to do that! But my commander preferred not to start anything now that we were being relieved. The Russians might start a continuous barrage and that would put an end to our relief. I understood what he was saying.

I was just sorry to have to leave the 200 rounds for our relief.

Then the individual squad leaders were briefed on the positions, observations were shared, and further information concerning the situation there, such as enemy strength, the Russian weapons and so on was passed on.

Our sentries were called in, our relief posted their own. We reported completion to the commander and carefully assembled our platoons in cover. The squad leaders reported everything ready, I went to the commander and reported: "Mortar platoon has handed everything over, ready to move out—all personnel and equipment accounted for!"

"Very good Rehfeldt, tell Obfw. Grosse that he is to lead the 8. Kp. back to G.M; he knows already." I walked out.

When I got outside I saw the company already marching; correct interval between men, no noise. The Russians fired blindly with anti-tank guns and mortars.

As I walked to my platoon several mortar rounds hissed overhead and exploded in the yard of the nearest farmhouse, causing a tumult there.

Four of our relief killed and three wounded! They had unwisely been standing together in a group. I shook my head, how is such a thing possible? Inexperience! They had no idea these boys.

We soon left behind us the village of Jäskeim, which we of the 8. Kp., together with elements of the 7. Kp., had defended—and held. We were accompanied by a sleigh carrying wounded, no one was left behind.

I went forward through the deep snow to Obfw. Grosse. As my platoon moved past I counted the people once again; just one casualty, I had been lucky.

Tired, the men trudged through the snow. Where might we be going now? Obfw. Grosse pulled his company out of the line; they were headed for Bohemia. And correctly: we were walking parallel to the main line of resistance. We met a soldier lying on guard in the snow. "What company?" we asked.

"11. Kp./III. Battalion. Outpost!" Aha!

We made a halt at an estate. There we received directions on the correct route and marched on. No sooner had we left when the Ivans showered the entire area with barrages.

After a seemingly endless march we arrived at the M... estate. There we had a brief rest and then our trucks arrived. Everyone climbed aboard. I loaded my platoon into two trucks and climbed into the cab of the Peugeot. It was freezing cold, for we were being towed by another truck—to conserve fuel. The engines roared to life. Where were we going? Where? The rocking of the truck put me to sleep.

When I awoke the city of Königsberg lay before us.

Soon we rolled across the big railway bridge into the city.

The 31st of January 1945 was used by the division in Pörschken to move in its remaining units, deploy the heavy weapons, undertake position improvements in certain sectors, and in general prepare the conditions for a forced breakthrough with a simultaneous widening of the very thin corridor along the coast road to Königsberg. To this end all available tanks, Tigers and self-propelled guns were readied in the Maulen area and the woods north of Waldburg. Attack units, especially the panzer-fusiliers on Reichsstraße 1, were relieved by alert companies and pulled out of the line.

The Div.Begl.Kp. GD under Oblt. Kollewe and the 2. Alarm-Kp./FEB under Lt. Krummel were committed for an advance through the Wundlacken Forest, south of Wundlacken.

During the night of 31 January elements of the Pz.Gren.Rgt. GD—in particular the II. Btl/Pz.Gren.Rgt. GD under Hptm. Mackert—were withdrawn from the previous positions in the Wesdehlen—Jäskeim area and were transferred behind the front over the coast road to Königsberg. There they took up quarters in houses at the southwest exit from the city. Arrival in Königsberg was at about 08:00 hours on 1 February. Meanwhile the fighting on the long side of the thin corridor in the area Maulen—Warthen—Kalgen to maintain communications with Königsberg went on with undiminished intensity. The Soviets repeatedly succeeded in advancing to the Baltic and blocking the coast road. But in each case the armored reconnaissance battalion succeeded in reopening the Warthen—Kalgen road in the direction of Königsberg, then the reinforced Div.Begl.Kp. GD conducted forceful advances toward Zu Warthen and Haffstrom. It was more due to luck than strength that the attempts to maintain communications with Königsberg were largely successful. In any case, in this way the Pz.A.A. GD succeeded in advancing past Haffstrom through Kalgen to Königsberg, where it joined the panzer-grenadiers. Finally, planning for the attack, on the one hand by the panzer-grenadiers and armored reconnaissance troops to break out of Königsberg, and on the other for the tanks and panzer-fusiliers to counterattack towards Königsberg, was so advanced that at about 03:30 hours on 3 February it was possible for the troops to leave their quarters in Königsberg and assemble near Kalgen. Their mission: (1) Gain the Reichsstraße 1 highway south of Haffstrom, and (2) advance south towards Warthen and take the town. With no fire support—probably to ensure the element of surprise—the companies of the II./Pz.Gren.Rgt. GD—the Pz.A.A. GD had not reached the assembly area in time—attacked south of Haffstrom. Very soon, however, they became bogged down in front of the well-prepared enemy positions under furious defensive fire. Oblt. Ochmann, who had just taken over the 6. Kp., was killed there, two non-commissioned officers and nine men were carried to the rear wounded. Nothing was achieved, the attack was a failure. The III./Pz.Gren.Rgt. GD, which was down to a combat strength of about 40-50 men, was placed under the command of the II./Pz.Gren.Rgt. GD. A line of security was taken up along the anti-tank ditch south of Haffstrom; without thorough artillery preparation taking the town of Warthen, which the Soviets had turned into a fortress, was simply impossible.

Enemy advances near the Maulen estate, some of which led to penetrations against the alert units deployed there, were eliminated as a result of the courageous efforts of the Lion Battalion (I. (SPW)/Pz.Füs.Rgt. GD). Several enemy tanks were destroyed in the process.

The second attack toward Königsberg was finally begun on 4 February. This time better prepared with strong artillery and tank support. Shortly after noon an armored group set out from the northeast towards Warthen; at about 05:00 hours this was followed by the panzer-grenadiers—in particular the II./Pz.Gren.Rgt. GD bolstered by the remnants of III. Btl.— plus several tanks of the 5. Pz.Div. The remnants of the 5. and 6. Kp. plus elements of III. Btl. were on the left, the 7.Kp. on the right. After the highway was reached in front of Warthen the attack force veered west and advanced along Reichsstraße 1. With heavy support from our artillery, the men entered and occupied Warthen. Casualties were very light.

Orders were immediately issued to occupy the line Maulen—Warthen with front facing east and to hold the positions at all costs. While the Pz.Gren.Rgt. GD established its command post in Heide Maulen, the new position was occupied with the help of four tanks, several anti-tank guns and 20-mm flak. The I.R. 975 of the 367 I.D. was placed in command in this sector and the reinforced II./Pz.Gren.Rgt. GD was placed under its command.

After a quick rest and reorganization the bulk of the panzer-grenadier division was transferred back into the Brandenburg area. Through its effort communications with fortress Königsberg had been reestablished and strengthened, and the enemy—in particular the Soviet XVI Guards Rifle Corps and the XXXVI Guards Rifle Corps—saw his plan to capture Haffstrom and advance along Reichsstraße 1 in the direction of Brandenburg frustrated.

The general line Colbnicken—Waldburg—Maulen—Warthen was held, with several corset stays in Kobbelbude and with the neighboring 562. V.G.D.

The Pz.Gren.Div. Großdeutschland's move from the Praschnitz area across East Prussia to the Baltic Sea was over. On its streets and roads lay the comrades who had paid for this effort with their lives. They and their graves in the southern areas of East Prussia are proof of their bravery in the battle for their homeland.

It was 4 February 1945.

Chapter 4
Panzer-Grenadier Division Brandenburg: In the Maelstrom of the Retreat from the Vistula to the Neiße

The virtually simultaneous attacks by the Soviet 1st White Russian Front under Marshall Zhukov (31 rifle divisions, 5 tank corps and 3 independent tank units) from the Magnuszew and Pulawy bridgeheads and the Soviet 1st Ukrainian Front under Marshall Koniev (60 rifle divisions, 9 tank corps and 8 independent tank units) from the Sandomierz—Baranow bridgehead on 13 January 1945 were aimed principally at the southern wing of the German 9. Armee as well as the entire length of front held by the 4. Pz.Armee under *General der Panzertruppe* Gräser. An artillery barrage of unprecedented fury lasting several hours left the German positions completely destroyed, and the few surviving German defenders were routed. The German front as such had ceased to exist. The immediate commitment of German operational reserves—those that were not attacked by Soviet armored spearheads in their assembly areas—did not provide any significant relief, especially since they had no time to deploy. They became caught up in the maelstrom of withdrawing German units: retreat became flight.

When, on 14 January, the scale of the Soviet breakthrough south of Warsaw became evident, *Führer* orders were issued for two divisions under the command of the Pz.Korps *Großdeutschland* to entrain with instructions to reach the area of Litzmannstadt (Lodz) and close the breach in Army Group A's front by immediately attacking towards the south. The two divisions, which began entraining on 13-14 January 1945, were *Panzer-Grenadier Division Brandenburg and Fsch.Pz.Div. 1 Hermann Göring*

Not included was the Panzer-Grenadier Division *Großdeutschland*, which was involved in heavy fighting near Praschnitz at this time. The attempt by *General* Wenck to utilize a *Führer* order to the 2. Armee in order to have the Pz.Gren.Div. GD, which was an organic part of the Pz.Korps GD, pulled out of the line and sent to the corps, was frustrated by developments in the situation in the Rozan—Pultusk bridgehead.

And so, beginning on the night of 14-15 January 1945, the transport trains carrying the Pz.Gren.Div. BR and HG 1 rolled out of northern East Prussia through Allenstein—Gnesen—Wreschen—Garotschin, passing close by the westwards-advancing Soviet spearheads, into the Kutno—

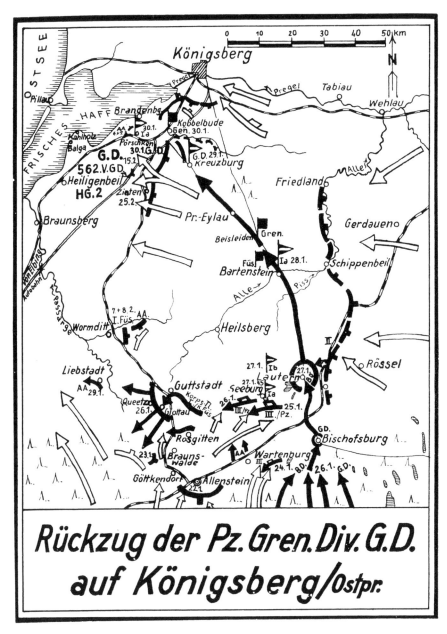

Rückzug der Pz.Gren.Div.G.D. auf Königsberg/Ostpr.

Withdrawal of Panzer-Grenadier-Division "Großdeutschland" to
Königsberg (East Prussia)

Lodz—Petrikau area, where the first elements arrived on 16-17 January.
Hitler's decision had deprived Army Group Center of its last capable

operational reserves. The result was that the German 2. Armee had nothing with which to meet the developing Soviet breakthrough into the area south of Praschnitz. Furthermore, the entraining of these two divisions at a time when the Soviet breakout from the Magnuszew bridgehead had already been achieved resulted in them not being available for at least two to three days. Thus the possibility of a timely intervention by Panzergruppe von Saucken and an eventual reversal of the overall situation in the area south of Warsaw was eliminated. And finally there was also the breakup of two panzer corps and the inevitable reduction in their fighting power, which had a significant effect on their subsequent operations.

The Pz.Korps *Großdeutschland*, with the Pz.Gren.Div. BR and the unfamiliar Fsch.Pz.Div. 1 HG, found itself back in the Lodz area; meanwhile, the *Fallschirmpanzerkorps Herman Göring* under Gen.Lt. Schmalz with its Fsch.Pz.Div. 2 HG and the unrelated Pz.Gren.Div. *Großdeutschland* continued to fight in northern East Prussia. An exchange had taken place which for GD at least had no solution and meant that its units were not brought together until the end. Invisible, yet felt by everyone, the words "too late" hung over the transports of the Pz.Korps GD, here principally the Pz.Gren.Div. BR and the few corps units travelling with it. And this in spite of the fact that not only the highest levels of the German command but also the population expected so much from its commitment.

Endless suffering accompanied these rail transports and this weighed heavily on the souls of the men who witnessed it. Trains of sorrow, packed with fleeing civilians perched on open wagons in the icy cold, including small children, old people and women. Everywhere there was collapse, chaos. The men on these transports became increasingly quiet, not knowing where it would end.

The situation became apparent at the detraining stations, which extended from south of Petrikau through Lodz to Kutno, distributed over an area of more than 60 kilometers.

When, during the night of 16-17 January, south of Petrikau the first trains were still venturing toward the makeshift loading ramps, the sound of combat was already audible in the near distance. The first security detachments south of Petrikau near Longinowka were provided by elements of Jäg.Rgt. 2 commanded by Obstlt. Oesterwitz, principally the I. Btl. The II./Jäg.Rgt. 2 under Oblt. Ahfeld, which also detrained in Petrikau, likewise got down from the trains unscathed and moved into quarters in a village southeast of Petrikau. This battalion, which depended too much on the security posted by others units there, also probably unaware of the dangerous proximity of Soviet armored spearheads, was surprised by enemy tanks in its quarters that same night. In the ensuing melee virtually the entire battalion was scattered, losing the bulk of its vehicles and almost all of its heavy weapons. On foot and in small groups, the

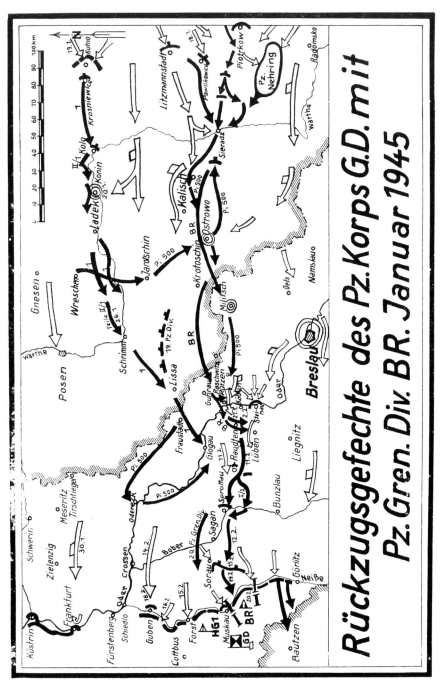

Fighting During the Withdrawal of Panzer-Korps "Großdeutschland" and
Panzer-Grenadier-Division "Brandenburg" in January 1945

175

men were able to take shelter in the surrounding forests and in some cases regroup. Nevertheless, considerable parts of the companies were missing. At the same time the striking power of this II. Btl/Jäg.Rgt. 2 had been reduced to zero. There was no contact whatever with the regiment; the survivors made their way west in the direction of Lask.

The uncertain enemy situation forced the next transport trains to be unloaded prematurely. There was no contact between trains and at the unloading stations the units were unable to learn anything about the situation north of Petrikau. So the 7. Kp./II./Jäg.Rgt. 2 disembarked in Baby, as did the Pz.Stu.Pi.Btl. BR under Hptm. Müller-Rochholz on 17 January. The latter was without its 3. Kp., however, which was on the transports carrying Jäg.Rgt. 1. Unloading in Baby took place under heavy enemy strafing attacks; damage was limited to vehicles with only a few minor wounds to unit personnel. The Ia of the Pz.Gren.Div. BR, General Staff *Oberst* G. Erasmus, who had joined one of the transports after completing an assignment in Berlin, also found himself in Baby, where he received from his O1 one of the first orders issued by the Headquarters, 9. Armee, which was in command in the Petrikau area. The order called for the Pz.Gren.Div. BR to assemble in the forest east of Petrikau.

For the recipient this was a crazy order given the uncertain situation in this area and based on the facts that enemy tanks were already driving around at the eastern outskirts of the city and that the bulk of the division's transport was still missing. Nevertheless Obstlt. Oesterwitz had security detachments posted on the outskirts of Petrikau and at first also assumed responsibility for the defense of the town from the local commander, who was leaving. Available to him for these tasks were elements of the Pz.Stu.Pi.Btl. BR less its 3. Kp., two batteries of the Pz.Art.Rgt. BR and elements of his regiment. When the first enemy attacks appeared at the east end of Petrikau on about the evening of 17 January, the line of security was withdrawn towards the northwest end of the city. It was also apparent that this group of *Brandenburgers* would have to withdraw in the direction of Lodz, where it was correctly assumed other elements of the division were. The city of Lodz gradually became a meeting and rendezvous point for the Pz.Gren.Div. BR and the transport carrying the GD corps headquarters also seemed to be headed there. There was no communications between units, not even with the BR division headquarters; so far only the Ia was present, but not the actual headquarters. No one knew where the other was or what he was supposed to be doing. Everyone tried to reach his own division in the confusion of retreating units and trains. In some cases this was not achieved until weeks later, this being due in large part to the rapid Soviet advance and the confusion it caused.

On the same day, 17 January, the assault guns of the Stu.Gesch.-Brigade GD under Hptm. Metzger, which was subordinate to the Pz.Gren.Div. BR, detrained in Lodz. The detraining procedure took until about 14:00 hours. There, too, the streets of this large city were filled with soldiers, civilians, refugee columns, and there too the mass flight toward the west had begun. The alarm had been raised: the Russians are at the gates of the city! Enemy tanks are coming! Tank cannon fired into the eastern suburbs. Volkssturm, just formed, moved in groups to the exit from the town to occupy positions, some prepared.

In a line, the 18 assault guns moved through the streets toward the south, from the southern suburbs in the direction of Pabianice. Enemy aircraft appeared frequently and strafed the column, however they did little damage to the assault guns. The vehicles on the streets, on the other hand, suffered more serious losses. By evening positions had been occupied at the edge of a wood south of Pabianice. This was only temporary, for a short time later there was a change of position to the south—to establish contact with the elements of the Pz.Gren.Div. BR advancing north of Petrikau. Together with the 2. Kp./I./Jäg.Rgt. 2, the village of Pawlikowice was occupied and secured. The crews and the *Jäger* remained there through all of 18 January with no contact of any kind with the enemy. According to reports from the next village to the east, Soviet cavalry had entered there.

At this time the Pz.Jäg.Abt. BR, less 2. Kp., which had been surprised and scattered by enemy tanks during transport in the Kutno area, was unloaded in Görnau, a suburb of Lodz, and as a result came into direct contact with the first Soviet armored spearheads. While they were still unloading, the anti-tank personnel fired wildly in all directions, destroying two of the attacking Soviet tanks with *Panzerfausts*. In the temporary quiet that followed, the unit was able to complete detraining and it set out to the south in the direction of Petrikau to seek contact with other BR units.

At about 01:00 hours on the same 18th of January the first transport trains carrying elements of Jäg.Rgt. 1 under *Oberst* von Brückner arrived in Kutno and could go no farther. The enemy was reported approaching from Warsaw, therefore the troops detrained immediately. The transport consisted of the regimental headquarters of Jäg.Rgt. 1 with the regimental headquarters company plus 6. and 7. Kp./II./Jäg.Rgt. 1. Immediately after the stop at Kutno station the units were alerted and ordered to prepare for action. All available forces were to be used to defend the city itself; available in addition to the elements of Jäg.Rgt. 1 were several units of the Transport Security Battalion 318 plus four assault guns, the only anti-tank weapons. After a brief issuing of orders in the base headquarters, the available companies, 6. and 7. Kp./Jäg.Rgt. 1, were deployed on the roads to Warsaw and Lodz respectively. Each of the two companies, which were equipped with twelve MG 42 light machine-guns and partly with assault rifles (*Maschinenkarabiner 43*), had a combat strength of approximately 140 men.

After scouting the area, Oblt. Röseke, commander of the 6. Kp./Jäg. Rgt. 1, deployed his company, which had been bolstered by four assault guns, at the east end of Kutno as follows:

I Platoon: Lt. Krosch—east end of Stara Wies, approximately 5 km east of Kutno, both sides of the Kutno—Warsaw road, approximately 300 m east of railway crossing. Tank-destroyer squad attached to I Platoon. Sector commander: Lt. Krosch.

II Platoon: Fw. Lämmerhirt—near Malina estate, 5 km northeast of Kutno, both sides of Zychlin—Kutno road.

III Platoon: Operational reserve (1 truck) in farm near Stara Wies railway crossing, 5 km east of Kutno. Leader: Oberjäger Haacke.

Company command post: Linesman's hut at the Stara Wies railway crossing. One platoon of Transport security Battalion 318 under the command of Lt. Holzinger subordinated to the 6. Kp., was moved into position in the open terrain between Stara Wies and the Malina estate.

Arriving from the east and southeast, numerous refugee columns poured into the city.

A patrol from the 7. Kp./Jäg.Rgt. 1 under Lt. Bürk, sent down the road in the direction of Lodz, was scattered by the enemy and was not seen again.

At about 20:00 hours Obgefr. Eckardt reported from his position approximately 4 kilometers east of Stara Wies that the enemy was approaching. A short time later enemy tanks made their first advance against the positions of the I. Zug/6. Kp./Jäg.Rgt. 1 near Stara Wies. One Sherman tank was knocked out by *Obergefreiter* Tröger and *Oberjäger* Hahmann using a *Panzerschreck*. Three more tanks were able to break through in the direction of the city.

Another attack by enemy tanks took place at about 22:00 hours; Gefr. Kofler knocked out one tank with a *Panzerfaust* while two more were destroyed by hand grenades and mines.

Toward evening the 7. Kp./Jäg.Rgt. 1, commanded by Oblt. Geisenberger, was also attacked by enemy tanks carrying infantry, and these attacks continued through most of the night. The company lost almost a third of its strength killed and wounded in these battles.

In this context the fate of the companies of II./Jäg.Rgt. 1 during the period from 16 January to 8 February 1945 should be described:

6 (Jäg.) Kp./II: Dispersed by Russian tanks approximately 15 km southwest of Poln. Slupca (Grenzhausen) together with 7. Kp.

7. (Jäg.) Kp.: Dispersed by Russian tanks approximately 15 km southwest of Pol. Slupca (Grenzhausen) together with 6. Kp.

8. (Jäg.) Kp.: Dispersed near Lodz.

9. (schw.Flachf.) Kp.: Got as far as the Lissa area, heavy casualties there.

10. (schw.Steilf.) Kp.: Missing in Posen area.

That is the fate of one of the two battalions of the Jäg.Rgt. 1, one that was shared by other companies of the Pz.Gren.Div. BR in this area.

The Pz.Korps Pi.Btl.500 GD, a corps unit under Hptm. Eicke, lost its entire 3. (Goliath) Kp. during transport from East Prussia. Since no 1. Kp. had yet been formed, the battalion consisted of just 2. *Kompanie* and the battalion headquarters, which detrained together in the area west of Kutno—at first without any contact with the GD Corps. Individual transports carrying the He.Flak-Abt. BR, elements of the Pz.Art.Rgt. BR, the supply troops and medical units had similar experiences.

Many units were missing; nothing was known of their location. They were searched for desperately in the chaos, but only a few were found, and then often only by chance.

General von Saucken had himself arrived in Lodz on 18 January, setting up his command post in a cloth mill on the outskirts of the city. He pondered over his mission to attack to the southeast and close the gaps in the front. It was clear to him that the mission could not be carried out, especially since his two divisions had not yet assembled. What had arrived was scattered over an area of 100 kilometers and the various units were attempting to establish contact with one another. The enemy was standing on a line from Kutno (evening of 18 January) to Pabianice (18 January) and Petrikau (evening of 17 January) without meeting much resistance from the German side. His objective was the Oder and the destruction of the remnants of the German armies still in that area.

Only a few Kampfgruppen had maintained their cohesion in this chaos and they were far behind enemy lines fighting their way through to the west. Among them was the XXIV. Pz.-Korps under *General* Nehring. Originally coming from the Baranow bridgehead, it fought its way into the Kielce area, followed by a rat's tail of shattered infantry and artillery units plus numerous refugee columns, all of which only hampered its movements. But Nehring had to take them into consideration in order to get them through relatively intact.

The leading elements of this Pz.-Gruppe Nehring, small advance guards, arrived in the Lodz area where they encountered the BR units positioned there; the general direction of march of this moving pocket was northwest.

In view of this situation, *General* von Saucken found himself forced to either allow his corps units that had arrived so far to immediately withdraw to the west, for that was the only hope for them to reach and cross the Warthe near Shieratz ahead of the enemy armored spearheads and thus escape again, —or to drive toward the moving Nehring pocket, join up with and reinforce it and together with it fight his way through to the west.

His decision was made all the more difficult when enemy advance groups appeared at the bridge near Shieratz and tried to eliminate this as a crossing for the German troops.

The decision was obvious: concentrating all of the units of the Pz.Gren.Div. BR and the Fsch.Pz.Div. 1 HG assembled in the area northwest of Petrikau and southwest of Lodz, *General* von Saucken decided to fight his way through to the west and establish a bridgehead over the Warthe at and on both sides of Shieratz in order to hold it open until the arrival of Pz.-Gruppe Nehring.

There was no contact with the northern group, meaning the elements of the Pz.Gren.Div. BR, in particular the Jäg.Rgt. 1 BR under *Oberst* von Brückner, which had detrained at and near Kutno; there the enemy situation forced further decisions. Kutno could not be held, at least not with the weak forces available—one battalion and several attached foreign units. On 19 January a force of almost fifty enemy tanks and masses of infantry approached the city. The courageous actions of individual tank killers resulted in the destruction of four enemy tanks, but then superior numbers forced a withdrawal towards the city limits. At about 08:30 hours the last *Jäger* of II./Jäg.Rgt. 1 withdrew and subsequently assembled near Kutno station. Together with elements of the regimental headquarters company and 3. Kp./Pz.Stu.Pi.Btl. BR, the regimental headquarters, Jäg.Rgt. 1 moved in the direction of the Warthe bridges. Orders to the *Jäger* in Kutno: fight your way through to the Kroschwitz (Krozniewice) area, approximately 10 kilometers west of Kutno. After arriving at the crossroads due west of this small town the leading vehicles spotted enemy forces on the outskirts of Kroschwitz. These were bypassed to the south. Destination: Warthbrücken.

Meanwhile the bridgehead position was expanded and manned in Warthebrücken, where one of the few bridges suitable for heavy armored vehicles crossed the Warthe. The Warthebrücken Volkssturm-Bataillon was placed under the command of the Jäg.Rgt. 1 BR, all men capable of fighting were taken from the fleeing columns and formed into alert units which were deployed in the bridgehead position. The sound of fighting drew ever nearer; the enemy spearheads might appear before the city at any time. In this situation it was questionable whether the elements of the regiment expected from Kroschwitz—a group from the 6. and 7. Kp.—would ever arrive in time.

But the vehicle columns coming from the east rolled over the Warthe bridges in a steady stream, harassed by Soviet aircraft which strafed and dropped bombs, seeking to take out the bridges. The river crossing was faced with chaos after several squads of infantry tasked with defending the bridgehead tried to flee across the Warthe ice. But it was already so thin in places that vehicles and groups of men went through. Cries for help rang out from the ice, scarcely audible in the noise of low-flying enemy aircraft—and death claimed another of the drowning men. No one knew who it was; no one knew him—he remained unknown, missing forever.

Meanwhile the elements of the Pz.Gren.Div. BR holding out between Lodz and Petrikau also left their positions and lines of security under over-whelming enemy pressure and withdrew towards the west—in the direction of Grabica. There, at a small river crossing, the units from Lodz and Petrikau were supposed to come together—from there the withdrawal toward Shieratz was to continue while screening to the east. The link-up was essentially successful, even though the assault guns of the Stu.Gesch.-Brigade GD and the *Jäger* of I./Jäg.Rgt. 2 were forced to fight fierce rear guard actions with Soviet cavalry and anti-tank units in the Pawlikowice area. Repeatedly outflanked through the woods, the assault guns and the *Jäger* had to fight their way through to the southwest. An armored troop carrier commanded by Fhj.-Uffz. von Kamptz and a truck carrying wounded received direct hits and burned out. Among those fatally wounded was Obgefr. Kamm.

And yet the assault guns succeeded in fighting their way through again, the *Jäger* riding on the armored vehicles. They finally established contact with the pioneers of the Pz.Stu.Pi.Btl. BR holding the bridge at Karezmy on the Gabria. The bridge was crossed and positions were occupied among the farm houses on the other side. The assault guns had barely enough fuel left for four or five kilometers and were almost out of ammunition.

Orders from division called for these bridges, including a new concrete bridge on the Petrikau—Lask road, to be prepared for demolition. Once the last elements—in this case the Pz.A.A. BR—had passed they were to be blown up. 1. Kp./Pz.Stu.Pi.Btl. BR subsequently set the necessary charges on the wooden bridges approximately three and eight kilometers northwest of Karezmy and then stood guard over them.

The commanding general arrived while work on the bridges was still going on and ordered that the explosive charges be removed immediately, because the bridges had to be saved for the Nehring armored group at all costs. Appropriate preparations were made. Meanwhile a reconnaissance platoon reported the approach of numerous enemy tanks with mounted infantry; the first of these then approached the concrete bridge in the evening twilight. Two Soviet tanks were knocked out by an anti-tank gun; one of them, a Stalin II, was left burning in the middle of the bridge.

The commander of the Pz.Stu.Pi.Btl. BR rushed to the division to get a decision—to blow the bridge or not. On the basis of the new situation he received orders to blow it at once.

By now it was dark, and the first Russians appeared to be on the bridge or already across it. The road on the near side was under enemy tank fire; Lt. Bätzing was wounded there. The pioneer commander and 12 men succeeded in getting to the bridge in three *Schwimmwagen*. A farmhouse right at the bridge was ablaze, however, illuminating the entire approach, where masses of Soviet troops were heading over the span. In spite of the inhuman fire one pioneer succeeded in reaching the bridge, however he was unable to set off the charges. With more luck than brains all of the pioneers got back, though two of them were wounded. The bridge remained standing. Both of the wooden bridges to the northwest were blown up and permanently destroyed. To make matters even worse, the assault guns sitting on the bridge were unable to engage the enemy; they were out of fuel and had little ammunition left. The fury of the *Jäger* standing guard was indescribable.

From there the retreat continued at a rapid pace, passing to the south of Lask in the direction of Shieratz, where elements of the regrouped II./Jäg.Rgt. 2 under Oblt. Ahfeld were standing by.

This retreat through Lask threatened to become a catastrophe for the *Jäger* of I. Btl. under Hptm. Steidl after the assault guns ran out of ammunition and were unable to pursuing enemy tanks, which in some cases had even outflanked them. The *Jäger* of I. Btl. riding on the assault guns found themselves in dangerous situations, which they were only able to escape by dashing into the dense woods. The pursuing Soviets found them there, however, and their march began to resemble a flight. The 1. Kp. under Oblt. Wirth and the 2. Kp. under Oblt. Gutweniger in particular were dispersed and could only make their way through the forests in small groups. Both company commanders went missing on 20 January 1945. Not until 24 hours later did elements of these companies rejoin their battalion. The pocket south of Szadeck had almost been the end of these *Jäger* of I./Jäg.Rgt. 2.

Meanwhile the GD Corps Headquarters had established itself in Shieratz. It set about preparing the bridgehead positions at the Warthe, while at the same time, with the help of pioneers, it sought suitable crossing places for the elements of Pz.-Gruppe Nehring already south of Lask. On 21 January reconnaissance revealed that, contrary to assumptions that it was already in Soviet hands, the bridge in the city of Shieratz itself was intact and passable. Another heavy military bridge in the Chojne area southwest of Shieratz, which was not shown on the maps, had been prepared for demolition by the pioneers but was still passable. The pioneers immediately took charge of it. The *Panzerkorps GD* received further orders to reconnoiter the bridges in the marsh and bog area around Marcenin southwest of Lask and likewise keep them open for Nehring. The entire corps was scoured for the fuel needed to carry out this task and it was made available for use by the Schwimmwagen of the Pz.Stu.Pi.Btl. BR's scout platoon and the 2. Kp./Pz.Stu.Pi.Btl. BR and its Maultier tracked trucks. In spite of heavy snow and icy roads, Marcenin was finally reached on 22 January. On the same day, soon after the arrival in the town (at about 11:00 hours), Hptm. Müller-Rochholz, commander of the Pz.Stu.Pi.Btl. BR, greeted the first elements of Pz.-Gruppe Nehring in Marcenin. In command was an older *Oberst*; the two officers hugged each other, overcome with joy that contact had been established at last.

As personnel from Pz.-Gruppe Nehring began taking over positions, the BR pioneers handed over the bridge at Chojne, while Shieratz at first remained in the hands of the Pz.Korps GD.

Meanwhile, the battle for the Warthe bridges had been raging since noon on 20 January. The Kampfgruppen of the 6. and 7. Kp./Jäg.Rgt. 1 BR had just arrived in the city, while the 3. Kp./Pz.Stu.Pi.Btl. BR, whose withdrawal orders failed to reach it in time, had been almost completely wiped out. The unit's commander, Oblt. Laurentz, was hit twice in the chest but was saved by his technical sergeant. Lt. Hertkorn was killed in the fighting. And the Soviets were already pressing into Warthe with tanks and artillery. Elements of the bridgehead garrison cracked and crossed the river to the west. The headquarters of Jäg.Rgt. 1 BR also left the city and headed west. After crossing the Warthe, elements of the Pi.Kp./Jäg.Rgt. 1 BR climbed aboard vehicles and drove away to the north. They were not seen again.

Since the bridge over the Warthe was already under heavy artillery fire, after an heroic scouting effort by the seventeen-year-old *Jäger* Hähnlein, the 6. Kp./Jäg.Rgt. 1 crossed the river on the ice, the 7. Kp./Jäg.Rgt. 1 followed on foot. Once again on their own, these two companies tried to fight their through to the west in the direction of Hohensalza as a single Kampfgruppe. Deutscheck was already occupied by the enemy.

The 3. Kp./Pz.Stu.Pi.Btl. BR, however, arrived at the crossing point in Warthebrücken just at the moment that a well-aimed stick of bombs rendered the bridge impassable. But then pioneers from other units succeeded in making at least temporary repairs to the bridge, and that under heavy fire. But, under pressure from the hard-pushing enemy, columns of vehicles began backing up before the bridge in four to five rows side by side, making escape almost impossible. Groups of men tried to get across the drifting pack ice to the other side of the Warthe. Only a few succeeded, however. Hundreds went under and drowned.

Meanwhile Soviet infantry in regiment strength with tank support tried to reduce the remaining bridgehead, which was about two kilometers wide and two deep, showering it with heavy fire. But the few remaining fighters held out bravely or gained breathing space through counterattack.

Finally elements of the 3. Kp./Pz.Stu.Pi.Btl. BR also withdrew from the bridgehead itself and sneaked across the bridge to the west bank. There they assembled and found that in addition to several wounded the crossing had cost the lives of four men who had fallen into the river and drowned. Their path led them on in the direction of Konin, the same one taken by the elements of the Jäg.Rgt. 1 BR. At about noon on 21 January, however, the city itself and the rail station to the north had been in enemy hands since the previous day. This meant deviating in a wide arc around the city to the south before heading west again.

Irresistibly the Soviet regiments and tank formations drove west, seemingly in great disorder but linked by a common will, toward their objective, the Oder. Where resistance was weak they rolled over everything; where resistance was stronger they outflanked the German positions, which cost them the time required to deploy their forces. Why lose time with these small groups of German defenders? If the Soviets had simply bypassed them and continued west they would eventually have given up on their own, tried to fight their way through to the west or been wiped out by the following infantry units.

The Soviets occupied the city of Konin on 20 January against little resistance; on 23 January Kalisch also fell into their hands without a struggle. The Soviet armored forces rolled on in the direction of Ostrowo, entering the town on 24 January. Various *Volkssturm* units tried to offer resistance, but most were blown away in the first attack.

On 23 January the leading Soviet elements reached the Oder between Oppeln and Ohlau and threatened the Silesian city of Breslau from the southeast.

Endless panye columns of Soviet infantry moved west through the large forested areas between Petrikau and Steinau an der Oder, using every forest road, footpath and raised roadway. They drove before them the civilian population, the local garrisons, the troops sent against them. In some places motorized German Kampfgruppen fought back, usually sticking to the main roads: pressured from behind, driving forwards, striking out to the sides against endless assaults from Soviet columns moving in the same direction, pressured and threatened by fuel shortages which were occasionally relieved through the chance discovery of an abandoned fuel truck or a depot.

Each of these German Kampfgruppen, whose will to break through kept them together, were followed by a trail of foreign infantry units eager to follow the armored wedge in hopes of yet reaching the safety of the Oder. Others tried to make their way in small groups through the forests, in constant danger of being discovered by the Soviets and destroyed.

But ahead—west and in particular the natural obstacle of the Oder—there were no combat units to receive the fleeing, often leaderless, beaten, demoralized troops or to halt Soviet units leading the advance.

Replacement units were rushed in from bases in central Germany, schools were reorganized into combat units and sent to the Oder, the *Volkssturm* was called up, equipped with rifles and sent to the front. At the same time the civilian population was called upon to resist, the Hitler Youth was armed and deployed in the villages along the Oder, the towns and villages were prepared for defense—all of this in great haste in a desperate attempt to once again halt the onrushing Soviet masses along the Oder.

Among the Kampfgruppen fighting their way back toward the west in moving pockets at this time were the von Saucken and Nehring groups, which after linking up at Shieratz had continued their westward trek together. Both formations were still strong as far as the will to fight and the desire to break through at any cost were concerned. Closely combined with the Pz.Korps GD, the Panzer-Grenadier Division *Brandenburg* fought its way back in the direction of Kalisch—Ostrowo in a continuous but planned withdrawal; the division had only the Jäg.Rgt. 2 but still had a strong armored formation, the Sturm-Gesch.-Brigade GD.

Repeatedly, attacks had to be made to the left and right in order to keep the flanks free and the parallel-moving enemy at the necessary distance. The breakthrough near Stören (Staw) on 23 January cost further heavy losses, especially to I./Jäg.Rgt. 2; among those killed were Lt. Langer and *Oberfähnrich* Albers, while the commander of the 1. Kp., Oblt. Wirth, was badly wounded and died during the night. In addition 1. Kp. alone had twelve wounded. Only at great cost, and with the support of two guns of the Pz.Jäg.Abt. BR under Lt. Kass, did they succeed in fighting their way through in the direction of Karlsbad—Schwarzau. Companies had to be combined on account of their low combat strengths, then the withdrawal in the direction of Zietenfelde succeeded without significant pressure from the enemy.

With resistance broken, the vehicles again rolled westward, the assault guns in front, then the *Jäger*, the headquarters, the columns. Parallel to this, Soviet T 34 tanks moved along the highway in the direction of Kalisch.

Farther to the southwest reconnaissance revealed that Ostrowo was already in enemy hands. A quick decision was made to fight through between the two places while screening toward the southwest and northeast. The pioneers advanced to the northern outskirts of Ostrowo and formed a thin line of security, behind which the withdrawal movements to the west were carried out. It succeeded, and during the night of 24 January the last vehicles had passed by the threat to the flanks—in the direction of Krotoschin.

Koppelstädt was driven through; the advance continued in the direction of the area south of Schmückert—on 26 January the first elements of von Saucken's Kampfgruppe reached the village of Waffendorf on German territory. The pace of the withdrawal increased as the Oder drew nearer, even though Kampfgruppen had to make repeated forays to the north and south in order to keep the Soviets at bay. It was also now possible to drive with fewer delays, because the withdrawing motorized and armored groups were all striving to reach designated bridgeheads across the Oder, therefore the retreat roads all came together at designated points. Column traffic on the highways had become extraordinarily heavy; numerous vehicles of the 20. Pz.Gren.Div., the 19. Pz.Div., the Fsch.Pz.Div. 1 HG, of *Brandenburg* and the Pz.Korps GD were all speeding towards the Oder.

Meanwhile, from the northeast the remnants of Jäg.Rgt. 1 BR under

Oberst von Brückner were fighting their way back through Schrimm toward Lissa in order to finally regain contact with the division. Little was left of II./Jäg. 1; only elements of the regiment's companies and almost all of I./Jäg, 1 were still together.

Hopes of reaching the Oder quickly and finding prepared positions on the other side, of a break to rest and reorganize the units, were very soon dashed, however. The situation as described in the noon situation report in headquarters on 27 January 1945 meant that the units would have to go back into action immediately:

Excerpts from Guderian's presentation:

The situation is difficult south of Steinau and near Köben, where this morning the enemy was able to achieve deep penetrations in the direction of Herzogswaldau and Raudten.

Deployed there are elements of a Kampfgruppe of the 408. under the direction of LVII. Pz.Korps, General Kirschner; preparations for a counterattack there have begun under the headquarters of the 16. Pz.Div., which had already been brought out of the pocket, with a number of armored troop carriers from the Glogau area. There are no confirmed reports that it has begun. It has only been ordered so far.

Hitler: *What is this here?*

Guderian: *That is the plan of the Saucken corps and of Jauer. Here they have reached the area of Koppelstädt, now they are to be directed into the Schmückert area and then turn south in order to smash the enemy forces here—especially the Soviet 4th Guards tank Army and the two tank corps that have already reached and crossed the river—and thus free the area north of Breslau.*

Today the Saucken group will attack from the south near Horle; 16 enemy tanks have been knocked out in this area.

The northern flank of the Saucken group is being covered by the 19. Pz.Div., which is in a relatively combat-capable state in the Gostyn and Storchnest area; it also has a number of assault guns and its artillery, so that it is to be hoped that this screen will suffice to cover the attack to the south.

The Saucken group—with the Reichsmarschall's and Brandenburg divisions—are to carry out this attack in order to destroy the entire enemy grouping in the Steinau bend of the Oder.

The enemy grouping in the Steinau bend of the Oder consisted of Koniev's tank corps and divisions, which had succeeded not only in reaching the Oder on both sides of Steinau but had also established a bridgehead across the Oder near Köben (north of Steinau) and thus set foot on the west bank of the river. The first enemy spearheads moved out of this bridgehead in the direction of Raudten on or about 31 January-1 February 1945.

Meanwhile, in the small city of Steinau the non-commissioned officer students of the Jauer NCO School were putting up a determined and stubborn defense and holding the city and the bank on both sides of the city. This struggle in Steinau against overwhelming odds was an heroic one; it cost hundreds of lives and was a selfless action in the best German military tradition with soldiers fighting a hopeless battle to the last drop of blood. This stubborn resistance forced Koniev and his armored spearheads to wait on the east bank of the Oder and seek another place to cross the river. This would be Köben, off the big highway to the west.

Kampfgruppe Nehring reached the Oder ahead of von Saucken's group and the bulk of it had already crossed to the west near Glogau. Its mission was to advance south without halting west of the Oder and to throw back or destroy the enemy forces near Köben advancing in the direction of Raudten.

However, when the leading elements of the von Saucken group, which was following close behind the Nehring group and striving toward the Glogau bridges, reached the Waffendorf—Geischen—Schätz area on about 29 January, orders were received not to continue in the direction of Glogau but to instead swing south while still east of the Oder and immediately attack Koniev's forces standing in the bend of the Oder near Steinau. The first objective was to capture the enemy crossing near Köben.

These movements were to be carried out simultaneously with those of the Nehring group on the west bank. Aware of his own weakness, *General der Panzertruppe* von Saucken carried out the order reluctantly, which caused strains between him and the army group. On 29 January the leading elements of the I./Jäg.Rgt. 2 fought their way toward Schlaube with the limited objective of winning a crossing over the Bartsch between Rützen and Wiersewitz.

At almost the same time a special operation was initiated against Rützen and the crossing over the Bartsch there from Kloden and Gross-Kloden. Leading a group of soldiers dressed in enemy uniforms, Oblt. Mischkeres, commander of the Div.Begl.Kp. BR, sought to seize the bridge site, however his force was ambushed and barely managed to extricate itself. At that moment, however, the SPW-Btl./Jäg.Rgt. 2 BR came to his aid together with several assault guns, these having driven cross-country toward Rützen, the moonlight reflecting off the snow-covered terrain. They opened fire at 100 meters. The response was heavy defensive fire, in particular from Rützen castle (Rützen castle belonged to Oblt. Count Carmer, the GD's O1, later O1 of Army Group Schörner). Behind its stout walls the Soviets defended bitterly, while resistance in the town itself was soon broken. The castle prevented our columns from passing and had to be taken. All attempts to force the enemy troops in the castle to surrender with heavy infantry weapons failed. An increasing number of wounded had to be carried off the battlefield, including Hptm. Schäfer, commander of the SPW-Btl./Jäg.Rgt. 2. Finally a number of 105-mm light field howitzers were moved into open firing position and the castle was bombarded with direct fire. Entire sections of the front castle wall were brought down by the force of the shells and opened up parts of the interior. The ensuing assault on the castle drove away the rest of the enemy troops inside.

At about this time the II./Jäg.Rgt. 2 under Oblt. Ahfeld set out in the direction of Wiersewitz in order to force another crossing over the Bartsch there. It succeeded. The elements deployed near Rützen were likewise ordered through the forest to Wiersewitz. The direct highway from Kloden also led through Wiersewitz to the south. The assault guns crossed immediately; unfortunately, one slipped off and two members of the crew were drowned. The river crossing proceeded rapidly, and, while elements of the regiment were advancing through the forest in the direction of the Oder, II./Jäg.Rgt. 2 under Oblt. Ahfeld attacked toward Neu-Wiersewitz; meanwhile the assault guns had advanced to Heidendorf and there made preparations for the attack against Neu-Wiersewitz.

At about 2300 hours on the night of 31 January the *Jäger* of II./Jäg.Rgt. BR 2 set out to attack the heavily-occupied village, closely bordering the forest. The 8. Kp. screened the northern flank, while the main assault against the village was carried out by the 6. Kp. along an anti-tank ditch. The 7. Kp. followed close behind as operational reserve with several assault guns. The attack initially proceeded as planned, with the leading elements of 6. Kp. under Oblt. Sauter reaching the entrance to the village, where a dug-in Stalin tank was destroyed. Other enemy tanks were knocked out by our assault guns, illuminated by burning houses and parachute flares. Elements of the Pz.Jäg.Abt. BR (four guns) under Lt. Kass also took part in the attack and these also destroyed several enemy tanks. Following the loss of the village, however, the enemy held the forest edge beyond it with about eight to ten tanks and fired wildly into the village. Further enemy tanks were destroyed when 6. Kp. moved in (now led by Fw. Hasenschwanz after all its officers had been put out of action) and the 7. Kp. was brought around under Lt. Salf, who was the heart and soul of the attack. At that very moment, however, orders were received to halt the attack and withdraw. After the loss of five officers and about sixty men in this attack the *Jäger* withdrew across the open field toward their departure positions. As had been foreseen, the attack by the von Saucken group led to a defeat on account of its own weakness and the overwhelming strength of the enemy forces attacking from the east. As a result the von Saucken group was placed in a dangerous position.

A way now had to be found through the narrow strip of forest, which was full of enemy infantry and tanks, to the nearest German-held bridge in order to cross the Oder in time. The columns moved down a road north toward Fähreichen, southeast of Glogau, so as to reach the opposite bank before the Soviets. On orders of the corps pioneer leader, *Major* Chrapkowski, part of the Pz.Stu.Pi.Btl. BR under Hptm. Müller-Rochholz moved forward to take over and strengthen a bridge thrown up by the Nehring group for the Pz.Korps GD. Built with B-bridge equipment, this 56-ton bridge was under the command of *Major* Wolff and the current had damaged the upstream trestle leg. This had given way and had to be repaired quickly in order to allow the tanks and assault guns to cross. The vehicles, tanks and trucks of the 19. Pz.Div., Fsch.Pz.Div. 1 HG, the Pz.Gren.Div. BR and other units became backed up in front of the bridge.

Under the most difficult conditions, and in spite of drifting ice and the fast current, during the night the trestle leg was reinforced sufficiently to allow traffic over the bridge to resume.

At this time the corps command post was in Nieder-Fähreichen, and when the sun came up over the banks on 1 February the Soviets also appeared in considerable strength on the east bank. The bridge ferries had left under cover of darkness and had been moved downstream in the direction of Glogau.

Elements of Jäg.Rgt. 2 BR were in position on the west bank, however both friend and foe remained quiet. A sigh of relief went through the ranks. Finally a break after weeks of retreat, always through the enemy. The men were given little time, however, for a new order had already reached the corps: immediately after crossing the Oder, the next day it was to attack the enemy bridgehead from an assembly area north of Raudten—Pilgramsdorf and drive it back to the bank of the Oder.

Chapter 5
Großdeutschland Kampfgruppen and Armor Hunter/Killer Units

So all of this had become fact: the rapid approach of Soviet forces to the Oder, the capture of a bridgehead north of Steinau near Köben by Koniev's units, the reaching of the entire upper course of the Oder from Breslau to the southeast and the readying of new Soviet attack forces in the bridgeheads between Brieg and Breslau—but also the rapid advance of Zhukov's forces into the Posen—Frankfurt/Oder area. The German high command was forced to adopt drastic measures to at least try to halt this enemy onslaught along the Oder. Realizing this intention was admittedly made more difficult, because the Soviets had already established several bridgeheads on the upper course of the Oder and there were no combat-ready German units there. The hastily formed units sent to the river line, *Volkssturm* battalions and replacement units, were in no position to offer serious resistance in the event of a new attack by the enemy. And yet in its distress the high command employed these means to at least delay the enemy advance until the units fighting their way back from the east had arrived. After a brief rest period they were sent back into action with the weapons they had brought with them and fresh replacements. New formations in the Reich, mainly from the reservoirs of the replacement units, were to further reinforce this improvised defense.

Among these units was the *Heeres-Panzerjagd-Verband Großdeutschland* (army anti-tank unit), which was hastily formed by the Pz.Gren.-Ersatz-Brigade GD in Cottbus under the command of Oblt. Herbig on 20 January. Its strength: 20 officers and 250 non-commissioned officers and enlisted men. Means of transport: bicycles. Just 24 hours after its formation the unit was transported by truck from Cottbus to Guben, from where it traveled by train to Liegnitz. There the unit was issued weapons, principally assault rifles, *Panzerfaust* anti-tank weapons, explosives and hand grenades. The mission of this army anti-tank unit was to attack advancing Soviet armored spearheads and destroy them using explosives and *Panzerfäuste*!

For this purpose the unit was divided into individual detachments, which were to occupy the area of operations strongpoint-style like a spider's web and attack enemy armor as it appeared. The strength of these anti-tank detachments was one officer and six men.

The first action by this Heeres-Pz.Jagd.-Verband GD took place on 26 January in the Stroppen—Winzig—Wohlau area, east of the Oder, just before the big bend in the river in front of Steinau. The collision between the anti-tank detachments and the advancing enemy armored spearheads was violent and led to the loss of two detachments. Nevertheless, this action caused some confusion among the Soviet formations, which benefited the brave defenders of Steinau. The Heeres-Pz.Jagd.-Verband GD was subsequently withdrawn over the Kloster Leubus bridge before it was completely scattered. During the night of 27 January it marched in the direction of Lüben in order to occupy new positions there. The anti-tank detachments were immediately deployed chessboard-style with the focus on both sides of the Lüben—Steinau road. There was no enemy contact at first, however. On the other hand anti-tank detachments did establish contact with the commander of the *Volkssturm* battalion which was defending the town of Raudten. On 30 January there was still no direct contact with the enemy. A further advance toward Steudelwitz, several kilometers west of Köben, resulted in heavy fighting with enemy tanks which had advanced into that area. While the *Volkssturm* battalion deployed there soon fled, the anti-tank detachments of the Heeres-Pz.Jagd.-Verband GD fought on for three days and nights and succeeded in inflicting serious losses on the westwards-advancing enemy.

The counterattacks by German units from the northwest at this time made it possible for the anti-tank detachments to disengage in the Steudelwitz area.

After establishing contact with the Pz.Korps GD in Nieder-Fähreichen, the Heeres-Pz.Jagd.-Verband GD, which was not under the command of the Pz.Korps GD, was pulled out of the line and deployed on both sides of Heerwegen to guard the Lüben—Glogau road. The Heeres-Pz.Jagd.-Verband GD was granted a brief period to rest and prepare for new missions before it was again caught up in the whirlpool of events.

No sooner had the men of the Heeres-Pz.Jagd.-Verband GD departed Cottbus on 21 January when another alert unit was formed from the Pz.Gren.Ersatz-Brigade GD under the command of Hptm. Schmelter. Its ostensible role was that of local defense, however it was more for the defense of the city of Cottbus itself. The unit consisted of five rifle companies, one machine-gun company and one pioneer company. Similar measures were also taken at Guben even though there was no immediate threat there, especially since to the east enemy armored spearheads had not yet reached the Oder. Formation of this "Alert Unit Schmelter," preparations for which had been under way for weeks, was initiated by the code-word "Gneisenau." There was a change of command even before the unit could depart. Hptm. Schmelter was replaced by the just returned *Major* Petereit.

During the night of 22-23 January, as part of a blocking plan by the OKH, the alert unit was placed on alert with orders to secure the Neisse near Forst. Its right boundary was the autobahn, left boundary approximately 7 kilometers north of Forst.

Following orders, the companies occupied their positions from the autobahn to the area north of Forst and immediately began building positions along the river line. At the same time *Major* Petereit was named battle commander of Forst.

Several days passed with no contact with the enemy. The latter was still on the other side of the Oder. On or about 26 January *Major* Petereit was ordered back to Cottbus by the commander of the Pz.Gren.Ausb.Rgt. GD, Obstlt. Schwarzrock. That night a command briefing took place during which orders were issued for the immediate formation of a "Kampfgruppe Langkeit." This was to be formed within 48 hours from all elements of the Pz.Gren.-Ersatz-Brigade GD and then transported as it was into the area east of Frankfurt/Oder to be committed against the westwards-advancing enemy. In well-chosen words it was stated that the enemy had to be driven back there by 30 January. The Schmelter unit, as it still called itself, was therefore to be withdrawn immediately and included in the establishment of this Kampfgruppe Langkeit. It subsequently also provided the foundation for the I./Pz.Gren.Rgt./Kampfgruppe Langkeit, which at this time was designated Pz.Gren.-Division Kurmark. At that time *Oberst* Langkeit was the commander of the Pz.Gren.-Ersatz-Brigade GD and was a well-known tank commander of the Pz.Gren.Div. GD.

But another Kampfgruppe was also founded in Cottbus in those last weeks of January 1945—like those that followed it under the pressure of events.

On Sunday, 21 January 1945 a group of men, drawn primarily from the Pz.Aufkl.-Schwadron Cottbus (armored reconnaissance troop), came together under Oblt. Gersdorf. Most were armored reconnaissance troops, radio operators, armored troop carrier drivers and eight-wheel reconnaissance vehicle crewmen. It was not yet clear to them what purpose their formation was supposed to have, although they were of course aware of the enemy's proximity to the Oder and assumed that they would be deployed there somewhere. But with whom and under whose command? There was talk of subordination to the *Führer-Grenadier-Division*, which was supposed to be heading east. Others were convinced that a completely new unit was to be formed from the replacement brigade, under the code-word "Gneisenau" in Cottbus and Guben and that they would form the basis of a new armored reconnaissance battalion.

The unit was transferred by rail into the Posen area with 15 to 20 armored troop carriers (3 ton and 1 ton) plus 2 four-wheel and 2 eight-wheel scout cars, all from the brigade's stocks. The city was not reached, however, instead the unit detrained in Buchenstadt, about 30 kilometers away. From there armored patrols were sent out to learn the precise whereabouts of the enemy's armored spearheads.

Reconnaissance between Moschin and Kosten revealed that enemy armor had been streaming in there since 25 January. As a result, on order of the local sector commander of the XXXX. Pz.Korps, the Kampfgruppe was ordered to conduct armed reconnaissance against the vastly superior enemy forces in this area. The result of this was the destruction of Kampfgruppe Gersdorf in a few days. Even though a number of enemy tanks were destroyed, defeat could not be averted. Elements of the Kampfgruppe were able to fight their way through to the southwest through Kosten, Lissa and Neusalz. Many vehicles were lost in the process; after the Kampfgruppe commander went missing the leaderless Kampfgruppe split up into several parts and tried to get back to our lines.

Only a few men with even fewer vehicles succeeded in this, returning to Cottbus and Guben in about mid-February. Others fought their way through Reppin straight to Frankfurt/Oder and were taken in by the Panzer-Grenadier Division Kurmark deployed north of the city and incorporated into the existing Pz.Aufkl.Abt. KmK. (armored reconnaissance battalion Kurmark).

Kampfgruppe Gersdorf had become another victim of the precipitous commitment of units formed from the replacement units which were neither prepared nor properly organized or fully armed but which were sent against the enemy anyway. Losses in men, whose names and origins remain unknown, increased shockingly in those weeks.

Chapter 6
The Brandenburg's Retreat toward the Lausitzer Neiße

Meanwhile orders had been issued for the von Saucken group (Pz.Korps GD, Pz.Gren.Div. BR plus Fsch.Pz.Div. 1 HG) to make preparations for an attack in the Raudten—Pilgramsdorf area. The objective was the destruction of the enemy forces that had crossed the Oder near Köben. For this purpose the Pz.A.A. BR under Major Bansen was deployed towards Pilgramsdorf and Raudten in order to determine the precise location of the leading enemy elements. On 1 February the armored patrols encountered the enemy before Pilgramsdorf, and in a rapid advance they were driven out of the town. In doing so they created a suitable assembly area between Pilgramsdorf, Polach and Raudten, but still north and northwest of the stream. Closer reconnaissance revealed, however, that an attack would have to be made to the southeast across open country against a rising slope on Hill 141. The enemy's strength was underestimated and the attack began early on 2 February. The plan of attack called for I./Jäg.Rgt. 2 to advance left of the Raudten brickworks and for II./Jäg.Rgt. 2 under Hptm. Zinkel (without Oblt. Ahfeld) to attack from Pilgramsdorf. The initial objective of our attack was Jauschwitz, to be followed by Mlitsch.

The advance was supported by a combined armored force comprising the Stu.Gesch.Brig. GD, I. (SPW) Btl./Jäg.Rgt. 1 under Hptm. Froboese and elements of the Pz.Jäg.Abt. BR with their self-propelled guns under Hptm. Königstein. It was to break through in the direction of the enemy bridgehead. At dawn on 2 February the *Jäger* moved out on the left wing, without supporting fire from the heavy infantry weapons in order to preserve the element of surprise. They advanced over open terrain, crisscrossed by marshy meadows, toward the line of hills on both sides of Hill 141 and the forest fortifications behind it in the direction of Mühle Polach and further toward the Alt-Raudten brickworks. Advancing on the left wing of the attack group, Fw. Peintner, platoon leader of III. Zug/1. Kp./I./Jäg.Rgt. 2 BR, was killed in front of the brickworks. The objective was taken after a fierce firefight; meanwhile, farther right the *Jäger* of II./Jäg.Rgt. 2 were spotted from the flank by the Soviets in their hill positions as they advanced along the edge of a ravine. As soon as they stepped into the open no less than ten men were wounded. Oblt. Planer, commander of the "Ninth," was killed and the 7. Kp. lost almost a third of its men; the battalion was pinned down at first. Meanwhile, farther to the southeast the assault guns and armored troop carriers of I. (SPW)/Jäg.Rgt. 1 BR pushed ahead, and, together with elements of the Pz.Jäg.Abt. BR under Lt. Kass and four anti-tank guns, they succeeded in advancing to the crossroads due north of Mlitsch, where they took up position. Immediate reconnaissance revealed the presence of almost twenty T 34 tanks with mounted infantry, which were in readiness positions near the crossroads.

Soon after midnight on 3 February the Soviet tanks made a surprise advance and overran Lt. Kass' anti-tank guns positioned at the crossroads. Seven of the approaching tanks were knocked out for the loss of two of our guns. The remaining six Soviet tanks, however, continued to drive toward the west.

The Pz.Stu.Pi.Btl. BR was moved in and after a quick regrouping the attack was resumed on the morning of 3 February. Advancing on the left, the I./Jäg.Rgt. 2 BR attacked in the direction of Töschwitz and entered the town in spite of fierce resistance. While the Pz.Stu.Pi.Btl. BR was moved up to Mlitsch, the *Jäger* of I./Jäg.Rgt. 2 BR moved north again and together-er with their sister battalion (II./Jäg.Rgt. 2 BR) advanced through densely wooded terrain toward Stein-Berge, due east of Raudten, in order to block the Soviet supply road leading through the forest. Several enemy supply columns were drawn into firefights and heavy losses were inflicted on them. Enemy counterattacks into the forest were repulsed. The village of Mlitsch was thoroughly mined by the combat engineers. The division commander, *Generalmajor* Schulte-Heuthaus, always in the front line with his attacking *Jäger*, was almost cut off in Töschwitz by advancing Soviet attack groups. Under enemy tank fire, he was rescued at the last minute by an eight-wheeled armored car.

On 4 February 1945 enemy counterattacks, especially in the difficult wooded terrain around the Stein-Berge, forced the abandonment of this area and a withdrawal toward better positions at the Gross-Rinnersdorf to the Raudten rail line. The attack was thus abandoned, having failed due to the weakness of our offensive power, which made it impossible for us to advance properly, especially the neighboring units. Having advanced quite a distance, the *Jäger* and the armored groups were left alone and without flanking cover and had to withstand the full force of the enemy advance there.

New defense positions were fortified and held in a rough line from the rail line to Hill 141 and Raudten. The enemy, however, increased the weight of his artillery, Stalin Organ and tank fire on to these open positions, which, visible to the enemy during the day, prevented contact from being made with other German units.

There was heavy fighting in the days that followed (around 6 February), especially for the village of Polach. The village changed hands three times. Holding out there were the remnants of II./Jäg.Rgt. 2 BR under the command of Lt. Stalf, himself the commander of the 7. Kp., who was the heart and soul of the defense. He received support from Lt. Kass' anti-tank guns, which repeatedly were able to intervene successfully in the battles between the opposing armored vehicles.

Finally, on the morning of 8 February, Soviet infantry launched an attack, especially against the positions of Jäg.Rgt. 2, following a heavy artillery bombardment of the German positions.

Accompanied by numerous tanks and assault guns, the earth-brown figures advanced on the German positions, which extended strongpoint-style between the two villages along a line of low hills from Raudten to about Gross-Rinnersdorf, roughly parallel to the line of communication. On the left wing, roughly level with the "toothbrush moustache," a small wood about 1 200 meters southwest of Raudten, the *Jäger* of I./Jäg.Rgt. 2 BR held their positions. The first enemy assault collapsed approximately 100 meters before them.

Against the neighboring 6. Kp./II./Jäg.Rgt. 2 BR, however, the enemy succeeded in penetrating into its positions, forcing that battalion's left wing to pull back toward Polach. The battalion command post was located in Gut Polach, where every subsequent attack was defeated in heavy house-to-house fighting. An enemy assault gun was captured there and, quickly manned under the command of Lt. Maier, within a short time it knocked out two enemy assault guns which had become stuck in a swamp.

Toward midday a courageous counterattack by the remnants of 6. and 7. Kp. succeeded in recapturing the old positions. Pressure from the enemy now abated there, but farther right the enemy was able to break into the forest against another division (a security division?). Soon afterwards endless enemy tank and vehicle columns were observed there, all driving west.

There was now a serious threat of being outflanked. Toward evening on 8 February the enemy entered Polach itself, from the right flank. At the same time he attacked into the gap between I. Btl. and II./Jäg.Rgt. 2 BR, placing the troops defending Polach in danger of being cut off. The companies' combat strengths had sunk alarmingly; the 6. Kp., which was being led by Fw. Hasenschwanz, was down to one *Feldwebel* and six enlisted men, one of them badly wounded. Everyone else was dead, wounded or had become separated.

Finally these few men withdrew to the southwest toward a hill near Pilgramsdorf and sought to hold new positions there. Two Kampfgruppen were formed, each with about 30 to 40 men. One was formed from the 6. and 7. Kp. under Lt. Stalf, the other from 8.-10. Kp. under Hptm. Zinkel plus the battalion headquarters of II./Jäg.Rgt. 2 BR. Obgefr. S. Rainer and Gefr. Kuhn of the 1. Kp./I./Jäg.Rgt. 2 had been killed in the fighting southwest of Raudten, many others were wounded or missing. During the night of 8-9 February the I./Jäg.Rgt. 2 also withdrew from the loose main line of resistance southwest of Raudten and took up new positions, also in Pilgramsdorf. At the same time, however, endless columns of Soviet tanks, artillery, mortars, panye wagons and infantry moved past Gross-Rinnersdorf into the forest and through Raudten to the west. The combat elements of the Pz.Gren.Div. BR, together with the elements of the Pz.Korps GD, but also those of the Fsch.Pz.Div. 1 HG and the 20. Pz.Div., had long since been outflanked and were in danger of being encircled.

The commanding general, *General* von Saucken, reported this state of affairs repeatedly to the army group and to the 4. Pz.Armee commanding there, pointing out the futility of holding out there any longer. In any case the superiority of the Soviets had made a continuation of the attack against the Köben area pointless.

Not until the afternoon did the elements of the Pz.Gren.Div. BR still holding out near Pilgramsdorf withdraw through the forest west in the direction of Dammer—Herbersdorf—Heerwegen. Fierce rear guard actions in the woods led to further casualties but were unable to halt the enemy. These battles went on well into the night, extending as far as the area of Forsthaus Dammer.

The units of the Pz.Gren.Div. BR had been outflanked and encircled in the woods south of Heerwegen. It was 10 February; in this situation the corps command post was outside the encircled group in the area of Herbersdorf. The commanding general made repeated attempts to reach his surrounded troops. Also separated from their encircled troops were the division commanders of the Fsch.Pz.Div. 1 HG and the 20. Pz.Div. Only Gen.Mj. Schulte-Heuthaus, commander of the Pz.Gren.Div. BR, was inside the pocket. When the army corps finally gave the order for the units to withdraw it was already too late. But nevertheless *General* von Saucken climbed into his command car and drove through the Soviet encircling ring into the pocket during the night.

There all was confusion. All of the officers sought to bring order to the units, which apart from the *Brandenburgers* were close to the point of disintegration. *Oberst* Stremmer-Johann was placed in command of the elements of the 20. Pz.Div., in which units of the Fsch.Pz.Div. 1 HG brought order. The *Brandenburgers* themselves maintained good order in their units and Kampfgruppen and covered the retreat. They also formed the spearhead of the breakthrough to the west. The march went through marshy meadows, along a poor built-up roadway. Vehicles were tipped over the side to make way for the serviceable vehicles and self-propelled guns. The *Jäger* and infantrymen made their way on foot through the woods on the left and right, repeatedly striking out to the side against approaching Soviet attack groups. Meanwhile artillery and mortar fire raked the forest, which echoed with the sound of explosions. Wounded screamed, ambulances made their way forward, everything pushed west—out of the encirclement. The commanding general von Saucken was a calming influence who organized the breakthrough to the west with iron determination. The *Jäger* of Jäg.Rgt. 2 BR assumed the point position and began the breakthrough.

Meanwhile around this pocket in the forest south of Heerwegen drove a column of vehicles led by a Volkswagen. It carried ammunition, fuel and food for the men trapped inside. Unable to find an open road into the pocket, the column, which was commanded by the Ib of the Pz.Gren.Div. BR, General Staff *Major* Spaeter, continued to circle.

However, it was unable to get through, not on the 10th and not on the 11th of February, when the battle against the Soviets, who attacked from all sides, went on in the woods northeast of Parchau. Many vehicles had to be left behind. The raised roadway between Heerwegen and the village of Herbersdorf, now in enemy hands, became the grave of countless vehicles of all kinds.

The units' reconnaissance vehicles were also constantly on the go seeking to find some kind of gap through the Soviets somewhere. Our spearheads repeatedly ran into the enemy, who appeared suddenly; the following column ground to a halt, pressured from behind—until finally several *Jäger* again set out under their commanders and chased the enemy away with hand grenades and *Panzerfausts*. Then everything streamed forward, in columns, vehicle after vehicle—until the next stop.

The Soviets in this area must have found it very unsettling to suddenly see a column coming toward them like a steamroller, which in spite of their fire did not lose a step and returned fire as soon as it reached the Soviet positions.

The column got past Parchau, where a vigorous attack drove the Soviets back. The endless column passed Weissig further into the Primkenauer forest, points out in front seeking passable bridges and roads. Then the column waited for hours, until finally movement returned. The crossing of the Weissig—Wolfersdorf—Primkenau road, which was already being used by the Soviets, took place under the protection of the II./Jäg.Rgt. 2 BR. During the night of 11 February it formed a hedgehog position, destroying Soviet columns in the process, and the entire length of the column was able to pass through this within six hours. It was followed by the rear guards, the 6. and 7. Kp. of this battalion, riding on Panthers of the Pz.Rgt. GD under *Major* Rossmann.

In the meantime, the Feld-Ersatz-Btl. BR had gone into position in Sprottisch-Waldau, where under the command of the BR's division adjutant, Hptm. Lau, it hindered the Soviet advance on the main road from Primkenau to Sprottau and farther west. But the stubborn defense of this position east of Sprottisch-Waldau also caused those in command of the pocket to advance out of the Primkenau forest north toward Sprottisch-Waldau, where the brave FEB/BR was picked up.

General Staff *Major* Spaeter immediately led his supply column there and waited for the moving pocket. During the night of 11-12 February the leading elements of the three encircled divisions under the command of *General* von Saucken finally reached the road near Sprottisch-Waldau and established contact with Hptm. Lau.

A sigh of relief went through the long ranks; finally, finally they had made it and were out. As they arrived they made a brief stop and then moved on in the direction of Sprottau for a quick rest and refit. Meanwhile the FEB/BR under Hptm. Lau remained in position near Sprottisch-Waldau, supported by several of *Major* Rossmann's Panthers.

Other elements of the column (I./Jäg.Rgt. 2) had headed through the Primkenau forest straight west to the Bober near Ober-Leschen in order to cross the stream there. During 12 February they also found their way to Sprottau to rest for several hours.

The cost of the struggle by the three divisions of the von Saucken group to break through to the west, which lasted almost three days, in killed, wounded and especially missing was considerable. A great deal of equipment was also lost because of poor road conditions in the forests, having to be abandoned after breaking down or becoming stuck.

But on that 12 February, when *General* von Saucken had regained his freedom of action—thanks to the personal bravery of the commanding general who had remained with the moving pocket and coolly led his troops out of this dilemma—he received the news that he was to immediately hand command of the Pz.Korps GD over to his already designated successor, *General der Artillerie* Jauer and report to the army group. On his way, *General der Panzertruppe* von Saucken stopped at the command post of the 4. Pz.Armee and paid a visit to its commander-in-chief. The latter expressed his gratitude for the accomplishments of von Saucken's corps and at the same time assured him that he had had nothing to do with the recall of the GD's commanding general nor did he know why the commander-in-chief of the army group had taken this step.

General der Panzertruppe von Saucken drove with his aide, Lt. Kohl, on to army group headquarters and reported to *Generalfeldmarschall* Schörner. The latter kept the GD's commanding general waiting for more than four hours. The conversation that followed lasted only a few minutes, after which an agitated and annoyed *General* von Saucken left the headquarters again with the words, "Now the both of us are driving to the personnel office!" The drive to Berlin passed through Dresden. *General* von Saucken made his way to *General* Burgdorf, described the actual situation in the combat zone and described the cause of the conflict between himself and Schörner from his point of view.

After a short leave on 23 March 1945 *General* von Saucken was placed in command of the German 2. Armee in the Danzig—Gotenhafen area. Once again the Pz.Gren.Div. GD was under his command. Also at this time Hitler presented him with the certificate for the award of the Swords to the Knight's Cross.

For the members of the Pz.Korps GD, however, the sudden departure of their universally revered and highly thought of commanding general was a shock which would remain in the minds of many for a long time. An outstanding commander, personally a gentleman and a Prussian, he had skill-fully led the Pz.Korps GD from November 1944 until mid-February 1945 during the critical weeks of the fight from the Vistula to the Oder and had earned the highest respect of all his men.

The new commander of the Pz.Korps GD, *General der Artillerie* Jauer, was no stranger; he had been the first commander of the Artillerie-Rgt. GD in the Infanterie-Division GD at the beginning and middle of 1942.

—

The battle for the small city of Primkenau on 10 and 11 February 1945 should not go unmentioned. It was from this small city that the Soviets launched fierce attacks against the von Saucken group, which at that time was still fighting its way west in the moving pocket. On or about 9 February anti-tank detachments of the Heeres-Pz.Jagd.-Verband GD under Oblt. Herbig moved into the city to give an appropriate greeting to the Soviet armored spearheads which were expected to appear at any time. With them, however, was what was left of the *Volkssturm-Bataillon Primkenau*, about 20 men. They, too, prepared to defend their home town. They were ready to hold their city at any cost, even the sacrifice of their own lives.

And one other group of men moved from Ottendorf, where they had detrained, in the direction of Primkenau in order to take up the struggle against the Soviet armored forces: Kampfgruppe Spornring, consisting of 51 officer cadets of the 2. Inspektion/IV. Abteilung of the OB.-Schule GD in Cottbus.

Independently, on 10 February these groups took up the battle with enemy tanks which appeared at the eastern outskirts of the city. The mur-derous close-quarters struggle began at about noon. The officer cadets, who had been sent without weapons to join the Pz.Gren.Div. BR, had to find what they could from among the discarded weapons. In the following bat-tle of man against tank, man against technology, but also men against Soviet infantry, almost all of the men of the *Volkssturm-Bataillon Primkenau* gave their lives. Of the 51 officer cadets only 13 reached the vil-lage of Petersdorf several kilometers west of Primkenau. The others were missing or had been wounded, captured or killed!

And there in Petersdorf they took up the battle again against the enemy tanks, destroying another five to seven with hand-held anti-tank weapons; the last members of the *Volkssturm-Bataillon Primkenau* were killed in action in Sprottisch-Waldau. They were hit after jumping up for joy at having just destroyed a T 34.

The anti-tank detachments of the Heeres-Pz.Jagd.-Verband GD were also able to account for several enemy tanks with their *Panzerfäuste* and then fought their way through to Sprottau, where they went into position at the airfield. This heroic struggle in and around Primkenau, in which many young and old men gave their lives in isolated actions, was just a side-line to the murderous struggle against the Soviet armies which flooded into the German homeland in those weeks.

The anti-tank detachments were now deployed in the area around Waltersdorf, in front of Sprottau. But they were no better able to withstand the enemy onslaught there than elsewhere. Falling back in the direction of Sagan, they took up position in front of the airfield there and together with a company of paratroopers defended it against all enemy attacks. Not until their positions were outflanked on both sides were they forced to abandon them and begin another retreat which took them behind the Queis.

There, however, they found the GD corps command post, where they received orders to repeatedly attack the enemy forces advancing through Sorau toward Forst, to create confusion and if possible to halt them.

This mission was carried out until 18 February, and it resulted in not inconsiderable losses to the Russians. Finally the unit was disengaged from the enemy and was transferred into the Muskau area to rest and refit.

There it was incorporated into the newly established *Heeres-Panzer-Jagd-Brigade I* under the command of General Staff *Major* Hoffmann. In addition to the Heeres-Pz.Jagd.-Verband GD, the new brigade also included the Heeres-Pz.Jagd.-Verband A under Hptm. Mayer and the Heeres-Pz.Jagd.-Verband G, neither of which included GD men.

The new organization of the Heeres-Pz.Jagd.-Verband GD under Oblt. Herbig was as follows:

1. Kp.   Lt. von Jürgensonn
2. Kp.   Lt. Bode
3. Kp.   Lt. Plitzkow
4. Kp.   Lt. Fuchs

Its future area of operations was to be the rear area of the Soviet units, which meant action behind enemy lines. Yet another unit was formed in the first days of February 1945, its companies and men recruited from the Wach-Regiment *Großdeutschland* in Berlin. Its origins can be traced back to a proposal made by *General* Guderian during a speech at the noon situation briefing on 27 January 1945. Guderian suggested that two companies of the Wach-Regiment Berlin be dispatched into the area due west of the Oder in order to establish a rear position under officers from other units to receive the fleeing units. The *Feldwach-Regiment GD (Hogrebe)*, a rather adventurous sounding name traceable to the *Wach-Regiment GD*, was formed in Berlin. Actually the word "formed" is a rather generous term for what went on there. Two battalions were formed; only a few of the men had seen combat and most were replacements from Denmark and recruits. The two battalions were at first supposed to be incorporated into the "Division Berlin." Morale was poor, especially since *Major* Hogrebe did not appear to be the right man for this unit. One of the two battalions was led by Hptm.

Schlee, a wearer of the Oak Leaves and a former member of the Wach-Rgt. GD Berlin.

When the departure order arrived several days later, issued by the military commander of Berlin, *General* Hoffmeister—the individual companies marched through a dark, rainy night to Putlitzstrasse Station to the accompaniment of the "Helenenmarsch" played by the Wach-Rgt. Berlin. Some of the horses had to be led by hand, since there was not enough harness available.

In spite of being less than ideally equipped, the mood of the men was good when they disembarked in the Golzow—Gusow area. In that area west of the Oder and the city of Küstrin they were able to obtain more horses and harness—slowly, very slowly, this collection of mercenaries became a unit. On or about 5-6 February the companies finally took up quarters in the Letschin area. Preparations were initiated for operations on the Oder.

On 8 February 1945 the unit was moved up to the Oder, where it was initially supposed to relieve a position battalion. It was a rainy night when the companies took over the strongpoints, which on account of the soggy subsurface were either under water or were built so high that they were under continuous enemy fire.

It turned out that the Soviets had already established a bridgehead, small at first, near Gross-Neuendorf and Kienitz. This was now to be eliminated through an attack by the Feldwach-Rgt. GD (Horgrebe).

The attack, which began on 10 February, was made across open terrain and proved a costly failure. The attacking companies were driven back to their starting positions by the Soviets, who had advanced to in front of Letschin. It required another attack on 12 February to eliminate the enemy salient near Kienitz, after which the German positions there were further fortified. Uffz. Seidenberg and an Obergefreiter particularly distinguished themselves in this attack against the enemy salient near Kienitz, destroying approximately forty Soviets with *Panzerfausts* while defending a bridge. Both men were awarded the Iron Cross, First Class for their actions.

The battalions of the Feldwach-Rgt. GD, now under the command of Obstlt. Müller with his command post in the Vossberg estate south of Letschin, remained in the positions they had captured and held them until 16 April 1945.

On 12 February elements of the Pz.Gren.Div. BR were rushed behind the Queis to provide flanking cover for the Sprottau—Sagan—Sorau retreat road. A new blocking line was built there from Dober through Tschiebsdorf to the Bober and to Silber. The BR command post, which had previously been in Mallmitz, was transferred behind the sector and the battalions immediately marched into their new positions.

The *Jäger* of Jäg.Rgt. 1 BR occupied their positions, to the Bober on the left and to Tschiebsdorf on the right, while Jäg.Rgt. 2 BR was stationed from Tschiebsdorf up to and including Dober. In Tschiebsdorf itself the new concrete bridge had been blown up by a local pioneer battalion, however the Soviets were still able to use the wreckage to form the basis of a crossing. Since one of the main supports was only wrecked on one side, the enemy succeeded in getting several squads of infantry and machine-guns to the west bank, where they dug in. All attempts to destroy what was left of the bridge from a distance, using Goliath remotely-controlled explosives carriers, failed. The Soviet infantry was therefore able to continue using the crossing. The result was fierce fighting in the first houses of Tschiebsdorf which proved costly to both sides. I. (SPW)/Jäg.Rgt. 1 BR fought numerous close quarters battles there. Finally the II./Jäg.Rgt. 2 BR was brought in as reinforcements; counterattacking with the assault guns and elements of the Pz.A.A. BR, it succeeded in driving the Soviets back toward the bridge. Thus on 13 February the old positions were returned to our hands.

But farther south near Dober heavy fighting was in progress with Soviet forces which had infiltrated there, mainly in the forests.

Between Tschiebsdorf and Dober the armored assault pioneers of the BR under Hptm. "Pioneer-Müller" battled Soviet Kampfgruppen that had infiltrated into the forest west of Tschiebsdorf. It was a tough, merciless close-quarters struggle in the forest, very costly for both sides, however the Soviets could not be dislodged.

Finally the Soviets succeeded in breaking into the positions of I./Jäg.Rgt. 2 BR near and in Dober, thus threatening our own positions. Counterattacks on 14 and 15 February at least sealed off the enemy penetration. But the enemy was steadily moving reinforcements across the Queis south of Dober, and pressure from the enemy ultimately resulted in the positions being abandoned. Early on 15 February, at about 03:30 hours, the *Jäger* disengaged from the enemy and fought their way back to the west in the direction of Hermsdorf. However the right wing, I./Jäg.Rgt. 2 BR positioned near Dober, stayed until early on 16 February, busy with counterattacks against the now outflanking enemy. Only with difficulty did it succeed in pulling back to the new defense line on both sides of Hermsdorf, along the Hammer Brook.

Everything now depended on getting our own units across and behind this line as quickly as possible and blowing the vital crossings, especially at Hermsdorf, before the Soviets arrived. For this purpose the commander of the Pz.Stu.Pi.Btl. BR, Hptm. Müller-Rochholz, immediately rushed to the road bridge east of Hermsdorf in order to prepare the walled arched bridge for demolition. Meanwhile the *Jäger* of the 2. Regiment under Obstlt. Oesterwitz occupied positions on both sides of the town.

The charges already on the arched bridge were a joke! "Pi.-Müller" therefore radioed his supply chief Michaelis: "Explosives, explosives to the front!!"

To the north in the forest there was a wooden bridge, whose charges were bolstered by the addition of hand grenade bundles. However the bridges had to be kept open for the last elements of the *Brandenburgers* prior to demolition.

The pioneers blew a footbridge south of the Hermsdorf road bridge immediately after the return of the last of the 2. Regiment. Meanwhile a combat engineer reconnaissance platoon conducted reconnaissance in the direction of Sagan, where the men found two or three German assault guns behind them, followed immediately by the first T 34s!

Farther northwest the enemy had already been in Sorau since 13 February. Where were the explosives? Where was Michaelis? The necessary electric and cord fuses had been laid. Only the most important part was still missing.

Then at the same moment, from the west a Studebaker came roaring around the curve in Hermsdorf. Ammunition boxes flew onto the bridge! Four large crates. The last assault gun passed; the first T 34 appeared close behind it.

Ignition. Boom...the bridge went up under the nose of the first T 34.

A sigh of relief went through the squads of *Jäger* lying there behind their machine-guns and carbines. The enemy had been stopped once again.

The Pz.Stu.Pi.Btl. BR then moved on to Wolfsdorf, where it remained as operational reserve.

In the days that followed, the Soviets successfully bridged this natural obstacle by going around and were soon in front of our main line of resistance again. In spite of heavy enemy artillery, mortar and tank fire, the positions in the heavily wooded area south of Wolfsdorf were held until about 19 February.

Then the order to retreat reached the units deployed there; they were to withdraw to the Neiße in one go. The withdrawal in the Wolfsdorf area was difficult, because the Soviets launched several counterattacks as the units left the positions and these had to be intercepted and beaten back first. At the last minute the *Jäger* and combat engineers were able to disengage, climb into their vehicles and race away to the west.

This withdrawal was covered by a screen provided by I./Jäg.Rgt. 2 BR, which, advancing in stages, had to hold off the advancing enemy for another 48 hours. Making skilful use of the terrain, and once again supported by the self-propelled guns of the *Panzerjäger* and several assault guns, they fought their way back toward the Neiße slowly and steadily.

There, however, the engineers were already at work, in spite of contradictory orders, preparing positions to receive the arriving elements of the Pz.Korps GD, especially the Pz.Stu.Pi.Btl. BR. The line ran from Steinbach to Priebus and Sagan to the outskirts of Muskau. In Muskau itself a bridgehead was held around the Muskau forest roughly in the Sagar—Braunsdorf area, primarily to take in units of the 20. Pz.Gren.Div. and the Fsch.Pz.Div. 1 HG arriving over the Sorau-Priebus—Muskau road. In the bridgehead there were combat engineers of the Pz.Korps Pi.Btl. 500 GD and 3. Kp./Pz.Stu.Pi.Btl. BR.

The entire width of the sector that the Pz.Gren.Div. BR had to defend was 32 kilometers. While the bulk of the division reached the Neiße river line via Pechern, including the I./Jäg.Rgt. 2 BR, the last elements in contact with the enemy, the armored patrols of the Pz.A.A. BR, returned by way of Muskau.

Meanwhile, from 19 February to roughly 25 February, the combat engineers of the Pz.Stu.Pi.Btl. BR carried out the following tasks, which were intended to strengthen our defensive positions: several roadblocks of felled trees protected by anti-tank and anti-personnel mines were set up on the road from Birkfähre to Priebus; explosive charges were placed on the bridges at Sagar, Pechern and Priebus, which were then blown up. Some of the charges were fabricated using powder from 88-mm shells brought from a munitions factory near Pattag.

The pioneers also cleared German minefields on this side of the Neiße in the area Sagar—Kaupenhäuser—Pechern—Neudorf. The combat engineers of the security units that had mined the forest roads had not followed any plan, which made their removal very difficult. Several days later *Major* Wandrey, commander of Jäg.Rgt. 1, drove over a mine in his VW and was killed.

In these days every last combat engineer, including those of the supply company, were constantly in action. Even when the Soviets appeared at the Neiße, as was the case in those days, the engineers still laid anti-personnel mines east of the Neiße. This forced the enemy to be cautious in his movements.

The positions along the Neiße were occupied, expanded and held by the battalions of the Pz.Gren.Div. BR.

The division command post was located in Heide, southeast of Weisskeissel, where the division Ib established himself. The corps command post was in Spreefurth.

At the Neiße, however, the enemy remained silent, also occupied positions and initially showed no intentions of continuing his attacks.

The enemy offensive, which had begun at the Vistula, initially ended along the Oder—Neiße line.

Once again—and for the last time—German troops occupied a continuous defense line.

Chapter 7
Alert Brigade Großdeutschland

In the last days of January 1945 the "Alert Unit Schmeltzer" had been withdrawn from its lines of security on both sides of Forst and recalled to Cottbus to be integrated into "Kampfgruppe Langkeit" (Pz.Gren.Div. KmK). Following the departure of the Kampfgruppe further new recruits for the Pz.Gren.-Ersatz-Brigade GD were taken in at Cottbus and Guben. Training began immediately and proceeded rapidly since most of the recruits already had pre-military training behind them.

It was clear to the brigade command, however, that the brigade, which was almost back up to strength in personnel, would have to continue carrying out security duties to the east of its bases. The makeshift outposts and defense lines along the Oder in no way guaranteed security against the advancing Soviet armies. News of the Pz.Korps GD's retreat from Raudten toward Sprottau, as well as reports of enemy armored spearheads reaching Sagan and Sorau on 12-13 February and the increased numbers of refugee columns passing through Cottbus, finally led the Pz.Gren.-Ersatz-Brigade GD to immediately establish a further alert unit at both of its bases. The unit, which was under the command of Obstlt. Schwarzrock's Pz.Gren.E.u.A.Rgt. GD (panzer-grenadier replacement and training regiment), was formed from all parts of the Pz.Gren.-Ersatz-Brigade GD and received the designation *"Alarm-Brigade GD (Schwarzrock)"*. The brigade was organized into two battalions commanded by *Major* Gerbener and *Major* Count Nayhaus and several heavy and reconnaissance companies (Hptm. von Bauer).

Elements in Guben, especially the III./Pz.Gren.E.u.A.Rgt GD, the Pz.Art.E.u.A.Abt. GD and other of the brigade's replacement units based there, did not take part in the formation process. These units were combined under the command of *Major* Theermann and were deployed to defend the city of Guben. Placed on alert on 12-13 February, they immediately formed themselves into Kampfgruppen and fortified their positions east of the city for all-round defense.

The Alarm-Brigade GD was placed under the sector command of the then brigade commander (*Oberst* von Gläsemer), who set up his command post in Gross-Kolzig, roughly between Forst and Muskau. Communications were established with the battle commander of Weisswasser-Muskau, *Sturmbannführer* Count von Egloffstein, as well as to his commanders in Guben (*Major* Theermann) and in the sector on both sides of the autobahn south of Forst and along the Neiße to just outside of Muskau.

The entire Alarm-Brigade GD left the base at Cottbus on 14 February, leaving behind only a few cadre personnel, convalescents and sick, and marched into its areas of operation (Gross-Bademeusel—autobahn—south along the Neiße to about Gross-Särchen), where its right wing was in contact with the elements of the Pz.Korps-Pi.Btl. 500 GD.

The departure of the brigade on 14 February left behind a Cottbus empty of soldiers, which was to prove fortunate, for at 11:00 hours on the following day the city was struck by the heaviest Allied air attack so far. The military hospital, which was in the main hospital, and two hospital and refugee trains in the station were hit, the city heavily damaged. The barracks sustained only minor bomb damage. The Alarm-Brigade GD itself arrived in its positions early on 15 February; it "pocketed" the *Volkssturm* men stationed there and distributed them among its various units. In the days that followed contact was made with the Soviets, who appeared on the east bank and periodically tried to establish several bridgeheads across the Neiße.

The subsequent battle between this replacement unit and the Soviets lasted about 25 days, dying down and flaring up again several times, and was described in detail in a report written by Obfw. Waldow:

The Alarm-Brigade GD's Battle near Gross-Bademeusel on the Autobahn near Forst on the Neiße in the Period 15-25 February 1945

I (Obfw. Waldow) had command of the 1st Platoon in the training company under Oblt. Hofsäß. With these people (16-year-olds) I moved out to defend Cottbus but was recalled on the second day. While marching through Dissenchen we were caught by surprise by the air raid on Cottbus and from there we marched further into the Neiße position. It was dark when we reached Forst and we were deployed in the Neiße bank position from the Gross-Bademeusel bridge to Kleine-Bademeusel on the right. My sector was Gross-Bademeusel to the right, including the bend in the Neiße, steep bank. On my left the Richter company held the line as far as the mill at Kleine-Bademeusel, while about 150 meters to my right the highway bridge over the Neiße had been blown. If I remember correctly Fw. Fischer was active in that sector at that time. My company was led by Lt. Trompeter. At that time about 96 Volkssturm men were assigned to me, so that there were always two of my men to a hole and between them two holes with two Volkssturm each. My entire sector was 1 800 meters wide; in command of my platoon command group was an Unteroffizier with the German Cross in Gold from another unit who had been assigned from the hospital in Cottbus. One morning Russians dressed in German uniforms (Free Germany) crossed over to the steep bank shouting, "Don't shoot, Germans coming!" From the water they walked to the bank and broke into our positions shouting loudly. My left wing was rolled up approximately 800 meters. At about 13:00 hours an assault pioneer company was committed from the area of Försterhaus and drove the enemy out of the forest back through my rear area. As they passed through I got about 35 men with the light machine-gun, the others (about 80 men) escaped across the Neiße. We immediately moved up and reoccupied the old main line of resistance.

After this first attack about sixteen of the Volkssturm men who had been placed under my command had disappeared. The next morning I sent six to eight men ahead of my right wing through the Neiße. Two days after the Russian's first penetration, using the same tactic they succeeded in breaking into the same sector and along the position on the bank, rolling up the company on my left (Richter Company) in the direction of Kleine-Bademeusel. They did not advance beyond the river embankment at first, however, instead they dug in and defended it tenaciously. During the following night, at about midnight, the regiment or division under whose command we were at that time sent an assault team from my platoon, about 24 men strong, to win back the embankment. After an hour it returned and the Feldwebel in command reported that it was impossible, the enemy was too strong. I sealed off the bank with two light machine-guns, rifle positions in front of and behind the embankment. The Russians succeeded in taking more of the embankment away from the Richter Company and sent further companies across the Neiße during the night. Thus in the morning the Russians had possession of about 1 400 to 1 600 meters of the Neiße embankment on our side. They dug into almost the entire embankment during the night, and during the day that followed we could see nothing in this steep embankment. The next morning I received orders from my battalion commander (Hptm. von Bauer), to attack the next night with an assault team, 24 men strong, and to retake and occupy the Neiße embankment at all costs. "Take the people you can depend on, begin the attack at 24:00 hours!" "My request: "I need one supply squad (3 men) each from the Richter and Trompeter companies to supply Panzerfausts, one supply squad from each for machine-gun and rifle ammunition, plus one each for hand grenades, submachine-gun ammunition and flares. I request that this ammunition be set aside and stored in the Richter Company's main line of resistance and in my platoon's sector. I need a Feldwebel I can rely on who will lead half of my assault team (12 men) from the Richter Company's positions. As well I need a combat engineer Feldwebel."

Uffz. Gensicke was the first of my people to volunteer, followed by the bulk of my men. A Feldwebel was sent to me from the Richter Company and at the same time it assumed responsibility for supplying the second half of the assault team and made available to me the necessary supply squads, as did Lt. Trompeter of my company. During the day I received the Feldwebel from the Richter Company, the pioneer Unteroffizier and an additional combat engineer. I assembled the entire assault team and discussed how the operation was to be carried out. In the evening both halves of the assault team moved into the sector, from which we set out at about 24:00 hours.

The Russians had now had the Neiße embankment in their hands for some time. It was thus clear to me that I would have to deal with a superior force of 250-300 men. I subsequently decided to blast our old position in the embankment as well as the area above or behind the embankment with Panzerfausts. Following my instructions, my half of the assault team and the other half crawled along, following the Feldwebel and me, about one meter below the upper edge. We rolled hand grenades over the embankment so that they would explode in the

208

holes behind it. On our side of the embankment we blasted every one of our old holes and all of the new Russian ones with Panzerfausts.

While I fired the Panzerfaust, Uffz. Gensicke stood up and threw his hand grenades into the old positions. So one hole after another and the new Russian position was taken. By about three in the morning we had forced the Russians back to within 350 to 400 meters of the embankment along its entire length. From there, however, we could get no further; we fought bitterly for every meter of ground and threatened to succumb to the enemy's superior force. For approximately one hour we made no forward progress at all. Right next to me a burst of submachine-gun fire stitched the chest of Uffz. Gensicke, who was standing with a live grenade in his hand. He fell and the hand grenade went off behind him. After firing my Panzerfaust I went over to him, but he died soon afterwards. I immediately jumped back into cover and a strange quiet and depression came over my people.

From there I was able to accurately determine the position of the other half of the assault team from Panzerfausts being fired, muzzle flashes and exploding hand grenades. I then made a decision to do something that was not part of the plan. Impulsively, I shouted "hurray!" several times, after which I said to my people, "I will count two, three and everyone shout hurray!" I repeated these numbers, whereupon everyone joined in. This was also heard by the other half of the assault team, which then began doing the same thing. All of a sudden we noticed that the Russians were becoming affected by fear; they probably believed that the same thing was about to happen to them that had happened to us two days before. As well there was the Neiße, which lay approximately 60 meters behind them; it was a well known fact that most of the Russians could not swim.

Now there was an eerie stillness among the Russians on the other side of the embankment. I reacted immediately and called for a flare pistol with which to shoot over the Neiße. In the light of the parachute flare, which lit up almost the entire strip of meadow from the embankment to the bank of the Neiße, I saw the Russians leaving the embankment in the hundreds. They ran to the bank and stopped. I immediately called out, "Machine-gun forward to the embankment! Open fire on the bank!" After this we fired parachute flare after parachute flare, the machine-guns fired everything they had. Now we could see that the Russians had completed a ferry link across the Neiße; the ferry was on the other side. We drove the entire mass back into and across the Neiße with machine-gun fire and the Panzerfausts as well as with rifle and submachine-gun fire. Only a few surrendered.

Afterwards the two halves of my assault team linked up, we immediately combed the holes of the old position behind the embankment and fetched several wounded from the holes; most had been wounded by fragments from the hand grenades we had rolled over the embankment. For most of the holes were one meter—three at most—from the upper rim of the embankment. I immediately discussed with the pioneer Unteroffizier how to take out the ferry, which we could not reach. There were two 76.2-mm anti-tank guns near the ferry and five on our side. Behind the embankment stood and lay six mortars, about 13 machine-guns, roughly 16 anti-tank rifles, hundreds of rifles and submachine-guns. While the main line of resistance was occupied from both sides, the assault team placed the captured mortars, heavy machine-guns plus about 3 000 meters of telephone cable and ammunition in safety behind the embankment. The light machine-guns fired constantly into the forest which reached the shore on the other side of the Neiße, so that we were able to work almost unhindered. The pioneer Unteroffizier and his man spiked the barrels of all the guns. After the anti-tank guns had been spiked too, we both fired at the ferry on the other side simultaneously with Panzerfausts until it was completely destroyed. I fired a total of 76 rounds of Panzerfaust ammunition during this operation, all I had apart from a small reserve. In some cases my young men fought more bravely here than the old soldiers. Casualties from my half of the assault team so far totaled four, as far as I remember the other half had about the same number, possibly one more. Four and a half hours of close combat had passed from the time we set out at 24:00 hours until the battle was over. Of my Volkssturm people, only the company commander and three men had been present for the second breakthrough, all the others had run away and did not return. I believe the unit came from Forst. According to statements made to me and the battalion by prisoners there had been more than 500 Russians on this side of the Neiße.

After the assault team was pulled back we were fed in the forester's house. I had to make a report to the unit commander. He said to me that it was impossible for me to drive more than 500 Russians across the Neiße with 24 men. At his request, the next night I had to count all the foxholes that the Russians had dug on the bank above the embankment. At that time I counted 526 one-man holes. I was told by Hptm. von Bauer, who had heard it from the Ia of the GD field division, that I had again been recommended for the Knight's Cross.

The system for supplying ammunition to the two companies worked perfectly. Thus, since there was no shortage, we were able to simulate a much larger force. This also had an effect.

The next day we finally had a quiet sector.

From there we went to the Brandenburg Division and I to the Korps-Begleit-Kp. in Reichwalde as leader of the first assault platoon.

Having fought their way out of the Soviet rear, an increasing number of units arrived in the new Neiße line and after a brief rest took over the positions held by the alert units.

On 19 February the Pz.Korps GD likewise began moving the Pz.Gren.Div. BR into its new positions along the Neiße south of Muskau; it was at this moment that the corps became interested in the Alarm-Brigade GD, which until then had been standing off to the side.

Finally, on 10 March 1945, the brigade was moved into the corps area and its companies were incorporated into the Pz.Gren.Div. BR to bolster that unit. Obstlt. Schwarzrock was placed in the command of the Lehr-

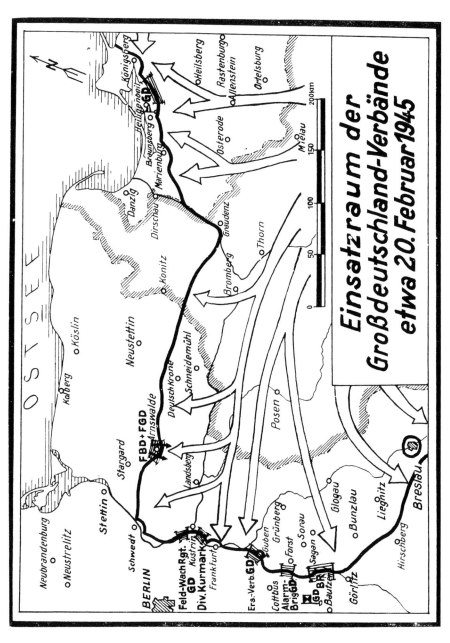

Operational Area of "Großdeutschland" Formations Around
20 February 1945

Rgt. *Brandenburg*, which was still at Oberkrain. *Oberst* von Gläsemer made preparations for moving the rest of the Pz.Gren.-Ersatz-Brigade GD to Schleswig, less the elements in Guben which at that time were already engaged in the initial battles for the Guben bridgehead.

The incorporation of the Alarm-Brigade GD into the Pz.Gren.Div. BR bolstered that unit in terms of men and materiel and enabled it to fill the gaps in several of its units and increase its defensive strength in the positions it had to hold at the Neiße.

This was also the first intentional joining of GD and BR men within a unit, which only improved their mutual respect and understanding. The positions along the Neiße were continually improved, further reinforcement was made in the rear of the defense zone, everything was readied for the final big offensive by the Soviets—which was sure to come one day.

Brandenburger Jäger on the Neiße—under the command of the Panzer-Korps *Großdeutschland*.

Part IV
In the Combat Zone East and West of the Oder Near Frankfurt

Chapter 1
Kampfgruppe Langkeit–
Pz.Gren.Div. "Kurmark":
Formation–Organization–Operations

At a nocturnal meeting of the commanders of the Pz.Gren.-Ersatz-Brigade GD on 26 January 1945 it was announced that "Kampfgruppe Langkeit" was being formed from all elements of the brigade. "Alert Unit Schmelter," which was at the front near Forst under the command of *Major* Petereit, was to be recalled to form the basis of this hasty establishment.

The code-words "Gneisenau a" (for the emergency formation of Kampfgruppen) and "Gneisenau b" (for the base at Guben) surely did not apply solely to the formation of an alert unit, but probably also for the drawing together of all available units for the special purpose of defending at the Oder in the event of approach by the enemy. Thus not only was the Alert Unit Schmelter created under this code-word, but also Kampfgruppe Gersdorf, Kampfgruppe Langkeit, the Alert-Brigade GD and others.

Formation of Kampfgruppe Langkeit from the Pz.Gren.-Ersatz-Brigade GD, which was relatively well off in terms of personnel, at its bases at Cottbus and Guben began on 26 January 1945. It was based on the awareness that a strong Kampfgruppe would achieve more in a defensive role than several smaller units with inadequate equipment and supply.

The situation at the front in the east—insofar as one could call it a front given its feeble state—showed the picture of constant movement by the advancing armies of the Soviet 1st White Russian Front under Zhukov south of Posen straight towards Frankfurt and the Oder, in order to reach the river ahead of the shattered German armies streaming back in disarray and establish several large bridgeheads from which they could launch the decisive battle for the Reich capital.

On the German side all hopes rested on the Tirschtiegel Position, which followed the chain of lakes from Kopnitz through Bentschen,

Tirschtiegel and Zetsche north to the Netze south of Driesen and which had hastily been placed in a defense-ready state through the addition of bunkers, field positions, anti-tank ditches and so forth. A second, similar position was under construction west of Schwiebus, Meseritz and Schwerin. But what use were positions and defense installations if the troops needed to man them were lacking? Several local alert and *Volkssturm* units were available, and these, inadequately armed and with limited fighting spirit, stood guard in these positions. But their value as combat units? What were they against Zhukov's armies with Stalin tanks, assault guns, Stalin Organs and masses of Soviet infantry?

The German high command used every possible means at its disposal to direct newly-formed units into this defense line, scraped together headquarters initially without troops, and tried at the last minute—but too late—to organize a new defense in this line. Kampfgruppe Langkeit was also earmarked for this; the command authorities increased the pace of its formation to the maximum. Cottbus was like a beehive. *Oberst* Langkeit, commander of the Pz.Gren.-Ersatz-Brigade GD since 1 November 1944, a senior tank commander and recipient of the Oakleaves, issued the necessary orders; General Staff *Major* Spaeter, just returned to Cottbus from the war academy and waiting for his next job, took over the duties of the "first general staff officer," selected suitable officers and men for a small headquarters staff and directed the work of establishing the unit. At first this looked quite simple, especially since the brigade's organization had for months taken into account the possible employment of Kampfgruppen at the front.

In the returning Alert Unit Schmelter the Pz.Gren.Ers.-u.-Ausb.Rgt. GD very quickly found the basis for the formation of the I./Pz.Gren.Rgt. with four to five companies which was formed under the command of *Major* Petereit. With his adjutant, Oblt. Wechmann, he formed three rifle companies and a machine-gun company, mainly from young recruits with veteran instructors providing experienced officers and non-commissioned officers. The unit was made mobile with vehicles of every conceivable type.

II./Pz.Gren.Rgt. was created under the command of *Major* Schöttler, adjutant Lt. Neher, with the 6.-8. Schtz.Kp., 9. (MG.) and 10. (Gr.We.) Kp., whose personnel consisted partly of trained replacement companies, convalescents, and in the case of 7. Kp. of men separated from their units and taken off trains in Cottbus. The brigade provided most of the non-commissioned officers. The majority of the vehicles were Opel Blitz radio trucks, some of whose wood-gas engines had to be replaced.

The artillery—a battalion at first—was formed at Guben by the Pz.Art.Ers.-und Ausb.Abt. GD. At first, however, no one knew whether it was being established for the Pz.Korps GD, for Kampfgruppe Langkeit or for the FBD (*Führer-Begleit-Division*). The numerous formation orders arriving for various GD units at this time were constantly changing.

An artillery regiment headquarters was created under the command of *Major* Hammerich with elements of a signals platoon. Adjutant was Oblt. Mahnke. Established next was a battalion headquarters under the command of Hptm. Buboltz, previously the commander of 1.(schw.) Art.Ers.u.Ausb.Abt. GD, with Lt. Vogel as adjutant.

In addition, Lt. Rolke put together a heavy battery with two heavy field howitzers from non-commissioned officers and enlisted men of the 1st battery, and Lt. Esslinger a light field howitzer battery with non-commissioned officers and enlisted men from the 4th Battery, while Oblt. Künkel raised a light anti-aircraft battery with four 20-mm single-barrel and four 20-mm quadruple-barrel weapons plus four single-barrel 37-mm flak mounted on prime movers. Also formed at Guben was the 3.(Stu.Gesch.) Batterie, something like an assault gun brigade, under the command of an *Oberleutnant*. While it was possible to take prime movers from the Pz.Art.Ers. u. Ausb.Abt.'s vehicle park, all other types of vehicles were absent and requisitioned civilian machines had to be used.

Obstlt. Klüver was initially employed as commander of the Pz.Gren.Rgt. and he saw to the task of forming the regimental companies. The 11.(IG.) Kp. under Lt. Dahlinger provided the regimental commander with heavy infantry weapons; its platoon leaders included Lt. Promalo and Obfw. Fey. The company's equipment included light and heavy infantry guns towed by various vehicles. Veteran soldiers filled the most important positions alongside young recruits.

For armored vehicles every training vehicle that was still in the vehicle hangars of the Pz.Ers. u. Ausb.Abt. GD in Cottbus was bought out: tanks powered by wood-gas engines, some without turrets, without guns, which had nothing but their armor. *Major* Hudel, commander of the training battalion, also an experienced tank commander, put together a dashing group of tankers whose initial organization was as follows:

Battle staff with signals platoon
1 tank company
1 armored patrol platoon
2 tank-destroyer squads with Panzerschreck anti-tank weapons
2 tank-destroyer squads with Panzerfaust anti-tank weapons
1 anti-tank company
1 motorcycle company

That was all there was in the beginning. When the Kampfgruppe's first unit set out for Frankfurt (I./Pz.Gren.Rgt. under *Major* Petereit) it was in fact more of a collection than a cohesive unit. But the mood and morale of these men was excellent; all were determined to give their all in the struggle against the superior enemy.

The initial destination for everyone was Frankfurt/Oder, where new orders were to be received. *Oberst* Langkeit, who had gone ahead with General Staff *Major* Spaeter, received his first assignment there:

Kampfgruppe Langkeit is to assemble in and around Reppen, attack the deep flank of the northeastwards-advancing enemy and reach the Tierschtiegel position near Zielenig...

Kampfgruppe headquarters immediately moved to Neuendorf—Gutshof and established its command post there. Information was gathered on the situation, the position of other units, and especially the enemy's movements. Slowly the Kampfgruppe assembled in the Reppen area and bit by bit established contact with the Kampfgruppe headquarters.

In Frankfurt *Major* Hammerich learned that he and his elements had been subordinated to Kampfgruppe Langkeit, and the Buboltz Battalion moved in from Guben, initially as far as Frankfurt-East. During the night of 29 January the Rolke Battery with the battery headquarters detail moved forward as far as Neuendorf, the prime movers followed through snow and over icy roads.

On 30 January 1945 not much was known about the enemy situation, especially for the Reppen—Sternberg area. All that was heard from refugees fleeing from the direction of Schwiebus was that the enemy was advancing with numerous tanks, driving isolated German Kampfgruppen before him, while away from the main advance route *Volkssturm* battalions continued to hold out in some towns. Furthermore, countless vehicles were heading toward Reppen—Frankfurt in order to cross the Oder ahead of the Russians. There were still *Waffen-SS* troops in or near Sternberg. An SS headquarters was also nearby, but troops, German troops? No, they hadn't seen many.

The pickets put out by I./Pz.Gren.Rgt. were immediately recalled, while the II./Pz.Gren.Rgt.'s 7. Kp. was sent down the road as point, initially as far as Pinnow. Mission: break through to Sternberg and liberate a Kampfgruppe of army elements and SS units encircled north of Sternberg. Apparently it was a special purpose corps headquarters under *General der Waffen-SS* Bittrich.

For this purpose the artillery battalion under Hptm. Buboltz was hastily deployed with its two batteries, with 2. Bttr. under Lt. Rolke taking up position northwest of Reppen and 3. Bttr. under Lt. Esslinger later occupying positions near Pinnow.

Everything proceeded smoothly as far as Pinnow; the battalions moved forward, the Pz.Gren.Rgt. command post was moved to Pinnow—Gutshof.

There two Kampfgruppen were formed from the regiment and these were to make a motorized advance in the direction of Sternberg. Only the 7. Kp. and one squad from each battalion remained in Pinnow for local defense.

Small arms and tank fire could be heard from the northeast, suggesting that the *Waffen-SS* had broken through. Anti-aircraft guns of the

Künkel Battery went into position near Pinnow.

Oberst Langkeit followed right behind the point in the direction of Sternberg. It was about noontime. Suddenly enemy tanks appeared from the northeast and began firing into Pinnow. One of the very first shells struck the manor's watchmaker's hut, causing it to collapse—almost on the head of Obstlt. Klüver, who had just stepped out in front of the house. Alarm! Enemy tanks in front of Pinnow! Report to *Oberst* Langkeit! Patrols found that enemy tanks and following infantry columns were passing north of Pinnow in the direction of Reppen! It was nearly evening. The point, which drove past *Volkssturm* in the villages, finally established contact with the surrounded *Waffen-SS* command post, which was in a manor house near Kerzenlicht. Its troops—apart from several SS units just alert units, *Volkssturm* and Reich Labor Service personnel—were scattered far to the east; but it was never certain where they were, where they were supposed to be or if they really were in position. All this was merely assumed. When contact was made with the SS corps headquarters an anti-tank company under the command of Oblt. Lützow appeared from out of nowhere. *Oberst* Langkeit immediately placed it under his command. This Pz.Jgd.Stu.Gesch.Kp. 1551 under Oblt. Lützow was not entirely unknown to the *Oberst*. In October 1944 near Schaulen his tanks (Pz.Rgt. GD) had rescued the company from a dangerous situation. The *Oberleutnant* and the *Oberst* had known each other since then. The company now came from Milowitz near Prague, where it had undergone rest and refit. Contact with Kampfgruppe Langkeit had been established at the very moment when the situation of the point units was somewhat less than rosy.

Meanwhile *General* Bittrich's SS-Korps-Stab z.b.V. withdrew from its unhappy situation and under the protection of Kampfgruppe Langkeit it hurriedly retreated westward to Frankfurt.

But the most forward elements of the Pz.Gren.Rgt. were now also pulled back. The plan to continue in the direction of Sternberg had to be abandoned, especially as the enemy was already advancing rapidly towards the Oder north of, but now also south of, Pinnow.

The I. Btl. under *Major* immediately moved to Reppen, followed closely by II. Btl., which also arrived in Reppen at about midnight. The latter occupied positions at the east end of town under the protection of 88-mm anti-aircraft guns deployed there in the anti-tank role, its front facing east and northeast. In the evening Lt. Rolke's Second Battery, which was stationed northwest of Reppen, also changed positions to Neuendorf, just as the first tank shells began falling on Reppen. The Kampfgruppe set up its command post in a manor house in Neu-Bischofsee. It was just north of the road at a bend in the road. And this road was jammed with refugee vehicles trying to get west and the eastwards-advancing columns of Kampfgruppe Langkeit which had not yet received the order to withdraw. It was mass confusion—into which enemy tanks, including the heaviest

Josef Stalin types, were now firing from the hills north of the road. The first vehicles were soon hit and set on fire and the light from the fires provided the enemy tanks with further targets.

There was no doubt: the enemy was not so worried about Kampfgruppe Langkeit on the Reppen—Kunersdorf road; his objective was the Oder, to win bridgeheads there ahead of the German troops and subsequently cut off the retreat of the German formations still to the east of Frankfurt.

For this purpose he had deployed the bulk of his tanks on the hills north of the Reppen road and in the favorable terrain, while the bulk of his foot troops advanced in the wooded terrain which ran parallel to Reichsstrasse 167 south of the road.

Meanwhile the last elements of II./Pz.Gren.Rgt. were still in Reppen with the stationary 88-mm anti-aircraft guns stationed there and a few *Volkssturm*. The point units of Kampfgruppe Langkeit—the bulk of whose vehicles were on the road in two columns—tried desperately to break through the enemy forces sitting astride the road between Kunersdorf and Neu-Bischofsee in order to allow the Kampfgruppe's vehicles to continue the withdrawal. The situation was more than unhappy. Endless columns of refugees, who were no more able to move ahead than the Kampfgruppe, hindered the forward movement of the heavy weapons toward the point, which was now facing southwest. They suffered considerable losses to Soviet infantry fire which repeatedly flared up from the woods south of the road, and to tank shells fired by T 34 and JS tanks from the north. These tanks shells fell both on the road and in the forest beyond, however. Loud cries could often be heard after shells fell among the Soviet infantry moving through that area.

The situation for Kampfgruppe Langkeit nevertheless remained very dangerous, faced as it was with destruction from all sides, with no possibility of deploying its own defensive strength. *Oberst* Langkeit was continually with the point southwest of Neu-Bischofsee, together with *Major* Hudel and his few tanks, trying desperately to drive back the enemy there. At the rear of the column the panzer-grenadiers remained in their positions in Reppen, where they were forced to endure the growing weight of artillery and mortar fire, mixed with tank fire, which fell among the positions and houses in the town. An advance against Reppen by ten enemy tanks was beaten off by the concentrated fire of the 88-mm guns and several tanks were destroyed; an attack against the positions of Oblt. Kühne's 6. Kp. by enemy infantry was also repulsed.

Finally, orders came for II./Pz.Gren.Rgt. to withdraw from Reppen during the night, after first destroying its vehicles, and fight its way through along the road to Neu-Bischofsee. This essentially senseless order was made necessary by the untenable situation in Reppen and on both sides of the road, causing *Oberst* Langkeit and his Ia to give consideration to having the entire Kampfgruppe make its way on foot through the forests in the direction of Frankfurt. The sole eight-wheeled armored car patrol still remaining was subsequently sent through the Reppen forest to scout roads and the necessary orders were prepared.

At about 23:00 hours on 31 January 1945 the vehicles and heavy weapons in Reppen were destroyed as quietly as possible. The foot march to the west was begun.

The available batteries of the Buboltz artillery battalion, whose firing positions were due south of Neuendorf, put down zone fire to all sides on forest roads and crossroads, observed fire on Drenzig and in the direction of Kunersdorf, while Lt. Esslinger provided fire control from near Neu-Bischofsee and attempted to support the breakout efforts toward Kunersdorf.

The situation was desperate. After the Stalin tanks to the north had put several shells through the roof of the manor house, the Kampfgruppe staff moved into the cellar, which also housed a makeshift dressing station for the wounded.

Everyone's hopes rested on the road scouting mission by the Grau armored patrol and its successful arrival in Frankfurt. The first radio reports sounded hopeful; everyone prepared for the foot march through the forests. Meanwhile on 1 February conditions on Reichsstrasse 167 between Neuendorf and Alt-Bischofsee became increasingly difficult; the unit's columns became completely entangled with the flood of refugees. The general nervousness was further aggravated by the continuous small arms fire from the southern edges of the forest. Tank shells whizzed from the north over the road and crashed into the forest. Drizzle, fog and mist lay over the entire area.

The flak combat teams formed in the cut lines, heavy machine-gun squads and anti-tank guns fired along the forest roads whenever they needed to get past another group of Russians.

Up front, before Kunersdorf, the previously unsuccessful breakthrough attempts were resumed. *Oberst* Rudel's tank-busting aircraft finally appeared in the sky, dropping bombs and firing armor-piercing ammunition at targets in the woods. And finally, finally, those outside had become aware of the Kampfgruppe's desperate situation. Rudel's aircraft brought some relief to those holding out on the road and not a little hope that a way out might yet be found. Meanwhile all of the heavy weapons were moved forward; the two batteries of artillery went into position just northeast of Neu-Bischof and opened fire on the surrounding woods. II./Pz.Gren.Rgt. was moved forward on foot as was the flak battery, at least those elements not deployed against the forest edges. Excessive nervousness reigned among the Kampfgruppe staff in the manor house near Neu-Bischofsee. The accursed Stalin tanks put another shell through the roof. The wife of the owner cared for the men in the house, making food, coffee and soup.

Her daughter went from room to room, taking care of the wounded in the cellar and trying to cheer them up.

Sometime on the evening of 2 February the Kampfgruppe commander, *Oberst* Langkeit, decided to call all of his commanders together for a conference. A way out had to be found—one way or another!

It was about 23:00 hours by the time all of the commanders were assembled in a wooden shed. They listened in silence to the brief situation report by the Ia, General Staff *Major* Spaeter; it offered little hope. Surrounded everywhere. And then there was the ammunition situation. The artillery was down to two shells per gun! Under these circumstances a breakthrough seemed hopeless; it was therefore decided to proceed on foot through the forest so as to at least save the men.

The *Oberst* quoted the *Führer* order: if any of the commanders present knew a better way out he might assume command of the unit. He had no means left with which to get out of this situation. It was 23:55 hours—just before midnight. Silent and exhausted, the commanders went their separate ways.

And yet they finally reached the conclusion that everything had to be committed to force a way through to Kunersdorf. Better that some men sacrifice themselves than everyone be killed there in the concentrated fire of the Soviets.

Kampfgruppe commander *Oberst* Langkeit had listened to the arguments of his commanders and now gave the breakout order—clearly and impartially. The attack was to take place early in the morning along the road with *Major* Hudel's few remaining armored vehicles. The attempt failed, however.

I./Pz.Gren.Rgt. under *Major* Petereit subsequently attacked again to the right of the road (to the northwest) into the forest in order to silence the enemy troops there firing into the Kampfgruppe's flank. Petereit, fighting at the side of his men, succeeded in gaining a foothold there, cleared the forest and eliminated the threat from the flank.

The Hetzer tank-destroyers of the Jagdpanzer-Kompanie were now moved forward and Hudel also attacked along the road. Finally, at about 14:00 hours, the enemy was dislodged. The first vehicles at the head of the column began moving, followed by the tanks, toward Kunersdorf. There there was another brief firefight at a Soviet tank barricade, in which *Feldwebel* Riedmüller distinguished himself by knocking out four T 34s. When the unfavorable terrain prevented him from reaching the other T 34s with his Hetzer, he climbed out of his vehicle and destroyed two more with a *Panzerfaust*. He was decorated with the Knight's Cross for this action.

More and more vehicles were rolling through Kunersdorf, past the airfield and into the suburbs of Frankfurt. II./Pz.Gren.Rgt. initially occupied flanking positions in Kunersdorf, while the artillery immediately changed positions to the first houses of Frankfurt so as to be able to watch over the movements from there. The bulk of Kampfgruppe Langkeit, however, initially stopped in the Frankfurt suburb of Damm, where it regrouped, assembled and then moved to the west bank into the barracks on the exit road to the west. Only the II./Pz.Gren.Rgt., the Art.Abt. Buboltz and the 11. (IG.) Kp. remained on the city's east bank, where they held a bridgehead around Damm, receiving a continuous flow of reinforcements from the fortress troops in Frankfurt.

II./Pz.Gren.Rgt. became engaged in heavy fighting at the Kunersdorf airfield, in which *Major* Schöttler was wounded. Hptm. Windeck, leader of the battalion supply company, assumed command. These battles in the Frankfurt bridgehead, which in the first days were fought solely by the men of the II./Pz.Gren.Rgt. together with a company of Croatian mountain troops of the 7. SS-Freiwilligen Gebirgs-Division Prinz Eugen with support from the 11. (IG.) Kp./Pz.Gren.Rgt. and the artillery battalion, prevented the surprise capture of the Damm bridgehead by the Soviets and also made it possible for this bridgehead to be reinforced and held until mid-April 1945. In addition they also made it possible for the Kampfgruppe to rest and regroup. The casualties suffered by this battalion were relatively heavy, especially in missing; they included Oblt. Kühne, commander of 6. Kp., and several squads from the same company.

In the barracks in Frankfurt, however, the companies and battalions rested, regrouped, received replacements, overhauled their weapons and equipment and hoped for a long break in the fighting.

On 3 February the new Ia arrived at the Kampfgruppe command post. He was General Staff *Major* von Hopffgarten, who was transferred to the Pz.Gren.Div. *Kurmark* effective 1 February. With him was General Staff *Major* Lingenthal, formerly of the 11. Pz.Div., who was to be his future second general staff officer (Ib). Thus the temporary assignment of the previous Ia, General Staff *Major* Spaeter, was over; he returned to Cottbus, where new orders were waiting.

The Panzer-Grenadier Division *Kurmark* (abbreviated KmK) was established. Its commander was *Oberst* Langkeit, although there were doubts about the nature of its organization. These were not alleviated even after the arrival of *Major* Count von Rothkirch, commander of I./Pz.Rgt. *Brandenburg* (formerly I./Pz.Rgt. 26), who together with his four companies of the latest Panzer V Panthers had been transferred to the KmK Division. This meant a considerable increase in fighting strength, which together with the tank-destroyers of the Pz.Jagd.Stu.Gesch.Kp 1551 represented a potent armored force.

Also arriving in these days were the first units for the Pz.Aufkl.Abt. KmK, one reconnaissance troop from Cottbus, then elements of Kampfgruppe Gersdorf. This new battalion slowly took shape with two armored troop carrier troops under the command of *Major* Baron von Albedyll.

Following the arrival of a second tank-destroyer company similar to Oblt. Lützow's existing Hetzer company, a panzer regiment headquarters was established and preparations made for the formation of a Pz.Rgt. KmK. *Major* Hudel was placed in command. The following units were created with new names:

I. (Pz.Jgd.)/1551/Pz.Rgt. Kurmark

II. (Pz. V)/(BR)/Pz.Rgt. Kurmark

(The departed *Major* Hudel was replaced by *Major* Frotscher, while Hptm. von dem Busche arrived to take the place of the missing *Major* Count Rothkirch as commander of II. Abt. (BR).)

Meanwhile the Art.Abt. KmK was bolstered by the arrival of another battery from Guben. It was the new 1. Bttr. under the command of Oblt. Jaeger, which, coming from the field division, was intended to form the foundation of the Pz.Korps-Art.Rgt. GD. Since the latter was never formed, however, the old battery was assigned to the Art.Abt. KmK.

The battalion's organization in those days was as follows:

Battalion commander: Hptm. Buboltz
Adjutant and leader of HQ battery: Lt. Vogel
1st Battery: Oblt. Jaeger (with 4 s.FH)
2nd Battery: Lt. Rolke (Oblt. Hoesch) (with 4 s.FH)
3rd Battery: Lt. Esslinger (with 4 l.FH)

Most of the non-commissioned officers came from the Pz.Art.Ers.-u. Ausb.Abt. GD at Guben and most of these were veterans of numerous actions in Russia. The enlisted men included new and old soldiers who quickly came to understand one another.

The officers—those who were not already members of the GD—were Lt. Vogel, Lt. Biesewig, Lt. Behn, lt. Puxkandl, Lt. Meier, Lt. Hielscher, Lt. Schwander—all transferred from the Gross-Born artillery school.

Chapter 2
Defensive Battles on the Oder Front

Soon the first tactical emblems appeared, familiar ones: it was the white steel helmet, which came from the Pz.Gren.ers.-Brigade GD. In some case the Kurmark eagle was added to the steel helmets. At first cuff titles were worn only by the veterans of the GD; later, however, they were presented to everyone. In spite of the military situation and the fact that it was 1945, everyone placed great value on being in a GD unit.

The events that followed 4 February 1945 are recorded in the writings of the Ia (Operations Officer), General Staff *Major* von Hopff-garten, which provide a good description of those turbulent times:

4 February 1945

General enemy situation:

The foremost elements of the Soviet 1st White Russian Front under Zhukov are closing in on the Oder, with the 69th Army between Frankfurt and Lebus, the 8th Guards Army on both sides of Göritz and the 5th Shock Army on both sides of Küstrin. Küstrin new city fell on 2-3 February.

Frankfurt—Kunersdorf sector:

Toward noon heavy enemy attacks with infantry and assault guns against Kunersdorf station and brickworks east of Kunersdorf, later also against the eastern outskirts of the town.

Successful counterattacks by II./Pz.Gren.Rgt. KmK initially restored the former front line. South of the Frankfurt—Reppen rail line enemy infantry and tanks advanced to the airfield and threatened the right flank of II. Btl.

Göritz sector:

With the help of frozen clumps of straw and bushes, 1 to 2 regiments of enemy troops crossed the ice-covered Oder west of Göritz, drove out the pickets of the Reagener Division (an RAD battalion) and in the early afternoon took the village of Reitwein. In the process they occupied an orphanage located at the exit from the village. This still housed children and nurses, which in later counterattacks precluded its destruction by tank fire.

Later the enemy continued his attack against the northeast end of Reitweiner Hill, which he reached at about 16:00 hours.

Numerous anti-tank guns, mortars and light field guns at the Göritz crossing point; the bulk of an enemy division in and on both sides of Göritz.

Orders and instructions by Raegener Division and Pz.Gren.Div. KmK:

At about 09:00 hours telephone call from Army Group Vistula (Himmler) to KmK stating that the KmK's Ia, General Staff Major von Hopffgarten, is to proceed to Regener Division immediately as that unit's Ia—command post in Podelzig..

At about 15:00 hours another telephone call from V. SS-Geb. A.K.: elements I./Pz.Gren.Rgt. KmK and II. Btl. (BR)/Pz.Rgt. are to immediately reach the area due south of Podelzig and are subordinated to the Raegener Division for a counterattack on the Göritz crossing site.

16:15 hours report by alert battalion to Raegener Division: battalion-strength enemy force has occupied north-east end of Reitweiner Hill.

16:20 hours order from Raegener Division to alert battalion and Feldherrnhalle Battalion: Feldherrnhalle Battalion to attack astride the Wuhden—Reitwein road, alert battalion along the Podelzig—Reitwein road. Attack enemy on Reitweiner Hill and initially take Reitwein. Main body of II. (BR)/Pz.Rgt. KmK (Panther battalion) will advance on Podelzig road, Hathenow as far as the brickworks, turn east and take the village of Reitwein by way of the Reitwein estate in cooperation with the alert battalion and the Feldherrnhalle Battalion. III./SS-Art.-Lehr-Rgt. to support the attack on Reitweiner Hill from positions in the Mallnow area.

Start of attack: 17:00 hours.

Except for operations staff, division headquarters Kurmark to transfer via Rathstock and Dolgelin to Libbenichen and set up new command post there. Operations staff initially to Podelzig estate.

Elements of Kurmark attached to Fortress Frankfurt:

I./Art.Rgt. KmK to support II./Pz.Gren.Rgt. KmK near Kunersdorf from positions on both sides of the road southwest of the exit from Frankfurt. Remaining elements of the Pz.Gren.Rgt. KmK to assemble at the Frankfurt barracks.

18:00 hours order from fortress commander Frankfurt to II./Pz.Gren.Rgt. KmK: at 18:00 hours withdraw into the Damm suburb position. A company of the SS-Geb.Div. Prinz Eugen will cover withdrawal in and near Kunersdorf.

Raegener Division/Ia:

18:00 hours order from Raegener Division to I./Pz.Gren.Rgt. KmK: I. Btl. is to advance via northern edge of Klessin toward the west bank of the Oder against the Göritz crossing point and barricade it.

Göritz sector:

At about 17:00 hours I./Pz.Gren.Rgt. KmK under Major Petereit reached the southern edge of Podelzig and then launched an attack on the Göritz crossing site. The attack bogged down in the darkness in the Oder meadows due south of the crossing point under heavy enemy anti-tank and machine-gun fire. The attack by the Feldherrnhalle Battalion ran into an enemy attack and also bogged down approximately 500 meters north of Wuhden. The battalion dug in there.

The attack by the alert battalion also failed and it ultimately dug in approximately 500 meters southwest of the forest's edge at Reitweiner Hill.

II. (BR)/Pz.Rgt. KmK reached the brickworks north of Podelzig at about 17:00 hours. Subsequent attack in darkness toward the burning village of Reitwein failed as a result of strong enemy anti-tank defense.

Stragglers from an RAD battalion, about a company strong, defended Gut Reitwein against weak enemy attacks.

On orders of the Raegener Division the II. (BR)/Pz.Rgt. KmK withdrew toward the brickworks and during the night guarded the division's open flank.

I./Pz.Gren.Rgt. KmK received orders to break off the attack on the crossing point and to stand by in Wuhden during the night of 4-5 February as counter-attack reserve.

Major Petereit withdrew the elements of his I. Btl. The men groaned beneath the weight of the ammunition boxes, base plates and carriages as they hauled them through the morass of the Oder meadows. Not until midnight was Wuhden reached, where the exhausted men threw themselves down in the first pile of straw they came across.

The consequences were clear: the committed battalions—with the exception of the I./Pz.Gren.Rgt. KmK, inadequate alert units unsuited to such an operation—were much too weak to dislodge an enemy prepared for counterattacks. Instead, he exploited the confusion on the German side to advance southwest toward Klessin, which could only be held as a result of a maximum effort. The fighting worth of the few alert units of the Raegener Division was virtually nil.

So passed the night of 4-5 February, which was to present the command of the Kurmark Division with missions as difficult of those the day before.

5 February 1945

Frankfurt sector:

Under heavy pressure from the enemy, at about noon our rear guards (a company of the SS-Geb.Div. Prinz Eugen) were forced to leave Kunersdorf. During the afternoon enemy attacks with assault guns and infantry against the Damm suburb position, which were repelled by II./Pz.Gren.Rgt. KmK. Toward evening on this day the commander of Fortress Frankfurt ordered II./Pz.Gren.Rgt. pulled out of the line and subordinated directly to the division. Its positions were taken over by fortress troops.

Göritz sector:

At dawn enemy expanded his bridgehead to the southwest and northwest with fresh forces. In the early morning hours one battalion attacked Klessin, another advanced unnoticed as far as Neu Manschnow. In Klessin there was fierce close-quarters fighting around the I./Pz.Gren.Rgt. KmK's dressing station, which was taken completely by surprise. Those wounded who could still fight defended themselves stubbornly under the outstanding leadership of their Oberarzt. Major Petereit and his battalion were able to rescue the people in Klessin at the last minute. The Oberarzt was later decorated with the Iron Cross, First Class. For the rest of the day no further attacks from the bridgehead.

Strong enemy anti-tank and mortar units already on the west bank of the Oder.

At the request of the Raegener Division the V. SS-Geb.A.K. placed I./Art.Rgt. KmK under the division's command. In the evening the III./SS-Art.Lehr.Rgt. with 7.-9. (l.FH) Bttr. was sent to the regiment and placed under its command. After initial difficulties cooperation was very good. Officers: SS-Stubaf. Schünemann, Major Petereit. The latter was wounded again and had to give up the command of his battalion. New commander of I./Pz.Gren.Rgt. KmK was Hptm. Pollmann, formerly of the Lehr-Rgt. BR. At about 09:00 hours radio message from V. SS-Geb.A.K. to the Raegener Division: at 10:00 hours Pz.Abt.(BR)/Pz.Rgt. KmK is to attack via Rathstock toward Neu Manschnow, clear the area Neu Manschnow—south edge of Kietz of weak enemy forces and subsequently establish contact with Fortress Küstrin.

At about 15:00 hours radio message from V. SS-Geb.A.K. to the Raegener Division: Inf.Rgt. Kriegsschule Dresden (abbr. KS Dresden) will arrive at Raegener Division during the night and will support its attack against Reitweiner Hill.

Repeated requests by the Kurmark division command to overturn the assignment of the 1st General Staff Officer, General Staff Major von Hopffgarten, to the Raegener Division were rejected by the corps. Similar requests were made to the Inspector-General of Armored Forces and HPA/P3.

Furthermore, the KmK division command submitted a request to commit the entire Pz.Gren.Div. KmK in the Raegener Division's sector in order to end the fragmentation of the division.

Göritz sector:

After the enemy had been driven from the eastern outskirts of Klessin by elements of I./Pz.Gren.Rgt. KmK, on order of the Raegener Division the latter was deployed in a defensive role in Klessin next to the Feldherrnhalle Battalion in Wuhden, simultaneously establishing contact with the RAD battalion in Lebus. Elements of the Volkssturm Battalion Potsdam were incorporated.

The attack by II. (BR)/Pz.Rgt. KmK ran into a strong anti-tank defense in Neu Manschnow and was beaten back. The regimental commander, Major Count Rothkirch, who accompanied the attack, was knocked out with his tank in Neu Manschnow and has been missing since. Four of our tanks sustained hits but were recovered during the night.

The Pz.Abt. (BR) withdrew toward Herzershof and Rathstock and on orders from the division covered its open left flank. Obstlt. Klüver, the commander of the Pz.Gren.Rgt., was seriously wounded in the upper arm during a scouting mission and had to go to the rear. The first elements of KS Dresden arrived in Niederjesar in the evening and received orders to send one battalion to Podelzig and another, later arriving battalion to Lebus. During the night leading elements of II./Pz.Gren.Rgt. KmK, which had meanwhile been pulled out of the line, arrived in the area of operations north of Frankfurt.

6 February—Enemy Situation:

The 1st White Russian Front has reached the Oder between Frankfurt and Küstrin with 3 to 4 divisions.

Weaker enemy forces apparently are only serving the purpose of improving the positions reached the previous day.

Our own bridgehead east of Frankfurt and the garrison of the old city of Küstrin were able to fend off repeated enemy attacks. The enemy is gradually completing his buildup of artillery and divisions between Frauendorf and Küstrin.

East of Lebus strong enemy patrols are attempting to approach the bank of the Oder.

Near Klessin, north of Wuhden and near Podelzig strong enemy offensive patrol activity.

North of Reitwein to southern edge of Kietz no combat activity. Enemy expanding his positions on Reitweiner Hill; enemy troops in front line estimated to be regiment strength. Neu-Manschnow area only weakly occupied, however numerous anti-tank guns. Enemy reinforcing the ice cover at the Göritz crossing.

Own Situation (Raegener Division and Kurmark)

In spite of subordination of elements of the KmK Div. on previous day the Raegener Division only able to occupy its front strongpoint-style. The division sees its primary mission as that of preventing the enemy from advancing further toward Podelzig, Wuhden and Klessin.

At the cost of consciously denuding the right and left division flanks, the Klessin—Wuhden—Podelzig triangle was strengthened through stricter organization and position building.

Apart from the I./Pz.Gren.Rgt. the combat value of the remaining alert units can only be seen as limited. With the troops at its disposal, the Raegener Division was also not in a position to carry out a successful attack on Reitweiner Hill on 6 February.

The RAD battalion west of Reitwein, the alert battalion and Feldherrnhalle Battalion suffered serious losses in the fighting on 4 and 5 February, which further degraded their value as fighting units.

The division expressed serious reservations about the V. SS-Geb.Korps' requested employment of the II. (BR)/Pz.Rgt. KmK from the direction of Podelzig against the heavily-wooded nose of Reitweiner Hill without its own escorting infantry and inadequate artillery support. In the division's opinion this plan of attack would result in crippling losses to the panzer battalion while failing to achieve its objective.

The arrival of the KSW Dresden at least represented a local reinforcement. In spite of this addition the Raegener Division's entire front—18 kilometers in a straight line from Burgwall to the south end of Kietz—was stretched extreme-

ly thin. The enforced use of the hodgepodge of inexperienced alert units and the piecemeal commitment of elements of the Pz.Gren.Div. KmK by the V. SS-Geb.Korps had an especially negative effect on the overall command of the battle. Since signals equipment and supply installations were lacking, there were grounds to fear that the enemy might be able to break into the division's front with an energetic attack.

Orders and instructions to the Raegener Division/1a KmK

02:00 hours. Order to KS Dresden:

By dawn KS Dresden is to take over the Podelzig sector with one battalion and prepare to defend there indefinitely. The remnants of the alert battalion is subordinated to the KS Dresden.

II./KS Dresden (division reserve in the Mallnow area) is to stand ready for a counterattack against a possible enemy penetration into the Klessin—Wuhden—Podelzig triangle as well as in the direction of Lebus.

03:00 hours order Ia to II. (BR)/Pz.Rgt. KmK:

As before, panzer battalion to secure the division's left flank in the Reitwein—Seelow road—Küstrin sector from the Rathstock—Herzershof area. One panzer company to reach southern edge of Podelzig by dawn and stand by at the division's disposal for possible counterattack into the Klessin—Wuhden—Podelzig triangle. For this purpose contact is to be established immediately with KS Dresden.

Approximately 03:30 hours division order to the Art.Rgt. KmK:

Art.Rgt. KmK to support the defensive battle from existing positions with main effort north of Podelzig. Barrage fire zones to be prepared in front of Wuhden and Podelzig sectors, harassing fire on Görlitz crossing site as ammunition stocks permit.

Morning radio message V. SS-Geb.A.K. to Raegener Division and Kurmark:

Relief of Raegener Division without troops by Pz.Gren.Div. KmK expected at noon on 7/2/1945. Begin preparations.

Pz.Gren.Div. KmK to SS-Korps:

KmK requests removal of subordination to Fortress Frankfurt and movement of all KmK elements in Frankfurt into the Raegener sector.

Order from V. SS-Geb.A.K. to Raegener Division:

Preparations for attack on Reitweiner Hill to begin immediately.

Apart from several enemy barrages on recognized positions the day was uneventful.

The following radio message from V. SS-Geb.A.K. was received at about midnight on 7 February 1945:

"At 12:00 hours on 7/2/1945 Pz.Gren.Div. KmK is to assume command of the sector and Raegener alert unit. No decision yet concerning subordination of remaining KmK units to Fortress Frankfurt."

Continuous enemy mortar fire and isolated surprise barrages on the entire front. Otherwise uneventful. At noon Pz.Gren.Div. Kurmark assumed command over the sector and troops of the Raegener Division. Kurmark command post in Libbenichen.

The tense situation on Reitweiner Hill and the fact that the approximately eight-kilometer-wide left flank is guarded by only II. (BR)/Pz.Rgt. KmK is causing the division command serious concern.

In the midmorning the defensive focal point northeast of Podelzig was bolstered by the insertion of I./KS Dresden. II./KS Dresden was not able to reach its assembly area east of Mallnow until dusk on 6 February.

In the afternoon the enemy launched a surprise attack against the positions of the I./KS Dresden northeast of Podelzig in regiment strength. The enemy then succeeded in breaking into the most forward positions on the Podelzig—Reitwein road. An immediate counterattack by the I./KS Dresden and the independent intervention by the Pz.Kp./II. (BR)/Pz.Rgt. KmK under the energetic command of Lt. Count Rothkirch (div. reserve) drove the enemy back into the forest on Reitweiner Hill.

In spite of an enemy anti-tank barrier Lt. Leopold Count Rothkirch and his five tanks were able to crush five enemy anti-tank guns and silence others with gunfire. Because of the onset of darkness the tanks had to break off their attack in the heavily wooded terrain and were able to return without loss. In addition to 200 killed the enemy lost several hundred wounded. A heavily fortified system of positions and large numbers of infantry were identified on Reitweiner Hill.

During the course of the counterattack I./KS Dresden was able to advance its positions as far as both sides of Hill 71—approximately 700 meters southwest of the forest edge. Exploiting the success of its neighbor to the left, the Feldherrnhalle Battalion was able to establish a strongpoint on the hill.

When the enemy attack began, on orders from the Kurmark Division Ia, II./KS Dresden was to attack immediately from its assembly area east of Mallnow toward Podelzig. On orders from division, it remained there in reserve and came under heavy enemy mortar fire.

The Pz.Gren.Div. Kurmark was now in command of a defensive sector north of Frankfurt approximately 18 kilometers wide. Equipped as a panzer division and ideally suited as an operational reserve, it instead found itself in a stationary defense because the situation left no other choice. It held its positions there, sometimes in heavy fighting, in which the names Wuhden, Klessin and Schloss Reitwein figured prominently. It stood and fought as a GD unit until mid-April without taking one step back. In these weeks it had succeeded in temporarily halting the Soviet advance. It was 7 February 1945.

Chapter 3
Replacement Units in the Battle for Guben

Only a few days later, on 13 February, farther south the units of III./Pz.Gren.Ers. u. Ausb.Rgt. GD, Pz.Art.Ers. u. Ausb.Abt. GD and other replacement units in Guben were placed on alert. The enemy was approaching, his armored spearheads were nearing Crossen, and his appearance at the gates of Guben had to be expected soon.

Guben, a typical city on the Lausitz, lay between Forst and the confluence of the Lausitzer Neiße on both sides of this small stream. Surrounded by forests, the southern approaches to the city were flat with fields and meadows, while the center of the city was hilly and to the east of the city the terrain changed over to low, mostly wooded hills. There were also higher hills, such as Ullrichs Hill, Adolph Wolf Hill and the hill with the Bismarck Tower. The city itself was divided by the Neiße, with approximately two-thirds of the city east of the river, and the railway station and the other third lying west of the Neiße in a flat depression.

Apart from occasional air raid alerts, life was still completely normal for the civilian population of Guben in January 1945. Naturally there was a tangible feeling of unrest with the first reports of the approach of the front. Some of the business people sold off their stocks, here and there families moved away, as did some of the soldiers based in Guben, who, based on a fixed plan, were transported west by truck or train. It must be stressed that the civilian population behaved magnificently and, trusting in their soldiers, stuck it out to the end. Later this went so far that requests for the setting up of command posts were only grudgingly accepted because it was seen as an infringement into the private area. Among the units based in the city at the beginning of 1945 were the Pz.Art.Ers. u. Ausb.Abt. GD and the San.Ers.Abt. (3) GD in the Mückenberg Barracks, and III./Pz.Gren.Ers. u. Ausb.Rgt. GD in the barracks at the north exit from the city, near the Bismarck Tower. In addition, other non-GD units were stationed in other buildings in the city.

In mid-January 1945 recruits were still being taken in; most were 16 or 17 years old. They came in small groups and not in the usual large numbers needed to fill the barracks. The shortage of suitable men was becoming noticeable. They were still full of enthusiasm about their infantry training, however, and were convinced that their efforts could still help avert the fate that was threatening Germany.

After just fourteen days of training they were sent to build positions in the defenses all around Guben. This defense line essentially followed the Neiße, bent in a northeast direction due north of Gubinchen (south of the city) following the border of the city, ran north past the Guben suburb, and then along the border of the city to the northwest, returning to the Neiße. Most of the positions were dug out of the earth, as well there were several underground fighting positions and braced tunnels. There was no continuous system of trenches, apart perhaps from a few individual sections.

A total of three lines had been scouted and these were to be occupied piece by piece. III./Pz.Gren.Ers. u. Ausb.Rgt. GD, commanded initially by Hptm. Weizenbeck then by *Major* Kriege, committed the following units:

9. Kp. – Oblt. Schonger: along the Neiße south of the city, including Gubinchen to roughly the crossing of the railroad and Road 112 (south of the Werder suburb).

10. Kp. – Hptm. Thormeyer: from rail crossing in a northeast direction toward Kiekebusch, to approximately the Gr. Bösitz—Guben City road.

11. Kp. – Oblt. Kelle: next to 10. Kp. at east end of East Cemetery, from the crematorium to the Crossener—Germersdorfer road fork.

3. Art.Kp. – Lt. Ambross: From there north along Reichsstrasse 97,

1. Art.Kp. – Lt. Kieslich: northwest to approximately Hill 105.4, where contact was made with

2. Art.Kp. – Lt. Loos: this unit had contact with elements of the SS-Brigade Dirlewanger, which held the positions as far as the Neiße.

The three artillery companies were under the command of the sector commander, Hptm. Kirsten, who had his command post in the Bürgerheim.

The military commander of Guben was *Major* Theermann, former commander of the Pz.Art.Ers. u. Ausb.Abt. GD, a wearer of the German Cross in Gold. His command post was in the revenue office near the Neiße, in the inner city.

Everyone was mobilization ready, to immediately occupy their designated positions on the issuing of a code-word. The practice was that each company would occupy the positions that it had fortified itself.

The alert was sounded on 13 February and the code-word was issued. The enemy was not there yet, but the prepared positions were occupied. The Mückenberg Barracks were hastily evacuated, the inventory was sent west, dispatch riders headed east to remain in constant contact with the troops at the front and bring back any reports on the enemy situation.

The troops were poorly equipped; modern weapons such as automatic rifles were scarce and there were few machine-guns. The heavy weapons situation was even worse; mortars and anti-aircraft guns, which were later used in a ground role, were all that was available to oppose the massed artillery of the Russians. There were almost no anti-tank guns; the *Panzerfaust* was the only defensive weapon against the expected enemy tanks.

The population was now systematically requested to leave the city. In not a single case did the authorities convince them to leave their cellars, some of which had been furnished as living quarters. Entire groups of civilians stayed and prepared to weather the storm.

The troops were on alert, however they continued to improve and fortify their positions.

At this time the city became the target of heavy enemy air raids. The first Soviet troops appeared on 17 February. They advanced in company strength from the area south of Schenkendorf (into the area of Oblt. Schonger's 9. Kp.) toward the forward strongpoint of Gubinchen, which was evacuated. However, after a brief but fierce exchange of fire, the enemy withdrew. Subsequent repeated night attacks by the Soviets were also repulsed, during the course of which one machine-gunner was killed after he and his second gunner had killed more than 20 Soviets.

Two days later, on 19 February, Soviet artillery fire began, concentrated on the city center. That same evening the Soviets launched an infantry attack along Crossener Street against the right wing of the 3. Art.Kp. (Lt. Ambross) which was defending there, resulting in a penetration into the positions. However, as hastily-organized counterattack by convalescents under the command of Lt. Kieslich drove the enemy out again and restored the old line.

One day later, on 20 February, the enemy renewed his attack at Crossener Street, this time with tanks, and made considerable inroads into the positions. Alert units thrown into the break-in point were able to prevent a deeper penetration, but only at the cost of heavy casualties. In the evening hours, however, our positions were pulled back to the third line held by elements of the San.Ers.Abt. (3) GD. These positions were inside the city, which led to fierce street fighting.

On 21 February the enemy attacked along Crossener Street again with tank support and in one go was able to advance as far as the Hindenburg School, the command post of the 1. Art.Kp. The defenders fought with *Panzerfausts* and destroyed one enemy tank from close range. In the days that followed, however, the enemy, suspecting a stronger garrison in Guben, slowed his advance and limited himself to offensive patrol activity. There was heavy small-scale fighting in the streets, from house to house. This also resulted in the situation of the Russians holding the house fronts on the left side of Seeckt Street and our troops those on the right side. By day the fighting died down, except for sniper activity, whereas at night there was much close-quarters fighting and patrol activity. This was the element of the lone fighter. The *Panzerfaust* proved ideal for ambushes against enemy machine-gun nests or snipers. In order to retain our freedom of movement, each night passages were knocked through house walls and cellar roofs, entire streets were equipped with underground passageways, until gradually all reporting and reinforcement traffic moved underground into the cellars and houses.

In those days too a young soldier, just 17, succeeded in destroying a T 34 with his *Panzerfaust* from a distance of just seven meters. He subsequently rendered the crew, which had bailed out, incapable of fighting.

The small-scale war continued until about 26 February. On that day there was suddenly heavy artillery and mortar fire, which was especially hard on our positions at the East Cemetery and the crematorium. This was followed by an infantry attack in such strength that the defending 10. Kp., whose ranks had already been seriously thinned, had to abandon the fiercely contested East Cemetery. New foxholes were dug in the open field at the foot of the crematorium hill under enemy fire. A further advance by the Soviets was halted.

Enemy tanks fired directly into the positions of the 1. Art.Kp. and in a short time inflicted more than 30 casualties.

The situation in the city of Guben became extremely critical and gave cause for serious concern. If the enemy wanted, a strong attack could take him to the Neiße—through the entire city. It was a miracle that he hadn't done so already.

Major Theermann, himself sitting in the revenue office and besieged with bad news hourly, no longer saw any possibility of holding the city as a bridgehead on the east bank. It may have been 26 or 27 February when he silently headed west into the woods on the far side of the Neiße and sought death with his family. He could no longer bear the nervous strain. An impetuous action? No one can say. None of his comrades thought it possible; but much was understandable at that point in time. Hptm. Kirsten, unaware of what had happened to *Major* Theermann, led the countermeasures in his sector, which was threatened by the Soviet attack. A courageous counterattack resulted in the regaining of a tenable position, and in the days that followed the Soviets did not initiate any large-scale offensive actions. Hptm. Kirsten was later awarded the Knight's Cross for his actions.

Gradually new units arrived, reinforcing our positions and regaining the old lines in joint counterattacks. Only at the airfield was this not possible.

The defenders now launched several operations of their own. Lt. Loos of the 2. Art.Kp. carried out an assault on the enemy-held Ullrichs Hill with a handful of OB. NCOs, capturing prisoners and weapons and driving the enemy off this commanding hill. Loos was subsequently awarded the Iron Cross, First Class.

Among the reinforcements that arrived was Brigade 100 under *General* Berger; its Silesian *Volkssturm* battalions significantly bolstered Guben's defenses. The brigade was subordinated to the GD replacement units; cooperation between the units was very good. In command of this sector of the Neiße was XXXX. Pz.Korps under *General der Panzertruppe* Siegfried

Henrici and his chief-of-staff General Staff *Oberst* Berlin.

On 1 March between 18: and 19:00 hours another daring but unfortunately questionable operation was initiated by the 1. and 2. Art. Kp. with the objective of reaching the Bismarck Tower, which was supposedly still being defended by a small group of about 70 German soldiers.

The Loos company was supposed to advance straight toward the Bismarck Tower, the Kieslich company against a neighboring hill, the lonely Fichte, in order to prevent Loos from being flanked.

Within twenty minutes the attackers stormed the Bismarck Tower and also took the neighboring hill, however the latter had to be abandoned again in the face of superior enemy forces. There was no sign of an encircled group of German soldiers. Finally the Bismarck Tower, which had been badly damaged by shellfire and explosives, was also abandoned when the Soviets began a counterattack. When at about midnight the two companies returned to their starting positions, both having unfortunately suffered considerable losses, they were informed laconically by the commanding SS-Brigade Dirlewanger that there had been no need to carry out this mission because the encircled group had already been captured in the afternoon.

On or about 10 March the enemy launched another general attack in an effort to take the part of Guben on the east bank of the Neiße. Supported by very heavy artillery and mortar fire, the Soviets stormed through the rows of houses to the bank of the Neiße. But this attempt by the enemy also failed in fierce street and house fighting. The enemy was stopped and later driven back to his starting positions.

After this the fighting died down and was limited to isolated operations, all of which continued to wear down the strength of the defenders.

On 16 March the elements of the Pz.Gren.-Ersatz-Brigade GD deployed in Guben were relieved by elements of the SS-Brigade Dirlewanger and pulled out of the line. While the bulk of the artillery companies returned to the Ersatz-Brigade in Cottbus and on to Silesia, on orders from above the III./Pz.Gren.Ers. u. Ausb.Rgt. GD under *Major* Kriege was incorporated into the *Führer*-Grenadier-Division, where it became II. Btl./F.Gren.Rgt. 4 (Sommer Regiment).

When the fighting in the Guben bridgehead was over, a total of 52 non-commissioned officers and enlisted men of the GD were buried in the village cemetery in Schenkendöbern. 11. Kp. alone had 23 of its number buried there.

The Guben bridgehead was an heroic episode in German military history, waged by young recruits and veterans of the *Großdeutschland* replacement units.

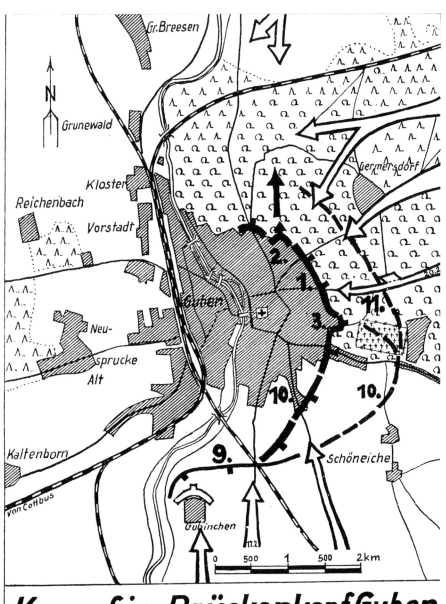

Kampf im Brückenkopf Guben
17.2. — 10.3.1945

Fighting in the Bridgehead at Guban
17 February to 10 March 1945

Part V
The Führer Divisions in the North and South of the Eastern Front

Chapter 1
FBD and FGD at Arnswalde – Lauban – Jägerndorf

In spite of the collapse of the German Eastern Front, following the Soviet breakthrough in January the German high command took desperate actions to put a stop to the Soviet spearheads that had advanced deepest into Germany. The hanging back of both flanks of the Soviet offensive—in the north roughly to Danzig, in the south roughly to Breslau—appeared to at least theoretically make possible the commitment of two attack groups from the area southeast of Stettin and from the Guben—Glogau area given sufficient reserves. That was the situation in the first days of February 1945.

The German side simply lacked the forces necessary for an operation of such scope, however. As well, there was the fact that against the wishes of his generals Hitler had sent the forces released from the western front to Hungary and Italy and did not make them available for this operation.

The few units left after the front had been stabilized were thus sufficient only for a limited flanking thrust from the Arnswalde area toward Landsberg/Warthe, which in the best case might take the Soviet forces north of Küstrin on the Oder in the rear.

By 15 February the forces earmarked for this operation had been assembled. Commanding this sector of the front was the headquarters of the 3. Pz.Armee under *Generaloberst* Rauss, the army having been pulled out of East Prussia.

Strong Soviet attacks against the line Pyritz—Arnswalde had been repulsed and the area southeast of Stettin, vital to our own buildup, was held.

Among the divisions earmarked to take part in the offensive were the *Führer-Grenadier-Division* and the *Führer-Begleit-Division*, which had only been reorganized into division formations during the rail transport. The order for these reorganizations, for which at least a few days of quiet were hoped, was issued by Hitler on 15 January and transmitted verbally by the *Führer*'s army adjutant, *Major* Johannmeyer. The commanders of both units, *Oberst* Mäder and *Oberst* Remer, were requested to appear in person at headquarters in Zossen. The two made their way separately to Berlin.

Oberst Remer, commander of the *Führer-Begleit-Division* (abbr. FBD), arrived in Berlin in the last days of January and reported to Hitler. There followed a detailed report on the course of the Ardennes offensive with open opinions as to the reason why it had to fail. Remer did not hide his feelings. Hitler, very impressed by what he had to say, dismissed Remer after assigning him his future area of operations and stressing the decisive importance of this offensive near Arnswalde.

From Berlin Remer threw all the switches necessary to drive on the expansion of his unit into a division, to obtain the additional required units as quickly as possible.

Oberst Mäder did not arrive in Berlin until 5 February and reported to the Reich Chancellery at about 10:00 hours. There he met the *Führer*'s army adjutant, *Major* Johannmeyer, who suggested that his arrival at such an usual hour, when everyone there was still sleeping, was not exactly desirable. Since Hitler always worked until about three in the morning, he used the morning hours to rest. This also applied to reports from headquarters, which could not arrive at *Führer* Headquarters until after midnight.

General Burgdorf, who happened to run into Mäder, asked in astonishment why he—Mäder—was not still in Pomerania. Mäder—it was now his turn to be astonished—merely said that he had not yet received a transport number, that instead the first elements of his brigade were just entraining on so-called free trains (non-assigned or surplus trains) of the SS-Pz.Div. "Das Reich" (without travel numbers!).

Mäder was shown in toward evening. After the SS had searched him for weapons, he was led by *Major* Johannmeyer to see Hitler.

Hitler: *My congratulations on your high decoration (Oak Leaves). As well I am awarding you the cuff title "Führer-Grenadier-Division" in honor of the fallen, in recognition of the living and to inspire those yet to come to the division!*

There was a brief pause, during which Hitler sat down on a stool, then he continued:

Why actually are you not in Pomerania?

Mäder: *I am having to use free trains because as of today I have still not received transport numbers.*

Hitler: *(standing up) Am I being lied to again?*

Jodl was summoned. **Hitler** *asked Mäder: Why do you think the offensive in the west failed?*

Mäder: *(in main points) The terrain not suited to tanks; not enough aircraft; no fuel for tanks, etc...*

Hitler: *I will tell you what I think...*

1. Army commander Dietrich has failed. I will give him an opportunity to make amends at Budapest. The 6. SS-Pz.Armee shall prove itself there. The attack by the 6. SS-Pz.Armee there must bring about the decision! On account of the bauxite! If it fails then the war is lost.

2. The Luftwaffe proved to be a failure!

3. I wanted a broad attack area. Model a narrow one. I allowed myself to be talked out of it by Model.

4. There was too much secrecy! (Secrecy was such that it proved to be a hindrance!)

But now we are facing another decisive battle in Pomerania.

Army Group Vistula, its right wing on the Oder, its left wing east of Arnswalde, is to attack south to the Netze, in order to smash the Russian buildup at the Oder (near and north of Frankfurt).

I expect that your division will perform as well as it did in the west. For we must get one back on the Russians!

You will have some time in Pomerania to rest and refit; you will not be committed without my express order! (Führer Order) It had also been reported to me that your replacements are on their way there."

With these words Mäder was dismissed.

On 6 February, one day after his conversation with Hitler, Mäder drove to Zossen, where he had a talk with *Generaloberst* Guderian. Guderian told him, "We must fight a great battle in Pomerania. If it goes wrong, the war is lost! Every officer of your division must know this before the attack begins. I demand the utmost effort! After the Netze is reached, the *Führer* divisions will be pulled out of the line and take part in the operation from the Breslau area to the northeast."

Mäder subsequently made his way to General Staff Obstlt. Litterscheid's organizational department to obtain further details of the division's reorganization. The new division was to be brought up to a strength of 10,000 men; replacements were to be provided by the GD. Based on his experience, Mäder suggested that the division's anti-tank and anti-aircraft defenses and the firepower of its artillery and infantry be increased. *Oberst* Mäder received authorization to organize his unit within the limits of what was available.

The ideas that motivated those in charge were that the two divisions were not—and should not—be identical in their organization. Experience under new commands and on various fronts was to be gathered first before deciding on the ideal organization.

Of course consideration was given as to whether these two GD units might be bound even closer to the existing Pz.Korps GD. It is also understandable that the Pz.Korps GD had an influence on the reorganization of these two divisions, especially since there was repeated talk of combining all divisions under the command of a Panzer-Armee *Großdeutschland*. However, Hitler seemed to be pursuing other ideas in reorganizing these two divisions: he wanted to have two point of main effort divisions which he could employ where he was seeking success. Therefore these divisions were always referred to as *Führer* divisions, which were to have their own cuff titles, not those of the GD.

Thought was also given to the tactical insignia of these units. These already existed but were to be supplemented:

Pz.Korps GD	black steel helmet on yellow field
Pz.Gren.Div. GD	white steel helmet
Pz.Gren.Div. BR	red eagle on white steel helmet
Führer-Begleit-Division	yellow steel helmet
Führer-Grenadier-Division	blue steel helmet

But there was not sufficient time for any of this. In fact no FGD or FBD cuff titles were ever issued to these two *Führer* Division, so that everyone continued to wear the old black and silver *Großdeutschland* cuff titles; even the newcomers and men from other units were issued them. The white steel helmet remained. The strength reports read out at the noon situation report on 27 January 1945 reveal the state of both units:

Führer-Grenadier-Brigade—before reorganization:
4,229 men daily strength
2 Panzer IV
3 in repair
8 Panzer V
10 in repair
5 assault guns
11 in repair
27 en route

Führer-Begleit-Brigade—before reorganization:
Approximately 7,000 men daily strength.

The division units were now formed with these strengths. Each of the two divisions received another Div.Begl.Kp. and general staff officers were assigned to make a complete division headquarters.

These were:

Führer-Grenadier-Division
Ia – General Staff Obstlt. Weitbrecht
Ib – General Staff *Major* Mohr

Führer-Begleit-Division
Ia – General Staff Obstlt. Reidel
Ib – General Staff *Major* Brandt

But the desired formation into division units was never concluded. The reasons: lack of personnel, inadequate access to weapons and equipment, a shortage of soft-skinned and armored vehicles, and the lack of time and quiet in which to proceed with this formation. There was some strengthening of the units, but this never proceeded beyond the realm of improvisation—in spite of all the skill and effort of the commanders.

On 30 January the two division commanders—*Oberst* Mäder and *Oberst* Remer—were promoted to the rank of *Generalmajor*.

Meanwhile the transports rolled northeast across Germany into the area of Stettin—Stargard, where the first elements of the *Führer-Grenadier-Division* detrained in the Ruhnow area near Wangerin, northeast of Stargard, on 8 February.

The first elements of the *Führer-Begleit-Division* were received by their commander in the Freienwalde area of Pomerania, where they received immediate orders to transfer to Gross-Silber. The situation in that combat zone, in which German attack formations were supposed to regain the initiative, was more than critical when the two divisions arrived. The Soviets were again on the attack to the northwest, towards their old objective, Stettin. Their spearheads were nearing the Stargard—Freienwalde—Labes rail line, over which rolled the bulk of the transports carrying the German attack units as well as all of the 3. Pz.Armee's supply.

Commanding the sector was the 11. Pz.Armee under *SS-Obergruppenführer* Steiner, who was placed in command of the attack based on his experience.

The army issued the first attack orders to the commanders of the arriving *Führer* divisions: these stated that the *Führer-Begleit-Division* was to attack south from the Freienwalde—Tornow area in the direction of Arnswalde, the *Führer-Grenadier-Division* from the area of Nördenberg south toward Liebenow. Objective: break through to the Netze and destroy the enemy spearheads which had advanced to the Oder in that area.

Both *Führer* divisions were to see action on the left wings of their respective attack lanes.

While the transports carrying the *Führer-Grenadier-Division* were slow in arriving and most were unloaded in the Wangerin—Ruhnow area, the *Führer-Begleit-Division* arrived rather more quickly in and around Freienwalde, Pomerania.

During the night of 8-9 February elements of I. (SPW)/Pz.Gren. Rgt. FBD under Hptm. Stoerk immediately received marching orders—depicted on a map—to Klein- and Gross-Silber, where the enemy was said to be already on the move to the north. It was vital that our assembly areas be protected, or in some cases taken from the enemy.

The first small Kampfgruppe to head south from Nördenberg in the direction of Gross-Silber consisted of 3. Kp., elements of 1. Kp./I. (SPW)/Pz.Gren.Rgt. FBD together with four tanks which had just detrained. Through binoculars it was possible to see Soviet infantry already marching north, which meant that our own front, which was being held by infantry, was already on the move. Enemy movements were visible on the Klein-Silber—Gross-Silber road.

A Polish farm worker, who had just come from Gross-Silber, reported to the leader of the point platoon that the enemy had been in Gross-Silber since early that morning, had become drunk in a local distillery and had treated the women in the town frightfully and misused them. He himself had fled to escape the massacre.

The vehicles immediately formed up to attack and moved out. The terrain was favorable; forest and gullies which led up to the village. The armored troop carriers were able to move up to the edge of Gross-Silber without being seen and then break into the village. It was cleared of the enemy in a few minutes. Pickets were immediately posted to the south and west. In the village street lay several dead women, including two with white hair. The scene was dreadful; each of the soldiers could picture for himself what had happened here hours ago.

No sooner had the commander of the 1. Kp./I. (SPW)/Pz.Gren.Rgt. FBD, Oblt. Seifert, arrived, than he ordered Obfw. Lischak, one of his platoon leaders, to take an armored patrol and scout as far as Klein-Silber that same evening. He drove off and had to drive south through a large wooded area in the dark, always expecting to be shot at from somewhere. Halfway there, however, he received orders by radio to return immediately. The enemy had attacked Gross-Silber from the southeast and north and had driven off the defenders. Obfw. Lischak, already on his way back, received another radioed order to stay where he was, as the bulk of I. (SPW)/Pz.Gren. Rgt. FBD was going to attack Gross- and then Klein-Silber with tanks early on 10 February. By 11 February the last elements of the *Führer-Begleit-Division* were unloaded in Freienwalde and immediately transferred into the area north of Nörenberg, which was not their planned area of operations.

The *Führer-Begleit-Division* established its command post in Nörenberg. It faced considerable supply difficulties, especially a shortage of fuel. The ammunition situation was still bearable. Early on 11 February the first measures were already affecting the FBD; with support from the 2. Kp./Pz.Rgt. FBD, the I. (SPW)/Pz.Gren.Rgt. FBD attacked Gross-Silber again. The town was taken quickly and, in a continuation of the advance, Klein-Silber also fell; there were no casualties. Klein-Spiegel was occupied by the same Kampfgruppe. III./Pz.Gren.Rgt. FBD advanced toward Gabbert, which was taken in a surprise attack. Elements of I. (SPW)/Pz.Gren.Rgt. FBD, together with Panthers and Panzer IVs, now attacked the village of Glambeck in cooperation with II./Pz.Gren. FBD. It, too, was captured after a fierce fight.

As a result of these actions, on 11 February a continuous line was established, running from roughly Klein-Silber in the west, east through Glambeck to Gabbert.

The FBD initially halted after this line was reached. The positions were improved and preparations made for the joint attack to the south. The enemy, at first surprised by the FBD's attack, regrouped and began determined efforts to retake the lost villages. The defending panzer-grenadiers of the FBD were repeatedly forced on to the defensive and had to fight off advances by Soviet tanks during the night.

At the same time there were regroupings on the German side which produced two powerful attack groups: one northwest of Arnswalde, to which was added another armored group from the *Führer-Begleit-Division*—I. (SPW)/Pz.Gren.Rgt. FBD and Stu. Gesch.Abt. FBD—in order to support the planned attack on Arnswalde by the SS-Polizei-Gren.Div. and the 10. SS-Pz.Div. "*Frundsberg.*" The other attack group comprised the bulk of the *Führer-Begleit-Division* plus the *Führer-Grenadier-Division*, which was in the process of assembling its units and which set up its command post in Zehrten on 16 February.

After two days the attack northwest of Arnswalde, which began on 12-13 February, ground to a halt in the face of the Soviet anti-tank barriers with little ground gained. Supported by Tigers and I. (SPW)/Pz. Gren.Rgt. *Führer-Begleit-Division*, our spearheads advanced to the village of Gut Marienburg, where they were forced on to the defensive before reaching the town. Arnswalde itself remained in enemy hands.

Meanwhile the bulk of the *Führer-Grenadier-Division* had assembled in the Nörenberg—Klein-Spiegel area, division command post still in Zehrten, where *Generalmajor* Remer (FBD) also established his command post on 16 February. At this time the *Führer* divisions, which made up the bulk of the attack force, were subordinated to *Generalmajor* Munzel's corps group. Munzel was the former commander of a tank-destroyer brigade and this was also a part of the corps group.

At about 16:00 hours on 16 February the panzer-grenadiers of the *Führer-Grenadier-Division* attacked south in the direction of Liebenow. While the attack was still under way, *Generalmajor* Munzel appeared at the FGD's command post, where he gave *Generalmajor* Mäder a brief situation briefing. He stated that the attack divisions at Arnswalde had not got far past their starting positions, having become bogged down in the face of stubborn enemy resistance. On the other hand, his own attack in the direction of Liebenow, made in cooperation with the FBD and with air support, had so far been successful. The armored units of the *Führer-Begleit-Division*, which were in the Klein-Silber—Steinberg area attacking toward Reetz, had made good progress, but had been forced to halt short of the objective through lack of fuel and ammunition. *Generalmajor* Mäder therefore suggested to *Generalmajor* Munzel that he ask the army group to commit the Tiger battalions at the army group's disposal on the left wing—in the FGD's attack lane toward Liebenow—and thus shift the main effort there. These proposals were rejected by the army group, however *General-*

major Munzel transferred the reconnaissance battalion and one or two Hetzer companies from his tank-destroyer brigade in order to exploit the success on the east wing of the attack. At the same time elements of the Pz.Rgt./FBD were temporarily placed under the command of the *Führer-Grenadier-Division*, in order to use their combined armored force to continue the attack toward Liebenow on 17 February.

FBD division command post: crossroads north of Nantikow.

FGD division command post: still in Zehrten, in the process of moving to Steinberg.

In spite of fierce Russian resistance, this joint attack by the two GD *Führer* divisions broke through on 17 February. Nantikow was taken and our armored spearheads reached Buchholz, which immediately went up in flames. The most forward elements were able to enter Liebenow by way of Buchholz and establish themselves there.

A nocturnal tank attack from the east by the enemy was repulsed. The night was very unsettled. The fighting flared up again everywhere, cut-off groups of enemy infantry made their presence felt, forcing our troops to remain at constant readiness.

Reetz was still in enemy hands, however it hindered our movements relatively little as the enemy troops there at first remained quiet. Pickets were put out to the west—toward Reetz—to protect the right flank.

Early on the morning of 18 February the enemy resumed his attacks from the east against Nantikow, and once again these were repulsed. The FBG brought heavy anti-aircraft guns, artillery and anti-tank weapons into position on both sides of Kreuz, allowing it to place fire on the enemy along the road from Hassendorf. Close-support aircraft of both sides very active; there were fierce air battles over the entire area.

The armored pickets abeam Kreuz were struck by heavy surprise artillery and mortar barrages. There were assaults by enemy tanks, resulting in fierce tank-versus-tank battles. In the afternoon the situation there became critical, with increased pressure from enemy armor against our positions.

At about 15:00 hours an order was sent to the FBD's armored elements still in Liebenow under the command of Obstlt. Schnappauf to withdraw his positions to Buchholz and occupy the new main line of resistance there along the Reetz—Buchholz road. Continuous attacks were made against the crossroads in Buchholz by enemy close-support aircraft, resulting in considerable losses in killed and wounded. A continuous main line of resistance was established, and by evening the enemy ceased further attacks.

The enemy had been brought to a temporary halt in this area. During the night elements of the *Führer-Begleit-Division* were relieved by the *Führer-Grenadier-Division*, which took over their positions.

On 20 February the FGD, still in the midst of preparations for its own attack from the recently won area north of Liebenow in the direction of the Zühlsdorf— Kölpin road, also received orders to transfer to the Nörenberg area. Its positions were turned over to an infantry division.

The planned attack operation in the direction of the Netze had thus been called off—and abandoned. Our forces were too weak to win out against the enemy south of Arnswalde—Liebenow; furthermore this operation came too late since the Soviets were already on the move again to the north, negating all our plans. Probably the only good thing about the operation in Pomerania was the appearance of the two *Führer* divisions, which prevented a Soviet breakthrough and temporarily brought them to a halt.

But for how long? This depended less on the defenders than on the Soviets, who were the stronger and who definitely wanted to take Stettin and with it the entire Oder line.

After the two divisions were entrained at Altdamm near Stettin— whose military commander at this time was *General der Infanterie* Hoernlein—and transported into the Stargard area (FGD), at least some elements continued on to Cottbus, where they were rested and brought up to strength.

Chapter 2
Lauban

In the last week of February the two divisions were partly en route to Cottbus by motor transport, partly on their way by train from Pomerania to the area east of Görlitz. It had been announced that a joint operation was being planned against Lauban, which had fallen into Soviet hands a few days earlier after a surprise attack. There was a danger that the enemy would also take Görlitz. The important rail center of Lauban had to be recaptured to ensure that the supply route to Breslau remained open.

The attack was set for 1 March. The plans called for the *Führer-Grenadier-Division* on the right and the 17. Pz.Div. on the left to attack from the Rachenau—Gruna area, both east of Görlitz, the *Führer-Begleit-Division* from the Cunzendorf area—below the forest north of Greiffenberg, together with the 8. Pz.Div. on its left, in such a way that after turning in their inner flanks the two attack spearheads would meet north of Lauban and link up there. At the same time the enemy forces trapped in the resulting pocket in and north of Lauban were to be destroyed.

Our own positions ran in a generally east-west direction—at and north of Cunzendorf—below the forest in an arc to Lauban, part of which was in Soviet hands the rest in our own, and from there in a northwest direction through Schreibersdorf—Rachenau.

For both divisions success depended on exploiting the element of surprise to break through the Soviet positions and then attack immediately toward the north—for the FGD toward Ober-Bielau, the FBD toward Neuland, in the direction of Naumburg. It was not known if enemy armored forces were operating in these areas; however, it was assumed that they were, especially since the Soviets viewed this forward area as a jump-off point for future operations.

The 9. Inf.Div. (later the 9. VGD) in position in the line Lauban—Rachenau under *General* Brücker reported no activity on the enemy side. Thank God one might say, especially since the majority of the members of this division suffered from various medical problems, making its combat worth questionable.

At the turn of the day from 1 to 2 March the two attack groups on both sides of Lauban launched their attacks toward the north almost simultaneously, led by their armored groups.

In the FGD's sector the tanks and armored troop carriers, followed by the Wischnath Regiment, advanced on both sides of Rachenau over open terrain in the direction of Ober-Bielau, which was entered against weak opposition. The advance continued immediately toward the woods north and northeast of the town, which were occupied after heavy fighting, especially at their edges. Attacking on the left, the tanks of the 17. Pz.Div. also reached the tips of the woods.

In the afternoon hours the FGD's division commander (Gen.Mj. Mäder) had to decide in which direction to continue the attack. According to orders he was now to head north toward Günthersdorf, which was known to be heavily defended by enemy anti-tank guns and tanks. An attack against that town would therefore cost numerous casualties and much precious time. On the other hand, veering east from north of Ober-Bielau was the shorter and thus faster way to link up with the *Führer-Begleit-Division* coming from the east; this option would, however, result in a smaller pocket and perhaps reduce the scale of the victory.

In this situation Gen.Mj. Mäder proposed to the commanding general of the special purpose corps, *General* Decker, to pass his plan to take the shorter route to Army Group Schörner. Gen.Feldm. Schörner himself appeared at the FGD's command post and merely said that *General* Nehring was in command of the overall operation there and that he should decide. A telephone call to Nehring resulted in the decision being left to *General* Decker. "Günthersdorf is the greater envelopment; you are up front—you decide together with Decker!"

No one wanted to take responsibility. In the end both *General* Decker and *Generalmajor* Mäder decided in favor of the smaller envelopment.

Preparations were made for the night, since darkness was to be used for the dash across the Queis. With this course of attack, which led over Butter Mountain, Fichtel Mountain, toward the center of Haugsdorf and across the stream line, the enemy in front of the 9. Inf.Div. was to be forced to retreat and the 8. Pz.Div.'s attack toward Linden Mountain made easier.

Meanwhile the Pz.Rgt. FBD, together with the armored troop carriers of I. (SPW)/Pz.Gren.Rgt. FBD, were advancing toward the Neuland crossroads in the *Führer-Begleit-Division*'s attack lane. Neuland station was first overrun against weak opposition, then the attack force headed toward the wooded area south of Kesseldorf. At the forest's edge there was heavy fighting with Soviet strongpoints and bunker positions.

II./Pz.Gren.Rgt. FBD was moved forward and it combed the forest south-southwest of Kesseldorf. After heavy fighting in the forest the battalion entered and occupied Kesseldorf. From the Neuland crossroads III./Pz.Gren.Rgt. FBD fought its way through to Alt-Neuland and took possession of it. This battalion quickly regrouped and continued the attack against the forest to the northwest. The Soviets had massed large numbers of anti-tank guns at the southern tip of the forest and the attack failed to get through. The battalion was stopped, and it secured for the night.

The *Führer-Begleit-Division*'s objective was Naumburg, however it was said to be strongly defended by enemy tank and anti-tank units.

The first day of the attack was over; the right attack group (the FBD) in particular had suffered from strong enemy flanking actions which time and again tied down considerable forces.

During the night the *Führer*-grenadiers of the Wischnath Regiment (Rgt. 4) together with combat engineers and elements of the Pz.Rgt. FGD continued the breakthrough toward the Queis, indeed they even established a small bridgehead across the stream with one grenadier company. The Soviets counterattacked immediately, however, and the bridgehead had to be abandoned. The tanks on the west bank of the Queis prevented the Soviets from streaming across and their fire prevented any movement by Soviet tanks to or from the area of Naumburg.

On the second day of the battle (2 March) the armored group of the *Führer-Begleit-Division* resumed its attack toward Naumburg in occasional snowshowers, but it was unable to force its way through because of the appearance of strong enemy tank forces. Its spearheads did reach the area east of Herzogswaldau, where it immediately went over to the defensive together with elements of I. (SPW)/Pz.Gren.Rgt. FBD in order to eliminate any flanking threat from the east.

The commander of III./Pz.Gren. FBD was hesitant in sending his battalion against the wood northwest of Alt-Neuland, for fear that it would be outflanked from the west. Committed against Gut Neuland, the Pz.Pi.Btl. FBD under Hptm. Knauer gained ground and was able to occupy the estate against stubborn opposition; there it immediately went over to the defensive on account of heavy enemy fire from the forest beyond the rail line.

The enemy was placing heavy artillery, mortar and Stalin Organ fire on to Cunzendorf and Neuland, at the crossroads were knocked out tanks and dead bodies. In spite of significant casualties—a *Leutnant* had both legs shattered at III. Btl.'s command post—III./Pz.Gren. FBD went to the attack again and its leading elements advanced through Nieder-Giessmannsdorf to the Löwenberg—Naumburg rail line. There was no significant resistance there, however the railway embankment beyond was heavily fortified.

The third day of the battle (3 March) also saw a great deal of air activity by the enemy in the area of the *Führer-Begleit-Division*, with waves of attacks on Cunzendorf, Giessmannsdorf, Neuland and the surrounding area. Visibility was excellent. White flares were fired from the crossroads beyond the Giessmannsdorf railway embankment; this was followed by a heavy bombing raid on the crossroads. III./Pz.Gren.Rgt. FBD was still pinned down behind the railway embankment, but it was preparing to attack into the forest in order to cross this. Two assault guns under Oblt. Welland were to provide support. The attack failed on account of the enemy's strong anti-tank defense from the wood; one assault gun was lost.

The armored group came under heavy attack from Naumburg and from the southwest; a maximum effort was required to fight off these attacks and several tanks were lost. II./Pz.Gren.Rgt. FBD was temporarily encircled in Kesseldorf but fought its way out again. The enemy was unable to fight his way through, however. But it was clear that his point of main effort was to the east and that he was moving in reserves from the north in spite of softened ground and almost bottomless forest lanes.

The division command realized that the pocket near Naumburg could not be closed and that it would instead have to take the shorter path to link up with the spearhead of the FGD attacking from the west.

During the night the *Führer-Grenadier-Division* was able to force a crossing of the Queis through the bold use of its pioneers and build the first footbridges and crossings while it was still dark. This small bridgehead was steadily reinforced, supported by the Pz.Rgt. under *Major* Schmidt, who used his tanks as artillery to keep the Lauban—Naumburg road under continuous fire. There was heavy Soviet column traffic on the road, with trucks trying to drive away to the north with booty from Lauban. They were shot to pieces. Meanwhile the Wischnath Regiment had penetrated as far as Sächsisch-Haugsdorf and defended it to the northeast with success. The II./Pz.Gren. FGD, meanwhile, advanced with elements of the 17.Pz.Div. towards Günthersdorf and occupied the edge of the forest south of the village.

The enemy, who was still sitting in his positions in front of the 9. I.D., which was also supposed to attack to the north but which refused to leave its holes, now withdrew slowly in a northeast direction, having realized that he was faced with the threat of encirclement. Our security outposts on Butter and Fichtel Mountains were handed over to the 9. I.D. The city of Lauban was free again after the Soviets had got wind of their imminent encirclement.

On 3-4 March, in the *Führer-Begleit-Division*'s lane, the armored spearhead near Naumburg was withdrawn and a general line Neuland station—Alt Neuland—center of Giessmannsdorf—Kastenwald—Timmendorfer Forest (wooded area west of Giessmannsdorf) was occupied. At the same time the rather battered II./Pz.Gren.Rgt. FBD under Hptm. Schmidt was withdrawn from Kesselsdorf and initially transferred to Stöckigt for a brief rest and refit. During the withdrawal of the armored group from east of Naumburg south through the east end of Herzogswaldau it came upon an enemy tank assembly area east of Giessmannsdorf, both sides being taken by surprise. By bringing in alert companies, the new main line of resistance was occupied at dawn; this move was necessary as II. and III./Pz.Gren.Rgt. FBD in particular had suffered heavy casualties which reduced their combat strengths.

Late on the afternoon of 4 March the enemy began strong armored attacks from the area of Kloster Simonishäuser past Neuland station in the direction of Alt-Neuland, placing the units of the FBD there in a critical situation. Resulting gaps in the main line of resistance were closed by committing the armored group, only in Alt-Neuland did the situation remain unclear. The town was ablaze from end to end, there was no sign of the 2. Kp./Pz.Pi. Btl. FBD deployed there. But contrary to expectations the enemy did not continue the pursuit; he seemed satisfied with what he had achieved and made no move to further exploit this opportunity. Elements of the Feldersatz-Bataillon FBD were rushed in to fully man the positions once again.

On 4 March the point units of the *Führer-Grenadier-Division* set out again across the Queis and with elements of the Pz.Pi.Btl. FGD occupied Linden Mountain, where it was able to establish first contact with the 8. Pz.Div. The pocket was closed, and while the number of prisoners was small, the booty and amount of destroyed weapons, equipment and vehicles was great. The fierce flanking battles fought by the FBD and the associated delay in linking up with the FGD had been just enough to allow the bulk of the Soviets to escape. It was a great moral victory, especially since Lauban had been relieved in spite of the fiercest fighting, and the Soviets had once again felt the force of the German offensive spirit.

On 5 March the III./Pz.Gren.Rgt. FBD moved west through soggy forest lanes and secondary roads and, in at times heavy fighting, was able to occupy the Silberberg near Schlesisch-Haugsdorf. In the days that followed, the wooded hills extending from north of Naumburg to the south changed hands several times in fierce fighting. At night the Soviets emerged from the forest and worked their way up the hill, and each day they were driven off again when the courageous grenadiers of III./Pz.Gren.Rgt. FBD counterattacked. The forest allowed the Soviets to approach unseen. The Silberberg was then incorporated into the new main line of resistance, which was occupied mainly by stationary infantry, but it continued to remain the key point in the entire system of positions.

The attack on Lauban was essentially over, even though further isolated actions had to be carried out to mop up the woods. The enemy also then quieted down and scarcely another shot was fired in the new main line of resistance.

Our own casualties had been relatively heavy, especially those of the *Führer-Begleit-Division* deployed on the right. At times it was only possible to hold the position by quickly moving in alert units. The efforts of the armored group—tanks and the armored troop carriers of I. (SPW)/Pz.Gren.Rgt. *Führer-Begleit-Division*—had been especially effective, clearing up many critical situations through their rapid intervention.

Only a few days after the taking of Lauban *Generalfeldmarschall* Schörner called the command post of the *Führer-Grenadier-Division* and instructed the division to immediately send a battalion to Lauban. It was to be part of a visit by Reichminister Goebbels to the town, especially since the minister wanted to give a speech to the front-line soldiers. After much to and fro about 100 men were assembled and these were driven in trucks to Lauban. Then on 8 March Goebbels gave his speech to the soldiers and *Volkssturm* members assembled in Lauban's marketplace. Praise for Schörner, praise for Goebbels, and as an aside the actions of the soldiers were also mentioned. Several members of the Hitler Youth were decorated with the Iron Cross, however none of the men of the units received a decoration.

Two days later, on 10 March, the *Führer*-grenadiers were put aboard trains in Ostritz near Görlitz for transport north in the direction of Angermünde. The units of the *Führer-Begleit-Division* moved by motor transport further south in the direction of Langenöls and remained there for a brief time to rest and refit.

The paths of the two GD *Führer* divisions parted forever at Lauban, after they had worked together from the Ardennes offensive through Pomerania to Lauban. The two divisions subsequently saw action on different fronts, the *Führer-Begleit-Division* on 24 March in the Ratibor—Troppau—Leobschütz—Jägerndorf area, the *Führer-Grenadier-Division* beginning on 15 March for several days near Stettin.

When the first trains carrying the *Führer-Grenadier-Division* rolled into the area west-southwest of Stettin, west of the Oder, on 15 March, they were already too late. It was supposed to see action against the Soviet forces which had been attacking northwest toward Stettin since the beginning of March and which were now making a maximum effort to also push their right wing to the Oder. But that had already happened when the *Führer*-grenadiers arrived before Stettin. Now—at the disposal of Army Group Vistula—its mission was to defend a bridgehead south of Altdamm on the east bank of the Oder, which was in danger of being lost under pressure from the Soviet attacks.

In the south of the bridgehead was a navy division, on its left and on both sides of the autobahn the 25. Pz.Div. Attacking from the south, the Soviets had broken through the navy unit and had driven straight through to the autobahn bridge, which they captured intact.

The *Führer-Grenadier-Division*'s mission: restore the situation by eliminating the enemy penetration. As well, it was to get the navy division out and secure its crossing to the west bank. Then it was to cross to the east bank itself over the autobahn bridge, which was then to be blown by combat engineers.

This mission, which was given at the command post of the 25. Pz.Div. on 15 March, required the division to attack from the move, channelized through the autobahn bridge in view of the now very small bridgehead.

The II./Pz.Gren.Rgt. FGD, led by *Major* Schmidt, made a sudden dash across the bridge, meeting surprisingly little resistance. The FGD's counterattack broke through immediately and the enemy elements which had broken into the German position were destroyed. Communication was restored with the split-up navy division. When darkness fell the navy division was pulled out and the autobahn bridge was crossed under ineffectual enemy artillery fire. In the early morning hours of the following day the *Führer*-grenadiers pulled back to the east bank to support the right wing (subordinated to the 25. Pz.Div.), leaving behind II./Pz.Gren.Rgt. FGD and an attached company of the Pz.Rgt. FGD. The withdrawal went unnoticed by the enemy.

II./Pz.Gren.Rgt. FGD under *Major* Schmidt remained with the units of the 25.Pz.Div. for a few more days and on more than one occasion distinguished itself through its bravery in the fighting near Klütz and Podejuch. It was later withdrawn over the Stettin bridge and returned to the division.

The first elements of the *Führer-Grenadier-Division* entrained again on 17 March for transport via Angermünde, Fürstenwalde and Briesen into the Seelow—Gusow area. It appeared that it was to see action against an enemy bridgehead west of Küstrin. The FGD set up its command post in Biegen near Jakobsdorf. The first operation in the new area, an attack toward the east by two SS divisions and the *Führer-Grenadier-Division* from the assembly area due south of Reichsstrasse 1 and the nearby woods on 23 March, became bogged down soon after it began when the attackers ran into a known but ignored Soviet minefield. The result was further senseless losses of men and tanks. Two days later the attack was repeated with the same result; after modest gains the attack bogged down in the face of stiffening Soviet resistance. Thus the last attempt by the 9. Armee to relieve the garrison of Küstrin had failed. Further attempts were abandoned, the units were withdrawn for new assignments. The *Führer-Grenadier-Division* was put aboard trains again—destination Bautzen.

Part VI
Balga – Kahlholz

Chapter 1
Last in the Bridgehead

Panzer-Grenadier Division
Großdeutschland
Ia

Div. Command Post, 5/2/1945

Division Order for 5 February 1945
(map 1 : 25,000)

Enemy facing the division: elements of the XVI Guards Rifle Corps (11th and 31st Guards Rifle Divisions), plus elements of the XXXVI Guards Rifle Corps (16th and 18th Guards Rifle Divisions) and remnants of the 26th Guards Rifle Division. Original plan to break through with the XVI Guards Rifle Corps from the Godrienen—Wundlacken—Maulen area to the Königsberger Haff and then swing southwest along the Königsberg—Brandenburg autobahn with the 11th Guards Rifle Division and elements of the XXXVI Guards Rifle Corps, has been hindered by our own attacks. In spite of extremely heavy losses, the enemy is sticking to his original plan of reaching the Königsberger Haff, if necessary at the cost of withdrawing forces from the southern Königsberg front.

The appearance of an assault gun battalion and Stalin tanks in the Warthen—Maulen—Waldburg area must still be expected.

Pz.Gren.Div. GD to hold the line Neu-Colbnicken—Waldburg—Maulen—Warthen with the intention, after rest and reorganization of various units, of attacking on 6 February 1945 in order to capture the Kobbelbude—Königsberg rail line.

Attached to the division are:

Gren.Rgt. 975 (367. I.D.) and

s.H.-Mörser-Abt. 816

assigned to cooperate are:

Werfer-Rgt. 81 and

I./Flak-Rgt.64

Deployed for defense on 5 February are:

Right: Pz.Füs.Rgt. GD – less I. Btl.

Left: Gren.Rgt. 975 with attached

I./Pz.Füs.Rgt. GD

II./Pz.Gren.Rgt. GD

Pak-u. Fla.Kp./Pz.Gren.Rgt. GD

1./Pz.Jäg.Abt. GD

Boundaries:

right: to 562. VGD:

Schoschen (562.) – Neu Colbnicken (GD) – Seepothen (GD) – Bergau (GD)

between Pz.Füs.Rgt. GD and Gren.Rgt. 975:

Factory 500 m east of Heide Waldburg (975.) – Point 0.5 (750 m northeast of Schloss Waldburg) – southwest corner of Maulen – VW Ludwigshof (Füs.)

To be transferred and placed at the division's disposal are:

Pz.Gren.Rgt. GD (less II. Btl. and without Pak-u.Fla-Kp.) to Brandenburg

II./Gren.Rgt. 975 to Heide Maulen

Btl. Brandenburg to Brandenburg

Pi. Units to Pokarben

Pz.A.A. GD into the Pörschken-Brandenburg area

Div.Begl.Kp. to Heide Waldburg

To clear up the main line of resistance, from which the attack is to be made on 6 February 1945, Maulen-North is to be taken by the Pz.Füs.Rgt. GD and Gren.Rgt. 975 during the night of 4-5 February and Gren.Rgt. 975 is to make preparations to retake Maulen-South.

Pz.Gren.Rgt. GD: support the grenadier regiments with armored group formed near the front and assigned to work with the grenadier regiments in the Honigbaum area, forest north of Waldburg, Heide-maulen and Warthen.

Communications between the regiment and battalion commanders and the leaders of the armored group are to be assured.

Pz.Art.Rgt. GD (with attached s.H.Mörs.Abt. 816 and assigned to cooperate Werfer-Rgt. 81) is to smash recognized enemy assembly areas and attacks, ensure cooperation by overlapping with both neighboring divisions,

artillery ammunition is not to be used for attacks by infantry alone; harassing fire and counter-artillery fire is to be avoided.

Assigned to cooperate are:

I./Pz.Art.Rgt. GD with Gren.Rgt. 975

II./Pz.Art.Rgt. GD with Pz.Füs.Rgt. GD

H.-Flak-Abt. GD is to instruct heavy batteries to cooperate with Pz.Art.Rgt. GD and deploy them in the area of the artillery firing positions so as to

protect the artillery positions against enemy air attacks,

be ready for use in a ground role on order of the Pz.Art.Rgt. GD in the event the threat of an enemy breakthrough,

leave the self-propelled guns of the light and medium batteries in the Heide-Maulen area with orders to cooperate with Gren.Rgt. 975

Anti-tank defense: Hptm. Rex, commander of Pz.Jäg.Abt. GD, is responsible for anti-tank defense in the division area. Pz.Jäg.Abt. GD to assign 1. Kp. to Gren.Rgt. 975 for action in the Maulen—Warthen area; keep 2. Kp. at the division's disposal in Ludwigsort.

Traffic control: Military Police Squad GD is to watch over traffic on the communications road to Königsberg and post signs (Brandenburg—Reichsstraße 1 – to Heide-Waldburg, Heide-Maulen, Haffstrom, Kalgen) See to it that the main road in the division area is cleared of all vehicles that might hinder traffic, position straggler assembly points around Brandenburg and mobile straggler patrols on the Königsberg road and on the Brandenburg—Pokarben road.

Communications:

Pz.Nachr.Abt. GD is to maintain telephone communications with all attached units and division reserves, radio to Fsch.Pz.-Korps HG, 562. VGD, 5. Pz.Div., Fortress commander Königsberg, Pz.Füs.Rgt. GD, Gren.Rgt. 975, Pz.Gren.Rgt. GD, Pz.Aufkl.Abt. GD, Pz.Art.Rgt. GD, II. Flak-Abt. GD and Ib.

In the event of loss of telephone communications all deployed units are to immediately dispatch communications officers to the division and make half-hourly radio reports.

Division command post: rest home south of Korschenruh, 2 km southwest of Brandenburg.

Signed LORENZ

Distribution: R

The order is to be destroyed after acknowledgement; report its destruction under the code word "Laubfrosch" ["Tree frog"] by 5 February.

The attack on 4 February in the direction of the Kobbelbude—Königsberg rail line, as prescribed in the division order, was proceeded by several operations with limited objectives which were carried out during the night of 4-5 February, their primary purpose being to improve our own positions. One of these involved two pioneer companies of the Pz.Pi.Btl. GD supported by three Tigers under Oblt. Leussing and three Panthers under Lt. Vogelsang in a small enveloping attack. The Tigers were to attack from Waldhaus north of Reichsstrasse 1 and take the group of farms left of the road, while south of the road the Panthers and both pioneer assault companies attacked the group of houses that was Maulen, with the final objective of freeing Reichsstrasse 1. The assault, which was planned for the night, misfired at the very outset when the pioneers fired white signal flares as they moved off, illuminating the battlefield and alerting the Soviets. Two Panthers were knocked out before they had fired a shot. The operation was called off.

Soon afterwards the I. (SPW)/Pz.Gren.Rgt. GD under Hptm. Pfau and II./Pz.Gren.Rgt. GD under Hptm. Mackert moved into assembly positions in order to attack from the Neu-Colbnicken area (enemy occupied) with I. (SPW) Btl. to the southwest against VW. Colbnicken, to be followed by II. Btl. from the Kamnicken assembly area, with subsequent continuation of the attack by I. (SPW) Btl. toward the Waldpothen brickworks in the direction of Seepothen.

Oberst Heesemann himself commanded the entire attack operation. He made his way to the Pistol Wood (also called Five Point Wood) west of Neu-Colbnicken, which had just been cleared of infiltrated Soviets. Friendly mortar fire roared overhead, enemy heavy mortars fired into the wood with dull thuds; all hell seemed to have broken loose there even before the attack began. *Oberst* Heesemann was standing at the telephone speaking to *Generalmajor* Lorenz when another heavy mortar salvo landed. The *Oberst* and commander of the Pz.Gren.Rgt. GD groaned and collapsed, struck in the heart by a splinter. Oblt. Jaenicke took the receiver from his hand and reported to *General* Lorenz: "*Herr Oberst* has just been killed. A sudden mortar barrage!"

The armored troop carriers of I. (SPW) Btl. drove forward and were able to enter Neu-Colbnicken, however only the right wing of II./Pz.Gren.Rgt. GD was able to follow. The bulk of the battalion continued to battle infiltrated Soviets in the "Pistol Wood." New positions with front facing northeast were occupied by the grenadiers of II. Btl., with 5. Kp. in reserve, 6. Kp. under the command of Lt. Hoffmann and 7. Kp. to its left. Quiet slowly came to this sector. The next day, which remained quiet, saw both sides improving their positions, in some cases laying wire and mines. The *Oberst* who had fallen the day before was buried. With him one of the bravest officers of the Pz.Gren.Div. GD left forever.

The days passed relatively quietly, with II./Pz.Gren.Rgt. GD moved farther south into a sector projecting eastwards, with its command post in VW. Wesdehlen. The artillery of both sides fired at identified and suspected targets, our rocket launchers—the only weapons still with adequate stocks of ammunition—fired repeated fiery salvoes at the enemy. Here and there there were sudden mortar barrages at Soviet troops entrenching or just walking around in the open; otherwise the days were uneventful.

The Pz.Aufkl.Abt. GD was temporarily placed under the command of another unit, conducting several advances into the Arnsdorf area in the following days or serving in a defensive role. I./Pz.Korps-Füs.Rgt. GD under Hptm. Buse, which was still not back with the division, continued to fight bitterly in the area northeast of Wormditt together with what was left of

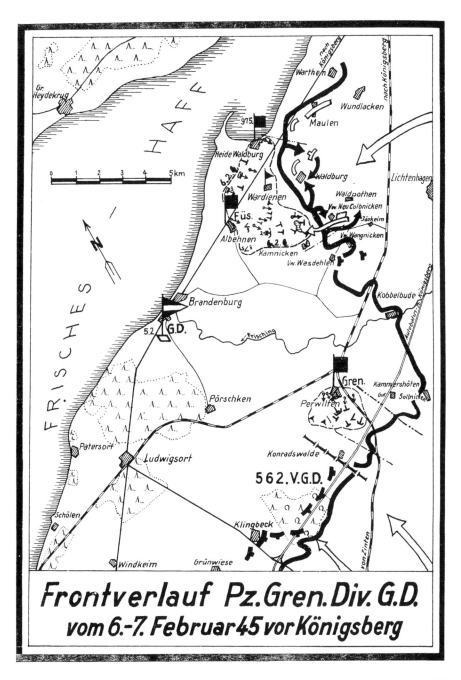

Frontverlauf Pz.Gren.Div.G.D. vom 6.-7. Februar45 vor Königsberg

Front-Line Trace of Panzer-Grenadier-Division "Großdeutschland"
From 6-7 February 1945 Outside of Königsberg

I./Pz.Korps-Art.Rgt. GD. Losses rose, combat strengths dropped. It was a battle with no chance of success, a battle of sacrifice and losses; and the group of old members of III. Btl., grenadiers who formed the core of I./Pz.Korps-Füs.Rgt. GD, grew ever smaller.

Hptm. Buse was wounded, as was Lt. Hentschel, leader of 1. Kp./ Pz.Korps-Füs.Rgt. GD; both had to be evacuated.

Oblt. Röder took over the remaining elements of I./Pz.Korps-Füs.Rgt. GD, which continued to be involved in the heavy fighting for the Dargels estate northeast of Wormditt. The fighting raged back and forth; on one occasion five enemy tanks, part of a Soviet penetration, were destroyed. There was close-quarters fighting for possession of the wrecked estate, changeable fighting for Hill 79.2, very heavy enemy anti-tank and mortar fire—but it was held. The Pz.Aufkl.Abt. GD, attached to the 49. Jäg.Div. in the area east of Mehlsack, also fought under an unfamiliar banner. It performed magnificently, repeatedly mastering dangerous situations. During the night of 12 February it was passed on to another division, now in the area south of Braunsberg at the autobahn. There it took part in fierce offensive fighting, capturing new positions at the rail crossing west of Pettelkau. In the days that followed there was fierce fighting for possession of Pettelkau, which was guarded by the Pz.A.A. GD. These battles were brought to a successful conclusion under Rittm. Schroedter. Deployed at the autobahn overhead crossing over the Passarge on 16 February, for the next few days it held a bridgehead there and defended it stubbornly with the help of an armored group. These battles were especially costly for the GD reconnaissance troops, the officer and non-commissioned officer corps in particular suffering heavy losses.

The struggle for the autobahn was in vain, the enemy gained a crossing over the Passarge near Schalmey and the Pz.A.A. GD was immediately sent there. Meanwhile, after changeable fighting which had taken it to Peterswalde, the I./Pz.Korps-Füs.Rgt. GD was withdrawn and transferred into the area north of Schönlinde to rest and refit. *Major* von Basse received orders to take over the regiment and reorganize it. This did not happen, however. On the evening of 22 February I. Btl.—now under Hptm. Knaub—was alerted and committed in an attack against enemy forces which had broken in to Lilienthal.

After this temporary commitment the I./Pz.Korps-Füs.Rgt. GD was pulled out of the line and transported by truck into the division's rear area near Ludwigsort. There the battalion was finally brought back up to strength and reorganized. Officers were flown in from the Reich.

The relative calm in the division's sectors made it possible to restore the fighting strengths of the battalions in the line; this was achieved by incorporating replacements and by combing the trains, rear services and other units for personnel.

12-13 February also saw the dismissal—one can scarcely call it anything else in this situation—of the commander of the Pz.Füs.Rgt. GD, *Oberst* von Breese-Viniary, and his adjutant Hptm. Boll, who had served continuously with the same regiment in headquarters and as regimental adjutant since 1942. The supposed reason was a difference in opinion over the employment of one of the panzer-fusilier battalions to stand guard on the boundary with the Pz.Gren.Rgt. GD. But that alone was not the actual reason. Gen.Mj. Lorenz had been the commander of the Pz.Gren.Rgt. GD for a long time and had achieved great success with it, but he had never cultivated close contacts with the other regiments. Even more, from the beginning there had been a certain competition between the two regiments, especially since the Pz.Füs.Rgt. GD had been established as a special formation in early 1942 and was not developed from a cadre of the former I.R. GD 1. Gen.Mj. Hoernlein was still division commander at that time and he, too, had previously commanded the Inf.Rgt. GD.

The soldiers of the two regiments had names for each other, "Eyeties" for the panzer-fusiliers, "Slugabeds" for the panzer-grenadiers. This typified the inner distance between the two units and their separate lives, which ultimately led to an explosion. That this happened in the final stages of their joint defensive struggle on German soil is especially regrettable. *Major* Fabich assumed command of the Pz.Fusilier.Rgt. GD.

On 13 February the enemy launched heavy attacks in the sector held by the Fsch.Pz.Gren.Div. 2 HG in the Zinten area. The Fsch.Pz.Korps HG, to which the Pz.Gren.Div. GD was subordinated, ordered II./Pz.Füs.Rgt. GD, which was in rest status, dispatched there. Oblt. Meinicke's armored Kampfgruppe (Panthers) also immediately dispatched several Panthers there and successfully intervened in the heavy fighting near Zinten. With just three tanks, on 16 February 1945 the Kampfgruppe destroyed 21 enemy tanks without loss.

Two days later, on 19 February, *Hauptmann* Meinicke was killed while leading the Kampfgruppe of I. (Panther) Abt. GD deployed near Zinten. At the same time there was trouble on the 562. VGD's left wing near Konradswalde, right on the boundary with the Pz.Gren.Div. GD. A Kampfgruppe comprised of elements of the Pz.Gren.Div. GD under *Hauptmann* Obermeier was sent there but was initially held in reserve near Konradswalde. The Div.Begl.Kp. GD under Oblt. Kollewe was also sent there, however, with the enemy attacks gradually threatening to smash the *Volksgrenadier* division.

Various enemy penetrations into the positions near Konradswalde were eliminated through counterattack, and after 48 hours peace returned. The elements of the Div.Begl.Kp. GD were withdrawn immediately on 20 February and then moved into the area of Heide Waldburg, relieving the panzer-fusiliers in those positions. II./Pz.Korps-Füs.Rgt. GD—called the "Brandenburg Battalion"—under Hptm. Sprengler took over similar duties in order to free up further elements of the Pz.Füs.Rgt. GD.

After a temporary quiet the situation near Zinten became acute again. On 20 February the few remaining Tigers of III. Abt./Pz.Rgt. GD were already fighting for the Heiligen Berg northwest of Zinten. The fighting raged back and forth in the city itself and on the outskirts. It was only because of the actions of the Sturm-Bataillon GD under *Major* Ostermeier that the city remained in our hands.

West of Königsberg, in Samland, German units had meanwhile launched an attack in the direction of Pillau in an effort to reestablish communications. It succeeded. Supplies for Fortress Königsberg again rolled through Pillau, bringing significant relief to the city.

Kobbelbude—which was still in our hands—was held mainly by the 5. (Pz.Jäg.)/Pz.Pi.Rgt. GD under heavy enemy artillery and mortar fire. On the railway embankment, which was about ten tracks wide and bordered on both sides by flooded fields, there still sat long rows of freight cars. In those to the west were our troops, 200 meters farther east the Soviets. All day long the men lay between the tracks and the bottoms of the cars; they were scarcely able to stir, because snipers on both sides fired at every movement. But the troops held on, even under such awful conditions. After heavy fighting, on 25 February the Soviets took Zinten and drove the soldiers of the Fsch.Pz.Gren.Div. 2 HG out of the town. New positions were occupied on both sides of and north of Zinten, however the enemy pressure remained considerable and also gave cause for concern for the future. The situation in the Pz.Gren.Div. GD's sector remained essentially unchanged until 1 March. The positions remained firmly in our hands, only—and this must be stressed—these positions were for the most part manned by alert units and infantry squads from other units, supported by self-propelled anti-aircraft guns, anti-tank guns, artillery and GD assault teams in the rear. The situation was especially bad in the Konradswalde and Zinten area; repeatedly, one battalion after another was pulled out of the positions southwest of Königsberg and taken from the Pz.Gren.Div. GD's area of command to serve as fire-brigades for other units. *Major* Fabich, commander of the Pz.Füs.Rgt. GD, still neighbor to Gren.Rgt. 975, had just one first-rate battalion under his command, the rest were foreign: artillery alert units, other alert units, sometimes the Div.Begl.Kp., sometimes II./Pz.Korps-Füs.Rgt. GD, elements of other infantry divisions, groups of stragglers—but not its own battle-tested battalions. It had been forced to give up two, including II./Pz.Füs.Rgt. GD at Zinten, subordinated to the HG. The same applied to the Pz.Gren.Rgt. GD, which after the death of *Oberst* Heesemann was commanded by *Major* Krützmann, the former commander of the Pz.Gren.Rgt. 51 of the disbanded 18. Pz.Gren.Div., and whose I. (SPW)/Pz.Gren.Rgt. GD was also released to the division's southern flank—to support the 562. VGD.

There were misgivings about this style of employment, about the splitting up of the division. It was bad enough that it was over-tasked in the belief that the name GD alone was sufficient to hold the front, which was nearly 20 kilometers wide. If the enemy should decide to attempt a break-through at this point, then it was up to the division command to hold as best it could while its battalions bled under foreign commands.

It must be stated here that all that was left of the panzer-grenadier division in this sector was the name *Großdeutschland*, while bit by bit it had to release the elements of its body to support other sectors of the front.

In the last days of February alone, the I. (SPW)/Pz.Gren.Rgt. GD had lost a total of eight officers, including four killed, near Tykrigehnen, south of Kobbelbude. The entire 2. Kp. had been wiped out, only Fw. Francke succeeded in making it back to our lines.

On or about 1 March the I./Pz.Korps-Art.Rgt. GD returned to the division command after having lost its way for some time. After having lost most of its guns and all of its vehicles, Hptm. Winkler set about rebuilding the battalion, even if part of it had to be horse-drawn. All three batteries, 10. to 12., were reestablished and were deployed near their sister batteries.

After its rest and refit, the Pz.Korps-Füs.Rgt. GD, now under the permanent command of *Major* von Basse, transferred to the autobahn crossing with the Zinten—Ludwigsort road, so to speak in the second line of defense against enemy attacks expected from Zinten. On 1 March the Tigers and Panthers attached to the Fsch.Pz.Gren.Div. 2 HG exchanged fire with marauding enemy tanks in the Gross-Klingbeck area. The Pz.Korps-Füs.Rgt. GD arrived just in time to avert the threat of an enemy penetration into the deep flank of the Pz.Gren.Div. GD, which would have posed a grave threat to its supply lines.

The Soviets now set about clearing the German-held Heiligenbeil pocket. All of their attacks and advances were part of this plan. Between artillery salvoes their propaganda loudspeakers warned the German troops manning the strongpoints that, "Five days from now (1 March) you will be chased into the Baltic Sea!"

But on 3 March the enemy ceased his attempts to break through the German lines; apart from occasional artillery fire the front became quiet. Had the steadfast German defense so weakened the Soviet offensive forces that they urgently needed a rest? Or was this the calm before the final storm?

On the German side preparations for the Soviet offensive that was surely to come went ahead. The men, in action without a break for weeks, were gradually transferred to rest stations; in recognition of their brave conduct they were each allowed to send home an East Prussian postcard. The defense was organized, the positions were further improved, mined, wired.

On the German side a plan to improve our positions was prepared for 5 March under the code-name "Operation Teutonic Knight." Its objective was to break through south of Konradswalde and then advance west of Zinten in order to destroy enemy groups that had advanced north to the autobahn.

For this purpose every unit of the Pz.Gren.Div. GD that could be spared was pulled out of its positions and replaced by alert units. As the unit with the best fighting spirit in this area, the GD was always expected to have success. The commander of the Pz.Gren.Div. GD, Gen.Mj. Lorenz, also proposed that the attack be made along Reichsstrasse 1 in order to widen the corridor linking Königsberg. The proposal was rejected by the 4. Armee, and instead it ordered the attack to take place from the area of Konradswalde to the south with the objective outlined above.

Plan of attack: advance through Amalienwalde wood—Kukehnen past Zinten to the west. Total distance 18 kilometers. But on closer examination it became apparent that the direction of attack specified by the 4. Armee ran directly parallel to the Soviet front, meaning that it ran behind this and depended on rolling up the enemy positions. From the very outset there were fears that it would go wrong.

The Pz.Füs.Rgt. GD, pulled out of its positions between Maulen and Waldburg, moved by motor transport into the area north of Konradswalde. II./Pz.Gren.Rgt. GD was likewise relieved from its positions north of Kobbelbude. It was to accompany the attack to the right. The troops moved into assembly areas: II./Pz.Gren.Rgt. GD due south of Konradswalde, the bulk of the Pz.Füs.Rgt. GD east of Konradswalde but still south of the autobahn.

Moving off at about 03:00 hours on 6 March, the Panzergrenadiere initially made good progress from their positions south of Konradswalde and moved toward the linesman's house. But then they came under furious defensive fire from the railway embankment, and shortly afterwards large numbers of Soviet infantry with assault guns launched a counterattack. *Feldwebel* Strassner and four men of the 6. Kp. were killed and more than twelve were wounded in a very short time. It was as if the enemy had smelled the attack. Much the same happened to the panzer-fusiliers, who were accompanied by the few remaining Tigers. They got as far as the wood north of Amalienwalde before they were met by fierce defensive fire. They were forced to fall back. Snow! Our own artillery barrage, which was supposed to precede the attack, stopped after the twelfth round. No more ammunition!

New order: attack again at 15:00 hours. It, too, failed. Finally the attack was called off and the troops returned to the old main line of resistance. Relieved by the Pz.Korps-Füs.Rgt. GD, the panzer-fusiliers were driven back to their old positions near Maulen.

If anything good came of this limited attack operation, it was that we became convinced more than before of the enemy's strength at this key point and now realized that there was a great danger of a breakthrough.

On or about 10 March *Major* Kraussold took the place of the former commander of the Pz.Korps-Füs.Rgt. GD, *Major* von Basse. After being relieved near Konradswalde, II./Pz.Gren.Rgt. GD returned to its old positions at Wesdehlen.

And then came the 13th of March, when the Soviets launched their major offensive to eliminate the Heiligenbeil pocket. The Soviets bombarded every recognized German position with a furious barrage and leveled them to the ground. It went on for hours. Then the earth-brown figures came running across the fields toward the German lines. They were met by the faithful, reliable MG 42s firing from collapsed foxholes, earth-covered machine-gun positions, collapsed observation posts in houses and ruins. Rocket launchers fired salvoes into the masses of infantry, mortars lobbed rounds against the enemy. The main effort appeared to be against II./Pz.Gren.Rgt. GD near Wesdehlen and to its north. But it held. North of Kalmnicken, however, in an area held by alert units, the enemy appeared to have broken through. The earth-brown masses poured in the direction of Honigbaum—Pokarben. Elements of the Div.Begl.Kp. GD and other alert units rushed there immediately. Was the enemy already there? Or was Honigbaum still in our hands? Halfway there soldiers lay in the open fields, on the edges of roads and fields. The sound of tank fire came from Honigbaum—enemy tanks were already in. Fall-back positions were occupied, Pokarben was still in our hands. The Tigers engaged the enemy, Lt. Doerr's was knocked out straightaway. Two members of the crew, the veteran Uffz. Schreier (11. Kp.) and the driver Fw. Giehl (formerly of 9. Kp.), wearer of the German Cross in Gold and previously driver of the commander's tank, were killed. Loader Gefr. Thoma was wounded.

And then the Soviets were there, young lads, elite troops, just arrived at the front. They used German Shepherd dogs to carry messages. Carrying red banners, they stormed forward, oblivious to the fire that reached out for them—accompanied by the heaviest Soviet assault guns.

While the battle still raged, while the positions were being lost and then retaken by counterattacking hunting platoons, the 4. Armee issued an order to the command of the Pz.Gren.Div. GD to immediately release an entire regiment for duty in the south—madness! But no protest did any good.

The Pz.Gren.Rgt. GD had to believe that. The Pz.Pi.Rgt. GD was in a relatively peaceful sector near Kobbelbude, one which had not been directly affected by the attack. It was now inserted into the Pz.Gren.Rgt. GD's sector in order to free up that unit. The Inf./ Pz.Rgt. GD, tank crews fighting as infantry, took over the positions. The Inf./Pz.Rgt. GD was commanded by Hptm. Zabel, while the 1., 2. and 3. Kp. were led by Oblt. Welke, Lt. Vogelsang and Lt. Pflästerer, respectively. It remained quiet on the tracks at Kobbelbude station. But gradually those there got cold feet; the din of battle which had been raging farther north since early morning seemed to be shifting to the northwest. What was happening? Toward evening on 14 March—after 48 hours—the order came for them to withdraw; they silently left their foxholes, crept along the railroad tracks to the west, withdrawing in the direction of Pörschken where they occupied new positions. Their dead were left behind: Uffz. Drescher, formerly of III./Pz.Rgt. GD, Gefr. Feldmann, Obgefr. Fischer.

The fighting also went on with undiminished fury in other sectors on that 14 March. It now also spread to the positions in the Waldburg—Maulen area, but these were more restraining than breakthrough attacks. Uffz. Hippauf's Tiger was knocked out there by a heavy assault gun. The commander was severely wounded and died that evening. Two of the enemy assault guns were destroyed.

The Soviet assault troops poured through Honigbaum in the direction of Pörschken with tanks and assault guns. To the north as well, on the road before Maulen and farther south of Kobbelbude, they streamed toward the northwest and west.

Early on 15 March elements of the Inf.Btl./Pz.Rgt. GD under Hotm. Zabel occupied positions at the east and south end of Pörschken. There were still rations vehicles and trains in the streets and in front of the houses, at the edge of town several dug-in 88-mm guns. The few men of the companies squatted in foxholes, one or two men every 50 meters. Their positions ran roughly parallel to the Pörschken—Brandenburg road. Due east of the village was the Welke company, beside it to roughly abeam Louisenhof the Pflästerer company, and then to the bend in the Frisching, a small stream in the direction of Brandenburg, east of VW. Neu-Cainen, the Vogelsang company. To the left there was contact with the last pioneers of the Pz.Pi.Rgt. GD under the command of Hptm. Warschnauer, who sought to defend the flooded area. GD units had created the flooded area by damming streams, but this now proved disadvantageous, in that only the higher roads could be used for the retreat to the west.

It remained quiet all day; only near Tengen were there indications of heavy fighting between the enemy and retreating panzer-fusiliers and pioneers. Gefr. Strohmeyer of the 5. (Pz.Jäg.) Kp./Pz.Pi.Rgt. GD was killed by artillery fire near Tengen, while three enemy tanks were knocked out by the company's anti-tank guns. Also killed were Fw. Hafner and Pioneer Müller. Farther south of Pörschken—in the Poplitten area—the panzer-grenadiers of II./Pz.Gren.Rgt. GD fought their way through from the direction of the railway embankment to Pörschken, during the course of which the companies became totally dispersed. Not until evening did they assemble in Pörschken. The men sought their fellow company members, knowing that alone they were lost.

North of Pörschken contact with the pioneers was lost when they withdrew toward Brandenburg. During the evening hours of that 16 March the Soviets opened fire on Pörschken with heavy artillery. They must have been at least 500-mm shells, such was the size of the craters and so tremendous the explosions. The impacts were similar to those of bombs. The effect was devastating.

As night changed to morning on 17 March the typical sounds of tank tracks and infantry could be heard; and by the time it became light there were already masses of Soviet infantry between our positions. Tank shells burst between the rows of houses, Stalin and T 34 tanks were approaching. The few surviving defenders abandoned their holes faster than ever before, ran around the corners of houses, now and then firing a few bursts of sub-machine-gun fire in the direction of the enemy, and south to escape in the direction of the forest north of Pörschken. But the enemy was there.

A single Tiger (C 12) was on its way from Brandenburg to the forest's edge near Pörschken. It joined the battle, defended itself desperately against the multitude of enemy tanks and was knocked out at about 14:00 hours. The crew, which included Obfw. Freiburg (10. Kp.), Müller (11. Kp.), Vogt (11. Kp.) and Gussone (11. Kp.) all escaped into the forest. The Tiger, one of the last three of the once so proud III. (Tiger)/Pz.Rgt. GD, had its left track shot up and was hit in the bow. When the enemy tanks reached positions abreast of the Tiger, it was blown up by its crew.

To the left (north) contact was lost with the pioneers; the Vogelsang company, which had been separated from the unit by the enemy penetration into Pörschken, also withdrew north towards Hill 27.6 where it occupied positions with the Pz.Pi.Rgt. GD.

Enemy attacks, made with strong air support, were in process against Brandenburg. Numerous vehicle columns were still making their way into the city and shells fired by enemy tanks struck again and again. Here a truck burned, there an ammunition load went up—a terrible scene.

The munitions dumps between Ludwigsort and Brandenburg were blown up; one munitions bunker after another went up, taking with them all of the precious ammunition which had been so absent in recent weeks. Brandenburg was evacuated toward evening, new positions were occupied farther to the west. The medical clearing station was moved to Patersort. The care of the wounded went on in spite of continuous air attacks on the passing columns. Finally it had to evacuate; things could not continue as they were.

Enemy tanks and infantry were now also in the forest west of Pörschken. The enemy sought to outflank and overtake the retreating grenadiers and pioneers. The pace of the retreat quickened, and nowhere was there an opportunity to establish a new defense line. Uffz. Adelhardt, Gefr. Kurzhahn and medic Zimmer, all of 5. (Pz.Jäg.)/ Pz.Pi.Rgt. GD, were killed by enemy antitank guns and Soviet tanks. Many of the wounded were left where they were, there was no one left to carry them. Their fate is unknown. One Muli (tracked truck) loaded with wounded was rammed by a Soviet tank, knocked over and crushed beneath its tracks.

The few still-intact units, now mixed with the HG and the 28. Jäg.Division, fought their way through to the west. The next objective was Schölen. But enemy tanks were already reported near Fedderau. The situation was desperate, command impossible—orders were passed by word of mouth: everyone back to Wolittnick. The pioneers under Hptm. Warschnauer formed the rear guard. They carried out their difficult task in fierce close-quarters fighting. Again and again they placed themselves in front of the pursuing enemy, held him up with fire, fought for every wooded corner, for every ruin—just to gain time. The number of wounded rose steadily. The 1. San.Kp. GD set up its O.P. (operations point) in a still-intact farmhouse in Wolitta. Many, many wounded and dead lay or sat in front of it, already stiff from the cold. Medics carried wounded inside and laid them on the operating table. The medic in his blood-stained smock had just amputated a leg, which lay beneath the table in a bucket. He lit a cigarette and stepped aside, his face like a mask, to where another doctor appeared to be waking up. Who knows for how many hours he had been witnessing all this suffering? Using a pair of scissors, a medic skillfully cut away the trousers and underwear from the thigh of a wounded man. Then the doctor came, saw the many splinter wounds, quickly cleaned them, pulled out bits of cloth and scab, and said something to the effect of, "There are too many small splinters, we can't get them out here, the leg appears to be still intact. Rivanol bandage, Kramer splint—have you had a tetanus shot?" – "Yes, in September 1942!" replied the wounded man. Meanwhile the medic placed the gauze bandage, dripping with yellow Rivanol, on the leg, fitted a splint from the thigh to the heel and the toes and wrapped it carefully with a paper binding.

Outside, enemy close-support aircraft roared overhead again; large numbers of small-caliber bombs fell nearby, then smoking rockets and finally, for moments at a time, the hammering and pounding of cannon. All of the soldiers outside took cover somewhere and stared at the Il 2s. Then several stray armor-piercing shells whizzed through the houses. The doctors continued to work; the wounded hoped again and waited patiently for treatment.

On 19 March Wolittnick returned to our hands; defending there were the Pz.Korps GD fusiliers under the command of *Major* Kraussold. Hptm. Warschnauer scraped together all the men he could find, took charge of the now idle bakers and butchers and launched courageous counterattacks at the linesman's house on the Wolittnick—Gross-Hoppenbruch rail line. Again and again he led his bakers and butchers against the onrushing enemy, fighting like a Beserker; determined to hold, no one gave an inch. The brave Lt. Höft was killed here. Losses were frightful, but they had to hold! Wolittnick—the railway embankment—it had to be held! The columns from the east were still streaming towards the shore of the Frische Haff, passing due north of Wolittnick toward the Balga—Kahlholz Peninsula, to where the ferries crossed the water to Pillau. In Rosenberg—

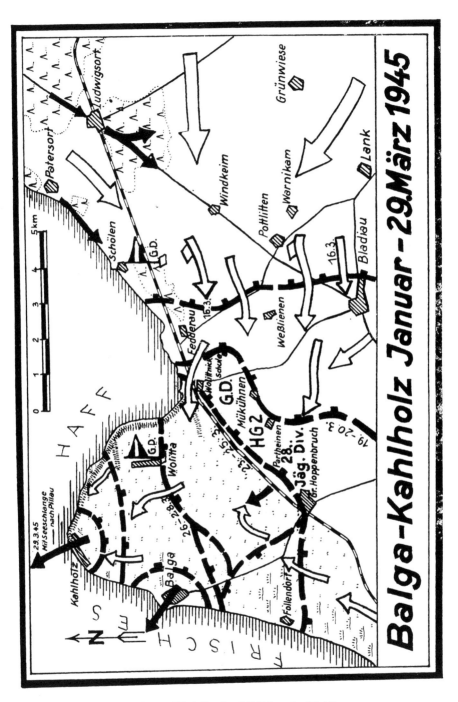

Balga—Kahlholz: 29 March 1945

267

Balga were the embarkation points for the trains, the wounded, for everything that was to go back.

In Balga, high on the sea wall, in the cemetery of the old church surrounded by trees, lay hundreds of wounded—on straw, on benches, on the bare ground. A steady stream of fresh wounded arrived, and then the din of approaching close-support aircraft, the thunderous impacts of shells fired by the "Black Pigs," the Soviet 152-mm guns, which threw up huge clouds of black smoke. The chaos was indescribable.

Near Rosenberg a single gangplank extended far out into the sea. It was the embarkation point for the wounded. Shells fell there, too—in the water, on the beach. Between the ruined houses deep bomb craters, against a tree a shattered ambulance, thrown there by the blast from a bomb, its back doors thrown open, inside shattered, dismembered bodies. The scene was the same in the next street. And again the cursed Il 2s came with their bombs and cannon.

A ship approached with a high bow wave, made a sharp turn, nearly rammed the gangplank and then docked with a hard jolt. Several sailors jumped off and tossed heavy hawsers over the posts. Quickly, quickly, they shouted. Then came the wounded, hobbling, helping drag each other, crawling. A man with a belly wound groaned loudly, the sailors dragged him onto the ship. Further above crates of ammunition were tossed over the side onto the gangplank. Keep moving, keep moving! But up front at the railway embankment the panzer-grenadiers, tank crews, the butchers and bakers, the Hermann Göring paratroopers, the panzer-fusiliers and the artillerymen continued to hold on, in cramped positions, weapons drawn. The machine-guns still fired, here and there an anti-aircraft or anti-tank gun. The last two Tigers and their brave crews under Uffz. Feuerpfeil and Uffz. Kroneis met their fates there. Fighting to the end, they were hit and went up in flames. Gefr. Brackmann died a hero's death, while Uffz. Feuerpfeil, Jürgens and Klickar were seriously wounded. They were the last of 11. Kp./III. (Tiger)/Pz.Rgt. GD to go down fighting—in the Balga pocket.

On 19 March *Major* Kraussold, who was in command, was hit by a shell splinter near the Wolittnick mill. Seriously wounded in the neck, he was evacuated to the rear. He was not seen again. But his men continued to resist—to the last! The Soviets assaulted the few German strongpoints without mercy and nevertheless were repeatedly forced to go to ground.

Everyone—the soldiers on the Balga Peninsula— was now fighting for his own life. Fsch.Pz.Gren.Div. 2 HG, 28. Jäg.Div., Pz.Rgt. GD, all together, even though the defenders numbers continued to dwindle. Wolottnick was held—*Major* von Basse was now leading the defensive forces of the Pz.Korps-Füs.Rgt. GD and fought with his men without regard to his own safety.

The artillery was in open firing positions in the swampy terrain east of

Balga—the Pz.Art.Rgt. GD alone still had more than 52 guns, and then there were the other units. All fired like mad, even though enemy aircraft, including American squadrons for the first time, and the much-feared Il 2s, bombed and strafed without letup. Casualties rose. It was difficult to know who had been killed and who was still alive. Even scouting new firing positions cost lives. Oblt. Robeck of the artillery lost his life, on 25 March Oblt. "Paule" Busch was killed by shell splinters while on a scouting mission.

At this time the GD division command post was still in Wolitta, deep in a cellar. The staff fed themselves from the food they found stored there. General Staff *Major* Adler, the Ia, was recalled and replaced by General Staff *Major* Clear. New order: the two bridgeheads at Balga and Kahlholz were to be held together under one command. The army group repeatedly radioed to hold the positions, hold the peninsula. Gen.Mj. Lorenz, in those days constantly outside with his men, radioed the situation the way it was. The army group ordered the rear guard to cover the 4. Armee to the last man! Fsch.Pz.Gren.Div. 2 HG and 28. Jäg.Div. were pulled out—GD continued to hold Balga and Kahlholz.

New positions were occupied in the night of 26-27 March; *Major* von Basse and his Pz.Korps fusiliers occupied the south tip of Wolitta as far as the Haff. Soviet infantry followed, but hesitantly; the terrain was now relatively tank-proof, the marshy subsurface prevented the passage of heavy armored vehicles. The fighting now increasingly centered around the few raised roadways and dam-top roads.

II./Pz.Rgt. GD continued to fight, now north of the railway embankment near Milchbude II—small Kampfgruppen which dug in and defended along the roads. The terrain was flooded all around, only the roads suggested the presence of a defense line. Little cover—too much open country.

Meanwhile, at Kahlholz and Balga the tank crews, elements of I. (SPW)/Pz.Rgt. GD, were loaded aboard navy landing craft, barges and small fishing craft. The vehicles stayed behind and were handed over to those who were left. II./Pz.Rgt. GD was still in position near Milchbude II; 5. and 7. Kp. were now led by senior non-commissioned officers, 8. (MG) Kp. by Oblt. Conschorek. In the evening the soldiers wounded during the day moved to the collection points and to the medical clearing station. At the same time more replacements were brought forward, mainly stragglers picked up in the rear, but also air force and navy personnel. At dawn most of these troops fled, the GD men remained behind and held their positions.

Defending against attacks by Soviet infantry were easier now, because they came without tanks. In almost every case the attacks were repulsed.

Meanwhile, in Balga, from all the wounded had been evacuated, elements of another division assumed the main defensive role. The GD fell back toward Kahlholz, the northernmost tip of the Balga Peninsula.

At about 14:00 hours on 28 March 1945 the army group radioed the following order: "All units on the Kahlholz Peninsula are hereby subordinated to the GD. The peninsula is to be held! Another regiment is being sent there. Submit ammunition requests."

Gen.Mj. Lorenz radioed back: "At best Kahlholz can be held until 05:00 hours on 29 March."

Everyone placed their hopes in the now famous "Sea Snake," which, operating from Pillau, had been picking up troops at Balga and Rosenberg and which was now earmarked to transport out the GD. Its creator, Gen.Mj. Henke, personally directed the "Sea Snake" from Pillau. It was approximately 65 meters long, consisted of landing craft lashed together and propelled by flak-armed lighters attached to the sides. Gen.Mj. Henke won acclaim for saving countless soldiers and civilians with this vehicle.

Toward evening on 28 March an order was received from the army corps: "GD withdraw!" Preparations were made immediately for the withdrawal and the picking up of the last from Kahlholz. The bridgehead around Kahlholz was becoming ever smaller as the Soviets pushed closer to the coast. But the bravery of the defenders, whose numbers shrank steadily as individual squads fell back, held them in check and dictated the pace of events. And that was what mattered now.

All heavy weapons, vehicles and guns were blown up one by one. Once again our artillery, which had just received ammunition, rose up and in regimental formation fired its last salvoes at recognized targets—it was nearing afternoon on 28 March. Then the last guns were spiked, the artillerymen climbed down the steep banks to the sea and waited to be picked up. Everything went exactly according to plan. When the last grenadiers and panzer-fusiliers sometimes looked anxiously for the landing craft, wondering if they had been left behind, they were comforted by Gen.Mj. Lorenz's words. They had faith in their command, even now. And then their machine-guns barked again, to hold the now tiny bridgehead and protect the embarkation.

Some tried to escape across the sea to Pillau on makeshift rafts, in amphibious Volkswagens, on fuel drums. The majority made the trip in navy landing craft. The sailors worked tirelessly to get everyone who was supposed to leave on board.

Only during the night of 28-29 March did the Sea Snake not come. It appeared to have failed to find the landing place. Had it become lost? It was almost midnight, the last machine-gun outposts waited at the steep bank. It was far beyond the appointed time. What was happening? Had something gone wrong? Were they still coming? At the point of desperation, several rowboats headed out to sea in the darkness to look for the "Sea Snake" and guide it to the landing place. They found it. The lighters pushed the cumbersome craft to the pier. Thank God! And soon the rows of men boarded the "Sea Snake" in good order, carrying their small arms and machine-guns.

Isolated anti-tank shells whizzed over their heads and landed in the sea; then once again the slow, monotone tacking of a Russian machine-gun, followed by the buzz of a rapid-firing MG 42. Quiet returned, only the soft tramping of feet on the pier suggested movement there down below.

It was almost 02:00 hours on 29 march 1945. Dense fog settled over the steep banks on to the sea. God himself had sent it. It saved the last men of the Pz.Gren.Div. GD.

Gen.Mj. Lorenz stood on the steps to the pier; repeatedly he nodded to someone, now and then counted, gave a few words of encouragement. Gradually the line of soldiers came to an end. Only a few more were coming, machine-guns shouldered, submachine-guns slung hunter style. The last of the Balga Peninsula, the last of Kahlholz; the last from the outposts at the steep banks.

It was deathly still when Gen.Mj. Lorenz gave the signal to cast off.

But…

The "Sea Snake" did not move; it remained stationary, did not pull away from the pier. Unrest among the men, soft curses. What was happening? The "Sea Snake" was not moving. Everyone down into the water—push, push! Relieved of some of its weight, the "Sea Snake" slowly rose from the bottom and began to move. The men in the water scrambled back aboard.

The engines of the lighters surged, pushing the "Sea Snake" away from the pier and out to sea—to freedom and safety. Somewhere on the Haff a lone Schwimmwagen, bullet-riddled but still watertight, chugged in the direction of Pillau. Alone and yet part of the whole. Under the command of Gen.Mj. Henke's pioneers, the "Sea Snake" sailed into Pillau harbor as the sun was rising in the east on 29 March. On board were the last survivors of Kahlholz, the last of the Panzer-Grenadier Division *Großdeutschland*.

*

The following numbers give some indication of the ferocity of the fighting there:

Losses from 15/1/45 to 29/3/45: 14,586 men, including 390 officers

Losses from 13/3/45 to 29/3/45: 5,653 men, including 120 officers.

During the period from 17/1/45 to 28/3/45, the 2. San.Kp. GD cared for 6,749 men.

From 20/3/45 to 29/3/45 the 1. San.Kp. GD cared for and evacuated from Kahlholz 18,467 wounded, including 2,392 non-ambulatory patients.

These figures include both GD men and soldiers from other units—but all were German soldiers.

The Panzer-Grenadier Division *Großdeutschland*'s total losses for the period from 15 January to 22 April 1945 were:

16,988 soldiers of all ranks.

No one can count their wounds, no one can measure their suffering, no one can minimize their sacrifice!

Part VII
The Panzer-Grenadier Division Kurmark's Fight for the Oder Bridgeheads at Lebus and Göritz

Chapter 1
Reitweiner Heights

The commanding massif of the Reitweiner Heights extends along the west bank of the Oder from Frankfurt through Lebus to Reitwein, gradually rising to the north to Point 81; on its decisive northern part lay three towns, which in addition to Lebus were to form key positions in the defense of the line of hills: Klessin, Wuhden and Podelzig.

While it was possible to see the upper course of the Oder between Lebus and Göritz from Klessin and Wuhden, Podelzig so to speak formed the backbone of the defense for both of these towns and was the key point for any major offensive to the west on the Oder plain north of Reitwein. Furthermore, possession of Lebus must have appeared vital to the enemy, since an attack from there northwest in the direction of Mallnow could potentially unhinge the Klessin—Wuhden—Podelzig triangle and the Mallnow—Seelow heights, which extended in a semicircle from Mallnow through Dolgelin to north of Seelow. In view of these facts the so-called Hardenberg position was also fortified and improved in the weeks that followed.

The objective of all the enemy's tactical measures in this sector must therefore be to gain possession of the Reitweiner Heights including Podelzig. But this could only be achieved by continuous attacks by the Soviet 8th Guards Army from the northern edge of the heights toward the south with simultaneous pressure by the Soviet 69th Army from Lebus in the direction of Mallnow. This also made it necessary for the Soviet 1st White Russian Front to establish a bridgehead for the 69th Army at Lebus.

With the capture of the Reitweiner Heights the Soviet side could be expected to launch a simultaneous secondary attack north of the heights into the plain as far as the Seelow—Küstrin road to create a buildup area for the first phase of the coming major offensive. The only possible objective of this first phase was to crack the Hardenberg position with superior infantry and artillery forces from the expanded bridgehead.

The main task of the few combat-capable divisions between Frankfurt and Küstrin was thus obvious: as per orders from corps headquarters, Pz.Gren.Div. KmK was to attack and capture the Reitweiner Heights as quickly as possible and smash the Göritz bridgehead. The division command had reservations about this mission, because it could only succeed if all forces—especially artillery—were employed in concentration. But apart from two battalions spread over an 18-kilometer-wide sector, the latter was absent. Furthermore, there was a shortage of infantry forces and those that were available had been in constant action for weeks with just one inexperienced battalion (II./Inf.Rgt. KS Dresden) in reserve. The division commander therefore demanded that all of his own units assigned elsewhere be returned plus the sending of additional infantry forces with which to carry out the attack, plus the sending of sufficient artillery to support the attack that had been ordered.

Attempts by the enemy on 8 February to send one or two companies across the Oder ice near Wüste Kunersdorf to establish a bridgehead were initially successful; however, immediate counterattacks by II./Pz.Gren.Div. KmK and elements of the Pz.Aufkl.Abt. KmK put paid to this plan. In any case, it was realized that further elements of the Soviet 69th Army were approaching the Oder north of Frankfurt, while the 8th Guards Army was taking advantage of the cover of darkness to steadily reinforce the Göritz bridgehead on the west bank. We proceeded from the assumption that there were already two Soviet divisions on the west bank.

On the German side the V. SS-Geb.-Korps, previously in command, had been relieved by the XI. SS-Korps under *SS-Obergruppen-führer* and *General der Waffen-SS* Kleinheisterkamp, who immediately established a stricter level of command in this sector. The corps command post was in Heinersdorf. The new command unit ordered the remaining elements of *Kurmark* brought in from the Frankfurt bridgehead plus the bringing in of additional infantry and artillery forces for the planned attack operation against the Reitweiner Heights.

The onset of enemy activity in the Lebus sector during the night of 8-9 February, and the threat this posed to the division's right flank, made it necessary for our dispositions to be changed for this and the following days. The change in our plans was mainly due to the increased ranging-in activity of enemy artillery from the areas south of Frauendorf. The enemy's targeting focus proved to be the Lebus area, Hill 55 to its north and Klessin. On the Reitweiner Heights the enemy kept up night attacks in company strength.

The *Kurmark* division command's desire for clear command conditions and a strong defense organization was frustrated by the situation, which forced it to spread out its units. Its own division reserves (initially just the Pz.Pi.Btl. KmK and I. (Pz.Jgd.) Abt. 1551/Pz.Rgt. KmK) were too weak to conduct offensive operations in addition to their defensive missions. The

Inf.Rgt. KS Potsdam, comprised of two battalions consisting mainly of senior officer cadets and in some cases *Leutnants*, had been promised and was in fact on its way. The unit's morale and spirit were excellent, however its command was miserable. Consisting of about 1,000 men, this regiment was now to finally relieve II. (BR)/Pz.Rgt. KmK in the Rathstock area with its regimental headquarters and one battalion. This would make it possible for the division command to establish an armored reserve. At the same time the other KS Potsdam battalion received orders to relieve the KS Dresden near Podelzig. The latter unit would then be inserted near Lebus as II. Btl. (BR)/Pz.Rgt. KmK was being withdrawn.

By bringing the Pz.Nachr.Abt. KmK and the Pz.Pi.Btl. KmK up to full strength and by bolstering the Pz.A.A. KmK's strength through the addition of an armored troop carrier company and supply companies, the division command was finally in a position to match the field telephone net, the building of positions and supply to the rising demands of the defensive struggle.

On 10 February two events took place which were to have unpredictable consequences for the Pz.Gren.Div. KmK.

Shortly after midnight the division command post at Libbenichen heard considerable battle noise from between the rail line and a sugar refinery. The enemy had apparently broken into the positions of the RAD battalion deployed there. Initial reports over the artillery net (forward observation posts—firing positions—battalions—regiment—division) spoke of enemy penetrations across the Podelzig—Küstrin rail line north in the direction of the Hathenow—Podelzig road.

The Pz.Pi.Btl. KmK and I. (Pz.Jgd.)/Pz.Rgt. KmK were immediately sent to counterattack, which began to have an effect at about 05:00 hours. These counterattack units succeeded in intercepting the enemy at the road due south of the sugar refinery and driving him back across the rail line. The Pz.Pi.Btl. KmK took up defensive positions there since all that was left of the RAD battalion was a few stragglers. I. (Pz.Jgd.) Abt. 1551/Pz.Rgt. KmK was moved back to the sugar refinery as reserve. Gradually the battle noise died down again.

At the same time (about 0500 hours), however, *SS-Standarten-führer* Fischer, sent by XI. SS-Korps and acting on a verbal order, appeared to take command of an attack against the Reitweiner Heights. In addition, a KS regiment and tanks were to be put as his disposal. Start of attack: 17:00 hours. The division command immediately objected to the lack of time to prepare for a twilight attack against the strongly fortified and occupied forest position of the Reitweiner Heights and refused to accept any responsibility for its failure. Furthermore, the attack unit was unfamiliar with the attack terrain, having just arrived from the officer school. In the division's opinion the use of panzer companies in a night attack into heavily wooded terrain without trained escorting infantry could only result in the senseless sacrifice of men and valuable armored equipment.

According to a radio message from XII. SS-A.K., the Pz.Art.Rgt. KmK was allocated 4,000 rounds of light and heavy howitzer ammunition for the attack plus sufficient mortar and infantry gun ammunition. It was to be delivered by 16:00 hours.

In command of the attack was *Standartenführer* Fischer, known as "Ghetto Fischer" for his destruction of the Warsaw ghetto. Following orders, the division command had to issue the necessary orders to the Inf.Rgt. KS Potsdam, Pz.Art.Rgt. KmK and II. (BR)/Pz.Rgt. KmK.

Standartenführer Fischer arrived at the division command post in Libbenichen at approximately 14:00 hours, was briefed on the enemy situation and his own forces, and then made his way to Podelzig to take over the attack force. He would soon finish off the few Russians were his words to his aides.

At about 17:00 hours the Pz.Art.Rgt. KmK began placing preparatory artillery fire on the designated break-in point. During this span of time, with dusk falling, the attack force reached its starting positions in I./Inf.Rgt. KS Dresden's lines and following another barrage attacked northwest toward the Podelzig—Reitwein road. The subordinated II. (BR)/Pz.Rgt. KmK reached the town of Podelzig via Dolgelin and Carzig on time and supported the attack, initially in the front attack waves. Displaying great courage, the officer cadets fought their way through to the wooded tip of the Reitweiner Heights (Mooshütte area) and inflicted heavy losses on the enemy.

Before the KS Potsdam battalion, now without tank support because of darkness and the trees, was able to reorganize its units and resume its attack toward the town of Reitwein, it was struck several times by furious enemy counterattacks from different directions. Having suffered heavy casualties, the KS Potsdam battalion was forced to retire in the direction of Podelzig, where it was taken in by the tanks and the I./Inf.Rgt. KS Dresden. Its total losses in killed and wounded, but especially missing, totaled more than 350 men!

Trying to exploiting this success, before midnight the enemy attacked in the direction of Podelzig. This night attack was beaten off by barrage fire from the Pz.Art.Rgt. KmK and the tanks.

It was not until the following day that the units of the KS Potsdam and KS Dresden, which had been thrown into disarray, were to some extent regrouped and reorganized.

Standartenführer Fischer left his attack troops at about midnight and, without any sort of report to the division, made his way back to his headquarters.

Chapter 2
11-13 February 1945

The situation in the Panzer-Grenadier Division *Kurmark*'s defense sector during the period 11-13 February 1945 can be summed up as follows: while the Soviet 8th Guards Army had clearly made the Reitweiner Heights a focal point, the continuing enemy attacks against the Frankfurt bridgehead and the absence of precise information on the enemy in the Lebus sector (Soviet 69th Army) made it impossible to determine where the point of main effort lay.

The initial portion of the boundary between the two Soviet armies had been positively identified as running from Frauendorf to due south of Klessin, however its subsequent path to the west was still unconfirmed. It was therefore impossible to say with certainty in which directions the two armies were likely to attack. An accurate assessment would not be possible until the bulk of the enemy units had been identified and located. Meanwhile both armies had largely completed their artillery buildups on the plateau east of the Oder from Gohlitz to north of Göritz. Aerial reconnaissance and the activities of the observation battalion had revealed that the Soviet artillery force to date totaled approximately 1,000 guns! Only a small part of the enemy artillery took part in the fighting for the Reitweiner Heights, however.

Still unknown was the whereabouts of the Soviet 1st and 2nd Guards Tank Armies, which had previously been part of the 1st White Russian Front. To them would fall the main responsibility for a future breakthrough operation, as soon as the Soviet 8th Guards and 69th Armies had created the conditions needed for a breakout from the Oder bridgeheads in the Frankfurt-Küstrin sector.

For the immediate future, therefore, the enemy's efforts would be concentrated mainly on taking the plateau from Lebus to Reitwein, since this was of vital importance for the building of large-scale bridgeheads in which to concentrate the two Soviet tank armies. All indications suggested that after creating these conditions the enemy would launch his ultimate offensive toward the west on both sides of the Küstrin—Seelow road. By night enemy patrols were extremely active on the river bank in the Lebus sector.

In the Göritz sector the enemy mounted repeated attacks in company to battalion strength; in each case these were repulsed with heavy losses to the enemy. As before, the focal point of these nocturnal attacks was the eastern edge of Klessin, the eastern edge of Wuhden and northeast of Wuhdin and Podelzig. North of Reitwein to the division's left boundary there was little activity apart from frequent nocturnal patrols.

So far the enemy artillery had not engaged in any counter-battery work against friendly artillery. The reason was probably the extreme range from the Gohlitz—Göritz area to the Mallnow area, which made effective fire questionable. Furthermore, it was to be assumed that the bulk of the enemy artillery would not intervene until just before the start of the actual offensive.

The friendly situation was improved through the insertion of the two battalions of the Inf.Rgt. KS Potsdam. This insertion also made it possible to finally employ the Inf.Rgt. KS Dresden as a complete unit instead of as separate battalions as before—in the Lebus sector. Even though there were no direct signs of enemy attacks in this sector, it was to be expected that the Soviet 69th Army would become much more active between Frankfurt and Lebus.

As a result of the widening of the Inf.Rgt. KS Dresden's sector, it was possible to withdraw II./Pz.Gren.Rgt. KmK from its sector near Wüste Kunersdorf on 12 February 1945. The battalion was initially positioned behind the focal point sector (the Reitweiner Heights) in Podelzig as division reserve. It was anticipated that it would subsequently see action as part of the Pz.Pi.Btl. KmK on the Klessin front. Unfortunately, due to a shortage of infantry forces, it was not possible to pull the Pz.Pi.Btl. KmK out of the front south of Hathenow.

The bulk of the Pz.A.A. KmK, which had meanwhile been brought up to strength in men and materiel, stood ready approximately three kilometers east of Libbenichen as a mobile reserve. Several armored patrols secured the division's right boundary near Burgwall and maintained contact with Fortress Frankfurt.

As a result of the great width of its sector, the KmK division command was forced to deploy the I. (Pz.Jgd.) Abt. 1551/Pz.Rgt. KmK in companies to the individual focal point sectors instead of in a body as hoped. This did, however, place the various sector commanders in the position of having tank support available immediately in the event of attack and being able to add their weight to every counterattack.

The choice of the Falkenhagen rear area for the division's supply services proved especially fortunate. On the one had there was a spacious barracks camp available there, on the other the distances to the army's installations were not great. Since the enemy had not yet committed his long-range artillery, transports on the Seelow to Schönfliess station section could be carried out at night without interruption. Through personal contact with the affected offices, the division Ib was eventually able to have the division's supply needs met directly from factories and warehouses in the home war zone.

In summing up the assessment of our own situation, as a result of reorganizations and the arrival of additional forces, the division command saw future developments as serious but not hopeless. The constant threat of a large and surprising enemy breakthrough appeared to have been averted.

True, given the unfavorable ratio of forces future local penetrations were unavoidable, however the division felt confident that it could deal with any major attack in the near future.

This assessment of the situation was based on the decisive ridge between north of Lebus and the tip of the Reitweiner Heights remaining in our hands. The fact that the enemy had established himself in the northern foothills of the Reitweiner Heights as well as at its eastern edges with relatively strong forces and sought to expand this area through persistent attacks was offset by our defensive effort, which received effective support from the artillery.

In the period that followed, the enemy had to be prevented from capturing all of the Reitweiner Heights through surprise attack. The elements of the Panzer-Grenadier Division *Kurmark* formed the backbone of the entire defensive effort, and these had to be continually shifted between the various hot spots.

Chapter 3
14 February 1945

On 14 February the formation of the Soviet 69th Army's point of main effort north of Frankfurt near Lebus was clearly recognized. On the afternoon of that same day, encouraged by hazy weather and the still-frozen Oder, it launched a surprise attack near Lebus with heavy forces. There was no special artillery preparation. The attack, spearheaded by several regiments, soon broke through the thinly-stretched and weakly-manned lines of the Inf.Rgt. KS Dresden. The Soviets took the town of Lebus and crossed the Lebus—Podelzig rail line in several places.

While the main assault by hastily moved-in tanks assumed threatening proportions, further strong enemy elements were able to expand the captured area to the north and south.

This posed a considerable threat to the regrouping and reorganization of the units completed in the previous days and with it the division's continuous, if loose front. All that the division could muster was small groups of reserves to give aid to the numerous points of main effort in the shortest time.

However, a possible broadening of the enemy attack near Lebus in the direction of Mallnow and its northeast made the situation in the Klessin—Wuhden—Podelzig triangle and the artillery area appear untenable. This assessment of the situation led the *Kurmark* division command to commit its sole substantial infantry reserve, the II./Pz. Gren.Rgt. KmK, to a counterattack from the Podelzig area toward the west part of Lebus. In the division's opinion this was the only way to effectively meet an enemy thrust in the direction of Mallnow, perhaps even bring the enemy to a halt at the railway line and at least temporarily close the ripped-open front. At about 17:00 hours on 14 February, therefore, orders were phoned to II./Pz.Gren.Rgt. KmK to immediately attack astride the rail line toward Lebus station and the western part of the town, prevent the further advance of the enemy to the north and northwest and reestablish communications with Inf.Rgt. KS Dresden at the west end of Lebus.

The more complete reports concerning the enemy penetration against KS Dresden at Lebus, which began coming in during the noon hour, showed that the positions held by the widely scattered companies of this regiment had been breached, especially at the eastern edge of Lebus. Since the enemy had rapidly moved reinforcements into the break-in position, by exploiting the confusion of KS Dresden as darkness was falling he was able to continue his main thrust along the Lebus—Schönfleiss station road as far as the railway line.

Several smaller attacks succeeded in driving the companies of the KS

Dresden, whose ranks had already been seriously thinned, at first to Elisenberg and in the northwest back through Lebus station.

Not until the evening hours did a counterattack by the II./Pz.Gren.Rgt. KmK (initially led by 7. Kp. under Lt. Schwing) make itself felt. It succeeded in heading the enemy off at Lebus station, and the enemy forces that had broken through across the rail line with tanks in the direction of Elisenheim were driven back across the rail line.

While the II./Pz.Gren.Rgt. KmK was able to establish a relatively continuous front roughly from the Lebus—Schönfliess station road to east of Elisenheim, the situation north and south of Lebus was still uncertain.

Not until about midnight on 14-15 February was it possible to see that the bulk of the Inf.Rgt. KS Dresden had been thrown back to the west and southwest by the enemy attack. Its units were completely mixed together, the bulk of the telephone lines from the regiment to the platoons had been knocked out. Because of the darkness it was impossible to estimate casualties. Isolated groups of KS Dresden soldiers did, however, manage to hold a line roughly along the rail line south of the Lebus—Schönfliess station road against persistent enemy attacks. The further development of the situation near Lebus was viewed with serious concern.

In conjunction with the attack near Lebus, in the Reitweiner Heights sector the Soviet 8th Guards Army now launched repeated night attacks in battalion strength. All of these attacks near Klessin, Wuhden and northeast of Podelzig were repulsed through the combined efforts of the infantry and artillery with heavy losses to the enemy.

On the other hand in the Reitwein sector as far as Kietz there was only active patrolling by both sides, which continued until about one hour before midnight. The enemy did not take advantage of the division's tense situation in this sector to launch a decisive attack operation.

By 14 February the armies of the Soviet 1st White Russian Front had succeeded in establishing a total of four bridgeheads across the Oder:

33rd Army	north of Fürstenberg
69th Army	near Lebus
8th Guards Army	near Göritz
5th Shock Army	near Schaumburg-Kienitz

On 15 February the ice covering the Oder began to melt and in the days that followed broke up into drifting ice; as a result the enemy immediately began building bridges.

The situation became especially critical on 15 February, however, especially since, beginning at dawn, the attack units of the Soviet 69th Army resumed their battalion- to regiment-strength attacks to expand their bridgehead to the west. Throughout the day they repeatedly succeeded in crossing the rail line to the west with tank support, but in each case they were thrown back again by weak reserves of the II./Pz.Gren.Rgt. KmK.

In spite of the fierce fighting the scattered elements of the Inf.Rgt. KS Dresden were gradually regrouped. A much-needed strengthening of the defending forces resulted from the insertion of the Pz.A.A. KmK's armored troop carrier troop due south of the Lebus—Schönfliess station road.

In addition to II./Pz.Gren.Rgt. KmK, that regiment's 11. (IG.) Kp. and a newly-arrived 320-mm rocket battalion played a major role in the defensive success on 15 February.

The Pz.Art.Rgt. KmK's forward observer reported that the enemy was beginning to build a bridge at the eastern edge of Lebus. He was helped in this by finding about 60 to 70 intact fishing boats in barns and sheds in the town.

In a surprise move, the previous evening the enemy had succeeded in putting about 30 to 50 T 34 and T 85 tanks across the Oder, and these became a factor in the advances across the rail line. Furthermore, the most forward enemy positions had been reinforced with numerous anti-tank guns. At first, however, no movement of artillery from the east to the west banks of the Oder could be detected; the size of the bridgehead may still have been too limited for this. On the other hand the Soviet attack units were supported by numerous mortars, which must have completed their change of position to the west side of the Oder during the night of 14-15 February.

In the Soviet 8th Guards Army's sector, the enemy also continued his attacks due south of Klessin in the Reitwein sector by day for the first time. These were unsuccessful, however.

Enemy artillery and mortars put down heavy fire near Wuhden, northeast of Podelzig and on the town of Podelzig itself, with the obvious intention of so grinding down our main line of resistance and reserve quartering areas by day that following night attacks would have a better chance of success.

In the Reitwein to Kietz sector the presence of II. (BR)/Pz.Rgt. KmK in the Sachsendorf area held the enemy back from attack operations of a serious nature. Furthermore, the 8th Guards Army seemed to regard the sure possession of the Reitweiner Heights as a precondition for a larger attack operation into the Oder lowlands.

Based on the observed behavior of the enemy, especially the Soviet 8th Guards Army, the enemy obviously rated the Panzer-Grenadier Division *Kurmark*'s fighting strength higher than it really was. This was probably due in large part to the unbroken fighting spirit of the front-line infantry and the appearance of our tanks and Hetzer tank-destroyers at the changing hot spots. According to statements by prisoners, the Soviets had suffered serious casualties in their mostly battalion-strength night attacks from the division's artillery (*Major* Hammerich), which had the precise range and was well-schooled in cooperating with the infantry. As well, the enemy had the misfortune of always attacking in the sectors in which the artillery was especially effective.

The approximately 2 000-meter gap in the lines between the northwest edge of Lebus and the town of Klessin, which for the time being could only be watched over by lone patrols, including a Tiger with attached infantry squad, caused the division command to press forcefully for the bringing in of further infantry forces. These demands were finally met by the commanding XI. SS-A.K. by subordinating to the division the Inf.Rgt. KS Wetzlar, which was on its way to the front. The leading elements of this regiment arrived in the Lebus area on the evening of 15 February and were immediately inserted between Lebus station and Podelzig, allowing the threatening gap to be closed. At the same time the II./Pz.Gren.Rgt. KmK was pulled out of the line. It was subsequently to see action south and west of Klessin as part of the lengthening of the Pz.Gren.Rgt. KmK's right wing.

Meanwhile, after further urgent pleas from the division, the corps promised that the Burgwall—Wüste Kunersdorf would be handed over to the newly inserted 712. I.D. The new division on the right side would become effective at midnight on 17 February.

The division command expressed the opinion that on the critical day of fighting (15 February) the division had succeeded in preventing an expansion of the enemy bridgehead, which would have threatened the entire sector.

The enemy had failed to exploit his big chance to unhinge the decisive hill position on the Reitweiner Heights by energetically continuing his attacks in the direction of Mallnow.

There was no doubt that since the beginning of February the Soviet 1st White Russian Front had halted its previous offensive to the west. Its main attack units—the Soviet 1st and 2nd Guards Tank Armies—had been diverted north into Pomerania, and consequently the forces necessary for a resumption of the offensive on Berlin were lacking on the Oder front.

As a result of the absence of the two Soviet tank armies, for the time being the Soviet 1st White Russian Front limited its offensive activities on the Oder to the winning or improvement of a series of at first tactical bridgeheads. This was a precondition for the resumption of the big offensive.

This also explains:

The bitter struggle to expand and fortify the bridgeheads;

the modest attack widths of both armies and the in-depth deployment of several divisions in the focal point sector at Lebus (Soviet 69th Army) and on the Reitweiner Heights (Soviet 8th Guards Army);

the unbroken offensive activity in these sectors and the concentrated employment of artillery.

The Soviet 69th Army appeared to have finally designated the Lebus bridgehead as the focal point of its offensive. The enemy had deployed at least two divisions and parts of a tank brigade there.

He had quickly improved the positions he had won and reinforced them with numerous anti-tank and mortar units. His infantry launched daily attacks west from the bridgehead in battalion, even regiment strength, with tank support. On the other hand there was no discernible offensive activity towards the south, in the direction of Frankfurt, so that it was assumed with a high degree of probability that the Soviet 69th Army's main direction of attack would be to the west and northwest. When the Oder ice began to melt it was found that the Soviets had begun building a bridge *beneath* the water.

In the Göritz bridgehead, in the attack area of the Soviet 8th Guards Army, the attacks were continued in the days that followed. As a rule these attacks were made at night in battalion to regiment strength, in order to allow the troops to quickly run under the accurate German barrage fire. As before, the point of main effort was near Klessin, Wuhden and northeast of Podelzig. On the other hand the enemy was noticeably quiet in the sector north of the Reitweiner Heights to the southern edge of Kietz.

A new offensive focal point emerged near Klessin. With the capture of this town the enemy was in the position to unhinge the German defense front northeast of Podelzig from the rear. The enemy had deployed one division and elements of a tank brigade in the Klessin sector. Together with several tanks, elements of this division had established themselves in the wood located 1 000 meters south of Klessin. From there the enemy undertook several attacks toward Klessin each day, breaking into the eastern and southern parts of the town repeatedly. He was, however, not capable of holding the ground that had been won against the immediately-launched counterattacks. Having been freed up by the insertion of the I.R. KS Wetzlar north of Lebus, II./Pz.Gren.Rgt. KmK had been deployed there in a line from Point 55 to the southern edge of the town, where it's positions bordered those of the I./Pz.Gren.Rgt. KmK.

The enemy kept up the pressure on Wuhden and the important positions northeast of Podelzig; however, our forces were able to fend off this pressure, smashing enemy attacks over the gently sloping, completely open terrain with concentrated defensive fire or employing local reserves to counterattack and eliminate minor penetrations.

According to reports by the *Luftwaffe*, the enemy was now building a second underwater bridge near Göritz.

Chapter 4
Situation on 17 and 18 February 1945

At the constant urging of Headquarters, 9. Armee and corps, on 18 February the KmK division command was forced to launch a counterattack with two battalions of the I.R. KS Wetzlar, which had only been inserted into the defense front on 17 February, and the Pz.Abt.(BR)/Pz.Rgt. KmK with the objective of reducing the Lebus bridgehead. The mission order: break through on both sides of the Podelzig—Lebus road to the crossroads in Lebus and split the enemy bridgehead. Focal point of the attack east of the road, also employment of our tanks there. Preparation and support of the attack by the bulk of our artillery and the rocket battalion as well as a squadron of Me 109s.

The infantry attacked at about 10:00 hours on 18 February and in spite of an half-hour preparatory barrage by the artillery it was only able to gain a few meters in a southerly direction in the face of the enemy's concentrated barrage fire and was forced to dig in. East of the road, however, the tanks of II. (BR)/Pz.Rgt. KmK managed to advance to within 1 500 meters of the northern edge of Lebus. Support by our tactical aircraft lasted just 30 minutes.

As a result of the enemy barrage fire, however, in the focal point sector east of the road our infantry soon became separated from the Panther battalion, which soon ran into an enemy anti-tank barricade. Under these circumstances the division command saw itself forced to break off the seemingly hopeless continuation of the attack and pull the Panther battalion back to its starting position.

The enemy then struck out in a counterattack in the evening hours of 18 February. In a subsequent night attack in regiment strength from the northern part of Lebus, he succeeded in breaking into the I.R. KS Wetzlar's positions at the Lebus—Podelzig road and directly to the west of it. The enemy gained a foothold in Lindenhof and achieved a deep penetration along the road to the north.

The division reserve in Podelzig was alerted immediately and without delay was sent to counterattack along the road from Podelzig to the south. Due south of Schäfergrund it ran into the leading enemy elements. This forceful counterattack in the early hour of 19 February drove the enemy back to the fork in the road two kilometers south of Schäfergrund. There, however, our counterattack was halted by freshly-committed enemy reserves.

The following days were largely quiet apart from repeated local attacks. Also contributing to the defense was an old heavy howitzer from the First World War, a museum piece from the arsenal in Berlin. It had been delivered to the sector in pieces and was accompanied by 100 to 150 rounds of ammunition.

After much hard work the big gun was set up in the area south of Podelzig. Approximately thirty minutes were required for loading and preparation between shots. Once ready, however, it could place shells with surprising accuracy and gave the Soviets something to think about. Their response, with Stalin Organs and mortars, was also nothing to sneeze at, however it failed to silence the howitzer.

The fighting to date near Lebus and on the Reitweiner Heights had led to heavy casualties among the front-line units. The daily total of killed, wounded and missing hovered around the 250 to 300 man mark. The Inf.Rgt. KS Dresden and II./Pz.Gren.Rgt. KmK had suffered especially heavy losses in the fighting for Lebus.

The continuous use by the enemy of artillery at the other key points also contributed to the high rate of loss.

At this period of time replacements were provided in a variety of ways:

From the remaining cadres of the Pz.Gren.-Ersatz-Brigade GD in Cottbus and Guben, at least until the beginning—middle of March 1945 when the brigade moved to Schleswig.

On the other hand the army also sent a steady flow replacements by way of the XI. SS-Korps. The bulk of these were soldiers who had been gleaned from the home bases and whose value as combat troops was minimal given the ferocity of the defensive struggle. It must be said, however, that in spite of many training shortcomings the replacements soon became accustomed to their difficult circumstances and fought bravely.

During this period the division was sent or formed the following complete units:

1 light and 1 heavy artillery battalion,
2 construction battalions, which had no combat value and could therefore be used only for building positions.

Promised and on still their way were:
1 100-mm cannon battalion,
2 heavy howitzer batteries,
1 heavy mortar battalion with approximately 36 120-mm mortars.

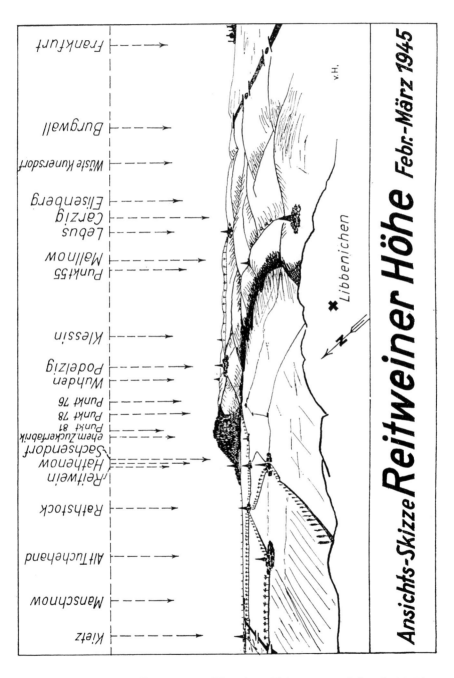

Panoramic View: Reitweiner Heights, February to March 1945

Chapter 5
18 to 25 February 1945

Enemy: During the course of almost three weeks the Soviet 1st White Russian Front had succeeded in so solidifying the bridgeheads of the Soviet 69th and 8th Guards Armies that only a major attack could destroy them. With the Soviets' inherent tenacity, the enemy infantry had immediately dug into every meter of ground and built strong positions.

Countless mortars and superior artillery supported the defense of the bridgeheads. In them since 15 February were elements of tank brigades which worked directly with the infantry.

The enemy's anti-tank resources were considerable. The Soviets undoubtedly wanted to quickly halt any armored attack by us aimed at splitting the bridgeheads.

Furthermore, they had concentrated large numbers of light and medium anti-aircraft guns at their bridge positions so that any approaching aircraft had to run a heavy gauntlet of anti-aircraft fire.

Three enemy divisions had so far been identified in the Soviet 69th Army's sector (Lebus bridgehead). In recent days these had begun launching a series of small-scale attacks whose apparent purpose was to improve the local positions for a later larger attack.

After the appearance of our Panther battalion the enemy tanks ceased fighting from the front lines, instead they were positioned at least 2 000 meters behind their infantry as mobile anti-tank guns.

In the northern sector of the Lebus bridgehead the enemy had placed numerous 76.2-mm anti-tank guns in masterfully camouflaged positions. This made it almost impossible for our artillery and aircraft to engage them effectively, especially since they did not open fire until German tanks attacked. In the Göritz bridgehead (Soviet 8th Guards Army's sector) the enemy attacks against the Reitweiner Heights went on without letup. They achieved little success, however.

Statements made by prisoners made it possible to positively identify the following units of the 8th Guards Army:

the Soviet 4th Rifle Division, including an assault gun brigade (SU) near Klessin,
a Soviet rifle division near Wuhden,
the Soviet Proletarian Division "8 November,"
the Soviet Proletarian Division "1 May" – both elite units, at the Reitweiner Nose,
at least one more rifle division between Reitweiner Nose and Kietz.

In general the strength of the enemy divisions was about 8,000 men. These were almost all combat soldiers, as the train was supplied by the army.

Friendly situation: Pz.Gren.Div. KmK: The division's front continued to be extremely tense. The division's sector was now almost 25 kilometers wide. Infantry available and in position: 8 battalions and the Pz.Pi.Btl. KmK. For infantry reserves the division had only two armored troop carrier troops of the Pz.A.A. KmK.

After the first counterattack (I.R. KS Wetzlar and II./Pz.Rgt. KmK) on 18 February had failed, the Panther battalion and the headquarters of Pz.Rgt. *Kurmark* were initially transferred to Altzeschdorf so as to be immediately ready to respond to a crisis situation in the Lebus—Klessin sector.

Meanwhile, the following had joined the division:

Two construction battalions, one mortar battalion, one 100-mm cannon battalion.

These assets were put to use in these days, with the construction battalions used mainly to improve the positions on account of their limited combat value.

The Reich Propaganda Minister was able to convince the XII. SS-A.K. that the Panzer-Grenadier Division *Kurmark* should launch another attack on Lebus. The reason for this was the East-Asian collection of the Kaiser Friedrich Museum which was stored in Lebus. This fact was not known to the division command and the attack was scheduled for 22 February.

The defensive struggle was seriously hindered by the *Gauleiter* of Kurmark's order for the civilian population to remain in the combat zone. Even if the towns involved in the fighting were evacuated, the civilian population remained in the villages behind the battalion command posts. Furthermore, the commanding corps issued a directive from Headquarters, 9th Army that the spring cultivation should go ahead in the combat zone.

Both the commanding general of the XI. SS-A.K., *General der Waffen-SS* Kleinheisterkamp, and the commander-in-chief of the 9. Armee, *General der Infanterie* Busse, visited the division command post several times. During this period of time the division was also visited by: the Inspector of Officer Replacement, *General* von Hellermann, who was responsible for reorganizing the officer candidate schools into infantry regiments; the Inspector-General of Armored Forces, *General* Thomale, who assisted the division in meeting its material needs; the adjutant of the SA high command, to which the Feldherrnhalle Battalion was subordinate for inspections; the commander of air forces in the area of Headquarters, 9. Armee; the senior artillery commander of Headquarters, 9. Armee and the artillery commander of the XI. SS-A.K.

For lack of space the Pz.Gren.Rgt. KmK's operations section (Ia, Ic and signals officer) moved out of the village of Libbenichen to the estate located approximately 500 meters east of Libbenichen station. From there it had a view of almost the entire division sector.

New to the division command was a National-Socialist political officer, with whom there was friction from the very start.

On the tactical plain the division commander and Ia were locked in a fierce struggle against the plans and efforts of the commanding corps, which was determined to commit the Pz.Rgt. KmK to an attack from Podelzig against the heavily wooded Reitweiner Nose.

On the one hand, in the opinion of the division command the Panzer regiment's main strengths—firepower and mobility—could not be exploited. In addition, the positions of the two Soviet elite divisions on the Reitweiner Nose were very heavily fortified and were literally studded with anti-tank guns. An attack by the regiment would probably result in heavy tank losses without being able to drive the enemy off the Reitweiner Nose. The response from the commanding corps (especially from its commander, *Standartenführer* Giese) to the division command was that no tanks were to be spared in this desperate hour! It was only a personal relationship between the Ia and the Inspector-General of Armored Forces that prevented this senseless waste of a panzer regiment.

Friendly units:

Following the counterattack on 18 February near Lebus, the Rgt. H.Q. and II. (BR)/Pz.Rgt. KmK were initially moved into the Altzeschdorf area.

In their place Inf.Rgt. KS Potsdam received a company of tank-destroyers from I. (Pz.Jgd.)/Pz.Rgt. KmK as counterattack reserve.

Pz.Pi.Btl. KmK had begun laying a deep mine belt approximately 1 200 meters east of Hathenow, bolstering the defensive strength of its positions there.

Pz.Jäg.Kp./I. (Pz.Jgd.)/Pz.Rgt. KmK was subordinated to the Inf.Rgt. KS Wetzlar.

The two remaining companies of the Hetzer battalion were deployed with one company in Podelzig at the division's disposal and another company at the disposal of the Pz.Gren.Rgt. KmK as counterattack reserve in the area southwest of Klessin—Wuhden.

H.Q. Pz.A.A. KmK including two armored troop carrier troops as division reserve in Libbenichen area.

Pz.Art.Rgt. KmK command post and H.Q. I. (Pz.Jgd.)/Pz.Rgt. KmK in Mallnow.

Planning for the attack on 22 February:

The division command expressed serious doubts about the attack on Lebus which the XI. SS-Korps had ordered for 22 February. With the extremely tight situation in the entire division sector, the only offensive units which it could provide to support the attack were II. (BR)/Pz.Rgt. KmK, two armored troop carrier troops of the Pz.A.A. KmK and elements of the artillery. On the other side the enemy forces in Lebus were numerically far superior and would be fighting from strongly fortified positions. The counterattack on 18 February had failed because of the materiel superiority of the enemy. The commanding corps made available for the attack:

1 squadron of Ju 87s to take out enemy anti-tank guns shortly before the start of the attack,

1 wing of Me 109s and Fw 190s for direct support of our tank attack,

1 air liaison detachment,

1 forward air control unit.

Organization of forces:

Command: division commander – *Oberst* Langkeit

Pz.Rgt. KmK – with II. (BR)/Pz.Rgt. KmK and a Jagd-Pz.Kp./I./Pz.Rgt. KmK, 2 armored troop carrier troops of the Pz.A.A. KmK.

II./Pz.Gren.Rgt. KmK in its position sector, from which the attack was to be made;

Artillery: In command artillery commander Pz.Art.Rgt. KmK with two heavy battalions, one rocket brigade, one mortar battalion.

Armored group to assemble in the area of the west part of Schäfergrund:

II./Pz.Gren.Rgt. KmK in its position sector in the area north of Point 55.

1st attack objective: Point 55. 2nd objective: northern edge of Lebus, east of the Lebus—Podelzig road. 3rd objective: communications road from middle of Lebus to bridge site.

At about the same time as the attack on the second objective the left wing of the I.R. KS Wetzlar is to attack astride the Lebus—Podelzig road toward the Lebus crossroads. II./Pz.Gren.Rgt. KmK to follow our tank attack and clear the captured territory of the enemy. Air-ground liaison detachment with the division Ia. Forward air control unit with the Pz.Rgt. KmK.

During the night of 20-21 February a pincer attack from the ravines east of Point 55 and from the Schäfergrund enabled the enemy to penetrate toward Point 55. In spite of an immediate counterattack, the elements of II./Pz.Gren.Rgt. KmK deployed there were driven back toward the hill 200 meters north of Point 55 by the superior enemy forces. Late in the afternoon on 21 February enemy troops in battalion strength attacked from the west part of Lebus west along the Lebus—Schönfleiss road, crossing the rail line in several places. The former front line was restored by an immediate counterattack by the local reserve of the Inf.Rgt. KS Dresden.

An offensive patrol operation by the Inf.Rgt. KS Wetzlar on the evening of 21 February aimed at improving its positions near Lindenhof failed. Continuous enemy artillery and mortar fire on the positions on the Reitweiner Heights, often bolstered by concentrations of fire.

Late on the night of 22 February the armored group reached the southern approaches to the Sichelgrund, and shortly before daybreak it assembled in the western approaches to the Schäfergrund.

The artillery barrage was followed by direct air support from our close-support units, and at 10:15 hours the armored group attacked from the northern approaches of the Hakengrund through the positions of II./Pz.Gren.Rgt. KmK north of Point 55.

The attack proceeded rapidly as far as the southern approaches to the Hakengrund and Point 55 was recaptured.

The enemy replied with mass barrages from the east bank of the Oder and placed a thick curtain of flak over the attack area. Southeast and southwest of Point 55 the enemy's camouflaged anti-tank guns opened fire on our advancing armor from the flanks. North of Lebus another anti-tank barricade engaged the armored group frontally.

Excellent camouflage and heavy anti-aircraft fire made it impossible for our artillery and air force to silence the enemy anti-tank guns. Faced with this fact, the division commander, who once again had personally taken part in the attack in the second wave of armor, decided to call off the attack. The hill at Point 55 was readied for defense by II./Pz.Gren.Rgt. KmK.

The committed tank units returned to their quarters.

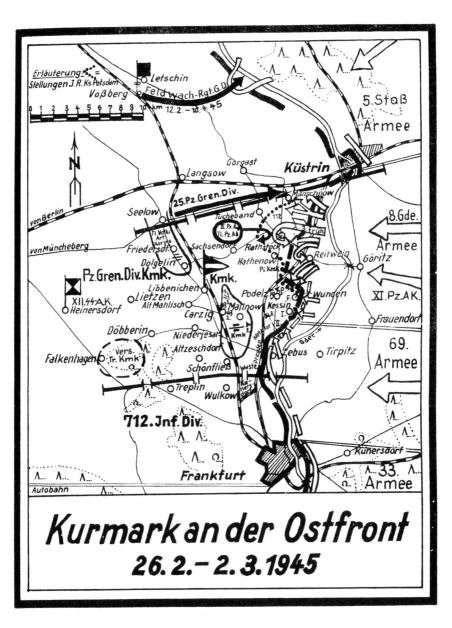

Kurmark on the Eastern Front: 26 February to 2 March 1945

PANZER-GRENADIER-DIVISION „KURMARK"
STAND: FEBRUAR 1945

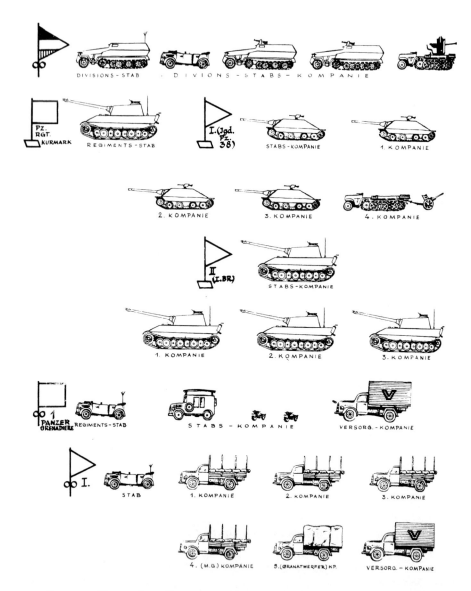

Panzer-Grenadier-Division "Kurmark" (as of February 1945)

Divisions-Stab = Divisional Staff; Divisions-Stabs-Kompanie = Divisional Headquarters Company; Regiments-Stab = Regimental Staff; Versorg.-Kompanie = Supply Compny; 4. (MG) Kompanie = 4th (Machine Gun) Company; 5. (Granatwerfer) Kp. = 4th (Mortar) Company

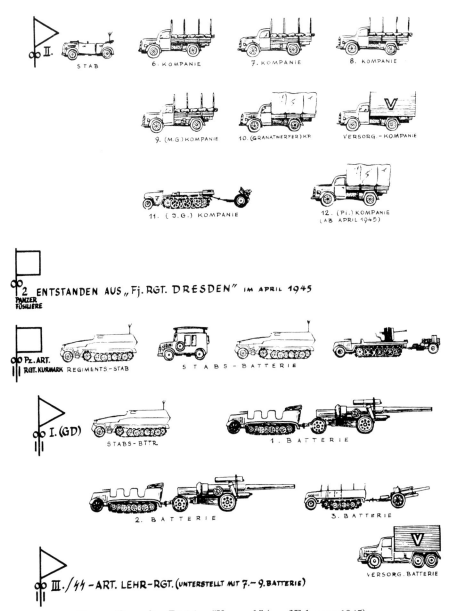

Panzer-Grenadier-Division "Kurmark" (as of February 1945)

Stab = Staff; 9. (MG) Kompanie = 9th (Machine Gun) Company; 10. (Granatwerfer) Kp. = 10th (Mortor) Company; Versorg.-Kompanie = Supply Company; 11. (IG) Kompanie = 11th (Infantry Support Gun) Company; 12. (Pi.) Kompanie (ab April 1945) = 12th (Pioneer) Company (starting April 1945); Entstanden aus "Fj. Rgt. Dresden" im April 1945 = Created out of "Officer Candidate Regiment Dresden" in April 1945; Stabs-Batterie = Headquarters Vattery; Versorg. Batterie = Supply Battery; and, III./SS-Art.Lehr-Rgt. (unterstellt mit 7. - 9. Batterie) = III./SS Artillery Intructional Regiment (attached with its 7th to 9th Batteries)

295

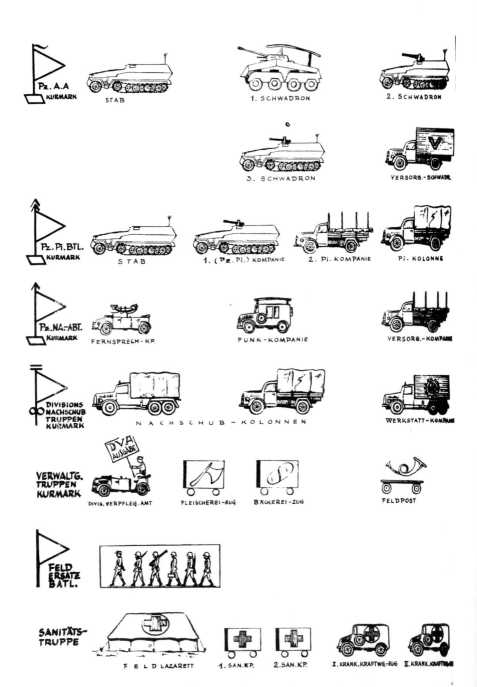

Panzer-Grenadier-Division "Kurmark" (as of February 1945)

Stab = Staff; 1. Schwadron = 1st Troop; Versorg.-Schwadron = Supply Troop; 1. (Pz.Pi.) Kompanie = 1st (Panzer-Pionier) Company; 2. Pi.Kompanie = 2nd Pioneer Company; Pi. Kolonne = Pioneer Support Detachment; Pz.NA.-Abt Kurmark = Armored Signals Battalion "Kurmark"; Fernsprech.-Kp. = Signals Company; Funk-Kompanie = Radio Signals Company; Versorg.-Kompanie = Supply

Chapter 6
The Situation from 26 February
to 2 March 1945

1. General Enemy Situation

The units of the 1st White Russian Front, which had taken part in the encirclement of Posen, had now probably reached the Oder. For this reason enemy offensive activity also increased at the Oder. However, the 1st and 2nd Guards Tank Armies had not yet been identified as being at the Oder front between Schaumburg and Fürstenberg.

The enemy's artillery buildup had already reached a considerable scale. Our air reconnaissance identified numerous large-caliber batteries with 15 to 20 guns each. So far, however, they had not intervened seriously in the fighting.

69th Army – Lebus

In addition to frequent, weak offensive patrol operations in company strength at the Frankfurt—Küstrin rail line, the 69th Army launched stronger attacks in a northerly direction at the Lebus—Podelzig road and to its east. During the course of these partial attacks the enemy succeeded in regaining the hill at Point 55 on 22 February. Astride the Lebus—Podelzig roads he made only minor gains.

8th Guards Army – Göritz Bridgehead

So far the 8th Guards Army had borne the main burden of the fighting in the area of the 1st White Russian Front. In the period that followed, it continued its continuous offensive activity at the same points of main effort.

Klessin: The enemy attacks, now by day as well, faced the defenders of Klessin with a difficult mission. As a rule these attacks were made in battalion strength. The enemy had undoubtedly realized that from the Klessin manor house it was possible to see the Oder and thus disrupt traffic over the military bridge located east of Klessin.

Wuhden—Podelzig: The enemy succeeded in carrying forward his

Company; Divisions-Nachschubtruppen Kurmark = Kurmark Divisional Supply Troops; Nachschub-Kolonnen = Supply Detachments; Werkstatt-Kompanie = Maintenance Company; Verwaltg-Truppen Kurmark = Administrative Services "Kurmark"; Fleischerei-Zug = Butcher Platoon; Bäckerei-Zug = Bakery Platoon; Feldpost = Field Post Office; Feld-Ersatz-Batl. = Field replacement Battalion; Sanitätstruppe = Medical Services; 1. San.Kp. = 1st Medical Company; I. Krank.Kraftwg.-Zug = 1st Ambulance Platoon.

attacks into the east part of Wuhden. He conducted further attacks on Wuhden from the northeast. Northeast of Podelzig the enemy achieved numerous penetrations. Following his success northwest of Reitwein on 2 March, the enemy gained some ground as a result of the planned withdrawal of the German front line (closer to Podelzig).

Northwest of Reitwein: In the last days of the month the enemy carried out several strong night offensive patrol operations against our positions near Strombrücke (2 km southwest of Neu Manschnow estate) and east of Hathenow.

At about 08:30 hours on 2 March the enemy launched a major attack operation northwest of Reitwein. After a 20 to 30 minute barrage, strong enemy forces attacked from his positions at the rail line north of Reitwein. The use of smoke enabled him to reduce the visibility and observation possibilities.

Behind a barrage creeping forward 200 to 300 meters at a time, the enemy attacked in division strength with several spearheads.

While the southern spearhead was halted in front of the positions east of Hathenow protected by a minefield, north of Hathenow another assault force succeeded in outflanking the Pz.Pi.Btl.'s left wing, after which it swung south.

The main thrust was made southeast of Rathstock. Supported by a guards tank brigade (KV 85 and Josef Stalin tanks), the enemy broke through our positions south of Sportplatz, crossed Reichsstrasse 112 and took Rathstock with strong infantry forces. Only there did our artillery succeed in separating the enemy infantry from its tanks, so that the guards tank brigades advanced alone through Rathstock to the west. The enemy was subsequently halted in the line due east of Sachsendorfer Loose, 800 meters southeast of Alt Tucheband.

A weaker enemy spearhead drove as far as the bridge over the old Oder (east-northeast of Herzersdorf).

With this attack the enemy had succeeded in significantly expanding the Göritz bridgehead.

2. Friendly Situation

Even though our counterattacks on 18-22 February failed, in the last weeks of February the situation in the division's sector had not developed the way that the division command feared it might.

In spite of a continuation of the enemy attacks at the previous points of main effort in undiminished strength, the two armies of the 1st White Russian Front did not achieve any great success. For the most part, every enemy gain was wiped out by the barrage fire which began immediately and by immediate counterattacks by local reserves.

With the beginning of the month of March, however, the Soviet offensive activities north of the Reitweiner Heights took on a more serious character. At the same time the enemy intensified his efforts toward the Reitweiner Heights in order to gain control of the key positions there. As in the weeks of the past February, the fighting there was extremely bitter and costly. In addition, the enemy attack north of the Reitweiner Heights on 2 March brought with it further losses of territory and casualties.

Arrival of New Units

At the beginning of March the division was sent four heavy howitzers (two 200-mm French guns and two 210-mm German) which were placed under its command.

Elements of the Volks-Artillerie-Korps arriving from the west went into position in the Seelow—Dolgelin area in such a way as to close the gaps in artillery coverage in the northern part of the division's sector. The affected battalions of the Volks-Artillerie-Korps were subordinated to the KmK's artillery commander for barrage fire missions, whereas for all other situations they were instructed to collaborate closely with the KmK Division.

Headquarters, 9. Armee temporarily committed frogmen against the enemy bridges near Lebus. Two Mistel aircraft—so-called piggyback combinations—were sent to destroy the same bridges. The Mistels consisted of a Ju 88 packed with explosives and a Me 109 guidance aircraft. Both were prevented from reaching their targets by the enemy's strong anti-aircraft defenses.

During the course of the month the division had received approximately 4,000 replacements.

3. Course of the Battle

Lebus sector:

While Inf.Rgt. KS Dresden was able to repulse all Soviet offensive patrol operations at the rail line near Lebus, the enemy did achieve penetrations into the main line of resistance against the I.R. KS Wetzlar and the right wing of the Pz.Gren.Rgt. KmK. On the last night of the month the group of houses 500 meters northeast of Lindenhof on the Lebus—Podelzig road was lost. The immediate counterattack by local reserves of the I.R. KS Wetzlar and the offensive patrol operations of the following night all failed.

In these days the enemy launched a dawn attack from the direction of Hakengrund and from the ravine due east of Point 55 and succeeded in taking that much fought over position. Since at the same time the Pz.Gren.Rgt. KmK's counterattack reserve was heavily committed with its I. Btl. in Klessin, II. Bataillon was not in a position to retake Point 55. From this point on II. Btl.'s positions ran along the rise 200 meters north of Point 55.

Klessin sector:

Again during the last weeks of February the Pz.Gren.Rgt. KmK's I. Btl. was engaged in fierce defensive fighting against the 4th Rifle Division for possession of the town of Klessin. The attacking enemy, supported by assault guns, succeeded in breaking into Klessin from the southeast on numerous occasions. In each case, however, the regiment counterattacked successfully and destroyed the enemy penetration.

A Hetzer of the Jagdpanzer-Abt. (Pz.Rgt.KmK) commanded by Uffz. Liepke positioned itself in the hall of Klessin castle in such a way that it was able to disrupt traffic on the bridge southeast of Klessin by day.

Tank in the Castle Hall

Klessin castle stood on a plateau which fell away steeply to the Oder. From its veranda one could see far across the Oder valley into the beautiful Sternberger Land. If the visibility was good, then the battlefield of Kunersdorf was visible in the slightly concealed depths beyond the rooftops of Frankfurt. In those days the Soviet onslaught struck the steadfast Damm suburb of Fortress Frankfurt.

The Soviets had dug into the earth on the steep slope of the castle plateau. Russian snipers had penetrated as far as the park; from the flanks and sunken side roads anti-tank and machine-gun bullets whipped against the barns and farm buildings. From time to time it was necessary to rush out of the castle cellar into the upper floors and drive the unabashedly approaching Bolsheviks back down the slope with bundles of hand-grenades.

It was a blessing that the walls were so thick!

During one recent night the Soviets had thrown a bridge across the Oder, over which their reinforcements flowed to Klessin with irritating regularity. For two kilometers they lay beneath the castle, which had been ripped apart by shells.

The commander of a tank—Unteroffizier Liepke—who gave the Oder bridge close beneath the plateau no rest, tried to push his way up to the corner of the plateau behind the castle. First right, then left. Pointless. Soviet tank and anti-tank shells soon chased him back into his safe hiding place.

But don't give up! That Oder bridge is too tempting and dangerous besides!

He made up his mind on the spot. He pointed his creaking and rumbling Panzerjäger up the few castle steps and forced his way through the portal. Then the steel giant was sitting at the veranda window, as terrible to look upon as the stone guest in Don Juan's hall. Close beneath it lay the bridge! The Soviets surely could not see into the room from outside, but the first shot would give him away. It didn't matter—the bridge was all that counted.

He loaded high-explosive ammunition, estimated the range at 2 000 meters. The first shot was short by 100 meters, the second came closer, the third was on target! The Soviet artillery, anti-tank guns too, now began seeking out the daring tank. But its commander did not give up. He fired fifteen shots through the rising firestorm of Soviet artillery, and more than 30 meters of the span splashed into the current and drifted down the Oder.

Newspaper article by war correspondent Eugen Skassa-Weiss

Note: The vehicle was a Hetzer tank-destroyer, which belonged to I. (Pz.Jgd.) Abt. 1551/Pz.Rgt. KmK commanded by Öblt. Lützow.

In three nights the *Kurmark* artillery commander succeeded in bringing the four heavy howitzers into position along the rail line near Klessin unnoticed by the Soviets. They were used with great success, primarily against the bridges near Lebus and east of Klessin as well as in support of local counterattacks in the Lebus sector. According to statements made by prisoners, the enemy found the presence of such heavy-caliber guns unsettling, however all his attempts to locate the positions of the heavy howitzers failed. Our mortars fired at the same time as the howitzers, preventing them from being pinpointed by sound locators.

Wuhden—Podelzig:

In Wuhden the combat strengths of the Feldherrnhalle Battalion deployed there continued to sink. During the course of his numerous night attacks there, the enemy succeeded in repeatedly gaining a foothold in the northeast part of the town. By the beginning of March the weak forces there were no longer able to drive the enemy out again.

Northeast of Podelzig the battalion of the Inf.Rgt. KS Potsdam deployed there and the attached remnants of the alert battalion repulsed the bulk of the enemy attacks. Only a few penetrations resulted in lost ground. Because of developments in the situation on 2 March, however, the main line of resistance had to be withdrawn from the area of the former sugar refinery 500 meters in the direction of Podelzig on the night of 2-3 March.

Each day Klessin, Wuhden and Podelzig continued to be scenes of fierce artillery duels.

Sector north of the Reitweiner Heights:

The main line of resistance ran (1 : 25,000) roughly as follows: northeast edge of Podelzig station—Point 13.5 (400 meters east of the former Podelzig sugar refinery)—Point 14 (750 meters southeast of Hathenow)—southeast edge of wood due south and northeast of Sportplatz—wood southeast of Strombrücke—west edge of Wiesenvorwerk—isolated groups of houses of Neu-Manschnow (east of Alte Oder) to 1 500 meters south of Reichsstrasse No. 1 Küstrin, Seelow.

The Pz.Pi.Btl. KmK had laid several minefields south of the Hathenow road, Reitwein estate.

The barrage and a general firing zone of the A.R. KmK (including attached battalions) stretched from the right division boundary to and including east of Hathenow. The adjacent sector north to Reichsstrasse 1 fell into the area of the Volks-Art.-Korps, which had been instructed to work closely with the A.R. KmK.

Because of the width of the sector, but also because of the relatively open and flat terrain, the positions could only be occupied strongpoint-style. The high water table (average height of terrain 12 to 14 meters above the water table) meant that foxholes could only be dug to a depth of 50 centimeters.

Commanding this sector was the Inf.Rgt. KS Potsdam, which had its command post in Sachsendorf. A KmK tank-destroyer company was attached to the regiment to reinforce the local counterattack reserve.

In the last days of February the Inf.Rgt. KS Potsdam had already been forced to fend off several night offensive patrol operations between the Rathstock—Reitwein road and Strom-Brücke. A counterattack was required to destroy the enemy, who had dug in near Strom-Brücke. Apart from these offensive patrol operations, until the morning of 2 March there were no confirmed indications of attack preparations by the enemy, especially since the high railway embankment and the town of Reitwein made it almost impossible to see into the enemy rear by day.

At about 08:30 hours on 2 March the enemy artillery opened up with a massed barrage which lasted for almost half an hour. Its focal point was the positions between the Rathstock—Reitwein road and Strom-Brücke. In a few minutes a cloud of smoke almost 100 meters high rose over this sector and it was intensified by the enemy's use of smoke shells. All telephone communications to the elements deployed at the front were soon knocked out. Furthermore, the enemy artillery fire and smoke shells prevented the forward positions from being seen from the rear.

Our own barrage fire began automatically, but it had to be broken off soon afterwards since the situation in the main line of resistance was completely uncertain.

After the initial barrage the enemy artillery fire moved west in leaps of about 250 meters, while the enemy attack groups advanced through open lanes toward Reichsstrasse 112.

The main assault came from due north of the village of Reitwein in the direction of Rathstock. There the enemy committed about 100 to 120 heavy tanks of a guards tank brigade. While behind the belts of mines the Pz.Pi.Btl. KmK was initially able to halt the enemy's left attack wedge, following the creeping barrage, by 10:30 hours the main spearhead broke through toward Rathstock. Rathstock was taken by enemy infantry. East of Rathstock, however, our own artillery had already succeeded in separating some of the escorting infantry from tanks, so that after Rathstock the guards tank brigade was totally isolated. From Rathstock the enemy tanks turned hard left and drove towards Sachsendorf.

Meanwhile the KmK's Panther battalion (II. (BR)/Pz.Rgt. KmK), bolstered by two armored troop carrier troops of the Pz.Aufkl.Abt. KmK, had arrived in the Sachsendorf area and at about 11:00 hours launched a counterattack in the direction of Rathstock. The enemy tanks were engaged near Sachsendorfer Loose and forced to retire in the direction of Rathstock. Our counterattack was subsequently foiled by a defensive barrier of enemy tanks, which turned to fight west of Rathstock. With the Panther battalion unable to dislodge the enemy, the division command ordered the attack broken off.

During our counterattack strong enemy infantry forces had outflanked the left wing of the Pz.Pi.Btl. KmK due north of Hathenow and turned into the deep flank toward Lehngut Hathenow. A subsequent frontal attack against the town of Hathenow drove the pioneer battalion's left wing back in a southerly direction. Attacking astride the Podelzig—Hathenow road, the local counterattack reserve was just able to halt the enemy infantry 500 meters south of Hathenow.

North of Rathstock the enemy took Herzersdorf and also reached Reichsstrasse 112.

During the afternoon (2 March) our artillery was able to prevent the enemy from gaining further ground to the west. By the evening of 2 March the makeshift front ran from south to north as follows: Podelzig station—former Podelzig sugar refinery—Lehngut Hathenow—east edge of Sachsendorfer Loose—east edge of Alt Tucheband.

The two armored troop carrier troops of the Pz.A.A. KmK initially remained in the Werder area as direct reserve and the Panther battalion in the Sachsendorf area.

The companies of Inf.Rgt. KS Potsdam had suffered serious casualties on 2 March; the same day the division IIa took immediate steps to make good these losses. Furthermore, as per orders from XI. SS-A.K., beginning at midnight, 3 March, the adjacent unit on the left, the 25. Pz.Gren.Div., took over the village of Alt Tucheband.

Other:

At the suggestion of XI. SS-A.K. and with Hitler's approval, the KmK division command was authorized to transfer its command post from Libbenichen to the Plötzenhof estate, its former location having become too exposed. The necessary preparations had already begun on 1 March.

In the last days of February the elements of the Pz.A.A. KmK assigned to the Petershagen area on orders from XI SS-A.K. were returned to the division.

Summary:

While the enemy was only able to make minor gains against the I.R. KS Wetzlar, Pz.Gren.Rgt. KmK and near Podelzig, his surprise attack on 2 March in at least division strength resulted in a penetration against the division's northern sector 5 kilometers deep and about 4 kilometers wide.

Even though the division was able to prevent the enemy from expanding his gains on the right wing through the excellent use of artillery, the counterattack by the reinforced Panther battalion and the stand made by the Pz.Pi.Btl. KmK, the Soviet 8th Guards Army did succeed in significantly enlarging its bridgehead and inflicting heavy losses on the Inf.Rgt. KS Potsdam deployed there on account of the latter's inadequately fortified positions.

While the fighting in the sector from Lebus to northeast of Podelzig was harder and more bitter than in the northern sector, the mass employment of tanks was not possible there. In general, therefore, the regiments deployed there were able to hold their key positions.

In keeping with Soviet tactics, offensive activity on the Reitweiner Heights could be expected to intensify even further in the immediate future, in order to finally unite the Lebus and Göritz bridgeheads into a single strategic bridgehead or completely eliminate the commanding Reitweiner Heights. Because of its over-stretched situation and the absence of serious reserves, the division was not in a position to conduct decisive counterattacks. The division command therefore looked toward future developments on the Reitweiner Heights with concern, should fresh, capable combat units be brought in quickly. The KmK division command made repeated requests of the commanding corps to be allowed to shorten its sector by having the adjacent divisions on both sides take over partial sectors on both wings.

Chapter 7
From 2 March 1945 until the End

The 8th Guards Army launched its first major attack with limited objectives early on 2 March 1945 in the direction of Rathstock—Alt Tucheband. It was obvious that in his southern sector the enemy hoped to eliminate from the front once and for all the two German strongpoints at Wuhden and Klessin. The almost simultaneous Soviet attacks against these two towns were probably intended first and foremost to divert attention from their plans farther north, but at the same time they were intended to unite their two bridgeheads on the west bank of the Oder at Lebus and Göritz.

The Soviet's efforts against Wuhden began slightly earlier than those against Klessin, however his attacks against Wuhden were made primarily from the northeast, while those against Klessin came from the woods south of the town. Ceaseless artillery fire pounded the defenders of Wuhden, which consisted mainly of the Feldherrnhalle Battalion (a trained replacement battalion of the Feldherrnhalle replacement unit which had been stopped on its way to Hungary) and elements of the I.R. KS Wetzlar. The ring around the defenders of Wuhden drew ever tighter and its defensive field within the town itself grew ever smaller. The Soviets were inside the first houses, and no counterattack was going to dislodge them. The garrison was too weakened by losses to be able to throw the enemy out again. On or about 4-5 March 1945 a counterattack supported by the tank-destroyers of I. (Pz.Jgd.) Abt. 1551/Pz.Rgt. KmK reestablished contact with Wuhden and also brought some relief. But as soon as the Hetzers withdrew, the ring closed around the town again. In the end the garrison had to be supplied from the air. Nevertheless, in the days that followed, the combat strengths of the encircled battalions quickly sank even further as a result of the constant artillery and mortar fire, and in the end the enemy attacks, mainly by night, could only be held off by employing every last man, including the sick and wounded.

The KmK division command repeatedly tried to have the strongpoint abandoned—passing its requests to the army via corps—but in vain. Hitler, who reserved every important decision concerning this front to himself, refused to authorize a breakout. And the officer cadets and men of the Feldherrnhalle continued to fight for their very existence—fully aware that holding this position meant nothing to the larger scheme of things but was vital to preserve their own existence. By the time permission to break out came, there were barely forty men left alive. The breakout succeeded after a superhuman effort, however the wounded had to be left behind. For them there was no path left to freedom.

At about the same time, but farther south right at the sector boundary of the Soviet 8th Guards Army, it was becoming apparent that a similar fate lay in store for the town and fortress of Klessin. There the II./Pz.Gren.Rgt. KmK (Hptm. Windeck) defended the castle on the left wing, while on the right wing the I./Pz.Gren.Rgt. KmK defended the estate and the town of Klessin. Both units focussed their main efforts on the inner wings, aware that the castle offered the only view of the Oder lowlands and the bridges. Also there were the artillery's forward observers, directing the fire of the heavy howitzers and cannon batteries on to Soviet traffic crossing the Oder. One of these was Lt. Puxkandl, transferred from the Gross-Born artillery school to 2. Bttr./Pz.Art.Rgt. KmK at the beginning of February 1945 and now a forward observer with a Type "g" backpack radio in Klessin Castle. His opposite number was the firing position of the 2. Batterie (Lt. Rolke), which placed its shells on the coordinates provided by him. After the fall of Wuhden the enemy now also pressed toward Klessin from the north, making total encirclement only a matter of days away.

Increasingly the enemy also concentrated his massed artillery and mortar fire on the castle itself; the owner's son was also the commander of the Pz.A.A. KmK—Count von Abydill. A direct hit struck the roof of the castle; it shook, but its stout walls prevented if from falling. A second shell, however, pierced the roof and landed in the cellar, where the forward observers' radio operators were sitting at their equipment. One radio operator and his equipment were buried, another was injured by splinters, his radio set damaged. And still the weight of the enemy artillery fire intensified, with shells up to 210-mm. The Volkssturm immediately occupied the upper floors of the castle, the contact company of I./Pz.Gren.Rgt. KmK the ground floor. Lt. Schwing of the 7.Kp./II./Pz.Gren.Rgt. KmK and his runners took shelter in the holes in the cellar.

Directly in front of the castle there was a small open area that fell away toward the enemy. And from there the enemy approached to within 150 meters of the castle. After a few meters, however, he was met with furious defensive fire and an increasing number of motionless brown forms dotted the open area. Three more times the enemy attacked there on this day—in vain; the defenders held their positions.

Farther south, however, the enemy had already broken in against 8./Pz.Gren.Rgt. KmK and was in the process of rolling up the positions in the direction of Klessin Castle. The enemy sent two self-propelled guns from the Oder, again accompanied by a mass of Soviet infantry. These now fired systematically into the ground and second floors of the castle. Those in the upper rooms who were not killed or wounded fled to the cellars. But when the brown figures again charged across the open area shouting their war cries, all of the windows, holes and look-outs were manned, and a furious fire met the attackers. Again the enemy was forced to turn back.

Despite their huge losses the Soviets refused to give up. The self-propelled guns rolled forward again and fired into the cellars from point-blank range. But the Soviets also advanced from the sides into the bordering farm buildings and tried to reach the castle from there. This was prevented by a raid from the castle carried out by a few men, with the small man's artillery, the *Panzerfaust*, achieving wonderful things. Casualties among the defenders were rising to shocking levels, however. Only by night was it possible to bring in supplies and fresh forces from Podelzig. An alert company under the command of an *Oberleutnant* was brought in to bolster the castle's defenses. The fighting raged on, including in the houses of Klessin, which were defended mainly by the men of the I./Pz.Gren.Rgt. KmK. House after house had to be abandoned as casualties mounted. Uffz. Teich was killed by a shot in the head moments after destroying a Russian self-propelled gun with a *Panzerfaust*. Hptm. Windeck and Lt. Schwing were wounded. There was fighting all day around I. Btl.'s command post, until finally rein-forcements from Podelzig created some breathing space again. A com-pany of officer cadets (I.R. KS Wetzlar) came in at night; they coun-terattacked along the road to Klessin and were able to open it for trans-port of supplies and evacuation of the wounded. The commander of the Pz.Gren.Rgt. KmK, *Major* von Courbière, himself went to Klessin to organize the defense and bolster the courage of the defenders.

Finally, during the night of 5-6 March, after eighteen days in com-bat, elements of the Pz.Gren.Rgt. KmK were relieved by a battalion of the I.R. KS Wetzlar and moved to the eastern edge of Podelzig. But no sooner were they in position when the Soviets attacked there and sought to force their way into Podelzig. Both battalions were brought up to strength while this fierce defensive fighting was going on, restor-ing their combat strengths. Soon afterward things quieted down there again.

Barely 24 hours after the relief of Klessin (on 7 March) the garri-son was surrounded for good, after which supplies had to be air-dropped. A *Führer* order declared Klessin a fortified place, meaning that it had to be defended to the last man.

A platoon of tank-destroyers of I. (Pz.Jgd.)/Pz.Rgt. KmK made one more attempt to break through from Podelzig to Klessin. The very first Hetzer was knocked out, another—the radio-equipped vehicle—got through, the third was destroyed before reaching the objective. But the radio-equipped Hetzer was in Klessin and this restored contact with our artillery. Its urgent appeals for a renewed barrage were answered promptly, and the artillery—which at times boasted up to 250 guns, including those of subordinate batteries and batteries assigned to cooperate with the division, plus the Volks-Artillerie-Korps—laid down a barrage fire which definitely got the enemy's attention. Without minimizing the bravery and courage of the defenders, it was the outstanding cooperation with the artillery which halted so many enemy attacks on Klessin before they could get started. Gefr. Pohl, the radio operator in the Hetzer which made it through to Klessin, performed a great service by maintaining communications with the firing positions and directing fire when required.

The battle for Klessin went on day after day; day after day the Soviets concentrated more and more guns, attack troops and finally tanks against Klessin—all in an attempt to take possession of this bastion of the German defense. Deliveries of supplies from the air soon had to be abandoned; the flak was simply too heavy. The area still held by the defenders had become so small that most of the small number of supply containers that were dropped fell amongst the enemy.

The radio reports sent by the radio-equipped Hetzer from Klessin were frightful. Not only did they tell of wounded racked by hunger and thirst, but also of the brave defenders—the officer cadets of the I.R. KS Wetzlar. They defended themselves grimly, even though there was no medicine for their wounds, no water to drink after the single well was buried by shellfire. Combat strength was down to about 150 men— from an original total of nearly 400. With them were brave Hitler Youths, members of the *Volkssturm*, outgrowing themselves. It was struggle in the best tradition of German soldiery, an heroic stand against impossible odds.

Faced with the shocking reports from Klessin, the rapidly sinking combat strengths there and especially the hopelessness of continuing to hold onto the fortress, the division command made repeated requests to corps and to headquarters for permission to evacuate, but in vain. Finally *Oberst* Langkeit decided, without waiting for further orders, to go ahead with a breakout on the night of 21-22 March. Assisted by his Ia, he did everything possible to put an end to this senseless sacrifice of such brave men. While appeal after appeal was still going up the chain of command, all preparations had been made for a breakout by the garrison of Klessin. Authorization to break out was received 24 hours after the actual breakout.

On the night of 21-22 March it was time; with one final surge the last survivors of Klessin fought their way through in the direction of Podelzig. There were approximately 70 to 80 men, none of them unwounded. They pierced the Russian lines in groups, in some cases had to fight for their lives, and with their last breaths reached the German lines. Fortunately the escape from Klessin cost only a few comrades wounded or missing (including Lt. Puxkandl). Once they had reached safety the exhausted soldiers collapsed. Among them was Gefr. Pohl, the Hetzer radio operator, who was later decorated with the Iron Cross, First Class for his courageous actions and who received a gold watch from the commander-in-chief of the 9. Armee in recognition. The 3. Batterie's forward observer, who together with the missing Lt. Puxhandl was one of the last in Klessin, Obgefr. Dittrich and Gefr. G. Meyer all received the Iron Cross, Second Class. All of those who escaped received fourteen days special leave. A *Führer* order declared that all of the officer cadets who survived were promoted to the rank of *Leutnant* effective the date of the breakout from Klessin. There were barely forty men. All the rest were still in Klessin or on their way out.

On that very day, early on 22 March, when the last survivors of Klessin reached the German lines again, the 25. Pz.Gren.Div. and the *Führer-Grenadier-Division* launched a counterattack along Reichsstraße 1 toward Küstrin under the command of XI. SS-A.K. to restore contact with the garrison. In spite of air and artillery support the attack failed in previously unknown minefields. In the subsequent advance the infantry became separated from the tanks, which succeeded in breaking into the enemy system of positions. These later had to be abandoned.

Headquarters, 9. Armee was ready to face the situation; further attacks appeared hopeless, the enemy having undoubtedly used the time to further fortify his positions in the captured areas. But in spite of all protests Hitler ordered the attack to go ahead again; as expected, it too bogged down, even though single German tanks did get to the first houses of Küstrin. Contrary to Hitler's order to hold, the courageous commander of the German garrison in Küstrin decided to break out during the night of 1 April, his situation having become virtually hopeless.

During the course of bringing in further German forces at the end of March, the Pz.Gren.Div. *Kurmark* was relieved, on the left by the 169. I.D. from Lapland and in the center by the Döberitz Division. It was then transferred to the Falkenhagener Forest to rest and serve as operational reserve. There it was once again able to take on replacements with which to restore its combat strengths, regroup and prepare for the coming Soviet major offensive.

In the last days of March there was another local attack operation in the Podelzig area on the left wing of the Soviet 8th Army against the positions of the Döberitz Division; its objective was to take the last town on the Reitweiner Heights still in German hands. Under an unprecedented artillery barrage the Soviets advanced to the eastern edge of Podelzig and finally broke into the town itself. Hastily alerted elements of the Pz.Gren.Div. *Kurmark*—especially II./Pz.Gren.Rgt. KmK under Hptm. Vehse—tried to hold in the casemates at the northern edge of the town and drive the enemy out again through counterattacks, but they were simply too weak. Podelzig had to be abandoned. New positions were occupied due west of the town. The Soviets now desisted from further attacks; things quieted down apart from daily artillery duels, especially near Podelzig, which the enemy was determined to hold on to. The Soviets had achieved what they wanted, though it took two months of heavy fighting and cost them heavy losses: an approximately five-kilometer-deep bridgehead between Lebus and Göritz which, after the enemy successes west of Küstrin, was linked to the approximately fifteen-kilometer-deep bridgehead there. This was sufficient in its entirety for the Russians to mass their armies in peace and partly out of sight for the coming great offensive. The German air force, which probably could still have interfered, was finished. It had only enough fuel and ammunition for three daylight missions by its remaining 200-300 aircraft. The German long-range artillery had to remain silent to conserve what little ammunition it had for the day of the enemy attack.

By 10 April German reconnaissance aircraft identified a total of 23 bridges and other crossings over the Oder in the enemy bridgehead. This was probably sufficient to transport the bulk of the Soviet attack troops to the west bank of the Oder in a single night.

The German units in position and in reserve could only be brought up to strength with reserves brought in from the rear. The attitude and morale of these replacements was no longer what it had once been—and daily training in close combat and defense was essential. Because of the absence of arms and ammunition, human bodies were to be thrown against the armored might of the Soviets.

Part VIII
Panzer-Grenadier Division Brandenburg
Defending on the Lausitzer Neiße

While during the course of February 1945, north of Frankfurt fierce battles raged around the enemy's Oder bridgeheads in which the Pz.Gren.Div. *Kurmark* was heavily involved, several hundred kilometers farther south along the Lausitzer Neiße, between Weisswasser and Göritz, a new defense line was being established by another GD unit, the Panzer-Grenadier Division *Brandenburg* under the command of Pz.Korps *Großdeutschland*.

After a weeks-long fighting withdrawal from the Vistula, the Pz.Korps GD with the attached Fsch.Pz.Div. 1 HG and the 20. Pz.Gren.Div. together with the Panzer-Grenadier Division *Brandenburg* had taken up new defensive positions along the Lausitzer Neiße from Forst through Muskau—Priebus to the Sänitz area. While the Soviets merely felt their way forward hesitantly in the southern sector, that of the Pz.Gren.Div. BR, and gave no indications of continuing the offensive across the river, in the northern sector held by the adjacent 20. Pz.Gren.Div. they struck at the German Muskau bridgehead with considerable forces at the division's boundary with its left neighbor. Not only were the Soviets trying to crush the bridgehead, they hoped to also gain the west bank of the Neiße in one go. They failed in their first objective at first; the Muskau bridgehead was held. In the second case, however, the Russians were able to cross the Neiße near Gross-Särchen—Köbeln and establish themselves on the west bank of the Neiße. The corps immediately committed the Pz.Korps.Pi.Btl. 500 GD to counterattacks in conjunction with the 20. Pz.Gren.Div.'s Pz.Pi.Btl. In a poorly-blown bridge the Soviets had found a way across the Neiße. This had to be destroyed permanently and those Soviets who had crossed the river wiped out. Committed in the last days of February were 2. Kp./Pz.Korps.Pi.Btl. 500 GD under Oblt. Wendt and elements of the 3. (Goliath) Kp., which fought their way through the dense forest to the Neiße. An initial attempt with Goliaths failed. A second effort at night surprised the Soviets and was a complete success; all of the enemy troops on the west side of the river were destroyed, possession of the old riverbank positions was regained. A fine success for this pioneer company under Oblt. Wendt.

While the fighting for the Muskau bridgehead was still going on, the bulk of the Pz.Gren.Div. *Brandenburg* was digging in along the Neiße from the southern edge of Muskau—Pechern—Grenzkirch to Steinbach, west of Sänitz, a distance of 32 kilometers. On the left was

Jäg.Rgt. 1, in the right sector Jäg.Rgt. 2. The BR division command post was in Heide, on the road from Muskau to Rietschen. The Muskau Forest extended almost right down to the Neiße in most of the division's sector; while this gave the defenders the advantage of camouflaged positions, there was also the inherent danger that the Soviets might cross the river at some unguarded spot and disappear into the forest.

At the end of February there was contact with the enemy everywhere on the Neiße front; the units of the Pz.Gren.Div. BR were in defensive positions, which the pioneers and construction units worked hard to improve, especially at night. To prepare for a Soviet attempt to cross the river bunkers were built, along with communications trenches, machine-gun posts and concealed positions. Such attempts by the Soviets were not long in coming, probably more to scout the German positions and their defensive strength than to establish a bridgehead by force. The enemy did not yet appear to be in a position to do so as his units had not yet closed ranks.

The *Brandenburgers* also sent their first patrols across the Neiße, usually at night, to likewise scout the enemy positions and bring back prisoners. Day after day the combat engineers worked to improve the *Jäger*'s positions and help establish lines of communication to the rear. Bunkers were manufactured using the production line method and at night they were transported by vehicle into the positions and set up. Local sawmills delivered beams and boards. The narrow-gauge railway was also made usable again and was soon able to supply the division, as it ran through the forest parallel to the Neiße.

A kilometer-long log road was built from Weisskeissel to Weisswasser to ensure passability in the event of rain. *Volkssturm* and a Cossack convalescent company helped with the construction.

All of the local foresters became soldiers; they retained their green foresters jackets and formed the so-called Forester Platoon in the Pz.Stu.Pi.Btl. BR. Taking advantage of their thorough knowledge of the terrain, a net of roads was scouted and marked precisely with numbers and letters. Supply routes, approach routes for reserves, tank tracks were laid down in this way. Corresponding maps were issued to all units.

With warmer weather the danger of forest fire became acute; an observation and reporting service was set up for the entire division area using existing fire watchtowers. A field telephone detachment was installed in each tower. Fire-fighting teams were assigned since there were fears that the enemy would at some point use phosphorous grenades to start forest fires. Everything was readied for a long-term defense.

Beginning in February, elements of a disbanded infantry regiment and its train were used to form a horse-drawn transport battalion. The first transport troop was formed under the command of Lt. Gruber and Hfw. Böhnke with two squads, each with ten horse-drawn wagons, mainly Hf 1 types. Its initial complement was about 80 personnel and 120 horses. The first transport troop was ready for operations just fourteen days later and it was employed by the division Ib for supply purposes, in particular from the town of Rietschen, from where supply goods, construction materials, fuel etc was delivered to the front-line positions of Jäg.Rgt. 2.

A second transport troop was formed on 23 February under the command of Lt. Göpfert (in Weisswasser) with panye horses and local vehicles. Obervet. Dr. Hein was appointed head veterinarian officer; he was responsible not just for the division's horses, whose number later reached nearly 600, but also for checking the hygiene of the butcher company. As per division order a Dept. IV e was officially established. With the formation of the third transport troop the *Brandenburg* Transport Battalion was established; it boasted 352 horses and had a transport capacity of 90 tons. In addition to this horse-drawn transport battalion, a GD cavalry battalion of three troops was also formed. The Pz.Korps GD gave command of the battalion to *Major* von O. The cavalry performed invaluable service in the heavily wooded areas west of the Neiße, conducting patrols, scouting missions and keeping an eye out for enemy patrols, paratroopers and watching over the corps' entire rear area.

Another very significant role in this combat zone was played by the industrial city of Weisswasser on the Berlin—Göritz rail line. Not only was it used as a transfer point for supplies to the front, the entire city was turned into a strongpoint. The city of about 15,000 inhabitants was home to the biggest glass industry in Europe; located there were the Osram-Werke, Vereinigte Lausitzer Hohlglas A.G., plus brown coal mines, porcelain factories, brickworks and so on. The city was surrounded by the Lausitz Heath with the open pit coal mines to the north, although these were now under water.

After handing over command to the Pz.Korps GD, the city's former military commander (Stubaf. Count von Egloffstein) volunteered to stay and the chief-of-staff, General Staff *Oberst* Bleicken, gave him the job of further bolstering the city's defenses for all-round defense while subsequently placing him under the command of the Pz.Gren.Div. BR.

In Weißwasser there was a *Volkssturm* battalion of local residents commanded by Oblt. Jilski. These volunteers were well trained and equipped and later fought extremely well. Elements of the Pz.Stu.Pi.Btl. BR arrived to watch over the defense installations plus a platoon of the Feldgendarmerie-Kp. BR under Lt. Feldmüller and several more. Close contact was maintained with the headquarters of the military commander of the city by way of telephone and teletype. Code name "Paladin." His staff included deputy commander Hptm. Berghoff-Ising, adjutant Oblt. Schwarzmann, *Wehrmacht* female auxiliary Gehlsdorf, Fw. Studerka in the quarters office, messengers, etc.

While the bulk of the inhabitants had been evacuated, the factories continued to work at full capacity, mainly with local members of the *Volkssturm*. Mayor Wenderoth remained. Cooperation with the party offices was not without some friction.

In general the Neiße front remained quiet, however from time to time the enemy intensified his artillery and mortar fire, a sign that he was moving up heavy weapons. On the division's right wing near Steinbach in the sector of I./Jäg.Rgt. 2 there was a small, indeed tiny bridgehead on the east bank of the Neiße, which was used primarily as a starting point for patrols. Unmanned by day and merely watched over by heavy machine-guns, when night came it was usually occupied by the battalion's 1. Kp. and expanded further. Night crossings were made with the pioneers' inflatable boats.

On 10 and 11 March all hell broke loose in the Fsch.Pz.Div. 1 HG's sector in the Muskau bridgehead. Supported by tanks, including Josef Stalins, a Soviet rifle division launched repeated attacks against the bridgehead positions. Seven enemy tanks were knocked out, some from close range, and the bridgehead was held. Roughly in mid-March elements of the Alarmbrigade GD arrived and were distributed between the BR and the GD Corps.

In about mid-March preparations were begun for a larger offensive patrol operation in the area of Jäg.Rgt. 2. Its objective was to destroy a house on the opposite side that had been turned into a bunker, but also to finally bring back some prisoners, earlier attempts having been unsuccessful.

Fw. Resch, platoon leader in the 1. Kp./I./Jäg.Rgt. 2, was placed in charge of the operation. Company leader was Lt. Esser, commander Hptm. Steidl. The target was the "Red House," so called on account of its color. Observations had revealed that it was being turned into a small fortress. Communication and rifle trenches had been identified in front of and beside the house, undoubtedly mines as well. Consequently combat engineers were also assigned to the patrol. "Stukas on foot," devastatingly effective 350-mm rocket launchers, arrived. They were to provide covering and preparatory fire.

On the night of 19-20 March Fw. Resch's men were transported in inflatable boats to our small bridgehead on the east bank, where they waited for first light. The order to open fire was given at about 05:00 hours, and the huge rockets roared toward the enemy-occupied village and the "Red House," trailing smoke and fire.

Friendly artillery placed barrage fire in the same direction, the heavy machine-guns placed pinpoint fire on positions and bunkers on the opposite shore. Meanwhile, Resch and his men had dashed to the "Red House" and placed their explosive charges. A thunderous roar and the house blew up. Resch had done it, all in a few minutes. Several prisoners were taken from the nearby trenches. Everything seemed to have succeeded, but on the way back to the crossing point the men walked into an unsuspected minefield laid by the Soviets. After leaving behind the prisoners and one fatally-wounded man, the rest of the patrol finally reached the bank of the Neiße, from where they crossed the river under Soviet fire.

The tally from this operation: the "Red House" destroyed; 20 to 30 Soviets killed. Our own losses outweighed our success. Killed while trying to recover wounded from the minefield were:

Obgefr. Hartmann	runner 1. Kp.
Objäg. Flick	pioneer
San.Sold. Brechtczenda	medic
Gefr. Jandl	1. Kp.
Gefr. Wittasek	squad leader

All had volunteered for this mission.

The front-line area become less quiet in the second half of March. The close-support aircraft came every day, and at night the "Night Owls" appeared to drop their fragmentation bombs. The enemy's heavy weapons became more active, also firing on the rear areas. It had started!

Further indications of increased Soviet activity were provided by radio intercepts and wiretaps. The Soviets were massing troops in their assembly areas in preparation for the big offensive.

On the German side the construction of positions went on with undiminished urgency; second and third lines of defense were scouted and improved, towns in the rear area became fortresses, replacements were fed into the positions—and finally the Pz.Gren.Div. *Brandenburg* was inserted in front of the anticipated spearhead of Soviet attack forces. All available information suggested that this would come in the Rothenburg area, and so the division was moved even farther south. This took place in the first days of April (roughly 2-3 April 1945). The division's former positions were taken over by so-called "sick battalions," which of course were of limited combat value.

The division's new sector ran from the Wehrkirch—Kohlfurt rail line on the right (forming the division's right boundary) north through Rothenburg and Zoblitz to Steinbach, which formed the division's left boundary. The military commander of Weisswasser was released from his subordinate position to the GD.

Division command post Ia in Heide, Div. Ib in See, west of Niesky. The regiments and artillery battalions moved again and settled into their new sectors. Once again work began on building positions, readying reserves and tanks; quarters were set up for the medical clearing station and all that went with it.

As usual, both *Jäger* regiments were at the front, Rgt. 2 with its command post in Kaltwasser, left Jäg.Rgt. 1 with command post in Forst Heide, due east of Spree.

Orders from army group rained down on the units almost daily, the moral equipment for the last battle to retain what was left of German territory.

Again the pioneers were in the field night and day, improving everything possible. Barricades of tree trunks were laid in the division's rear area, while anti-tank detachments consisting of Hitler Youth members under the command of proven non-commissioned officers were organized to meet the anticipated Soviet tanks. The trains of the various units had been assigned to various towns and villages, and they now outfitted these for all-round defense, built new rear positions, dug anti-tank ditches, constructed bunkers and machine-gun positions. The entire land became covered by a net of small and smaller defense installations. There was no tree that was not an observation post, no house whose cellar was not equipped with rifle ports, no hole that was not also a machine-gun position. There was digging everywhere, preparations for the last attack in the east. Things became more lively in the various combat sectors: increased sniper activity on both sides, which always claimed victims, increased patrol activity which cost a man here, another there. The German side became increasingly aware that there were fresh Siberian troops on the other side of the Neiße—the new attack troops, young, excellently equipped, with outstanding morale. And so the nervousness increased. Air attacks on the station at Rietschen, former end station on the railway, made it necessary to abandon this stopping point, while some residents from the west returned to their villages. And so the typical rushing about near the front began, relieved by the almost hourly combat activity.

At this time the radio reported on the advance of the Western Allies, as on 13 April: British troops in Wittenberge, American units in Jena, American troops and tanks advancing on Dresden and the Elbe. Everyone had the same thoughts: what will happen next, where is my family, where will it all end? And yet the men stood iron-firm and together in comradeship. Desertions were extremely rare, instead many men still returned to the front from leave—to take the last walk with the others.

Increased fighter-bomber activity, a growing weight of artillery fire and the ranging in of new enemy guns of many batteries previously not seen—all of these were indications of a coming Soviet offensive whose objective would be Dresden and the Elbe.

Everyone waited for what was to come. Alerts were called, alerts were cancelled. It went back and forth. There was still something to drink. Every evening a new bottle was opened and once again the men drank to health, survival—or a quick death.

And finally on the afternoon of the first warm sunny Sunday—15 April 1945—it was announced that the Soviet offensive was expected to begin on Monday, 16 April. The Muskau bridgehead was being emptied to spare forces and release reserves.

The events early on 15 April in the right of the division's sector, manned by I./Jäg.Rgt. 2, were largely responsible for the precise reports on the start of the Soviet offensive on the Neiße.

In the battalion sector near Kahle Meile the Neiße was not exactly a serious obstacle. It was scarcely more than 15 meters wide, in many places its water was little more than a meter deep. Early on that Sunday morning the Soviets attempted to cross in front of 1. Kp.'s sector (Lt. Esser), bringing boards and beams with which to throw up a footbridge over the Neiße. Only a rapid counterattack by Lt. Korte's second platoon was able to prevent this.

The enemy did not give up, however; in the late afternoon he tried to cross again at the same place, this time accompanied by heavier mortar fire which forced the defenders to take cover. This time the defenders were unable to prevent the Soviets from building the footbridge over the river. One of the greatest hindrances was a lack of ammunition which prevented our artillery from firing.

The alarm was raised immediately, but it came too late. By nightfall the Soviets had completed their crossing. Under cover of heavy artillery fire they streamed across toward the west bank and drove into the first foxholes of the 1. Kp.'s third platoon. As soon as the enemy fire let up a little the men of the platoon counterattacked and drove the Soviets back to the bridge. The enemy tried again at another place under cover of smoke, finally driving into the positions and splitting the third platoon in two.

Major Steidl hurried forward with Lt. Esser, went into the company command post there and instructed Lt. Huesker to immediately lead a patrol against the crossing point. However, Huesker was caught in barrage fire from the other side of the river and was killed. The Soviets were already established on the west bank in numbers and sought to expand their bridgehead to both sides. The result was bitter close-quarters fighting; it did no good, for the enemy was already too strong. The objective now was to seal off the bridgehead and, if possible, clear it the next morning after reserves arrived. A company of II./

Jäg.Rgt. 2 (*Major* Renner) was moved forward and readied. Meanwhile, in the dark of night and under continued heavy enemy mortar fire, the men of 1.Kp. tried to contain the enemy bridgehead. Lt. Stolf was fatally wounded almost immediately, others were split off, making it difficult to hold the company together. The first platoon (Obfw. Ascher) continued to hold in its positions; it was the pillar at the point of penetration.

Not until about 23:00 hours did the fighting die down somewhat; it became quiet in the sector where the Soviets had won their bridgehead. The Renner Battalion's reserve company moved forward and together with remaining elements of 1. Kp. occupied new positions along the road.

It was the last night before the big Soviet offensive. Midnight passed. It was Monday, 16 April 1945.

Note: General Remer, commander of the Führer-Begleit-Division, visited the command post of the Pz.Gren.Div. BR in Heide on 13-14 April 1945.

The Führer-Begleit-Division transferred out of the Jägerndorf area via Göritz to the Muna Schleife/Spremberg area, where it was stationed at alert readiness west of Muskau as operational reserve.

Führer-Begleit-Division in the Jägerndorf Combat Zone

By mid-March 1945 the Eastern Front had solidified somewhat in the north and in the center—along the Oder and the Lausitzer Neiße—except for the German Courland and Heiligenbeil—Samland bridgeheads. On the upper Oder in the area of the German 1. Pz.-Armee the Soviet 4th Ukrainian Front had failed to match the success of the other Soviet armies. Undoubtedly there was also no point of main effort formed there. After the Soviet armies had reached their jump-off positions on the Oder—Neiße line, it was the lagging 4th Ukrainian Front's turn to attack with its outer wings in an effort to break through toward the Moravian Depression in the Ratibor—Troppau—Leobschütz area.

Concentrated in a small area, the armies of the 4th Ukrainian Front advanced in a generally southwest direction toward the line Troppau—Jägerndorf without meeting serious German resistance. The German front line—once again depleted in favor of other sectors—was split apart, the enemy's armored spearheads were soon advancing irresistibly. All available reserves were thrown against them.

This included the *Führer-Begleit-Division* commanded by *General* Remer, one of the *Führer* units, which was again forced into a fire-brigade role. Coming from the Lauban area, where it had a few days to rest and refit and just enough time to regroup after its last deployment, its transports now rolled into the Jägerndorf area to be thrown against the onslaught of Soviet armor and infantry as a last resort. The division went into action in totally foreign terrain, with no knowledge of the enemy or our own situation. The units of the division were thrown into action piecemeal as they detrained, rather than as a complete division. Success was therefore questionable from the very start.

The first hastily-loaded trains carrying the *Führer-Begleit-Division* arrived in Jägerndorf late on the afternoon of 23 March and were unloaded immediately. The division Ib had already gone ahead by motor car and had set up his command post in Bleichwitz so as to settle all supply questions before the division arrived. Haste was the order of the day. Enemy tanks were advancing west on a broad front unopposed. The unloading of the division—under a continuous hail of bombs—took until 25 March. Jägerndorf was ablaze from end to end.

Bleichwitz was already under enemy artillery fire on 24 March, and the division Ib was slightly wounded. Lt. Wimmen was hit in the head by splinters and died in hospital that evening. The town of Lindau was in flames—the enemy was at the gates of Jägerndorf. The division units would have to come straight off the loading ramps and fight for their assembly areas.

On 25 March the first elements of I./Pz.Gren.Rgt. FBD under Hptm. Schulz, together with the Stu.Gesch.Abt. FBD under Hptm. Franz, moved out of Bleichwitz in a northeasterly direction and formed a security screen on Hills 379 to 382, behind which the artillery of the Pz.Art.Rgt. occupied firing positions.

During the afternoon communication the units sought to establish contact with the 17. Pz.Div., which was supposed to be in the Bratsch—Mocker area on their left.

After driving over Hill 382 in a northeasterly direction, the leading vehicles of 1. Kp./I. (SPW) Btl./Pz.Gren.Rgt. FBD spotted a Soviet battalion attacking south accompanied by seven T 34 tanks. The armored troop carriers immediately opened fire with their cannon and machine-guns, and within a short time three T 34s had been knocked out by the escorting assault guns. The Soviet force disappeared again quickly. Contact was established with a company from the 17. Pz.Div. and position was held there until evening.

At the same time the remaining companies of I. (SPW) Btl./Pz. Gren.Rgt. FBD together with the Pz.Rgt. FBD under Obstlt. Schnappauf advanced toward Löwitz and from there on toward Hennerwitz, occupying both villages against negligible resistance. During the night they were relieved in these two villages by troops from other units, since the *Führer-Begleit-Division* was supposed to attack to the southeast.

In spite of heavy enemy fighter-bomber activity, on the following day the advance to the east continued and Hill 305 due west of Paulinenhof was occupied. The tanks immediately went into position there, as enemy counterattacks against this commanding chain of hills were inevitable. In fact the position was held until 29 March and every assault by enemy tanks was beaten off. Oblt. Geisberg of the Pz.Rgt. FBD distinguished himself and was later awarded the Knight's Cross.

The main line of resistance was now relatively stable; in the first day of combat on 26 March it ran: Hennerwitz—Possnitz—Hill 305—Paulinenhof. Under sunny spring weather the enemy massed more and more tanks in the area north of Paulinenhof, where heavy fighting had to be expected soon Enemy fighter-bombers and bombers were constantly in the air, attacking our positions and vehicle concentrations.

Meanwhile contact had been established to the southeast, where elements of a *Ski-Jäger-Division* were in position. These were mainly in the line Bauerwitz—Troppau rail line, or the area south of Alstedt. There were again signs of a continuous main line of resistance. The danger of an enemy breakthrough to the west was not yet gone, the enemy had probably only been forced to halt temporarily.

Small groups of enemy tanks repeatedly felt their way toward the strongpoints held by the FBD, seeking weak spots. These were usually forced to turn back after several T 34s had been knocked out. Given the stubborn determination of the Soviet tank crews, it is no wonder that the number of kills recorded by the FBD continued to climb. More than 30 enemy tanks were destroyed near Hill 305 in a single day of fighting.

The forward command post was in a sanitarium in Branitz which offered an excellent all-round view to the east. Heavy attacks by enemy infantry with tank support were in progress against Hill 305 and Paulinenhof, with associated heavy artillery and mortar fire. The infantry of the Pz.Gren.Rgt. FBD suffered mounting casualties, thinning the ranks manning the positions.

As a precaution two of Hptm. Knauper's pioneer companies were placed in rear positions south of Hochkretzscham. And it was a good thing. For the enemy, attacking en masse, succeeded in driving through the gullies from the north into Hochkretzscham, where fierce close-quarters fighting developed.

The town had to be abandoned during the night of 28-29 March. A crisis was developing, as our infantry forces were no longer sufficient to offer serious resistance everywhere.

The last infantry forces were immediately assembled on 29 March and committed to a counterattack against Hochkretzscham. The attack failed; in the town itself were masses of Soviet tanks, while south of the town enemy infantry was already advancing south.

The FBD hastily occupied fall-back positions, strongpoint-style—in a line from Neuhof estate—line of hills north of Osterdorf Kaldaun. The grenadiers were shaken; there was much nervousness on account of the massing of enemy tanks in Hochkretzscham. Hptm. Knauper, commander of the Pz.Pi.Btl. FBD, brought up his last combat engineers. Oblt. Arnold, the O1, assembled stragglers to man new fall-back positions. Panic! And as well the enemy fighter-bombers, bombing and strafing everything that moved, and the artillery and mortar fire. Chaos! The enemy now resumed his attacks with masses of tanks and infantry from the north in the direction of Osterdorf—Neuhof estate—Fasanerie. No holding now, the men fell back. Only here and there did isolated machine-gun nets hold on and try to defend themselves. But they were swept away or blasted out of their holes.

The Mother of God at the Crossroads
(Account by Oblt. Arnold, Div. O1)
30 March 1945:

I stood in the ditch several meters away from the statue and looked over to the Neuhof estate, which our III. Btl. had attacked from the area around Kaldaun a few hours before. The attack had bogged down since the enemy was too strongly massed in the estate.

A simultaneous attack with tanks and armored troop carriers from the direction of Osterdorf toward the estate by Obstlt. Wulf, commander Pz.Gren.Rgt. FBD, and I had likewise been unsuccessful, the Russians having placed all their tanks in well-camouflaged defensive positions in the buildings on the estate.

We were too weak to be able to press the attack across the open fields to the edge of the estate. During the two-hour attack enemy fighter-bombers hailed bombs on us without inflicting any serious damage.

Obstlt. Wulf feared that the enemy in front of III. Btl.'s sector was gathering his forces for defense and eventual counterattack.

We therefore drove to the crossroads so as to be able to intervene from there if III. Btl. should pull back.

The enemy had to be prevented from reaching the road at all costs.

We were both completely exhausted after the heavy fighting of recent days. The grenadiers were in a similar state. It was a miracle that they were still able to attack at all.

Scattered mortar shells were falling where III. Btl. had dug in, about 300 meters in front of us. The Russians swept the terrain with machine-gun fire, forcing us to take cover in the ditches.

Suddenly I saw movement in III. Btl.'s positions. Singly at first, then more, the men were getting up and beginning to stream towards the rear. Something must be up over there. I stared across at the edge of the estate and saw T 34s.

What we had feared was happening. The Russians were also massing their tanks in this sector.

The grenadiers could not be stopped. The first of them had already reached the road. We stopped them and had them go into position in the ditches to our left and right. If the Russians counterattacked, the front line at the road would have to be held.

I kept my eye on the T 34s at the edge of the estate. Suddenly there was flash from one of the tanks. I pulled Obstlt. Wulf, who was squatting half erect beside me, to the ground, and seconds later the first shell exploded in front of us on the other side of the road. Fragments whizzed past. Shot now followed shot, impact followed impact. Between impacts I repeatedly raised my head to see whether the tanks were moving. Then we pressed our faces into the damp, cold earth again.

Something seemed to be going on over by the statue.

I stood up and ran over.

Suddenly, a shell exploded beside me.

Something dark, the size of a fist, whizzed past my face, struck the side of the chapel and fell to the ground. It was just a large fragment.

The chapel had already been hit.

Several people were wounded, one would not be moving again. Concerned, I continued to stare over at the edge of the estate. Would the T 34s begin to move, would they attack?

Where was our artillery?

They must have noticed that something was happening here. The entire side of the road was under enemy tank fire. Impact followed impact. Bursts of machine-gun fire chirped past. High-explosive shells exploded everywhere.

Time passed slowly. Was it the remaining seconds of our lives ticking away, or was it just our heartbeats, our blood, which pulsed so irregularly?

Would the tanks attack?

They could be here in three minutes and overrun us! We would have to let it happen and fire at the following infantry.

Next to me a wounded man groaned.

I calmed him and again stared over at the tanks, which fired without pause, as if they were trying to throw up a bridge to us with the tracers from their shells. A shining bridge, on which death and destruction rode over to us!

Suddenly there was an impact on one of the estate buildings, then another and another. Roofing tiles and beams flew in all directions, smoke rose high, the roof caught fire. Our artillery was shooting!

Now I heard the deep howling of the shells as they passed high overhead on their way to the enemy. The tanks became uneasy and pulled back into cover behind the buildings.

Slowly our tension eased.

An attack was now unlikely. I walked over to the statue, where the medic was applying the first emergency dressings. The dead man was still lying as he had fallen.

His eyes stared glazed into the sky. His right hand had scratched into the earth, as if he had been trying to hold on.

Above him sat the Mother of God with her child. Silently she bowed over the tiny creature in her arms. She seemed wrapped up in herself, unaffected by the events of the past hours.

Endless peace surrounded her—no conflict touched her. She stood above things, as we stood in them. Nothing else mattered to her but the life in her arms—she protected it, we destroyed it!

Holy Mother, pray for us!

The grenadiers of II./Pz.Gren.Rgt. FBD held on in Kaldaun, scratched into the earth behind the ruins and fired everything their machine-guns could give. Then one cried out. A medic crawled over to him, pulled out a packet dressing, wrapped it around the wound, placed his canteen to the thirsty lips. They took heavy casualties, but they held Kaldaun, often in close combat. Their commander, Hptm. Zamnow, was killed when he ventured outside his command post, which was suddenly ringed by brown-clad figures. The runners, telephonists and radio operators attacked with spades and pistols—to avenge their commander, to force the enemy to flee. Kaldaun was held. Night came; the cursed tanks came again and blasted everything in their path. Then, finally, Kaldaun had to be abandoned. The few grenadiers occupied positions along the Branitz—Osterdof road, now reinforced by hastily brought in alert companies of train and headquarters personnel. But what good was that! There were simply not enough men, enough bearers of arms, for the main line of resistance to be held.

The 6. Kp./II./Pz.Gren.Rgt. FBD was stopped in Jakobsfelde, led forward again by Oblt. Schmied in the direction of Kahle Kuhle, a small wood halfway to the front. It had to be held, contact had to be maintained with I. (SPW) Btl. Any gap in our defenses carried in it the danger of an enemy breakthrough.

Then, during the night of 30-31 March, a commander's briefing for a flanking attack by all elements of the FBD from the west against the southwards-advancing enemy. With tanks, assault guns, grenadiers, pioneers. The enemy would be stopped now, come what may!

The plan called for the attack to begin at 06:00 hours on 31 March from the area east of Branitz, initially east to the area of Osterdorf, followed by a swing north to attack and drive back the enemy. Elements of I. (SPW) Btl. were to take part with their armored troop carriers. General Staff Obstlt. Knoopen-Wulf, the division Ia, would himself lead the Pz.Gren.Rgt. FBD.

And it worked. Obstlt. Schnappauf's tanks began to roll. They were followed by the assault guns, which were to guard the flanks, then the armored troop carriers of I. (SPW) Btl. The armored vehicles drove through bombs dropped by Il 2s and mortar fire between Osterdorf (where the I. (SPW) Btl. took up positions facing Fasanerie) and the Neuhof estate. Farther right riflemen of a pioneer company from the *Ski-Jäger-Division* joined the advance on the right flank. Oblt. Dyckerhoff appeared with several of 4. Kp.'s vehicles mounting 75-mm guns, plus several more of 5. Kp. mounting three weapons, reinforcing the armored troop carriers which were soon able to drive into Fasanerie. Our tanks from the east and our assault guns from the north, all streamed toward Neuhof estate and Hill 320 to its west. Both were taken.

Grenadiers followed up immediately and, protected by the tanks, occupied new positions facing north and northeast; to the right there was continuous contact with the ski infantry again. The enemy had been halted!

The FBD's command post was moved to Skrochowitz when the enemy pressure increased again. I. (SPW)/Pz.Gren.Rgt. FBD in positions north and northeast of Burgfeld, heavy enemy artillery and mortar fire on the center of the town and positions at the edge of town. Farther to the northwest contact with II./Pz.Gren.Rgt. FBD near field barns in front of Lindau. Farther northwest on 1 April heavy tank fire; enemy tanks breaking through to the west there, Turmitz area. Our tanks immediately moved forward to counterattack. Seventeen enemy tanks were destroyed, and thus the enemy breakthrough was halted at the last minute.

In the 48 hours that followed, there was furious defensive fighting in Burgfeld as I. (SPW) Btl., now under the command of Rittmeister Seibold, tried to hold the town. It was held in spite of heavy enemy tank, artillery and Stalin Organ fire. The enemy was determined to commit whatever was required to achieve a breakthrough there. Burgfeld was ablaze from end to end, while in its midst the armored troop carriers and grenadiers continued to hold, even though their numbers steadily decreased. At night alert companies were moved in, and once again the last man was sent up to prevent an enemy breakthrough. The men were badly exhausted, they slept while standing or behind cover—in spite of the fact that there was no letup in the enemy fire. This went on day and night, and it was already day three, 3 April 1945.

The Soviets tried to sneak through the depressions, especially at night; and by day the grenadiers had to cope with enemy machine-guns which had infiltrated between their scattered strongpoints during the night. No one knew if the man next to him was friend or foe. It was a battle to all sides.

Finally everything settled itself. The first reinforcements arrived from the rear. They were the leading elements of the 10. Pz.Div., which, as if by some miracle, were to relieve the *Führer*-grenadiers of the *Führer-Begleit-Division*. And at that very moment the enemy pressure subsided. It became quieter, the enemy fire weaker. The Soviet breakthrough toward Troppau had failed, stopped by the bravery of the men of the *Führer-Begleit-Division*, who had held on in spite of grievous losses.

In these fourteen indescribably tough days of defense and counterattack in the Jägerndorf combat zone, the division destroyed a total of 231 enemy tanks for the loss of 23 of its own. Its losses had been heavy, but those of the enemy were even heavier!

But there was no respite with which to close the gaps and rest. The division was loaded aboard trains again during the night of 5-6 April. Its destination was the Hirschberg/Riesengebirge area.

New operations lay ahead. The big Soviet offensive was imminent. The *Führer-Begleit-Division* was to be positioned behind the center of the Eastern Front, in the Muskau—Spremberg area, as operational reserve.

Part IX
Großdeutschland in Action in the West
From Cottbus to Schleswig-Rendsburg

Chapter 1

The Allied bombing raid on Cottbus on 15 February 1945, the surprising speed with which the enemy neared the Oder—Neiße line, the threat posed to the training of recruits and the provision of replacements for the front-line units, and finally the final mobilization of all German men to defend the homeland: these were the reasons why the GD replacement units were transferred to less threatened areas of Germany.

For the commanders school in Cottbus, being quartered in wooden barracks was no longer satisfactory in view of the expected further Allied air raids. The presence of high-grade replacement officers in the direct vicinity of the front and the fact that command agencies were searching everywhere for available reserves regardless of their qualifications for use in alert units with which to plug gaps in the front—these conditions threatened to simply cause the schools output to be frittered away. Repeatedly pointing to this situation, the commander of the GD's replacement officer school, *Major* Poeschmann, was able to have the facility transferred out of Cottbus. The SS officer candidate school at Bad Tölz was the initial choice; but then the school was sent in the direction of Zwickau-Lauterbach. Beginning with advance detachments on 9 February, the bulk of the officer candidates reached their new base during the period 15 to 20 February. Two trains carried the men and all their training materials. Their new quarters were the König-Albert Barracks in Zwickau, and training resumed soon after their arrival. Just two nights after their arrival, however, more than 1,000 Allied bombers overflew the city, so that it had to be expected that its railway installations would soon be the target of a major attack. The commander of the GD's replacement officer school therefore decided to spread his classes among the surrounding villages, but at the same time to try to join up with the Pz.Gren.-Ersatz-Brigade GD in Schleswig as soon as possible. On 25 February the replacement officer school was in fact put aboard two trains for transport right across Germany to Rendsburg in Schleswig-Holstein.

Once again the families of the married instructors were taken along and they found permanent quarters in the Rendsburg area.

Soon the school was functioning normally again in the Wrangel

Barracks in Rendburg, its tough and determined training ensuring a steady flow of replacement officers. Training continued until the last days of March 1945 without further hindrance from bombing raids or the approach of enemy forces.

Only a few days after the replacement officer school's advance detachment left Cottbus—on or about 16 February—the advance guard of the Pz.Gren.-Ersatz-Brigade GD also left the bomb-battered city for Schleswig-Holstein. A few days later six trains were loaded with the brigade's remaining personnel, the rest of the training weapons and equipment, the remaining vehicles, orderly rooms, etc. These departed Drebkau station near Cottbus bound for Schleswig-Holstein. The last transport, which departed at about 10:00 hours on 22 February, carried Abt. V (k), the brigade's photo section, and several medics.

Only clean-up and base detachments were left at Cottbus, and these sought to restore some semblance of order to the hastily abandoned barracks and quarters.

On account of the defenses set up by the GD, the city of Cottbus was very soon declared a fortress. Gen.Mj. Sodan was later named its commander. Not many more than 100 men of the GD clean-up detachments were kept within the walls of the city.

Arriving in Schleswig-Holstein on 20 February, the brigade headquarters and its commander, *Oberst* Glaesemer, set up quarters in Gottorf Castle. The various units moved into the nearby towns and villages. The first steps toward the resumption of training were taken immediately, especially since a batch of recruits had been received just prior to departure. Convalescents from hospitals, the recovered and men declared medically fit for front-line service again were placed in special units. Soon the first replacements were on their way to field units.

No more replacements reached East Prussia, which had been cut off from the outside world since March 1945 and could only be reached by air or sea.

Since officers and non-commissioned officers could no longer reach the Pz.Gren.Div. GD by land and after initial attempts to fly them in failed, a plan was conceived to create a further replacement unit as a catch-basin for returning convalescents.

More or less with the knowledge of the brigade, on 20 February the Pz.Gren.Ers. u. Ausb.Rgt. GD issued the order for the formation of an E. und A.-Abteilung GD (Replacement and Training Battalion) in Denmark. Its first commander was Hptm. Neudahm. The battalion initially comprised three training companies and a convalescent company. The units were quartered in Odder, near Argus, Jutland. A completely mixed convalescent company under the command of Oblt. Müller and company officer Lt. Rohlandt left the Cottbus area by express train for Odder—

Copenhagen. These people, who were again fit for combat, were retrained as infantry and after about six weeks were exchanged.

At the time of the arrival of the first elements of the new GD replacement and training battalion the only military presence in Odder, a small Danish town, was a small vehicle repair group. The arriving personnel moved into temporary quarters at first, sleeping on bags of straw in school classrooms, gymnasiums, etc. Finally, on 26 February, Hptm. Weizenbeck arrived from Guben and took over command of the GD replacement battalion. More and more men found their way to Odder, including Lt. Buchhagen and Kaufmann, both BR officers, who were soon employed as company officers in training the now steady influx of convalescents.

In the following weeks until March 1945 the duty schedule frequently called for "training of non-commissioned officers and setting up of quarters." The training of convalescents for the infantry role also proceeded at a leisurely pace. Meanwhile, however, German evacuees from enemy-occupied areas had also begun to arrive, and these had to be housed somewhere. This was done with the help of the E.- u. A.-Abt. GD in Odder, which requisitioned summer houses for the refugees.

In general, relationships with the Danes, who continued to remain neutral, were cool and correct. Here and there they did show human feelings for the plight of the refugees. Gradually, however, the feeling of freedom began to be felt on Danish territory, which toward the end of the war led to several confrontations with the German garrison.

Until January 1945, the *Brandenburg* Home Headquarters, a unit of the *Brandenburg* Division, was based in Brandenburg on the Havel near Berlin—in the General-Feldzeugmeister Barracks. Some time in the first half of January, this unit was renamed the "*Ausbildungs-Bataillon Brandenburg.*" It received recruits from Cottbus for GD and BR and was finally placed under the command of Hptm. Schewe (GD). It was reorganized into a panzer-grenadier replacement and training battalion, as had been done at Cottbus, with the incorporation of training, convalescent and trained replacement companies. The recruits were sworn in on 6 January in the presence of the Wach-Rgt. GD Berlin's band, and on 26 January all officers, non-commissioned officers and enlisted men were presented the *Brandenburg* cuff band; GD insignia were worn on shoulder straps and boards.

The battalion's personnel strength soon reached about 2,500 men, all of whom were housed in the barracks—which normally accommodated just 500 men—on straw and mattresses. Air raid shelters, gymnasiums, barns, gas mask testing rooms—all were occupied.

In addition to the front-line units, primarily the GD and BR, replacements were also sent to the Wach-Rgt. GD Berlin.

On the evening of 12 March the alarm was sounded in Brandenburg.

It was soon announced that the Pz.Gren. E.- u. A.-Abt. GD would soon have to depart for combat duty. Departure was delayed. Finally, at about 03:00 on 13 March, the troops headed to the station to board trains. Their destination was Schleswig-Holstein. After an uneventful 24-hour journey the transports arrived in Eckernförde and finally were unloaded on 14 March in Rieseby, where temporary quarters were occupied.

The battalion's organization and quarters were as follows:

III. (Brandenburg) Btl./Pz.Gren.E.- u. A.-Rgt.
Großdeutschland

Quarters: (also organization)

Btl. command post	Rieseby
9. (A.) Kp.	Waabs
10. (A.) Kp.	Norby
11. (A.) Kp.	Loose
12. (A.) Kp. (MG.)	Grünholz
Spec. Purpose Training Company	Blumenthal
1. Umschul.-Kp.	Kosel
2. Umschul.-Kp.	Barkelsby
Trained Replacement Company	Bohnert

Command Positions:

Battalion commander	Hptm. Schewe
Battalion adjutant	Lt. Gerving
Battalion medical officer	Oberarzt Dr. Hoffmann
Abt. IVa	Oberzahlm. Kohls
Abt. Vk	Tech.Insp. Ramboldt
	Oberschirrm. Prien
Ia steno	Obfw. Korthaus
IIa steno	Fw. Trebschek
Ib steno	Uffz. Knieper
9. (A.) Kp.	Lt. von Bülow
10. (A.) Kp.	Lt. Feinauer
11. (A.) Kp.	Lt. Becker
12. (A.-MG.) Kp.	Lt. Steinmann
Special Purpose Training Company	Lt. Braun
1. Umschul.-Kp.	Oblt. Kappel
2. Umschul.-Kp.	Oblt.Horsthemke
Trained Replacement Company	Oblt. Hälbig

The skeleton detachment in Brandenburg, one convalescent and one trained replacement company, was ordered to send all capable soldiers to the front. It thus was no longer under the command of the Pz.Gren.-Ersatz-Brigade GD.

The total strength of the Pz.Gren.-Ersatz-Brigade GD now assembled in the Schleswig area—not counting the replacement officer school—is revealed in the following strength return:

Rations and combat strengths of the Pz.Gren.Ers. u. Ausb.Rgt. *Großdeutschland* (prior to departure of the Ersatz-Brigade GD).

Rations Headcount:	Officers	NCOs	Men
I. Btl.	(—)	(—)	1043
II. Btl.	17	81	888
III. Btl.	13	98	1058
Res. NCO Comp.	6	31	146
KFA Comp.	3	31	53
Rgt. H.Q.	5	7	33
Totals:	44	248	3221

Actual Strength:

Combat Strengths	Officers	NCOs	Men
I. Btl.	8	41	436
II. Btl.	8	38	482
III. Btl.	7	51	460
Totals:	23	130	1378

Reserve Units	Officers	NCOs	Men
I. Btl.	5	60	472
II. Btl.	5	35	365
III. Btl.	8	46	588
Totals:	18	141	1425

Chapter 2
Lingen—Rheine—-Cloppenburg
Panzergrenadier-Einsatz-Brigade GD

On 22 March 1945 the leading elements of the united Allied armies stood along the entire length of the Rhine—from the mouth of the Main to the mouth of the Rhine. They had established several bridgeheads, especially on the middle Rhine, such as those at Oppenheim and Remagen. It was Eisenhower's objective to establish one large bridgehead across the Rhine extending from the mouth of the Neckar near Heidelberg to the Sieg and east to Hanau, Giessen and Siegen.

On the lower course of the Rhine the 21st Army Group under Field Marshall Montgomery had likewise massed its forces and was preparing for the much more difficult task of winning bridgeheads across the broad lower part of the river near Rheinberg (by the Americans) and near Wesel and Rees (by the British and Canadians). Facing them there were four parachute divisions and three infantry divisions, with two weak panzer divisions stationed near Emmerich as operational reserve. These forces were under the command of *Generaloberst* Student's 1. Fsch.Jäg.Armee. Both bridgeheads were established during the night of 23-24 March, then expanded by paratroops 24 hours later, and finally on 28 March were united into one large bridgehead which extended from Bottrop through Dorsten and Bocholt to just short of Emmerich.

But this was also the first step in the encirclement of the German 5. and 15. Panzer-Armee in the Ruhr region. On 1 April the 1st American Army from the Remagen bridgehead linked up near Lippstadt with the 9th American Army which had attacked north of the Ruhr and then turned east toward the Elbe. The crossing of the Rhine by the U.S. 9th Army in the Rheinberg area and its subsequent advance to the north also resulted in contact being severed between the German 1st Parachute Army on the lower Rhine and the 15th Army on its left, which was now caught inside the Ruhr pocket. The left wing of the German 1st Parachute Army was forced by the Allied operations to swing its left wing to the northwest and, under pressure from the British 21st Army Group, which had now also gone to the attack, it was driven north in fierce, continuous fighting. The British army group continued to face the divisions of the German 1st Parachute Army, with the veteran parachute divisions of II. Fsch.-Korps under *General der Fallschirmtruppen* Meindl in the north and the equally capable 9. Pz.Div. and 15. Pz.Gren.Div. in the south. All of these units put up a determined resistance to the British advance.

In this final stage of the struggle in western Germany, the Pz.Gren.-Ersatz-Brigade GD, which was now based in the Rendsburg area of

Schleswig with the E.- u. A.-Rgt. GD and the Replacement Officer School GD, plus all other smaller units, was called upon to form a combat unit and stand ready. The preparations for this were carried out under the most unfavorable circumstances. The first order of battle soon revealed itself:

Panzer-Grenadier-E. u. A.-Regiment Großdeutschland

C.O.   Major Wackernagel (disabled)
Adjutant   Oblt. Bensinger
O.O.   Lt. König, Lt. Slaner
Ops. Section   Lt. Schardt
(operational platoon, dispatch rider squad, bicycle messenger squad)
Ib   Lt. Rehrmann
Signals Platoon   Lt. Bauer

I./Pz.Gren.E. u. A.Rgt. GD   II./Pz.Gren.E. u. A.Rgt. GD
1.-3. (Schtz.) Kp.   5.-7. (Schtz.) Kp.
4. (MG.) Kp.   8. (MG.) Kp.
Major Gerbener   Hptm. Goeldel
Hptm. Blumenthal   Hptm. Schmidt

III. (BR)/Pz.Gren.E. u. A.Rgt. GD
9.-11. (Schtz.) Kp.
12. (MG.) Kp.
Hptm. Schewe
RUB-Kp.   Hptm. Schmidt
Platoon leader   Lt. Baumgarter
Platoon leader   Lt. Bieniussa
                             Lt. Schönbrunn
Platoon leader   Lt. Nolting
Operational Panzer Battalion   Hptm. Bauer
                             Hptm. Franke
1 armored scout troop   Oblt. Schmarbeck (GD)
1 armored pioneer company (GD)
1 armored company (GD)
1 assault gun company (not GD, added later)
Rations Strengths (as of 31 March 1945)

	Officers	NCOs	Men
Rgt. H.Q.	5	7	33
I. Btl.	12	95	907
II. Btl.	?	?	?
III. Btl.	13	98	1058
RUB Comp.	6	31	146
KFA Comp.	3	31	53
Field Combat School	1	6	1

Concerning combat strengths, it can be said that these were about 50% lower than the rations strengths, since each battalion had to form so-called reserve units with half of its men, including those made instructors on

333

account of handicaps, illness or disability and the recruits. There was no question of using these as first-use combat units, instead it was anticipated that they would be trained as field replacement battalions and later incorporated into the fighting units.

Here are several combat strengths with which the battalion went into action:

	Officers	NCOs	Men
I. Btl.	8	41	436
II. Btl.	4	18	234
III. Btl. (BR)	7	51	460

At this point the regiment consisted mainly of recruits and new draftees who had been soldiers for just eight days. Some had not been sworn in yet; obviously there could be no question of using them in the field. After having released so much to the previous new formations, the weapons and equipment state was such that there were shortages of steel helmets, boots were second-hand, ammunition had to be carried in jacket pockets, and so on and so on. The only vehicles available were several old motorcycles and one or two wood-gas-powered trucks—that was all!

Some of the squad, platoon and company leaders were highly-decorated and experienced soldiers. Of course some of them had been serving as instructors in the homeland for a long time and were no longer used to combat. Most of them were also handicapped as a result of wounds.

The orders for *Major* Poeschmann's replacement officer school were different; it was to continue its training, in another place where it was also to serve as the garrison. On order of the OKW march readiness was to be achieved by the end of March for transfer by rail into northern Holland. The order expressly called for the transfer of the "training unit," which meant that instructional material, training equipment and female office personnel were to go too.

On the evening of 23 March elements of the Pz.Gren.-Ersatz-Brigade GD were placed on alert. The rail transfer was to begin at noon on the following day. The orders given the brigade commander, *Oberst* Glaesemer, called for the selected combat units to go to the area due east of Bremen, the GD's replacement officer school into the Roden area, south of Grooningen.

The first elements of the *OB-Schule GD* , the 2, 3 and 6th sections, boarded the train in Rendsburg under the command of Hptm. Menzner. Departure followed at 00:45 hours on 25 March 1945. The second transport, comprising the 1st, 4th and 5th sections plus the school headquarters under the command of Hptm. Erdmann, which included the female personnel, loaded on the morning of 25 March and departed the same evening.

Detraining in Ottersberg, about 10 kilometers east of Bremen, and quarters in villages northeast of Bremen such as Falkenberg (2nd sect.), Lilienthal (3rd sect.) and Heidberg (1st sect.).

By 28 March the Pz.Gren.-Ersatz-Brigade combat units had gathered northeast, southeast and east of Bremen and were preparing to march into the Weener—Papenburg area on the Ems. Since there were no vehicles a foot march was planned, mainly at night since enemy fighter-bombers posed a serious threat in this area.

Horses and wagons were requisitioned in the quarters and villages, harness was purchased. There was soon a good relationship with the population; cattle were bought to improve the rations and some uniforms were found in the clothing stores at Varrelbusch airfield. Everyone prepared to move into the new area.

Meanwhile, in the former quarters in Schleswig—Rendsburg inventory was taken, the remaining elements were combined and in part reorganized. Oblt. Schlüter of the staff formed new trained replacement and convalescent companies with the soldiers arriving from the hospitals. The quarters personnel were soon organized as follows:

Rgt. H.Q. (skeleton crew Pz.Gren.Ers. u. Ausb.Rgt. GD) in Tolk	
I. Btl.	Westerackeby area
II. Btl.	Böklund area
III. Btl.	Moldenit area
Special Purpose Training Company	Schaalby-Glensby area
Trained Replacement Company	Kaleby area

After several days *Major* Everth was placed in command of the remaining elements of the Ersatz-Brigade GD still stationed in the Schleswig area.

These elements were in possession of the following weapons (31 March):

339 rifles
702 bayonets
9 pistols
20 submachine-guns
28 assault rifles
14 machine-guns
1 anti-aircraft machine-gun
1 mortar

More men from the hospitals gradually found their way there, including officers and non-commissioned officers, some of whom were sent back to their units after recuperating. Preparations were also made for the formation of new operational units.

On 28 March movement orders were issued for the combat units of the Pz.Gren.-Ersatz-Brigade and the OB-Schule GD, with march routes, march times and march organization.

The following units were combined into march groups:

North Route: (tank route)	Center Route:	South Route:
Bergedorf	Leeste	Syke (Riede)
Sandkotten	Ganderkeese	Wildershausen
Oberlethe	Wardenburg	Garrel (Sage)
Bösel	Holtange	Gehlenberg
Lorup	Esterwegen	Surwald
Dorpen	Papenburg	Heede
Vlagtwedde	Wedde	
OB-Schule GD	I./Rgt.	Pz.Abt. GD
Nachr.Abt. GD	II./Rgt.	III. (BR)/Rgt.
Pz.Jäg.Abt. 20	Pz.Abt. 20	Pi.Btl. GD
Art.Abt. GD		
Lehr-Btl.		

In addition to the specified march groups for the Pz.Gren.-Ersatz-Brigade GD, the individual sections of the replacement officer school also went on the march, forming two march groups as they had for rail transport:

March Group I commander: Hptm. Menzner
March Group II commander: Hptm. Erdmann

All excess material, training materials, office records and the female personnel were left at the base in Lilienthal. For no one believed that any kind of training course could be held in the Roden area. Instead the officer cadets got used to the idea that they would soon be going into action.

The march was also used to increase the combat readiness of the sections, however; it was associated with small exercises, served to improve equipment and weapons and to strengthen the feeling of community.

The general direction of march was west at first, direction Holland. Because of the enemy situation, during the night of 31 March-1 April it was changed to southwest in the direction of Lingen—Rheine. It was expected that all elements, including the replacement officer school, would soon see action. The march columns were hit by the first fighter-bomber attacks, their movements having been spotted in the darkness.

On 1 April 1945, Easter Sunday, more became known about the enemy situation: leading elements of a British unit had advanced into the area west of Rheine and were threatening to cross the Ems to the east. Along the Ems itself there were only weak German units, mostly alert formations from the surrounding airfields of *Luftgau-Kommando XI*.

In order to be able to meet the threat of an enemy crossing of the Ems in time, and with a unit whose combat worth was still highly thought of by the high command, during the night of 1-2 April the I./Pz.Gren.Ers. u. Ausb.Rgt. GD was loaded aboard trucks and driven into the area due east of Rheine. There it was quartered with Kampfgruppe Knaust already in position there. Early on 2 April the first elements of *Major* Gerbener's I. Btl. were already in position on the east bank of the Ems—between the river and the Dortmund—Ems Canal. There was no contact with the enemy, however the first enemy tanks were observed in the rail yards south of Rheine.

On 2 April 1945 the commander of the Pz.Gren.Ers. u. Ausb.Rgt. GD issued the following order for subsequent march movements:

Pz.Gren.Ers. u. Ausb.Rgt. GD   *Rgt. Command Post, 2/4/1945*

Großdeutschland   *12:50 hours*

Abt. Ia

Order for further movements by the Rgt. into the area of operations.

I. Enemy

No enemy contact so far according to reports by 1. Bataillon already deployed in the Rheine area. Weak enemy point units with some tanks are said to have reached the rail yards south of Rheine. Yesterday enemy artillery fired a few rounds into the town of Rheine.

II. To be transferred

(a) on the night of 2-3/4/1945:

I. Bataillon: reserve headquarters

1. and 4. Res.Kp. by Lt. Schumann's transport column from the Wardenburg area into the area of operations. Report to I. Btl.'s message center, Lt. Krüger, in Altenlünne. Mission orders there.

(b) on the night of 2-3/4/1945:

II. Bataillon: — headquarters

1.-4. Combat units from the Sage/Grosskneten area via Altenlünne into the area of operations by Lt. Schumann's transport column.

Btl. C.O. ahead to Altenlünne to receive detailed operations order from regimental commander.

Rest of II. Bataillon (reserve unit) foot march from the Sage/Grosskneten area into the Stapelfeld area.

During the night of 3-4/4/1945:

Further transfer of the remaining elements of II. Bataillon by Schumann transport column via Altenlünne into the area of operations.

(c). On the night of 2-3/4/1945:

III. Bataillon: foot march from the Stapelfeld area into the Kettenkamp area.

(d). on 2/4/1945…

Rgt. H.Q.: with rest of operations section and anti-tank detachment RUB-Kp. by motor transport to Altenlünne.

(e). UB-Kompanie to prepare for change of position by 18:00 hours on 2/4/1945, transportation probably by motor transport company.

March and mission orders to follow.

(f). KFA-Company and 1b section prepare for change of position and during the night of 3-4/4/1945 transfer into the Schale area, southwest of Fürstenau.

(g). Horse sections I. to III. Bataillon follow III. Btl.'s march route and assemble in Basum area, 3 km south of Kettenkamp, early on 3/4/1945.

III. Movement by motorized units to be completely without lights. Air attack interval to be maintained, in every vehicle second driver on the fender.

IV. New regimental command post: as of 21:00 hours on 2/4/1945 in Altenlünne. Telephone: Altenlünne 101. Reports on completed transfers to be sent there.

I myself will leave for Rheine at 13:00 hours, from approximately 18:00 hours I may be reached through I. Bataillon reporting center, Altenlünne 101!

Wackernagel

At the same time (evening of 2/4/45) the command post of the Pz.Gren.-Ersatz-Brigade GD was moved to Freren. After another regimental order a Field Replacement Battalion of the Pz.Gren.Ers. u. Ausb.Rgt. GD was formed under the command of Hptm. Schmidt. It consisted mainly of untrained men from the reserve units, with officer candidates and cadets as instructors. The RUB Company was disbanded and its personnel divided among the regiment and the replacement officer school. It in turn assigned its officer cadets and candidates to the various battalions as squad, train and section leaders. This move was intended to prevent all command personnel, which were in short supply, from being concentrated in one unit in the expected event that the replacement officer school saw action.

On 2 April there was an adjutants' conference at which the formation of a Field Replacement Battalion (Feldersatz-Btl. GD) of the Pz.Gren.Ers. u. Ausb.Rgt. GD was ordered. Its commander was Hptm. Schmidt (formerly of the RUB Company). (RUB Company was divided among the Pz.Gren.Ers. u. Ausb.Rgt. GD and replacement officer school.)

The following detachments were provided by the various units for the formation of the Feldersatz-Btl. GD:

OB-Schule: 1st section including officer candidates, taken in on 1 April.

Strength: 4 officers, 20 NCOs and 145 enlisted men, no previous training.

Trained Replacement Company:

Strength: 3 officers, 14 non-commissioned officers and 180 enlisted men. Only 2/3 of the assembled sick, stragglers, hangers-on had any weapons at all.

Pz.-Abt.: Had approximately 80 men near Bippen. Crews for assault gun "Clausewitz."

Nachr.Abt.: Strength: 2 officers, 13 NCOs and 178 enlisted men; these were retrained as grenadiers and were also earmarked to bolster the division's signals battalion.

Pi.Btl.: Strength: 2 officers, 7 NCOs and 147 enlisted men, untrained recruits, meaning they had only been soldiers for three days. They, too, were planned as pioneer replacements for "Clausewitz."

Rgt.: Strength: 11 officers, 43 NCOs, 50 assistant instructors, 492 enlisted men. Enlisted men not trained, poor physical shape.

Armament: 6 machine-guns, 2 medium mortars, all with rifles.

The two march groups of the replacement officer school, which were on foot, reached the Liener—Lindern area on the night of 2-3 April.

At about 18:00 hours on 2 April 1945 Hptm. Schewe, commander III. Btl. (BR) received a call from his regimental adjutant, Oblt. Bensinger, in his quarters in Kneheim, 10 kilometer southwest of Cloppenburg. His message: "Enemy at the gates of Lingen! On order of the army group (Gen.Oberst von Blaskowitz) 1,000 men of the *Großdeutschland* unit are to be transported to Lingen via the fastest means possible for employment there." Reply: the regiment has nothing left in hand, since I. Btl. is already in action near Rheine, II. Btl. is en route there by motor transport, the brigade commander cannot be reached.

Predicted loading on Hptm. Schwelmer's transport column in Essen, north of Quakenbrück, at about 24:00 hours. Hptm. Schewe made immediate preparations to continue the march in the direction of Essen, separating the reserve and combat units. The latter had a combat strength of:

III. (BR)/Pz.Gren.Ers. u. Ausb.Rgt. GD: 7 officers, 51 NCOs and 460 enlisted men.

At about 23:30 hours on that 2 April III. Btl. (BR) met the Schwelmer transport column at Essen station and boarded for transport to Lingen.

During that night the units of the Pz.Gren.-Ersatz-Brigade GD less III. Btl. came under the command of the 15. Pz.Gren.Div., command post at the southern entrance to Beesten, approximately 20 kilometers north of Rheine. This division was in command of the Lingen sector. Commanding the 15. Pz.Gren.Div. was Gen.Lt. Rodt, 1st General Staff Officer was General Staff *Major* Monshausen who had served as Ib in the Inf.Div.(mot.) GD in the winter of 1942-43.

At this time the 15. Pz.Gren.Div. was subordinate to the II. Fsch.-Korps commanded by *General der Fallschirmtruppen* Meindl, which was part of von Blaskowitz's Army Group H.

At the same time, on the night of 2-3 April the combat units of the

Pz.Gren.-Ersatz-Brigade GD were renamed as follows:

Pz.Gren.-Ersatz-Brigade GD became Pz.Gren.-Einsatz-Brigade GD.

Pz.Gren.Ers. u. Ausb.Rgt. GD became Regiment Wackernagel

OB-Schule GD became Regiment Poeschmann

At the time that the elements of the Pz.Gren.-Einsatz-Brigade GD were subordinated to the 15. Pz.Gren.Div. the situation was as follows: Wackernagel Rgt. command post: northern exit from Dreierwalde, northeast of Rheine. Kampfgruppe Knaust—a unit of recruits, handicapped, leg amputees—in position at the Dortmund-Ems Canal. I./Wackernagel Regiment on the west bank of the canal with pickets in and east of Rheine. Command post also in Dreierwalde. II./Wackernagel Regiment under the command of Hptm. Goeldel still on its way, with orders to go into position on I./Wackernagel Regiment's right at the Dortmund-Ems Canal. Battalion command post: Spelle. III. (BR)/Wackernagel Regiment— removed from the unit, arrival at eastern entrance to Lingen on morning of 3 April for special mission from II. Fsch.Korps. Poeschmann Regiment (OB-Schule GD) with two battalions still on foot march, now also diverted toward Lingen to reinforce the III./Wackernagel Regiment there.

Enemy: leading elements entered Rheine on morning of 3 April, linked up with British XII Corps in and on both sides of Rheine, preparing major attack across the Dortmund-Ems Canal to the east and northeast. The British XXX Corps, whose leading elements were just outside of Lingen, was already firing into the city with artillery. Farther north, near and west of Meppen, advance detachments of the Canadian 4th Armoured Division, probably with orders to also cross the Dortmund-Ems Canal to the east.

On the German side all available reserves were rushed to the Dortmund-Ems Canal to bolster the alert units positioned there and to prevent a crossing by the enemy. It was a race against time and troop shortages—although both could still be won. Time was short, but the race could still be won, however the troops were inadequately armed and equipped and had little mobility. The latter prevented them from reaching the canal in time, there simply were no vehicles.

In this context several orders:

I./Wackernagel Regiment (Gerbener Battalion)   *Command post*
3/4/45

To 1., 2., 3. and 4. Kp.

Beginning at 03:00 hours withdraw to new line Dortmund-Ems Canal, leaving behind rear guards to harass the enemy.

Right boundary: Rheine—Spelle railway line.

Left boundary: Small bridge southeast of Altenrheine, 1 km southeast of Altenrheine, above the woods at Hafenrheine. Rheine—Dreierwalde road bridge still intact, boats still there.

2. Kompanie: From the right boundary to 1 km southeast of Point 36 (left boundary).

1. Kompanie: From there to and including the Altenrheine road bridge.

3. Kompanie: exclusive of Altenrheine road bridge to the left boundary. 3. Kp. will march across the Rhiene—Altenrheine road and leave a rear guard of four men in the southern group of houses.

1. and 2. Kp.: also to leave four men each at same place on road.

These people subordinated themselves to the SS tank-destroyers there. They have orders to guard the battalion's withdrawal and subsequently provide covering fire for the building of the new main line of resistance.

Gerbener command post now needs back all members of the staff on detached duty. These will stay directly behind the Altenrheine road bridge and will be picked up by us there.

Location: Battalion command post cannot be revealed until tomorrow morning. I will establish contact with the companies myself. Attached heavy weapons are to travel with the companies.

Leutnant Reinartz is to be informed by the company he was with that he is to report to the road with his company headquarters section.

Leave no wounded comrades behind!

Take the weapons of the killed and wounded!

Withdraw quickly, but no panic!

Gerbener

Major and battalion commander.

The detailed battalion order issued to the companies of I./Wackernagel Regiment show the first steps in the positioning of forces along the Dortmund-Ems Canal which were carried out early on 3 April.

The following regimental order reveals further details of the establishment of a continuous defense line along the canal:

Wackernagel Regiment   *Command post, 3/4/1945*

Ia

The Pz.Gren.Ers. u. Ausb.Rgt. GD is directly subordinated to the 15. Pz.Gren.Div. I. Btl. thus leaves the command of Kampfgruppe Knaust. Close contact is to be maintained as before, however. The timing of the battalion's departure from Kampfgruppe Knaust is yet to be determined. Probably 08:00 hours on 4/4/1945. The battalion will establish itself in defensive positions in its former sector and prevent the enemy from crossing the canal. For this purpose a Marder company (tank-destroyer, 75-mm long, self-propelled) will be placed under the battalion's command. To be sent this night. I. Btl. to provide guide. Guns are to be positioned directly north of the canal on both sides of the

Altenrhein—Dreierwalde road in such a way that armored advances and amphibious tanks can be engaged effectively and the battalion's defensive effort against crossing attempts can be supported.

II. Btl., Goeldel battalion, with attached SS tank-destroyer company, has the mission of advancing our main line of resistance. Link-up point: position 36. The regiment is instructed to cooperate with Flak-Abt. I/31 with firing position in Varenrode. The battalion has orders to place harassing fire on the areas depicted on the map. In the event of an enemy attack requests for fire to be made through the regiment.

During the night battalions to send volunteer tank-killing squads ahead of the main line of resistance to seek out armored vehicles and other worthwhile targets.

The night's events are to be reported to the regiment by 06:00 hours.

Signed Wackernagel

Regimental commander

Still lagging behind, II./Wackernagel Regiment (Goeldel battalion) was put aboard trucks early on the evening of 3 April and rushed to the new positions west of Spelle on the Dortmund-Ems Canal. No contact with the enemy there, positions were occupied and prepared for defense.

Meanwhile, III. Btl. (BR) under Hptm. Schewe had reached Lingen and dismounted in the city market place early in the morning. The young men, most of whom were recruits, were so happy and determined to fight that they sang as they got out of the trucks. Hptm. Schewe immediately deployed his companies to secure the area and himself established contact with the local military commander to organize a joint defense. There he learned that the bridges over the Ems (Lingen was east of the Ems) had already been blown and that the enemy had reached the east bank of the river. Repeated mortar barrages on the city made it difficult for the battalion to go into position.

The nearer the battalion's companies came to the Ems, in order to occupy their positions, the more they were bothered by enemy snipers and tank fire from the east bank. The moment a man showed himself on the west bank he was fired on by several guns simultaneously. The first casualties were taken; 9.Kp. had three seriously wounded and two slightly wounded. The less seriously wounded did not want to leave the positions, however, preferring to remain with their comrades.

According to information from the city's military commander, there was supposed be an even larger number of units in defensive positions in and near Lingen. There was no sign of them, however. Then on the afternoon of 3 April an order came from army group to blow all the bridges over the canal between Lingen and Meppen. The execution was done on foot, with the disadvantage that the III. (BR)/Wackernagel Regiment now had no crossings to the east except for a small footbridge south of Lingen (in

9. Kp.'s sector).

Casualties among the ranks of the defenders increased steadily as enemy tanks drew nearer to the Ems. Difficulties were already being encountered in evacuating the wounded to the rear.

At about 23:00 hours on the night of 3-4 April the following order was received from II. Fsch.-Korps (Meindl):

H.Q., II. Fallschirm-Korps   Corps command post, 3/4/1945

Command group Ia No. 1064/45 secret

To the military commander of Lingen!

Effective immediately all troops, including III./Brandenburg Regiment, are placed under your command.

Mission: Occupy a bridgehead (see map) and prevent an enemy break-through along the road toward Lingen from the south and west. In the event of heavy enemy pressure, in the west the bridgehead may be withdrawn to the canal line. This line is to be held to the last man!

In the event of a withdrawal to the canal line, all bridges over the Ems and the Dortmund-Ems Canal inside the bridgehead are to be blown.

As commander, you are responsible for holding Lingen.

Signed Meindl

Almost simultaneously, the military commander of Lingen informed Hptm. Schewe that he had been called away for other duties by the army group and that he—Schewe—was the military commander of Lingen effective immediately. The hand-over was very rushed. In spite of his best efforts, Hptm. Schewe, who had been reassured repeatedly that there were other units in Lingen, was unable to find any, apart from an anti-aircraft combat team in the northern part of the city. And so he and his battalion were now sitting almost alone in Lingen, awaiting heavy enemy attacks which would surely begin early on 4 April.

During the night of 3-4 April the enemy appeared to complete his preparations along the Ems. The continuous sound of tanks from the opposite bank and the ranging-in of the British artillery died away. The calm before the storm!

The first radio report reached the division headquarters at about 06:50 hours on 4 April 1945: from the Wackernagel Regiment in position along the Dortmund-Ems Canal opposite Rheine.

0650: Firing continues. Flame-thrower tanks between road bridge and locks, south of the canal—in front of I. Btl.'s sector. Urgently request artillery fire there.

Wackernagel

0740: Enemy had broken into main line of resistance between Altenrheine road bridge and lock under heavy covering fire from across the canal by artillery

343

and flame-thrower tanks. Once again urgently request forward artillery liaison detachment or observer.

Panzer-Abt. has not joined regiment.

Wackernagel

0745: Report by II./Wackernagel Regiment (Goeldel battalion)

Strength: 5 officers, 16 NCOs, 254 enlisted men.

During the night enemy patrols felt their way forward to our positions. Company patrols determined that there were enemy pickets at the rail tunnel to Rheine.

Beginning at 07:00 hours sound of enemy tanks in Rheine.

So far only one of the three self-propelled guns allocated has arrived.

Goeldel

0930: report by Kampfgruppe Knaust to Wackernagel Regiment:

Enemy across the canal near Altenrheine at the Rheine—Dreierwalde bridge, already with 1 to 2 companies, after heavy artillery preparation and use of flame-thrower tanks. Situation still unclear. No reserves yet available. Message was given to Korück with request that it be passed on to the 15. Pz.Gren.Div.

Knaust

This was the last report received for some time concerning the enemy attacks east of Rheine. The battle there raged back and forth. *Major* Gerbener and several men tried to seal off the enemy bridgehead; however, the enemy tank and artillery fire from the west side of the canal forced everyone to take cover. Every movement on the German side was immediately answered with a hail of fire. The situation was becoming desperate. Everyone prayed for night to come. Heavy enemy artillery fire on the surrounding villages of Dreierwalde, Neuhaus and Spelle.

Finally, on the evening of 4 April, the first reports were received containing more details:

1830: To Wackernagel Regiment!

Enemy broken through against 3. Kp. left of the lock. Sound of combat can already be heard. 18:30 hours!

Road from the lock to Wischemeier barricaded by reserve platoon with Lt. Hoffmann (rifles only!)

He can definitely not hold!

1945: Can RUB-Kp. help? Bad there otherwise!!

Almost simultaneously a report from I. Btl. to the military commander of Rheine, Obstlt. Knaust:

To military commander!

Penetration left of the lock – 18:35 hours!

The reserve platoon has gone into position on the road from the lock to Wischemeier—has only rifles!

Anti-tank gun was briefed by me. Solidly dug in!

1935   4. Have no more people!

Gerbener, I. Btl.

The regiment immediately issued its first orders for countermeasures.

Wackernagel Regiment   Regimental command post, 4/4/1945

Commander

To Commander I. Btl.

On order of the division all available forces are to be concentrated and all means employed to halt the enemy so as to prevent a further expansion of the bridgehead—especially to the northwest.

I instruct Major Gerbener, with the regiment's anti-tank platoon and all other available soldiers and the attached Marder platoon, to evict the enemy from the farmhouse.

The RUB-Company is to be committed immediately to seal off the bridge-head.

Wackernagel

Major

These countermeasures were taken as quickly as possible as darkness was falling; *Major* Gerbener ran around, gathering men together with which to advance against the enemy.

But the latter was also not asleep: he used the darkness and continuous artillery fire to cover his intentions so as to move more infantry forces across the canal and quickly make preparations for a crossing by his light tanks.

Meanwhile, fighting had also broken out in the town of Lingen. Initial reports reached Hptm. Schewe at about 04:00 on 4 April that the enemy had crossed the canal north of Lingen. A member of the Todt Organization in full uniform had forded a shallow spot in the river, showing the enemy the way across.

Patrols were sent there immediately and they were only able to confirm what had happened; the enemy was crossing the canal to the east. The enemy was throwing a bridge across the canal. The 11. Kp. tried sending its hunting platoon against the bridge site, however it was hit by enemy artillery and anti-tank fire and was completely wiped out.

At the same time other British infantry with tanks was advancing toward the city from the northwest. Hptm. Schewe scraped together runners, dispatch riders, etc and rushed there to meet the enemy. His desperate effort succeeded in stopping him for a time.

The remaining companies were ordered to leave the Ems and pull back behind the canal into the interior of the city. 9. Kp. was first to arrive at the battalion command post; it launched an immediate counterattack to the northwest and gained ground at the cost of serious casualties. The other companies were organized into strong assault teams and sent into position. The other companies were slow in reaching the battalion command post; 11. Kp. was still missing, the British were already in its positions. In the northern part of the city the 9. Kp. fought desperately against the enemy's crushing superiority, but the British finally broke through and soon reached the command post. The battalion train was lost after it blundered into the enemy.

Friendly defense was now concentrated in the houses around the command post, and it was due to the determined actions of everyone that what was left of the battalion was not overrun straightaway. *Panzerfäuste* were used against enemy machine-gun nests, and a counterattack by just five men caused the enemy to waver and finally drove him back to the marketplace. The 9. and 12. Kp., which did not make it back to the command post in time and which took up hedgehog positions elsewhere, were almost out of ammunition. Smaller groups did make it through to the command post, which had been set up for all-round defense.

Hptm. Schewe gave his operations officer a detailed situation report and ordered him to try and get through to the regiment with it. He succeeded and was also able to make his way back—with an order from the army group: Lingen is to be held. No troops are to leave the city!

Meanwhile two British armored divisions were in the city with the intention of crushing the isolated III. (BR)/Wackernagel Regiment.

Hptm. Schewe wrote a new report to the regiment, his last, which his operations officer was able to get to *Major* Wackernagel:

Lingen, 4/4/1945

Herr Major!

I am carrying out the order of Headquarters, II. Fallschirm-Korps to hold Lingen.

The forces still available to me do not make it possible to hold the city. I am forming a hedgehog around my command post and will fight to the last cartridge.

Unfortunately, the brigade will thus lose a battalion that knows how to fight and die.

III. (BR)/Pz.Gren.Ers. u. Ausb.Rgt. GD salutes the other battalions!

Long live the Führer!

Long live the proud Großdeutschland units!

Schewe

It was nearly 23:00 hours. There was still no sign of the 10. Kp., the 9. Kp. had just under 60 men. The heavy machine-guns and mortars of 12. (schw.) Kp. had all been knocked out, lost or destroyed.

Quiet had settled over the strongpoints. Approximately 150 wounded lay at the aid station in the cellar of a nearby house, brave young soldiers of the III. (BR)/Wackernagel Regiment.

Finally, at about 24:00 hours, the company of 10. Kp., Lt. Feinauer, arrived. It was decided to break through the enemy ring in the interior of the city, as there was still a narrow opening to the south. The necessary preparations were made. There were almost no heavy weapons, many of the men were out of ammunition. The British resumed their attacks early on 5 April, overran several strongpoints and finally reached the houses opposite the battalion command post. Our planned attack could not be carried out. From houses and windows the enemy was forced into cover with the last of the ammunition. Then a force of five enemy tanks, two Shermans in front, a flame-thrower tank in the middle and two more Shermans bringing up the rear, came along the street. A young battalion runner grabbed the last remaining *Panzerfaust*, armed it, but was too excited to fire. It went off, killing the young man who was caught in the jet of flame.

Finally there were just twelve men left in the cellar, which the enemy had identified as the command post. With all ammunition gone, further resistance was pointless. They had to surrender to the stronger, satisfied in the knowledge that there in Lingen their brave resistance had held up two enemy armored divisions and an infantry division for three days.

III. (BR)/Pz.Gren.Ers. u. Ausb.Rgt. GD was no more. Some soldiers managed to make their way out, others held out for another 24 hours in small groups—but the majority were taken prisoner. Just as the last German resistance in Lingen was being extinguished on 5 April 1945, in the Dreierwalde—Hopsten area the battle was just beginning. During the night the enemy had brought strong forces across the Dortmund-Ems Canal and had also thrown up a bridge beside the road bridge. The first enemy tanks reached the east bank.

Early in the morning, with strong artillery support and escorted by the leading tanks, the enemy attacked toward the northeast. His initial thrust breached the positions of I./Wackernagel Regiment (Gerbener battalion). Isolated groups of men from the battalion were able to break through in the direction of Dreierwalde and occupy new strongpoints at the edge of town. All was confusion, it was almost impossible to gather even a few men together. *Major* Gerbener was captured but later managed to escape. Hptm. Blumenthal, formerly on the staff of the Wackernagel Regiment, received orders to go immediately to Dreierwalde and assemble what was left of the shattered I. Btl. Together with the remaining elements of I./Wackernagel Regiment, isolated assault teams of Pz.Gren.Rgt. 115 of the 15. Pz.Gren.Div., which was operating in the same area, sought desperately to hold onto Dreierwalde. II./Wackernagel Regiment (Goeldel battalion) was also caught up in the maelstrom of the enemy attack and was forced to draw in its left wing to the north. At almost the same time the leading British elements were advancing on Spelle, where they engaged II./Wackernagel Regiment, most of which was still in its old positions, in fierce fighting.

And so the front began to move; the battalion conducted a fighting withdrawal to the northwest, although its right wing continued to hold at the Dortmund-Ems Canal.

Meanwhile the Poeschmann Regiment (OB-Schule GD) had been placed on alert, and, based on the brigade order of about 16:30 hours, was dispatched to Hopsten to establish a fall-back line there.

There in the Hopsten area the Poeschmann Regiment would see its first action. The following is its table of organization:

C.O.	Major Poeschmann
Adj.	Oblt. Geist
Ops. Off.	Lt. Henrich
Liaison Off.	Hptm. Ritter
Special Duties	Lt. P. Klüver (02)
Rgt. H.Q. Comp.	
Comp. C.O.	Hptm. Roscher
Signals Platoon	Oblt. Barck
Pioneer Platoon	Lt. Schröder
Medium mortar platoon	Obfw. Gmind
Recce platoon	Owm. Roth
VIb	Ass.-Arzt Miedok
IVa	Zahlm.Anw. Volz
V (k)	Onsp.Anw. Borer
I./P.	Hptm. Menzner
II./P.	Hptm. Erdmann
Adj.	Oblt. Alberti
Adj.	Lt. Schmid
Ops.Officer	Lt. Rotter
Ops.Officer	Lt. Hasenschwanz
1. Kp.	Lt. von Bülow
2. Kp.	Oblt. Beckers
3. Kp.	Oblt. Gnärig
4. Kp.	Oblt. von Kleist
5. Kp.	Oblt. Wechmann
6. Kp.	Lt. Wokek
H.Q. Plat.	Lt. Eilnberger
H.Q. Plat.	Lt. von Waldow
Sigs.Squad	Lt. Germann

Supply Squad   ?

Most of the Poeschmann Regiment's company commanders and some of its platoon leaders were former instructors of the OB-Schule GD, the former guardians of the officer cadets and candidates. Each of these instructors now got the chance to observe his boys in combat and determine whether their training and personality formation had been correct.

Strength on the first day of action: 30 officers, 150 NCOs, 700 enlisted men.

On the first day of the battle in the Dreierwalde—Spelle—Hopsten area Pz.Gren.Rgt. 115 (commanded by Knight's Cross wearer *Oberst* Haucke) of the 15 Pz.Gren.Div. (commanded by Gen.Lt. Rodt, command post east of Settrup on 5 April) bore the brunt of the fighting. As a veteran front-line division it sought to assemble and shore up the newly-established battalions of the Wackernagel Regiment.

In the evening hours of 5 April the Poeschmann Regiment, now also under the command of the 15 Pz.Gren.Div., went into position roughly in a line along the Hoppstener Aa south and southwest of Hopsten with I./P. on the right, II./P. on the left and the regimental command post in Borken. Both battalions made defensive preparations. Heavy harassing fire on Hopsten by enemy artillery. Toward evening our patrols found the northern edge of Dreierwalde still free of the enemy.

During the night the scattered I./Wackernagel Regiment was reassembled and transferred into the Ruschendorf area, north of Hopsten, to the left of II./Wackernagel Regiment, which was establishing a new defense line behind the positions of the Poeschmann Regiment.

On 6 April the situation demanded of the division's hard-fighting battalions and of the Pz.Eins.Brigade GD that the division command post remain far to the front, in direct contravention of the rules for fighting a delaying action, so as to provide a calming influence for the fighting units and guarantee that its orders were executed plus orderly movements. This became all the more important when on this day the loss of all communication made it almost impossible for Gen. Meindl to command his II. Fsch.-Korps. The commanding general was forced to remain at the command post of the 15th Pz.Gren.Div. and use its radio communications. Another important factor in the *General's* decision was the fact that the division's operations section had the enemy's cipher codes, and with seven radio stations was monitoring communications by the enemy units, making it possible to determine what measures they would take next. The position of the division command post, together with the monitoring of enemy communications, proved invaluable in those days as it did in the fighting on the west bank of the Rhine in the Krefeld area. Not without reason did the British intelligence service characterize the reinforced 15. Panzer-Grenadier Division as the only unit in northwest Germany still offering serious resistance.

The forward sector held by the Poeschmann Regiment was quiet during the morning hours.

Not until about 11:45 hours were small numbers of British tanks and troop carriers sighted on the Dreierwalde—Hopsten road; soon afterwards they appeared in front of the position. Our anti-tank guns knocked out two of the Shermans and forced the rest to retire.

Meanwhile the enemy was putting together an assembly area south of Hopsten and, after heavy preparatory artillery fire, the first advances were made from there against the left wing of II./Rgt. Poeschmann. The enemy infantry and flame-thrower tanks broke through the thin lines of security into Hopsten, where fierce house-to-house fighting broke out. The officer cadets and candidates fought with cool courage. Repeatedly they regrouped, launched counterattacks, defended house by house, took one ruin after another, destroyed enemy machine-gun nests and blew up enemy tanks. Many streets were recaptured. Oblt. von Kleist, wounded three times already, continued to lead his men and stormed house after house.

The following report on this action was made by the battalion commander:

II./Rgt. Poeschmann Battalion command post, 17 April

In the late afternoon hours of 5 April 1945 the battalion received orders to march to Dreierwalde to bring relief to the Wackernagel Regiment, which was heavily engaged there, and to relieve it. On the way there, however, the battalion was diverted to Hopsten, 7 kilometers from Dreierwalde, since it was already obvious that Dreierwalde could not be held. Instead an attempt was to be made to throw up a barricade in front of Hopsten in order to prevent the enemy from breaking through to the north and northwest.

The battalion went into position in Hopsten along the stream bed, with 5. Kp. on the right with orders to barricade the southern and southeastern exits from Hopsten, to defend the anti-tank barricade and secure the road to Dreierwalde against enemy tanks and advancing infantry. The 4. Kompanie was on the left, with instructions to block the road in the direction of Ibbenbüren. On the battalion's right was I./Wackernagel Regiment. The battalion's left flank was open. The 6. Kp., as reserve company and operational reserve, was positioned abeam the battalion command post.

The following heavy weapons were deployed in the battalion's sector:

Two 88-mm flak battalions with forward observer in Hopsten's church tower, and a battery of light field howitzers with forward observer in the mill. The following anti-tank weapons were deployed in 4. Kp.'s sector:

Three 50-mm anti-tank guns of the Waffen-SS and two self-propelled 75-mm guns of Pz.Jäg.Abt.20. In the 5. Kp.'s sector were two 75-mm anti-tank guns of an SS anti-tank company commanded by Obersturmführer Kämmler; their mission was to guard the anti-tank barricade and the bridges in the direction of Dreierwalde, which had been prepared for demolition. The night passed quietly, patrols reached almost as far as the northern edge of Dreierwalde without contacting the enemy. The results of patrols on the morning of 6 April 1945 were similarly negative until about 10:30 hours.

At that time the enemy opened fire with artillery from the direction of Dreierwalde; the church, and with it the center of town and the entire battalion sector, came under fire. At the same time I. Bataillon, which was in flanking positions on the road to Dreierwalde, reported six tanks and several armored troop carriers approaching the southwest exit of the town from the direction of Dreierwalde. These armored vehicles represented the first enemy contact for the battalion's right wing. After initial artillery fire, which now pounded the main line of resistance without letup, the enemy tried to seize the southwest exit of the town in the initial rush. This attack was totally beaten off and two Shermans were knocked out. The enemy subsequently disengaged, but 45 minutes later he attacked the right wing again, this time with infantry on foot protected by tank machine-gun fire, clearly recognizing the boundary between I. and II. Bataillon.

This attack was also repulsed, however 5. Kompanie suffered serious casualties, the majority as a result of artillery and tank machine-gun fire.

These losses seriously weakened the right wing of the 5.Kompanie and as a result a renewed enemy attack was successful. Under covering tank fire, the infantry broke into the main line of resistance on the company's right wing and took two prisoners.

Our artillery recognized the situation and blanketed the enemy tanks with well-aimed fire, causing them to leave the infantry and withdraw to the south.

Leutnant Järschke used this moment to lead two men in a counterattack on his threatened wing. His action inspired his men who, though out of ammunition, had nevertheless stayed in their holes singing "Watch on the Rhine", and they advanced with him and cleared the break-in point in hand-to-hand combat. Forty-two enemy dead were counted after this engagement.

After these considerable losses the enemy abandoned his plan to force in the southwest entrance so as to gain control of the direct route to the north and northeast. He know launched a frontal attack against the 4. Kp., which was in position along the stream bed on the road to Ibbenbüren. Once again the attack was preceded by a fierce artillery bombardment of our positions, after which the enemy felt his way forward along the entire main line of resistance. Here, too, however, he failed to break into the main line of resistance during the entire afternoon. Not until evening, when he massed against the left wing and advanced on the company's open left flank, was he able to break into 4. Kp.'s positions, suffering heavy losses in the process. Though three times wounded, Oberleutnant von Kleist and his company headquarters squad held out against the enemy's massed firepower, although they were unable to halt him.

The battalion subsequently committed the reserve company under the command of Leutnant Wokek and thus restored the main line of resistance with the exception of two houses on the left wing which were held by the enemy.

It appears that the enemy reported to his command immediately following this initial success and now intended to seek a breakthrough at this supposedly weak spot. This intention became obvious when he immediately concentrated heavy artillery fire on this sector, set all the houses on fire, and fired red signal flares to call in an attack by fighter-bombers.

His plan was foiled, however, by a quickly initiated counterattack under the command of Leutnant Wokek, which was launched against the two lost houses at about 21:00 hours. The attack was a success; both houses were retaken, two machine-guns and one medium mortar were captured, and eleven prisoners were brought in. According to statements made by these prisoners, this was the first planned, serious resistance the enemy had met since January. The stresses of the day and the fright from our tough defense was clearly visible in the faces of the prisoners.

After this successful counterattack, the main line of resistance was in our hands again. The old positions were occupied again and, as it was already dark, night pickets were posted.

In the end the sacrificial struggle in front of and on the outskirts of Hopsten, especially by II./Poeschmann Regiment, was for nothing. The enemy's direct advance had been held up for hours, but then enemy tanks and infantry outflanked these positions to the east and attacked Staden, which was guarded by II./Wackernagel Regiment positioned in the second line. After crossing the Dortmund-Ems Canal at numerous places, the enemy's armored spearheads fanned out over the entire area. Farther east, where Kampfgruppe Knaust should have been on guard, enemy armored spearheads streamed north across the Mittelland Canal, through Steinbeck toward Recke. It was becoming apparent that we were being outflanked by the advancing British, especially since elements of the British XXX Corps were now advancing east from Lingen, sweeping aside what little resistance they met.

For the elements of the Pz.Gren.Eins.-Brigade GD the danger of being cut off, especially from the north, was drawing nearer. In the rear— if one could call it that—dreadful things were happening. All main and secondary roads were clogged with vehicles seeking to escape the marauding enemy tanks by fleeing north. And in the skies above them were the fighter-bombers, using their speed to appear suddenly and attack the columns with bombs and guns, spreading death, confusion and destruction. No one knew any longer where to go; it was headlong flight from the enemy tanks approaching from the south and southwest. There was no stopping; save yourself if you can was the order of the day.

To add to the misfortune, the following order was issued on the night of 6-7 April: 15. Pz.Gren.Div. to transfer as quickly as possible into the Bremen area. The Poeschmann Regiment was thus deprived of its supporting artillery on the very night that at least twenty enemy tanks were attacking the left wing of its II. Btl.

Once again a report by the battalion commander:

The front was quiet until 01:20 hours on 7 April. The 6. Kp., whose sector was still being reinforced by the remaining elements of 4. Kp., reported loud tank noises in front of its main line of resistance, which suggested a night operation by the enemy

At about 01:20 the enemy began pounding 6. Kompanie's sector with heavy artillery fire. All attention was now focused on this sector, since the artillery preparation was obviously the prelude to an enemy operation. The surprise was all the greater when, after thirty minutes of artillery fire, approximately 22 flame-thrower tanks guarded by conventional tanks suddenly placed the 6. Kp.'s entire sector under concentrated fire. The entire main line of resistance was set ablaze, and many soldiers were burned to death when they did not have time to get out of their holes.

Leutnant Wokek took the rest of the company behind the village edge of his sector and with them sealed off the broad point of penetration as best he could. Nevertheless, the breach in the main line of resistance could not be closed, even though another company of the Wackernagel Regiment was placed under the battalion's command. It consisted of six- and twelve-day recruits, who were totally unsuited for this scarcely still necessary counterattack, lacking any combat experience or command.

The battalion fought hard and bravely and held out until the early morning hours against the numerically and materially far superior enemy. An attempt to bend back the left wing of the 5. Kp. and attach the remaining elements of the battalion to it in order to establish a new main line of resistance was doomed to failure because of the continuous pressure from the enemy. Leutnant von Waldow was captured by the British near the cemetery while seeking contact to the right during establishment of the new main line of resistance.

Together with the Wackernagel Regiment, during the course of the day a new main line of resistance was established under heavy pressure from the enemy. It ran approximately as follows: Hopstener Aa (I./P.)—Hof Giegel—Hof Keimer—Hof Feldmann for II./P.—subsequently line Droste—Ruschendorf (I./W.)—elements of II./W still near Staden.

This line was not held for long, however; at about 17:00 hours came another order to withdraw to the Hollenstede area, leaving behind strong rear guards. While the positions were being evacuated, Obfw. Paul and his third platoon of the 2. Kp. were caught in an ambush and obliged to surrender.

The enemy had now broken out of his canal bridgeheads toward the east and northeast on a broad front. His spearheads were already moving into the area (from north to south) of: Herzlake—west of Menslage—Handrup—(west of Bippen)—west of Fürstenau—Hopsten—Weese. The advance was led by strong tank forces, motorized infantry and self-propelled artillery. Large numbers of fighter-bombers were constantly in the air, bombing and strafing targets on the ground.

The German units, if one could still speak of such, were battered, harried from place to place. Weak in numbers and weapons, here and there they sought to offer resistance, more as loose groups than as cohesive units, in order to at least slow the enemy's advance.

The strongest morally among them probably saw the end coming, but they continued to hold on and followed the orders that were given them.

The two regiments of the Pz.Gren.Einsatz-Brigade GD, of whose command little is said in general, since both units usually operated under the direct command of a division, fell back toward the north as best they could. One time it was the officer cadets and candidates in position at the front, the next time the grenadiers of the Wackernagel Regiment—and so it went, back step by step, chases, forced out of their positions or outflanked. The number of missing rose, those who could not be informed of a withdrawal, who walked into traps, individuals who could not go on and preferred captivity to an uncertain future. The latter were relatively few in the GD units, but there were some.

On the evening of 9 April the enemy situation in front of the 15. Pz.Gren.Div., which, reinforced by the regiments of the Pz.Gren. Einsatz-Brigade GD, was deployed on the left wing of the parachute army, was roughly as follows:

Canadian 4th Armoured Division advancing on Papenburg, south of Leer (on the Ems).

British 43rd Infantry Division attacking from the southwest in the direction of Cloppenburg.

British 51st (Highland) Division advancing out of the Vechta area toward the north.

British 3rd Infantry Division had taken Bassum and its advance guard was south of Wildeshausen.

The 15. Pz.Gren.Div.'s assignment remained the same, to move into the area west of Bremen and there seek contact with the SS units under the military commander of Bremen, in order to prevent the parachute army from being cut off from the south by advancing enemy forces. In the process strong elements of the Pz.Korps-Art.Rgt. GD were to conduct a fighting withdrawal at the side of the 8. Fsch.Jäg.Div., initially to the Hase, later to a line at the south end of Cloppenburg.

On April 9 the I./Pz.Gren.Rgt. 115, which had been sent ahead into the area west of Bremen the day before, had contact with the enemy in the line Bassum—Syke. During the night of 8-9 April the bulk of the still fully mobile 15. Pz.Gren.Div. reached the Harpstedt—Nordwohlde—Fahrenhorst—Ippener area and secured the area to the south.

The withdrawal of the 15. Pz.Gren.Div. was covered by the

Pz.Gren.Eins.-Brigade GD, which in those days had to fight fierce defensive battles against the hard-pressing enemy. Fighting a sacrificial battle, it repeatedly succeeded in frustrating the enemy's attempts to break through and enabling the initiated march movements to proceed.

Early on 9 April the enemy broke through along the Gross-Hase Canal to Menslage and became involved in fierce close-quarters fighting with the elements of the 8. Fsch.Jäg.Div. defending there.

Even though elements of the paratroopers were preparing to withdraw, counterattacks allowed the town of Menslage to be held until the night of 10 April. Still farther to the south, in the forest west of Bippen, the men of the Pz.-Einsatz-Abt. GD fought just as bravely against enemy forces advancing from the west. They were unable to hold, however, and were forced to retire to the northeast.

Elements of II./Rgt. P. also continued to hold out in Fürstenau against enemy forces streaming in from the west, however they were gradually forced to give ground. New positions were occupied in the Sussum—Bassum area and at the southwestern edge of Kettenkamp. The combat brigade's command post was in the Suttrup area, also elements of the Wackernagel Regiment. In no case was it still possible to go into position without harassment from the enemy; 1. Kp., which continued to hold out in Schwagstorf and cover the retreat of I./Wackernagel Regiment, fought to the point of self-sacrifice for every house, finally abandoning what was left of the town in small groups and making its way to the north. Only its selfless courage enabled the bulk of I./Rgt. W. to reach Gross-Mimmenlage relatively intact. Meanwhile, in expectation of the enemy, the II./Rgt. W. had again occupied intermediate positions at the crossroads west of Suttrup. Still in front of it at that point, the evening of 9 April, were elements of the Poeschmann Regiment, whose I. Btl. was barricading the southern edge of Kettenkamp, while its II. Btl. secured the area near Bassum—Sussum. On the right to Döthen was the Pi.Kp.GD, which was holding that town. The mission of all the GD units there: prevent enemy tanks and infantry from breaking through to the north.

During the course of the movements by the 15. Pz.Gren.Div., which had meanwhile occupied new defense lines between Bremen and Wildeshausen with contact with the Fsch.Korps Meindl in Menslage, the units of the Pz.Gren.Eins.-Brigade GD, which were now subordinate to the parachute corps on its left wing, were withdrawn to the line Menslage to Quackenbrück and inserted into new defensive positions along the Kleine-Hase. These security positions, which were occupied during the night of 10-11 April with almost no pressure from the enemy, enabled an attack group of the 15. Pz.Gren.Div. to attack from the woods north of Nordwohlde southeast into the enemy's flank (who was attacking northwards from Syke in the direction of Bremen) and throw him back. The "Hohe Berg" on the road was taken, while radio monitoring revealed that additional enemy forces were being fed into the Syke—Bassum area. Gren.Rgt. 857 was also able to establish a new defense line north of Wildeshausen. It was subsequently extended through Ippener and Brinkum (contact there with an SS training unit) to the Bremen bridgehead.

But the attempt to reorganize the defense along the Hase—Hase Canal was frustrated by a morning breakthrough across the canal near Menslage by enemy tanks. There was already heavy fighting in the Felsen—Herzlake area along the road to Löningen and north of Menslage, as well as north of Menslage along the road to Löningen.

The Feldersatz-Btl. GD under Hptm. Schmidt was alerted in its quarters and, on 10 April, attached to the 8. Fsch.Jäg.Div. (Fsch.Jäg.Rgt. 61), was deployed along the Hase near Werve—Evenkamp. On the right and already engaged in heavy fighting was the 7. Fsch.Jäg.Div. in the Westrum—Herzlake area. As a result of these enemy threats to the right flank, the elements of the Wackernagel Regiment and the Poeschmann Regiment still between Menslage and Quakenbrück were pulled out and inserted into a new defense line along the Hase: Lodbergen (II./Rgt. P.)—Altenbrunnen (I./Rgt. P.)—Herbergen (I./Rgt. W.)—south and west edge of Essen (II./Rgt. W.). The necessary marching orders were to be carried out during the night of 10-11 April. Brigade command post was in Suhle. But there was no holding now; while the enemy pressure abated noticeably in the left sector near Essen, at about 1000 hours on 11 April enemy tanks and armored infantry advanced irresistibly against weak resistance from parachute troops against Boen and Bokah and established bridgeheads over the Hase near these towns. Spearheads had penetrated north into the Buren-Tannen area. Their apparent objective was Cloppenburg.

Strong British armored forces were also already on Reichsstrasse 213, due north of Löningen, heading northeast. Withdraw! No time to lose! Withdraw again! Finally find a position somewhere that is not being outflanked.

New defense lines were occupied on the evening of 11 April. From the right in Lastrup II./Rgt. P., wooded area southeast of Lastrup to Hamstrup I./Rgt. P., bear Knokerei contact on the left with Pz.Eins.Abt. Bauer. Next there was the Kampfgruppe of III. (BR)/ Wackernagel Regiment. I./Rgt. W. in Herbergen, II. Btl. still in Essen. The night of 11-12 April was spent in this line. By early, morning, however, the enemy was there, firing artillery into the towns and readying his tanks to attack. The focal point now appeared to lie along Reichsstraße 213. At about 11:00 hours the enemy attacked the town of Lastrup with tanks and forced II./Rgt. P. to withdraw to Schmertheim. I./Rgt. P. also lost Hamstrup. It was necessary to retreat in the direction of Vahren. These movements left the Pz.Gren.Eins.-Brigade GD's left wing, and especially that of the Wackernagel Regiment, hanging, which resulted in hasty withdrawals without further pressure from the enemy.

Movements were begun on the afternoon of 12 April and these began to have an effect to the southeast on Kampfgruppe Knaust positioned there. The task facing the Pz.Gren.Eins.-Brigade GD was to once again establish a continuous defense line in front of Cloppenburg in order to gain time to organize the defense of the city.

While II./Rgt. P. set up the first pickets along the Soeste in Cloppenburg, the remaining GD units occupied their positions roughly in a line from Matrum to Kneheim with the defensive focal point on Reichsstrasse 213 by I./Rgt. P., then to the southeast the Pz.Eins.Abt. Bauer and what was left of I./Wackernagel Regiment in the woods southwest of Hof Brinker. Next to it was the Kampfgruppe of III. (BR)/Rgt. W. to Hemmelte, where by the evening of 12 April the II./Rgt. W. under Hptm. Goeldel had established itself.

But the enemy reached this line rather quickly, once again concentrating on Reichsstrasse 213. He undoubtedly intended to enter the city of Cloppenburg at the same time as the defenders. Lt. Hasenschwanz, already sent by the commander of II./Rgt. P. to Cloppenburg to search out suitable defensive positions (and fall-back positions) at about noon on 12 April, found that the southern edge of Cloppenburg was totally unsuited for the defense ordered there. It would be better to defend along the Soeste, which ran through the middle of the city. Furthermore Cloppenburg had been devastated by bombs and the civilian population was almost all gone.

All crossings over the Soeste had been prepared for demolition. The plan was for one battalion and anti-tank weapons to go into position at the southern edge of Cloppenburg. The other battalions were to occupy fall-back positions behind the Soeste. When the enemy pressure became too great, the first battalion would also withdraw behind the Soeste and defend the river line with the other battalions.

While these movements were carried out by the evening of 12 April, the remaining elements of the Wackernagel Regiment were fighting the hardest battle of its existence to gain time for the defense of Cloppenburg to be set up. I./Rgt. W. was outflanked in its forest—meadow positions in front of Hof Brinker and almost encircled. Not until darkness fell were these elements able to disengage in small groups and filter through to the north west of the city. It was several days before Hptm. Blumenthal and these remnants of I./Rgt. W. found their way to the brigade command post north of the city.

On the other hand II./Wackernagel Regiment, commanded by Hptm. Goeldel, was encircled in Hemmelte and fought a hopeless battle there against a vastly superior force of enemy tanks and infantry supported by heavy artillery. The fighting there raged until far into the night, and Goeldel's men succeeded in holding up the enemy tanks along Reichsstrasse 213 between Hemmelte and Cloppenburg. The remaining elements of III. (BR)/Rgt. W. and Pz.Eins.Abt. GD also fought their way north in small groups, regrouping in the Varrelbusch area. By the evening of 12 April it was obvious that none of the battalions of the Pz.Gren.Eins.-Brigade GD were still intact apart from those of the Poeschmann Regiment, and that the brigade was hopelessly scattered. To what degree the brigade command had failed and orders were poorly carried out remains a matter of conjecture.

During the night of 12-13 April the enemy began firing on Cloppenburg with heavy artillery. At various points to the south, southwest and west he massed his tanks for the decisive attack on the city. Isolated Kampfgruppen of the 8. Fsch.Jäg.Div. still held out to the west and northwest, while the 490. I.D. was supposed to be somewhere there. In any case there was no contact with the latter units.

Regiment Poeschmann   **Regimental Command Post, 17/4/1945**
Combat report 12-13 April 1945, Cloppenburg
12/4/1945

Tired and hungry, both battalions saw the towns of Schmertheim and Vahren, where reserve positions were to be occupied, just in front of them. Just one main line of resistance between the intersection near Schmertheim, along the stream to Cloppenburg, to the left boundary at the railway crossing, south of "C" from Cloppenburg was still to be reconnoitered. There was nothing else to do.

But things always turn out differently than one hopes. So it was here too. I. Btl. was diverted just before Vahren. Direction Matrum, and the commander of II. Btl. was ordered to reconnoiter the regiment's entire sector. As favorable as the main line of resistance along the stream was, it still had a weak point on the left wing: Cloppenburg!

The situation on the main road from Lastrup to Cloppenburg was serious. So II. Btl. received orders to leave the quarters it had just occupied and take over the regiment's left sector near Cloppenburg. Since the main line of resistance went through the middle of the town, at the suggestion of the commander of II. Btl., so as to use the Soeste as an anti-tank barrier, at 23:55 hours the brigade ordered:

"I. Btl. to block the Cloppenburg-Vahren and Cloppenburg—Lastrup roads at the southwestern edge of Krapendorf with two companies and not withdraw toward II. Btl. until enemy pressure becomes stronger."

Regiment ordered:

"1. Kp. remain as reserve in the area 'by the straw' east of Cloppenburg."

13/4/1945

By about 22:00 hours II. Btl. had occupied the sector, no contact on the left or right. At about 07:00 on 13 April 1945 I. Btl. reported "assigned positions occupied."

The regimental pioneer and reconnaissance platoon received orders to go into position near Bühraner-Kämpe as reserve and to scout counterattacks at the boundary between II. Btl. and the Wackernagel Regiment.

The regimental command post was set up 500 meters north of the north church at 03:00 hours.

Artillery fire began falling on the town when the operations section arrived in Cloppenburg. One of the Tommy's batteries fired harassing fire onto Reichsstrasse 213 all night at intervals of 2 to 3 minutes. Secure cellars were scouted immediately. A bombing attack on the previous day had wrecked the windows and ventilated the houses very well. Careful residents had used six years of war to ferret away enough supplies, alcohol and tobacco for the defenders of the city. Their physical well-being was thus very well looked after.

The late morning was suspiciously quiet. The peace was only interrupted by the harassing fire and our own demolitions. At about 10:00 hours the enemy artillery began pounding the main line of resistance and the city center with two battalions, one light, about 75-mm, and a heavy 172-mm battalion.

The regiment lay among the houses of the city and was taking a brief rest after the exertions of the recent days and nights, when a clear order was received from the brigade:

"Cloppenburg is to be held at all costs."

At 11:30 hours the fire of the Tommy's heavy weapons began to intensify, with the result that the leading elements of the regiment made their way to the cellars and the remaining elements took cover in foxholes. After the experience of recent actions everyone could imagine what would happen if the British attacked seriously. Then it would be soldierly virtue against the firestorm and brave spirits against flame-thrower tanks again; for the regiment had no heavy weapons.

At 13:00 the artillery liaison detachment (Oblt. Schulze) from I./84 reported and received a warm welcome as the representative of nine artillery pieces and eight Flak-88s. At 12:00 2. Kp. reported: "Enemy attacking with tanks and infantry after heavy artillery preparation." 2. Kp. was unable to withstand the pressure of the attack any longer and as per orders withdrew toward II. Btl.'s main line of resistance. The company's losses were heavy.

Thus the British attack on Cloppenburg began. A short while later the 3. Kp. reported an attack by seven tanks and armored troop carriers along the Lastrup—Cloppenburg road. The enemy attacked the regiment's entire front, seeking a weak point and a crossing over the Soeste.

At about 14:00 hours the pressure on 3. Kp. became so strong that it likewise followed orders and withdrew toward the 5. Kp.'s main line of resistance. Enemy tanks, armored troop carriers and infantry on foot advanced into the abandoned suburb.

At 14:15 hours the enemy pounded the Muhlenbach—Brücke area and massed his tanks there. Our own line was pinned down by continuous tank machine-gun fire. Under cover of a wall of smoke, the enemy moved up infantry, supporting these with anti-tank and mortar barrages and continuous tank *machine-gun fire. In this way he blasted a hole in the front and succeeded in crossing the Mühlenbach with infantry. The tanks remained behind the infantry and did not come within Panzerfaust range.*

Moving two anti-tank guns forward, the enemy advanced deeper into the gap. The enemy infantry took up positions in and near the church, brought several machine-guns into position and occupied the hospital, which II. Btl. had intentionally not included in its main line of resistance, placing snipers in the roof hatches and windows.

The regiment's right wing reported strong infantry forces just in front of the main line of resistance. Two assaults were repulsed. The threat arose of being outflanked from the right through the gap near Bühren, into which I. Btl. of the Wackernagel Regiment had not yet moved. Consequently at 14:18 hours 3. Kp., which had just been pulled out, received orders to immediately go into position in the sector west of Cloppenburg between the southern edge of Bühren—school and south of Schmertheim. The company on the regiment's left wing also reported enemy advances and tank sounds in front of the main line of resistance.

The sound of fighting in the town grew louder and louder. Enemy tank cannon, tank machine-guns and artillery fired without letup. The mortar fire intensified. 1. Kp. (Lt. v. Bülow) received orders to go to the command post at once.

Counterattacks by weak forces against the enemy forces that had broken in to the north church crumbled under heavy defensive fire.

In order to prevent a breakthrough to the north, Lt. Klüver received the order to launch a counterattack with the regiment's messenger section. The latter set out immediately, but at the main street it came under such heavy machine-gun fire that it was impossible to cross. Lt. Klüver subsequently tried to initiate the counterattack via II. Btl.'s command post, so as to seal off the church until 1. Kp. had arrived.

The pioneer platoon under the command of Lt. Schröder, which had meanwhile been moved forward, received orders to advance to the church with a squad of tank killers to destroy the enemy tanks there with Panzerfäuste.

1. Kp. arrived at 1530 hours and went to the counterattack. A platoon from the 4. Kp. arrived from the left at the same time. The pioneer squad worked its way to within 50 meters of the church, however any further movement was impossible. It did succeed in smoking the enemy out of the church with its Panzerfausts and also knocked out two Sherman tanks. The enemy became aware of the preparations for a counterattack and sealed off the area with uninterrupted artillery fire. He continued to use a great deal of smoke and under its cover brought more tanks across the Mühlenbach.

Thus in spite of committing all of its reserves, the regiment was unable to completely close the gap in the front. Movement was now scarcely possible. There was no support at all from our anti-tank weapons. On account of lack of ammunition and the absence of forward observers, our artillery fire was too weak and inaccurate to effectively suppress the enemy.

The artillery and mortar fire on the right wing grew steadily heavier. 3. Kp. reported: "An advance by day to the Soestebach is not possible, since the enemy has the area sealed off with fire." The company therefore remained where it was on the path south of the Cloppenburg—Bühren road before moving into its assigned sector after nightfall.

At about 19:30 hours enemy tanks were reported from the left wing, firing into the rear of 6. Kp.'s front. The enemy succeeded in breaking through, because the unit on the left had not yet been able to occupy its assigned sector, leaving a large gap. Our resulting losses were considerable. On the right wing the enemy put further forces across the Soestebach under cover of smoke. From there he advanced with strong forces on the road to Bühren, splitting apart the 3. Kp. from the 5. Kp. and the battalion headquarters. The companies had heavy casualties. 3. Kp. immediately established a new main line of resistance, and, with the help of the II. Btl.'s headquarters platoon under the command of Obfhr. Werner, the road to Bühren and Bührener Kämpe was sealed off.

So the regiment was threatened with encirclement. The commander reported the situation to the brigade. The brigade commander ordered:

"Cloppenburg is to be held at all costs."

At the regimental command post there was a conference of commanders and several company commanders. The situation was portrayed in stark terms: the penetrations made by the enemy could not be eliminated by the seriously weakened companies without tank, anti-tank and artillery support. In order to prevent a breakthrough by enemy tanks to Bethen, the brigade subordinated five Hetzers to the regiment; however, these were less than ideally suited to supporting the hard-pressed regiment among the houses. The Hetzers were therefore ordered to guard the Cloppenburg—Bethen road and the north exit from the town.

The enemy steadily reinforced his troops among the houses, making the restoration of a continuous main line of resistance with the forces available out of the question.

In addition, the enemy began setting some houses afire with smoke and incendiary ammunition, thus illuminating the decisive break-in area near the church almost as bright as day. Brave advances by several non-commissioned officers and forward observers into enemy-held houses only increased the certainty that the enemy was sure to resume his attack after briefly regrouping his leading elements.

The last chance to take advantage of a brief and deceptively-quiet pause in the fighting at about 21:00 hours to pull the companies out of their predicament could not be exploited. When the regimental commander again reported that Cloppenburg could not be held with the available forces the brigade commander confirmed the existing order:

"Cloppenburg must be held at all costs."

The regimental commander then turned to the commanders and company commanders who were present and ordered:

"Everyone hold where he stands. If the enemy pressure becomes too strong, fighting withdrawal toward the regimental command post and hold there."

Then he dismissed the officers.

The atmosphere in the regimental command post was calm. The necessary orders to destroy all documents that might be of use to the enemy and secret files were given and carried out. The commander ordered the drivers and dispatch riders to make their way over the north road, which might still be open, to the brigade command post and thus save their cars and motorcycles. The men followed orders, but it was against their will. The five Hetzers likewise received orders to pull back to Bethen, since their use in the narrow streets was out of the question.

There was an amazing quiet in flame-illuminated Cloppenburg. The enemy searchlights shone through the fires to the north. From several houses came jazz music, played by the overconfident British, who were certain that Cloppenburg was already theirs. Everyone in the command post realized that soon the regiment would no longer exist.

In spite of the bravery of all the soldiers, who made repeated minor assaults and shortly after 21:30 hours destroyed two tanks from close range, one by Obfhr. Werner, the other by Gren. Giessler, there were insufficient forces for a large-scale counterattack. There was nothing left to do but wait for the Tommies to attack. And they came.

At 21:45 hours the enemy laid down a heavy barrage on the regiment's right sector. The enemy's heavy machine-guns opened up again with sustained fire. The regimental commander got on the wire to brigade again and in the presence of his battalion commanders informed the commanding officer that this was the end of his regiment. Soon afterwards the wire was cut by shellfire. The sound of fighting increased in the entire sector.

The remaining elements of the regiment fought bravely and with determination for every house and fought their way back to the regimental command post. Soon a perimeter about 200 meters across was formed around the command post, and it gradually shrank further. The Tommies were in the houses surrounding the regimental command post, in which the commanders of both battalions were present.

At 23:40 hours the two dispatch riders of II. Btl., Pz.Schtz. Kriechler and Kan. Schewior, who had also been ordered to brigade by their battalion commander, rushed into the command post, almost out of breath. Bathed in sweat and out of breath, Pz.Schtz. Kriechler cried out:

"Herr Major, I bring the withdrawal order from the brigade."

The order also called for the surviving elements to occupy a blocking line at the southern edge of Bethen.

The last orders for the withdrawal were quickly issued and the time set. The *enemy artillery and infantry weapons increased their fire to the maximum. It was as if the British had overheard the order to withdraw and wanted to make it impossible for the remaining elements of the regiment to pull back.*

In small groups the soldiers retired toward the north under the command of their officers.

The British immediately set out in pursuit of the withdrawing elements with strong infantry forces and flame-thrower tanks. But under cover of darkness they succeeded in reaching the Cloppenburg—Bethen road and the forest edge near Ambühren. Given the enemy's tremendous material superiority, it was only his hesitancy that had allowed the surviving elements of the regiment to escape to the north and rejoin the Großdeutschland Brigade for the subsequent battles.

Oblt. Reinhold Geist (Adj.)

and Lt. Horst Henrich (O1)

Report by the 1. (O.B.) Kp./Poeschmann Regiment
The Day of Cloppenburg

13 April 1945. Five years ago we had taken off in Ju 52s for the airborne landing in Norway. This time the day began shortly after midnight with a march to Cloppenburg. The O.B.-Regiment, or more accurately what was left of the regiment, reached Cloppenburg while it was still dark. Dig in again! We were supposed to build a dummy position and convince the English, who were expected in the morning, that they were facing a strong fortification and considerable numbers of troops. When it was light, I received orders to take up quarters with my company near the rail line on the far side of the marshalling yard. We were to stand by as reserve, which meant that we would be employed as a flying company wherever things were hottest. A battalion runner briefed us. The way—as always we marched widely spaced—led us through the marshalling yard. Then suddenly from out of the clear blue sky a furious artillery barrage! Beside me my company headquarters squad leader was hit by several shell splinters and collapsed covered in blood. I was struck between the shoulder blades by a shell fragment. I felt the pain of the hot iron. Then it was quiet again. We dressed the squad leader's wounds; they looked bad, but they appeared to be only flesh wounds, even though we had a hard time stopping the blood flowing from five different places with our packet dressings. My wound did not appear too bad. A man inspected the site. My raincoat was torn, my tunic as well. The shell fragment was stuck in my sweater! I had been lucky. But now into the quarters, quickly! I stayed up, waiting for what was to come. The field telephone team ran a line to my room. It was not yet complete when a runner came in: "To the regimental command post immediately!" We ran through the city, which had been evacuated by its inhabitants. Artillery salvoes forced us to repeatedly take cover. Dead horses and dogs lay in the streets. The sun was out, it was a fine spring day. Major Poeschmann greeted me in the cellar of his house, "Good to see you old boy!" (Old boy! At 36 I was by far the oldest in the entire regiment.) And then came my mission: the English had broken through and taken up position in the main street. My company was to drive them out again. They had tanks. And then he wished me good luck. Poeschmann passed me a bottle of Moselle wine that he had found somewhere. "Best you drink it straight away; then nothing will happen to it on the way!" And since they apparently had plenty of Moselle at the command post and no one wanted to share, I drank the bottle down. It did me good, what with the heat and having been awake all night. But now to the company. Listing slightly, I ran through the streets, but I was completely sober when I arrived. The hardest thing was waking the exhausted boys. It took an entire hour to get the company on its feet. I gave a quick briefing on our mission and instructions on street and house fighting, for our mission would take us there.

I divided the company near the English-occupied main street: 1st Platoon took the left row of houses, 2nd Platoon the right row of houses, 3rd Platoon followed 1st Platoon as reserve. I myself assumed command of the 1st Platoon. And then off we went. Since enemy tanks commanded the street, we had to approach the houses from the back. This worked extremely well for my 1st Platoon. House after house was taken, and the English pulled back, offering little resistance. We stormed into another house (a hardware store). The English fled up the stairs. I went after them with two men. On the top floor they skillfully swung themselves through the window into the hall window of the next house, which was only a few meters away. We scoured the top floor of the hardware store: no more English there. On into the next house. One of the men with me passed the hall window on his way to the stairs. As he did so a bullet grazed his head; he came back with a bleeding ear lobe. The other was hit in the arm in the same attempt. We were sitting in a trap! While trying to attract 2nd Platoon's attention out the window, a burst of machine-gun fire was directed at us, probably by one of the British tanks. We could not reach the back of the house facing the garden, for the only door out of the room led to the hall with the fire-spitting window. But the Tommies saw to it that we did not get bored. First they threw hand grenades into the apartment. (Luckily the windows were open, allowing the blast to dissipate!) Then they lobbed smoke and incendiary grenades. The air was almost unbreathable and we didn't want to get closer to the window and give up our cover from the hand grenades. Tricky situation! Now small flames began spurting up from the floor. Were we to suffocate or burn to death here? What was 1st Platoon doing? From the garden we heard the rattle of machine-guns. Obviously the British infantry was advancing again. We had to get down! Perhaps the dense smoke was just as thick in the hall and we could get past the window unseen. A quick and fervent prayer to heaven and we were through.

Below I found the company rather desperate. It was impossible to go any farther, indeed it was already extremely difficult to stay where we were. Report to battalion! The answer came quickly. I was to lead the company back in the direction of the regimental command post. When I arrived in Poeschmann's cellar all of the other company commanders were already sitting there. My company had held the longest! But it was senseless. The city was surrounded by the English on all sides; what was left to us. A hedgehog position and fight to the last round.

I briefed my men, and we built what we thought would be our last anti-

tank foxholes. Via the platoon leaders I advised my men that when the English attacked they should fire off all their ammunition as quickly as possible and then wait out everything that followed under cover. I convinced myself that the holes really were deep, and then we waited. Twilight fell. Then it became dark. Tommy did not attack, and based on our experience we knew that he would now not attack until later in the morning. Quite unlike the Russians, who preferred the twilight of the morning or evening for their attacks, the English were obviously shy of uncertain situations. We waited, fell asleep. Someone shook my foot. It was the battalion runner, who came creeping to me in my foxhole: "Herr Leutnant! Order from battalion: the companies are to break through the enemy encirclement on their own. Direction: north!" "Nothing else?" "No, nothing else." I passed the order through my runners to the three platoons and wished them good luck. The runners returned. They did not need to tell me that the order was being carried out. There was shooting everywhere. Noise, screams and flashes of fire in the dark night. The four of us orientated ourselves by compass. I took my pistol in hand, safety off, and off we went. It was a terrific mix-up. The night was pitch black. Then an English flame-thrower lit up the terrain: there were scarcely any German soldiers to be seen, but the place was swarming with Tommies. Nearby there was a barn. Inside!

Breathing heavily, we stood inside the barn door. Darkness around us. But not for long. A flame-thrower had set a hay rick on fire. In an instant the hayloft was lit brightly. It was full of Tommies. That's all we needed!

What happened next took place more quickly than one can describe it. Now, while writing it down, I try to place myself back in my then frame of mind. I probably didn't think at all, instead I acted purely out of the instinct of the front-line soldier, and a front-line soldier did not give himself up, even when the situation looked completely hopeless!

A second: astonished faces! Then I shouted: "Hands up!" Reply? An outburst of laughter from the 40 or 50 Tommies. "No hands up! You! Hands up!" Then I was seized by rage: they were laughing at a Leutnant of the Brandenburgers? I snatched the rifle from the hands of the Englishman nearest me and threw it out the barn door. But then a bullet whistled past my head and struck the door frame. Good, you'd rather have it that way? I fired my pistol at the three Tommies standing nearest me. "Out!" I shouted to my runners. And in no time we were left out the door, running as fast as we could along the outside of the barn. I remembered from that morning that the barn must be near the street, and the street ran north! We heard English voices ahead of us. Breathing heavily, we stopped. Only a few meters to our right a jet from a flame-thrower hissed past us. Would they see us? Apparently not. The jet stopped. We had to carry on. A wire fence barred our way. Over we go! Oh dear, the noise. And the English voices from the flame-thrower were right in front of us. Lucky they were talking so loudly. They didn't hear us. All four of us got over the fence and—there was the road. We stopped in the ditch. On the road English soldiers. How far north might the road be held by the enemy? With extreme caution we crept and crawled along the ditch. Blessed be the darkness! Then across the road into the ditch on the right. And beyond it was open field. The Tommies certainly weren't there. We were through! After about 30 minutes the first hail in German. An anti-tank position. We had made it!

The scattered elements of the Wackernagel Regiment had still not reassembled by after midnight on 13-14 April, and thus they could not be deployed in the forward line and in fall-back positions for the shattered Poeschmann Regiment.

Instead the Feldersatz-Btl. GD under Hptm. Schmidt, with a strength of 6 officers, 22 NCOs and 237 enlisted men, was ordered to hastily establish a blocking line south of Little, far in the rear.

The gathering remnants of the Poeschmann Regiment had no other choice but to secure both sides of the Bethel—Cloppenburg road. It was about 01:00 hour on 4 April when a brigade order reached the regiment, instructing it to immediately occupy a new main line of resistance approximately 1.5 kilometers south of Beverbruch and cover the road from Cloppenburg to the north. Persistent machine-gun and artillery fire could still be heard from Cloppenburg; it seemed that small groups of soldiers that had been unable to withdraw—or which had failed to receive the order to do so—were still putting up resistance. So it was initially quiet in the new position, however weak enemy forces were feeling their way forward in the direction of Bethel, which was occupied without resistance. Additional elements slowly arrived; to the right of the Poeschmann Regiment small groups from the Pz.Eins.Abt. Bauer went into position, and these were initially placed under the Poeschmann Regiment's command. Finally, in the Varrelbusch area contact was established with Fsch.Jäg.Rgt. 24. On the left the first elements of Kampfgruppe Knaust arrived and secured there in loose formation.

The Wackernagel Regiment—without the lost I. Btl. under Hptm. Blumenthal—received orders by radio to assemble behind the Poeschmann Regiment's main line of resistance and occupy a new line of security (2nd line) from the Nikolausdorf church to the word "Moor" in Heiter-Moor. This was done only by the regrouped II./Wackernagel Regiment under Hptm. Goeldel, which on 14 April had a combat strength of 4 officers, 18 NCOs and 181 enlisted men. The entire 6. Kp. with 1 officer, 7 NCOs and 51 enlisted men had been missing since the action south of Essen.

The morning report by the 8. Fsch.Jäg.Div. on 14 April 1945 made it clear to every single participant of these past 48 hours once again the extent of the superior force against which this small band of brave men had held out for two days.

Morning Report 8. Fsch.Jäg.Div. of 14 April 1945

At about 11:00 hours on 13 April 1945 the enemy launched his expected breakthrough attack against the division's front with strong tank support. The attack was preceded by very heavy mortar and artillery fire. During the previous night (12-13) Cloppenburg had been bombarded by heavy artillery. The

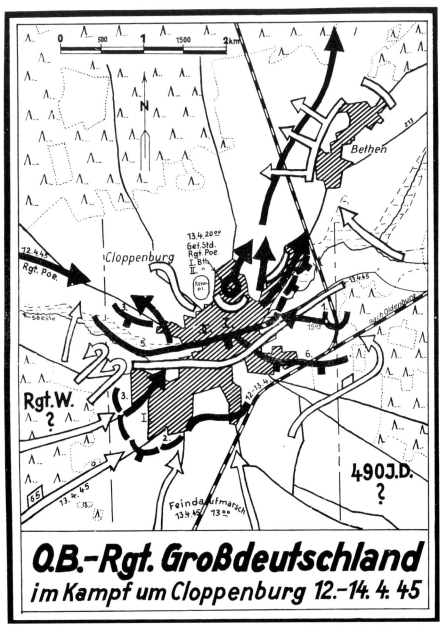

O.B.-Rgt. Großdeutschland
im Kampf um Cloppenburg 12.-14. 4. 45

Officer-Candidate Regiment "Großdeutschland" in the Fighitng for
Cloppenburg (12 - 14 February 1945)

main attack force came out of the Stapelfeld area from the southwest with an initial wave of sixty tanks. A breakthrough along the road was inevitable. At the
same time a second group of enemy tanks reached Tegelrieden from the south. In
a self-sacrificing battle which lasted six hours, the Pz.Ausb.-Brigade GD pre-

vented the enemy from entering Cloppenburg.

After the Wackernagel Regiment was completely surrounded near Hemmelte and the Poeschmann Regiment was nearly wiped out while defending the east ring, the overpowering enemy succeeded in entering the town.

The remaining GD soldiers prevented the enemy from achieving the desired result in six hours of fierce house-to-house fighting. In spite of low strengths, repeated counterattacks were launched and according to initial reports about 15 tanks were destroyed in close combat (detailed report will follow). Simultaneous with the attack on Cloppenburg, the enemy advanced out of the Peheim area towards Grönheim and in spite of fierce resistance reached Molbergen with about thirty tanks. According to initial reports Fallschirmregiment 24 destroyed four tanks with close-range weapons and 2 with mines.

The third assault came from the Matrum area against Vahren.

After Pi.Btl. 21 and I./61 (last division reserve) were moved in, a counterattack was made against the enemy forces in Cloppenburg with the support of all anti-tank weapons. It did not succeed on account of the weak forces available. The line south Büren—Kämpe, south edge Bethen remains the main line of resistance. Counterattacks gained 1 000 meters to all sides, the town was placed firmly in the GD Brigade's hands. On the right wing as per orders in spite of inadequate forces, the enemy also pressed toward the line Dwergte, Stedingsmühle, Stahlvörden.

Barrage fire on Bühren and Bethen since midnight.

8 Fsch.Jäg.Div.

Pz.Gren.-Ersatz-Brigade   Brigade Command Post, 15 April 1945
Großdeutschland
Abt. Ia

Distribution:

Wackernagel Regiment
Poeschmann Regiment
Pz.Abt. GD, Pi.Btl. GD
Nachr.Abt. GD, Art.Abt. GD
Pz.Abt. 20, SS-Pz.Jäg.A.Abt. 2
Pi.Btl. GD (Brigade)

On 15 April 1945 the enemy from Cloppenburg appeared to be concentrating his fast armored forces on Reichsstrasse 213, moving east through Ahlhorn, or almost parallel to the German front. Coming from the Markhausen and Molbergen area, initially weak armored forces reached the Varrelbusch— Friesoythe road (about 12:35 hours) and are now advancing with infantry toward Garrel and America airfield, south of Garrel. The parachute troops previously holding this line are withdrawing without offering significant resistance and are occupying new fall-back positions farther north. Near Garrel and Friesoythe the enemy has therefore once again reached the deep flank of the ele-

ments of the Pz.Gren.Eins.-Brigade GD still holding south of Beverbruch, which means that they will have to withdraw from these positions on 16 April. Unit strengths, particularly of the Wackernagel Regiment, are not sufficient to offer serious resistance against the superiority of the British–Canadian tanks.

Combat strengths Wackernagel Regiment:
I. Btl. – lost, so far not returned from march.

	Officers	NCOs	Enlisted Men
II. Btl.	4	17	181
III. Btl. (BR)	2	6	31
SS-Pz.Jäg.	1	3	35

Weapons complement:
II. Btl.: 4 medium mortars, 7 machine-guns, 118 rifles, 26 assault rifles
III. Btl (BR): 22 hand grenades, 4 submachine-guns, 2 assault rifles.

The Einsatz-Brigade GD therefore once again issued orders to withdraw for the evening of 16 April under the code-word "Cigar." These applied first and foremost to the Poeschmann Regiment and the new line (2nd line) was specified as Haschelbrock—"Keller Hill"—hills north of Döhlen. After enemy tanks entered Garrel the Poeschmann Regiment conducted its withdrawal movements without significant pressure from the enemy. The Wackernagel Regiment was now back up front, manning the line: Nikolausdorf—Sager Lake—south edge of Bissel—southwest end of Sage. There was no enemy contact at first. The Pz.Gren.Eins.-Brigade GD's command post and that of the Wackernagel Regiment were in Halenhorst. In the days that followed the enemy activity lessened significantly, which suggested that the enemy was stopping in this area and forming a new point of main effort. The enemy subsequently shifted the bulk of his units northwest in the direction of Bremen with the objective of clearing out the German Bremen—Bremerhave bridgehead then being formed.

Thus the elements of the Pz.Gren.Eins.-Brigade GD in their positions at Nikolausdorf—Sage were also without meaning to the conduct of battle and could therefore be put to much better use elsewhere.

With the renewed subordination of the Pz.Gren.Eins.-Brigade GD to the 15. Pz.Gren.Div., whose command post was in Gifhorn, during the night of 19-20 April 1945 also came the order for the brigade to disband. It was the intention of Headquarters, Ems Army Corps to ready the reinforced 15. Pz.Gren.Div. for an attack toward the southeast (Rotenburg—Soltau) in order to relieve an encircled Kampfgruppe in the Soltau—Munster area and to sever the lines of communication of the enemy forces fighting northeast of Rotenburg.

The order to disband the Pz.Gren.Eins.-Brigade GD surprised and stunned the members of both regiments. It meant that they would be forced to join strange units and required them to give up their fighting community. Why this apparently senseless order? Why the brigade? Why not disband other, less cohesive units and preserve the GD? Many questions lay on the lips of the men who were affected.

The comments from the troops were quick and harsh: the senior command of the regiment is taking its leave! They are leaving us to our fate! They are selling us to strangers!

But what were the real reasons? There is no doubt that the brigade command never really had a chance; senior commands had always subordinated the two regiments to other units. Was the brigade command unable to get its way? Did it in the end play only a shadow existence and worry more about supply than the fighting troops? Did it show itself to be unequal to the conditions when it and its freshly-established force were thrown into a major battle at Rheine and Lingen? Or was the awareness of the senselessness of this struggle in the last minute more dominant in its methods of action than its bonds to those under its command, the bravely-fighting troops?

Question after question, which can scarcely be answered. There is no doubt, however, that not inconsiderable differences in command by the different command offices did lead to the decision to order the brigade disbanded and incorporated into the 15. Pz.Gren.Div.

During the night of 19-20 April it was determined that the Wackernagel Regiment would remain in existence and be incorporated as the division's third regiment. This happened as recognition of the unit's behavior in the recent fighting. II./Poeschmann Regiment was incorporated as a whole into the regiment to reinforce the "Regimental Group Wackernagel," as it was now called. The former I./Poeschmann Regiment was disbanded and was incorporated by companies into the 115. Panzer-Grenadier Regiment. The regimental command and headquarters of the Poeschmann Regiment were disbanded; *Major* Poeschmann went back to the Pz.Gren.-Ersatz-Brigade GD Schles-wig. The brigade command was also disbanded. *Oberst* Glaeser left and was transferred.

A completely new unit, Panzer-Füsilier-Bataillon 115 under the command of Hptm. Weizenbeck, was formed from the remaining elements of the Pz.Gren.Eins.-Brigade GD—in particular from what was left of the Pz.-Einsatz-Abt. GD (Bauer), the Pi. Kp., etc—and was placed under the tactical control of the 15. Pz.Gren.Div. All of these elements of the Pz.Gren.Eins.-Brigade GD were transferred across the Weser into the Mayenburg—Schwanewede—Eggenstedt area.

Thus on 20 April 1945 the Pz.Gren.Eins.-Brigade GD, most of which had come from the Pz.Gren.-Ersatz-Brigade GD, ceased to exist. The disbandment of this unit of recruits, disabled, instructors and stragglers was not in keeping with their wish for an honorable departure. The conditions had made it necessary, however. The men fought and died, even in a hopeless situation. And after all a battle is only hopeless if it has to be fought alone and without the help of others.

By now, with their backs to the sea, many of the soldiers, perhaps the majority of them, realized the futility of the struggle. The realization of this fact carried within it the seed of inner surrender, of letting slide, of an attempt to withdraw from this chaos; doubts arose as to whether risking one's life was still worth it.

Should one stay and carry on? Was it the years of instilled obedience to stay where one was put? Was it the blind following of orders from one's superiors, who in the end were in the same situation as every man? Was it the easy way out, to stay rather than take the decision to seek a way out? Or, was GD "home," where for weeks, months or even years one had lived, suffered and fought with a community of men who were the same age, acted alike and thought alike? Many, indeed most, decided to go into the dark future with this community of men, no matter what it looked like.

Chapter 3
The GD's Last Battles in the Northwest of the Reich

The men of the various GD Kampfgruppen went into action once again, now as part of the 15. Pz.Gren.Div.—in Pz.Gren.Rgt. 115, the first to return to action, in the independent Regimental Group Wackernagel, in Pz.Füs.Btl 115. It was a battle for the line Zeven to Bremervörde against enemy forces attacking west, to hold one of the last large bridgeheads east of the Weser estuary. Indeed, it was almost a battle to retain a tiny piece of German mother earth, on which there might somewhere finally be a break in the fighting.

The Pz.-Füsilier-Btl. 115 formed under Hptm. Weizenbeck brought the following companies into action again:

C.O.	Hptm. Weizenbeck
Adj.	Lt. K. Langenfeld
H.Q. Comp. and	Lt. H. Breskow
Signals Platoon	
1. Stu.Gesch.Kp.	Hptm. K. Buckel (not a GD unit)
2. Pz.Füs.Kp.	Oblt. A. Kloft (GD unit)
3. Pz.Späh-Schwadron	Oblt. E. Schmarbeck (GD unit)
4. Pz.Pi.Kp.	Lt. R. Roloff (GD unit)
5.s.Flak-Bttr. 162	Oberst-Feldmeister Fr. Kaeble (RAD unit)
6. Versorg.Kp.	Hptm. K. Hartmann (GD unit)

The enemy situation on 21 April 1945 was as follows: east of Bremen Headquarters, Army Group Ems was about to be encircled as a result of the rapid advance by British guards divisions to the line Tostedt—Stensen and the veering of strong enemy tank forces in the direction of Zeven. A successful enemy attack from the east through Zeven toward Osterholz—Scharmbeck would overrun the corps command post in Hepstedt and settle the fate of the German troops still south of the Hamme—Oste line in a few days. At the suggestion of the commander of the 15. Pz.Gren.Div., Gen.Lt. Rodt, at the command post the commanding general therefore ordered all attack preparations halted and instructed his units to go over to the defensive in a line from Rotenburg to Zeven, since the Pz.Gren.Rgt. 115 was already engaged in heavy fighting at and south of Zeven anyway.

On 22 April the enemy launched concentric attacks, with the main effort from the northeast, and entered Rotenburg.

The GD-bolstered 15. Pz.Gren.Div. subsequently received orders to go over to the defensive in the line from the road fork northwest of Rotenburg through Abbendorf and Gyhum to Zeven, simultaneously readying attack groups in the areas southwest of Gyhum and west of Brüttendorf. The pincer-style attack launched eastwards from Gyhum and Brüttendorf led to the recapture of Wistedt, which was taken in a surprise raid by Lt. von Bülow and his men (formerly 1. Kp./Poeschmann Regiment). On the other hand Elsdorf, which was defended stubbornly, remained in enemy hands.

Lt. von Bülow described this day:

6. Kp./II./Pz.Gren.Rgt. 115 – 15. Pz.Gren.Div. – formerly 1. OB. Kp. GD

21 April, the Day of Wistedt!

I woke up. Five AM. By this time we were already supposed to be with the battalion in Wehldorf! Heinous deed! But we were supposed to be picked up! I walked onto the dark road. It was pouring rain. No trucks. Only a tractor far behind. Really! And hooked to it were two milk wagons. It was supposed to take the Bülow company to Wehldorf. Where was it? It couldn't have found it. Lovely state of affairs. My men snored and slept, trying to outdo each other. The stresses of the last weeks and the cognac had done their work. But it didn't matter: Up! And still half asleep they climbed onto the wagons, and the slow tractor towed us calmly and pleasantly to Wehldorf. What would the commander say? I was ready for anything, including court-martial! But things always work out differently than one expects. When we finally arrived at battalion the commander was standing in front of the door, and when I went up to report I was struck by his curiously pale face and his slightly swaying figure. Aha. So the battalion had also become aware of the flowing wine in Zeven. "Good that you're here, Bülow. Come right in!" And then I received my orders: the enemy's tank battalion was sitting in the village of Wistedt, and my company and I were to drive it out again. I was assigned three assault guns as support. And then he wished me good luck. The assault guns were already sitting in front of the door. After quickly briefing my platoon leaders, I assigned the three platoons to the three assault guns and climbed onto the first vehicle myself. And with a wild rattling and clattering we set off toward Wistedt, still in pouring rain. We soon turned left off the road onto a secondary road, then we crossed a wooden bridge and—crash! The beams had been unable to support the assault gun's weight, we were stuck. The driver told me that going any farther was out of the question. What now? Runner to battalion. I moved the company up; to the left and right of the road were more or less marshy meadows to the railway embankment bearing the Zeven—Rotenburg line. Approximately 250 meters in front of us to the northeast lay Wistedt. The slightly raised railway embankment provided excellent cover. Widely spaced, the company waited for what was to come. And it came: the adjutant! The old man was furious—why wasn't I attacking? If the assault guns were out of action then I would just have to attack alone. I tried to convince him that it was suicide to attack an English armored battalion with a pure rifle company armed with a few machine-guns and Panzerfausts. Yes, he saw that too, but the commander was insisting on it. I tried to make clear to him the pointlessness of storming a village here when almost every big German city was already in the hands of the Allies. "Order from battalion!" "Fine, please tell them I am attacking!"

"Platoon leaders!" I explained the order. If we fulfilled this mission we would owe it all to: the grace of God, the sleepiness of the victory-drunk English and the speed of our men! Beautiful. We tried the age-old trick from Caesar's *Bellum gallicum*: "Move your squad another 100 meters up the railway embankment, then cross it and the Zeven—Wistedt road under cover. Go wide and then appear suddenly northeast of Wistedt, act like the first men and draw fire before taking cover and waiting to see what happens. Our three platoons will cross the embankment 200 meters in front of us in one rush, silently of course, and stop at the bushes in front of the village (it was too far to crawl, furthermore it was much too wet; there was little cover anywhere). If we get across unseen, then we will storm the village on a broad front, but silently, with no shooting unless we meet resistance, but then with everything we have in order to simulate a major attack.

The platoon leaders were fire and flame! The chosen group moved off. Time seemed to stop. Then, after about 45 minutes, rattling at the far side of the village. Terrific! Get ready! Go! Everyone give his all! I was shocked at how much noise our spades and gas masks made in spite of the precautions we had taken: but—not a shot was fired! Breathing heavily, we reached the cover of the bushes at the outskirts of the village. Now we had to be fast and quiet. A fervent prayer: God, look after my men. The agreed-upon signal, and in to the village we went—at the enemy.

We had run less than 20 meters when some idiot suddenly began to shout, and this infected everyone. Shouting war cries, the Bülow company stormed the village of Wistedt, just as in the days of Old Fritz. But it worked. Only a very few of the tank crews got to their vehicles. An enemy machine-gun plastered us with steady fire. One or two tanks fired incendiary shells, and in no time the entire village was in flames, with dark clouds of smoke often reducing visibility to zero. But—we advanced. Our Panzerfäuste howled into the enemy tanks. Oberfeldwebel Brackert, the East Prussian, a bull of a man, fired his Panzerfaust at a tank but missed. Furious, he leapt onto the tank, banged on the hatch with his entrenching tool and shouted: "Get out! Get out!" And in fact the Tommies came out! And raised their arms! From all sides they came with arms raised. The enemy machine-gun fell silent. Wistedt was ours! Eight tanks destroyed. 68 prisoners. My company had suffered none killed, just three slightly wounded.

We spent some time disarming the prisoners. We did not treat each other like the enemy. Indeed, a sergeant congratulated me on my success; we had really done a fine job! The Tommies offered us cigarettes and showed us how their machine-gun was operated.

But now we had to get out of the village quickly. The enemy artillery would come with deadly certainty, if not a counterattack. We quickly helped ourselves to chocolate, cake, candy and preserves from the tanks and then went into position at the edge of the village.

A small house which was somewhat off to the side and undamaged by fire became my company command post. The Tommy's hot coffee and buttered bread were still on the table, wonderful refreshments. One of the men of the company headquarters squad found a gramophone and put on a record: In the Sanssouci Rose Garden! It was spring, sunny spring, in the Sanssouci rose garden. The rain had stopped; the sun came out. Spring, sunny spring! But, a burnt-out village: the result of this senseless order in what had become a senseless war in the year 1945.

Two men from the company headquarters squad asked for permission to run back into the village to examine the tanks before other companies arrived. I said to them, "But be back here in ten minutes at most! There will be an enemy artillery barrage as sure as the amen in church." They stayed past their time. The first shells exploded in the village. One came back in one piece, the other with a shattered arm. Our only serious wound of this day!

By about evening it had become quiet. I moved the company command post into the likewise intact teacher's house. Two other companies moved in; they were supposed to support us in the defense. But it stayed quiet..

At this time the Rgt.-Gruppe Wackernagel was still approaching via Wallhöven, Kuhstedt, Karlshöfen, Rhade and Selsingen before assembling in Selsingen prior to returning to action. The regimental group arrived early on 23 April. I./Rgt.-Gruppe Wackernagel commanded by Hptm. Blumenthal was inserted along the Twist to secure the northern flank of the 15. Pz.Gren.Div. which was engaged in heavy fighting on both sides of Zeven. At first there was no direct contact with the enemy in the Meinstedt—Sassenholz—Anderlingen area.

On the night of 23-24 April 1945 the Rgt.-Gruppe Wackernagel/15. Pz.Gren.Div. issued the following order:

Rgt.-Gruppe Wackernagel/15. Pz.Gren.Div.
Command Post, 24/4/1945

Ia

Order by the Rgt.-Gruppe Wackernagel for defense of the Zeven—Twiste sector.

The enemy has brought the Brit. 52nd I.D. into action on the east bank of the Weser, bringing the total forces operating opposite the corps front to three divisions, the 52nd and 53rd I.D. and the Guards Armored Division. The former enemy situation suggests an enveloping attack from the Achim area as well as Rotenburg—Schesel aimed at encircling our forces southeast of the autobahn.

While further enemy attacks toward the west will come from the area of Elsdorf—Hesslingen in order to force back our front, since 22 April the enemy has been moving strong forces into the Zeven and Elbe area. His previous direction of reconnaissance suggests that these will be used in an advance towards Bremervörde and the lower course of the Oste.

Rgt.-Gruppe Wackernagel, to which I./Blumenthal is once again subordinated effective immediately, is to defend the area on both sides of Zeven and the Twiste river line on the right of Pz.Gren.Rgt. 115. Right boundary: Badenstedt (incl.) – Frankenbostel (excl.) Left boundary: Wense (excl.) and Grafel (excl.)

Detailed orders for the defense: (a) II. Btl. to defend on both sides of Zeven with point of main effort at Forst Zeven crossroads; road fork near Point 26; road intersection Offensen, Zeven—Heeslingen, Offensen. (b) I. Btl. to defend strongpoint-style along the Twiste, with focal points at the Twiste crossings, especially on both sides of Twistenbostel and the Anderlingen—Sassenholz road, as well as network of roads 2 km east of Anderlingen. Boundary line: between I. and II. Btl. = Selsingen—Offensen—Heeslingen road (to II./)

Mortar Company: instructed to cooperate with II./, position heavy mortar platoon near tip of wood, approximately 1 km south of Brauel. Infantry platoon to form strongpoint in area of wooded point 300 m east of mortar position. Medium mortar platoon to go into position in such a way as to be able to give supporting fire to II./— strongpoint at eastern edge of Offensen. *Special-Purpose Jäger-Kp.*: to move into west part of Dungelwald as regimental reserve with orders to scout counterattack possibilities in the direction of Zeven, Offensen and Twistenbostel. In event of enemy attack Jäg.Kp. to occupy blocking position in scouted positions at east end of Dungelwald with mission of blocking Heeslingen—Selsingen road. *Jagd-Zug*: (hunting platoon, Lt. Käs): under II./— for use in counterattacks with attached assault guns. *Pioneer Platoon*: establish strongpoint at east edge of Seedorf, with front to east and southeast. To the extent possible Pioneer Platoon to carry out blocking missions and demolitions at request of the battalions.

The following are directed to collaborate with the regiment:

II./AR 33

elements Panzer-Abt. 115 (with II. Btl.)

elements Heeres-Flak-Abt. 315 (with II. Btl.)

Luftwaffe Flak-Abt. 939 (with II. Btl.); one battery in Anderlingen, one battery in Hassel, one battery requested to go into position in area of Point 31, 4.3 km southeast of Hassel.

A forward observer of II./A.R. 33 with I. Btl. in area of Twistenbostel. One observation post II./A.R. 33 in area 800 meters south of east part of Brauel, with forward observer in Offensen and on the Zeven—Heeslingen road, approximately 500 m east of east edge of Zeven. II./A.R. 33 liaison detachment with regiment.

Reconnaissance: to be conducted day and night, especially in the morning, by a few enthusiastic volunteer soldiers equipped with Panzerfausts and assault rifles to unsettle the enemy. Special-Purpose Jäger Company to carry out operations on the Heeslingen—Steddorf—Ahrenswalde road with mission of harassing enemy supply on that road.

Pickets: are to be pushed far forward as far as possible, well-camouflaged, in the battalion sectors in order to eliminate surprises. It is vital, first that no position be recognized by the enemy, and second that every man makes full use of his weapon's firepower.

Intended Conduct of Battle: In spite of the width of the sector, the objective is to repulse the expected enemy attack toward Zeven and in the direction of Selsingen toward Bremervörde east of Zeven—Dungelwald—Twiste river line in the specified sectors by exploiting the depth of the combat zone and employing well-prepared firing plans.

Signals communication by wire to the two battalions backed up by radio. I. Btl. to establish wire communications with Special-Purpose Jäger Company.

Vehicle parking area: Seedorf.

Regimental-Headquarters Company: Lavenstedt.

12. Forward Ib Command Post: Rhade.

13. Regimental Command Post: Lavenstedt (occupied from 22:30 hours).

14. I expect that after being incorporated into the 15. Pz.Gren.Div. the regiment will continue to bring honor to the name Großdeutschland and in Germany's most difficult time will continue to fight ruthlessly and bravely true to the tradition of our GD units within the 15. Pz.Gren.Div.

Original signed by Wackernagel

Major and regimental commander

While the I./Rgt.-Gruppe Wackernagel was in position, with command post in Hassel, 3. Kp. in and due east-southeast of Anderlingen, 1. and 2. Kp. along the Twiste near Twistenbostel and the (east end of) Brauel forest, II./Rgt.-Gruppe Wackernagel secured at the forest edge east of the Brauel—Zeven road, with elements also at the Zeven station. The hunting detachment under Lt. Käs was in position with two assault guns at the east edge of Zeven, attached to II. Btl.

Regimental command post: Selsingen. Special-Purpose *Jäger* Company as reserve in the forest on the Zeven—Selsingen road.

On the right, forward elements II./Pz.Gren.Rgt. 115 (6. Kp., formerly 1. Kp./Poeschmann Regiment under Lt. von Bülow) held in Wistedt and further line to Elsdorf station.

Increasingly heavy British artillery and mortar fire on Zeven since early morning hours of 24 April. At about 10:00 hours this intensified into barrage fire, finally at about 11:30 hours came the expected infantry attack in battalion strength, supported by 8 to 10 tanks and flame-thrower tanks.

Taking advantage of the terrain—mainly woods and bushes—the enemy approached the town of Zeven relatively quickly. II./Rgt.-Gruppe Wackernagel, which was deployed east of and on both sides of Zeven under the command of Hptm. Goeldel, withdrew to the west and northwest under heavy enemy pressure. In Zeven itself the men of the Jagd-Kdo. Under Lt. Käs continued to defend with two assault guns, however it, too, was forced to give ground. Four to six enemy tanks were destroyed, some with *Panzerfausts*. However, in this house fighting the entire 7. Kp./II. Btl. Goeldel under the command of Lt. Richter was lost; apparently it was wiped out.

II. Btl. Goeldel established itself in new positions along the rail line west and northwest of Zeven. At the Twiste river line held by I./Rgt.-Gruppe Wackernagel there was little contact with the enemy at first; he made only weak advances, which were repulsed along the Twiste.

An advance against Anderlingen in the afternoon by about sixteen enemy tanks was largely repulsed in collaboration between I./Rgt.-Gruppe Wackernagel and 2./1.Flak-Abt. 939. Anderlingen burned. At about 17:00 hours further enemy tanks suddenly broke through in the direction of Selsingen, threatening the Rgt.-Gruppe Wackernagel's command post there. It managed to flee the town to the west, however. It turned out that a French prisoner of war had revealed the presence of the regimental command post to the British tanks.

It was now certain that the British had launched a major offensive against Bremen and they had succeeded in advancing to the city's inner defensive ring.

The 15. Pz.Gren.Div., reinforced by the GD elements, occupied a new blocking position in the line Botersen—Mülmshorn—Bockel—Dehldorf—Brüttendorf—Oldendorf—Forst Zeven—Godenstedt. This was also the beginning of a withdrawal by the entire Headquarters, Ems Army Corps toward the Hammer-Oste line. Simultaneously the 15. Pz.Gren.Div., the Pz.Pi.Btl. 33 and the Pz.Füs.Btl. 115 (GD) transferred into the area between Zeven and Elbe following the Aue river line. Their orders were to prevent enemy reconnaissance to the north and any advance against the Oste river line.

The *Wehrmacht* communiqué of 25 April 1945 makes some mention of the fighting in the northwest and other fronts:

From Führer Headquarters, 25 April 1945 (excerpts)

Breakthrough attempts repulsed on both sides of the lower Weser, Delmenhorst area. Horneburg retaken. Berlin main line of resistance: Babelsberg—Zehlendorf—Neuköln. Nauen, Ketzin and Oranienburg held. Penetrations near Eberswalde.

Elbe reached between Risa and Torgau. Advance into Bavarian forest near Cham.

In Italy main line of resistance at the Po. Attacks by American V Army repulsed. Communist bandits advanced to Fiume. Southeast front firmed up.

Deep penetrations near Brünn. All attacks on Breslau repulsed since 17 February 1945. Counterattacks in Bautzen area, Görlitz and Kamenz gained ground. Weissenburg was liberated. Enemy attacks at the Oder north of Gartz to west of Tantow. Heavy forest fighting near Pillau. Weak bomber units over southern Germany by day. Night attacks on Kiel.

A navy tank-destroying detachment under Korv.Kapitän Kremer destroyed 24 tanks within a few days.

Today the Allied nations convened a conference in San Francisco which is supposed to bring peace. In Berlin yesterday 50 Soviet tanks were knocked out in the Frankfurter Allee.

On 26 April, after a preparatory artillery bombardment, the enemy attacked from the Zeven area with his main effort in a southwesterly direction. Because of our seriously reduced combat strengths "Grosses Holz Zeven" was lost in a few hours. A new defense line was set up between Badenstedt and Badenmühlen. Badenstedt subsequently also fell into enemy hands. Our tanks were still holding east of Ostertimke. Radio monitoring gave running reports on enemy spearheads, successes by our artillery and further attack plans by the enemy, for example that a direct hit by German artillery destroyed a truck on the bridge over the Bade, that a new bridge was to be completed by the enemy by 17:30 hours and so on.

This day brought a crisis for the reinforced 15. Pz.Gren.Div. It was due to the excellent work of our radio monitoring service that the enemy attempt to break through was prevented and that new lines of resistance could be set up at the decisive spots.

The 15. Pz.Gren.Div. sent emissaries to negotiate the surrender of the prisoner of war camp at Westertimke. Their progress was monitored by radio, since all enemy offices reported their arrival. From the same source the division also learned that the commander of the British Guards Tank Division was holding the emissaries as prisoners of war and was planning an attack through Ostertimke toward Westertimke with all armored elements at 18:00 hours on 26 April. Since the military bridge north of Badenstedt was supposed to be completed by 17:00 hours, the enemy issued an order for the attack to begin at 17:30.

Based on this intelligence the German anti-tank defense was immediately reorganized.

The attack toward Ostertimke by tanks, personnel carriers and infantry, which followed an artillery bombardment, broke down under German defensive fire with heavy losses to the enemy, who subsequently withdrew to Badenstedt.

This was the decisive success of the day; knowing what was at stake there, our own tank crews performed well and earned high praise.

Enemy organization in front of the sector of the 15. Pz.Gren.Div.:

Canadian division west of Delmenhorst
51st (H) Division southeast of Delmenhorst
British 3rd I.D. south of Bremen

British 9th Armoured Division east of the Weser, SE of Bremen
British 52nd I.D. Achim area
British 43rd I.D. area south of Hellwege
British 53rd I.D. around and north of Rotenburg
British Guards Armoured Division north and northeast of Zeven
British 7th Armoured Division area south of Buxtehude
British 58th I.D. area east of Buchholz

Combat strengths of Rgt.-Gruppe Wackernagel as of evening 25 April 1945:

I./— Blumenthal

	Officers	NCOs	Enlisted
HQ	4	19	58
1. Kp.	2	14	90
2. Kp.	1	19	75
3. Kp.	2	18	78
4. Kp.	1	12	74
Totals	10	82	375

II./— Goeldel

HQ	4	7	30
Supply Co	1	9	51
5. Kp.	1	2	1
6. Kp.	2	12	79
7. Kp.	0	5	12
8. Kp.	2	9	51
Totals	10	44	224
Rgt. HQ Co	5	23	134
Mortar Co	2	20	86
Spec.Purpose Jäger Co	2	25	87
Totals	29	194	906

Casualties as of evening of 25 April:

	Officers K/W/M	NCOs K/W/M	Enlisted K/W/M
I./—	0/0/0	0/0/2	0/0/21
II./—	0/1/3	0/3/17	1/3/182
Rgt. H.Q. Co	0/0/1	1/0/7	0/1/18
Mortar Co	0/0/0	0/0/0	0/3/0
Spec.Purp. Jäger Co	0/0/0	0/0/0	0/0/0
Totals	0/1/4	3/26/1	1/7/224

I. Btl. of the regimental group under Hptm. Blumenthal held the town of Rahde, having withdrawn from the east sector under heavy enemy pressure. II. Btl. under Hptm. Goeldel lay behind—in Glindstedt—under no pressure for the time being. Regimental command post in Karlshöfen. The ability to resist of the Kampfgruppen still deployed there was dropping noticeably, morale was sinking. There was no more supply—no one wanted to die a hero's death at the last minute. Only where there was still heavy weapons like anti-aircraft guns and tanks was resistance temporarily offered, but as soon as the enemy artillery began ranging in the positions were hastily abandoned. The enemy used the opportunity and made repeated attempts to make surprise advances with small groups of armored cars and infantry. These usually succeeded in chasing away or capturing whatever German troops were present.

Major Wackernagel was put out of action by an outbreak of jaundice; Hptm. Goeldel took over command of the regimental group. Gradually everything forward of the line Hepstedt—Breddorf—Glinstedt moved back toward the Hamme-Oste Canal, where another continuous defense line was to be built. All that was left of the Rgt.-Gruppe Wackernagel in the 15. Pz.Gren.Div. was II. Btl., now under the command of Hptm. Schmidt, which held the front line of outposts in this sector. Everything else pulled back behind the canal on 29-30 April. Even though the feeling of cohesiveness was still quite good in the GD units, some of the other units were beginning to show signs of disintegration. Requests for surrender were already having success; a similar request directed to the 15. Pz.Gren.Div. and its former GD units was rejected by the division commander Gen.Lt. Rodt on 29 April. It seemed that this division was the only large combat unit still fighting in this area.

The Rgt.-Gruppe Wackernagel under the command of Hptm. Goeldel continued to see action at the Hamme-Oste Canal on both sides of Gnarrenburg, with II. Btl. still in Glinstedt. The enemy pushed ahead slowly. He seemed to have shifted his main effort farther to the south, when on 30 April it was reported that the enemy had entered Tarmstedt with tanks and was advancing north against little resistance.

On the same day German radio announced that Adolf Hitler was dead. Grand Admiral Doenitz was his successor.

This news affected the men very little, as they had concerns of their own. The initial shock passed quickly. But they had to realize that time had run out, the end had come.

On the release of the code-word "Gotenzug" on 1 May the entire 15. Pz.Gren.Div. withdrew to the west bank of the Hamme-Oste Canal and took up defensive positions. II. Btl. under Hptm. Schmidt remained in Glinstedt on 2 May, now with more contact with the enemy and heavy artillery fire. On the whole, however, there was no increase in enemy pressure in front of the canal.

On the other hand, a force consisting of the British 51st Infantry Division and the Guards Armoured Division bolstered by an armored brigade broke through out of the Bremervörde area.

This made a joke of our defensive position along the Hamme-Oste Canal, since the loss of Bremervörde was the beginning of the outflanking of this sector. Pz.Gren.Rgt. 115 was thrown into the area, and on 3 May it was able to head off the advancing enemy in the line Ebersdorf—Lindorf, with the reinforced Pz.Füs.Btl. 115 even reaching the road junction at Glinde, then advancing to west of Bremervörde and digging in there. An attempt in the evening by the enemy to seize this crossroads behind a creeping barrage failed thanks to the bravery of the GD men of the Pz.Füs.Btl. 115. The still unbroken morale of the former GD soldiers enabled them to launch a successful counterattack against the crossroads during the night of 3-4 May. 36 British soldiers were captured and four enemy tanks destroyed; the battalion's losses totaled 12 killed and wounded and one assault gun knocked out. When first light came on 4 May the last survivors of the Pz.Füs.Btl. 115 were still at the Glinde crossroads. Only then did they have to disengage. The battalion made its way west, where at the same time the 15. Pz.Gren.Div. was conducting an ordered withdrawal into the line Kirchwistedt—Appeln—Frelsdorfermühlen, part of Headquarters, Ems Army Corps' plan to withdraw to the outer fortified area of the Weser estuary and Geeste—Edd Canal should its current positions be breached. In the course of these joint withdrawal movements the Rgt.-Gruppe Wackernagel reached the Kirchwistedt area without pressure from the enemy. I. Btl. was positioned there, with II. Btl. in Beverstedt, and the regimental group's command post in Heyerhöfen. Positions were occupied there; there was enemy artillery fire but no attacks.

There was no doubt that the enemy was rapidly approaching his goal. His success in the recent weeks and months was based on several factors:

embarrassingly detailed preparation as well as carefully thought-out and purposeful cooperation between ground and air forces;

clear materiel superiority;

better trained replacements compared to the recruits, home defense troops and so on on the German side.

All that the German command had to offer against this superiority was improvisation on an unprecedented scale, which, while able to delay the outcome, could not prevent it. When such improvisation became the rule, it bore within it the seed of collapse.

At precisely 2014 hours on the evening of 4 May 1945 the Rgt.-Gruppe Wackernagel received the following message from the division radio center: "Cease-fire reached until 2200 hours. Open fire after 22:00 or if enemy approaches. Div. Ia, 15. Pz.Gren.Div."

Combat operations had been halted—and they would not be revived.

When the radio message reached the regimental group it was disposed as follows:

Command post Rgt.-Gruppe Wackernagel	Heyerhöfen
Command post I. Btl./—	Kirchwistedt
Command post II. Btl./—	Beverstedt
Command post 15. Pz.Gren.Div.	Sellstedt

A follow-up radio message was received during the night:

To battalions, tanks, etc...

At 08:00 hours German summer time on 5 May 1945 cease-fire with the Allied forces. It encompasses all units of the army, the navy, air force and Waffen-SS in the areas of the Netherlands, Friesland (including Ostfriesland, East Friesian Islands and Helgoland), Schleswig-Holstein and Denmark.

Signature on receipt and report transmission to all of the division's subordinate units.

I expect maximum discipline and in particular monitoring of the issuing of alcohol so as to avoid incidents.

Signed Rodt

This was supplemented by a statement on the surrender by the OKW on 5 May:

We are laying down our weapons in northwestern Germany, Denmark and Holland, because the war against the western powers no longer makes sense. In the east, however, the war goes on in order to save as many German people as possible from Bolshevism and enslavement.

After discussions with British representatives revealed that the enemy was interested in former *Brandenburgers* (members of the Pz.Gren.Eins.-Brigade GD), the 15. Pz.Gren.Div. ordered all former GD members (including the Ia, General Staff *Major* Monshausen, a member of the GD in 1942-43) to remove their cuff titles. This was passed on to the officers of the division, whose ranks included members of the GD. New pay books were issued, making it impossible to identify the former identities of GD-BR men. The division stressed that it was carrying out this order on its own responsibility, since the units were still under German military law and could and should give whatever orders were necessary to ensure the safety of the troops. Even if this order did not receive the full approval of every former GD-BR member, it was later acknowledged to have been fully justified.

During the night of 5 to 6 May elements of the Rgt.-Gruppe Wackernagel became involved in a skirmish with British troops in which about twenty enemy soldiers were captured and twelve killed.

Then the cease-fire took effect in the northwest area, causing everyone to reflect on what had happened in the past. Only a very few had any illusions about the future; from 15 May 1945 on they found themselves in British prisoner of war camps in the Westerode—Hemmor area.

The cease-fire also took effect in the Schleswig-Holstein area, where the last elements of the Pz.Gren.Ers.-Brigade GD were quartered.

Once again the Pz.Gren.-Ersatz-Brigade GD was issued orders to use its reserves of personnel to form new units for use in central Germany. A regiment of three battalions under the command of the recovered *Major*

Krieg was formed on or about 17 April. As part of the new formations for *General* Wenck's 12. Armee, together with other units from tank schools, officer schools, the Reich Labor Service and so on, it was to see action in the relief of the Reich capital. While being transported by rail via Hamburg to Neu-Brandenburg—Neu Strehlitz, the last train was captured by the British near Hamburg. As a result just one over-strength battalion of this Krieg Regiment ever reached its intended area of operations, where it went under in the general collapse.

Much the same fate was suffered by the reformed Pz.Jäg.Abt. *Großdeutschland* under the command of *Major* Wolle. While on its way to the field division the completely reequipped unit came under the command of the "Clausewitz Division," likewise made up of thrown-together remnants, and with it took part in a relief drive (*General* Blumentritt and *General* Unrein) along the Uelzen—Gifhorn—Brunswick road. During the night of 15-16 April there was a fierce fight in the town of Nettelkamp, about 15 kilometers south of Uelzen, with about sixty American tanks, in which *Major* Walle alone destroyed nine with close-range weapons. He was seriously wounded in the engagement. Finally the end of the battalion came on 21 April in the area northwest of Brunswick.

In general, everyone remained in their quarters when the cease-fire took effect on 5 May. Schleswig was handed over to the British and all weapons and equipment were surrendered. Otherwise they pretty much left the men alone. Daily roll calls gradually began to wear on their nerves. The 1. and 2. Mil.Pol.Kp. were formed under the command of Hptm. Haase to maintain law and order among the GD units, which were not watched over by the British at all. Their main duties were watching over the stores of bread, grain, meat and ammunition. Houses were also searched for *Wehrmacht* property, and in each case the patrol consisted of a British officer with six German and six British soldiers. They were transported by a former combat train vehicle.

The change from soldier to prisoner did not always go so smoothly, however, even if the respect of the British for the defeated allowed them a certain degree of freedom. The GD elements assigned to maintain order by the British approached their task with interest, however this did not prevent the former officer reserve of the Pz.Gren.-Ersatz-Brigade GD, almost 65 men, from being suddenly arrested on 22 May. They were transported to Gottorf Castle, which had been set up as a prison for members of the SS.

After being delivered to the castle courtyard the men were drawn up in long rows. Each spread out his personal things in front of him. The demand to surrender weapons was unsuccessful, since while being transported by truck all ammunition had been fired off and the parts of the remaining pistols thrown overboard.

And while the two long rows were being frisked—each was subjected to an intensive interrogation—two GD men—a Hauptfeldwebel and a *Feldwebel*—were suddenly led to one of the guard huts that flanked the main entrance. A short while later they returned, each with two pails…filled with latrine contents…in their hands. They were then led under guard past the long rows of officers standing there. Chance or intentional?

When the two men reached the front of the row of officers, both turned as if on a signal and marched past on both sides carrying the pails.

This demonstration brought tears to the eyes of many of the GD officers standing there. Tears of frustration over such unworthy treatment—tears of pride over this demonstration of the relationship between the men and their officers.

Part X
The Beginning of the Soviet Major Offensive on 16 April 1945

Chapter 1
Defense at the Neiße
Panzer-Grenadier Division Brandenburg

From Führer Headquarters, 16 April 1945:

Soldiers of the German Eastern Front! The Jewish–Bolshevik mortal enemy has gone to the attack en masse for the last time. He is trying to wreck Germany and destroy our people. Most of you soldiers from the east already know the threat facing German women, girls and children. While the old men and children will be murdered, the women and girls will be degraded to camp whores. The rest they will send to Siberia.

We have anticipated this thrust, and since January of this year everything has been done to build up a strong front. A huge artillery force awaits the enemy. The losses sustained by our infantry have been made good by countless new units. Alert units, new formations and Volkssturm bolster our front. This time the Bolsheviks will experience Asia's old fate, which means that he must and will bleed to death before the capital of the German Reich. Anyone who does not do his duty at this moment is a traitor to our people. The regiment or division which leaves its position is behaving so disgracefully that it should be ashamed to face the women and children who stand fast through the bombing terror in the cities.

Watch out especially for the few treacherous officers and soldiers who, to save their pitiful lives, will fight against us in the pay of the Russians, perhaps even in German uniforms. Anyone you do not know who issues you the order to retreat is to be arrested immediately and if necessary forcibly detained, no matter what his rank.

If every soldier on the Eastern Front does his duty in the days and weeks to come, Asia's last assault will collapse, just as the invasion by our enemy in the west will fail in spite of everything. Berlin remains German. Vienna will be German again and Europe never Russian.

Build a sworn community to defend, not the empty concept of a fatherland, but to defend your homes, your women, your children and thus our future.

My eastern warriors, the entire German people looks to you in this hour, and its only hope is that through your steadfastness, your fanaticism, through your

weapons and under your command the Bolshevik onslaught will end in a blood-
bath. At the moment in which fate has taken the greatest war criminal of all
times from this earth, the turn of events will decide this war.

Adolf Hitler

The *Jäger* was still studying the contents of this order of the day in his foxhole, it having been brought to him with his food during the night, when at a few minutes before five in the morning on 16 April the flood-gates of a furious barrage opened above them. Like a distant thunder at first, an eerie howling, the roaring from the far side of the Neiße—and then the raging inferno all around them. He ducked, stretched out in his hole, made himself smaller and then smaller again; he scratched into the dirt, pressed himself against the wall of the hole—moaned and cried in protest. Shells fell all around, the earth shook and heaved, fountains of dirt rising and falling back again. It was like a giant plough, which meter by meter threw the ground out of the earth and let it fall back again. And above him? Cracking and splintering, the crash of tree crowns and the beams of shat-tered bunkers, the whizzing and buzzing of splinters and shrapnel. Where were the other lads of the platoon? Where was the *Oberjäger*, the platoon leader? Were they still alive? Had they been hit? Just the continuous, pounding din in the air, which made further thought impossible. Minute after minute passed, and still the shells continued to rain down. Minutes became hours, hours passed and still more, still more!

This barrage unleashed by the Soviets early on 16 April 1945 from hundreds of guns of every caliber, mixed with the roaring Stalin Organs and smoke shells, went on for hours, lasting until after 08:00 hours.

Then there they were, at first the outlines of lone brown figures, as if they had appeared from nowhere—then hundreds, thousands. Gesticulating wildly, rising up, running, then dropping again—toward the chaos which their artillery had prepared for them. There was no resistance at the forest's edge; scarcely a shot fired. The light machine-guns were silent, there was no coughing of mortars or the hammering of light anti-aircraft weapons. All destroyed, wiped out, eliminated? Had the barrage wiped out every living thing at the forest's edge—or was it just shock that had silenced everything human?

The groups of armed Soviets drove deeper into the shattered darkness of the forest. Then a flash, a hand grenade, an explosion. Down, take cover, then up again.

The Soviets drove into the forest with all their strength, like a steam-roller, into the forest southeast of Kahle Meile where the *Jäger* of I./Jäg.Rgt. 2 BR commanded by *Major* Steidl were in position. Finding lit-tle resistance, they formed into groups and advanced to the road and approached the rail line.

A *Jäger* machine-gun opened fire, here a burst of fire from a submachine-gun, and farther to the rear the detonation of a hand grenade. From the Neiße the sound of the first T 34s, which had already reached the west bank of the river. The roar of their engines, the rattle of their tracks, iron slapping against iron—tank after tank now rolled behind the Soviet infantry, making their way to the front, their guns pointing straight ahead threateningly.

The concentrated Soviet thrust had struck the entire sector of I./ Jäg.Rgt. 2 BR and farther north beyond the regiment's boundary also the positions of I./1244, a "sick battalion." From the small bridgehead in the sector of 1. Kp./I./Jäg.Rgt. 2 BR that had been won the night before, the Soviet mass now rumbled westward, while following elements turned north in order to roll up the German positions.

It was not possible to establish a new defense immediately. The elements of I. Btl. Steidl had been shattered, scattered to the winds, wounded or lost in the insane barrage even before the full scale of the enemy breakthrough was known. Only small groups were able to make their way to the west, but they were overtaken and picked up by the Soviets. Others cowered in their holes and waited for rescue—but those who can should help themselves. Obfw. Ascher was still holding in his sector with the men of his 1st Platoon of 1st Company, firing everything he had into the flanks of the mass of earth-brown forms. Not until they turned against him as well, seeking to ferret him out from behind, did he, too, have to yield and make his way to the west behind the enemy spearheads.

Obgefr. Bonke, runner—killed; *Oberjäger* Burkhart—dead, and this one gone, that one gone—soon there was no one in the forest, not even in the holes. In spite of a serious leg wound Lt. Esser had dragged them to the rear.

The first attempt to reestablish a line—with men sent to the front, radio operators, mortar people of the 5. (Gr.We.) Kp./I. Btl./Steidl— failed; they were simply brushed aside and attacked from the rear, like those other groups of *Jäger* who, without orders, stopped at some favorable position, threw themselves down and opened fire. But it was completely futile; the Soviets were everywhere and in particular already far to the west. What mattered here was not building a new positions—what mattered there was being faster than the enemy spearheads, digging in and holding.

The assault pioneers of the Pz.Stu.Pi.Btl. BR under Hptm. Müller-Rochholz, known simply as "Pi.-Müller," of the 3. Kp. were still battling the Russians somewhere in the forest in front of Geheege. "Pi.-Müller" rushed to bring in his 1. and 2. Kp. situated farther to the north, to get his men of the 3. Kp. out. A young pioneer rushed a T 34 from the side and blew it up with a *Panzerfaust*. Radio-equipped armored troop carriers from the rear were already reporting dense masses of enemy troops accompanied by T 34s advancing against the vineyard on Hill 199 from the direction of Biehain. Oblt. Schlosser immediately led all available runners, including those of 2. Kp., staff people and the reconnaissance platoon there, and set up defensive positions in the vineyard. There they had to hold, had to force this flood of Soviet soldiers to halt.

It appeared as if the Soviets were already outflanking to the south, moving elements toward the south part of Ober-Wehrkirch. On the estate and in the castle there was He.Flak-Abt. BR under *Major* Vosshage with three 88-mm guns. The other platoons and batteries were still up front with the regiments in the anti-tank role. They could not be reached now, some having already engaged the enemy while others were standing guard farther north in Ndr.-Wehrkirch. The castle itself was in the middle of the town of Wehrkirch, but the nearest houses were some distance away because the estate park extended around the entire castle. A strong, massive wall closed the park off to the east, leaving open just one opening. Heavy enemy artillery fire was falling on the park and the castle, making it necessary to evacuate the upper floors. The Soviets surely suspected that it housed a defense command center, and they were not entirely wrong. *Major* Vosshage was holding there with his flak artillerymen, and he intended to offer resistance with his guns. Pi-Müller made contact with him and agreed that his pioneers would fall back toward the castle if the enemy suddenly pressed hard. The positions near Geheege could not be held, the pioneers were outflanked and had to get out. It was almost noon. *Major* Steidl, commander of I./Jäg.Rgt. 2 BR, met Gen. Schulte-Heuthaus, who was driving around at the front in his armored troop carrier, organizing the defense, assembling the men, giving orders to hold on. He instructed *Major* Steidl to immediately lead the men with him back to Kaltwasser and reestablish positions there. Also headed there was Obstlt. Oesterwitz with elements of his II./Jäg.Rgt. 2 under *Major* Renner. Train and alert units were already crouching in their holes around Kaltwasser, expecting the Soviets at any minute. It wasn't long before they were there, the T 34s; they came from the right from out of the forest and headed straight for the houses of Kaltwasser. In waves, accompanied by masses of Soviet infantry. Their engines roared, their machine-guns spat out bursts of fire. Then one tank went up, a jet of flame shot from its turret. There a cloud of smoke—another T 34 from which all life had been extinguished. But it was for nothing, there were just too many. And they were already in the town. A few continued to exchange fire with the Soviets, the rest fled across open fields.

It was afternoon, the sun was shining straight down, dust lay in the lungs; the heat was enough to drive one mad. Dripping sweat, the *Jäger* dashed back to the forest's edge. But there were Soviets there too, whole groups, even columns, all moving west. They were already in the attacker's rear, forced to give up, to withdraw. Where weren't the Soviets? Where could one stop and rest? They were everywhere!

The soldiers fell back on foot, machine-gun boxes on their backs, mortar baseplates, barrels. Back—back!! To Mückenhain through dense undergrowth across the rail line. New pickets along the tracks, new positions at the edge of the town—when would the Soviets be there? Kodersdorf was the next fall-back point, the place where they were supposed to regroup if outflanked. Jäg.Rgt. 2's command post was there with Obstlt. Oesterwitz.

Where was II./Jäg.Rgt. 2 under *Major* Renner? It was battling the Soviets farther north. No contact with it—runner up, dispatch rider: assemble II. Bataillon here and there, get back here no matter what!

Patrols reported strong enemy columns with T 34s, panye wagons and guns on the Rothenburg—Dunkelhäuser—Uhsmannsdorf road—already north of Wehrkirch. The Soviets seemed to be bypassing Wehrkirch. Under the protection of the pioneers the few remaining *Jäger* and men of I./1244 withdrew towards Wehrkirch; but too late: the earth-brown figures were already in the northern part of Wehrkirch and pushing south. They also came along the rail line and drove toward Wehrkirch station. Oblt. Schlosser was still battling desperately in the vineyard (Hill 188), fighting beside his men of 2. Kp./Pz.Stu.Pi.Btl. BR. He was fatally hit, several of his men were killed; wounded dragged themselves to the rear, west into the forest—hoping that they would find someone to take them in. The vineyard could not be held, by evening the enemy was on the hill and had surrounded the last pioneers still holding out.

Pi-Müller abandoned his positions at the edge of the forest west of Geheege, fought his way through to Ndr.-Wehrkirch, stormed the houses, which had been occupied by the enemy, and drove him back to the station. *Major* Vosshage was still in Wehrkirch castle, now engaged in a fierce firefight with Soviet infantry and tanks advancing on the park. The men of the He.Flak-Abt. BR had knocked embrasures out of the walls; they placed their machine-guns in these and fired for all they were worth. All the while the 20-mm flak spat out streams of shells. Men attacked tanks with explosives, with *Panzerfäuste. Major* Vosshage himself knocked out two armored transport vehicles with his *Panzerfaust.* All the while heavy artillery fire continued to fall in the park. After the loss of several of their tanks, the Soviets pulled back to the bordering houses until the darkness concealed their T 34s. But they were in all the houses; Wehrkirch was occupied. Only to the west, in the rear, did there still appear to be an open path, though probably under Soviet fire.

It was almost 1800 hours. The 1. and 2. Bttr./He.Flak-Abt. BR had arrived and were positioned behind the village (west of Wehrkirch) in such a way as to be able to provide flanking covering fire. Some reassurance at least. Pi-Müller's combat engineers also now arrived, perhaps forty men, and took up position in the park. They strengthened our defense. Counterattacks to both sides from the park placed part of Wehrkirch back in our hands. More pioneers arrived and were moved into position. It was almost 20:00 and getting dark.

The resistance was organized. 3. Bttr./He.Flak-Abt. BR was also there, and it was deployed in the town itself for all-round defense. Two batteries of the Pz.Art.Rgt. BR provided badly needed reinforcement, they too positioned their guns for direct firing. More groups of *Jäger* and infantry arrived, having made their way through to Wehrkirch from somewhere in the darkness. They further bolstered the defense, which was now under the unified command of *Major* Vosshage. All was quiet; scarcely a shot was fired in the darkness. The men at the park's east wall in Wehrkirch lay in wait.

Meanwhile, roads were scouted beyond the park to the west in the event that a retreat became necessary. During the night the engineers fortified bridges for the tractors, the guns. The sound of battle had also died down elsewhere; the only sound was that of a steamroller somewhere in the distance. The Soviets were apparently building bridges, crossings. It would start again in the morning.

Least affected so far was Jäg.Rgt. 1 BR, whose positions extended between Rotenburg and Steinbach; it had not been touched all morning. Its men also heard the heavy barrage fire falling on their neighbor to the right, and during the morning they took in the first stragglers from I./1244. Nothing was heard from I. (SPW)/Jäg.Rgt. 1 BR under Hptm. Schuster, which had been ordered into Jäg.Rgt. 2's sector by the division commander. Jäg.Rgt. 1 BR continued to hold its positions at the Neiße; diversionary measures by the enemy in the form of offensive patrols were spotted early and wiped out. The commander and *Jäger* operations officer one drove into the right sector in their car. The situation was clear: the enemy had crossed the Neiße, broken through I./1244 and the adjacent I./Jäg.Rgt. 2 BR and was advancing west. There was no contact; it appeared that the division had been struck in the center of its sector and rent asunder. Jäg.Rgt. 1 BR was in danger of being cut off. I. (SPW) Btl. was not available, having probably become caught in the maelstrom.

Heavy air attacks were reported from Hähnichen and Spree, where Jäg.Rgt. 1 BR's supply units were stationed, then the first casualties. Finally, late in the morning, the first reports on the enemy situation, enemy tanks before Spree, situation also unclear in Rotenburg; elements of I./1244 were apparently still holding on there. The town had apparently been outflanked, however, for II./Jäg.Rgt. 1 BR's right wing company was being attacked in the area of the northern edge of Bleichenau from Rotenburg and had to bend its positions back to the north. A short time later there was a firefight at the southern edge of Rotenburg; Soviet artillery and tank columns were observed on the Rotenburg—Schlangenhäuser road. There was no sign of either our own defense or artillery; the enemy columns were able to head west undisturbed. Schlangenhäuser was evacuated after a brief but fierce street battle. The enemy had already penetrated deep into our area.

By the evening of this eventful day, 16 April 1945, the overall situation was as follows:

The enemy had driven through with strong armored forces on a width of 8 kilometers and had penetrated to a depth of up to about 15 kilometers. In our own sector I./1244 (south of and at Rotenburg) had been shattered and scattered. I. (SPW)/Jäg.Rgt. 1 BR had been moved by the division and deployed in the sector of the neighbor regiment. II./Jäg.Rgt. 1 BR had to bend its right wing company, which had to stay in contact with 6. Kp., north, resulting in positions facing south. Bremenhain was abandoned toward evening in order to shorten the front line and prevent being outflanked. The enemy was on the move to the west just west of the Jäg.Rgt. 1 BR's command post (only about 1 000 meters). Behind our strongpoints the enemy was already in front of Spree, which was evacuated by the 1. Rgt.'s supply units, leaving it undefended.

Wire communication to division were gone, the radio was silent—no more communications.

As before, even in the darkness of the falling night (16-17 April) the regimental headquarters staff was still in its old command post. It had prepared for an all-round defense.

The commander, *Major* Bansen (former commander of the Pz.A.A. BR) sat in his bunker and brooded over the situation leaping from the map, which was covered in red blots and thick arrows, thin blue lines and circles and many question marks. All the blue places on the map were surrounded by red, open flanks, wings hanging in the air and enemy in the rear marked the situation of Jäg.Rgt. 1 BR. And tomorrow morning? Encircled? Outflanked?

How to master the situation? Where were the reserves? Who would commit them? These were the questions that went through the regimental commander's head. And over all these questions stood the *Führer* order which had been issued to the troops barely 24 hours ago: not one step back! This battle would decide the war. And then the supplementary order from *Generalfeldmarschall* Schörner to the commanders: "I do not recognize concepts such as withdrawal, fighting retreat, folding up…"

How to act now—in this situation? To leave this place and fold up the front to the south was contrary to orders. Unless reserves arrived in time with sufficient strength to head off the enemy breakthrough and close the gaps in the front, to stay in place and wait for the enemy meant destruction, senseless loss of blood and the wasteful loss of human life.

What decision was to be made? In the hands of the commanding officer were the lives of several hundred men under his command. Also in his hands was the responsibility for the sector of front entrusted to him; but perhaps even more than that lay in his hands, namely whether by holding desperately to the positions, perhaps just for a few hours after daybreak, strong reserves might yet close the gap in the front. On the other hand, a premature withdrawal could destroy this opportunity for all time. Who could show him the right path in this situation?

The mood in the bunker was eerie. Everything, especially time, made a decision imperative. Although the men around the commander had been completely exhausted by the trying events of the day, the time was nearing midnight and weary heads drooped from sleepiness, the ingrained sense of responsibility rose high. A decision had to be made. We could not hold the positions any longer—that was an absolute certainty. But the order remained: hold to the end! This battle would decide the outcome of the war. The division was no longer reporting. So no one could release the commander from this order—he had to follow his own instincts.

The words of *Major* Bansen, commander of Jäg.Rgt. 1 BR, were hard: "We will swing south and thus establish a continuous line. There is no point in leaving anyone here. Reason demands this solution. The regimental headquarters will stay here until dawn and if necessary cover the building of the new defense line. They shall not be able to reproach us for lack of personal courage."

The tremendous tension eased. For a moment the commander lowered himself onto the couch and lay there, exhausted. His eyes stared at the roof but he could not sleep. His brain began working again and his thoughts about the coming battle became a firm plan which forced aside his doubts about the decision he had just taken.

The first orders with which to execute these thoughts were issued to the troops.

What the hard-pressed commander of Jäg.Rgt. 1 BR did not know about at that hour was the equally serious situation facing the Div. z.b.V. 615 north of his sector near Steinbach. After clearing the Muskau bridgehead in the evening hours of 15 April, the Soviets had also gone into action there as part of their general offensive on the morning of 16 April. They succeeded in crossing on both sides of Sagar, which prompted an immediate counterattack by a Kampfgruppe from the Pz.Korps.Pi.Btl. 500 GD. The Soviets had also broken through farther north in the Köbeln area, where their leading elements were now moving west. But very much more dangerous seeming was the breakthrough on both sides of, but particularly south of Forst, roughly at the autobahn, which was undoubtedly another point of main effort for the enemy. After destroying the German alert units stationed there, by evening—at precisely 16:00 hours—the Soviet forces had already made contact with the leading elements of the *Führer-Begleit-Division* holding a line Trebendorf—Halbendorf—Gross-Düben. This immediately led to unexpectedly heavy fighting. Even before the entire *Führer-Begleit-Division* had arrived as the 4. Pz.Armee's operational reserve its leading elements were already in heated battles. This unexpectedly deep breakthrough by the enemy and the premature enemy contact were the first indications of the tragic fate that awaited the *Führer-Begleit-*

Division.

In contrast to the previous day, the night of 17 April was relatively quiet. On the side of the defenders the officers tried on the one hand to regroup their totally shattered units, to assemble them and restore their sense of fighting community, to get a picture of the extent of the destruction, to ascertain the losses in men, weapons and equipment and build new defense lines. On the other they tried to become clear as to where all this was leading. Almost every battalion was on its own, sometimes with no contact with regiment. The bulk of Jäg.Rgt. 2 BR was holding in the Kodersdorf—Mückenhain area, Kampfgruppe Vosshage with elements of the Pz.Art.Rgt. BR, He.Flak-Abt. BR and the Pz.Stu.Pi.Btl. BR in Wehrkirch, Jäg.Rgt. 1 BR (less I. (SPW) Btl.) in the forest east of Hähnichen, the Pz.Korps.Pi.Btl. 500 in and near Sagar—each unit was thus isolated deep in the rear area with no contact to the sides. The corps command post was still in Spreefurth, also there and farther northeast the Stu.Gesch.Brig. GD (attached to the BR). The division's supply units under the Ib, General Staff *Major* Spaeter, together with the battalion trains were mostly still in their old places, though ready to withdraw west at any moment.

That night saw hardly any of the *Jäger* or their officers or commanders get any sleep; and it was followed in the early morning hours of 17 April by fresh movements. Fierce fighting was already raging in and around Kodersdorf (elements of I./Jäg.Rgt. 2 BR), placing the 5. (schw.) Kp. under Oblt. Gabel in a perilous situation. The company was surrounded in the few houses in Kodersdorf and fought desperately to hold its positions. The other units of the same battalion fought their way back towards Ullersdorf to establish new fall-back lines there. In Mückenhain, Obstlt. Oesterwitz and the III. Btl. were facing a similar fate as in Kodersdorf; he and his few men were also in danger of being encircled and just managed to disengage at the cost of heavy casualties. Stabsarzt Dr. Wolf Backhausen was killed; many dead or wounded *Jäger* had to be left behind under the pressure of the enemy's superiority. There at least there was contact, albeit tenuous, with elements of the 20. Pz.Div. fighting on the right. That unit had not been struck so directly by the Soviet assault. It also bent its wing to the west, however with the help of reserves it sought to prop up its left wing—and thus the BR's right wing—and initiate counterattacks.

In Wehrkirch, which was still in our hands like a rock in the flood of the Soviet offensive, a heavy enemy tank attack had been in progress against the defenders of the castle park since 03:00 hours. The battle lasted for hours and nearly forty enemy tanks were destroyed; the enemy was beaten off outside the castle wall. The light and heavy anti-aircraft guns played a decisive role in this; the pioneers also accounted for a large number of tanks with explosives and *Panzerfausts*. Ultimately the Soviet attack foundered on the personal bravery of these men. The quiet that followed was brief; at about 09:00 the enemy began a heavy preparatory bombardment intended to grind down the defenders, but they held on. Initial preparations for the abandonment of Wehrkirch were begun, the wounded were evacuated to the wood west of the town by Oberarzt Dr. Braun of He.Flak-Abt. BR. Finally, at about 13:00 hours, the division gave the order to abandon Wehrkirch, whose defense had been made pointless by the Soviet advance deep into our territory. The guns of the He.Flak-Abt. BR withdrew in stages, initially to the forest edge. The pioneers fell back step by step, making it possible to evacuate the town and castle of Wehrkirch with no losses in weapons or equipment and without leaving any wounded behind. Fall-back positions were occupied; the anti-aircraft guns were withdrawn another 800 meters. Once again it was the pioneers who had to make the last dash across open terrain, finally reaching the safety of the woods. There, however, our losses increased; the heavy, continuous artillery and mortar fire forced the men to go to ground, and yet everyone had to fall back. Again and again this cost blood, wounded, dead. Nevertheless, the dash to the rear was a success and the forest covered everything and gave time for a quick assembly. Division orders called for a new defense line to be established in the area of Niesky—Neuhof—road to Rietschen. Pz.Stu.Pi.Btl. BR was to go to Niesky, where it would be subordinated to the 4. Pz.-Armee's assault regiment. That evening the companies reached Niesky by separate ways and were immediately put into position at the edge of town. The battalion command post was in the Niesky theater. The men were still not in position when two T 34s appeared at the outskirts of town on the Neu-Särchen—Niesky road (from the southeast). These were taken out from close range. Enemy infantry were surprised while looting at the east end of town and were initially driven off. Under pressure from the enemy, new positions had to be taken up at the eastern end of town; the few companies of the panzer army's assault regiment played little role in this, especially since their low morale did not promise a successful outcome. Once again the pioneers were the core of the German defense. Meanwhile, farther southwest the He.Flak-Abt. BR assembled in See and elements went into position along the road to Rietschen (Reichsstrasse 115) with their front facing east. Even though there was no direct contact on the left (north), there were indications of a continuous line. Kodersdorf and Ullersdorf were still in our hands. The enemy was known to be in Oedernitz and already through south of Niesky. Our troops were in Niesky with loose contact to the north along Reichsstrasse 115. There somewhere, in addition to the He.Flak-Abt. BR, was the Stu.Gesch.-Brigade GD. Hähnichen was still in our hands. Rietschen too, however the situation there was uncertain.

During the course of 17 April the enemy took Weisswasser. Corps Group Kohlsdörfer withdrew farther to the west. On the same day Jäg.Rgt. 1 BR transferred its command post to Heidehaus, north of Quolsdorf. Spree was still in our hands, however there was continuous enemy contact. Kampfgruppe Kappel was engaged with attacking enemy elements there.

Spree could not be held. The defenders withdrew towards Hähnichen, where there were six assault guns under Oblt. Duncker. But all hell soon broke loose near Hähnichen too; advancing under cover of the forest east of the town, and causing confusion by hailing in German, even wearing German uniforms (apparently members of the Committee for a Free Germany wearing white armbands), enemy elements infiltrated to the outskirts of Hähnichen. The companies of the remnant battalion of I./1244, which were supposed to cover there, gave up after the first exchange of fire. The enemy pressed toward Hähnichen, however it remained in our hands, probably thanks to the assault guns positioned there. At the Hähnichen station was an abandoned fuel train. In spite of the continuous enemy fire, fuel trucks drove there and during the night emptied the cars so as to save this precious commodity.

On the whole, however, the situation in Hähnichen was completely unclear, especially in the woods east and west of the town. There, too, the enemy appeared to be preparing to advance on Rietschen. Farther northwest, near Weisswasser, the enemy was already advancing in a generally southwest direction toward the Spree. Once again the forces still holding at the Neiße between Steinbach and Sagar faced the threat of encirclement; these included elements of the Div. z.b.V. 615, the bulk of Jäg.Rgt. 1 BR and the Pz.Korps.Pi.Btl. 500 GD, the latter in and near Sagar. Realizing that Jäg.Rgt. 1 BR was now completely out of touch with the division, its commander, *Major* Bansen, subordinated himself to the Div. z.b.V. 615 so as to build and hold a common defense line under a unified command.

Early on 18 April reports began flooding in concerning new enemy movements. Once again it appeared that there were two points of main effort in the Panzer-Grenadier Division *Brandenburg*'s area. On the one hand, north and south of Niesky the enemy was advancing west across Reichsstrasse 115 through the woods toward Bautzen, which seemed to be the objective of his movements. German troops were still in Niesky, without contact with other units. See was evacuated, Quitzdorf too. He.Flak-Abt. BR was already withdrawing toward Gr.-Radisch. North of this town enemy columns in the Petershain area moving southwest. At about 16:00 hours the Ib staff was blasted out of Steinerlen, the enemy was there now too. The masses of enemy columns, the waves of tanks moved west and southwest like a tidal wave. Where resistance flared up they simply blasted their way through. If this did not succeed on the first attempt they simply went past to the right or left and continued on. The forces coming behind could take care of the nest of resistance.

For the German defenders still fighting in small groups—out of contact with the command, other units, with no knowledge of the situation—it seemed increasingly hopeless to stand against this flood of enemy tanks and columns. It was impossible to help out anyone else; everyone had to look after himself. This meant giving up and fighting one's way through until a new, common line was found. That was the only possibility in this situation.

And so all organized resistance ceased in the area between the Neiße and Bautzen; individual Kampfgruppen still held on in Niesky, in Kodersdorf and Ullersdorf, in Spreefurth, held on because they had been outflanked and were now deep in enemy territory. They, too, would one day have to fight their way through or surrender.

The commanders of the Pz.Korps GD and of the BR Division were still bound by the *Führer* order not to retire. This rigid command from above forced the units to hold senselessly everywhere while being unable to damage the enemy, who continued westward unimpaired. The chances of establishing a new continuous defense line were slipping away. There simply were not enough troops; those that had not been destroyed were holding out in their fortified places, sitting immobile, surrounded by the enemy masses rolling past them.

Still not in radio or telephone communication with all of its units, the Pz.Korps. GD in Spreefurth could not evacuate its command post in Spreeforth, even though enemy forces were already approaching the Spree from the northeast. The first enemy tanks appeared in the Boxberg area in the afternoon. The Stu.Gesch.Brig. GD and the Pz.Korps.-Pi.Btl. 500 GD were moving along the road from Weisswasser to Spreefurth, the enemy in front of and behind them. In the corps command post in beautiful Spreefurth castle, defensive preparations were being made. The enemy was said to be already by to the southeast; enemy patrols were in the Mönau area. *Major* Bethke, corps IIa and adjutant, rushed out; this would not do much longer. Several available alert units were put together, non GD units whose fighting worth could not be rated very high. Bethke placed himself at their head, hurried out with them to quickly establish a strongpoint-style defense line around Spreefurth in order to try and halt the enemy spearheads. Evening came. The enemy approached the town across the fields, unhindered; there was no resistance, hardly a shot. *Major* Bethke scraped together these unfamiliar groups of weapons bearing men, quickly organized them for the attack and led them against the enemy.

Armed with just a submachine-gun, he walked through small arms fire toward the enemy positions at the forest's edge, hoping that the men would follow him. Left alone in the middle of the field, he was hit and fell. But he rose to a crouching position, screamed at his men, stood up and began walking toward the enemy positions again. No one followed him; none of them recognized the spirit of sacrifice of this German officer, who finally collapsed in the enemy fire.

As darkness was falling the severely-wounded *Major* Bethke was recovered from the field and was taken to the rear. He was still alive when he reached the operating table of a BR medical company, 2. Korps-San.Kp. GD. The doctors tried to save his life, but in vain. This brave officer died under their hands.

The following are the division commander's words about Theo Bethke:

Theo Bethke stands before us as a man one seldom meets: a person with unsurpassed strength of character. Well raised in a modest home, he was destined from an early age to be a leader of men. He first distinguished himself in an independent position as commander of 8./I.R. GD. He accepted his forced employment as regimental adjutant only grudgingly; soon, however, he convinced himself that he had found an area of work which gave him an opportunity to fully develop his abilities. And he used this opportunity so well that his name is virtually inseparable from that of the GD. Without Bethke the GD would never have become what it was supposed to and eventually was.

His office work was exemplary; his clear insights into the career of a soldier, into his duties and rights, never wavered. He worried about everyone and never wavered in his tireless concern, in his search for ways to ease the burden of the troops and the individual. For this reason he was constantly driven to be with the fighting troops, to whom he had a natural attachment and who always expected and welcomed him. His intelligence and bravery constantly took him to where things were hottest. The knowledge he acquired during these visits to the front were then put to use immediately and effectively.

His very special strength lay in his ability to gain the full confidence in those around him in a very short time. Thus he did not remain someone who dealt in the personal affairs of officers, non-commissioned officers and enlisted men, rather an advisor, indeed in many cases even a friend of the commander and company commanders and not least of the division commander.

I welcome this opportunity to honor my dead adjutant and friend Theo Bethke, because to me his loss will always be irreplaceable. When I met him for the first time in August 1941, it took only a very short time for us to get to know each other. But our relationship soon became more personal and finally developed into a close friendship. Thanks to his sense of tact the great difference in our ages was irrelevant. I was with him daily, often we lived in the same space for days and weeks. There were frequent open exchanges of opinions, which left me with a deep impression of his inner feelings and allowed me to see all the questions of life from his point of view. Such conversations were always a joy for me and a gain. With his clear view he recognized early on the unavoidable dangers approaching us and growing steadily. In spite of this knowledge he continued to do his duty as a soldier without allowing those around him to sense the worries that burdened him. The fact that he shared his personal burdens with me as a friend drew us even closer together.

In every conversation he revealed his high moral values and his awareness that these morals were the basis for the troops' performance. With his unique gift for educating and influencing officers, non-commissioned officers and enlisted men, he was able to make use of this knowledge in an ideal way. Thanks to his vigor and sureness, his warm-heartedness and true comradeship, he soon had human contact with everyone around him. In this way he created and fostered the sense of volunteerism which so contributed to our success.

Everyone who knew Theo Bethke mourns his death. I mourn his death to a special degree.

Hoernlein

General der Infanterie, Rtd.

By the evening hours the Pz.Korps.-Pi.Btl. 500 GD had occupied a line of security around Spreefurth, while a pioneer company cleared the enemy from the east bank of the Spree in the Mönau area. In Niesky, already surrounded on all sides, the assault pioneers under Hptm. Müller-Rochholz, together with the weak elements of the 4. Pz.Armee's assault regiment, defended a tiny area against increasingly strong enemy forces. Artillery and mortar fire, occasionally mixed with tank fire, pounded the edge of the town. Groups of Russian infantry made repeated assaults from the southeast, mainly along the road from Neu-Särchen, against the defenders in Niesky. The machine-guns of 2. Kp./Pz.Stu.Pi.Btl. BR played a decisive role in preventing the Soviet infantry from advancing. Several T 34s broke through, blasted the barricades of trees west of the theater and entered the town, where they were destroyed. Smaller penetrations into our positions were also eliminated by courageous counterattacks by the pioneers. New, more favorable positions were occupied right at the edge of town, while assault teams recaptured several forward-lying houses. It was a continuous back and forth, but the men held everywhere. Admittedly, the enemy ring around the defenders became ever tighter, the concentric fire ever stronger and more effective. 1. Kp. continued to hold at the north and northeast edge; the enemy had infiltrated west through the forest between the watchtower and the C&U Company buildings, contact to the south with 2. Kp. was lost. Two attempts to reestablish contact between the houses on Reichsstrasse 115 failed. The Soviets were now thick in the houses; continuous enemy attacks from the inner town near the baths in the direction of the watchtower were repulsed.

2. Kp., plus several men of the 1. and some of the Sturm-Rgt. 4, occupied the dug positions near the watchtower.

A truce delegate, a German *Feldwebel* carrying a white flag, appeared at the tree barricade on the road, which ran from the market in the direction of the watchtower; he requested that the defenders surrender, stating that resistance was futile. He was shot.

The attacks continued, now also from the north from the pine forest. The defenders displayed excellent discipline in opening fire. The attacking Russians were allowed to come to within 40 meters before the first *Panzerfaust* was fired. Its effect among the trees was frightful. Then the machine-guns and assault rifles opened up with well-aimed fire. Some of the Soviets fled in panic; wounded screamed. Then five or six pioneers counterattacked in order to reach the enemy's flank. It worked: everyone was back in their old holes.

Casualties rose, however, caused by mortar rounds exploding in the trees. Many comrades were lost here; the wounded lay in cellars, dressings were already in short supply. But Niesky was held.

Farther south, completely out of contact, on 19 April elements of the Jäg.Rgt. 2 BR, reinforced by the rear guard of the 20. Pz.Div., fought due west of Kodersdorf and near Ullersdorf. Both towns had to be abandoned after fierce fighting; the remnants of I./Jäg.Rgt. 2 withdrew towards Altmarkt (Altwiese?), assembled there next to elements of the 20. Pz.Div. and linked up with Panzergruppe von Wietersheim, which provided it with the necessary armored support.

Farther north, where Jäg.Rgt. 1 was, it was obvious that the Division z.b.V. 615 group was being encircled and decisive measures were required. After shortening the front, especially in the south of the developing pocket, roughly in line with the former regimental command post on either side of Heidehaus, the panzer corps finally gave the order releasing the regiment from the command of the Div. z.b.V. 615 and instructing it to withdraw via Daubitz—Rietschen to take up a new defense line east of Spreefurth. The order was to be carried out on the night of 19-20 April. The Div. z.b.V. 615 was also to withdraw to the west while these measures were being carried out. Leaving behind rear guards in the Heidehaus area, during the night of 19-20 April the bulk of the Jäg.Rgt. 1 BR withdrew via Daubitz—Rietschen through the Forst Muskau in the direction of Boxberg—Spreefurth, where the leading elements encountered the enemy in Boxberg early on 21 April. The center of Boxberg was traversed by a rather deep and wide stream, the Schw. Schöps. The Jäg.Rgt. 1 BR initially set up its command post in a house on the near side of the stream, regardless of what was happening on the enemy side. The first arriving elements of the regimental headquarters company and the 8.Kp. under Lt. Klaus immediately set about clearing up the situation on the east side of the Schw. Schöps and chased the enemy into the bordering forests. Contact was immediately sought with Spreefurth, where the Pz.Korps.-Pi.Btl. 500 GD was still in position. The corps itself had since transferred its command post to Lohsa, since it could not effect an orderly command while surrounded by the enemy. The Ia of the Div. z.b.V. 615 under *Oberst* von Bülow, to whom the Jäg.Rgt. 1 BR was again subordinated, immediately issued orders demanding the recapture of Klitten as well as the holding of a defense line from Spreefurth to Boxberg. However, it was well into the afternoon hours before all elements of Jäg.Rgt. 1 BR and the attached I./Pz.Art.Rgt. BR had assembled in the Boxberg area. At this time there was no major activity on the enemy side. The assembly of Jäg.Rgt. 1 BR and preparations for the attack on Klitten were completed by evening. In preparation for this attack, Jäg.Rgt. 1 BR moved its command post farther forward, into the forester's house in Wilhelmsfeld, so as to be better able to command from there. Dusk was already falling when the reinforced

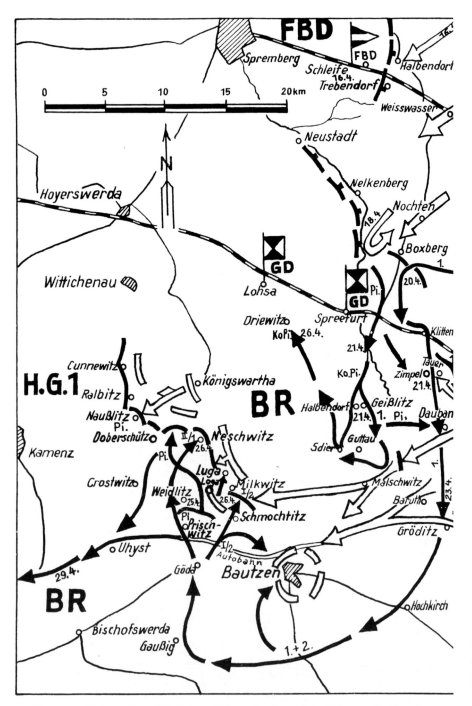

Panzer-Grenadier-Division "Brandenburg" in Heavy Defensive

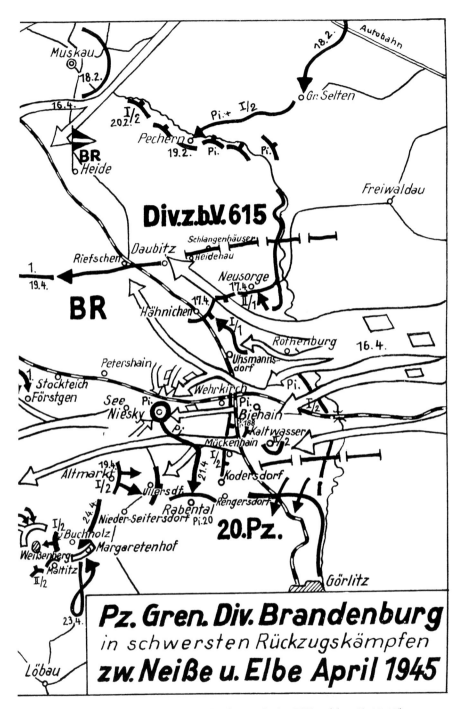

Fighting Between the Neiße and the Elbe (April 1945)

Jäg.Rgt. 1 BR launched its attack. There was a brief, fierce struggle in which three enemy tanks were knocked out. Klitten was back in our hands, pickets were posted for the night. A continuous, strongpoint-style line of positions had been established from Spreefurth to Klitten. All preparations during the night were devoted to the anticipated continuation of the attack to the south, which was to be met by a corresponding operation in the Radisch—Altmarkt—Ullersdorf area.

An attack by elements of Jäg.Rgt. 2 BR with the support of Pz.Gruppe Wietersheim against Ullersdorf and Jänkendorf had been under way since early on 20 April. Ullersdorf was taken in this very heavy and costly battle against Polish troops and units of the Committee for a Free Germany. The town was completely destroyed and burnt out; *Major* Steidl went there with his I./Jäg.Rgt. 2 BR command post. Jänkendorf remained in enemy hands. In Niesky, however, the battle by the surrounded defenders—the bulk of the Pz.Stu.Pi.Btl. BR under Hptm. Müller-Rochholz was nearing its climax. There had been no peace all night, not even for the slightly wounded. There was no letup in the mortar fire. Bringing wounded from the trench, which was only 100 to 150 meters from the command post, into the cellar with the other wounded cost further casualties. For two hours on the morning of 20 April things quieted down somewhat, and the reason why was known. The Soviets were waiting for reserves. These finally arrived in German trucks. At least one battalion of infantry was unloaded onto the street of Neu-Särchen in front of the theater. This was noticed immediately by the German side, because it was possible to see into the town along a street from the watchtower. One of the three remaining assault guns, which had already beaten off several attacks in the brush near the watchtower, was pulled back 250 meters, from where it was able to fire directly at the trucks. High-explosive shells were fired into the column. It worked. The Soviet reserves were put out of action before they could be used.

The Pz.Stu.Pi.Btl. BR's radio-equipped armored troop carrier was now in the corner of a house near the command post, with the antenna installed above on the roof of the house. There was good communication with the division. *Hauptmann* Müller-Rochholz advised by radio that he had assumed command in Niesky. The division Ic radioed back that the Soviets in their radio reports were complaining bitterly about the resistance being put up by the garrison of Niesky and demanding additional units.

In the late morning it was reported from Kreishaus that Cossacks were attacking from the forest to the south. They were almost completely wiped out by machine-guns firing from windows.

But the Soviets were also eager to stop the dying. The defenders could easily spot their attack preparations, for the Soviet officers only shouted so when they had to rally the attackers. The pioneer's recipe for this: first *Panzerfaust* from close range, then open fire with machine-guns and assault rifles. This was very effective. The Soviet attackers were stumbling over their dead from previous attacks before they could even see the defenders. The north slope of the watchtower was littered with Soviet bodies. Toward midday (20/4) someone lost his nerve. He threw his rifle away and ran down the south slope. The pioneer *Hauptmann* ran after him. They reached the fence 80 meters in front of our position on the slope at the same time. Luckily Pioneer-Müller got through the fence faster than the fleeing soldier. He was killed! He had failed to reach the Soviets, only 20 meters away in the trees. It was found that he was not one of the pioneers, but was from another unit.

In the afternoon there was an enemy attack every hour, but never on the entire front simultaneously.

At the watchtower the three assault guns sat under the command of an excellent *Oberleutnant* and waited calmly until the Soviets had worked their way up to the slope from the west. When the first reached the small pines—a stand about one meter high—the assault guns moved forward five to six meters, their barrels depressed to the maximum. The vehicles had to be in nose-down positions themselves in order to reach the enemy. When they did open fire there were explosions among the trees, followed by screams and shouts, and there was no further need for the pioneers to position more riflemen there.

The defense district commander of Niesky, who was in the houses due east of the pioneer command post with several of his people and civilians, came and asked if there would be a breakout at all. Pi-Müller promised to let him know when the time came.

At noon the pioneer doctor ran out of dressings. Whatever cloth could be found in the houses was used instead. The number of men manning the trench dropped steadily; it seemed certain that they would not be able to hold out for even another day.

The *Major* of Sturm-Rgt. 4 sat on the steps to the cellar, the cries of the wounded making him even more desperate. In the evening he told the commander of the *Brandenburg* pioneers that they were going to break out that night. Then the defense district commander, a *Luftwaffe Oberstleutnant*, came again. It was a difficult conversation, for he wanted to take along approximately 200 civilians, women and children. Müller had to refuse, for the pioneers would have to fight and could not have any women and children with them. Far behind them, yes, but not among the fighting men. Everyone was angry over this hard decision by the pioneer commander, but it was the only one possible and Müller would be proved correct.

Every detail was discussed with the *Oberleutnant* in command of the assault guns. A terrific chap! Shot-up trucks were hooked to the assault guns and towed on their rims and axles. In these were placed all the wounded, approximately 80 men. That was the safest place. By evening all the dead had been buried in spite of continuous enemy fire.

The breakout was set for two in the morning (21/4). Everyone knew what was at stake. There had to be no noise, no one was allowed to smoke, no one could fire without orders to do so.

A small Kampfgruppe was to lead the way, then the two pioneer companies under Oblt. Bank (3. Kp. had meanwhile been shared out), then the assault guns with their attached trucks, in them the wounded, and several armored troop carriers.

The breakout spot was scouted at about 01:00 hours. The route was to lead south. The small road which led 400 meters to Reichsstrasse 115 was reached without contacting the enemy. It had been strangely quiet since midnight. One might suggest that the Soviets had noticed the withdrawal and were obviously happy to have German resistance cease in this way.

It was almost 02:00 when they set out. Final volleys of fire from the trench, then everyone moved onto the road. There was one row on each side of the road, men walking silently in single file. When they finally reached Reichsstrasse 115 the assault guns could be heard approaching. The axles and rims of the attached trucks squeaked loudly and crunched on the stones.

To the right and left of the retiring pioneers cigarettes glimmered everywhere; it literally stank of Soviets, of machorka. Did they not see this unusual procession, or did they want to see? Perhaps they thought they were their own. In any case they were allowed to pass, even the trucks. And so this breakout procession finally got to a position about 300 meters north of the big intersection in the planned marching order. The *Sturmgeschütze* had joined up; four men went to the crossroads, were challenged and threw themselves down in the ditch. The Ivans opened fire. A machine-gun, deployed to guard the intersection. The Soviet muzzle flashes were visible; the four at the crossroads fired their assault rifles, a *Panzerfaust* was set off. Meanwhile other groups of pioneers outflanked the machine-gun through the woods and attacked from behind—again with a *Panzerfaust*. The crossroads was clear.

Radio message to the point: move up, crossroads clear. The assault guns were still 300 meters south of the crossroads when Soviet vehicles approached from behind. The wheelless trucks pulled over to the right. The Soviets rolled past. Also past the German assault guns, past German soldiers marching left and right of the road. The Soviets were long used to seeing captured German vehicles. Had they turned on a light—the pioneers had their fingers on the triggers.

It was already getting light when the column emerged from the forest southwest of Oedernitz. To the northeast a Soviet battery was in position. The men and pioneers, followed by the civilians, now turned off the road due south. The motorized elements drove on—there was no choice now but to go through, for German troops could already be seen south of Särchen, near Wilhelminenthal, waving them on.

Radio message to everyone: "To armored troop carriers, to assault guns with attached trucks: through! Through! German troops in front of us!" Abeam Oerernizt, on the road being used by the motorized elements, a German Opel Blitz with limbered 88-mm flak overtook the column. And since the armored troop carrier was also at full throttle, it drove side by side with it for some distance. The truck was full of Soviets. As they raced onwards both vehicles drove into a bomb crater in the middle of the road. The armored troop carrier shifted in the truest sense of the word—namely backwards. It did it! The Opel Blitz ran into the armored troop carrier, which dropped its square nose into the crater, allowing the truck to fall in. By the time the Soviets realized what was happening the third assault gun with the wounded in tow had already passed in the field to the side of the road.

Finally they reached the first German troops. They were elements of Pi.Btl. 20 of the 20. Pz.Div. The civilians also made it. Everyone had got away. The sun was slowly rising in the east when the escaped men regrouped and headed off to find quarters. They were supposed to be in Rabenthal—where there was supposed to be some BR units. All of the wounded were evacuated immediately. While the pioneers were still settling in in Rabenthal, falling into a dreamless sleep, the commander of the Pz.Stu.Pi.Btl. BR, Hptm. Müller-Rochholz, rushed to the division command post in Bischdorf to report his return. There he learned of the attack operation from the north begun that morning by the reinforced Jäg.Rgt. 1 BR in the Klitten area, and of the attack by the reinforced Jäg.Rgt. 2 BR with the Wietersheim armored group from Ullersdorf toward the south. The objective of this combined operation was to cut off the enemy forces that had broken through in the direction of Bautzen and establish a continuous defense line.

After readying Panzergruppe Wietersheim and the available heavy weapons of Jäg.Rgt. 2 BR in the area southwest of Ullersdorf, the *Jäger*, primarily those of I. Btl., advanced out of the ruined houses of southern Ullersdorf toward the north in order to break the stubborn enemy resistance in the northern part and on the commanding hill. The enemy-held hill was taken quickly with the aid of the tanks, however in northern Ullersdorf the attackers soon became bogged down before the fortified bunkers, machine-gun positions and barricaded ruins. It came down to hand-to-hand fighting, and the enemy's superior numbers soon placed the brave *Jäger* in a difficult position. For hours the battle raged in the ruins, houses and barns in the northern part of Ullersdorf, bringing the attackers heavy casualties. The enemy soon recognized the German weakness and himself went over to the attack. This forced the *Jäger* of Jäg.Rgt. 2 BR onto the defensive, which became increasingly difficult as losses mounted. As well, the fighting was hampered by heavy downpours. Finally the *Jäger* were fighting just to hold on to their own positions. It required an extreme effort to hold onto the southern edge of Ullersdorf. When the fighting finally died down in the darkness, the few survivors crawled into cellars and ruins, where they were able to dig in for the night.

On the other hand the attack by the northern group, the reinforced Jäg.Rgt. 1 BR from the Klitten area with the Pz.Korps.-Pi.Btl. 500 GD on its right, which had begun in the morning, had made significant gains.

At noon on 21 April II. Btl./Hptm. Hunold, together with two batteries of the Stu.Gesch.Brig. GD and Kampfgruppe Kappel (elements of I./1244), launched a frontal attack on Zimpel. These attack elements encountered stubborn resistance at the outskirts of the town and fierce close-quarters fighting developed. Five to seven enemy tanks in the town made things difficult, because they could only be approached with explosives and *Panzerfausts*. For while Hptm. Hunold's *Jäger* were still struggling in Zimpel, the assault guns moved in a arc around the town in the direction of Tauer in order to attack this enemy-held town, from which the enemy resistance in Zimpel was undoubtedly being nourished. Together with Oblt. Kappel's men, Hptm. Hunold succeeded in taking Zimpel and then advanced toward Tauer. The fighting was fierce and several enemy tanks were destroyed. When the Soviets recognized the threat they opened fire from every nook and cranny. The assault guns were just as active, however. Several houses went up in flames, illuminating the picture of destruction in the approaching twilight. The *Jäger* broke into the town of Tauen. Fierce close-quarters fighting broke out which eventually ended in favor of the attackers. Losses were significant. Stabsarzt Dr. Fischer had his hands full caring for the wounded in the town school. At first the wounded could not be evacuated to the rear because the Soviets had cut the north road again. Contact was restored during the night, however, and the wounded were taken out. In Tauer itself everyone prepared for all-round defense, since the situation in the Daubaner Forest was uncertain. The bulk of the Soviets had to still be there, having taken cover while it was dark.

During the day the Pz.Korps.-Pi.Btl. 500 GD, which had attacked from the Spreefurth area on Jäg.Rgt. 1 BR's right, advanced south through Halbendorf and reached the village of Guttau with elements of an assault platoon under Uffz. Gebhardt. A small force of Soviet guards was cut down or chased away. The bulk of the battalion moved through the forest toward Dauban with orders to cut the Stockteich—Malschwitz—Bautzen road, which was seen as a supply road for the advancing Soviet spearheads. This mission was accomplished. In the evening Oblt. Wendt's 2. Kp. occupied its defensive position with front facing southeast in expectation of the effects of the attack by the reinforced Jäg.Rgt. 1 BR. The headquarters of the Pz.Korps.-Pi.Btl. 500 GD also set up its command post in Dauban. There was no doubt that the advance by Jäg.Rgt. 1 BR toward the road from Stockteich was also leading to the encirclement of the Soviet group suspected in the forest, which demanded that the corps pioneers exercise extra vigilance toward the east. Throughout the night of 21-22 April there were wild shootouts, continuous unrest and constant banging in Dauban and in Guttau, caused by the surprised and fleeing Soviets who were unaware that there were German troops in Dauban.

During the night of 21-22 April the Jäg.Rgt. 1 BR (Hptm. Hunold's II. Btl.) and Kampfgruppe Kappel regrouped for another attack—this time against Förstgen, which was to be attacked early on 22 April. Forward observers from several artillery and rocket battalions arrived looking for target assignments. In terms of terrain, the only problem facing the attackers was the chain of lakes in front of Förstgen, which allowed only a narrow opening to the south. The attackers would have to strive to cover this critical area with artillery fire. This formed the basis of *Major* Bansen's plan, who left a weak group south of Tauer, with the bulk of II. Btl. and Hptm. Metzger's assault guns advancing through the forest in order to reach the northeast flank of Förstgen.

The *Jäger* and the assault guns passed through the forest unhindered,, although they were kept under a constant watch by Cossacks. II. Btl. slowly approached the town of Förstgen, which lay in a valley, while the assault guns continued on and appeared before the town almost from the southeast.

Förstgen itself was heavily occupied by the enemy; numerous tanks could be seen, while engine and track noises suggested a strong enemy presence. Hptm. Hunold reached the northeast edge of the forest at about noon and pressed for the attack. It was almost 14:30 hours when there was a heavy outburst of firing from the other end of Förstgen. The *Jäger* could be seen storming down the slope to the village. Hptm. Hunold had not wanted to wait any longer for the assault guns. The 20-mm flak fired into the town, the assault guns rolled into firing positions, and soon a wild battle was in progress. The *Jäger* were soon in the town. Several Soviet trucks and tanks sat across the village street, while the houses burned. Armor-piercing shells exploded, here and there a tank blew apart.. The assault guns in their firing positions were watchful, repeatedly striking recognized targets with their shells.

As soon as the village was entered one company advanced toward the forest's edge on the other slope to eliminate any flanking threat from there. From there the scale of the success could be seen. More than fifty enemy tanks had been knocked out or destroyed. More than 100 vehicles of all kinds were destroyed, while huge quantities of weapons, equipment, food, fuel and vehicles, the latest American types, fell into the hands of the attackers.

Those Soviets not killed or wounded fled in all directions, including west. But there, in and near Dauban, the corps pioneers barred the way, and they soon felt the effects of the attack at Förstgen.

During the afternoon of 22 April, after the sound of battle had increased in the east, several T 34s with infantry riding on them suddenly broke out of the Daubaner Forest and rolled down the road in the direction of the "Public House" at the crossroads south of the actual town of Dauban. The unit deployed there, 1. Kp./Pz.Korps.-Pi.Btl. 500 GD under Oblt. Meyer, reacted immediately and opened fire at the tanks. The Soviet infantry was soon forced to jump down, while the lone Panther attached to the company blew up the trailing T 34 from a reverse slope position. A jet of flame shot high into the air as it blew apart. But now all hell broke loose; the tank cannon barked, ammunition exploded. In no time the Soviet infantry had taken cover and opened fire on the corps pioneers. But slowly the Soviets began to lose hope, seeing their tanks being blown up one after another. The corps pioneers stood up in their holes and fired at the retreating enemy. Panic broke out and the Soviets fled in all directions.

Meanwhile, at the "Public House" at the crossroads south of Dauban, there was fierce close-quarters fighting with Soviet infantry, who after their armored carriages had been knocked out had begun firing wildly in all directions. By the time darkness was falling the situation there had been cleared up, however; the flew surviving enemy fled in all directions in the twilight.

The situation at the Daubaner Forest remained uncertain, however, as fragments of Soviet units were still suspected there. As a result, the elements of Pz.Korps.-Pi.Btl. 500 GD remained in their positions for the night of 22-23 April—expecting to make contact with Jäg.Rgt. 1 BR in the Förstgen area. This took place early on 23 April when a young *Leutnant* and several *Jäger* of the regiment arrived. There was great joy and much relating of recent events; everyone stood in a group near the public house.

Then, suddenly, submachine-gun fire; the *Leutnant* was hit and dropped to the ground. The rest immediately spread out and dragged the wounded man into the entrance of the public house. Nothing to be seen. Where had the shots come from? Soviet stragglers? But where?

Hptm. Eicke, commander of the Pz.Korps.-Pi.Btl. 500 GD, ordered the public house searched again immediately, especially the cellar and the upper floor. An *Unteroffizier* and several corps pioneers set out to do so. After a few minutes there was a wild shoot-out in the barn—so there were stragglers. Supported by a pioneer, the *Unteroffizier*, who had been wounded in the arm, staggered down the steps of the neighboring house and reported that he had suddenly been fired on while searching the loft. In order to prevent further casualties, the remaining personnel left the public house and at first waited to see what would happen. The house was then encircled at a distance of 100 meters and set on fire with *Panzerfaust* rounds. A Russian staggered out. When questioned by the interpreter he said that when the tanks attacked he and four men had jumped into the house and had waited for an opportune moment to escape. The other Soviet soldiers had met their ends in the burning house.

Meanwhile the battalion set about inspecting the booty in trucks and weapons and supplementing its vehicle complement with the latest American models. Jeeps, heavy Studebakers, every one that was usable was requisitioned and loaded with booty.

Soon an order arrived from corps to advance west through Guttau and reconnoiter toward Sdier. Because of the completely uncertain situation north of this line the battalion turned north toward Dreiwitz, southeast of Lohsa.

The reinforced Jäg.Rgt. 1 BR also received orders on the afternoon of 23 April, to rejoin the division and seek contact to the south, in the direction of the autobahn. The initial march destination was Grödnitz, northwest of Weissenberg. The regiment's vehicles moved south into the approaching darkness, through enemy-occupied territory, uncertain of the location of the Soviet units. But all went well; during the night of 23-24 April the regimental headquarters took up station in Grödnitz Castle. Weissenberg, on the other hand, was enemy-occupied; this was found out the hard way, when several trucks from the train drove unsuspectingly into the town and were fired on by the Soviets there. Then orders were received from the division Ia for 24 April. In collaboration with Jäg.Rgt. 2 BR (which was in the Buchholz-Margaretenhof and Maltitz area), an enveloping attack was to be made against the apparently strongly-held village of Weissenberg and the enemy forces there destroyed. They apparently intended to break out of the German encirclement to the east.

In Weissenberg itself, which could be seen easily from the hills, there were countless enemy tanks, guns and vehicles, all standing close together on the village streets and scarcely able to move. Assault guns and heavy weapons were immediately moved into position, and the artillery opened fire. Almost from off the move, the *Jäger*, spurred to hurry, went to the attack against Weissenberg. The battalions of Jäg.Rgt. 2 BR, on the other hand, initially remained in their blocking positions near Buchholz and Maltitz in order to prevent the enemy from fleeing to the east and southeast. The right wing of this formation, I./Jäg.Rgt. 2 BR, joined the attack movements of Jäg.Rgt. 1 BR coming from the northeast and likewise stormed into Weissenberg. Panic broke out among the Soviets in the village as it came under attack from all sides; they all tried to break out in some direction, especially to the southeast. They fled in droves across an open plain, the only way out of Weissenberg. Quadruple flak, machineguns and mortars fired everything they had. Hundreds of panye wagons raced across the plain, overturned and broke apart, their wreckage littering the field. Hundreds of enemy infantry were mown down. Finally the *Jäger* charged into the village and took hundreds of prisoners. Another huge haul of fuel and weapons fell into their hands. Almost 1,500 vehicles were counted in and around the village. The Soviet formation, about the size of a division, had been wiped out.

But even this action, one of the last successful attacks, did nothing to alter the overall situation in the Bautzen area. The Soviets had entered the city itself with strong forces; approaching from the northeast, their northern attack spearheads were already northwest. The Soviet advance northwest of Bautzen was again threatening to encircle the German units still northeast of the city and force them to retreat without a battle.

Orders came for the units to move south around Bautzen and assemble west of the city, and in the planned German attack by several divisions against Bautzen to continue our own attack to the north.

After a brief rest and refit, on 25 April the two companies of the Pz.Stu.Pi.Btl. BR under Hptm. Müller-Rochholz went into position north of Prischwitz, north of the Bautzen—Dresden autobahn. The battalion command post was in Solschwitz. The battalion had orders to prepare to attack north towards Storcha—Loga (Storcha was a commanding line of hills on which there was a well-known white church) together with Panzergruppe Wietersheim on 26 April. The same order was waiting for Jäg.Rgt. 2 BR, which on 25 April was directed into the Schmochtitz area in a lone drive around Bautzen (arrived there during the night of 25-26 April).

In Schmochtitz itself the enemy was already in the manor house. The arriving *Jäger* of I./Jäg.Rgt. 2 BR drove them out again and chased them away.

The attack to the north was ordered to commence during the night of 25-26 April, precisely at 01:00 hours; there was little time left for preparations.

The plan called for the 20. and 21. Pz.Div. to attack the city itself from the area south of Bautzen. The Panzer-Grenadier Division *Brandenburg* on the left wing would advance north and cut off the flanks of the enemy force attacking towards Dresden. Associated with this attack was the hope that contact could be made with our units still along the Spree west of Königswartha, including the Fsch.Pz.Div. 1 HG, thus establishing a new, continuous defense line in a general north-south direction.

In the course of this attack operation the Jäg.Rgt. 2 BR moved off on the right, the Pz.Stu.Pi.Btl. BR bolstered by Panzergruppe Wietersheim on the left, and Jäg.Rgt. 1 BR, initially following the left wing, to the north. On the right the *Jäger* advanced steadily, although there was fierce fighting for the heavily-fortified hill positions, through Klein- and Gross-Brösern toward Milkwitz, which was finally retaken towards evening. There was heavy enemy traffic out of Bautzen north on Reichsstrasse 96 in the direction of Kleinwartha.

In Schmochtitz itself the enemy was already in the manor house. The arriving *Jäger* of I./Jäg.Rgt. 2 BR drove them out again and chased them away.

The attack to the north was ordered to commence during the night of 25-26 April, precisely at 01:00 hours; there was little time left for preparations.

The plan called for the 20. and 21. Pz.Div. to attack the city itself from the area south of Bautzen. The Panzer-Grenadier Division *Brandenburg* on the left wing would advance north and cut off the flanks of the enemy force attacking towards Dresden. Associated with this attack was the hope that contact could be made with our units still along the Spree west of Königswartha, including the Fsch.Pz.Div. 1 HG, thus establishing a new, continuous defense line in a general north-south direction.

In the course of this attack operation the Jäg.Rgt. 2 BR moved off on the right, the Pz.Stu.Pi.Btl. BR bolstered by Panzergruppe Wietersheim on the left, and Jäg.Rgt. 1 BR, initially following the left wing, to the north. On the right the *Jäger* advanced steadily, although there was fierce fighting for the heavily-fortified hill positions, through Klein- and Gross-Brösern toward Milkwitz, which was finally retaken towards evening. There was heavy enemy traffic out of Bautzen north on Reichsstrasse 96 in the direction of Kleinwartha.

On the left the assault pioneers under Hptm. Müller-Rochholz advanced through Dreikretscham towards the towns of Loga, Storcha and Weidlitz, in which enemy troops, mainly Poles under Soviet command, tried to hold. There were truly huge numbers of enemy soldiers, who had positioned themselves in barns, on hills and in the bushes. They were basically weak, however, and with the help of the Wietersheim group's tanks they were blasted out of their positions and put to flight. The 1. Kp. under Oblt. Michaelis, which was equipped with aircraft machine-guns mounted on armored troop carriers, sprayed the enemy positions and forced the last hold-outs to flee. Numerous dead lay on the battlefield. Accompanied by the tanks, the company's armored troop carriers advanced irresistibly to the north. More than 600 prisoners were assembled in a meadow north of Dreikretscham.

It was vital to exploit the situation there. T 34s fired into the flanks of the attacking *Jäger* of 2. Regiment from Loga and Luga. The pioneers immediately continued their attack against Loga to eliminate this threat from the flank. Pannewitz was taken, Loga fell into our hands, the Poles ran like hares. The pioneers had the bit between their teeth. 1. Kp. advanced from the southwest toward Krinitz, 2. Kp. from the south toward Luga. Luga was taken after an half-hour of house-to-house fighting, however enemy resistance, especially from Stalin and T 34 tanks in the woods north of Luga, slowed progress. Preparations were made to resume the attack the next day. Meanwhile Jäg.Rgt. 1 BR had been moved up from the left (west) and sent into action from Neschwitz (the bulk of II. Btl./1 under Hptm. Hunold) farther west into Lomske and the surrounding woods. The enemy's point of main effort was now near Neschwitz. The enemy was determined to force a crossing of the Schwarzwasser in order to continue his attack to the southwest from there. There was soon fierce fighting for the castle and castle park, especially at the northern exit from Neschwitz, and these changed hands several times. This critical point, which offered a view of Reichsstrasse 96, became the focus of the battle. Hptm. Hunold and his *Jäger* were soon in a difficult position.

In recognition of the situation at Neschwitz, early on 27 April the Pz.Stu.Pi.Btl. BR was pulled out of the Luga area and its positions taken over by Jäg.Rgt. 2 BR. The assault pioneers were sent via Neupuschwitz to the forest southeast of Doberschütz. Doberschütz itself, held by weak enemy forces, was overrun and held by the pioneers.

Further mission for the assault pioneers: attack strongly-held Casslau in order to establish a continuous defense line to the northwest to the German strongpoint still holding in Nausslitz. Reconnaissance towards Casslau revealed that the town was crammed with T 34s, Stalin IIs and the latest Soviet super-heavy assault guns. Prisoners stated that the bulk of the Soviet 22nd Guards Tank Brigade was there with orders to hold at all costs.

The first attack by the pioneers failed. A second at about 22:00 hours on 27 April, begun with the attached Sick Battalion 1244, reached the first houses of Casslau, but was then stopped by heavy defensive fire.

The establishing of contact with the 20. Pz.Div.'s armored group in Nausslitz early on 28 April resulted in a new plan. A combined attack from Nausslitz and from the south was to place the town of Casslau in our hands. Meanwhile the fierce battle for Neschwitz went on. In the afternoon the enemy broke into the northern part of the town. Mistakenly assuming that all of Neschwitz was in enemy hands, artillery of the Fsch.Pz.Div. 1 HG fired into the town, seriously wounding the commander of II./Jäg.Rgt. 1 BR, Hptm. Hunold. The *Hauptmann's* entire lower jaw was blown away; he was recovered, still alive, and transported to the rear. The *Jäger* were stunned, but they continued to hold the town. Rittmeister Sandmeyer, formerly of the Pz.A.A. BR, was brought forward to assume command of II./Jäg.Rgt. 1.

Meanwhile the bulk of Jäg.Rgt. 2 had been relieved from its positions on both sides of Milkwitz and had initially been moved into the forest south of Casslau. Elements were inserted into the positions in the Doberschütz area next to Jäg.Rgt. 1 BR.

In the meantime, at about 10:00 hours on 28 April, the assault pioneers under Pi-Müller attacked strongly-defended Casslau for the third time. Under the protection of their artillery, the two assault pioneer companies advanced from the south, followed by the men of Sick Battalion 1244. Meanwhile the valiant men of the 20. Pz.Div.'s armored group, accompanied by Wespe and Hummel self-propelled guns, were approaching from the west, almost the northwest. Casslau was entered within fifteen minutes. More than 15 enemy tanks were destroyed. Numerous dead and wounded lay among the houses, the survivors fled down the slope to the north and northeast, pursued by machine-gun fire.

Casslau was immediately prepared for defense. The 20. Pz.Div.'s armored group was withdrawn, and the sector to and including Nausslitz was taken over. A battery of the He.Flak-Abt. BR was subordinated. East of Casslau contact was established with I./Jäg.Rgt. 2 BR and a joint defense of the achieved line coordinated. Command post in Doberschütz, which at about 15:00 hours was bombed by Soviet aircraft. Fw. Fischer of the assault pioneer battalion staff was killed, Lt. Puls was seriously wounded, several men of the staff were fatally hit. At the same time the enemy began launching heavy counterattacks with numerous tanks near Nausslitz, which was held by Lt. Koch and his pioneers. Lt. Koch defended the village desperately, but was finally driven out by superior force. The assault pioneers dug in again at the edge of the forest. Tanks of Panzergruppe Wietersheim were dispatched there but were unable to help; Nausslitz was in enemy hands. Our counterattacks failed; waves of T 34s prevented any approach. While the fighting was still raging in Neschwitz (II./Jäg.Rgt. 1 BR), Casslau (I./Jäg.Rgt. 2 BR) and Nausslitz (Pz.Stu.Pi.Btl. BR), in the command posts preparations were already being made for the Pz.Gren. Div. BR to be relieved. The division was to be relieved by elements of the 269. I.D. during the night of 28-29 April and transferred into the Dresden—Meissen area for a new mission. The orders were hastily issued to the units, the trains had already left for the new area, guides were assigned to direct the relieving units. But the men, the *Branden-burgers*, were pleased by this unexpected relief, for they could expect at least several days of rest.

Still under cover of darkness, the march columns moved to the autobahn and drove to their assigned quarters. The troops were quartered in the area north and northeast of Dresden, where they rested. Finally a chance to sleep, to restore order, to regroup. Meanwhile, new orders were received from the Pz.Korps GD command post in Moritzburg. The deployment in the Dresden area had been cancelled, instead the Panzer-Grenadier Division *Brandenburg* was to leave the corps for transport by rail to Czechoslovakia to Army Group Schörner. Further details to follow. Once again preparations were made to entrain; the first elements were to board on Monday, 30 April. Entraining stations: Radeberg and Klotzsche. All the units were still in their quarters on the morning of 1 May, although these were close to the stations where loading was to begin later that day.

It was reported that the Supreme Commander of the German Armed Forces, Adolf Hitler, had died in Berlin on the evening of 30 April. The men were mustered to receive the news, and as per orders their oath was transferred to Grand Admiral Doenitz.

The men dwelled on this news; they knew that the Pz.Gren.Div. *Brandenburg* was still intact, in fighting trim, ready for any mission. But where? What for? The Americans were at the Elbe, the Soviets in Berlin and farther north at the Elbe. Only in Czechoslovakia were there German troops, under *Generalfeldmarschall* Schörner. The last organized German resistance seemed to be taking place there and that was where the *Brandenburgers* were being sent. Incidentally, the chief-of-staff of Army Group Schörner was Gen.Lt. von Natzmer, Ia of the Pz.Gren.Div. *Großdeutschland* in 1942-43.

With the departure of the Pz.Gren.Div. *Brandenburg* from the Pz.Korps GD on 1 May, the corps lost its last GD unit. It was left only the few GD corps troops as well as the Pz.Korps.-Pi.Btl. 500 GD under Hptm. Eicke, the Feldersatz-Btl. BR and the Korps-San.Kp. GD, all of which were grouped in the Dresden area.

After Hitler's plan to carry out a relief attack toward Berlin with all of the scraped-together elements of the 4. Pz.Armee in the area between the Elbe and the Mulde came to nothing before it ever got started, only the Pz.Korps.-Pi.Btl. 500 GD having conducted several reconnaissance advances to the north, the Pz.Korps GD with the foreign units, Kampfgruppen and alert units under its command initially remained in this area without being pressured by the enemy. After reaching the Elbe, and in some places crossing and advancing toward the Mulde, the enemy initially made no further moves to attack the northern flank of the 4. Pz.Armee, which was held by the Pz.Korps GD north and northwest of Dresden. The Americans had also halted in the Chemnitz and Leipzig area, so that the line of security was under no serious pressure at first.

The absence of further enemy activity to the south caused the 4. Pz.Armee to withdraw its northern wing back towards the Erz Mountains in order to occupy better defensive positions at the edge of this natural obstacle. With this the last GD troops of the Pz.Korps GD began their move south. The countryside resembled an abandoned army camp; columns on foot, unfamiliar units, civilians—all moving around aimlessly, with no guiding hand to intervene in the beginning chaos. The roads were clogged with countless vehicles, making it difficult for columns to proceed. But the soldiers picked up refugees whenever possible and took them along in their vehicles.

No further halts were made until the foot of the Elbsandstein Mountains and later on the top of this chain of mountains. There an attempt was made to erect barricades, prepare roads for demolition, build defensive positions. The Pz.Korps.-Pi.Btl. 500 GD completed its final missions there, principally to cover the retreat to the south. Even though there was no direct enemy contact, its columns came under repeated air attacks which inflicted casualties in these final days. A *Feldwebel* who took a motorcycle-sidecar combination to scout off the main road was shot when he entered what was supposedly an enemy-free village.

For the last days of the war the Pz.Korps GD's command post was located in Tetschen-Bidenbach. After a futile attempt to rejoin the Pz.Gren.Div. BR in the Olmütz area, the Feldersatz-Btl. BR likewise took up station outside this town, while the Korps-San.Kp. GD was quartered nearby in a spa hotel.

On or about 6 May there were signs of disintegration, brought about by the renewed attack on the part of Soviet units along the Upper Elbe towards the south and southeast in order to reach the rear of Army Group Center and cut it off from the west. While in some cases this generated panic, the few GD units held firm in the Tetschen-Bodenbach area. As before, they remained firmly in the hands of their commanders. There was discipline and order there. The men remained together and trusted their officers, none joined those taking flight.

Finally, on the evening of 8 May, the surrender was announced, not via senior posts, but by radio, after communications between Army Group Center and the 4. Pz.Armee were severed. The order for everyone was to stay together to the extent possible, cross the Elbe to the west and try to reach American-held territory.

Carrying out this last order was much more difficult than was thought. On both sides of the Elbe the Soviets drove south against negligible resistance, seeking the retreating German units and refugees desperately trying to reach the west bank of the Elbe in time. Only a few crossings remained; it was the goal of everyone to reach them ahead of the Soviets. During the night of 8-9 May the Korps-San.Kp. GD tried to reach Karlsbad. At about 05:00 hours, however, it could go no farther than the north exit from Aussig, since all through streets were blocked by columns, refugees, burning vehicles and overturned wagons. From the bushes Czech partisans fired into the vehicles on the road. Panic and chaos dictated the events. As an unarmed medical unit, the Korps-San.Kp. GD finally managed to get through in the direction of Lobositz. But barricades of all kinds erected during the night by partisans forced the company to make numerous detours. It slowly became obvious that continuing on as a column was hopeless. Off the main roads the Korps-San.Kp. GD was assembled once again, each member of the company was handed his service record book and released to make his way to the west alone or as a member of a small group. Everyone was issued food, dry rations and tobacco from the stores. A final handshake and then they set off, alone, in groups, on foot. Some of the wounded were placed in the care of the local inhabitants.

Each of these men of the Korps-San.Kp. GD now left the community of which he had been a member for years into a lone fate which had been forced upon him by conditions.

This was also the bitterest hour for the Pz.Korps.-Pi.Btl. 500 GD, which was quartered in various towns when the news of the surrender was released. Here, too, the officers sought to keep their men, their platoons and companies together, and together with them escape their fate. All

417

unserviceable or unnecessary vehicles were destroyed, just enough were kept to transport the men. Small arms and machine-guns were retained, personal baggage was kept to a minimum.

Then they set out in one long column, slipping into the numerous lines of vehicles on the main road. The pioneer column became separated in the process, the leading elements were split off from the main body. They drove ever southwards, hoping to find a crossing over the Elbe still free of the enemy. Fewer and fewer vehicles followed the leaders, separated from the command and left to their own devices.

And so the Pz.Korps.-Pi.Btl. 500 GD, which had set out together, became separated in the last hours—on 9 May 1945, Alone and in small groups the men sought their way home, out of the threat of encirclement by the Soviets.

The GD corps headquarters itself initially remained in Tetschen-Bodenbach. After the last orders were issued at about 21:00 hours on 8 May it, too, disbanded, after first destroying all documents. It headed in the direction of Karlsbad. Czech partisans were already everywhere, their barricades, check points and firing making fast driving impossible. Everywhere they met German soldiers with white armbands, without weapons, also members of the disbanded Vlasov Army and refugees.

Finally a halt was called off to the side of the road. Civilian clothes were obtained in a village, the vehicles were destroyed—the march to the west was continued on foot.

Chapter 2
The Meadow of Death near Neu-Petershain
The End of the Führer-Begleit-Division in the Spremberg Pocket

The thunderclap with which the Soviet artillery opened the great offensive along the Lausitzer Neiße on the morning of 16 April fizzled out, at least in front of the German Muskau bridgehead. Expecting a Soviet attack, the units inside the bridgehead had abandoned it during the night of 15-16 April. At this time the *Führer-Begleit-Division* was positioned east of Spremberg as the operational reserve of the 4. Pz.Armee, with a thin security screen roughly in a line Trebendorf—Halbendorf—Gross-Düben, command post in Muna Schleife. The wide-ranging enemy artillery fire struck as deep as the division's rest areas—a foretaste of the events to come.

Early that morning the units of the *Führer-Begleit-Division*, which had been at constant readiness for the past 24 hours in expectation of the Soviet offensive, were placed on alert. The assigned patrols of the division's reconnaissance company immediately set off for the front at the Neiße, in order to scout the enemy's probable focal point and observe the behavior of the stationary units. Since the start of the Soviet barrage fire their will to resist had been badly shaken, in some cases shattered, and their communications with the rear severed. Retreating soldiers, RAD groups and train vehicles soon showed that some of our positions had already been abandoned. It could only be a matter of hours before the first Soviets appeared on the rear communications roads.

The FBD's radio station received running reports from its patrols and gave the division command a complete picture of the situation up front—but it left it increasingly uncertain as to where our own counterattack focal point should be. Soon the radio messages were mixed with situation reports which spoke of enemy advance, waves of enemy tanks, of endless panye columns.

Everything suggested that the Soviets had breached the entire line and that the German defense had been eliminated except for isolated nests of resistance. How could it be any different, with hastily formed, poorly equipped infantry units in widely-spaced strongpoints facing a massive enemy force of heavy artillery, infantry and tanks? It truly was the last reserve which was assembled there on the Oder—Neiße line to face the expected enemy offensive.

Now this last reserve was on the run, unrestrained, interested only in saving its own life.

By the evening of that first day in the area east of Spremberg, the *Führer-Begleit-Division* had contact with the enemy all along its hastily improvised defense line, giving it no time to organize a counterattack. It was already practically tied down everywhere. Our defense had collapsed much too quickly, the enemy's tanks had already appeared in the division's rest area. By evening the enemy artillery and Stalin Organs had already reached the town of Schleife and set it on fire. The first close-quarters fighting was already in progress with the westwards-streaming enemy.

The situation remained completely uncertain until well into the night, especially the location of the enemy spearheads. It could only be assumed that the stubborn resistance in the area east of Schleife had led them to outflank this area, especially in the north. Armored patrols reported that to the south Weisswasser was still in our hands. But for how long?

During the night radio messages were received imploring the division to hold at any cost.

At first light on 17 April the patrols were sent out again and these merely confirmed the suspicion that the enemy was long past our positions, especially in the north, and was advancing west. In the southeast there was heavy fighting for Weisswasser; it had to be assumed that the city would be abandoned sometime on the 17th. Recognizing the threatening situation facing his division, namely encirclement, *General* Remer regrouped his forces, reinforcing his northern flank and extending it to the west. Remer stayed at his command post until the evening of that day; however, as darkness was falling he abandoned it with enemy infantry less than 2 000 meters away and a further threat obvious from the rear left. His new command post was on the Eichberg, in the forest right beside the Weisswasser—Spremberg rail line. This area, too, was already under enemy artillery fire, and the situation in the Muskau forest was uncertain. Officers, non-commissioned officers and groups of infantry from other units, part of the stationary force at the front, began arriving at the FBD's command post in larger numbers. They joined any unit that still felt strong enough to offer organized resistance to the advancing enemy. Weisswasser was about to be abandoned, with the enemy now advancing west through the forest south of the town. But Remer's division continued to hold its positions on both sides of Schleife, repulsing every enemy attack.

During the night of 18-19 April at the command post of the *Führer-Begleit-Division* there were heated arguments between the Kampfgruppe and division commanders arriving there and Remer. The former tried to convince him that they were encircled, that the enemy was long since in their rear, that they were running the danger of losing communications with the west. Finally, impressed by these arguments, but primarily to get his division out of this encirclement—but contrary to his orders to hold at all costs—Remer finally gave the order to move position into the area due west of Spremberg. The correctness of this decision was underlined by the report at noon on 19 April that the enemy had broken through a battalion of paratroopers just brought in and had cut the Hoyerswerda—Spremberg road. There was already heavy fighting in progress for Trattendorf, while the town of Spremberg was still in our hands.

Spremberg was under heavy enemy air attack; the city was in flames.

All units of the *Führer-Begleit-Division* prepared for all-round defense in their new positions due west of Spremberg in anticipation of renewed enemy attacks following the capture of Spremberg.

Meanwhile, a growing number of reports were being received that the enemy had already reached the Cottbus—Drebkau—Senftenberg road in a sweeping envelopment and was advancing southwest on it. Other enemy groupings were southwest of Spremberg advancing on Senftenberg. But *General* Remer received orders to hold in the new line with all available means as a counterattack by the SS divisions "Das Reich" and "Frundsberg" had been initiated to reopen the Senftenberg—Spremberg road. The men held out in spite of fierce enemy artillery fire, sustaining heavy casualties, in the hope that by holding they were lending support to our counterattack from the southwest.

In the evening, with the *Führer-Begleit-Division* unable to see any effect from our counterattack, which had barely got started, *General* Remer assembled all available unit commanders and officers. He informed them, as well as the officers of foreign divisions who were present, that they would have to maintain the strictest discipline now that they were encircled in a small area and that joint action was their only possible way out of this encirclement.

The heavy forest fighting of 20 April continued unabated throughout the night. The state of the troops, who did their duty without knowing the situation in which they were in, was bad.

At about 09:00 hours on 21 April 1945 a radio message was received from 4. Pz.Armee: breakout to the west. The unit commanders were quickly informed and two Kampfgruppen were formed for the breakout. The Soviets attacked with tanks from all sides while preparations for this operation were still under way. The situation became untenable, and the breakout to the southwest began sooner than desired. It was to initially proceed through the forest in the direction of Kausche, then on to Neu-Petershain to the Cottbus—Senftenberg road. Secret files and documents were destroyed. It was a matter of life and death.

The entire march route of the *Führer-Begleit-Division* lay under heavy artillery and mortar fire; the division first had to fight its way to Kausche through difficult wooded terrain.

Finally, in the afternoon, Kausche was taken against fierce enemy resistance. But the men of the *Führer-Begleit-Division*, supported by only a few tanks and armored vehicles (fuel was in short supply, and more and more armored vehicles were left behind and had to be blown up; as well there were heavy losses due to enemy action), fought in the knowledge that only a forceful breakthrough from the pocket offered even a slight chance for them to escape alive. By evening the armored spearhead reached Neu-Petershain and gained a foothold there. Its situation was more than ticklish, however, since the Soviet were already using this main road as a supply road and one column after another was heading for Neu-Petershain.

Neu-Petershain was evacuated during the night on account of the untenable situation there, and the Kampfgruppen of the *Führer-Begleit-Division* withdrew into the woods northeast of Neu-Peterhain to wait for morning. The Ivans, well aware of the desperate situation facing this German Kampfgruppe, were everywhere. They were intent on grinding it down with concentrated Stalin Organ, artillery, mortar and anti-tank fire from all sides.

There in the wood between Neu-Petershain and Kausche, both long since in enemy hands, the *Führer-Begleit-Division* fought its last action.

On that night of 21-22 April a war council was held in a lonely forest hut. Generals Harmel, Jolasse—both leaders of infantry Kampf-gruppen—and *General* Remer of the FBD decided that Remer and the bulk of his division should lead a breakout to the southwest on the morning of 22 April. The remaining units would screen this breakout and as soon as the spearhead was through follow at once. This was the last chance, especially since Remer had only a few tanks and armored vehicles and little fuel left with which to carry out the breakthrough.

Everything was prepared in the darkness. The soldiers were briefed to follow the armored spearhead in small groups, to load the wounded on to the remaining vehicles and to try and get their weapons and vehicles out of the encirclement. The mist and darkness had still not risen when the enemy began pounding the wood with heavy artillery and mortar fire.

The Meadow of Death
Oblt. Arnold, O4/FBD

During the last years of the war I often had a strange dream.

I dreamed of a large, gently rising meadow, covered in flowers, spanned by a sky of unusual purity.

I stood before it lost in thought, not knowing what the flowers meant.

A strange, indescribable feeling enveloped me. Then I woke up.

22 April 1945. It was the hour between day and night, when a filmy mist spread itself over nature like a diaphanous screen and the light of day, growing ever stronger, pushed back the darkness.

I stood at the edge of a small wood and peered across to Neu-Petershain, where the Russians were just bringing two anti-tank guns into position.

We had already been in the town during the night and had met no significant resistance.

Then on orders of the command we had pulled back into this wood, where we now stood assembled with our combat vehicles in a very small area.

Our advance road led through the forest toward Neu-Petershain.

Five-hundred meters separated us from the town, whose farmsteads stood out ever more sharply from the brightening sky. General Remer ordered an 88-mm flak to go into position and open fire on the anti-tank gun position.

No one knew exactly what was supposed to happen now. There was no communication with higher command. There was a great deal of confusion.

The gun had just reached the edge of the forest when there were several flashes in quick succession over at the edge of the town. Instinctively I took cover.

The first shot was too short, the second struck the tractor, which immediately burst into flames, and the third knocked out the gun itself.

The driver of the tractor, who was killed instantly, was tossed into the ditch by the blast of the exploding shell, while a member of the gun crew lay writhing in pain on the asphalt with a shattered leg and frightful burns.

Everyone else had suffered more or less serious wounds.

I wanted to traverse the seventy meters to recover the seriously wounded; but I did not get far, for suddenly there were bullets whizzing about me. The Russians were spraying the edge of the forest and the burning tractor with machine-gun fire. The seriously wounded man was suddenly still. He must have been fatally hit. At the same time hellish mortar fire began falling on the entire wood. I dashed back into the forest, where our armored troop carriers and tanks were sitting and there I encountered Geisberg, Remer and the others, who had sought cover among the vehicles.

"Wilhelm, the shit has started," I called to Geisberg. He nodded his head, he was strangely bright. We had experienced many terrible hours together in the last three years. But so? I still did not know him!

Nevertheless, we both knew well enough what a frightful situation we were in.

But let ourselves be taken prisoner by the Russians?

Never!

We would rather blow ourselves up!

We could not retreat, for the village at our back, where we had forced a breakthrough yesterday in heavy fighting and where my armored troop carrier had been knocked out twice in quick succession, had been reoccupied by the Russians during the night.

And we lacked the necessary ammunition, but especially the fuel, with which to make a frontal attack against Neu-Petershain, which was likewise heavily defended by anti-tank weapons. We therefore had only one possibility of getting out of this witch's cauldron.

We would have to try and break out over the large meadow to the south.

That would cost blood, a great deal of blood, for the meadow was flanked by these two towns to the east and west.

The mortar fire grew steadily in intensity. Ricochets whizzed just over our heads. Branches broke. Wounded cried out.

After a brief conference the generals decided in favor of the breakout across the meadow.

Soon afterwards I was with Geisberg at the southern edge of the forest. Before us several hundred grenadiers, armored troop carriers and tanks had already set off across the meadow. Mortar shells fell among them and among the vehicles. Several tanks and armored troop carriers were already burning. On the left a tank was stuck in a marshy spot. It was hit, caught fire, while the crew bailed out. From the east and west the tracers of the anti-tank and machine-gun ammunition reached out for the grenadiers and vehicles like long, illuminated fingers.

Dead lay strewn all around. Wounded staggered, screaming; more and more vehicles were knocked out, human bodies whirled through the air, shattered, burned. A frightful scene!

And the breakout had only just started!

It was all or nothing!

But it didn't matter; we had to get through! A thought flashed through my mind: God, have mercy on us!

Geisberg lay beside me. An armored troop carrier pulled up behind us. Half turning, I saw General Remer standing inside. The engine roared, then the vehicle moved forward.

I bit my lip. We waited a second, then suddenly we were already 30 meters into the meadow, 30 of the 600 we would have to cover to reach the edge of the forest on the opposite side.

We worked our way forward in stages. The air around us was filled with the hiss of machine-gun bullets, anti-tank rounds howled, heavy mortar rounds detonated with a sharp, dry crack. Splinters whizzed past.

The fire grew ever more intense.

It was hell!

I had regained my old composure; the horror of before was gone. My body was like a machine being driven forward.

Seconds later I was lying in a foul, water-filled trench. Geisberg lay beside me, breathing heavily.

I looked to the right and to the left, from where the tracer was hissing towards us.

Wilhelm was anxious; he jumped up.

"Wilhelm, don't expose yourself," I called to him. But he didn't hear and raced on.

Soon he was about 50 meters away from me. Then I couldn't see him any more. I worked my way farther forward in short dashes. To my right, about 15 meters in front of me, someone jumped up. He appeared to be an Unteroffizier. Then, suddenly, a shell fell right beside him.

As I dropped I saw the Unteroffizier fall. Splinters whizzed past, dangerously close.

I should probably have called out.

The entire meadow was littered with dead, wounded and burning combat vehicles.

An armored troop carrier carrying women and children was hit. Bodies whirled through the air.

I ran on.

In front of me someone fell in the tracer from a burst of machine-gun fire. He pulled his pistol from its holster, placed it against his forehead and collapsed, while a fine, gray cloud of smoke dissipated over his body.

Through the smoke I saw General Jolasse beside me trying to jump onto an armored troop carrier which was overtaking us. He failed; he slid, fell, got up again and hurried on.

In his right hand he held a thick walking stick.

My lungs felt as if they must burst. Laboriously I worked my way forward, passing shattered bodies, tripped over something, pressed myself close to the ground.

Anything else, just don't get wounded on this damned meadow, I thought.

I summoned all my strength, dashed onwards again, expecting to be hit and killed at any minute. The blood pounded in my temples.

And all around me the air hummed and buzzed.

Death reached out for me with glowing fingers!

Lie down—lie down and sleep; no, I mustn't do that!

I raced on towards the edge of the forest. Forty meters to go.

In front of me a shallow ditch. I threw myself in, crawled forward, got up again and with the last of my strength I dashed to the forest. There I sank to the ground, exhausted, shells bursting in the treetops above me.

The meadow was behind me now.

"Medic, medic," someone called in a curious, high-pitched voice,

It was the first thing I heard again with certainty. I stood up and saw a young, wounded SS man coming toward me.

425

His right sleeve was torn and bloody. His face was encrusted with blood.

But he wasn't bleeding any more, and he did not appear to be wounded very seriously.

Since I had no bandages with me, I took him with me a way toward the west.

I followed the tracks of an armored troop carrier, which had probably headed into the undergrowth in the same direction a short time before. After about 150 meters the forest thinned out and soon I had reached the western edge.

Dismayed, I stood and stared at the meadow which spread out in front of the forest to the south. The same spectacle was being played out as on the one I had just crossed.

This meadow also lay under very heavy anti-tank, mortar and machine-gun fire.

Grenadiers and a few armored troop carriers were trying to break out to the south.

Almost all of the tanks had been knocked out in the first meadow. There were dead everywhere, armored troop carriers burned.

The meadow before me was as flat as a board, with no cover, rising slightly at the other end, which bordered a forest.

I hopped into a foxhole, as this wood was also under mortar fire.

Suddenly Oberfeldwebel Schneider appeared next to me.

"Herr Oberleutnant, I've been hit in the ass!" he called to me. I asked him if he could still walk.

He said that he could.

I walked along the edge of the forest. Fifty meters farther south I came upon Lt. Jochen Friedrich of the pioneer battalion. We decided to cross the meadow together, and a little later we worked our way forward in stages. Meanwhile, all hell seemed to have broken loose around us again.

I consciously stayed away from the main body of grenadiers, since the fire was heaviest where they were moving forward en masse.

We took turns advancing. Once Friedrich was in front of me, then I was at the front again.

Our breath came in whistles, our legs refused to go on; we stumbled, fell, got up again and staggered on towards the distant edge of the forest.

Some time later, it seemed to me like hours, we reached a field planted with clover.

Exhausted, we pressed our glowing faces into the cooling mass of leaves. All the while shells and bullets whizzed and howled overhead. My left leg hurt badly. I didn't know if I had been wounded and I cautiously bent my knee. I could still move it; that was the main thing.

And then we got up and ran again. How many times now?

I don't know.

How slowly the time passed! Had we been in this meadow for hours, or was it only minutes?

I don't know!

We were still about 30 meters from the edge of the forest. We pressed ourselves close to the earth and gathered our strength for the last dash. Heart and lungs seemed ready to burst.

I went first—and collapsed.

Seconds later Friedrich was lying beside me.

"Are you wounded, Herr Oberleutnant?" he asked.

"No, leave me here—I can't go on," I replied. What had happened to my left leg? The pain was almost unbearable, although I could still bend it.

I didn't care any more.

I wanted to sleep, lie and sleep, nothing but sleep! Then Friedrich grabbed my arm; he pulled me up and dragged me to the edge of the forest, where we both finally collapsed. Behind us in the meadow the work of destruction went on.

I do not know how long we lay there like that.

Friedrich was the first to regain his strength.

"What do you have on your coat?" he asked suddenly.

Small blood-red bits of flesh and fibers were stuck to my right side. Human flesh, I think.

I tore off my coat and threw it away.

It shook me; I wiped my face with my hand.

Hours after the event had passed, we met General Remer in a large forest. He was resting there with several survivors.

Obergefreiter Nax informed me that Oberleutnant Geisberg had been killed.

Nax had called to him, but he lay outstretched in the short grass, his face half turned to the earth, not moving.

His tunic was drenched in blood.

He must have been dead!

That was almost two years ago. But I cannot forget the events of that 22 April 1945, which for so many soldiers was the day they died. I think of the dream again. Perhaps what had once been only a dream had become reality.

Perhaps I once stood pensive, reflective, before the meadow of death, the deep blue sky arching above me, countless flowers smiling up at it.

How can it be otherwise then, that flowers will spring from every pain-filled drop of blood shed by the dead?

That the spirits of the dead have a rendezvous there on moonlit nights?

That they will never leave this patch of earth which they soaked with their blood?

Yes, there must be very many flowers blooming there!

For the *Führer-Begleit-Division* the end came on the meadow of death near Neu-Petershain, brave and loyal to the end. This was its last action, there it fought for its existence.

Waiting on the other side of the meadow was *General* Remer, who had gathered approximately 400 men around him. No more came; the others were dead, wounded, captured, missing. Only small groups had escaped this hare hunt; only a few men were able to get through and escape. They found themselves somewhere on the Elbe—in small groups, alone. They crossed the river on empty fuel drums, tree trunks or they swam to the safety of the other bank.

But *General* Remer and his 400 men moved in the direction of the main Senftenberg—Calau road and there came upon an armored group from the SS-Division Frundsberg. The wounded were loaded aboard vehicles for transport to safety, but *General* Remer insisted in continuing on foot with the rest.

A short time later there was an encounter with the Soviets which resulted in the march group becoming split up. *General* Remer was alone. He and his driver disappeared into the darkness of the forests—to make their way through to the south alone.

Finally, on 3 May, he was back; he reported to the command post of the Pz.Korps GD near Dresden, still in the civilian clothes he had worn for the past few days. It was his right to travel in civilian clothes as long as he was just trying to reach his unit. All means were allowed here; but everyone was free to seek the path to freedom any way possible. Better to reach the German lines in civilian clothes than be captured by the Soviets in a German uniform.

More men of the *Führer-Begleit-Division* turned up at the GD message center in Dresden. Obstlt. Schnappauf, commander of the Pz.Rgt. FBD, had already reassembled his men and was fighting with a Kampfgruppe in the Kamenz area; the Ia, General Staff Obstlt. Reidel, had also turned up; many other soldiers and officers found their way back to the unit which *General* Remer was reassembling around him.

On 6 May 1945 the men of the *Führer-Begleit-Division* who had been assembled into a "Kampfgruppe Remer" were still fighting against the attacking Soviets in the Pennrich area near Dresden. Taking heavy losses against the overwhelming force of tanks and infantry, they fought their way back slowly to the south over the Erz Mountains to far south of Teplitz-Schönau. There the trail of the Kampfgruppe, the last fighting men of the *Führer-Begleit-Division*, disappears.

In reality, however, that division, which was created in autumn 1944 and came to feel the full weight of the war, was destroyed on the meadow of death near Neu-Petershain. Numerous dead and wounded were left upon it; Oblt. Geisberg, commander of a panzer company, Lt. Famula, leader of a Kampfgruppe, both wearers of the Knight's Cross, *Feldwebel* Dittmar, Gefr. Schnackerts and so many unnamed. They all loved life—and yet they were soldiers. They all knew their duty—and acted according to it. They all knew loyalty—and died in it on the meadow of death at Neu-Petershain.

Chapter 3
The End of the Pz.Gren.Div. Kurmark at the Elbe

The deceptive calm along the Oder between Frankfurt and Küstrin lasted until 10 April 1945. Apart from the daily artillery duels, most of which were waged one-sidedly by the Soviets, and the day and night patrol operations in the various sectors, the days since the end of March had largely been uneventful. The German side was aware of the enemy's steadily growing strength. More and more artillery went into position, more and more guns carried out adjustment fire. New, previously unknown infantry units appeared. Vehicle traffic over the known Oder bridges from the east became livelier. There was little that the German side could do about it. Apart from our infantry—most of which consisted of inexperienced replacement men and officers—our artillery and heavy weapons remained silent beneath their camouflage. There was just enough ammunition for them to be effective at least on the first day of the big attack. That's all there was, for there was nothing else available.

Day and night the men dug new positions, bunkers, foxholes, anti-tank ditches and barricades at the front and further in the rear; however, there were no defensive weapons with which to arm them. Only here and there, mainly at the front, were heavy flak batteries dug in, manned by young men of the Reich Labor Service. The barrels of anti-tank guns projected from their camouflaged positions, pointed in very specific directions. Tank-killing squads of the two anti-tank brigades waiting in the army's rear area, equipped with *Panzerfausts* and close-range weapons in anticipation of the waves of enemy tanks, from which they would claim their victims. But what else? What did the individual know of the preparations on the other side? Of the massed employment of enemy tanks? Of the Soviet artillery buildup, gun after gun, so many that there was hardly room left for the firing positions. It was clear to him that this would be a battle of life and death, that here it would be man against machine, the individual against technology—and that hopes of emerging victorious were damned slim.

And yet everyone remained at his post, because orders demanded it, because this was home, one's comrades were right and left. Only a few preferred cowardice to the expected inferno.

The Panzer-Grenadier Division *Kurmark*, still in the Falkenhagen-er Forest as operational reserve, was ready. Once again it had done everything possible to prepare its troops for what was coming; scouting of approach routes, assembly areas and firing positions, organization of supply, repair of the armored vehicles, laying of communication lines; everything was ready. The division was ready for action.

It seemed about ready to begin on 12 April. The Soviet artillery was more active than usual, and it began to pound the positions of the defending German infantry. But there were no actual attacks—at least between Frankfurt and Küstrin. Farther north the Soviets did attack the positions of the 303. I.D. and the southern wing of the 616. I.D., as if they intended to increase their offensive activity in stages. On 13 April they expanded their initially local attacks to the south, but the main purpose of this was to improve their basis for the main attack.

On 14 April the enemy shifted these still local attacks to the area north of Lebus, which brought them into the area of the Pz.Gren.Div. *Kurmark* waiting in reserve. On release of the code-word "Herrenpartie" just the Pz.Gren.Div. *Kurmark* was alerted and during the day it was moved into the sector of the "Döberitz Division" in and near Dolgelin.

The reason for this was an enemy penetration farther north of Sachsendorf toward the high ground southeast of Seelow. There on the commanding high ground west of Küstrin was the former second defense position, which after the enemy's success at the end of March had become the front line. In it with forward combat outposts were elements of the 169. I.D., which linked up with the 9. Fsch.-Division to the north near Seelow. Something had been up there east of Seelow continuously since 12 April, and the enemy was able move closer to the hill positions.

The Pz.Gren.Div. *Kurmark* went into position east of and on both sides of Dolgelin station and the rail line, immediately relieving the 169. I.D., in such a way that it could have an effect deep into the Oder break from the high bank positions. At this time Sachsendorf was still in our hands, with elements of the "Döberitz Division" there. At first there was little combat activity apart from enemy artillery fire, which concentrated itself mainly on these hill positions. 11. (IG.) Kp. was in position near Alt-Mahlisch, the artillery's observation post was in Dolgelin.

As expected, based on experience with the enemy's methods of attack, the enemy attacks were not continued on 15 April. It was clear that the enemy was making final preparations, moving his attack divisions forward and preparing the final blow. During the night of 15-16 April the forward outposts were withdrawn from the break to the hill positions, at least those that had not become part of the main line of resistance after the previous day's losses of ground. The code-word "Herrenpartie" was also issued for the remaining elements of the Pz.Gren.Div. *Kurmark* in the rear; all moved from the west closer to the heights so as to be available to counterattack immediately and anywhere, in particular with the armored elements. The 11. (IG.) Kp. went into prepared firing positions south of Dolgelin, the artillery placed harassing fire on designated fire zones. Everyone was wide awake and ready to respond energetically to the first enemy attack. During the final hours of that day the order of the day "To the Soldiers of the Eastern Front" was distributed to the most forward holes and machine-gun posts. It stressed the decisive importance of holding the Oder—Neiße front.

At about four o'clock on the clear, breaking morning of 16 April thousands of Soviet guns opened up a barrage on the suspected German positions in the Oder break, but also far above the actual hill positions to deep in the rear. Salvo after salvo rolled over the bunker positions of the defenders, there were casualties, increasing as the barrage went on. Its tremendous scale had a demoralizing effect. A direct hit struck the observation post of 1. Bttr./Pz.Art.Rgt. KmK and killed almost the entire observation post crew. Killed were Uffz. Sommerlade, Obgefr. Witt and Kanonier Tobaben. The armored troop carriers of the KmK's armored reconnaissance battalion, which set out to prepare for counterattacks toward Libbenichen as soon as the Soviet artillery fire began, were repeatedly held up by hits; Uffz. Sohler was fatally wounded by shell splinters. Enemy artillery blanketed Nieder-Jesar with heavy fire; the church tower, which the enemy suspected to house an observation post, blazed like a torch. Enemy bomber squadrons and tactical aircraft filled the sky, attacking recognized and suspected artillery and other firing positions.

Not until about 08:00 hours did the first brown-clad forms of Soviet infantry appear before the German positions, too late, because they found the more forward positions unoccupied. But this was not the main body of Soviet troops—rather their strength was hardly greater than that of a battalion. Advance groups? Or just a diversionary maneuver? They were met by heavy machine-gun fire from the positions, the infantry guns fired, the artillery fired on the designated areas. Smoke lay over the entire section of land, restricting visibility and forcing the defenders to lay down unobserved fire. At first there were no enemy penetrations, even though there was contact almost everywhere.

Not until about midday did the real Soviet attack come. In the positions near Dolgelin repeated enemy attacks were repulsed, the panzergrenadiers remained in their holes at the rail line on the high ground east of Dolgelin. Farther north, however, the enemy had broken through against the division's left neighbor. Some enemy tanks had broken through, and the 6. Kp. deployed on the left destroyed three with close-range weapons. There was heavy fire on the positions there, the sound of infantry combat and occasionally tank fire. Fierce close-quarters fighting was soon in progress.

Farther south, in the neighboring sector on the right, at about noon enemy tanks appeared out of the smoke around Schönfleiss—Libbenichen, but they were stopped by the German anti-tank defense. Instead, they swung north from Schönfleiss station towards Mallnow and began rolling up the foremost holes of the main line of resistance there. Was Schönfleiß still in our hands? Were the guns of an artillery battalion near Carzig still in position? Situation completely unclear. Enemy tanks appeared to have penetrated into Mallnow itself. Flak fire and the crack of tank cannon in rapid succession.

Meanwhile, German reserves were already marching from the west in long columns on both sides of the main and secondary roads. *Volkssturm*, men of the Volksgrenadier divisions, *Waffen-SS*, all heading to the front to reinforce the positions and fill the gaps torn by the fierce artillery fire. Was this part of the enemy's plan when he attacked with just weak advance groups in the late morning? By doing so did he hope to draw out the German reserves and force the command agencies to prematurely fill the front lines with their last reserves? Perhaps…

If that was what the Soviets intended, then they had largely succeeded. For by evening almost all available reserves had been sent forward. They now felt the full weight of the Soviet attack, especially where the enemy had achieved the first penetrations into the German main line of resistance the day before; in the south near Schönfleiss and Mallnow, in the north on both sides of Seelow, while at Frankfurt the enemy attacks died down as a result of the brave defense mounted by the garrison.

But there seemed to be a Soviet point of main effort north of Dolgelin; the first big wave of enemy tanks also appeared there on 17 April, seeking to expand the point of penetration to both sides. For II./ Pz.Gren.Rgt. KmK, deployed on the left wing of the defensive position northeast of Dolgelin, on the boundary with the neighboring division on the left, it became necessary to swing south and at the same time defend to the north. South of Seelow enemy tanks reached the Seelow —Müncheberg road and advanced along it to the southwest. The elements of the Pz.Gren.Rgt. KmK in Dolgelin were in great danger. All enemy attacks against the regiment's front itself were repulsed with heavy losses to the attacker. Lt.. Doost was killed there, Lt. von Gersum was wounded. Casualties mounted.

On 18 April 1945 the German units gradually began to weaken in the face of the enemy's overpowering attack, especially in the sector between Dolgelin through Seelow to Neu-Hardenberg. The force of the enemy assault swept away the last nests of resistance. Like a spring flood, south of Seelow the wave of enemy tanks now rushed forward in the direction of Müncheberg, destroying everything in its path. This included the gun crews of the stationary 88-mm anti-aircraft guns dug in somewhere between Seelow and Dolgelin; they fought to the last gun, knocking out tank after tank until they were themselves destroyed. Here and there some brave groups of infantry still held out. But it was senseless, they were simply crushed. The left wing of the Pz.Gren.Rgt. KmK, II. Btl. under Hptm. Vehse, stood in the ruins of Dolgelin, by then also defending to the northwest. Like a pillar at the break-in points, the *Kurmark* grenadiers fought desperately against a hundred-fold superiority, increasingly running the danger of being outflanked and encircled. The enemy was already pressing into the ruins from the west, driving into the defenders' rear, when the order to withdraw finally came on the evening of 18 April. After destroying almost all their vehicles, the men disengaged, unnoticed by the enemy, and withdrew south along the rail line in the direction of Libbenichen, where they were to link up with I. Btl. and continue the retreat towards Arensdorf. A battered aid station was picked up as they passed Libbenichen, the wounded were recovered and taken along. The first T 34s now appeared in the area of Neu-Mahlisch and Lietzen, where they were placed under direct fire by the guns of I./Pz.Art.Rgt. KmK. They turned away. But when darkness fell it became necessary for this battalion to evacuate its firing positions and join the retreat. It moved southwest into the Hasenfelde area, where it went into position again.

During the day other elements—the bulk of the armored vehicles, the tanks and the Hetzer tank-destroyers plus the pioneers—had been sent north to occupy a flanking position in the Diedersdorf—Neuentemmel area. Everything depended on keeping the enemy's breakthrough wedge as narrow as possible, in order to cut it off with fresh reserves. Our own counterattacks north toward the Seelow—Müncheberg failed in the face of stubborn enemy resistance; the enemy's armored spearheads could not be prevented from entering Müncheberg. In fierce fighting the 18. Pz.Gren.Rgt., which approached from the northwest, succeeded in halting the enemy armored spearhead northwest of Müncheberg together with an anti-tank brigade. Farther southwest, however, there remained a gap into which enemy tanks advanced in the direction of Heinersdorf and Tempelberg in the evening. Hastily mobilized reserves, including elements of the Pz.Gren.Rgt. KmK, counterattacked and drove the enemy back to the northwest and finally secured on Reichsstraße 167 in the direction of Müncheberg. I./Pz.Art.Rgt. KmK went into position near Hasenfelde in such a way that it could fire to the north and northwest.

By the evening of 18 April it was apparent that the enemy had broken through on both sides of Seelow and to its north and had thus began splitting the 9. Armee in two. Elements of the Pz.Gren.Rgt. KmK were still holding on the southern flank of this breakthrough, seeking to prevent the enemy from advancing to the southwest, and the 18. Pz.Gren.Div. was still fighting northwest of Müncheberg, the last obstacle in the path of the spearheads of the 1st and 2nd Guards Tank Armies, but our forces were simply too weak to be able to present a continuous, tenable defense line to face the mass of the enemy. Southwest of Müncheberg, for example, there were no troops at all.

Its right wing holding firm at the defensive installations of Frankfurt, the XII. SS-Korps had been forced to fold back its left wing toward Heinersdorf. The LVI. Pz.Korps had been forced back to Müncheberg and its northwest, while the LI. A.K. was being forced around its steadfast left wing to the northwest on both sides of Eberswalde.

Farther south in the 9. Armee's area the enemy was already due south of Lübben. The left wing corps of the 4. Pz.Armee (V. A.K.) had been able to throw up a line of security against him at the northern edge of the Spree forest.

The German command's thoughts were now preoccupied with restoring contact between the XII. SS-Korps and the LVI. Pz.Korps, while holding out on both sides of Müncheberg and plugging the gap to the LI. A.K. through an attack by elements of the 23. SS-Freiw.-Pz.Gren.Div. "Nederland" which were en route to the front.

These notions were brought to a premature end, however, when the enemy launched fresh attacks on 19 April. Early on the morning of 19 April a few enemy tanks appeared before the firing positions of I./Pz. Art.Rgt. KmK near Hasenfelde. These turned away after being fired on by the light howitzers, however their presence indicated that the enemy had entered Heinersdorf. Near and west of Müncheberg the enemy continued to attack with undiminished ferocity and his waves of tanks drove west in the direction of Fürstenwalde, driving the 18. Pz.Gren.Div. before them. The gap in the front still loomed large—the Soviets' goal was the direct route to Berlin. The elements of the Pz.Gren.Div. KmK withdrew due southeast of Fürstenwalde, in order to reach the Spree, which was to be the new defense line, before the Soviets entered Fürstenwalde. In orderly columns the vehicles moved through Steinhöfel and Berkenbrück to the autobahn on Dehm Lake, where a new fall-back position facing north and east was to be occupied. It was to be held in order to take in the SS formations coming from the north. Several reconnaissance advances in the direction of Fürstenwalde resulted in contact with the enemy at the southern end of the city; weak enemy screening forces were already on the autobahn access at Ketschendorf. A reconnaissance advance by KmK tanks and SS troops went over and under the autobahn toward Ketschendorf and drove weak enemy forces back to the north. Contact was established with *Volkssturm* troops at the southeastern edge of Fürstenwalde. I./Pz.Art.Rgt. KmK positioned observation posts in a cable factory near the Spree to provide artillery support. Firing positions in the Streitberg area. The enemy had meanwhile taken up position all along the east bank of the Spree, preparing to cross to the west. The Spree river line was defended by *Volkssturm* men every 100 meters or more—nothing else. It appeared that the enemy intended to regroup at the Spree, therefore there was no serious enemy activity for 24 hours.

Trains of the Pz.Gren.Div. *Kurmark* meanwhile moved to the southern tip of Scharmützel Lake, into the wooded area north of Bugk, while combat elements of the division pushed pickets across the Spree and, mainly with infantry, attacked along the autobahn to the west and across the autobahn to the south. The armored troop carriers, together with the tanks and Hetzers, made repeated forays north into the dense forest to prevent the enemy from filtering through. This effort was in vain, for with the weakness on the German side the enemy was always able to get through to the south and southwest. There was heavy fighting in Colpin Forest, however the enemy could not be prevented from occupying the village of Colpin on 23 April. Counterattacks achieved nothing there. All that was left now was to keep open the Bad Saarow road to the south along Scharmützel Lake in order to assure the orderly withdrawal of the *Kurmark* elements to the northeast. During the night of 23-24 April the artillery was ordered to move to new firing positions southeast of Neu-Golm in order to bring the heavy weapons closer. All road movements attracted enemy aircraft; but otherwise the enemy activity northeast of Scharmützel Lake gradually died down. The reason for this was the steady advance by the enemy's armored spearheads along the autobahn to the west and other elements in a south-westerly direction towards Storkow. During the night of 24-25 April, therefore, the elements of the Pz.Gren.Div. *Kurmark* still deployed south-east of Fürstenwalde moved south along Scharmützel Lake to intervene in the fighting near Storkow. The artillery of the Pz.Art.Rgt. KmK also joined in from firing positions southeast of Storkow, with observation posts at the edge of the town.

The fighting units were completely in the dark as to the overall enemy situation; enemy groupings were encountered everywhere. Then the men received the order to withdraw in a generally southwest direction. It appeared as if our movements were to pass south of Berlin. And that was what Headquarters, 9. Armee had in mind, to split its army into three groups while retreating in a generally westerly direction. In the north the LI. A.K. was forced off to the northwest; it reached the area of the 3. Pz.-Armee and was subordinated to it for command reasons.

The LVI. Pz.A.K., which was moving in the middle of the area west of Fürstenwalde as a mobile pocket, was turned toward Berlin without the knowledge of Headquarters, 9. Armee and placed under the direct com-mand of the OKH. The southern group, which included the XII. SS-A.K. and the Pz.Gren.Div. *Kurmark*, was still in contact with the brave defend-ers of Fortress Frankfurt, which on 22 April 1945 had been given permis-sion to break out of the fortress. Together with V. A.K.—which left the area of the 4. Pz.-Armee—it conducted a fighting withdrawal to the south-west. Its orders now were to withdraw toward *General* Wenck's 12. Armee standing between Wittenberg and Belzig, link up with it near Jüterbog and with it attack toward Berlin from the south.

The Soviet 1st Ukrainian Front, which had begun its attack on both sides of the autobahn near Forst on 16 April, had advanced far to the west through Calau—Luckau after destroying the *Führer-Begleit-Division* in the Spremberg area and now, west of Lübben, it turned north for the deci-sive attack on Berlin. On 24-25 April enemy spearheads were already in front of Teupitz engaged in heavy fighting with the 21. Pz.Div. which had been sent there to hold the Teupitz—Priros line. Farther north meanwhile, the armored spearheads of the Soviet 1st White Russian Front had advanced as far as Erkner, thus reaching the outer districts of the Reich capital. But the rest of the 9. Armee was surrounded, its way to the west barred.

For these elements of the 9. Armee, which had been ordered to link up with *General* Wenck's 12. Armee, it was now imperative that they break through the rear communications of the northern wing of the Soviet 1st Ukrainian Front in the direction of Märkisch-Buchholz and further toward the Jüterbog—Luckenwalde line in order to bring about the linking-up of the two armies in this area.

To this end it was necessary for the 9. Armee to complete its movements in the direction of Märkisch-Buchholz as quickly as possible in order to prevent the enemy from taking effective countermeasures. Most importantly, the effects of enemy aircraft and tanks on the marching columns had to be minimized, which meant a march through heavily-wooded terrain. The broad belt of forest between Teupitz and north of Lückenwalde was ideal for this—with the condition that the enemy encircling ring would have to be breached in the Märkisch-Buchholz area.

In carrying out the now known intentions on the German side, the columns of the Pz.Gren.Div. *Kurmark* moved out of their former area of operations between Bugk and Storkow south through the wooded terrain. They passed through Bugk, initially leaving the train there, before occupying new positions in the Selchow—Schwerin area. On 26-27 April the enemy was advancing from Storkow in the direction of Priros, apparently with the intention of linking up with his spearheads in the Tornow—Teupitz area. Fierce fighting developed in the Selchow area, during the course of which the enemy was forced away to the north.

Meanwhile the fact that the division and army were encircled was becoming known. Like a creeping poison the word went from man to man, paralyzing our actions and forcing the question how to get out of the pocket.

During the night of 26-27 April commanders everywhere issued the official order for the breakthrough from the pocket, associated with the destruction of all vehicles not needed for the transport of the men and their small arms in order to conserve the fuel for the tanks and armored vehicles. Further, half of all the heavy weapons were to be destroyed, the light and heavy field howitzers, the infantry guns and others. All that mattered now was getting the men safely out of the shrinking pocket to the southwest. More and more vehicles, interspersed with horse-drawn wagons carrying refugees, column after column, drove over the forest roads towards Halbe, where the breakthrough was to take place. Enemy aircraft were constantly over these processions, strafing the groups of people and vehicles. Casualties mounted. Human bodies flew through the air, here and there vehicles began to burn, ammunition trucks exploded. The chaos was beginning, everyone pressed toward the front—everyone wanted to stay with the column, not lose contact.

The vehicles rolled down the road from Bugk to Schwerin and on through the forest toward Münchehofe in the direction of Halbe. The Soviet's tactical aircraft spotted the self-propelled guns and tractors of the artillery and bombed them, spreading death and destruction. Gefr. Bartolomäus Irlinger and Gefr. Rudi Klunker were killed by bombs, while Uffz. G. Hennemann, Obgefr. A May, Kanonier G. Holm and an *Oberwachtmeister* were seriously wounded. (All were members of I./Pz.Art.Rgt. KmK.) One tractor loaded with ammunition was set afire and threatened to explode at any minute. Quite near it was another tractor with ammunition; the driver, an Obergefreiter, saw the flames coming from the other machine, jumped behind the wheel of his own vehicle and cooly drove it out of the danger area amid the falling bombs. Thus the battery's last ammunition was saved. Only a few minutes later the other burning tractor blew up. Thus the gunners continued to fulfil their duty even at this time!

Late on the afternoon of 27 April the stream of vehicles gradually dried up, only a few still coming from behind. That was it, it appeared that the main body had arrived before Halbe. An armored group succeeded in breaking through Halbe to the south without waiting for the foot troops. Instead the tanks had already disappeared into the forest south of Halbe when the infantry set out to follow. The Soviets, however, fired from their ring and prevented them from doing so. There were terrible scenes at the northern edge of the Halbe Forest, where the bulk of the vehicles sought to save themselves under a hail of shells from Soviet mortars and Stalin Organs.

Meanwhile, the Pz.Gren.Div. *Kurmark*, which had formed the rear guard during the night of 27-28 April, arrived near the Hammer forester's house. But all hell was loose there! A wild mix-up of men, vehicles, shooting and explosions—everyone against everyone. It appeared that everyone wanted to destroy the other.

Gefreiter Kermann, a member of 11. (IG.) Kp./KmK described what took place there:

Halbe!
28 and 29 April 1945
On the retreat from the costly defensive battles on the Eastern Front, the 11. (IG.) Kp./Pz.Gren.Div. KmK went into firing position in the forests north of Halbe in order to break enemy resistance in and near the Hammer forester's house. The forester's house sat beside a passable forest road which led to Halbe. Russian units had taken up position in the house itself and all around it so as to hinder the retreat of German troops.

On the German side there were already serious signs of disintegration. When we arrived in good order in our assembly area, we found in the forest in front of the Hammer forester's house large groups of soldiers—parachute troops, SS-

438

Nederland, Volkssturm, Luftwaffe ground units, etc. They were sitting behind trees or wandering around leaderless in the forest in large groups, there apparently being no officers present. Everyone was afraid of being captured by the Russians. Everyone sought safety in flight, ruthless and brutal. Panic! And the way home led through Halbe, which was to be the undoing of us.

The Pz.Gren.Div. Kurmark was still in an orderly state; complete units with officers and a clear command. As soon as we arrived in our assembly area we saw in the faces of the soldiers wandering about the woods that they wanted to leave the work of breaking through to us, and that is what happened. Kurmark was to lead the way; Kurmark was to undertake the breakthrough, these and similar thoughts were voiced loudly.

Everywhere where soldiers of the Kurmark Division wearing the GD armband appeared, the soldiers hid in groups out of fear that they might have to fight on.

In order to clear the way to Halbe, the leading Kurmark units fired on the Hammer forester's house with anti-aircraft guns and infantry weapons. Among them was 11. (IG.) Kp. under the command of Leutnant Dahlinger, which had just one infantry gun. Under the concentrated fire of the German units the weak Russian pickets withdrew into the forester's house and the road to Halbe was open. Everyone climbed onto the vehicles and raced past the forester's house, from which the Russians were still firing, in the direction of Halbe. Given the uncertain circumstances everyone in the vehicles fired into the forest, and hand grenades were lobbed into the forester's house as we drove past. Among the German vehicles were a few Panthers, which helped clear the path to Halbe. Lying on these tanks were numerous wounded, most with belly wounds. Their cries for a drop of water echoed through the forests. There was nothing anyone could do to make their final hours somewhat more bearable, for in this situation adequate help was out of the question. It struck me as very comforting that in this dreadful situation where no one knew if he would make it, Kurmark always took along its wounded, while other groups of soldiers did precious little to look after their comrades. They were forced to die somewhere in the forest, alone, without help, unless they wanted to end their own lives. Beyond the forester's house everyone formed up into a sort of column; then the drive to Halbe continued. Through the forests, which was crisscrossed by forest roads, crept groups of soldiers, all heading for Halbe. Now and then Russian machine-guns fired into them from some corner of the forest—what disarray!

It was about noon on 28 April 1945.

Tanks of the KmK and rocket launchers on armored troop carriers formed the point of the column on the forest road to Halbe. The vehicles of our 11. (IG.) Kp. drove right behind the rocket launchers.

Early in the afternoon the point reached the edge of the forest in front of Halbe. The village itself lay in a large forest clearing, the bulk of the houses were grouped along the right side of the main street (seen from our direction of march—west), roughly in the center of the village a church. On the main street, roughly abeam the church, there was an anti-tank barricade. It left a narrow passage open, but not until about 100 meters did it become apparent that it was built behind a gentle curve.

Led by the tanks (on them the countless wounded), the vehicles left the edge of the forest and rolled down the main street toward the village of Halbe. Not a shot was fired—all was quiet. The tanks, with the rocket launchers on armored troop carriers behind them then the vehicles of the infantry gun company, drove into the village, past the first houses toward the anti-tank barricade. Under cover of the tanks our infantry advanced into the village on both sides of the street. Everyone followed.

When the tanks were about 150 meters from the anti-tank barricade, with the infantry gun company just passing the first houses, suddenly and without warning we were hit by a murderous enemy barrage coming directly at us from all sides. The Ivans were firing 120-mm mortars, Stalin Organs, machine-guns and so on. In the center of the surprise barrage was 11. (IG.) Kp. Tremendous panic broke out among the infantry accompanying us on foot and this made the chaos complete. Everyone rushed forward in wild gangs. Everyone wanted to reach the cover of the tanks which had stopped up ahead.

The Russian barrage increased in intensity and the Ivan's shells fell among the soldiers crowded onto the main street. It was a scene of horror, one could scarcely imagine anything worse. Hundreds of German soldiers lost their lives and the number of wounded lying on the street, often lying beneath dead comrades and crying pitifully for help, was incalculable. But only a very few could be helped, because the Russians fired at anything that moved from the houses on both sides of the street, and all the while shells from Stalin Organs and other Russian heavy weapons continued to fall. While at the beginning most of the Russian fire had come from the left side (meadow), it now began pouring in from all sides. We had definitely walked into a trap. In desperate assaults soldiers tried to take this or that house from the Ivans, resulting in vicious close-quarters fighting. Meanwhile Ivan's shells continued to strike the main street without letup, fountains of earth flew up from gardens, roofing beams, bricks and windows flew through the air, and the number of comrades lying dead or wounded on the street became ever larger. The fire from Russian infantry in the church, the church tower and the bordering houses became especially heavy, raking the tanks and groups of soldiers bunched up in front of the anti-tank barricade. Death reaped a rich harvest there.

I lay down in the tracks of a Panther (right side), behind which some 50 to 60 men were seeking shelter from the enemy fire. Under fire from all sides, the soldiers fled to the right into a garden, only to come under fire from the houses! They soon had no idea where to go, for we were squeezed into a tiny area. And then there were the many wounded on the tanks, who could not move, had no protection and lay exposed in the open. No one helped them, no one concerned himself with them. The men who had run into the garden dashed back to the cover of the tank, and just as a whole group was standing there a Russian shell

440

scored a direct hit, inflicting frightful casualties. Pieces of bodies flew through the air, blood-curdling cries rang out from the wounded. It was frightful! More than 70% were hit—the road was now completely blocked. The tank backed up a bit, probably out of nervousness, and in doing so drove over some of the many wounded. And still the Stalin Organs and heavy weapons continued to pound the main street, which had become a road of death.

The soldiers streamed back from the barricade—they had to, for there was simply no other way to get over the dead and wounded—and shouted: "The Russian are attacking!" Once again there was panic.

The few officers assembled everyone still able to fight for an immediate counterattack in the direction of the anti-tank barricade. We had to get through or else we would all be stuck in the trap. The tanks were to blast the anti-tank barricade.

The dismounted elements of 11. (IG.) Kp. under Lt. Dahlinger assembled on the left side of the street, roughly abeam the anti-tank barricade, where a few houses right on the street were in our hands. Meter by meter we fought our way forward in bitter close-quarters fighting, but the houses changed hands several times; first the Russians were inside, then the Germans. While this house fighting was going on the Russians continued to fire their heavy weapons at the main street, and many comrades were wounded several times in succession.

Dusk began falling (28 April 1945).

Under Lt. Dahlinger a house with adjoining chicken coop was taken with hand grenades and several dead Russians were found there. Our small arms (we were almost all carrying assault rifles) failed frequently, being prone to jamming. But in this situation we were not hard up, for on and near the street lay all sorts of small arms, most belonging to fallen comrades. And so we changed weapons frequently. The wounded, rolling in pain on the street, almost never gave up their weapons, and we often saw a seriously-wounded comrade still firing. It was a desperate struggle in the truest sense of the word. Women from the refugee columns, who had hoped to get through more easily this way, fought at our side in Halbe in full uniform, with steel helmet, hand grenades and assault rifle. They displayed a reckless bravery and determination which experienced soldiers simply could not surpass. I saw several women killed in battle in Halbe. One of the survivors was still with us when we reached the German lines near Salzbrunn on 1 May 1945. The church represented a particular source of danger. This was still in Russian hands and the fire coming from there prevented any further movement. Then the rocket launchers mounted on armored troop carriers were moved forward to smoke out the church with direct fire. These rocket launchers opened fire from 70 to 80 meters, whole sections of roof flew away—terrific! At the same time the tanks blasted the barricade and created an opening. But our own losses were incalculable, burning vehicles and armored troop carriers blocked the street and increased the chaos. Among them the many wounded, about which no one still cared. Everyone was trying to get out of this hole as quickly as possible.

The men of the infantry gun company wanted to be as near to the front of *our breakthrough as possible, since there was a danger that the soldiers in the town would not get out of the Russian encirclement before darkness fell.*

The vehicles and soldiers stood out ghost-like against the burning vehicles and houses. Then Russian infantry attacked the village from the forest on the right, almost from behind. The Russians reached the first houses, but a desperate counterattack gained us some breathing space.

Then suddenly a runner turned up among the men of the infantry gun company and reported that the first elements had reached the far side of the village— we were finally through Halbe.

The vehicles—armored troop carriers and tanks—were to advance individually; the infantry along the houses on foot. The men of the infantry gun company were fighting their way through when fire began coming in from the left again. This we soon silenced with our weapons. As we left the town in a westerly direction we again came under furious fire from the right flank. Our infantry, which was about to leave the village, went back to the first houses. There was no getting through!

Courageous Kurmark officers and non-commissioned officers advanced against this enemy with their few men who were still in one piece. The resistance had to be broken at all costs, otherwise it had all been in vain! The assault teams stormed the Russian machine-gun positions and took them out from behind. At the same time we broke through again from the east end of the village. Russian heavy machine-guns and anti-tank guns were still placing pretty accurate fire on to the main street, and everyone ran for his life to get out of there. In the village of Halbe itself one could see that there was an opening up front and that the breakthrough had succeeded. Everyone pushed forward blindly. The surviving soldiers suffered further heavy casualties to the pinpoint fire of the Russian heavy machine-guns, which could see everything in the light of the burning houses and vehicles. It was pure target practice!

Finally, after a 600 to 700 meter race against death across open ground, we were through.

Lt. Dahlinger assembled his men of the infantry gun company in the forest at the fork in the road. Most did not turn up. In my estimation there were no more than about forty men compared to the 160 to 180 at Falkenhagen.

It was dawn on 29 April 1945.

The infantry gun company had only a few vehicles left and we placed our wounded comrades in these. All baggage was thrown away, no one else was allowed to ride, no matter how tired he was. Meanwhile a Stalin Organ began firing into the forest, the Ivan having realized that our breakthrough had succeeded.

In Halbe itself heavy fighting went on all day long. The Russians were squeezing the troops surrounded there tighter and tighter, resulting in desperate close-quarters fighting. A comrade who got out of Halbe on that day later told me that even the wounded had fought like animals—it was a real bloodbath.

Older comrades later told us that they had never seen such a slaughter dur-ing the entire war in Russia.

One more sketch from burning Halbe: an Unteroffizier with a serious shoul-der wound sent a comrade who wanted to help him away, to the front, contin-ued to fire his submachine-gun at the Russians with his remaining good hand, then put a hand grenade beneath him, set it off and blew himself up.

Such and similar cases were common in the fighting in Halbe. Many wounded shot themselves in order to escape the sadism of the Russians.

After regrouping, the 11. (IG.) Kp. under the command of Lt. Dahlinger, to whom most of the men of the company owe their escape, for he repeatedly urged us to stay as far to the front as possible so as to be able to exploit the element of surprise when the breakthrough came, marched through the forest in the direction of the autobahn.

There in the Halbe pocket the Panzer-Grenadier Division *Kurmark* met its end along with thousands of German soldiers and civilians. What managed to escape was individual groups and remnants of units, which fate now scattered in all directions. Where they found each other they joined together again; others, however, avoided large groups and sought safety alone.

The larger groups moved through the forest toward the autobahn, where they were stopped again by advancing Soviets. Machine-gun fire reached out for them in the forest, but scarcely anyone took notice. The survivors grimly joined together and stormed this obstacle too, driving the Soviet troops back and finally reaching the autobahn. Anyone who could not keep up was left behind. Scarcely anyone paid attention to the wound-ed. The only goal was to get out of this encirclement and find a place where one could be among his own again.

The groups filtered through the Baruth Forest to the west—repeated-ly fired on from the flanks or from ahead, repeatedly mustering their strength to chase away the enemy or find a detour. Stronger enemy resist-ance was met along the line Baruth—Wünsdorf—Zossen, on the big through road to Berlin. Once again the groups assembled under coura-geous officers and squad leaders and formed up to attack. They charged out of the woods against the enemy, attacking machine-gun bunkers and mor-tar positions, and with desperate courage these obstacles were cleared. Just get through! Through at any price!

Somewhere behind other soldiers, including wounded determined to go along or be taken along, assembled in the dense undergrowth. They debated the best path to the west—to freedom. Their number included three generals. Some spoke of giving up, of putting an end to it. The mood was excited, men grumbled, finally cried out loud. The majority was against ending it; better to try to get through somehow, to have a little hope of yet regaining freedom. With a heavy heart it was decided to leave the wounded behind. What was at stake there was a breakthrough at any cost. Several medical officers and NCOs remained with the hundreds of wounded, ready to share their fate. On it went at another place—in the area of the Wunder forester's house, northwest of Baruth, members of the *Waffen-SS*, the *Luftwaffe*, elements of II./ Pz.Gren.Rgt. KmK and of the 11. (IG.) Kp. under Lt. Dahlinger, several hundred men, some tracked vehicles and trucks—all were ready, all moved by the will to break through to the west. In the midst of a conference involving several officers an officer appeared whom no one knew. An *Oberst*? A *General*? He finally identified himself as having come from headquarters. He was going to lead them out, with detours, unseen by the Soviets, and implored the men to follow him. Once again there were fierce arguments—finally it was discovered that the man was a member of the Committee for a Free Germany, sent into the rear by the Soviets to send the various groups of fleeing soldiers in the wrong direction and into Soviet hands. There were shots—no one knows from where—and the *Oberst* fell dead to the ground.

The same thing happened in other places, sometimes it was a *Feldwebel* or an *Unteroffizier*, it was hard to tell them apart from the real thing. Who knew whom there? Who knew who was true and who had adopted the red banner?

Finally, on 30 April, the Schönfeld—Sperenberg—Zossen rail line was reached, due south of Kummersdorf. Who didn't know the place? The tank firing range, southern offshoot off the Wünsdorf training grounds? How often had they conducted tank firing exercises there; in peacetime, with no interference from the enemy? And now? On the run, enemy everywhere, outflanked, surrounded! Nowhere a bit of earth where one could rest. Pursued, fired on from the flanks, from ahead, from behind, from above!

And then that road of horror, the shattering scene of the destruction of men and materiel; upset trucks, smoldering wagons, overturned guns, shattered gun tractors—and among them incalculable numbers of dead and wounded. They had been there all day; the wounded were barely able to still move, to attract attention to themselves. Some had the worst kinds of wound: belly wounds, shattered legs, head wounds. And no help; no one to bandage them, to care for them, to at least give them some water to wet their lips. Many of the wounded asked the passers-by for a pistol with which to end their lives, to free themselves from all this suffering.

And on it went—and on! Parts of the march group turned north, including elements of the KmK's armored reconnaissance battalion, hoping to meet friendly troops there. Others moved straight across the training grounds to the northwest—attacked repeatedly, ambushed, fired on. With them was a *Leutnant* of the *Kurmark* together with *Stabsgefreiter* Alfred Schmidt and *Gefreiter* Steuber. All had been wounded in a mortar barrage somewhere. The *Leutnant*, who only had a grazing wound, helped the other two carry on, hoping to finally find a vehicle which could pick them up. Nothing! Vehicles passed by, but none stopped, everyone was thinking only of himself. It took many attempts before the crew of one truck were convinced to take the two wounded men.

Somewhere else in the forests southwest of Halbe. Lt. Schwander, formerly, of I./Pz.Art.Rgt. KmK, on the run with *Wachtmeister* Hempel. There were only a few men left together, the rest having vanished. It was nearing evening, about 18:00 hours. They suddenly realized that they were being pursued by Soviets. Several of the escapees stopped running and abandoned themselves to their fate. But the *Leutnant* and *Wachtmeister* Hempel suddenly jumped from cover and ran away, deeper into the forest. The race lasted more than an hour, the Soviets always behind them. Then, suddenly, not 20 meters in front of them, a Soviet captain standing by an oak tree with submachine-gun raised. He fired and missed. Suddenly Hempel screamed: "Submachine-gun down—man behind!" And that was it. The Russians caught up with them in no time. The captain stepped toward the two escapees, obviously pleased to have won the race. He offered them cigarettes, even gave the two now prisoners back their pocket maps. Captivity!

And again and again the individual march groups gathered themselves together and moved west, breaking resistance, attacked by bombers and close-support aircraft. The north railway was crossed somewhere north of Lückenwalde on 1 May. Remaining in the cover of the forest, they passed south of Wiesenhagen. There were repeated, sudden outbursts of anti-tank or mortar fire; each time the remaining self-propelled anti-aircraft guns were moved forward to fire their shells at the suspected targets. Their firepower was still able to create breathing space, sometimes even clear a path at the last minute.

Somewhere between Zauchwitz and Rieben—it was now 2 May—groups of soldiers rolled west, not all led by *Unteroffiziere* and *Feldwebel*. There were no more officers to be seen. Now and then the call came back: "*Panzerfäuste* to the front!" And then the meadow just in front of Zauchwitz—it had to be crossed in order to reach the forest on the other side. The mass of people was exactly in the middle of the meadow when, suddenly, heavy machine-gun fire! As fast as it began all was quiet again. When the first soldiers dared rise up from cover they found themselves surrounded by Soviet infantry, submachine-guns at the ready. Captured! The wounded remained on the ground, those who were still whole assembled at the tip of the wood.

While the men were still walking there, they heard several German NCOs call: "So, they're gone now; let's get the others out of the bushes." There were also several Soviet officers present; they spoke to the non-commissioned officers, pointed to the east—and the non-commissioned officers walked in that direction. They were Seydlitz troops! Members of the Committee for a Free Germany!

Others went toward Elsholz; another enemy anti-tank gun tried to bar the way. The last anti-aircraft gun was rushed forward. Continuous fire. There—a direct hit on the anti-tank gun. The Soviet anti-tank position was stormed with fixed bayonets, the crew killed. Heavy enemy air raid south of Rieben; another march column there. The bulk of II./Pz.Gren.Rgt. KmK; dead, wounded. The enemy aircraft made pass after pass, strafing visible targets. Oberarzt Dr. Falk, the well-known battalion medical officer, ran here and there tending to the wounded. As he ran around in the open he was hit and fell. Killed while carrying out his duty, caring for his soldiers.

Then suddenly another big through road—according to the map it led from Treuenbritzen north in the direction of Salzbrunn—Beelitz. The column stopped. Was it the enemy, or German soldiers? Brown color? But German helmets? Through the binoculars it was clear that they were German! Due west of Salzbrunn. Reich Labor Service. They were in cover in a thin line of security, observing to the east. Germans! Thank God! Saved! Finally out of the mess, finally no more enemy ambushes! Free!

Truly summoning the last of their strength, the men moved toward Salzbrunn in individual groups.

All was so peaceful there; no more shooting! No screaming! No aircraft! Just don't stop, just don't let anyone order us into position here. Keep moving, keep moving, farther to the west, find shelter somewhere, assemble, rest! They crossed the autobahn again near Borkheide and at last halted. The men immediately crawled into the nearest houses. A sign was quickly hung outside: "11. (IG.) Kp. *Kurmark* assemble here," or "I./Pz.Art.Rgt. KmK assemble here." And then they slept. But the interlude was a brief one. The men moved on, urged by rumors that the Soviets were approaching. Their next goal: the Elbe. Using the available vehicles, they now moved down the autobahn through Lüsse to Belzig. There were German troops there, but all was confusion.

Other elements of *Kurmark* heard that the GD was supposed to assemble in Schleswig, and these now tried to get through to the north so as to establish contact somewhere. Rathenow was reached, then on in the direction of Havelberg. Enemy contact there, the breakthrough to the north failed. And so it was back to the Elbe. More and more vehicles had to be left behind, out of fuel. Most were blown up.

Görzke was reached on 3-4 May. There was a brief stop, fuel was transferred, some vehicles were left behind. The march continued to the Elbe, where the Americans were already supposed to be—but not the Russians! Rottstock—Ziesar—Tuchheim. The column split up near Dretzel. The bulk continued toward the north, other elements headed west, both parts seeking a usable crossing over the Elbe.

And where were the Soviets? Rumors abounded. Their spearheads were said to be advancing toward the Elbe from the direction of West

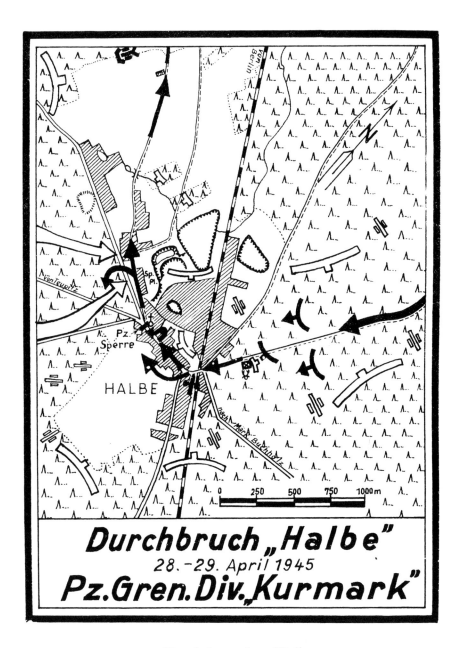

Breakthrough at Halbe
28 - 29 April 1945
Panzer-Grenadier-Division "Kurmark"

447

Berlin, or from the northeast. The situation called for speed. Move, move, just don't become engaged in combat with the Soviets again, don't be captured so near to the end!

Genthin was passed on 4 May 1945; to the north, then the northwest, they must come to the Elbe soon. The sound of fighting could already be heard from the north. Soviets? Enemy tanks were said to be near Buckow.

Finally Jerichow was reached. It was 5 May 1945. Near Fischbeck the Americans erected a makeshift footbridge on the wreckage of the blown Elbe bridge. There was a German reception headquarters in Jerichow; it was supposed to restore order to the columns streaming in, and organize a crossing of the bridge. Others were to immediately take up defensive positions, establish a bridgehead—just in case.

Thousands and thousands of vehicles of all kinds assembled near Fischbeck and sat drawn up close together in front of the bridge, which was still under construction. Everyone loitered about, soldiers and generals, officers and enlisted men. No one lifted a finger to help. Everyone waited impatiently, until finally on the afternoon of 6 May the temporary bridge was finished. But most had waited in vain; only a little more than two meters wide, it was useless to vehicles. But who cared; the bulk of the vehicles and equipment were left where they were. It was a real graveyard. Thousands of vehicles, bridging equipment, guns—all spread out over the Elbe basin, on both sides of and in front of the makeshift bridge. The Americans had placed Red Cross flags on the east bank to prevent enemy air attacks. Nevertheless, Soviet aircraft repeatedly dove on the mass of abandoned vehicles and opened fire. The men fled across the bridge. But waiting on the west side were American negro soldiers. It was the same old story—as soon as they reached the other side the men were frisked, watches were taken.

Standing at a fueling station somewhere near the eastern approach to the makeshift bridge was a German general. Lost in himself, he let the units and individuals pass as they arrived.

Many members of *Kurmark* heard his words:

He had commanded many units; but he had seldom seen such courageous soldiers as those of Kurmark and SS-Nederland. It was only because of these men that they were there. He thanked them for their efforts and their loyalty.

Then it was on to Tangermünde, where the men from the other side gathered. The civilian population lined the streets through which the soldiers passed. Here they passed a bar of chocolate, there a loaf of bread. Letters were passed on to the locals with requests to forward them. The letters had been written while on the march from the bridge, sometimes on the back of the man in front or on a map case. They provided news, the first in weeks, that they were alive and well and prisoners of the west.

Finally they gathered at Tangermünde station; from there the transport trains were supposed to leave. But nothing came of it. On foot—with no food and under the blows of their guards—they went to Stendal, where they boarded trains for transport to the actual prisoner of war camps.

The war was over. Thousands of comrades of the Panzer-Grenadier Division *Kurmark* had been left behind on the road from the Oder—killed, missing, died—alone. The Märkisch forests rustle as ever, they cover countless nameless men who never saw their homes again.

Chapter 4
Samland – Pillau – Neutief
The Last Battle of Panzer-Grenadier Division
Großdeutschland

30/3/1945 – 12/4/1945: Armee reserve in Samland
13/4/1945 – 30/4/1945: Fighting withdrawal in Samland and on the Frische Nehrung.

With the arrival of the "Sea Snake," that famous vehicle of last resort, in Pillau harbor on the morning of 29 March 1945, the last of the Panzer-Grenadier Division Großdeutschland went ashore. All in all, including the preceding transports, it may have been less than 4,000 men who set foot on the coast of Samland. Among them was the division commander, Generalmajor Lorenz. Almost all still had their small arms with them; machine-guns shouldered, ammunition boxes and belts in their hands, assault rifles on short slings over their backs. But there were no heavy weapons, scarcely any vehicles, no field kitchens, no equipment and no ammunition vehicles.

The men of the GD assembled with their officers and non-commissioned officers in Pillau itself—the last access to the sea and the last landing port for the remnants of the combat units in Samland, the very last loading port for thousands of refugees and wounded from northern East Prussia and Königsberg. Hastily manufactured signs gave directions to the assembly point, showing the soldiers the way to their units. "Pz.Art.Rgt. GD here!" "Inf.Btl.Pz.Rgt. GD assemble at the silo." These were typical inscriptions. But really there were only remnants left of once proud units; the losses of the past weeks, the heavy casualties during the fighting on the Balga Peninsula, the evacuation of specialists by sea to the Reich—all these had reduced the division's strength to barely 4,000 men. There were only Kampfgruppen, even if they still carried the old familiar names out of pride. But this could not conceal the fact that they no longer represented a complete division. And yet the officers pulled themselves together again and sought ways and means to equip these remnant units with what they needed—food, weapons, ammunition, heavy weapons, vehicles and so on—in order to increase their defensive capability as much as possible. But it was clear to all of these men that in the coming days they would be facing the final battle against the vastly superior power of the Soviets and that there would be no going back. Behind them was the sea, in front of them the thin line of German positions, roughly in a line from Rantau on the northern coast of Samland south through Pobethen and Wiekau towards Gross-Heidekrug on the Königsberg Lake Canal, which was also manned by worn-out Kampfgruppen and shattered divisions. None of the units, not the veteran 95.I.D. or the 5. Pz.Div. or any of the other names entered on the situation maps, were still what they had once been. They were simply thrown-together groups of men who were in the currently quiet positions. The Panzer-Grenadier Division *Großdeutschland* was another such unit which in the few days remaining before the Soviet attack tried to assemble what was left, to regroup and establish order.

Using the still functioning narrow-gauge railway from Pillau to Fischhausen, the various groups and the GD division headquarters (Div. H.Q. GD and remnants of the Pz.Art.Rgt. GD), moved into the Palmnicken area in the first days of April 1945, the Pz.-Musketier-Rgt. GD (former Pz.Korps-Füs.Rgt. GD) under the command of *Major* von Basse to Rothenen, likewise the Pz.Füs.Rgt. GD. The Pz.Gren. Rgt. GD moved into Kraam, including the regiment's II. Btl., while I./Pz.Gren.Rgt. GD assembled in Gremau, southeast of Palmnicken. The last of the Pz.Rgt. GD, which had once consisted of three battalions, combined into an Inf.Btl.Pz.Rgt. GD under the command of Oblt. Pohl, went into security positions along the west Samland coast—roughly along a line from Palmnicken to Pillau—to guard against an eventual enemy landing. In general the deployment of the GD Division was in keeping with its role as the 4. Armee's operational reserve behind the German main line of resistance.

The April days were quiet at first, apart from occasional incursions by enemy bombers, whose primary target was the busy shipping traffic in Pillau. In keeping with the situation there was also little happening at the front, most of all because the Soviets had launched their final assault against the surrounded fortress of Königsberg in the first days of April. Heavy artillery was already pounding Königsberg day and night, while waves of Soviet bombers dropped their loads on the ruins of the city. The commander of the fortress, *General* Lasch, defended bitterly with the few surrounded *Wehrmacht* and *Volkssturm* units available to him, however on 7 and 8 April the Soviets broke into the outer districts and thus the actual fortress area. *General* Lasch requested permission for the entire garrison of the fortress to break out to the west in order to put an end to the murder in the burning city. Hitler refused; the battle continued towards its inevitable end. *General* Lasch finally surrendered on 9 April 1945 after a relief attempt from the west had failed.

This sacrificial battle for Fortress Königsberg did, however, give the Kampfgruppen in Samland the opportunity to use the days of quiet to raise their level of defensive readiness. The troops of the Pz.Gren.Div. GD were regrouped with what was left. No supplies of men or materiel could be expected from outside, from the Reich; the Samland fighters were thus completely on their own. But there were troops enough in Samland, even if they were thrown together from countless units: *Luftwaffe*, navy, infantry, supply, trains, rear-echelon services, *Volkssturm* and many others. Their fighting spirit was low and those who nevertheless felt strongly in this hopeless situation attached themselves to the combat-ready units such as the 5. Pz.Div. and the Panzer-Grenadier Division *Großdeutschland*. It is not surprising, therefore, that most of the replacements for the various regimental groups came from these homeless men, who were incorporated into the existing units—most of them because they were ordered, a minority as volunteers. Only it was not *Großdeutschland* any more, that fighting community of loyalty and comradeship to the death, instead it was a band of mercenaries in which the GD men were a minority, filling the positions of company commander, platoon and squad leader, machine-gunner. It was the last reserve of the German armed services, which came together there under the command of GD men and organized itself for defense.

There was no shortage of light infantry weapons. Indeed it even proved possible to procure several field howitzers, anti-tank guns and vehicles for the fighting troops, meaning they were taken from others or were found and repaired.

Tank-killing squads were formed and equipped with *Panzerfaust* and "Stovepipe" anti-tank weapons. The Pz.-Musketier-Rgt. GD was even able to put together an entire 16. (Pz.Zerst.) Kp., which was equipped with hand-held anti-tank weapons. These were all stop-gaps, because there were no anti-tank guns left. But better this type of anti-tank defense than none at all.

The remaining elements of the Pz.Aufkl.Abt. GD, now on foot and without its beloved armored scout cars and armored troop carriers, formed a Kampfgruppe, filled it out and trained it. It, too, had to expect to be employed purely in an infantry role when the action started.

The regimental groups conducted training, focusing on defense, constructed positions, constructed second and third lines of obstacles and anti-tank barricades, and prepared towns and quarters for all-round defense.

Rations were poor, were very one-sided and did little to raise the morale of the already battered fighting troops. The noon meal was always the same in those days: turnip with barley and horse meat. There were too many civilians and refugees in Samland; the killing of cows was forbidden on penalty of death so that the milk could be given to the children. Potatoes could also not be consumed because they were being saved as seed for the spring planting. It was only human that one or the other of these bans was silently ignored.

On or about 4 and 5 April elements of the GD Division were moved into areas near the front to serve as operational reserve in the main line of resistance. I./Pz.Gren.Rgt. GD went to Grebieten, the headquarters of the Pz.-Musketier-Rgt. GD moved to the Pinken estate west of Kraam, the Pz.Füs.Rgt. GD remained in Rothenen and was taken over by *Hauptmann* Nebel after illness forced *Major* Fabich to leave for Germany. An order was issued for everyone to occupy and defend scouted fall-back and blocking positions as soon as the expected Soviet attack began.

The last heavy units of the remnant division were also disbanded in these days; the tank crewmen, heavy infantry gun crews, specialists of the Pz.Beob.Bttr. GD (armored observation battery), train people and functionaries were assigned to the infantry units. On the other hand certain valuable specialists were sent home where, according to hazy declarations, a new *Großdeutschland* Division was to be formed. It may also be that by shipping these men out the division command was simply seeking to save as many lives as possible. For the division command had no doubts that no front could be held there in Samland and that it would only take the Soviets a few days to be in Pillau. But it also knew that the sole purpose of this last battle by the GD and others was to allow as many civilians and refugees as possible to be evacuated from Pillau by sea and escape the coming hell. This was the only thing that motivated the men to carry on in their hopeless situation.

In Pillau, however, on the quays and loading ramps, countless unfortunate people, wounded, malingerers and those being sent home, fought for space on the ships. Everyone wanted to be taken along, in their fear everyone did whatever he could to escape. The seamen took aboard an unbroken succession of people—men, women, children—more than the ships could carry. Loading was accompanied by indescribable scenes, it was a tragedy of great proportion. But, nevertheless, countless people were saved, thanks to the bravery and willingness to sacrifice of the ships' crews.

General der Panzertruppen von Saucken, former commanding general of the Pz.Korps *Großdeutschland*, was placed in command of *Gruppe Ostpreussen*, the remnants of the 4. Armee in East Prussia to the Vistula delta.

Then it was time: Fortress Königsberg had fallen, and the Soviets turned their attacks against the German Samland front so as to crush the last resistance in East Prussia. During the night of 12-13 April the massive Soviet artillery force, in conjunction with countless bombers and close-support aircraft, began bombarding the narrow strip of coast still in German hands. Soviet batteries also fired into Pillau from the Baltic coast, from the Brandenburg area and from the Balga-Kahlholz Peninsula, attempting to interdict the shipping operating there day and night.

The Soviet air force was in the air constantly, bombing and strafing known and suspected targets. Nothing escaped the hail of bombs—no wood, no ruin. Jammed with vehicles of all types, trucks and cars, guns, ammunition, soldiers, stragglers, wounded, bunkers and positions, the Neuhäuser Forest was one of the few wooded areas northeast of Pillau to offer some cover. It was later plowed up in the truest sense of the word by fragmentation and large-caliber high-explosive bombs and became a graveyard for men, weapons and equipment of the German Samland force.

All GD elements were immediately placed on alert and moved into scouted, and in some cases fortified, positions, mainly in the 6th or 8th lines behind the main line of resistance. There was still hope that the Soviets would become bogged down in the numerous German defense lines. It was to turn out differently, however; the Soviets were already crossing the fields in vast numbers, unstoppable, meeting little resistance.

Forward, where the German main line of resistance once lay, the *Volkssturm* and alert units had stood up in their holes, waved white flags, raised their hands and resigned themselves to their fate. The heavy Soviet bombardment, the awareness of the futility of the struggle, the shattered will to resist: all were factors which had led to this desperate step. Hundreds, even thousands, had given up. The German defense line had disintegrated in no time.

Behind them the few still combat ready Kampfgruppen sougth to save what could be saved. There were elements of the 5. Pz.Div. which, having lost their operations section, were subordinated to the *Großdeutschland* Division. There were the Kampfgruppen of II./Pz.Gren. Rgt. GD under *Hauptmann* Mackert, which were rushed forward via Germau, Rothenen and Godnicken in the direction of Norgau to halt the enemy forces which had broken through south of Thierenberg near Norgau. There were remnant elements of the Inf.Btl.Pz.Rgt. GD, approximately 120 men under Oblt. Pohl, which were deployed from their security positions on the coast to both sides of Reichsstrasse 431 with front to the east. There were Kampfgruppen of the Pz.-Musketier-Rgt. GD and Pz.Füs.Rgt. GD, which, combined under the command of *Major* von Basse, occupied the Polennen—Powayen line under the command of another division headquarters.

It was the beginning of the dissolution of units, for there were only certain Kampfgruppen which, gathered round their officers and non-commissioned officers, held onto various points of terrain and tried to offer resistance. It was as good as hopeless; the Soviet infantry, accompanied by tanks, was everywhere, streaming in masses from the northeast towards Pillau, the last port still in German hands. The Soviet points of main effort—if one could still speak of such—lay near Rauschen in the north, near and south of Thierenberg in the center and along Reichsstrasse 431 west of Gross-Heidekrug in the south. The situation became especially difficult in the center near Norgau along the rail line to Fischhausen, since a Soviet breakthrough at that point would have cut off the German Kampfgruppe still fighting to the north. West of Norgau (the town itself was already in Soviet hands) the men of II./Pz.Gren.Rgt. GD assembled once again for a counterattack. It made its preparations in the Antonienhöhe area, south of Norgau and on both sides of Point 63, with the panzer-fusiliers to the northwest. The following is an account of the counterattack, which was carried out on the moonlit night of 13-14 April:

6. Kp./II./Pz.Gren.Rgt. GD
My attack lane ran from the trench west of Norgau to Hill 60, where I had

contact with a panzer-fusilier battalion. To the right of the trench across Hill 63 ran the attack lanes of the 5. and 7. Kp. During the night our attack got to within almost 50 meters of the first houses of Norgau. However, since we had just one light machine-gun and no other heavy weapons to support us, in spite of the use of Panzerfausts we were unable to evict the Soviets from their entrenched positions in the houses. My company (6. Kp.) advanced with elan, which was especially spurred on by the screams of women being tormented in the town. But we were unable to enter; the men were halted in front of the town by heavy mortar and machine-gun fire. By going around the large bog west of the town, however, the 5. and 7. Kp. were able to enter the first houses of Norgau. They could not hold out there for long, however; enemy tanks forced them to give up and withdraw to their starting positions.

The Soviets also came to a halt west of Norgau. Throughout 14 April fierce fighting raged in the Germau area and north of Polennen, with little gain to the attackers. The few defenders held out in their hastily-dug foxholes, all the while under heavy air attack which severely restricted movement. Their number diminished steadily. Already the wounded could no longer be evacuated; under the hail of fire they dragged themselves or were helped by comrades in the direction of Pillau, to Dargen, where the 1. San.Kp. GD had its medical clearing station.

In Pillau itself the wounded, transferred, refugees, railway workers and others continued to crowd the quays, under constant air attack and heavy artillery fire, seeking places on the last ships and landing craft.

Mercifully, on that 14 April the sky was cloudy and gray, making it difficult for the Soviet airmen to acquire their targets. Their bombs fell haphazardly on the ruins of the city. The last big ship, the Balkan, landed that evening, once again taking on a load of people which exceeded its capacity. It cast off at about 20:00 hours. After its departure there were only several navy landing craft at anchor in Pillau, taking on passengers in spite of heavy enemy fire.

It was still relatively quiet on the morning of 15 April; however, the enemy artillery and mortar fire grew heavier, the first attacks in the area due north of Polennen forced the few defenders back to the northern edge of the town where they were able to hold on. Fighting in this area were the last remnants of the Pz.-Musketier-Rgt. GD and Pz.Füs.Rgt. GD, which had been combined into a Kampfgruppe under the command of *Major* von Basse. Other elements of the Pz.Füs.Rgt. GD were still holding out in the area west of Norgau adjacent to II./Pz.Gren. Rgt. GD, where the weak Kampfgruppe under Hptm. Mackert, now reinforced by the 16. (Pz.Zerst.Kp.)/Pz.-Musketier-Rgt. GD under Lt. Apel, was in position in front of the town. There, too, it was quiet in the morning, apart from the unbearable air attacks by the enemy. Wherever a few men still stood there was digging, the defense was organized, cover established.

But there were no heavy weapons; one triple flak near the battalion command post and several *Panzerfäuste*—that was all. There were no anti-tank guns, no heavy anti-aircraft guns, little artillery—all areas were lacking. And up front in Norgau something was going on again. Tanks rumbled, shouts and curses suggested that the enemy was preparing something new. It was approaching midday when the enemy's artillery, Stalin Organs, mortars, anti-tank guns and tanks opened up with a withering barrage which forced the few defenders to take maximum cover. It was beginning—no doubt! Losses mounted, weakening our lines; the last of the company headquarters personnel, the trains, were added to the already weakly manned lines, however losses far exceeded this help.

And then the enemy attack broke loose; Soviet tanks and infantry advanced from the southern edge of Norgau in the direction of Antonien Hill, shattered the thin defense line and streamed through to the southwest.

Once again an account from the ranks of 6. Kp./II. Btl. (Mackert):

While I was with the neighboring battalion (a panzer-fusilier battalion), the Ivans began pounding our positions with barrage fire (mortars and Stalin Organs). With the greatest effort I managed to regain my command post, which consisted of an anti-tank hole. During this barrage I suddenly saw the neighboring battalion fleeing to the rear through my first platoon's trench. My platoon leader was still trying to halt the soldiers, but he was simply overwhelmed by the panic caused by the barrage and the resulting heavy casualties. My company was also caught up in this panic. My attempts to hold the company together with threats failed. The people preferred to let themselves be shot down rather than remain in the positions. I cannot explain what caused this panic, especially since the Ivans had not attacked yet. In any event, my company headquarters squad leader, a runner, two radio operators and I found ourselves all alone. Only a squad leader with a light machine-gun reported in from the next hole. Meanwhile I saw that the 5. and 7. Kp. were running away from Hill 63. A machine-gun manned by a Feldwebel and an officer was still firing from Hill 60. When the battalion began to run I sent the following radio message to battalion, I had no telephone link: "Company running, please stop and send back; Russians not attacking." But I soon saw that the people were not fleeing in the direction of the battalion command post. In the meantime the Ivans emerged from their entrenchments and moved toward us. I then transmitted the following radio message: "Russians attacking, cannot hold position with three men, request further orders." Enciphering and deciphering took a great deal of time, and in spite of our defensive fire the Ivans were much nearer. I had to decide for myself now, especially since we had to cover an open stretch of 100 meters if we were to retreat. I first ordered the two radio operators to fall back under our covering fire. Then I ordered the squad leader with the machine-gun to provide covering fire for our withdrawal. After the headquarters squad and I had reached the trench we provided covering fire for the squad leader to retire. In this way we reached the battalion command post without loss. There I met the leader of my 1st Platoon. Of the rest of the company I saw nothing. A three-barreled anti-aircraft gun was still in position near the battalion command post. It opened fire when the Russians drew nearer, and the Ivans fled in panic. Soon afterwards came the order to reoccupy Hill 63 together with a tank that had arrived in the meantime. We formed an assault team from the available officers, what was left of the battalion and part of 8. Kompanie for the attack on the hill.

Halfway there we suddenly came under heavy mortar fire which seriously wounded my platoon leader and me. One officer was killed, others escaped with minor wounds. My runner and another officer helped bring me back to the command post and from there I was transported to the medical clearing station in Dargen.

Hand-to-hand combat raged in the impenetrable forest around Antonien Hill. Brave men continued to hold on there and fire their machine-guns, while others fell back, pursued by the Soviets. No one knew where the enemy was, where were friends. Communications were severed. Everyone defended himself as best he could until well into the night. Then finally the last defenders broke contact and left the field to the Soviets. The surviving defenders assembled near and east of the Linkau estate; here an officer, a radio team, several runners, there several non-commissioned officers and men, a machine-gun crew—but no more units.

On learning of the desperate situation somewhere up front, at the division command post in a farm house near Fischhausen the adjutant, Hptm. Haus, formed an alert company from all available staff personnel. Hfw. Kaufmann assumed command of a platoon. Retreating soldiers were stopped and added to this ad hoc unit. These men were deployed to defend the mine field in front of the Fischhausen heights against the Soviets, who were expected soon. Holes were quickly dug everywhere, several machine-gun positions set up—then they waited.

Only small Kampfgruppen under brave non-commissioned officers and officers continued to hold out near the Linkau estate and on both sides of Godnicken and Rothenen. There had not been a continuous defense line for some time.

The destruction of the last *Großdeutschland* Kampfgruppen began at daybreak on 16 April. Somewhere south of Rothenen groups of soldiers belonging to I./Pz.Gren.Rgt. GD were still fighting a lonely battle. About forty men of the Pz.Füs.Rgt. GD—the messenger section, several radio operators and clerks with Oblt. Jung and *Major* von Basse—were still holding on at the north exit. The last survivors of II./ Pz.Gren.Rgt. GD and Pz.-Musketier-Rgt. GD had established themselves on the Linkau estate and now watched as their positions were smashed. Heavy artillery, mortar and tank fire rained down on Linkau, Soviet infantry forced their way into the positions. Some stood up and surrendered. At the moment that the enemy broke into our positions others disengaged again and fell back to positions somewhere in the rear. Others ran away. Massed attacks by close-support aircraft on anything that moved made the roads to the rear scenes of horror.

Somewhere in the Kallen and Bludau area the last units of the 5. Pz.Div. were scattered for good.

Nevertheless, panzer-fusiliers under their commander *Major* von Basse continued to fight at the north entrance to Godnicken, even though they were outflanked on every side. At about 11:00 hours runners reported that enemy infantry were already advancing south on the road to Gaffken. It was time to break out and try to regain contact with friendly forces.

On reaching the south exit from Godnicken, approximately 200 meters to the side, the few men surrounding *Major* von Basse were forced into cover by well-aimed small arms fire. Most were wounded and *Major* von Basse was fatally wounded. Only a few meters further an officer and several men were caught by the Soviets. The others ran in all directions and sought to escape to Gaffken. But there too the few survivors of the shattered Pz.Füs.Rgt. *Großdeutschland* were met by enemy machine-gun fire.

Division adjutant Hptm. Sanken, at 21 the youngest captain in the division, and the O1 Oblt. Hübner, scraped together whatever personnel they could find at division headquarters and led a counterattack against the Gaffken estate, which was strongly manned by the Soviets. Sanken was killed.

Gaffken estate, a yellow patch widely visible in the East Prussian countryside, the manor house more than 100 years old, with walls over a meter thick, stood up to the enemy artillery fire. The handful of men held out there to the end.

Farther southwest, in Sanglienen, the last assault pioneers of the Pz.Stu.Pi.Btl. GD sat in hastily-dug holes and waited for the enemy. The estate itself was untouched, the manor house intact. But this changed as the day went on: enemy bombers, mainly American-built twin-engined types, called "the stubborn ones" by the men, and close-support aircraft soon appeared and began their work of destruction. As they flew away the first enemy tanks and brown-clad forms appeared and attacked the makeshift positions of the GD assault pioneers. As long as the machine-guns and the few anti-tank guns fired, everyone kept his place. Heavy artillery fire began falling on the positions but the assault pioneers held.

It was almost noon; ammunition was running low. The rifle and machine-gun fire became sporadic, the anti-tank guns had long been silent. Then they came—the Soviet infantry—advancing cautiously, guns raised. They advanced among the positions of the pioneers and called them out. The last survivors of the Pz.Stu.Pi.Btl. GD were forced to surrender, out of ammunition and overwhelmed by a superior foe. It was over in Sanglienen.

Everywhere a few brave men pulled themselves together to establish a new defense line and hold off the rapidly pursuing enemy. Fischhausen was

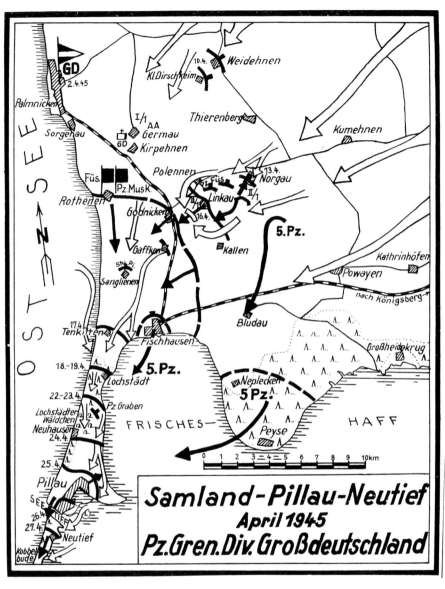

Samland — Pillau — Neutief
April 1945
Panzer-Grenadier-Division "Großdeutschland"

---

abandoned after all efforts by the division headquarters to hold it failed. New positions in the so-called Tenkitten Line, which Korps Wuthmann reported was manned by infantry. In reality the positions on both sides of Tenkitten were not occupied. Nevertheless, the remaining groups from the

Pz.A.A. GD, the panzer-fusiliers and –musketeers, the panzer-grenadiers and tank crews assembled there. There were perhaps several hundred GD people. The rest were from other units—from the 5. Pz.Div., the 551. Volks-Gren.Div., railway workers, *Volkssturm*—but the majority of those trying to hold the Tenkitten Line were still GD men.

Meanwhile a tragedy was played out in Fischhausen. On 16 April the 5. Pz.Div., or what was left of it, was driven back to the sea. The men used every available means of transport to try and reach safety: tree trunks, rafts, fuel drums. Others leapt into the cold water and tried to swim to the Neuhäuser shore. Hundreds were captured.

In the meantime, in the children's hospital in Lochstädter Wood, the doctors of the combined 1. and 2. San.Kp. GD fought to save the lives of the hundreds of wounded that had been brought there. They worked under a steady hail of enemy bombs and shells, and yet they stood at their operating tables and tried to save the lives of those with even a spark of hope.

18 April 1945. The GD division command under *General* Lorenz succeeded in assembling all remaining GD units behind the Tenkitten Line and returning them to action at the Lochstedt anti-tank ditch. That position was to be held at all costs on 18 April so as to allow the last civilians and wounded, but also the troops in Pillau, to escape by sea to Neutief. The anti-tank ditch at Lochstedt had been bombed heavily and was leveled in several places. Only a few men were still up front, with as many officers as possible in the front line in order to avoid panic.

But the Soviet tactic was to feel their way toward suspected German positions until these opened fire. Then they pulled back and their artillery began a destructive barrage fire. When there was no more German defensive fire they advanced again, usually meeting little resistance. Therefore, German defenders now adopted the tactic of leaving a handful of officers and men forward while positioning the bulk of the defenders further to the rear.

Oblt. Zühlke and his men had established themselves in Lochstädt Castle itself, intending to employ every trick in the book to defend it. The days passed until 20 April. The defenders were still in the Lochstädt anti-tank ditch and repelled all enemy advances. The enemy barrage—produced by artillery, captured German rocket launchers, aircraft—went on without end, slowly wearing down the morale of the defenders. It seemed as if the Soviets were intent on minimizing bloodshed, allowing their artillery and air force to do the work. The German defenders, mainly GD people and brave members of the 5. Pz.Div., were still fighting only to keep the rear free for the evacuation of the men and wounded to the Frische Nehrung. For that only! Everything else seemed senseless. The positions at the Lochstädt wood had to be given up during the night of 23-24 April; new positions were occupied along the anti-tank ditch south of Neuhäuser in the dark of night.

That night also saw the printing of the last edition of the GD's front-line newspaper *Die Feuerwehr*, almost 1,000 copies of this two-page edition were put out by a printer in Pillau and distributed.

The 1. San.Kp. GD was already preparing to move to Neutief, the unremitting hail of bombs having made its work impossible. Taking the wounded with it, the company withdrew in groups to Pillau, waited in the ruins until the arrival of darkness and then crossed to Neutief on a ferry.

Up front, however, at the anti-tank ditch south of Neuhäuser, the last members of the GD were still fighting to hold onto their positions. Mainly it was individuals and small groups who pulled themselves together and launched counterattacks to take out nests of enemy resistance among their own positions. They attacked with unbelievable courage, battle cries emitting from their parched throats. Their plans were aided by the heavy coastal guns (280 mm) firing from Neutief, whose courageous forward observers remained up front with the infantry.

During the night of 24-25 April the fighting troops south of Neuhäuser were ordered to withdraw in stages to Pillau and there assemble and cross to Neutief according to plan. The remnants of the Pz.Gren.Rgt. GD assembled in the ruins of Pillau, which were illuminated by parachute flares, at about 23:00 hours; the first elements crossed at about 02:30 on 25 April. Elements of II. Btl. under Hptm. Mackert remained in the citadel of Pillau as rear guard against the approaching Soviets. The commander of Pillau, *General* Chill, sought to ensure a relatively orderly evacuation of the remaining troops from Pillau to Neutief. This proved impossible, however; the Soviets committed all available aircraft. These bombed and strafed the city, which became the scene of a frightful tragedy.

Infantry units were moved back into position at the northern edge of the city to cover the withdrawal of the remaining Kampfgruppen. Their ability to hold was minimal, their fear of being left behind great. They did not hold up the enemy, who entered the city of Pillau early on 25 April. There was heavy close-quarters fighting everywhere between the fiercely-defending rearguards and the Soviets, who wanted to snap up the German soldiers pressing into the southern part of Pillau. There was panic—everyone south to flee to Neutief. The few ferries cast off and headed across the shallows toward the Frische Nehrung. Some soldiers jumped into the sea and began to swim. Some drowned in the icy water. Most were unable to escape and resigned themselves to their fate as prisoners of war.

There was still shooting at various places in Pillau on 25 April, a sign that there was still resistance. Hptm. Mackert and his few men held out in the citadel, probably knowing that they could not get out in the light of day. Other elements, such as the approximately 30 men of the Pz.A.A. GD under Rttm. Düvel and Hptm. Stier, likewise battled in the ruins of the city and were able to hold out until night.

The last of the GD, those who had not been taken prisoner, were finally able to cross to Neutief during the night of 25-26 April.

There, however, they were met again by heavy artillery and machine-
gun fire. The Soviets had already landed in their rear and sought to cut off
the men on the Nehrung.

They had landed between Neutief and "Gull Hook" in landing craft
escorted by destroyers. Those near Neutief and at the airfield were cut off;
their only option was to break through and regain contact in the rear. The
enemy, mainly infantry, kept the highway under machine-gun fire. It had
to be crossed, however, in order to reach open ground.

Several soldiers gathered in a hollow. An *Oberst* came and urged the
GD officer present to undertake a breakthrough. He led the way across the
autobahn and the others followed. But by now the Soviets had noticed
what was happening and opened fire. One at a time, soldiers raced through.
Some were hit and fell. Others were hit while falling; they got up again and
with the last of their strength ran for the safety of the bushes. Then—an
embankment. It was inspected carefully; only a few meters farther several
Russians, but they had seen nothing. The handful of German soldiers
formed up and charged, shouting battle cries. Startled, the Soviets began to
run and fled—the men were through! Finally, at the north beach, there was
quiet. The men assembled there and set off along the beach to the south.

Speed was the watchword—away from the Soviets as quickly as possible. Lt. Dornia was killed, shot in the stomach, and had to be left behind.
Others went the same way. It was a hard war, common and ruthless.

The defenders fell back from line to line, named only for kilometer
stones. The enemy continued to put troops ashore behind the defenders,
forcing them to break through again and again. New positions were occupied at Kobbelbude, north of Waldhalle. Back again. Narmeln, a small
cluster of houses on the south beach—another blocking position, somewhere at the "Forsthaus Grenzhaus." Hold again—there were only remnants of Kampfgruppen left. Also there, as if by a miracle, a lone Tiger
under Lt. Peter. From which unit? That didn't matter any more. Also there
was the legal officer of the 5. Pz.Div., *Hauptmann* Tilse, always the last to
disengage from the enemy. Then there was Lt. Leyse and Hptm. Winkler
of the Korps-Art.Abt. GD, the GD's last artillery battalion, who had even
managed to save three guns from Pillau to Neutief. They had long since
been smashed, destroyed by bombs. But Winkler, wounded for the fifth
time near Neutief, was one of the last on the beach of the Frische Nehrung.
The *General*, too, was with them.

On 29 April enemy troops landed near kilometer 32.5. The GD men
there put up a fierce fight. Two gunboats and 12 landing craft were
destroyed, more than 80 prisoners taken. Everyone was fighting for his life,
everyone wanted to get out. The Kahlberg—Liep line was held—and then
the withdrawal went on. Pröbbernau, Neue Welt, Vogelsang...

Hptm. Haus was wounded, but not seriously. Gen. Lorenz sent him back with the leader of *Gruppe Ostpreussen* to establish contact with *General der Panzertruppen* von Saucken, their old commander. Haus was to describe the true situation to him, to tell him that only a few GD officers and men were still holding on and were fighting their way through. Finally *General* Lorenz himself reported to *General* von Saucken, who had words of appreciation for the stand made by the men. *General* von Saucken gave orders for the rest of the GD to embark on 30 April in Kahlberg for transport to Hela. Meanwhile, the 28. Jäg.Div. took over the positions near Vogelsang and the tiny remnant of the GD, about two companies strong, was subordinated to this division. The GD's message center was in the forest near Hela; rations were issued there and the men assembled. Other GD men, including the Ib, boarded landing craft at Stutthof and were transported to Hela. The remnants of the GD, a few hundred men, mostly of the two medical companies and supply units, gathered there. The fighting units were less well represented, with just two officers from the Pz.Gren.Rgt. GD, Oblt. Baumhoff and Oblt. von Prittwitz. After a brief rest the personnel were put aboard navy landing craft, which sailed through heavy seas and rain to Bornholm. The destination there was Rönne, where the troops were quartered.

For all those who were there, the march through this small Danish city was unforgettable: 800 more or less tattered figures, weapons shouldered, with the words of the old song on their lips once more: "The world's rotten bones tremble before the great war." There was grim irony in the words: "We will go on marching when everything falls to pieces."

The division headquarters, however, remained in Hela in order to send through the last members of the GD. Oblt. Hauptmann held on there with the men of his II./Pz.Gren.Rgt. GD and several anti-aircraft guns, guarding the port and supply dump. He and his men had been deployed by the von Saucken group to defend the headquarters.

The evacuation by sea to the Danish island of Bornholm continued on 3 and 4 May; the naval commander assumed that the island would lay in the British sphere of influence and that they would thus come under British control. *General* Lorenz was of a different mind, however, and the frequent appearance of Soviet reconnaissance aircraft convinced him further. The Soviets were planning a landing; he had to prevent further landings on Bornholm and direct the next convoys to proceed directly to Copenhagen. The German troops, including the GD remnants, would have to get away from Bornholm as quickly as possible.

General Lorenz, who had landed on Bornholm with the rest of his division staff, did everything he could to get his men out in one piece. During the evening hours of 8 May *General* Wuthmann, the last commander in Samland, gave his approval for the GD's departure with the words:

I agree with your assessment of the situation. I have ordered a tug and a navy landing craft readied for your people and you in the harbor. I don't know if I am doing you any good, because I do not know what conditions you will find in Schleswig-Holstein. Accept my offer as thanks for the bravery of your men.

The landing craft arrived in Fehmarn at about 18:30 hours on 9 May, at almost the same time as the Soviets landed on Bornholm. From Fehmarn they continued to Flensburg, where the men from Samland were reunited with those of the replacement brigade and other units in British prisoner of war camps. Some reached "Korpsgruppe von Stockhausen" in the internment area between Fehmarn and Eutin. *General* von Stockhausen had been the first commander of our Inf.Rgt. *Großdeutschland!* Others landed in Denmark or Odder, where the Ausb.Abt. GD was stationed.

Night settled over the Danish land. Sentries walked around the quarters of a training company. There was still a light in the office. The senior NCO, a reddish-blonde Oberfeldwebel, sat at a table, writing. Every time the sentry passed, those inside raised their heads and counted the steps around the house.

A few hundred meters farther two officers—a Major and an Oberleutnant— sat at a radio in the winterized beach house of a well-to-do Dane. The Major, a bandage on his chin, said something. The other listened attentively because the Major's wound made it hard for him to be understood. From somewhere there came women's voices, the radio softly underlined the conversation between the two officers. It was interrupted abruptly; the two officers stood up and stared at the radio; one turned up the volume. Bits of words reached my ears—surrendered. Music blared, then silence. The two stared at one another, faces pale. This was the end! The Oberleutnant left the other, his steps along the beach neared our quarters. "Halt! Password!" A brief exchange of words. The office door opened, the senior NCO and the commander faced each other. Just a few words, then the voice of the officer of the watch rang out: alarm!

In the rooms sleep-drunk men jumped up, young hands reached for weapons, steel helmets were thrown on. There was much rushing about.

The company formed up behind the house. Right and left two torches cast their light on steel helmets and rifle barrels; the senior NCO's voice rang out clear in the night when he reported the company present.

There they stood before me, the last reserve, the youngest. Their eyes stared wide, the sound of the Baltic could be heard through the silence that now hung over everything. The commander said: "I have to tell you that radio reports indicate that the surrender has been signed. This is the end, my young soldiers. You have been spared experiencing the misery, suffering and death of a terrible war. Perhaps you have experienced the bombing terror or the death of a father and brother. We older ones have five years of war behind us, and nothing was spared us. Even the bitterness of defeat will not upset us. Something is collapsing in all of us at this hour. We have believed, trusted and fought again and again, and now we stand before nothing. I ask that you be aware of the fact that many men have fallen, many officers have fallen, that generals have fallen. But they all fell more or less not for an idea or for one man, but they all fell in true fulfillment of duty for their nation, their people and their home. They lived, fought and died for Germany! But you, my young soldiers, are the inheritors of this great legacy. The defeat weighs heavier on your young shoulders than on we battle-tested old ones. We still remember the time before the assumption of power, we will find our way into much which lies before you, which lies before all of us. You will have to relearn, and it will be much more difficult because you know nothing but the world view in which you were raised. Remember during all that is to come that you were the last to assume the beliefs, the strength and the will of those who died before you in the same uniform.

Leaders fall, officers fall, soldiers fall...but Germany will live in you!

The voice died away slowly in the distance. The two torches blazed. The sea sang its song again. The faces of the young ones were fixed; some were sniffling suspiciously. The shadows of the steel helmets over their eyes hid much. The thoughts of the few older ones rushed to those comrades resting in the earth somewhere far away, rushed to their destroyed, shattered homeland. Everything was dark. And once again the voice of the *Oberleutnant*: "Let us sing together..."

Hesitantly at first, the tightened throats joined in, but then the hymn rose into the Danish night:

"Germany, holy word, you are endless,
across the ages, you are blessed!"

Chapter 5
From Vienna to Stockerau...
from Trakwein into Captivity

Bautzen was the destination of the transports carrying the Führer-Grenadier-Division, which in the last days of the month had departed Küstrin and once again traveled along the Eastern Front for deployment in a new combat zone. This time it appeared that it was supposed to be assembled in the rear area of the German 4. Pz.Armee as operational reserve for counterattack in the event of a major Soviet offensive. Several days of rest were expected, yet all forces were mobilized in order to finally complete the reorganization into a division formation, something that had been interrupted several times by operational commitments.

The Feldersatz-Bataillon FGD and the Feldausbildungs-Bataillon FGD provided soldiers for this purpose; they had been hastily trained in numerous courses. The Panzer-Radfahr-Regiment Sommer, which was in the formation process, assembled with its new I. Btl. in the area east and southeast of Fürstenwalde. This unit consisted of recruits, elements of the Feldersatz-Btl. FGD, NCO students of the Potsdam-Eiche NCO school, and with these it formed the:

1. (Schtz.) Kp.	under Oblt. Zacher
	platoon leader Lt. Steller
2. (Schtz.) Kp.	under Oblt. Harald Wunsch
	platoon leader Lt. Schöfeld
3. (Schtz.) Kp.	under Oblt. Hans-Joachim Osthues
	platoon leader Lt. Unruh
4. (schw.) Kp.	under Oblt. Zöschbauer
Supply Company	under Oblt. Grotewohl, Lt. Kauert

Commander of this I./Pz.Radf.Rgt. Sommer was *Hauptmann* Schorn, however because of a special assignment he did not assume command of his battalion until in the Vienna area.

II. Btl. was formed from the former "Bataillon Kriege," formerly III./Pz.Gren.Ers. u. Ausb.Rgt. GD, which had gained its first combat experience in the Guben bridgehead. After taking on replacement personnel, *Major* Kriege, released with his unit from Guben in mid-March 1945, led his battalion into the Vienna area, where it joined the regiment in the first days of April. II./Pz.Radf.Rgt. was organized into four companies (5.-8.) and a supply company. The 8. (schw.) Kp. consisted of three platoons (anti-tank, flak and light infantry gun). The 9. and 10. Kp. of this armored bicycle regiment were regimental units in the hands of the commanding officer, *Major* and Knight's Cross wearer Sommer.

The Panzer-Grenadier Regiment FGD was under the command of *Major* Schmidt, while the Panzer-Regiment FGD was led by Obstlt. Schmidt. The latter had one panzer and one armored troop carrier battalion combined under his command.

In addition to its original batteries, the He.Flak.Abt. FGD, now increased to regiment size, had the Luftwaffe-Flak-Lehr-Abt. under its command.

As of 1 April 1945 all these units of the *Führer-Grenadier-Division*, apart from the infantry regiments, added the number two to their designations in order to differentiate them from those of their sister unit, the *Führer-Begleit-Division*, whose unit number was one. This meant, for example, that the FGD's artillery bore the designation Fü.Pz.Art. Rgt. FGD 2, and the former Pz.Gren.Rgt. the designation Fü.Pz. Gren.Rgt. FGD 2.

On the other hand, effective 1 April 1945, the infantry regiments were renumbered as follows:

Fü.Pz.Gren.Rgt. FGD 2	former Pz.Radf.Rgt. Sommer
Fü.Pz.Gren.Rgt. FGD 3	former Pz.Gren.Rgt. FGD under Major Schmidt
Fü.Pz.Gren.Rgt. FGD 4	new designation for the former Fü.Pz.Gren.Rgt. 2 –see above
Fü.Pz.Gren.Rgt. FGD 5	created from the bulk of Lehr-Rgt. BR Obstlt. Schwarzrock

But the hastily initiated reorganization, manning and equipping of this large number of regiments was halted almost as soon as it began. In fact only two regiments, the Fü.Pz.Gren.Rgt. FGD 3, commanded by *Major* Schmidt, and the Fü.Pz.Gren.Rgt. FGD 4 (formerly No.2), commanded by *Major* Sommer, became available, plus Fü.Pz.Gren. Rgt. FGD 5 under Obstlt. Schwarzrock in the last days of April 1945. This regiment consisted of the recently reorganized Lehr-Regiment *Brandenburg* based in Oberkrain less one battalion. In early April it was transferred by rail into the Stockerau-Krems area; at that time it consisted of three battalions.

By chance the division commander of the *Führer-Grenadier-Division*, *Generalmajor* Maeder, learned that the transports carrying his division were being diverted in another direction. Maeder drove to headquarters at Zossen, essentially because of the expansion of his unit and not to receive new orders, and there heard that the division was being transferred into the Vienna area.

The situation in this battle zone in Army Group South's sector had not changed since the unsuccessful counterattack by the 6. SS-Pz.Armee under *SS-Oberstgruppenführer* Sepp Dietrich with the I. and II. SS.Pz.Korps and the army's III. Pz.Korps between Lake Balaton and Lake Veleme in the first days of March. In the extreme south the 2. Pz.Armee was still between the Drau and Lake Balaton; next to it the 6. Armee covered the area as far as the Danube, where it linked up with the 8. Armee along the Gran river line.

These three armies of the German Army Group South faced the Soviet 3rd Ukrainian Front under Tolbuchin in the area of Lake Balaton and the Soviet 2nd Ukrainian Front under Malinovski on both sides of the Danube. So far these had not shown any signs of joining the assault by the Soviet armies farther to the north. Instead, the objective of these two Soviet army groups remained to link up with the western allies via Vienna. It was also certain that the Soviets intended to reach Vienna before the Allies.

This may have been the reason why the Soviet armies finally launched their last great offensive in the final days of March. *Generalmajor* Maeder learned of the first effects of this Soviet attack between Lake Balaton and the Danube during his visit to Zossen on 1 April 1945, Easter Sunday. It also gave cause for the diversion of the FGD's transports into the Vienna area, especially since the Neiße combat zone remained quiet. For the initial reports from the southeast were less than rosy. German units were fighting a delaying action as they withdrew northwest toward Vienna. The *Waffen-SS*, too, had been caught up in the maelstrom of the general retreat. The first signs of disintegration were visible in Vienna; there were uprisings by foreign workers and some unrest among the Austrian population. In addition to the GD convalescent company, Reichsleiter Baldur von Schirach had only a few *Volkssturm* units, rear-echelon services and replacement units with which to maintain order.

After crossing the Austro-Hungarian border on 29 March, the spearheads of the two Soviet fronts quickly gained ground. As the supreme commander's main effort division, the *Führer-Grenadier-Division* was ordered to assemble in the area northeast of Vienna. The change of direction toward Vienna resulted in the last units of the FGD to entrain arriving there first, as they received the order in time and proceeded directly south. These were the regiment trains and the Fu.Pz.Pi.Btl. FGD under *Hauptmann* Horn with two pioneer companies. The other transports arrived later, including those bearing elements of the Fü.Pz.Rgt. FGD.

While the FGD division headquarters moved into Breitenlee, east of Vienna and thus north of the Danube, *Generalmajor* Maeder sought to make contact with the senior commands. At this time Army Group South had its headquarters in Mauerbach, west-northwest of Vienna. There Gen.Mj. Maeder learned that he had been subordinated to SS-Korps Bittrich. He was able to learn few details of the enemy situation, but on 3 April news filtered down from refugees that enemy spearheads had already been sighted in the area of Payerbach—Reichenau west of Gloggnitz on the Schwarza and that Malinowski's forces were at the gates of Pressburg

(Bratislava).

At this time the following German units were southwest of Vienna in the area of Rosenhügel: the 3. SS-Panzer Division, the 12. SS-Panzer Division "*Hitlerjugend*" and the army's 49. I.D. Nothing more could be learned given the growing confusion in that area. The impression left by the drive through Vienna was depressing. In the city a throng of soldiers, Cossacks, *Volkssturm*; here and there obstacles, barricades and bunkers were being built, there was tension and agitation everywhere, recalcitrance and muttering among the population. On the walls of houses and other prominent places posters proclaimed that Vienna had been declared a defensive zone; that women and children were to leave the city as soon as possible; that all men were being called upon to make themselves available for the defense of the city.

On about 4 April the commander of the *Führer-Grenadier-Division*, *Generalmajor* Maeder, received orders from SS-A.K. Bittrich to immediately conduct reconnaissance towards Klosterneuburg, as enemy forces were allegedly already there, having supposedly infiltrated through the Vienna woods. The patrols dispatched there by the Pz.Aufkl.Kp. FGD found no sign of the enemy, however. Klosterneuburg lay north of Vienna on the Danube—thus still in the rear; the fact that the enemy was already suspected there shows all too clearly the uncertainty that already prevailed in the senior command authorities. But the fact is that on 4 April enemy advance guards had already crossed the Schwarza—Leitha line south of Vienna and had reached the area of Sooss south of Baden and Schwechat on the Danube. Thus the leading Soviet forces were already in the outer districts of the city of Vienna.

Two factors—the standing *Führer* order to defend the city to the outmost, and the limited number of units available for the defense—two badly battered *Waffen-SS* divisions and one army infantry division—led the senior command authorities to move into the city of Vienna the *Führer-Grenadier-Division*, which was still assembling north of the Danube. In terms of equipment and armament the division was the only really combat-capable unit in this area. Hitler himself ordered its diversion and subordination to the command of the city defense. On the evening of 5 April advance groups of Soviet tanks reached the suburbs of Vienna.

The first units to respond to the order were the Fü.Pz.Rgt. FGD 2 which moved into the Prater, and the Fü.Pz.Pi.Btl. FGD 2 which transferred into the area of the central cemetery in the southeast part of Vienna. On 6 April uncertainty as to the position of Soviet advance guards believed to be advancing from the south and southeast led the II. SS-A.K. to order the FGD to attack with the bulk of its units in a southerly direction through the *Waffen-SS* units standing guard on the Rosenhügel. The mission order still spoke of isolated German Kampfgruppen supposedly operating in the Vienna Woods, and contact was to be established with these.

As well, there were numerous German hospitals in the no-man's-land between the German defenders and the Soviet spearheads containing a large number of sick and wounded, and these were to be rescued if possible.

The order was carried out. *Generalmajor* Maeder ordered the units to come to march readiness and move out. They passed through the security positions on the Rosenhügel and entered no-man's-land to the south, resulting in the recovery of several German hospitals, which were evacuated before the Soviets arrived with the courageous assistance of the Vienna fire brigade. Soon afterwards, however, orders were received by radio to cease all movement to the south at once and immediately advance in the direction of the city of Klosterneuburg, which had been entered by enemy forces coming out of the Vienna Woods. All units of the *Führer-Grenadier-Division* were halted and directed north.

The Fü.Pz.Rgt. FGD 2 formed the point and the lead tank was commanded by *Leutnant* Reinsberger. His tank rolled slowly through the streets of Vienna, then turned onto Maria-Hilf-Strasse—but suddenly it was met by anti-tank or tank fire from the direction of the West Station. Surprised, the driver of this lead tank stepped on the brake, immediately backed up and then proceeded around the nearest street corner. Well? Was it perhaps friendly gunners firing out of nervousness? Or was it the enemy already?

Reconnaissance revealed the presence of at least 20 to 30 enemy tanks in the area of the west station which were being reinforced steadily by motor vehicles carrying Soviet infantry. It was also quickly learned that local people had guided the enemy vanguards, which were apparently receiving reinforcements from the Vienna Woods, through side streets to the area of the west station, avoiding German pickets and the *Waffen-SS* troops on the Rosenhügel.

The units of the FGD, which were in a long column on the street, immediately spread out and went into position facing west. Since the Soviets were also spreading out more to the north, the FGD was forced to extend its lines parallel to these to the north. The result was a main line of resistance which extended roughly along the rail line to the north. Finally, by evening the extreme right wing of the FGD reached the Danube Canal, while the provisional division command post was established in Augarten.

From there it was not far to the Hofburg, where Reichsleiter Baldur von Schirach had set up his command post. Also deployed there was the GD's convalescent company, now motorized with vehicles of the NSKK and designated Headquarters Company GD of Operations Staff "S"; its main role was guard duty. Meanwhile, in Vienna itself the feared rebellion had broken out. Not only did some treacherous persons guide an increasing number of Soviet troops through underground passages to positions behind the German lines, now shots were being fired from windows and cellar entrances, killing German sentries. Patrols using side streets were fired on and suffered losses. Runners fell victim to bullets, while some soldiers disappeared never to be seen again.

Where German infantry squads moved through the streets there were sudden attacks from houses with stones, boiling water and even hand grenades. Even the wounded became targets; their hospitals were attacked several times by hostile-minded rebels.

The battle raged in Vienna's streets and alleys. Shells and rockets exploded, there was house-to-house fighting in many places. The situation in the city became ever more fatal—and Hitler had ordered it defended to the last.

The following is an account by a gun commander of the Pz.Jäg.Kp. FGD, Uffz. W. Putzmann:

Combat Zone Vienna

Many comrades suffered from general nervousness over the coming street fight in Vienna. Uncertainty lurked around every corner and behind every window, and the city was an unfamiliar battleground for the Eastern Front veterans.

Gradually we had to get accustomed to our increasingly uncomfortable environment. The rifle and machine-gun fire had grown heavier and one often did not know who was firing—friend or foe!

We were in the area of the eighth district of Vienna, in the area of the Lerchenfelder Belt, and it appeared as if the main line of resistance was stabilizing there. Correct. Lt. Daffner appeared by our gun, the fourth gun of the 2nd Platoon, and instructed us to go into position at the next street corner. It was where the Tiger-Gasse opened into Josefstadt Street. The tractor and gun moved forward quickly. The gun was unlimbered, ammunition unloaded and the vehicle sent to the rear into cover. Immediately the burning question arose for us: how to dig in the gun's trails? How would we find resistance for the gun's recoil? Hesitation was not part of the profession of soldier. Should we let the trails strike the curbstones or the house front behind us? That would mean depriving the gun and crew of any cover. There was only one other choice: move the gun up to the corner of the house facing the enemy, which offered cover, leave the trails closed and fire from the side using the lanyard. What to load? For now high-explosive was the only choice. The first shell went into the throat of the barrel and the breech closed with a metallic click. The man assigned as gunner was a former Luftwaffe Obergefreiter. The gun commander (Uffz. W. Putzmann) therefore thought it advisable to once again point out to his most important man the impossibility of remaining sitting on the trail when the gun was fired, and that it was best that the remaining crew leap to the gun as soon as it was fired to move it back into firing position again.

Thank God—we did not remain alone. A rifle squad was also there, its light machine-gun positioned in such a way as to provide our gun with the necessary infantry support.

Now the Ivans could come; a fitting reception was guaranteed.

Meanwhile it had begun to get dark, and the rifle fire gradually died down. It was therefore sufficient to leave a single sentry at the gun, since the rifle squad's man at the light machine-gun—which was between the cannon and the corner of the house—was also watching. The members of the rifle squad not on watch had meanwhile gone looking for shelter in the immediate vicinity. A roomy hall-way in the ground floor of a house located 20 paces from the firing position offered the best solution. There was much coming and going through the portal-like entrance. The absolute darkness—there was a new moon—made it necessary for everyone to stay especially alert and ready for action. Of all our senses only our ears could give us some inkling as to what was happening on the enemy side. The utmost silence was required on our side in order to reveal as little about our pres-ence as possible. The only sounds heard in the featureless space were the crunching of soldiers' boots on the sandstone tiles, mixed with muffled curses when there was a change of guard or the squad or platoon leader made his rounds. This in turn caused fresh unrest among the men of the gun crew or rifle squad who were try-ing to get some sleep.

And so the 23rd hour approached. And then something inconceivable hap-pened; suddenly, from nowhere!

At about this hour a Russian machine-gun squad worked its way in our direction. At the same time our gunner, Obergefreiter Willi Kremer, was stand-ing guard by our gun, which meant that he was sitting on the gun trail and star-ing intently into the night over the armored shield. The enemy soldiers were still invisible, shrouded in the darkness. And yet they were already within about 30 paces of our gun. At that moment the attention of our brave gunner was attract-ed by soft tapping and gentle whispering. Alarm!! The men of the rifle squad rushed to our quarters. But the danger facing our two men on guard was already tremendous. Now the brain of our calm Obergefreiter reacted lightning quick. The most reasonable solution was to have the machine-gunner beside him go into action, and he immediately tried to transmit this to him by nudging him hard. No reaction! Why wasn't the fellow shooting? The squad's young machine-gun-ner was dead to the world, apparently exhausted by the previous deprivations and exertions. But he had to do something now! The Russians would be there at any minute.

Then the anti-tank gunner, my Obergefreiter, came up with a unique solu-tion. Still sitting on the trail, he pressed the firing button.

A red flash and an ear-shattering crack greeted our comrades as they poured out of the house; they dropped on the spot! But they soon picked themselves up again. Their only thoughts: the gun! Willi! The gun commander, an Obergefreiter but already an experienced anti-tank man, at first thought it was a direct hit by an enemy tank cannon.

"Willi, Willi, are you alright?"

Screams and shouts—some from the enemy—rang out through the night. Suddenly the gun commander's foot struck something soft and he heard a stifled moan.

"Willi, where have you been hit? Say something!"

"Ouch, my head, my head—I didn't think that something like that—I couldn't do anything else—ouch, ouch..."

"Yes, yes, what then? Is it enemy tanks?"

"It was something—I, I fired at it!"

At that moment tremendous amazement overcame the gun commander. But at the same time joy and relief seized him and his men when they realized that their gun was intact and back in position. So Willi had fired! We were masters of the situation. We had fired first and had the upper hand. We helped the injured man from the scene of the battle. His entire body had to be covered with scrapes and bruises. He was surely knocked out for a while! No one—not even he—will likely ever be in the position to be able to adequately describe his wild ride, for it is not contained in any service manual nor has it been tested at any training ground!

The rest of the night now passed quietly. No more enemy soldiers dared enter our area.

At dawn the infantry squad posted an observer in the window of the corner house above our gun. As it grew lighter, what he saw before him in the intersection caused his eyes to widen. He could now see with grim certainty the horribly mutilated bodies of several Soviet soldiers, mixed in with items of kit and a shattered machine-gun...above them a bent lamppost. A shocking scene. Had the blindly fired shot from our gun bounced off the lamppost resulting in this immense effect? There was no longer any doubt that it had.

While the situation of the German defenders in the city of Vienna became ever more unbearable, with both the attacking Soviet troops and ambushes and internal unrest to deal with, after crossing the Danube over a newly erected bridge near Hainburg other Soviet troops began advancing north, north of the river, in order to encircle the city of Vienna and deprive the defenders of their last contact with their northern neighbors.

The weak pickets along the Danube were incapable of offering serious resistance to the growing enemy pressure; their thin lines of security threatened simply to burst. Faced with the fact of the likely pinching off of Vienna and its German defenders, the commander-in-chief of Army Group South, *Generaloberst* Rendulic, with the agreement of the commander of the 6. SS-Pz.Armee, gave instructions to begin the abandonment and evacuation of Vienna.

Once again, as the most capable unit, the *Führer-Grenadier-Division* received orders to disengage immediately from its positions in the city and cross to the north bank of the Danube during 8 April. New positions were to be occupied and the enemy forces advancing on the north side of the Danube were to be halted at all costs.

The division's command post was in Breitenless, while that of II. SS-A.K. Bittrich was in Leobendorf, north of Klosterneuburg. All that was left in the city itself was units of the *Waffen-SS*, which withdrew toward the Danube canal under pressure from the attacking enemy. On that 8 April the enemy reached the Ring, a broad avenue encircling the actual city core. The last German units still held a bridgehead there on the south bank of the Danube in order to assure the evacuation of the wounded and cover the flow of troops across the Reich Bridge to the north.

The units of the *Führer-Grenadier-Division* occupied the specified line in loose formation with the focal point in the southern sector, where the bulk of the tanks and regiments were located. Farther north, where the terrain was hillier but more complex, there were only reconnaissance forces. These could report the approach of the enemy but could do nothing about it. Still farther north, or north of Grossengersdorf, there were apparently no more German units. Thus the left (northern) flank of the FGD was open.

The last battalions of the *Waffen-SS* left the city during the night of 12-13 April, crossing the Reich Bridge to the north bank, and took up position in a line from Stockerau to Klosterneuburg.

Already on 12 April there was heavy fighting with leading Soviet elements, which were attempting to force a passage through to the Danube with tanks. Through skillful maneuvering and outstanding bravery, the Fü.Pz.Rgt. FGD under Obstlt. Schmidt destroyed a total of 57 enemy tanks—a success which caused the Soviets to initially halt their attacks. The German tank-destroyers and their long-barreled 88-mm guns proved particularly effective in this engagement, being able to destroy even the heavily-armored Josef Stalin tanks from maximum range.

The main line of resistance ran from Königsbrunn in the north (I./Fü.Pz.Gren.Rgt. FGD 4 under Hptm. Schorn plus a GD battery which had come from somewhere) to Gross-Engersdorf (forward patrols), south through Raasdorf and Essling to the Danube. Another division was finally inserted on the left wing, roughly in the Wolkersdorf—Königsbrunn area, finally ending the danger of an open left flank.

Nevertheless, the *Führer-Grenadier-Division*'s situation was less than ideal; it was in a long tube whose only remaining opening was to the northwest. Meanwhile the Soviets had appeared on the west bank of the Danube, forcing *Generalmajor* Maeder to also position security forces—mainly *Volkssturm* and alert units—at his back, along the east side of the Danube.

After the Soviet spearheads had been halted on both sides of Raasdorf and held there by stubborn resistance, they shifted the focus of their attack to the north, having detected the open area there. For this reason the Fü.Pz.Gren.Rgt. FGD 4 under *Major* Sommer was withdrawn to a shorter line, roughly in the Gerasdorf—Stammersdorf area, with its left wing on the Danube.

On 14-15 April the division command post was in the area of Steinern Kreuz, northwest of Stammersdorf.

But it also became apparent that following the abandoning of Vienna holding the southwards-pointing salient, with southern pickets still abeam the Prater on the Danube, no longer made any sense. Consequently initial preparations were made to evacuate to the northwest. First, however, it was necessary to withdraw the heavy artillery, some of which was in fixed emplacements, and the mobile corps artillery to the northwest without being seen; this was accomplished during the night.

At this point the Reich Bridge (now the Red Army Bridge) was still intact, making it possible for the Soviets to use it as a crossing. The bridge itself had been prepared for demolition. Pioneers lay in cover and waited for the order to blow the span. A message was sent to Berlin asking for permission to detonate. Reply: detonate! No sooner was the order issued to the pioneers when a counter-order was received. This happened seven times: order to detonate—counter-order.

Meanwhile the Soviets had positioned anti-tank guns right at the western approach to the bridge and were firing on and over the bridge—apparently in order to prevent it being blown.

There was obviously a great danger of the partly exposed explosive charges being hit and set off prematurely. In order to prevent this, during the night the pioneers removed the exposed charges and disarmed them. No sooner had this happened when the ultimate order to detonate arrived from Berlin. And the Reich bridge was not blown!

Night after night everything between the front line—held by the *Führer-Grenadier-Division*—and the Danube withdrew north into the area of Leobendorf, first the artillery and flak units and the rear-echelon services.

Finally the FGD also received orders to withdraw in a single movement that night to abeam Bisamberg, southeast of Kornneuburg. This would be followed by another movement as far as Leobendorf. Then, however, the bad news was received that the enemy had already entered Kornneuburg, and that the leading Soviets spearheads had crossed the Danube. The danger that the retreat would be interrupted as it was beginning and the road to Leobendorf severed, cutting off the units withdrawing to the north, was huge.

All of the units subordinate to the FGD, including the *Begleit-Bataillon Reichsführer SS* in Leobendorf, were alerted and deployed to screen toward Kornneuburg. The assault gun brigade under Hptm. Tornau rushed to the Bisamberg area, went into position there and engaged recognized enemy targets in Kornneuburg and on the west bank of the Danube. Several enemy tanks were destroyed.

No sooner was the initial threat averted than a new, more alarming report was received: the enemy had now also broken through in the area north of Königsbrunn, at the boundary with the division on the left and was advancing west. The enemy's plan was thus clear: cut off the German units still east of Vienna in the Kornneuburg—Leobendorf area. Faced with these conditions, the defenders were forced to empty the sack more quickly than anticipated; the necessary orders were issued. At the same time the 3. SS-Panzer Division Totenkopf was directed to attack from the Leobendorf area toward Kornneuburg and encircle and seal off the town so that the final withdrawal movements could take place behind this screen.

Finally, during the night of 25-26 April, all the remaining German troops were pulled out of the salient and moved into position in the area on both sides of Leobendorf with front to the east and south. This was an outstanding tactical accomplishment by the command of the *Führer-Grenadier-Division*.

By early on 27 April the same troops were already in a defensive position roughly in a line from the Danube (right) through Leobendorf and Rückersdorf to the adjacent division. The FGD's command post was on the Dobler-Berg.

Fü.Pz.Gren.Rgt. FGD 5 under Obstlt. Schwarzrock had made preparations to receive the withdrawing troops, with elements in the front line east of Stockerau, roughly between the road and the Danube. To the north with its defenses concentrated on both side of the Stockerau—Kornneuburg road was I./Fü.Pz.Gren.Rgt. FGD 4 under Hptm. Schorn: south of the road in a sparsely wooded area the 2. Kp., left of the road in favorable terrain the 3. Kp., behind it the 1. Kp. as operational reserve. Then to the north the II./Fü.Pz.Gren.Rgt. FGD 4 under *Major* Kriege, which in turn had contact with Fü.Pz.Gren.Rgt. FGD 3.

The *Führer-Grenadier-Division* remained in these positions, where there was soon contact with the enemy again, until 7 May 1945. Its main opponent was the Soviet 49th Guards Rifle Division, with which there was at times heavy fighting in the days that followed.

On the German side the positions were now fortified further. Bunkers were built, along with barricades and machine-gun posts. Penetrations by the enemy were eliminated through counterattacks or rendered ineffective by timely withdrawals to fall-back positions. Seen as a whole, however, the line held until May 1945.

Work also began on a second line which was to serve as a fall-back position in case of a breakthrough. It ran along the Muhlbach to the east end of Stockerau and from there to Hatzenbach and Senning.

Even while these preparations were under way, the general situation dictated subsequent events.

During the evening hours of 6 May 1945 Army Group South sent the following radio message to the units under its command:

H.Q., Army Group South, 6 May 1945, 20:00 hours

To Pz.A.O.K.2, A.O.K 6, Pz.A.O.K. 6, A.O.K. 8

Hostilities against the Americans are to cease at 08:00 hours on 7 May.

After nightfall on 7 May the armies are to disengage from the enemy on the Eastern Front and withdraw toward the west.

Details of implementation, if they could be considered such, stated that the *Führer-Grenadier-Division* was to form the rear guard for these withdrawal movements while simultaneously assuming command of all remaining German troops in the Stockerau—Leobendorf—Obergänserndorf area.

Fü.Pz.Gren.Rgt. FGD 5 under Obstlt. Schwarzrock, which had meanwhile been withdrawn from its positions, received orders to take up a receiving position on both sides of Krem with its right wing on the Danube and hold this until all elements of the FGD had passed through.

During the night of 7-8 May the units of the FGD left their positions unnoticed and withdrew to the west. As so often, at dawn the enemy began firing into the area east of Stockerau—Leobendorf—this time at abandoned positions.

The roads leading west were scenes of panic and disintegration, with everyone fleeing to escape Soviet captivity. Column after column, vehicles of every kind, raced west—just to get away from there and reach the Americans in time. The *Führer-Grenadier-Division* carried out its mission in an orderly fashion, true to its orders, and was not affected by this chaos for even a minute.

Generalmajor Maeder, since awarded the Knight's Cross with Swords, pressed ahead to establish contact with the corps. It, however, was already breaking up. Only the Ia of the SS-A.K. Bittrich was still manning his position. *Generalmajor* Maeder took over command of the corps on the spot and issued orders for the *Führer-Grenadier-Division* and the units of the *Waffen-SS* to move west through the specified combat position. His main concern was for the lives of his men, whom he badly wanted to place in the hands of the Americans. The premature withdrawal of the *Waffen-SS* forced him to take this difficult decision.

Finally on 9 May *Generalmajor* Maeder was reunited with the elements of his division in a meadow near Trakwein, where by now approximately 30,000 men were camped. The meadow was being used by the Americans as an assembly point for all of the German units arriving from the east. It was there that *Generalmajor* Maeder first learned that the surrender had been signed. Not present were several division trains and the Ib staff of the FGD under General Staff *Major* Westhoven, which had already moved west.

Generalmajor Maeder reported to the American camp commander, who merely told him that he was a prisoner and that his division would be moved farther west in a few days. The elements of the *Führer-Grenadier-Division* remained in the meadow under American command until 12 May, armed but with no armored vehicles, which had been driven into a swamp somewhere by night.

Then, during the night of 12-13 May, something unimaginable happened: in the darkness the American guards disappeared and early on the morning of the 13th the entire camp was surrounded by Soviet guards!

It had all been in vain; all attempts to save the men from the Soviets and captivity in their hands had failed. *Generalmajor* Maeder remained with his men. He had them fall in by units one last time, spoke to them, reminded them of their common struggles and sacrifices, and asked them to maintain discipline even in this difficult situation and remain true to themselves.

The next night *Generalmajor* Maeder assembled the entire officer corps of the *Führer-Grenadier-Division* in an old mill near the meadow at Trakwein and following a brief speech said goodbye to each with a handshake. The Soviets officers who were present watched in silence; when the last officer was about to leave the room and turned to go, one of the Soviet officers walked up to the German general and in broken German said:

I served at sea as a sailor in the last war. Every time a ship sank the captain remained on board and went down with the ship; his officers followed this example and followed him into death. I experienced this twice—such discipline!

And here I have seen the same thing. What discipline! Politics is nothing— discipline is everything!

The officers of the *Führer-Grenadier-Division* assembled before their commander once again in the coming days, when the commanding general of the Soviet forces addressed them; in fluent German he said:

I express my admiration to the division for its outstanding fighting performance and soldierly bearing. I give you my word of honor that you will be sent to another camp, there you will be registered and then released to go home. Officers may retain their sidearms.

Based on these promises by the Soviet officer, the departure for the camp at Zwettl took place quickly and uneventfully. In spite of the depressing end, discipline was exemplary. Everyone believed the victor's promises.

And then the promises were "redeemed": released from the camp at Zwettl, the men were loaded aboard trains in groups and transported to the east! Among those sent into the vast spaces or Russia was the division commander of the *Führer-Grenadier-Division*, *Generalmajor* Maeder.

Chapter 6
The Road to Captivity for the Panzer-Grenadier Division Brandenburg

The transports carrying the Panzer-Grenadier Division Brandenburg rolled through the protectorate of Bohemia-Moravia, which was in revolt. Coming from the loading stations near Dresden, they headed via Glatz and Prague in the direction of Olmütz, which was their designated target station. The Ib, General Staff Major Spaeter, had gone ahead with a few vehicles to make preparations for the division's arrival in Olmütz. He was also under orders to find out as much as he could about the Brandenburgers' next mission. He therefore sought contact with XLIX. Geb.A.K., which was engaged in fierce defensive fighting east of Olmütz in the industrial region of Mährisch-Ostrau. Like a narrow tube to the east, the mountain corps' Jäger divisions stood back to back along the Mährisch-Weisskirchen road to Olmütz. The only contact with the general Eastern Front was near Sternberk north of Olmütz and in the area southwest of Leipnik to the south of it.

The order to withdraw this exposed position had long since been issued when the first units of the Pz.Gren.Div. *Brandenburg* arrived in Olmütz. At the same time, 2 and 3 May 1945, the Soviets were desperately trying to break into the city and sever the last avenue of retreat into the city from the east. Already on 2 May tank shells whistled over the city, mainly fired from the northeast. Endless infantry and vehicle columns rolled through Olmütz toward the west; to their credit in good order, although under pressure from the intensifying enemy fire. However the slow walking pace of the now horse-drawn units caused the defenders on the flanks north and south of the city grave concern. Would they withstand the constantly growing pressure until the last of the infantry's vehicles was through? Was there still enough time to bring in all the units of the Pz.Gren.Div. *Brandenburg*, with whose help a stable defense could be erected against these flanking attacks?

Everything depended on the timely arrival of the *Brandenburg* fighting units, the bulk of which were still on the rails.

Many soldiers asked themselves repeatedly what the reason had been for taking them out of the Dresden area and the command of the Panzerkorps GD and sending them more than a hundred kilometers into what was obviously a pocket forming around Army Group Center. Was it the fact that Army Group Schörner was the only complete, self-supplying army group capable of offering effective resistance to the Soviets and thus at the same time a catch basin for all combat-capable fighting units, especially since the rumors that the Reich government under Dönitz was considering a move to Prague refused to die?

Was it the fact that the behavior of the Soviets in the Bautzen—Dresden area in the last days of April which made possible a withdrawal of German units from that front? Or was it perhaps concern on the part of Gen.Lt. von Natzmer, the chief-of-staff of Army Group Schörner, for his GD Division and a desire to place it under his care and thus offer it a chance of survival? Or was the Panzer-Grenadier Division *Brandenburg*, which could still be counted on in those days, to cover the retreat of Army Group Center?

The latter explanation must probably be accepted, although the average soldier knew little about any plans. In the previous war years he had seen action in so many places, had experienced the thrill of victory and the burden of defense, had lost count of former comrades now lying somewhere in Russian earth, scarcely remembered the names of those who had once gone into battle with him. Only one thing had remained with him: the community of his squad, his company, his comrades!

There was no more retreating; anyway, where could they go? He shared the isolation that surrounded him with those in his unit, and only in it did he still have a tiny chance of survival.

But what kept him going, what led him to go into battle again and again, to take up his weapon, to risk his life? Was it the orders issued to him by his superiors? Was it a sense of duty? If so, then toward what? Or was it a vague hope of a turn for the better?

Perhaps the answer may be found in the words of the commander of the Pz.Stu.Pi.Btl. BR, *Hauptmann* Müller-Rochholz, a few days before the transfer into the Olmütz area:

The war cannot last much longer; there will be chaos. In these days we wish to be true to ourselves and follow our fate through to the end. The spirit of our battalion, our comradeship and our dead obligate us. Our shield shall remain pure to the last minute! No one will run away. All our battles have proved that we do not go under if we stand together as one man.

So it will remain until the final order!

So it will remain until the final order; only a few commanders would be still capable of giving it. This applied to the assault pioneers as well. Their transport was the last planned, at least the directed rest for the battalion was to be exploited to the full. This order by the division commander was a Greek gift to the men, however: only one of the three transport trains reached the Olmütz area, the others came to grief. The 1. Kp. and headquarters Pz.Stu.Pi.Btl. BR landed in Hansdorf, the point at which the Soviets forced the pioneer group to turn west.

Things went much the same for the Fahr-Abt. BR under Stubaf. Count Eggloffstein. Two trains carrying the 1. and 2. Fahrschwadron reached their assigned destinations, however the third carrying the head-

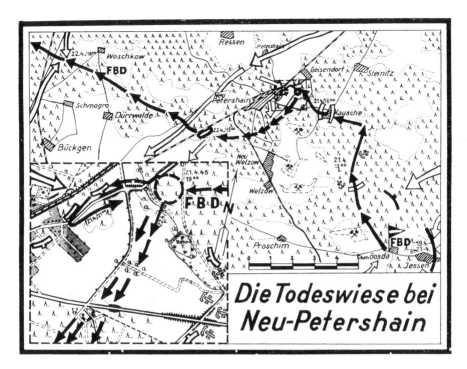

Die Todeswiese bei
Neu-Petershain

The Meadow of Death at Neu-Petershain

quarters and 3. Schwadron was forced to turn back in the Glatz area. Its fate, like that of the other transports and groups which departed last and drove into the midst of the uprising by Czech partisans and advancing Soviet tank spearheads, was the beginning of that which would befall most of Army Group Center: the road into Soviet captivity!

The majority of the Panzer-Grenadier Division *Brandenburg*'s combat units—the two regiments, the artillery, the armored reconnaissance battalion, the assault gun brigade and several supply units—did reach Olmütz, arriving piecemeal and going into action from there. Of the division headquarters all that was on the spot was one radio section and the Second General Staff Officer; the Ia, General Staff Obstlt. Erasmus, lay wounded somewhere in an ambulance of the San.Kp. BR on one of the transport trains. The division commander, Gen.Lt. Schulte-Heuthaus, was pacing the trains in his Kübel and could not be reached. The command of the division was thus in the hands of the Ib, General Staff *Major* Spaeter. Beginning on 2 May, he received the arriving units in Olmütz, issued their orders and assembled all of *Brandenburg* around him.

The Panzer-Grenadier Division *Brandenburg*'s mission was dictated by the situation on both sides of Olmütz: cover the passage of German infantry units through the city by defending against all enemy attacks,

481

eliminate all enemy penetrations into the weak German lines of security north and south of the city, and finally cover the retreat of the 1. Pz.-Armee.

There was no time to assemble the division; the approaching sound of battle, the tank fire into the city and the bad news from the passing infantry columns made it imperative that the BR units go into action at once as their transports arrived. Elements of the Pz.A.A. BR left the ramps of the detraining station and deployed in a northeasterly direction. On the evening of 2 May the arriving I./Jäg.Rgt. 2 under Hptm. Steidl left the city and headed south to close a gap somewhere southeast of the city. Uncertainty about the situation and the darkness forced the battalion to halt and wait for daylight.

While the first transports were unloading at Olmütz station, the last units of the Pz.Gren.Div. *Brandenburg* were waiting at the loading ramps in Klotzsche and Radebeul. There were not enough cars. It really was a joke: the units still waiting there went searching for railway cars in an effort to somehow join the rest of the division. The last did not leave the stations near Dresden until 4 and 5 May, having acquired the necessary trains, in some cases by force. The situation around Olmütz was becoming critical; in the city itself numerous infantry and vehicle columns passed through from the east. The enemy had already reached the area north of Sternberk, some armored forces were advancing south; the thin German security lines there tried desperately to hold. Enemy spearheads had already reached the Tscheitzitsch area southeast of the city; some tanks were prowling around somewhere near the rail line, causing more than a little consternation.

German units included the infantry formations streaming west as well as arriving motorized units, among them the Pz.Gren.Div. Feld-herrnhalle 1, which went into position somewhere south of Olmütz with its front facing east. It took some time to establish a continuous line, which was significantly strengthened with the arrival of the BR units.

Meanwhile Obstlt. Oesterwitz, the commander of the Jäg.Rgt. 2 BR, arrived, with II./Jäg.Rgt. 2 BR coming almost simultaneously. He took over command south and southeast of the city. Meanwhile the Steidl battalion had worked its way over rain-soaked roads right up to the town of Tscheitzirtch, where it was met by a hail of shells of every caliber. This was not fire in the usual sense, instead it was the showering of a small group of men with a series of light, medium and heavy shells which did not leave even a small patch of earth unturned. The first impacts inflicted casualties in the ranks of the arriving troops. This was not combat, it was the destruction of the weaker by the superior force.

It was also not courage that impelled a man to get up and carry on; it was simply desperation, a desire to somehow get away from this inferno, to find a place where his life was not in danger. Only the old hands, following their own system and orders, still advanced on the enemy. They were the veterans of numerous battles. Only in this way did I./Jäg.Rgt. 2 BR and its brave commander Hptm. Steidl succeed in entering Tscheitzitsch, where they established themselves in the ruins of houses and behind shattered walls. In spite of the fury of the enemy barrage they held on.

No one asked why—it really didn't matter. They fought, carrying those who wavered with them, held the positions—and remained together, one way or another.

Meanwhile, farther to the rear—somewhere on the rail lines—the last transports carrying the Pz.Gren.Div. *Brandenburg* were rolling through the countryside; this meant that they were stopped more than they were moving. Even if the railways were operating more or less according to plan, many Czech railway workers, sensing that Soviet troops were near, did their best to sabotage the German effort. Some trains were sent the wrong way. In some cases trains found themselves back at the same station they had left hours before. Others stopped on the tracks, allegedly because the coal or water had run out. Hours passed and nothing happened. Slowly, very slowly, other elements of the division arrived. The cars carrying the He.-Flak.Abt. BR under *Major* Vosshagen finally arrived at the platforms of Olmütz station early on 5 May. Unloading began. The battalion initially moved east, toward Blaze, where it assumed responsibility for the air defense of the retreat road. Soon afterwards it transferred to Krönau in the area northwest of Olmütz. Only hours later the first trains carrying Jäg.Rgt. 1 BR pulled up in front of Stefanau and detrained there. No more trains could stop in Olmütz because the platforms had been destroyed. No one knew what was actually going on. Shellfire continued to land in the city, on the other hand an increasing number of infantry columns continued to move through the streets of Olmütz to the west. Whole squadrons of Soviet bombers dropped their loads on the city. Fortunately the division commander and his Ia arrived at this time; the division command was able to resume its tasks. Its first step was to deploy the elements of Jäg.Rgt. 1 BR which had just arrived to secure along the Olmütz—Stefanau—Hohenstadt rail line. Their sector was approximately 15 kilometers wide and was initially held by II./Jäg.Rgt. 1 BR commanded by *Rittmeister* Sandmeyer. The town of Stefanau was already occupied by the enemy, and infantry fire was striking the rail station located approximately 2 000 meters west of the town. *Major* Bansen set up his command post near Nakel, where he met *Rittmeister* Frey with elements of the Pz.A.A. BR. Soon afterwards *Hauptmann* Metzger also assembled the *Sturmgeschütz-Brigade GD*, which was equipped with the latest assault guns, representing a considerable armored force. Thus reassured, the *Jäger* set about building and occupying a loose line of fortified strongpoints and machine-gun nests.

On 5 May the enemy situation northeast of Olmütz was as follows: the town of Stefanau was in enemy hands, but with infantry only at first. A continuous flow of reinforcements was arriving from the hills east of the town. Column after column of motorized units accompanied by tanks streamed into the valley, especially on the road from Sternberk. These movements were particularly noticeable at night, as the vehicles were driving with all lights on. It appeared, however, that the bulk of the Soviets were moving past Olmütz to the south, at least the sound of battle suggested this.

On the afternoon of 5 May a makeshift hospital train steamed into Olmütz station. The locomotive uncoupled and disappeared to the west. Alone and abandoned, the cars full of seriously wounded men sat on the tracks, enemy infantry fire already striking among them. Then three salvoes of Stalin Organ fire which fell in the middle of the stopped train with terrible effect.

By the next evening the *Jäger*, under the direction of the battalion medical officers, succeeded in rescuing the survivors. This was not without problems, for the Soviets repeatedly attacked Stefanau station and the defenders were only just able to keep them at bay. The doctors and medics were forced to work under awful conditions. Each car in the train had been hit at least once by the Stalin Organs, which continued firing. The cars were filled with bodies, while those left alive were half mad and scarcely conscious from horror and dismay.

Farther south near Olmütz the *Jäger* of the 2. Regiment were still fighting stubbornly, especially I. Btl. under Hptm. Steidl. The main line of resistance now ran along the outskirts of Tschahovic, the Soviets having succeeded in advancing past the positions on both sides. And yet the defense line stabilized; anti-aircraft guns were in Bedihorst, other elements of German motorized units bolstered the defense. Finally it was possible to relieve the units of the Jäg.Rgt. 2 BR deployed there and pull them out of the line. The task now was to assemble the *Brandenburg* units in one combat zone. During the night of 6 May, therefore, these elements moved via Olmütz and Nakel into the area just west of the rail line near Stefanau station.

The German divisions there were showing the first signs of disintegration, however. Word got around, many listened to the other side's radio broadcasts: the Soviets were in Vienna and near Leobendorf. The German units deployed in the west of the Reich and those in Denmark and Norway had surrendered. Street fighting was already raging in Prague. The end was near. And with this coming end first individuals, then entire squads, companies and independent units separated themselves from their units and headed west. Entire divisions disintegrated, left their positions and disappeared into the dead of night. Others commandeered trucks and fled fully armed without regard for their comrades up front in the holes.

The latter now had to draw even closer together, to stand together even more than before. Only together might they yet find a way home. The command, the officers and non-commissioned officers considered, seeking a way out of the coming chaos, a way to escape the collapse.

The last Order of the Day from the commander-in-chief of Army Group Center, *Generalfeldmarschall* Schörner, promising an orderly withdrawal to the west by all of his units and dated 5 May 1945, came too late.

Schörner's Last Order of the Day

The commander-in-chief of Army Group Center   *H.Q., 5 May 1945*

Soldiers of Army Group Center!

After six years of bitter struggle the superior strength of our enemy has succeeded in bringing about the fall of one part of our fronts. The front held by the southern army groups on the Eastern Front alone still stands unbroken. This is due to your bravery and steadfastness.

The war is approaching its end. In keeping with the order from the Führer's chosen head of state and supreme commander of the German armed services, Grossadmiral Doenitz, we are to fight on until the most valuable German people have been saved.

After completing this mission it is my intention to send you, my soldiers, back to the homeland together and proudly. This noble mission of command can only be accomplished with an obedient and capable force. In these most difficult days for our Reich we must not lose our nerve or our courage, most of all we must not listen to the enemy's skillfully distributed rumors. We must have faith that our command is doing the right thing in this situation.

For six long years we have stayed together and defied the enemy. In the final weeks we must not show the world a picture of disintegration and thus shatter the negotiations that have begun. Every unauthorized absence, every attempt to find a way home on one's own, is an honorless betrayal of comrades and our people and must be punished accordingly.

Our discipline and the weapons in our hands are our pledge to exit this war decently and bravely. Our honor and the heroic deaths of so many of our comrades obligate us to do this. Only someone who gives up on himself is truly lost.

Soldiers of my army group!

Together we have mastered so many serious crises in many sectors of the east. You can trust in me to lead you out of this crisis too; and I have faith that you will stand by people, state and head of state. But we must stand together and in spite of some traitors and cowards employ our last strength in these final hours of this war for the fulfillment of our mission. Only iron unity, unshakable will to resist and an always continuous front will lead us straight and true on the soil of the protectorate to the homeland.

Schörner

Generalfeldmarschall

Everything depended on the withdrawal on the evening of 4 May 1945 contained in Army Group Center's order, on it being carried out according to plan in an orderly fashion. According to the so-called "Operation Flower" this was to be accomplished by sectors, with the withdrawal by the

17. Armee in the east and the 1. Pz.Armee on its right setting the pace of the retreat. With its foot infantry divisions the 17. Armee could not disengage from the enemy quickly and its neighbor divisions had to hold their positions until they had done so. Only then could the subsequent, general withdrawal commence, with the fronts being held strictly together. Everything depended on keeping the 17. Armee from the clutches of the Soviets; it was vital that the positions farther south and on both sides of Olmütz be held.

On the evening of 5 May the first units quietly left their positions, and as a result on the morning of 6 May the enemy found a gaping open space in the German main line of resistance. Only the bravery and loyalty of the motorized units made it possible to overcame this danger. And even though there were only the armored patrols of the armored reconnaissance battalions, a few armored troop carriers of an SPW battalion and a handful of tanks and assault guns, the main line of resistance remained in our hands for another 48 hours.

Not until 6 May did the defensive battle being fought by the *Jäger* of 1. Rgt. near Stefanau and the rail line reach the crisis point, when the first enemy tanks, including Josef Stalins, drove through their thin lines and caused confusion in the regiment's rear sector. *Hauptmann* Metzger called up his assault guns and these succeeded in knocking out three of these armored giants. Even though the danger was not gone, the actions of the assault guns did give a warning to the attackers to exercise caution when they came again. I./Jäg.Rgt. 2 BR was now deployed at the rail line near Stefanau station, further strengthening our defense line. 3. Bttr./He.Flak-Abt. BR was also in action; the other batteries were dug in on both sides of Nakel.

The early morning hours of 7 May, the day which was to bring a decisive turn in the battle around Olmütz, saw the beginning of fighting for the city itself. The city, in fact a fortress, had no garrison, as it had withdrawn with the infantry units days earlier. The fortress artillery was weakly manned and seldom was it heard to fire. It was impossible to determine who was defending the city; in any case there was some firing there, which at first delayed the Soviet entry into Olmütz. The bunkers and positions in the approaches were locked, their keys had disappeared. They still contained weapons and ammunition which could not now be used. Somewhere in the big storehouses in the city there were enormous stocks of food which, locked until the last minute, ended up falling into enemy hands.

The Pz.Gren.Div. *Brandenburg* also encountered the first cases of desertion. First it was several clerks from the trains, then the entire crew of an infantry gun abandoned their weapon and fled west in their truck.

Rumors circulated; there was to be an immediate withdrawal toward the American lines. The motorized and panzer divisions were to cover the retreat. Early the next day the Pz.Gren.Div. *Brandenburg* was to fall back by approximately 100 kilometers. Armored patrols and armored troop carrier crews of the Pz.A.A. BR were directed into the positions along the rail line on both sides of Stefanau station—the Pz.Aufkl.Abt. BR was to take over the positions formerly held by the bulk of the Jäg.Rgt. 1 BR and screen the division's withdrawal. Fortunately the Russians did not initiate any major actions during the afternoon of 7 May. There was some firing and artillery and Stalin Organ barrages but no attacks.

Meanwhile all excess baggage was destroyed, office material was burned. The vehicles were lightened to make room for the men. The night of 8 May passed; early on the morning of this last day of the war the men rose from their holes. Dirty, cold and aware that the great war was over, the various groups made their way to the assembly point. Machine-guns on their shoulders, ammunition canisters in their hands, the men trotted to their vehicles and climbed aboard. The drive began; over roads and past anti-tank barricades, the vehicles rolled west in good order. Behind them the din of the battle being fought by the elements of the Panzer-Aufklärungs-Abteilung *Brandenburg* deployed northwest of Olmütz. They were the last in contact with the enemy, covering their comrades' withdrawal even though they knew that their own escape became more and more doubtful as each hour passed.

All day long the vehicles of the Pz.Gren.Div. *Brandenburg* rolled west, covering hundreds of kilometers, and assembled in and near Bistrau. The combat elements, the heavy weapons and assault guns went into position west of the city. The Ib took up station in a house in Bistrau, seeing to it that the vehicles and supply units took cover behind houses. Czech partisans were doing some shooting; soldiers from other units roamed the streets, unarmed, some already in civilian clothes, some wearing white armbands. In a school there was a German hospital with some seriously wounded men plus a few medics. Runners and dispatch riders were on the move to establish contact with the division command post in Svitava Valley. They had to keep to the forests, were driven out of these by enemy fire, one returned with a wounded arm. The order was issued to travel only in column, never alone. Another dead man was found on the road, shot from ambush.

The division commander and his Ia were in a house by a road in the Svitava Valley. Next to the wall was a radio set, the radio operator transmitting messages—to the corps, to the Pz.A.A. BR fighting up front. The division's combat vehicles were parked under trees, next to houses, beside bushes. The sound of battle could still be heard from the east.

It was nearing evening on 8 May; the last rays of sunshine fell on the soldiers as they set up camp. Sitting in the Kübelwagen of Jäg.Rgt. 2's signals officer were Oblt. Schmalbruch and Oblt. Brauschmidt, the signals officer. They fumbled with the radio set, listening to news reports on

German radio. Then they listened. The word surrender was heard, names like Keitel and Jodl. Signed, the surrender was being signed—over! Obstlt. Oesterwitz heard the news and ran back into the house to tell Gen.Lt. Schulte-Heuthaus. Silence! Here and there an officer wiped his eyes as if a fly were bothering him. Others left the house in silence, walked onto the road and off to the side. Then the Ia got up, he wanted to say something. But the division commander swept away the still unspoken words with a wave of his hand.

Radio message—immediately to the corps, to the army group; to everyone:

Jodl and Keitel have betrayed us; Panzer-Grenadier Division Brandenburg is marching!

His words fell heavy in the room, picked up by those present and passed on to everyone:

All vehicles, weapons, ammunition, tanks and assault guns are to be destroyed immediately! Panzer-Grenadier Division Brandenburg to retain only those vehicles necessary for the transport of men and small arms, assemble near Bistrau and break through to the Bavarian Forest!

Now it was out, the decision made: it was 18:05 hours on 8 May 1945. It went through the room like a sigh of relief and then made its way outside. Runners raced off, the first vehicles carrying staff officers set out to scout roads, officers rushed to their units and issued orders to destroy weapons and equipment.

Less than 30 minutes later the first explosions rang out in the narrow valley, echoing along the forest's edge. The engines of the assault guns roared to life for the last time before the vehicles were driven into a ravine somewhere. The men assembled, armed with machine-guns, submachine-guns, rifles and assault rifles, picked out a spot by a tree and waited.

Cars and trucks raced to Bistrau, prepared for departure, and also blew up countless vehicles there. The Ib oversaw the loading of fuel, the vital fluid for the long journey west. Fires began, the most effective means of destroying vehicles and equipment.

Darkness fell. It was already 20:00 hours when the front of the column passed through Bistrau headed west. In the lead were several cars, Oblt. Bröker (the O1) and several other officers, with a radio truck. Their task was to report on the usability of the roads as quickly as possible. Truck after truck joined the column—no more guns, no tanks or assault guns, no heavy prime movers—just trucks and more trucks, now and then a car or Kübel, in them the *Jäger* and other troops, tent squares around their shoulders, weapons between their knees. They were going home. Back to where they had first set out from.

Would they succeed? Would all of these men get through enemy territory?

It was night—the night of 8 May 1945. The road was hopelessly clogged; two columns stood on it side by side. An eerie light bathed this urgent, excited, in some places already panicky scene. Rumors spread through the columns: the Soviets are on our heels! Save yourself if you can! We have been betrayed and sold out!

The banks on both sides of the road were littered with burning vehicles, abandoned and destroyed. An awful scene, the start of the breakdown. But it was not yet over.

Officers with pistols drawn finally cleared the road. Vehicles which were in the way were pushed over the bank. The frightful tangle of vehicles unraveled and dispersed. The drive continued slowly through the night. There were repeated tie-ups, more waiting, nervous pacing. Then another horse-drawn column; the horses strained nervously against their harnesses. Curses from the drivers added to the din. In a field to the right several vehicles were burning. Parachute flares. The animals became spooked, could scarcely be held. Teams and wagons stood across the road. Then there were two columns side by side again. It took an hour to untangle this mess.

Finally the *Brandenburgers'* motorized column turned off onto a side road. There it proceeded rapidly, but soon an anti-tank barricade was encountered which halted all progress. More than 30 minutes of hard labor were required before movement was restored. But the joy was short-lived. Ten stout tree trunks lay across the road. Cursing, the men moved in to clear away this obstacle too. The trunks were sawed, hacked and finally dragged to the side.

The journey resumed. At last a fine, broad asphalt road. The vehicles increased speed. Morning was dawning, it was between 05:00 and 07:00 hours.

In front of Frauenthal the point once again found the road clogged with traffic. There was I. (SPW)/Jäg.Rgt. 1 BR. But the armored troop carriers pushed the obstacles aside and the column moved forward again. Then another halt—some other column had pushed its way into the line. Some elements lost contact. Curses and shouts. Then everything stopped again. Ahead was a village, that wouldn't work. Officers, commanders, runners and unit leaders jumped onto motorcycles and drove along the halted column to a hill, before which spread a flat valley. There the town of Deutschbrod. Incomprendingly the men saw before them Soviet tanks and vehicles. Too late! The Russians were already there; coming from somewhere in the north or south they had closed the first ring around the German armies.

Driving through Deutschbrod itself with just trucks and machine-guns, with just small arms and no tanks or assault guns, was out of the question.

And there at a crossroads on the hill before Deutschbrod, in the middle of an open field, the end came for the Panzer-Grenadier Division *Brandenburg*. There it dispersed to the four winds, there the community of men, some of whom had been together since 1938, parted ways. Over! Finished!

Early on 9 May 1945 division commander Gen.Lt. Schulte-Heuthaus sent the following fateful radio message: "Deutschbrod occupied by the enemy! Division diverting to the north!" Only the remaining radio stations picked up this message and passed it on to the units. No one else heard it and no one else could follow it. The fighting units split up at this crossroads. Some headed north, others south, others followed the leaders in the direction of Deutschbrod. And in the midst of this decision Soviet bombers attacked the clusters of vehicles at the crossroads, bringing death, chaos, destruction and panic to the columns. Men ran in all directions, seeking desperately to get away.

Off to the side of the crossroads sat a plain Volkswagen; in it was the division Ib, General Staff *Major* Spaeter, together with several signals men and one or two officers. They watched the end, experienced it in shock, for they were always at the end of the column in order to help anyone faced with vehicle breakdown or fuel shortage. So far they had been successful, now it was over; all help was too late here. With tears in their eyes the last eyewitnesses of this scene of death turned and drove away alone—home.

What would become of them? Of the Panzer-Grenadier Division *Brandenburg* there at the crossroads before Deutschbrod on 9 May 1945? The following accounts tell how the various units tried to get home. There are only a few, but they are representative of all:

Jäger-Regiment 1 Brandenburg: the O1, Lt. Grosser, wrote:

The column stopped again. We were in front of Deutschbrod. The commander and I drove ahead in the motorcycle-sidecar. We reached the hill, from where we could see into Deutschbrod. Russian tanks in the town! This discovery struck us like a blow! Paralyzed, we looked at each other for a moment. Then we collected ourselves. We would have to act quickly if we still wished to get through. The Major issued the order: "Divert north toward Caslau and get across via the Deutschbrod—Caslau road before the Russians arrive!" The commander specified another assembly point for the regiment. He remained with I. Btl. I drove back down the road as fast as I could to the armored troop carrier, sent a runner to II. Btl. with the necessary orders. At the same time there was radio activity. An order from the division was passed to me from the division radio vehicle, which was still with me. Its contents were as follows: "Deutschbrod occupied by the enemy, division diverting to the north." II. Btl. received the division order. Rittmeister Sandmeyer had already turned the battalion north. I decided also to drive north with the two armored troop carriers and the dispatch riders so as to be able to organize the regiment as soon as it reached the assembly point. Furthermore I would rejoin the commander there. We were about to drive away when the division armored troop carrier threw a track. We hastily repaired the thing. The armored troop carrier began moving under tow on its tracks again. But a cotter pin had broken. It took some time until a new one was fitted. But the crew would have to help themselves now. I drove away. I never saw the division armored troop carrier again.

We drove north across open fields. We came upon a road again, just outside a town. Long, unbroken column. I was reluctant to drive into a town, the danger of a traffic jam was too great. The vehicles were already becoming backed up on the road. I followed a narrow path into the bushes and meadows. When I was abeam the village in question, truly hellish firing broke out in it. Damn it, the Russians were already there, that could get ticklish. Or perhaps it was Czech partisans. Only where had they got all the arms? We also now came under fire in the open. We had to turn around in a marshy meadow. The armored troop carrier had to pull the dispatch riders' motorcycles out of the mud. We followed a steep path down into a ravine and away.

We continued to drive, always north, through many small villages. Our weapons and Panzerfausts lay ready across the sides of the vehicles. But all the villages were as dead. No Czechs to be seen. Now and then we saw a woman pushing her child away from the street in fear.

Our rapid zigzag drive made orientation very difficult. I repeatedly became lost. On the way we picked up a Czech who also wanted to reach the west. He was carrying a small case. He told us that he expected little from his countrymen in the future. I was distrustful of him at first, but he guided us well.

We came upon a column of Volkswagens, with a general, a wearer of the Oak Leaves. Like us he was headed north, but he was unsure which way to go now since columns could be seen on the main road moving north parallel to us. They included tanks. It had to be Russians. They were fatally quick.

We stopped in a small village. Vehicles dashed back and forth. It was said that the enemy held the other exit from the village. There were Czechs standing there and in a friendly way they called upon us to lay down our weapons and surrender. It was enough to drive one to despair. But I hadn't reached that point yet. Then Rittmeister Sandmeyer and Feigle arrived in a motorcycle-sidecar combination. "Go, Grosser. We have to cross the road now or never, otherwise we will be sitting in a mousetrap." So I climbed back into my vehicle. The Rittmeister led the way with his motorcycle. He went so fast that I had trouble keeping up with the armored troop carrier. Finally it was done. The Rittmeister was gone. I drove out of a valley onto a level area, on which there was a farm. Anti-tank or tank fire landed among the vehicles parked around the farm house. Nevertheless, I drove up to see whether the Rittmeister was there. He was not to be found. The enemy fire was damned accurate. Beside me a vehicle took a direct hit and blew up. I subsequently left this inhospitable place. The choking dust made my eyes water. I could barely see, it was awful. I had to repeatedly wash out my eyes with cold coffee from a canteen so as to be able to see at all. We made another dash to the north. We entered a town with a high-sitting estate or castle. Tanks were firing into the town. I drove down the street from the estate into the town. To my surprise, down below I found our Ia and division adjutant. They, too, had tried to get through but had failed. We discussed the situation. The Ia was of the opinion that we should try to force our way through. Major Lau definitely wanted to get to the general so as to avoid leaving him in the lurch. We therefore decided to try and assemble strong elements of the division rather than try and sneak through again. We drove south a ways and soon met the general. My commanding officer was also there. It was desperately hot and there was not a drop left to drink. I crawled into the clay culvert to get out of the sun. Finally, some water. I poured a bucket over my head, in my eyes and down my collar. How refreshing it was! To complete my joy I found a crushed cigarette in my pants pocket. Refreshed and satisfied, I crawled back into my culvert.

The commanders of the other regiments and independent battalions had also found their way there. The only one missing was Rittmeister Frey, the commander of the reconnaissance battalion. He and his battalion were covering the division's retreat. He was said to have been killed or badly wounded. Our Hauptmann Schuster was also there. He had the bulk of the armored troop carrier battalion with him. My Horch was also there with my faithful batman Krehan. He gave me something to eat. Our radio-equipped armored troop carrier was also there.

The commanders gathered for a conference. We were all tense to the point of bursting about what was to come. Shooting broke out in the woods behind us. In front of us on the road the sound of fighting.

Krehan told me what was going on behind us. Russian close-support aircraft had caught the column and worked it over. Many vehicles had been left in flames. The road was completely blocked. It must have been a chaotic mess. Our medical officer, Dr. Fischer, was last seen when, with tears in his eyes, he blew up his vehicle, which was blocking the road. The commanders talked endlessly, at least it seemed so to me. Finally they were finished. What had they decided?

The general came toward us. In the past hours he had escaped the Russians by a hair's breadth. His armored troop carrier had driven three meters in front of a Russian anti-tank gun. He had managed to escape to the west, but had been ordered to turn around. The anti-tank gun fired at him from close range and he jumped from the armored troop carrier. In the confusion he jumped onto a motorcycle at the last minute and got away from the Russians.

"Gentlemen, it is a difficult hour. I can not get the division through in one piece!" The blood ran ice cold through my veins and a shudder went through me. "An attempt must be made to get through in small groups, with or without vehicles, it's up to the individual. Small groups, lieutenants with their platoons or companies. The commanders with their headquarters. Gentlemen, don't leave the men who believe in you. I cannot say whether we will reach the west. I must leave it to each man's luck and fate. The American are on the Moldau."

The Ia, General Staff Oberstleutnant Erasmus, was of the opinion that it would be best to try to get through farther south during the night. The Russian armored spearheads must have advanced as far as Caslau. In his opinion, the *only possibility was to cross the road behind these and their following infantry.*

Those of us gathered there shook hands one last time before going our ways into an uncertain future. The general said goodbye with a firm handshake and a gaze into the eyes: *God be with you!* The division was no more… It was incomprehensible and I was barely able to hold back my tears at the thought of this tragic end of our proud unit. It was simply incomprehensible.

Hauptmann Metzger and a medical officer, who were driving a Schwimmwagen, attached themselves to our group. Several other officers, including Oblt. Mücke of the reconnaissance battalion, also joined us with a number of men. Our vehicles were overfilled with people. We drove off to try our luck.

Everywhere the fields swarmed with men and vehicles. A shattered army. When they saw our armored troop carriers they tagged along, hoping that the armored vehicles would dare to break through.

Within five minutes we had a train of more than fifty vehicles behind us. This wouldn't work; we would never get through with such a dust-raising column. We zigged and zagged in an effort to shake our appendage. But it was quite impossible. So we drove into a group of bushes, parked the vehicles and lay down to rest. Everyone who came and asked if we could take them along we told that we were not going to risk a breakthrough and instead were going to surrender to the Russian here. It was a bitter thing to put people off in this way, but our vehicles were already overfilled. Again and again we were sought out and assailed with every possible plan.

Slowly, slowly, they left us alone and abandoned us as hopeless idiots. Only a Hauptmann Pösch, commander of a ski battalion, a tank man, stubbornly remained with us in his car and was thus taken into our ranks.

Meanwhile the Russians were fanning out from the road. The shooting was already uncomfortably close. By now it was late afternoon. For an hour already we had been observing an unbroken stream of vehicles approaching from the northwest. We expected that the whole bunch would start flowing back at any minute. But it had been flowing smoothly for an hour already. Was there a gap in the enemy's blocking line? I was in favor of going along. The commander, however, was against the idea of joining such a large group. But finally we agreed to try it again.

We pulled on our jackets and packed out things. Everyone had readied a small emergency kit in case we had to leave the vehicles. Climb in, move out! Our hearts beat higher again.

We joined the stream of vehicles, with some skepticism at first. But we moved ever farther to the west, zigzagging back and forth, over meadows, fields and ditches. To our right in front of us lay Caslau.

Although there were many vehicles under way, there were no stoppages for we were driving cross-country, not on roads.

We crossed the rail line and shortly afterwards the road. Done it! A sigh of

493

relief; we had achieved that which we scarcely dared to hope. We had escaped encirclement. Now we must make it!

Our armored troop carrier had dropped a track, the old problem. We stopped by a hedge. It was still frightfully hot. Like a man dying of thirst I bent over a small rivulet to fill my stomach with water.

Finally finished! We continued on our way. Often one did not know which way to turn for the vehicles in front of us headed off in different directions. Several times I saw several hundred meters farther the column heading in exactly the opposite direction. Swampy areas had to be skirted, bridges sought.

We came to a small stream. About 50 vehicles were stopped in front of the bridge, down to which led a short stretch of sunken road. They sat wedged together, their radiators facing the bridge in a star pattern. A truck had tried to force its way into the column farther ahead in the defile. It half toppled down the embankment and was now blocking the road even more. There was much pushing and shoving. There was no consideration. It would have been senseless to intervene as an officer. Panicky fear of the Russians was in everyone's bones and showed in almost every face. Everyone wanted to be first to get away to the west. Après mois le déluge!

We tried to get across the river at another place. We drove along the water. But we could not find another way across, as the bank on our side fell away vertically 8 to 10 meters straight to the river. There was nothing else to do but force our way through the crush at the bridge too.

Scarcely a few minutes had passed, during which the mass of vehicles became even more crammed together, when a shout came from a vehicle that had raced up behind us: Russian tanks! It was as if the devil were loose! The vehicles pushed out and in some cases into each other, some drivers fled on foot. Beside us one set his truck on fire and it immediately began to burn fiercely. A frightful panic had broken out. We tore the Panzerfausts from their racks. Several of our men were positioned along the embankment so as to engage the tanks with Panzerfausts if need be. The panic did achieve one thing, however; it restored forward movement. Like an icebreaker our armored troop carrier pushed its way through the tangle of vehicles, creating a lane for our other vehicles.

Finally we were on the bridge. The report of tanks proved to be false, or at least exaggerated. Russian tanks had appeared two or three kilometers back on the road and had cut off the stream of vehicles there. But it would be a while before they got to the bridge.

We continued on our way. It wasn't long before we came to the big Caslau—Tabor road. We were able to go quite fast and covered a lot of ground.

When dusk came we stopped in a forest to rest both men and machines. After about five minutes our pioneer platoon came driving up. We were happy to have found someone from our own unit. Except for them, only Lt. Herzog and Lt. Kröner had joined us in a VW. So we had become a nice, exclusive bunch. If not us, then who would succeed in getting through to the Americans?

It was dark. Let's go! There was again plenty of traffic on the road and after a while we were in an endless column again. We drove with headlights on full. As we drove up a hill we saw behind us another string of pearls, light after light. It was Russian columns coming from Iglau.

The column stopped in front of a town. Czech partisans were said to have occupied it. We were to hand over our weapons. We could already see rifles and so on flying out of several vehicles in front of us.

We cocked the machine-guns, picked up our assault rifles and several hand grenades and placed a Panzerfaust over each side of the vehicle. Using hand signals, we let our other vehicles know what we were doing. No halt, in no event allow our weapons to be taken away, otherwise they would be able to do with us whatever they wanted, and we would be betrayed and sold out.

The commanding officer was impatient. "Go, get moving!" We sheared out of the column and drove forward. Three Czechs on a blacked-out motorcycle-side-car combination came driving towards us and tried to stop us. One called to us: "Put down your weapons, war over!" Our driver shifted down. The engine roared. I swung the machine-gun around toward the Czechs, so that there would be no doubt as to our reply to their suggestion. The boys immediately turned around and cleared the road in front of us. In the town they drove at our side and gave us directions. When we drove past them and raised our hands to say thanks, they saluted us. So they still had respect if one showed them his teeth!

And somewhere in that battle zone of Czechoslovakia the paths of various units and fleeing groups of the Pz.Gren.Div. *Brandenburg* crossed again. The Pz.Stu.Pi.Btl. BR under its commander Hptm. Müller-Rochholz was known to have been the last battalion to entrain in the Dresden area and the bulk of its men never reached the division's area of operations. They probably tried everything in their means to link up with it, however it was unable to do so. In the Caslau area, where they were on the day of the surrender, they met the first members of the Panzer-Grenadier Division *Brandenburg* to have broken through.

"Pi-Müller," the commander of the Pz.Stu.Pi.Btl. BR, described the end of the unit as he experienced it:

Panzer-Sturm-Pionier-Bataillon *Brandenburg*
9 May 1945

The column in which we were approaching Caslau halted for good before noon. It was still about four kilometers to Caslau. The red flag waved from a prominent castle on a hill. The road before us snaked down into the valley, and down below T 34s were disarming the column. For us this meant veer off. Driving through fields, we headed back along the column and turned south. Using forest and field roads we reached the broad valley south of Caslau. It, too, swarmed with German troops and vehicles trying to get to the west. For the first time we again saw vehicles bearing the white helmet and red eagle. There were no answers to our pressing questions: "Where is our general? Have you seen any vehicles of the pioneer battalion?" Here, too, all was confusion. We learned that General Schulte-Heuthaus had given the order to try to reach the Bavarian Forest in small groups. Our initial objective was Tabor. Our decision in Handorf had been right. Hopefully we would find the general or Erasmus!

There was no time to lose now. We reached the stream called Doubrava. Everyone pressed toward the bridge. Shooting to our west. We linked up with several armored troop carriers from other units, two assault guns and a Panther in order to force our way through, but there was no way to reason with the gathering in front of the bridge. No one wanted to let us through, but they also did not want to fight any more. We advanced on foot and behind a railway embankment, less than a few hundred meters from the Caslau—Deutschbrod road, we found an Oberst with a white flag. He wanted to parlay with the Russians and Czechs, who were barring the way with T 34s, anti-tank guns and a few infantry! He made us sick. I spat at the Oberst's feet and we walked back. We had to find another crossing. A reporting point was established and the scout platoon set off for the last time. Mission: find a bridge over the Doubrava somewhere and look for our 2. Kp. and supply company. After a lengthy search we found a crossing near a small mill. Just beyond the stream the road climbed steeply. Above it was only about 1 500 meters to the Prague—Brünn highway, which was held by Russians and Czechs together. The T 34s shuttled down the road at intervals of about 45 minutes. It was thus not difficult to get through. The assault guns and tank came with us. The 1. Kp. (SPW) was moved forward. Attack. When we opened fire the Czechs ran away. The scout platoon reported: "2. Kp. and supply company found, given directions to us." As everywhere, a trail of various units had attached itself to us and now was first to drive through the gap. The assault guns and 1. Kp. kept the gap open, then the first vehicles of 2. Kp. arrived. Our mood was excellent. It was a miracle that we were all together again at exactly the right moment. Like in peacetime, the 2. Kp. moved quickly past me followed by the supply company. I had to stay behind with the assault guns, otherwise they might yet knock us off. We waved and laughed. Behind this hole we have the Russians at our backs, and we will drive! Drive! There was nothing to be seen of Russians or Czechs. Lt. Clemeur remained at the breakthrough point and I drove back to Lt. Küper (communications officer), having promised to pick him up there. We had left him with five abandoned trucks. He and a few men were supposed to get these going again, as they were loaded with fuel and rations. Küper was waiting, engines running. "Follow me!" We drove back to the breakthrough point. All hell was loose there, the tank and assault guns had taken off. Russian infantry—truck after truck had driven up, the road was closed again. I simply didn't want to believe it, but soon I was forced to take cover and fall back. Masses of Russians had already deployed and were advancing towards us. Still on the road were the master armorer's vehicle, our ambulance and several cars. Lt. Clemeur, Küper and about 30 men of the battalion had missed making contact. Everyone else was through. Our rage was indescribable.

We drove farther in a southerly direction and hoped to break through there, but the Russians were already in the villages everywhere and firing, whereas in *the morning they had only been shuttling along the road. Several times we drove up to occupied villages and increased speed, in order to rid ourselves of the long train of motor vehicles behind us; finally we were left with a small group of vehicles. In a forest we turned off the road to get out of sight. We would never get through with a long column We had to be a small, determined band. A Leutnant in an armored troop carrier had stayed with us and in his Schwimmwagen General Klatt, commander of the 3. Geb.Div. He was also a pioneer and determined to break through with us. We scouted from our wood. As soon as it was twilight we would drive at full speed from the hill into the small village of Friedenau, through and immediately into the high forest to the west of it. If necessary, we would fire from every buttonhole. Two Schwimmwagen brought up the rear. They were to pick up the drivers of the rations trucks should these fail to get through the town.*

We set out at 22:00 hours. The Russians were surprised. There was shooting, but we made it through to the edge of the forest. The drivers of the trucks had climbed out and approached. There was wild but inaccurate tank firing behind us. Shells exploded in the forest to our left and right. Soon we were deep enough and thus safe. For a time it looked as if everyone would become stuck in a swampy forest lane. We were forced to turn on lights and wriggle through. Then came better lanes, a poor road and a village in the forest. Czech sentries fired and tried to stop us. We drove up to them, fingers on triggers. I shone the swiveling lamp of our armored troop carrier in the face of the first, seized him by the collar and pulled him onto the nose of our vehicle. We had a guide. "You will take us to a bridge over the Sazau or…" He looked at the pistol and did as I asked. According to our 1:300,000 map his directions looked right. And they were.

10 May 1945

After the breakthrough south of Tschaslau the bulk of the battalion probably reached the Tabor area and some elements were taken prisoner there. I only met a few in captivity, because after I was arrested by the Czechs the Russians held me back in Brünn for a long time and most of the pioneers had probably headed off to Russia before me.

The last thing I heard from the division headquarters was a radioed order: I was to report to the general. This was told to me by a radio station of Jäg.Rgt. 2 which, also lacking contact with Oesterwitz, could not tell me where the general was. That was at the breakthrough point on 9 May 1945.

And here an account by the commander of I./Jäg.Rgt. 2 BR, *Major* Steidl, who later succeeded in getting home with a few of his men, but not before, like so many others, falling into Soviet hands.

Wednesday, 9 May 1945: *I met Oesterwitz in the morning. The general drove point with the armored troop carrier battalion. We advanced slowly beneath a brilliant blue sky, through hilly, fallow countryside. Vehicles from other units pushed their way into the long, endless column. There were halts every minute. I promoted my driver Wallner to Unteroffizier. I climbed onto a motorcycle and drove to the head of the column to speak to Oesterwitz. Our advance* *came to a halt in a small place. Soviet bombers and fighters suddenly roared over the column, shooting up everything. Many dead and wounded littered the road, vehicles blazed, ammunition exploded.*

I cowered next to a thatched hut. The blast waves from exploding bombs pressed me against the ground. Bombs dropped for hours.

The men scattered into the countryside. A wild panic broke out. I looked for my people in the hail of bombs. I did not find them. They must have turned off onto another road. I drove ahead again and met my senior NCO Diesel on a motorcycle. We both got on the motorcycle and drove several kilometers further in the direction of the west. We stopped in a Czech village to get our bearings. We two stood alone, surrounded by Czech civilians.. Some unfamiliar vehicles came through and became lost in the town. The Czechs had closed the anti-tank barricades at the exits. We turned around and searched in vain for our column. While seeking the way to the next town Diesel was overpowered by civilians, who took away his motorcycle and his weapon. In the same town I met the regiment's armored troop carrier with Oblt. Brauschmidt. I went with them. Several vehicles joined us. We hoped to get through to the west on our own. No trace of our people. Confusion everywhere. Columns drove here and there, were fired on in many villages and could not turn around. Staying to small forest roads we drove cross-country and gained some ground toward the west. But toward evening all forward progress came to an end. Thousands of vehicles sat everywhere, the roads were jammed. We were stuck. We decided to wait until nightfall. We put together an armored Kampfgruppe and planned to break through the Russian cordon. But there was no getting through with vehicles. The Russians bracketed us with armor-piercing shells. The last attempt had failed. I decided to break through to the west in the dark with the crew of the armored troop carrier. We left the vehicle and took only the most important equipment. Before us the Russian columns were driving on the highway with lights on. Only here could we get through. There were about 20 men with me. We felt our way ahead to the highway, weapons in hand and ready to fire. We succeeded in crossing the road through a small gap in the column. In the dark of night we pressed on over damp stubble fields and through gloomy forests, several times passing Russian bivouac camps and groups of tanks. At dawn, dead tired, we came to a rail line. In a small wood in front of it we dropped and slept.

Thursday, 10 May 1945: *After a brief rest we were jolted out of our sleep by a swarm of Cossacks. We thought they were Russians, but they were Vlasov people trying to get through to Poland on their horses.*

We forded a stream and in the late morning hours reached a wood, from which we could see German columns rolling down a road. From the soldiers we learned that the Russians were allowing free passage in the direction of Prague and that our release would take place there. We squeezed into a truck and went along. We drove west through various Czech villages. Czech policemen directed our column through larger towns. We were in good spirits, believing that all was OK. We had not yet seen any Russians. But suddenly there was a halt in a vil-

498

lage, and from a nearby gasthaus came Russian voices and singing. We jumped from the vehicle, but in an instant we were surrounded by brown figures who immediately took everything away from us. We stood there almost naked and startled at this turn of events. A commissar told us that we were to go to the station immediately and take the next train to Vienna. "Dawai!" he screamed, meaning: go home! We trudged to the station and in spite of everything still believed that we were going home.

The great collapse had come. Only now did we realize it. The people celebrated the Russian liberators in the streets, the locomotives bore wreaths and were adorned with pictures of Stalin and Soviet stars. A mass of disarmed soldiers had gathered at the station, all waiting for the next train. They gave us a train ticket, and in one hour we were in fact sitting in a train departing for Vienna.

We gnawed on our last crispbread, for we were very hungry. We passed main roads, Russian tank columns stormed forwards—endless—endless, applauded by all the people. We saw this from the windows of the car and scarcely had time to consider that we were travelling as prisoners—beggars—and that we were dependent on the favor or disfavor of the people. At one station—it was called Vlaschim—there was suddenly a murderous screaming. "German swine out!" The next thing we knew they were shoving us with rifle butts and submachine-guns out onto the platform. Waiting was a Czech mob. They spat in our faces, struck us with fists and threw rocks at us. Avoiding it was impossible. We stood drawn up in a column, about 80 men, all units mixed together. Beside every two men stood Czech civilians, some drunk, holding the muzzles of their weapons in front of our foreheads. These moments were not particularly elevating. They led us into the town and made us stop in front of a sand pit, again tormented by the mob. Machine-guns were moved into position. I was standing in the last third of the column. Beside me Oblt. Brauschmidt, pale and green in the face. We had an idea of what they were going to do: shoot us. The first were led away and from behind the wooden wall came the famous neck shots. Escape was impossible. To the left and right were rows of houses, heavily manned by civilians. Brauschmidt lost his nerve. I tried to calm him even though I was not too optimistic in this situation.

Suddenly the sound of tanks. A Russian column rolled up and stopped in front of us. Shouting loudly, the commissar put an end to the proceedings and told the Czechs that we were to be sent to the nearest camp immediately. A sigh of relief went through our ranks, we felt reborn. We trudged on over hard paving stones and came upon a large, endless column of prisoners, in whose ranks we continued to march. At the same time an endless column of Russian guards troops marched alongside us.

We went as far as Beneschau. They stuffed us into a barn, which was so crowded that we could barely squat. We dropped onto hard stones and dozed for a few hours, stomachs growling. But our thirst would not let us rest. The water line into the barn was closely guarded and we were not allowed even one drink of water. We were no longer humans.

Yes, we were no longer humans...the path to captivity for the Jäger of the Panzer-Grenadier Division Brandenburg was not the end, but the beginning of a new ordeal. The last of them returned home after eleven years.

With them also came the last of the Brandenburgers—from that division whose special missions had scattered them all over the world and did not bring them back into a fighting community until the end of 1944, where they would meet their fate.

Chapter 7
Wachregiment Großdeutschland – Berlin
The Final Battle for the Reich Capital

From Adolf Hitler's order of the day to the soldiers of the German eastern front...

This time the Bolsheviks will suffer Asia's old fate, which means that they must and will be bled white before the capital of the Reich. Berlin remains German, Vienna will be German again, and Europe will never be Russian. Form a sworn community to defend not the empty concept of a fatherland, but to defend your home, your women, your children and thus our future. In this hour the entire German people looks to you, my eastern fighters, and only hopes that through your steadfastness, your fanaticism, through your arms and through your command the Bolshevik onslaught will suffocate in a bloodbath.

From the *Wehrmacht* communiqué of 16 April 1945:

After futile attacks yesterday, following a heavy bombardment the Russians this morning launched a major assault between the mouth of the Neiße and the Oderbruch with strong infantry, tank and air forces. Bitter fighting is in progress on the entire front.

With this major assault on the Oder—Neiße line on 16 April 1945 the Soviets began the last round of the battle for the Reich. Their objective was the capital city of Berlin, the last bulwark of German resistance, the last stronghold of German command in this war. The vast metropolitan area had been devastated by air raids in recent years and was on the point of collapse. Millions vegetated in its walls, more in cellars and ruins than in wrecked apartments. The people of the city were exposed to the fury of war. The Soviets masses were approaching inexorably, carrying with them the torch of death, of destruction, or murder and devastation. Like a torrent they rolled over everything in their path, swatting aside all resistance.

But a call went out in this city to defend to the last; everyone who could carry or even serve a weapon was rushed to the defensive hotspots. Hitler Youths, the elderly, children—everyone, everyone, was mobilized, placed in groups, equipped with weapons and sent into action. Characterizing this lost group as the last reserve is charitable indeed.

There were only a few regular *Wehrmacht* troops within the walls of the city. The remains of the 9. Armee which had escaped from the west, guard units, *Volkssturm*, Hitler Youth, offices and gunners of the Reich capital's air defense, plus Kampfgruppen of the Pz.Gren.Div. *Kurmark*, sent there from its retreat from the Oder, and elements of the *Wachregiment Großdeutschland Berlin*, which had found its way back to Moabit after the collapse at the Oder west of Küstrin. *Major* Lehnhoff, the regiment's commanding officer, had once again succeeded in regrouping his two battalions. As well, he had procured weapons from the Borsig factories plus vehicles and equipment. Replacements from the navy and air force, from the Hitler Youth and anti-aircraft crews, were used to bring the units up to strength.

The Reich capital was divided into combat sectors, for whose defense Kampfgruppen, *Volkssturm*, Hitler Youth and all sorts of people were mobilized and deployed. The companies of the *Wachregiment Großdeutschland Berlin* were to act as corset stays in various sectors, shoring up the defenses there. Only in the area along the south station railway embankment (Schönhauser Allee—Prenzlauer Allee—central stock yard) did the regiment hold a continuous defense line, and in the fighting to come this was to be held without interruption until 2 May.

The military commander of Berlin, *General* Weidling, had his command post in an air raid bunker in the Bendler-Strasse, from where he tried to organize resistance against the Soviet forces driving into Berlin. Young *Leutnante* of the OKH's officer reserve who had voluntarily flown into the city assumed command of Kampfgruppen, which they led into the thick of the fighting. One such officer was Lt. Thater (GD), whose 76 veterans of the GD occupied positions at the Bendler-Block, at the Shell-Haus and near Potsdamer Strasse. The House of Tourism became the guard house, MG 42s were set up on the sidewalks and commanded entire blocks. As well there was Lt. Scheerer (GD), who assumed command of a *Volkssturm* unit from the Spandau district and led it in the battles for the city streets.

On 23 April 1945 the headquarters company left the Moabiter Block, the last of the *Wachregiment Großdeutschland Berlin*'s units to do so, and moved into the area of Lietzensee. It was led by *Hauptmann* Hoss. It was not directly involved in the fighting; instead it was used to supply the regiment's various Kampfgruppen. On 26 April *Unteroffizier* Franke of the *Wachregiment* rose above the mass of lone fighters in Berlin by single-handedly destroying seven T 34s. He was later wounded at the Friedrichshain. Hitler spoke with this brave GD man for twenty minutes in his command center in the bunker of the Reich Chancellery and then awarded him the Knight's Cross, one of the last to be awarded in the Reich capital.

Twenty-four hours later the *Wehrmacht* communiqué reported that Potsdam was in enemy hands and that the Soviets had broken into the city center, including the government quarter, from three sides.

The battle zone in the Reich capital steadily diminished in size under the pressure of the Soviet masses. The following account details the experiences of a small group of men:

The Last Days of a GD Kampfgruppe in Action in Berlin
28 April 1945 – 20:00 hours
After the recent actions there was much activity in the command post of the

sector commander of the second defense ring around Berlin in the Friedrichshain—Frankfurter Allee—Schultheiss Brewery—cemetery sector. The reports of the individual Kampfgruppe commanders were received personally, as well new orders and directives were issued, so as to gain a complete picture of the current defense belt. The previous hours had been hard ones for the men of the GD Kampfgruppe, but they were tough and determined grenadiers with many battles already behind them. Many of them, decorated with the Iron Cross, First and Second Classes, were experienced fighters, and knew well the kind of opponent, the sort of pitiless enemy they were facing. It was the lone fighting man who contested every foot of ground, who knew what was at stake: Germany's capital, his family, his home. Many of them had been wounded several times and wore the Wound Badge in Gold. They were assault soldiers, volunteers from every German district, greater German grenadiers.

The civilian population, too, came out of the air raid shelters, from the bunkers, to breathe fresh air. Food was distributed. Water was brought in. In spite of the hardships of recent days one could see how happy they were to have German soldiers nearby. A calming word often worked wonders, and many sought to find out about the situation as they hurried past. "Impossible!" one heard from the command post. This exclamation came from the second sector commander, an officer, wearer of the German Cross in Gold and the Honor Roll Clasp, a tough, veteran fighter who had a name in the division and who always turned up where it was the most dangerous. The Leutnant drew a circle in red pencil on the map in front of him and declared: "Contact with our neighbor on the left absolutely must be maintained, otherwise the assault guns on street X will be left hanging in the wind."

Orders and directives were issued for the group leaders present. The machine-gun positions were assigned to provide the necessary support. The Leutnant himself directed the operation, put together the groups of volunteers equipped with assault rifles, hand grenades and explosive charges. Contact with the unit on the left had to be restored as quickly as possible, before the enemy became aware of the gap. Messengers with orders for the rear group roared off. The group itself, led by a mission commander, set off through cellars, ruins and back yards to its departure position, a huge bomb crater. "It's always good to have the night as your friend," the light machine-gunner whispered softly to his comrade. "I wish we were already over there," replied the other.

"Stay close," said the leader softly—and in no time the grenadiers were swallowed up by the darkness.

"It seems to be going well," the leader of the company headquarters squad, an Oberfeldwebel and wearer of the Knight's Cross, whispered to the Leutnant. The Leutnant said nothing, he just stared into the darkness. But what was that? An unfamiliar voice suddenly reached the ears of the two men in the bomb crater. Muzzle flashes, bullets whizzed through the night, hand grenades exploded. The Kampfgruppe had encountered resistance. The sector commander rushed out of the bomb crater, dashed through the darkness to the reserve squad and moved it *forward.*

"Take cover immediately," he ordered, "and eyes open." Up ahead the squad fought its way with determination. Suddenly the sound of fighting was joined by the grinding of caterpillar tracks. Tanks? No, they were Russian assault guns! They were shooting blindly at anything suspicious.

"Don't be afraid!" the Leutnant admonished his men, "they can't hurt us, we are lying lower."

A loud explosion drowned out the sound of fighting. The Leutnant looked up and saw an assault gun burning, and from the near side came a shout of hurray from the dry throats of German soldiers, the signal that the squad was through.

The reserve squad moved up slowly, filled the gap, and anything that was seen in the glare of the burning assault gun was fired on. The second assault gun had been crippled by a Hetzer. Brightly lit, it crawled behind cover just in time. Brave boys, they returned and reported: "Mission accomplished, contact with left group established—two slightly wounded." "And the enemy assault gun, who…?" "I did, Herr Leutnant," declared a fifteen-year-old member of the Hitler Youth. "I would like to stay here with you." The boy had come from the neighboring group, the squad leader informed the Leutnant. The latter took the Iron Cross ribbon from the button hole of his tunic and pressed it into the boy's hand. The young man's eyes beamed.

Arriving at the command post, the sector commander was presented with an unidentified officer who had been caught snooping around in front of the positions. Although he wore a German uniform, the Leutnant stood out because he wore the national symbol on his right breast. He was taken under guard to the regimental command post. There he was found to be a member of the NKFD (National Committee for a Free Germany).

That same night we were transferred by regimental order to the southern defense belt after we were relieved by Volkssturm units. The general line: Alexanderplatz, Weibergstrasse, women's prison and farther west. The regiment's operations officer, Leutnant R., briefed us. Positions were improved, roadblocks used as cover, holes in cellars fitted out as listening posts…the enemy was not going to take us by surprise. We had arrived at a key point which was vital to the defense of the Zoo bunker.

Contact there was established by a flak officer, who promised us all possible support. Before dawn we considered feeling our way forward in groups, to seek contact with the enemy in small teams. Officers and grenadiers familiar with the local area were brought together for this purpose.

Only one group in the forward part succeeded in starting out before the sector commander's order reached them. It completed its mission in exemplary fashion, but more of that later.

The enemy fire grew in intensity, and many harsh words were spoken about so many blessings from above. Many hours had already passed and the enemy was neither to be seen nor heard. The sector commander was concerned about his men and one could see that he was worried about them. A runner came with news that contact had been lost with the unit on the right. The reserve squad was deployed there immediately to restore communications.

The enemy fire finally abated somewhat and the Leutnant made his way to his forward positions to see the situation for himself. Suddenly, from the side street in front of them, the sound of rattling tracks and engines reached the ears of the Leutnant and his grenadiers.

The first tank pushed its way around the corner of the houses and rotated its gun alarmingly toward the roadblock in front of it. It neared the anti-tank barricade slowly, too slowly. A second tank turned in, followed by a third and a fourth. We were in good cover. "They can't hurt us," said a grenadier to the Leutnant lying next to him. The first tank was now within 50 meters of the barricade, the fifth monster turning around the corner, when a terrible explosion shook the air. The Leutnant raised his head for a moment and looked and shouted: "The last one's burning, let's get them!" Cautiously, remaining in cover, the Leutnant and four grenadiers stalked into an opposite-lying ruin, armed with Panzerfausts and grenades. A second explosion followed and the Leutnant saw another tank burning. The other three now reacted violently, turning their turrets like a top and firing into the apartment buildings, the leader at the roadblock. The Leutnant and the grenadiers had already reached the ruins when there was another explosion...the third tank was out of action. The Leutnant now went after the first tank with his Panzerfaust, a shot, explosion...the tank fired no more. The crew bailed out, sought cover behind the second tank, was placed under fire by the grenadiers. The Leutnant fired another Panzerfaust and the second tank was no more.

But now back to the position, ordered the Leutnant, for the smoke and the exploding shells from the tanks threatened him and his men. The squad literally danced for joy when he returned with his four grenadiers. The position had to be pulled back 100 meters. During the withdrawal there was another explosion which the Leutnant could not explain. After about an hour the squad that had set out first also returned, and, beaming with joy, the Unteroffizier reported the destruction of an enemy anti-tank gun and three T 34 tanks, no casualties.

The report was passed via the Zoo bunker to the regimental command post, where the regimental commanding officer, Major L., expressed his appreciation to his grenadiers and the Leutnant.

From the Wehrmacht communiqué of 29 April 1945:
In the heroic battle for the capital city Berlin the fateful struggle of the German people against Bolshevism has once again found its highest expression. While this unprecedented battle rages, our troops on the Elbe have turned their backs to the American forces in order to come to the aid of Berlin's defenders.

The enemy has broken into the inner defense ring, into Charlottenburg from the north and Tempelhof from the south. Heavy fighting is taking place in the Alexanderplatz and near the Halleschen Tor. The East-West Axis is under heavy fire.

This assistance from the Elbe consisted of a few divisions of the 12. Armee under *General* Wenck, which was supposed to carry out a relief attack northeast of Berlin aimed at allowing the shattered remnants of the 9. Armee to break through to Berlin. Only after these two formations had linked up was a joint attack to be made against Berlin. The Wenck army did succeed in advancing northeast out of the Belzig area early on 29 April. It broke through the rear echelons of the surprised Soviets, freed about 3,000 wounded in Beelitz, and its left wing reached the Ferch area on Lake Schwielow. After heavy fighting the remnants of the 9. Armee were able to break through the Soviet ring in the Beelitz—Ferch area.

The planned relief drive towards Berlin did not take place, however, due to lack of forces. The hopes of those still fighting in Berlin were buried in the forests around Oranienburg.

Meanwhile, in the inner districts of Berlin the final battle was being fought over houses and ruins, in cellars and subway tunnels. Heavy shells rained down on the East-West Axis, from which small aircraft continued to take off and land until the end, maintaining a tenuous link with the out-side world. Columns of vehicles, Kübels and cars, trucks and a few horse-drawn vehicles, lined both sides of the once magnificent street beneath the trees of the Tiergarten. Foxholes, bunkers of earth and wood, barracks-like quarters, some draped with camouflage nets—all lay under Soviet artillery fire. Waiting there—exhausted, bitter, hopeless—were soldiers, men of the *Volkssturm*, a few women, girls and Hitler Youths—waiting for the inevitable. The Soviets raised the red banner on the Reichstag building, heavy fighting already raged on upper Friedrich-Strasse, and Stalin Organ fire pounded the gardens of the Reich President's palace and the Reich Chancellery.

In the bunker of the Reich Chancellery Adolf Hitler's life ended dur-ing the afternoon hours of 30 April 1945.

General Weidling, last military commander of the Reich capital, learned of this during the night of 1 May 1945 and made preparations to surrender. Messengers hurried through the streets of Berlin to the sector commanders with orders for them to disengage from the enemy and try to break through in small groups.

Major Lehnhoff gave orders for his Kampfgruppen of the *Wachregiment Großdeutschland Berlin* to assemble in the Kastanien-Allee at 23:00 hours on 1 May 1945 in preparation for a breakout attempt through Rathenow to the west. The tanks of the remaining vehicles were filled, mil-lions of Reichsmarks were distributed to the men, the last rations allot-ted—and then they set off. The Soviet lines were pierced at the Schönhauser Allee train station, although Stalin Organ and tank fire inflicted heavy casualties. With five tanks and 65 men, *Major* Lehnhoff succeeded in breaking out of the city into the Oranienburg area. There, however, the tanks had to be blown up, out of fuel. Divided into four groups, the men continued on in the direction of the Elbe and Schleswig-Holstein, while Oblt. Kralack and Hptm. Hauck remained in Berlin. They were probably the only officers of the *Wachregiment Großdeutschland Berlin* to experience the end in the Reich capital.

Shortly after midnight on 2 May 1945 the military commander of Berlin, *General* Weidling, transmitted radio messages from a radio center of the LVI. Pz.A.K. situated near the command center

"LVI. German Panzerkorps here, LVI. German Panzerkorps. We request cease-fire. We will send emissaries to the Potsdamer Bridge at 1230 hours Berlin time. Recognition signal white flag in front of a red light. We request reply. We are waiting.

LVI. German Panzerkorps here. LVI. German Panzerkorps here…

The message was transmitted five more times. Then the Soviet radio stations took notice of it. Contact was established at about 0530 hours. The surrender took place at about 1500 hours on 2 May 1945.

Hauptmann Hoss gathered the last of his men around him in the *Wachregiment Großdeutschland Berlin*'s barracks and said to them: "The city of Berlin has been surrendered!"

Quietly the men removed their equipment and laid their weapons and ammunition aside. Then they went their separate ways. The war was over.

Since midnight the weapons have been silent on all fronts. The Wehrmacht has ceased the hopeless struggle on order of the grand admiral. Thus the almost six-year-long heroic conflict has come to an end. It brought us great victories, but also severe defeats. In the end the German Armed Services succumbed honorably to superior force.

True to his oath, the German soldier has done his utmost for his people, something that will never be forgotten.

The unparalleled accomplishments of front and home will later find their ultimate justification in a later, fair assessment of history.

The enemy, too, will come to respect the deeds and sacrifices of the German soldiers on land, sea and in the air. Every soldier can therefore lay down his weapons with pride and in this most difficult hour in our history go to work bravely and confidently for the eternal life of our people.

At this hour the Wehrmacht honors those comrades killed on the battlefield.

The dead obligate us to show unconditional loyalty, obedience and discipline to our bleeding fatherland.

From the last Wehrmacht communiqué

9 May 1945

507